THE
HORIZON
HISTORY
OF
AFRICA

At right, a Fulani woman
VICTOR ENGLEBERT

∾ Contents of Volume Two

260 *Chapter Seven:* INNER AFRICA

304 *Chapter Eight:* THE COMING OF THE EUROPEANS

352 *Chapter Nine:* TIME OF TROUBLES

400 *Chapter Ten:* WARS OF RESISTANCE

448 *Chapter Eleven:* UNDER COLONIAL RULE

496 *Chapter Twelve:* AFRICA FOR THE AFRICANS

530 Acknowledgments and Index

THE
HORIZON
HISTORY
OF
AFRICA

INNER AFRICA

(c. A.D. 500–1800)

by

Jan Vansina

INNER AFRICA ENTERS HISTORY on the tide of a huge migration that covered a subcontinent—all of Africa south of a line from the Bight of Benin to southern Somalia. This invasion of Bantu-speaking people was one of the great upheavals of all time because of the area affected, the time span covered, and above all, because of the linguistic and cultural tradition it left.

Among the results of the migrations was the formation of four-hundred-odd different languages, all as closely related to each other as are the Romance languages. Just as the peoples speaking Romance languages inherited many features of Rome's civilization, shaping it by their indigenous cultures and their subsequent history, so the Bantu speakers inherited the civilization of their common ancestors and diversified the common inheritance in similar ways.

The original people are called the Bantu, and in recognition of the great cultural and physical mixing that has since occurred, their descendants are most properly known as Bantu speakers. The word *bantu* means "the people," plural of *muntu*, "a person." It is still found in this form in all the Bantu languages and comes from the ancestral speech, the proto-Bantu language. Much of the vocabulary of proto-Bantu has thus survived, and from this as well as from the geographical distribution of languages scholars can tell how the original Bantu lived, where they came from, and how they migrated; but they cannot date with any exactitude their coming.

The original home of the Bantu was territory south of the middle Benue River valley in eastern Nigeria, an area well watered, fertile, rich in fauna and flora because it lay on the fringes of forest and savanna. The people were principally fishermen. They used dug-out canoes, nets, lines, and fishhooks in their business. They also hunted big and

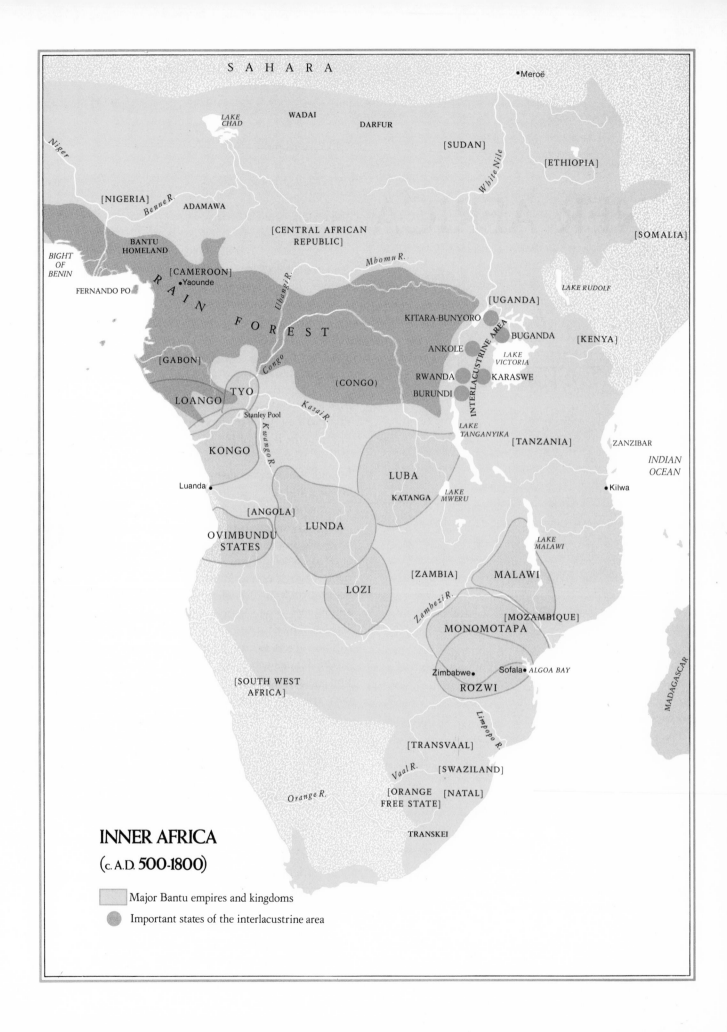

SAHARA

•Meroë

LAKE
CHAD

WADAI

DARFUR

[SUDAN]

[ETHIOPIA]

Niger

[NIGERIA]

Benue R.

ADAMAWA

[CENTRAL AFRICAN
REPUBLIC]

[SOMALIA]

BIGHT
OF
BENIN

BANTU
HOMELAND

Mbomu R.

LAKE RUDOLF

FERNANDO PO

[CAMEROON]
•Yaounde

Ubangi R.

R
A
I
N

KITARA-BUNYORO

[UGANDA]

[GABON]

F
O
R
E
S
T

Congo

(CONGO)

ANKOLE

BUGANDA

INTERLACUSTRINE AREA

[KENYA]

LAKE
VICTORIA

TYO

LOANGO

Kasai R.

RWANDA

BURUNDI

KARASWE

KONGO

Stanley Pool

Kwango R.

LAKE
TANGANYIKA

[TANZANIA]

ZANZIBAR

INDIAN
OCEAN

Luanda •

LUBA

[ANGOLA]

KATANGA

LAKE
MWERU

•Kilwa

OVIMBUNDU
STATES

LUNDA

LAKE
MALAWI

LOZI

[ZAMBIA]

MALAWI

[MOZAMBIQUE]

Zambezi R.

[SOUTH WEST
AFRICA]

MONOMOTAPA

MADAGASCAR

Zimbabwe•

Sofala• ALGOA BAY

ROZWI

Limpopo R.

[TRANSVAAL]

Vaal R.

[SWAZILAND]

Orange R.

[ORANGE
FREE STATE]

[NATAL]

TRANSKEI

INNER AFRICA

(c. A.D. 500-1800)

Major Bantu empires and kingdoms

Important states of the interlacustrine area

small game, and cultivated African yams and palm trees as well as some millet and sorghum. They made pottery, used bark cloth, and perhaps already wove fibers of the raffia tree on wide looms. They bred goats, perhaps sheep, and some cattle. (But the last could not thrive near the forest, so they would leave them behind during the migration.) Iron was not worked; rather, tools were fashioned out of wood or stone.

These fishermen were sedentary and lived in compact villages of unknown size. Their communities were organized in part on a basis of kinship. The leaders were the older men, and all others obeyed them because the elders were their grandfathers, fathers, uncles, and granduncles. The right to exercise authority was legitimized by common ties of blood, and in matters of succession and inheritance, kinship among them was matrilineal. Thus a man's estate went to the son of his sister, not to his own son. Polygyny was common. Because of the nature of the descent system and the fact that women left their villages to follow their husbands, the descent groups, or lineages, were dispersed over different villages. As a result, village organization could not be based entirely on kinship; rather, the settlement may have been governed by a council. Certainly, chiefs were recognized and had territorial power, but we do not know if they ruled over one or several villages.

The Bantu also had religious specialists, acting as both medicine men and diviners, though the roles were often performed by the same person. The Bantu believed that witchcraft was a major cause of misfortune. They may have believed as well in the influence on the lives of men of nature spirits or ancestors. Nothing is known about their arts, and no archeological sites traceable to them have yet been found. They must, however, have been excellent wood-carvers, and they may have produced terra-cotta sculpture.

The Bantu expansion was triggered probably by a great influx of population in Nigeria, which itself was the result of the arrival of many people who had gradually been driven out of the increasingly arid Sahara after 2500 B.C. At first the population pressure found an exit eastward by expanding along the forest fringes as far as the present border of the Republic of Sudan. The invaders were farmers of the savanna; they spoke a language belonging to the Adamawa Eastern group that spoke a Central Sudanese language and had lived in those areas before them. The older inhabitants were scattered north, east, and south until an equilibrium of forces was reached.

Then the pressure in Nigeria built up once again. It was relieved this time by the Bantu southward migrations, which were made easier because of their ability to adapt successfully to life in the forest near the rivers. The forest became their home and it was a good home. It furnished as much timber as was needed for housing and canoes, and the people could fell trees without woodsmen's tools, by burning them at the base of the trunk.

The forest was rich in game, and the marshes and rivers were well stocked with fish. It was more pleasant than the savanna because it was cool, provided a more temperate climate, and was never dusty. It also contained scattered huge patches of savanna called the *esobe*, where flora and fauna typical of the savanna could be found. Within the forest the Bantu could find all the advantages they had known in the mixed environment of the forest fringe.

As for the Bantu's means and manner of migration, being fishermen, they were able to load themselves, their goods, and livestock aboard canoes. The larger boats could take as much as a ton and a half, and the Bantu were carried along rivers and thence along the Atlantic coast, settling the island of Fernando Po early on. They knew where to go because scouting comes naturally to fishermen, whose quests take them many miles from home.

The migration was not a single mass movement, but a gradual process. People packed and went farther on when they felt they had too many neighbors or when there had been quarrels or when they feared witchcraft at work in their village. Because the waterways made travel relatively easy, a village might, in a single move, migrate a substantial distance. Reckoned in centuries, the rate of Bantu dispersion was relatively rapid, and thus at the end of the first phase the people had come to occupy most of the equatorial forest, mixing with the indigenous peoples, including Pygmies and Negroid hunters of a larger stature, about whom nothing more is known.

The movement slowed down for a time when the Bantu encountered new environments on the far sides of the forest and were forced to adapt their economies accordingly. To the east a different sort of forest—more tropical in its vegetation and providing no *esobe*, or clearings—was reached. There the tropical forest covered the great mountain range west of the Great Rift Valley, and the society based on fishing had to transform itself into a hunting and agricultural community. Similarly, where open savanna was reached again in the south, the cultivation of cereals became more important.

Another consequence of these adaptations was a differentiation in the Bantu language as it was spoken among the increasingly dispersed migrants. Thus one can later distinguish between western and eastern subgroups of Bantu speech, the more marked innovations appearing in the east, where other aspects of the Bantu culture would also undergo considerable changes through the influence of a substantial autochthonous population there. But no certain trace of these aborigines has remained to give a clue to their racial identities.

Once the adaptation to the savanna had been made, the southern migrations gained momentum again. The Bantu speakers still stuck to the rivers where possible, not only for the fish found there but also because something approaching the ideal conditions of the savanna-forest fringe could be found in the less dense gallery forests that grew along the river banks. One migratory route seems to have gone downriver on the Congo and then eastward and southward on the Kasai River and other Congo affluents. Following a network of lesser rivers and occasionally traveling overland, this group reached the headwaters of the Zambezi River, from whence they could float downriver to the Indian Ocean and the island of Zanzibar, and then paddle north along the coast as far as Somalia.

At the same time the mass of Bantu migrators that had initially taken a more direct route eastward toward the Great Rift Valley and the interlacustrine area was making much slower headway. The terrain of the Great Lakes area was difficult, and the eastern Bantu had adapted to the social organization of the indigenous population living in relatively dense, well-defined societies. So these Bantu, traveling along their more obstructed route, may have reached Lake Victoria at about the same time the southern wave reached Zanzibar.

During the later part of this second period of expansion some remarkable technological changes percolated throughout the whole Bantu world. First, they learned how to smelt and work iron. The new technology came to them from several sources. This author concludes that the art had spread south from Meroë after 500 B.C., reaching East Africa shortly after the beginning of the Christian era. It reached northern Nigeria around 300 B.C., perhaps from North Africa. So the northwestern Bantu—those who joined the later waves of migrations—acquired the knowledge from Nigeria; the Bantu who moved through the interlacustrine area received it from pre-existing populations in East Africa; and those who moved southeastward and then up the coast were introduced to ironworking by sailors from southern Arabia, perhaps in the first century A.D. or earlier. From all these sources the knowledge spread to other Bantu speakers. In the equatorial forest excellent charcoal could be manufactured, and soon the metal produced there, probably from ore bought in trade for other goods, surpassed what was made anywhere else in inner Africa. It is a sign of the cohesion of the Bantu world that the terminology for working iron developed homogeneously over the whole area occupied by Bantu speakers.

Other innovations at first produced more dramatic results than the knowledge of iron smelting. Banana and taro, crops of southeast Asian origin, had been introduced in East Africa late in the first millennium B.C. By way of the Zambezi valley and the Great Rift regions the new crops spread all over Central Africa, becoming the staples for the forest populations as well as for the peoples of the interlacustrine area. If it was the Bantu peoples who picked up these crops along the coast and transported them inland, they must have migrated there before the birth of Christ.

Lastly, the eastern and southeastern Bantu reacquired cattle. (Their ancestors had lost their incidental herds to the ravages of the tsetse fly when they first entered the forests.) They met with cattle-keeping people in East Africa and perhaps Zambia, and learned the art of husbandry from them. So at the end of this phase the Bantu peoples had acquired a totally new mode of life. They were now farmers and herdsmen rather than fishermen, grew banana and taro as well as cereals, and smelted iron—with consequent changes in social organization. The lapse of time required to change the old way of life must have lasted well over a century and probably much longer.

And then the expansion began once again. Between the first and the fifth century A.D. the Bantu speakers, with their cattle, went from the Zambezi valley all the way to the Transvaal (in the northeastern region of what is now the Republic of South Africa) and continued southward. By the thirteenth century A.D. at the latest they were in the Transkei (a territory within South Africa's Cape Province); but there is evidence that they may have completed their move much earlier. During this last period they also moved into the regions of southern Angola and South West Africa (known to its indigenous inhabitants as Namibia).

In East Africa further gains of territory were slow, even though Bantu speakers advanced from the west, south, and east into the interior of Kenya and Tanzania. Progress was slow because the Eastern Rift of Kenya and Tanzania and large parts of northern Kenya and Uganda were not sufficiently fertile to support sedentary farmers, but were well suited to support pastoral nomads; peoples engaged in herding were already occupying these lands. So the Bantu farmers could not deeply penetrate those areas. Then there were places in the region of Tanzania with a fairly dense population and established cultural patterns, which did not allow for Bantu speech or customs to assert themselves.

However, as a general rule, the Bantu immigrants assimilated the native peoples they encountered, transmitting not only speech but often their whole civilization; the Bantu and successive autochthones often merged, becoming one population. How did this happen?

The Bantu civilization was generally not much more complex or appealing than the civilizations of the local peoples. This was not comparable to the spread of Rome's superior civilization over much of barbaric Europe. Rather, the process of Bantuization seems to have been similar to that of urbanization. The immigrants lived in compact settlements that acted as centers or "towns" for the more dispersed nomadic camps of the non-Bantu peoples around them. The aboriginal hunters and/or farmers came to these centers to exchange produce with the Bantu, married with them, took gradually to their speech, and through it, adopted the Bantu civilization. And, to a lesser extent, the Bantu took on features of the aboriginal peoples as well.

Since the Bantu villages were small, the difference between "town" and "country" was slight, and the process of assimilation went on very slowly. Still slower was the Bantuization of indigenous hunters, whose nomadic life brought only intermittent contacts with the villagers. Examples in Zambia show that Bantu farmers and autochthonous hunters lived side by side without amalgamating until the thirteenth or perhaps even the fifteenth century.

Bantuization, then, did not take just a few centuries, but covered almost two millenniums. The process was completed only in the western and central equatorial forests and in the savanna as far south as southern Angola and Rhodesia. Pockets of hunters surviving in the forest in southern Africa and even in parts of East Africa represent specialized populations that have adopted Bantu speech and live in a symbiotic economic relationship with the Bantu. But among others assimilation never happened (for example, the Pygmy hunters living in the oriental parts of the great equatorial forest).

And so the Bantu civilizations evolved from a mixture of proto-Bantu culture and of features produced after the migrations by internal invention and even more by contact with neighboring groups. The Bantu languages cannot be classified in clearly recognizable genetic subgroups. Languages grow only in relative isolation from each other. A particular language first develops dialects, and these become daughter languages of the ancestral mother language

after the passage of some centuries. But if the communities that speak those dialects are not sufficiently isolated, as happened among the English in Great Britain, it then becomes impossible to find out in what way the daughter languages descended from the ancestral tongue. This is obviously what happened with the Bantu languages. One can recognize that the original Bantu divided into two languages called Proto-Bantu A and Proto-Bantu B. One can also see that the four-hundred-odd languages that are spoken now stem from eighty to ninety mother languages. But the relations between them cannot be determined with precision, which proves that at all times since the original expansion Bantu speakers have kept up a great deal of communication with each other all over the huge subcontinent they occupied.

The relatively constant communication between these people must be attributed above all to the development of trade. Everywhere fishing folk exchanged pottery, fish, game, and vegetal and cereal foods. Areas blessed with the required raw materials exported such goods as ironware, copper, salt, basketry, mats, and sometimes even canoes and wooden tools. Trade was fueled not only by the needs of people but by their tastes. Thus a householder in the southern Congo might add imported woven ware to his store of locally made baskets and mats simply because the designs or shapes appealed to him.

If trade was of great importance in opening avenues of contact between near and distant neighbors, the accompanying spread of technological skills was also of major significance in the Bantuization process. The effects are visible both from linguistic evidence and the diffusion of items found. Among the objects and techniques that came into use over wide parts of the Bantu-speaking area, perhaps the most important set of items is the shaft furnace and its associated technology, which between A.D. 700 and 1200 ushered in the later iron age for inner Africa. These had been developed in the forests of the Congo, mainly because the hardwoods growing there produced a charcoal that allowed iron to be treated at much higher temperatures. This area remained foremost in the quality of its iron and steel products well into the twentieth century. Other, lesser centers of metallurgical skills were in Katanga, where evidence of the later iron age is attested as early as the eighth century and somewhat later in central Angola. This new technology allowed men to fashion large iron tools, both for peace and war. These broad-bladed hoes, heavy axes, and large spears enabled people to carry out their tasks much more effectively than did the brittle and clumsy small iron tools they had used before this time.

Also, archeological evidence tells us that by A.D. 1200 the Bantu civilizations had reached the point at which one finds in each region a set of different but related cultures, and no further differentiation occurred. Even though the major proof for this development stems from an examination of pottery, it is sufficiently established that the regional Bantu cultures of 1200 are the direct forerunners of those ethnic cultures that began to be identifiable by 1800. From this time on, the history of the continent is best told by geographical areas: the savanna north of the equatorial forest, the forest itself, the southern savanna, Africa south of the Zambezi River, and East Africa.

The peoples of the northern savanna, both the autochthonous Central Sudanese speakers and the Adamawa Eastern speakers who had invaded the area, never lost touch completely with the culture of the Sahel (between Lake Chad and the Nile), and the Bantu never made any imprint here. The early evolution of this area is still shrouded in mystery. A complicated set of population movements resulted in the present crazy quilt of language groups, but a fairly uniform culture pattern was preserved over most of the area now occupied by the Central African Republic, the northern Congo, southern Sudan, and parts of Cameroon. The people were skilled farmers, living in dispersed homesteads that were organized into tiny kinship groups, and they recognized leaders only in time of war.

On the upper Ubangi River one group of people began to organize a kinship system that included many hundreds of relatives or supposed relatives and brought them under the control of a tribal patriarch. By 1600 the concept of territorial kingship had been introduced, and a fairly small kingdom was born. The first tiny states were led by members of the Bandia clan, whose kinsmen, the Avongara, also developed a microkingdom. By 1750 one of these proto-states began a career of conquest, pushing farther eastward with each generation. (This was to become the Zande nation in the nineteenth century.) The result of the expansion was the adoption by the new inhabitants of an incredible range of objects, techniques, behavior, and values, producing in their fusion an extraordinarily complex new civilization. They took over every indigenous crop cultivated by the people they subjugated, adding them to their own repertoire. This could only be accomplished by altering the rotation of crops, and it ultimately produced a wholly new type of agriculture that relied on the growing of perhaps forty crops rather than two or three staples.

Trade between this northern savanna and other areas may have remained negligible before the eighteenth century, though the existence of ancient underground iron mines not far from the Ubangi Bend indicates a brisk trade in iron. Traders from Darfur and even distant Egypt reached the Mbomu by traveling directly south. From then on the relative isolation of the area was completely shattered. The mystery is why influences from the Sahel had not percolated much sooner all over these great grasslands, especially along the fourteen-hundred-mile-long Chari River, whose many tributaries linked parts of Central Africa with the Lake Chad region.

As stated earlier, a major consequence of the Bantu migrations was a change in their way of life as they entered new vegetation zones. Following their arrival in the forest zone, the Bantu began very slowly to specialize. Some groups turned to farming and hunting, while others remained fishermen. In the Congo Bend area, where the specialization was most marked, the fishermen, owing to their greater mobility, took on additional roles as traders. The local trading networks grew bigger and bigger with the passage of time as one group of fishermen made contact with other groups and markets arose among them.

There was no lack of products to trade. People outside the forest needed ironware, red camwood for ornamentation and medicine, copal (a kind of resin obtained from trees), canoes, and later even such particularized items as sugar-cane wine, certain types of knives, and certain kinds of caterpillars to eat. In exchange, people in the forest sought such goods as copper and copperware, coastal salt or salt from Katanga, iron ore (probably from the Ubangi region), and later, raffia cloth, ornaments, and certain types of seashells used in monetary exchange. In a general sense the same situation prevailed all along the coast, from the Niger delta to the mouth of the Congo and up the estuaries of the rivers there. The trade can be attested by such traces as the strong similarities found in polychrome sculpture from Yorubaland to the Congo. Just before 1700 a European trader even claimed that African sailors from the Gold Coast traveled all along the coast southward, reaching as far as Loango, near the mouth of the Congo.

But in the area roughly equivalent to the mountainous parts of southern Cameroon, Gabon, and eastern Congo there was no such specialization between Bantu fishermen-traders and farmers. There, especially in the northeastern Congo, the intermixture with autochthonous hunting bands became very pronounced. By the thirteenth century A.D. new Bantu-speaking immigrants from the area of the Great Lakes arrived in the hospitable country. In some cases their superior social and political structures enabled them to wrest the leadership from the autochthones. In most cases, however, the newcomers lost their own cultural background almost totally and blended with the cultures they found. In the northeastern Congo the process was less complex and happened on a much smaller scale, but still many Bantu groups there began to take on Pygmy physical features. But the effect was rendered less distinct when the mighty nineteenth-century invasion of the Bantu-speaking Fang overran the area, adding still another element to the culture.

In the central portions of the forest, all along the affluents of the Congo, an institution of ritual chieftainship arose between perhaps the thirteenth and the seventeenth centuries. This was an important change in the whole way of life because it replaced the notion of authority by virtue of superior age in the kinship system with the notion of authority based on territory. The new system also led to a great flowering of rituals, all of which are related in their oral tradition.

Thus the spread of ideas, intense trade, and local migrations brought about a remarkable uniformity of civilization over equatorial Africa. The influence of the forest environment is particularly noticeable in the realm of religion. For the Pygmies there was only one god: the forest. The Bantu speakers observed a more complex set of beliefs, wherein the banks of pools and the thickets were the abode of nature spirits whose whims controlled life; but ancestors and forms of magic also had a place in the system.

In other aspects of their cultural life as well, the Bantu speakers achieved a high degree of sophistication. The popular image of tiny settlements lost in the awesome majesty of unending depths of foliage could not be more wrong. The people were neither lost nor barbarous, and some of the most original monuments of African civilization originate with the forest peoples. From the lake regions of the Great Rift Valley to Cameroon, the forest was the home of great epics, literary masterpieces of a scope and length unequaled elsewhere in Africa. In the eastern Congo and Gabon a rich and delicate tradition of sculpture existed, and in the central forest the arts of dancing and polyphonic song achieved great distinction.

By the eighteenth century the increase in trade and the linkage of more and more local networks into large commercial systems led to the fusion of all into one far-reaching system for the purpose of exporting slaves and ivory to the coast. By 1800 the network that fed into Stanley Pool (a lakelike expansion of the Congo some three hundred fifty miles from its mouth), and thence to the Atlantic, spanned a thousand miles, reaching to the Central African Republic, the Adamawa plateau in Cameroon, and to the Stanley Falls in the Democratic Republic of the Congo. Indeed, the northern affluents of the Congo connected with Darfur and Egypt. A systematic study of this far-flung and complex commerce still remains to be done.

In the southern savanna two areas stand out as centers of Bantu evolution: northern Katanga and the lower Congo. Archeological finds from the former area show that by the eighth or ninth century a complex culture existed there. Several earlier cultures had fused together, as evidenced from pottery, and both potters' art and metalwork had reached amazing virtuosity. The distribution of the population was dense; there can be no doubt that a political structure based on the occupation of common territory had evolved and that a form of chieftainship had developed. By the twelfth century long-distance trade in copper was under way, differences in wealth between poor and rich had increased, and chiefs or kings ruled over larger areas than earlier. The territorial structure had expanded so that certain chiefs had authority over headmen of villages, but themselves became subjected to overlords, whom we can call kings. With the development of this type of kingship came an increase in the complexity of the ideology of kingship, the etiquette connected with it, the quality and number of regalia that expressed it.

Descendants of these twelfth-century chiefs arose to lead great kingdoms, perhaps in the sixteenth century, if not somewhat earlier. The renowned Luba kingdom was created by Kalala Ilunga, whose deeds are recorded in Luba oral history. Kalala Ilunga introduced the notion of *bulopwe*, a form of sacred kingship. All the descendants of his line were supposed to have a special sort of blood, and its virtues were such that anyone endowed with this blood had a right to rule. Only people with *bulopwe* could mystically protect the country against harm and promote the fertility of crops and of women or ensure the success of the hunt—the central concerns of all Luba.

Well before 1600, but after the foundation of the Luba kingdom, a prince from that realm introduced the Luba concept of *bulopwe* to the Lunda people to the west. Tradition has it that the Lunda were then governed by a young queen, Rweej. She met the handsome Kibinda Ilunga, a Luba hunter, at a camp near an idyllic brook, married him, and let him rule. Her twin brothers, dissatisfied with the arrangement, left for the interior of Angola to carve out new chiefdoms for themselves.

The Luba kingdom proper did not expand beyond the plains of the upper Lomami River before the eighteenth century, and even then the territories added were lost again by 1850. The kingdom was a collection of hereditary chiefdoms of all sizes, joined by a common allegiance to the sovereign. Despite the theory of *bulopwe*, or rather beyond it, the kings in practice enforced their government by the use of a small bureaucracy of titled officers and the threat of force against recalcitrant chiefs, who were never fully welcomed into the system of Luba kinship.

The Lunda adopted a modified form of this, blending it with a political institution of their own. Their earlier form of government had fused in an original way the idea of ties by blood with territorial authority and structure. Everyone in the family was supposed to obey senior members and also to collaborate with junior members (that is, men of equal status). From this it evolved that chiefs were considered to be members of a family headed by the Lunda king or queen. So chiefs were related to one another as brothers, cousins, nephews, and the like, at least fictionally. To preserve the fiction it became practice that a successor took over the name of the deceased chief and his whole personality so that he, too, now was the brother, nephew, cousin, and so on, of other chiefs. Even the wives of the deceased became his wives; so much did the successor "become" the dead man.

It was easy to adapt this principle to the titled bureaucracy introduced by the Luba. It allowed the whole political system to function, whatever the social structure of a people might be, since it could be adapted to any system of political succession. The Luba system, by contrast, could not. The Luba were patrilineal, and offices were inherited either by the brothers of the deceased or by their male children. This hampered the diffusion of the Luba model of government whenever societies were organized matrilineally (for example, whenever their practice was to have nephews rather than sons as heirs). In addition, the Luba system meant that with the passing of each generation the ties between chiefs weakened, and attempts at breaking away from the realm or wars between chiefdoms in the kingdom became more and more probable as time passed.

The difference between the Lunda and Luba systems explains why large numbers of peoples actually subjected themselves to the rule of Lunda chiefs. These chiefs still remained in touch with the Lunda emperor. By 1750 the Lunda had created an empire stretching from the Kwango River in the west to the Luapula River and Lake Mweru in the east, ruling over a million inhabitants or more.

The net effect of the Luba and Lunda expansion was to establish transcontinental long-distance trading routes from Angola to Mozambique and to leave a powerful imprint upon the civilizations of all the peoples living in the southern savanna east of the Kwango, as will be shown later in this chapter. The commodities traded were mainly slaves, but also included ivory, copper, salt, European goods, as well as items of local produce. Ramifications of the trade routes covered the whole savanna and linked up with the forest peoples' network.

As for the cultural influence, all sorts of institutions were diffused—from initiation rituals for girls to veneration of a special tree in ancestor worship. The most remarkable facet of this was perhaps the extraordinary efflorescence of a system of common symbols. Using these symbols, the southern savanna peoples elaborated a complex philosophy applicable both to an investigation of reality and to the ordering of societal relationships. But the diffusion was not total; in some fields there was none. For instance, the Luba homeland and central Angola were two centers where very distinct styles of sculpture developed before 1600. Not only did these two styles not influence one another, but the Lunda, who lived between the centers, did not take to sculpture at all. The example of sculpture brings home the point that diffusion is not an automatic process. The societies that are exposed to new objects, behavior, or ideas are selective, taking only those things that complement their own traditions well.

North of the lower Congo river chiefdoms began to form primitive states perhaps as early as the twelfth century. Continuing growth led to the establishment of three major kingdoms, Congo, Loango, and Tio—all by the fifteenth century at the latest. Of these, Congo became the most famous. Congo civilization encompassed the kingdoms of Congo and Loango, and stretched from there through northern Angola to the Kwanza River and beyond; east of the Kwango River, Congo influence mingled with Lunda features. The Tio type of civilization asserted itself on all the high and drier plateaus around the Stanley Pool and toward the lower Kasai River.

By 1480 Congo was a flourishing state. Initially, the staple crops were millet and banana, superseded in the sixteenth century by maize and a hundred years later by cassava. A rich and highly accomplished technology flourished. Pottery making, weaving, smithing, and other crafts were fully established, and a brisk trade brought products from all parts of the kingdom and beyond to its major markets. The arts were well developed, especially sculpture.

Stone statues of chiefs, dating to the seventeenth century, have survived.

There was state-controlled currency, based on the exchange of a small seashell found only near the coastal town of Luanda, and it was controlled by the state's treasurer. Government was somewhat more centralized than elsewhere in Central Africa, in part because the king could depose any chief, and hereditary succession was not recognized except for kingship. All lesser officers served at the pleasure of the rulers, at least in theory. In practice the relations between a territorial chief and a king were determined by power politics, and there are many instances in which the sovereign could not oust some of his lesser officers. Despite the fact then that Congo was perhaps the most centralized of the Central African kingdoms, the structure of the state was still unimpressive when compared with the West African states.

Conflicts developed between the aristocracy and the farmers, and the system of royal succession worked poorly. Finally, contact with the Portuguese brought about the state's downfall after 1665. The increased slave trade that followed in the whole area, unhampered by political checks and balances, allowed individual entrepreneurs to become wealthy and powerful men. They invested their profit in guns and armed guards, made up of slaves and poorer kinsmen. Thus the very fact that power could be achieved by anyone who was successful in trade undermined the belief that only the nobility should or could rule and indirectly undermined the basis for any royal authority itself. For the authority of a monarchy was based ultimately on the belief that the king ruled because it was preordained by his birth into a royal lineage, and the royal lineage ruled as if preordained by natural law. The emergence of powerful merchants changed all this. The monarchies survived, but after 1800 the major states had either fallen apart or had become hollow shells, mere shadows of a former structure.

Two other influential Bantu-speaking civilizations were those of the Lozi and the Ovimbundu. Lunda migrants to the upper Zambezi blended with the locals to form the Lozi kingdom, in which a new, unique culture arose. The Ovimbundu civilization grew out of a mixture of Lunda and Congo elements, with some southwestern cattle-keeping Bantu intermingled in the Angolan highlands. Cattle raids by the Ovimbundu chiefdoms kept them perennially at war until their restlessness was turned toward the acquisition of wealth through trade after 1750. The Ovimbundu became, especially in the nineteenth century, the most successful long-distance traders in the interior.

In southern Africa, even before 1200, the development of localized cultures resulted in the establishment of the main distinct civilizations that have since dominated there: the *bantu botatwe*, or "the three-people group" in Zambia; the Malawi, living in what is now the Republic of Malawi; the Shona in Rhodesia; and the Sotho and perhaps the Nguni speakers (including the Xhosa, Zulu, and Swazi) of South Africa. All of these are set apart from the civilizations discussed so far by their emphasis on cattle: possession meant wealth and power. The transfer of cattle regulated all intergroup relations: tribute to the king was paid in cattle; bridewealth was paid in cattle to the father of the prospective bride by the father of the groom; important sacrifices required the slaughtering of cattle.

The great importance cattle assumed in these societies is called the cattle complex. Historically, the complex originated in East Africa. Cattle were not sacred animals as in India, but there was an intimate bond between cattle and people. Men had their favorite single steer or ox and identified with the animal even more than some Western people do with their pets. Cattle were considered the most beautiful creations of nature, and much of the poetry in East Africa and also in southern Africa describes the beauty of the hides, horns, and behavior of herds or individual beasts. Cattle were also the intermediaries between man and the spirits. When an ox was sacrificed, one often told the animal before it was killed what to say to the ancestors in the next world. Cattle produced wealth for their owners by producing offspring or by being hired out. In addition, men could be made vassals of a lord simply because they were entrusted with his herd. There is no aspect of life in which cattle did not figure prominently.

The civilizations south of the Zambezi did not only absorb features from East and Central Africa, they interacted daily and for a full millennium with non-Bantu peoples: the Khoikhoi (Hottentots) and San (Bushmen). The former were nomadic pastoralists; the latter hunters and gatherers. The farther one goes from the Zambezi to the south or to the west, the more one finds the imprint of Khoi or San ways of life on the cultures of the Bantu speakers. Thus in the region of South West Africa the black and Bantu-speaking Herero are culturally pastoralists like the Khoikhoi, whereas the black and Khoi-speaking Bergdama took over a Bushman way of life. Thus one can show that language, culture, and race do not necessarily go together at all. The Herero took over only a Khoi way of life, but kept their language; the Bergdama took over a Khoi language and a San way of life. Both Herero and Bergdama are black, and different from the yellowish Khoi or San.

After 1300 the influence of the Luba civilization began to affect the technology and political organization of the area. Luba emigrants founded a large kingdom in Malawi, while the Shona, new settlers in Rhodesia, founded the states that were to fuse into the empire of Monomotapa by 1450. Even before the Luba's arrival, however, trade had developed with ports along the Indian Ocean. Gold had been mined in Rhodesia perhaps as early as the fifth century A.D. As discussed in Chapter Four, the precious ore became a major export around A.D. 1100, being sought after by Arab and Portuguese traders, and it rapidly turned into the keystone of the prosperity of all the Swahili cities on the east coast. The gold trade brought through the harbor of Sofala such imports as cloth, beads, and porcelain. The presence of foreign traders also stimulated the export of other commodities along the Zambezi, mainly ivory, leading to the creation of a dense network of local exchange in all manner of minerals, household goods, and luxury items. With the arrival of the Portuguese in Mozambique the patterns and volume of trade did not change much, but the routes did. A steady expansion continued until the eighteenth century, when even north Transvaal had become a major trading area. By the end of the eighteenth century the goods, including many slaves now, went from Lake Malawi to the Portuguese coastal settlements at Kilwa, the Zambezi estuary, and Algoa Bay.

The Malawi kingdom did not long outlast the arrival of the Portuguese. It was a loose confederation, and the power of the monarch was linked directly to the control of trade. The state reached its zenith in the seventeenth century with Portuguese help and then fell apart when the Yao, a Bantu-speaking people dwelling in Mozambique and southern Tanzania, managed to wrest the commerce in ivory and slaves.

Meanwhile, the Monomotapa empire had gradually grown from a set of chiefdoms into a very large state. But after fifty-odd years, in about 1475, its southern half broke away and became the kingdom of the Rozwi, a Shona clan. The Shona people are responsible for some spectacular stone ruins in Rhodesia; but these do not include the ruins at Zimbabwe, a site that antedated the empire of Monomotapa. The size of the walls, the wealth in gold, stone sculpture, and oriental porcelain, led to wild speculations as to when the site was founded. Some even held that this was the land of the Queen of Sheba! Now it is evident that the place was occupied over a very long period by Bantu speakers and that it developed along with the growth of local states.

The Rozwi were skilled builders in stone, and their art was passed on to peoples in South Africa, where builders copied the forms in wattle and daub as well as wood. Their empty villages are still found from the Zambezi River to the Orange Free State.

Beyond statecraft and architecture, the Shona were remarkable for their spiritual beliefs and organization. There was an official religion invoking royal and lordly ancestors by oracle, in the person of a chief priest, who transmitted to kings and commoners the wishes of Mwari, the creator-god. The oracle's authority extended throughout the kingdom, and lower priests were linked to him in a loose hierarchy.

Of the peoples living in what is now South Africa, little is yet known of the period before colonial rule was established. The stone ruins probably belonged to the Sotho; traces of Nguni settlement have not yet been found, even though the Nguni were presumed to have reached Natal by the eleventh century and are known to have developed chiefdoms there by the fourteenth. All evidence indicates that there was a slow growth of territorial chiefdoms over a long period of time. These political units were not welded into kingdoms, perhaps because there always was room for further expansion in unoccupied or sparsely settled territory, a situation to which political practice among the Nguni had adapted itself. Whenever a quarrel for the succession to a chieftainship broke out among two contenders, one could always move out of settled territory with his followers and set up a brand-new chiefdom. When no further expansion was possible, however, weaker chiefdoms were incorporated into bigger states, and the process culminated with the creation of the Zulu nation in what is now the South African province of Natal.

Meanwhile, the San and Khoikhoi lived on in western South Africa, where desert conditions made farming impossible. The Bantu who arrived in this environment adapted to it and were unable to Bantuize the original inhabitants, who kept their traditional ways. These civilizations have been remarkable not only for the skills exhibited by Bushmen rock painters and engravers but especially for the mythology and religious beliefs that they developed. The myths are richer, more varied, and infinitely more poetic than those of the agricultural peoples, and the mythology influenced deeply the oral literature of both the southwestern and southeastern Bantu peoples.

In East Africa the evolution of the societies turned out to be more complex than in any other part of inner Africa. The great variety of environments in the area, including the ex-

These Watusi dancers are members of an elite corps of professional entertainers that performs for the Burundi court. Chosen for exceptional height—they average well over six feet—these scions of the aristocracy have been given rigorous training not only in dance but also in military sciences, law, oral history, and the social graces. While performing, they wear leopard skins and headdresses made of fur from the rare colobus monkey. The Watusi people have for centuries been the overlords of Burundi and Rwanda and hold the Bantu-speaking Bahutu and the Pygmy Batwa people in servitude. The Watusi, themselves, are cattle owners who measure wealth in the size of a man's herd.

PHOTO RESEARCHERS—THOMAS D. W. FRIEDMANN

ceptionally arid Great Rift Valley of central Kenya and Tanzania, can be held responsible in part for the complexity. The pattern of immigration further complicated matters.

Sometime before 1500 B.C. the indigenous Khoikhoi and San hunters encountered migrations of peoples of Ethiopian origin, who made pots and owned cattle. These farmers occupied the fringes of the Rift Valley and dispersed over southern Tanzania. Next, there appeared a group of truly nomadic pastoralists, speaking kindred tongues known technically as the Nilotic languages. These people originated in the area between the White Nile and the Ethiopian highlands well over two thousand years ago. By the time of the birth of Christ their languages had split into three branches: Western, Eastern, and Southern Nilotic. The speakers of Western Nilotic migrated toward the White Nile, while the speakers of Eastern Nilotic stayed in the area of their collective origin. Southern Nilotic speakers moved toward the Great Rift Valley of East Africa, where they became the first people to perfect a pastoral economy suitable to the arid environment of the Rift Valley. There they were able to maintain a social organization that allowed nomadic life and yet provided an orderly society on a fairly large scale.

The basis of the specific institutions by which this feat was achieved were systems of age grades, which guided the males of a society as they passed, with other males of their generation, through a succession of duties and roles within the community. Each age set, recognizing leaders within its number, entered the system as boys, when they underwent initiation. After a fixed number of years the young men moved from one grade to the next. The most junior grade was that of the warriors. At the next level the men founded households; at the next they formed councils and directed the group; and at the most senior level the old men were advisers to the leaders. On this pattern each society embroidered its own arabesques to make the system even more effective. Most of the Southern Nilotic speakers remained in Kenya, the exception being the Tatog, who occupied the fertile plains south of Lake Victoria. This, therefore, was the mixture of people the Bantu found on their arrival in the area.

The Bantu first absorbed the Ethiopian farmers of southern Tanzania and chased the Tatog away from the fertile parts of the eastern Tanzanian plateau. Near the Great Rift Valley, however, both the hunters and the Ethiopian farmers stood their ground, and a very complicated interaction with the Bantu followed. Some of the farmers began to take over Bantu speech, as happened perhaps with the Gogo and Iramba, while in other cases the Bantu speakers lost the speech of their ancestors and for a time adopted that of the farmers of Ethiopian origin, as was evidently the case with the Iraqw. The way of life of the incoming Bantu speakers and that of the aboriginal farmers was equally well adapted to the environment and equally complex, which explains this pattern of mutual interaction. By 1500, however, the whole of eastern and southern Tanzania was Bantu speaking, and the highlands of Kenya east of the Great Rift were also occupied by Bantu speakers. On the coast itself, where the Bantu had arrived sometime earlier (as indicated previously), they accepted many features of the Persian and Arab ways of life, and by A.D. 800 Swahili civilization was already formed there. A major influence is evident in the language; nearly half the vocabulary is borrowed from these foreign sources. Such observances as Nauruz, the New Year's festival, are also of Middle Eastern origin.

After Bantu settlement, development in southern and eastern Tanzania came about much more slowly than in the southern Congo, yet on the same lines. Internal trade in salt, pottery, basketry, and iron developed locally. The dominant form of government was the chiefdom; but as in South Africa, chiefdoms did not amalgamate into kingdoms. Whenever they attained a certain size, they split, and by 1750 there were hundreds of these microstates on the plains. True, clusters could be recognized among them wherever people followed the same customs or spoke similar dialects or where their chiefs claimed descent from a common ancestor. But growth into bigger states would not come here until the nineteenth century. Only in parts of northeastern Tanzania do kingdoms form before 1880—near the Kenya-Tanzania border part of the Pare Mountain people were united under one dynasty as early as the sixteenth century, and the neighboring Shambaa were welded into one monarchy around 1700. In eastern Kenya the Bantu adopted age-grade organizations, similar to those recognized by the Southern Nilotic speakers, and thus remained on the whole loosely structured.

All this stands in sharp contrast to the interlacustrine area, where the population was growing fast because of the great fertility of the soil, for which banana and beans as well as millet were very well suited. Around A.D. 1000 pastoralists of unknown cultural affiliation from northern Kenya or southern Ethiopia arrived in the area, occupying the less fertile and consequently almost unpopulated land that they prized for their cattle.

Being more mobile and better able to call up greater numbers of men at a shorter notice than the Bantu-speaking chiefdoms they encountered, they finally became lords over most of the Bantu speakers, adopting Bantu rituals and sacred kingships. In Uganda the large state of Kitara grew and survives in legend. Founded perhaps before 1300, it was overrun around 1450 by Western Nilotic speakers, who moved upstream from the White Nile. The Chwezi, rulers of Kitara, were defeated; they were replaced by invaders, the Kitara Bunyoro, who also gave dynasties to two tiny states in the vicinity, one of which was to become Buganda.

The defeated Chwezi, or at least a group of them, went south and founded a host of smaller states on the western shore of Lake Victoria. Among these, Ankole and Karagwe were to become the biggest. From 1500 to 1800 the two major developments in the area were the unending struggles between Buganda and Bunyoro, in which the former gradually took the lead, and the emergence of Rwanda as the leading state in the south. After 1800 Burundi was to become as powerful as Rwanda, and these two kingdoms are the only ones that survived the colonial period to become independent nations.

Every one of the four major states was organized in a somewhat different manner. For most of the period Bunyoro was the greatest in territory, but its population, principally millet farmers, was small. A significant part of the aristocracy was seminomadic, and consequently, royal control remained limited. In Buganda agriculture was based on the cultivation of bananas, which are land-intensive but labor-extensive crops, thus freeing relatively more men to perform other duties such as warfare. Buganda saw the power of its king grow all during this period, and by the end of the nineteenth century its bureaucracy was the tightest and most centralized of all kingdoms, with its state encompassing about one million inhabitants. The Rwanda monarchy followed the example of Buganda in strengthening the powers of the king. However, the internal caste structure of the country meant that the nobility remained much more dominant than in Buganda, and the bureaucracy was less well developed, even though Rwanda controlled perhaps two million inhabitants. As for Burundi, it was a major power only for a relatively short time, and its kings never succeeded in asserting their power over that of their own relatives in most of the country. It, too, controlled over two million inhabitants.

The contrasting civilizations that existed and the caste systems that have developed out of them are reflections of this history. The three major castes are: Pygmy hunters, Bantu-speaking agriculturalists, and Nilotic or other pastoral rulers. The complicated set of values linked with the cattle complex was the main ingredient brought by the pastoralists, whereas the complex rites of kingship were a Bantu inheritance. A peculiar effect of the downfall of the Chwezi was their transformation in the memory of their former subjects into glorious heroes around whom a religious cult arose. This spread over the whole interlacustrine area and even into eastern Tanzania. Despite a great many local variations, there remains everywhere a common core of myth and ritual as well as an ideology of equality that clashes violently with the fundamental inequality inherent in the caste system. In time each of the civilizations developed further by internal growth. Thus the political structures, especially the particular forms of landholding and rights over cattle, evolved in different ways.

The invaders of Kitara had only been a fraction of the Western Nilotic speakers. The others continued their trek in northern Uganda and then along the eastern shore of Lake Victoria. They settled in all these lands and turned to a mixed economy. In some places Bantu speech ousted Nilotic, whereas in others Nilotic dominated. But the cultures were quite comparable blends of Bantu, Western Nilotic, and some Southern and Eastern Nilotic features. This process of settlement lasted from 1450 to the end of the nineteenth century. The Eastern Nilotic speakers moved southward from the cradle lands of all Nilotic speakers into what is now Kenya and adjacent parts of Uganda, probably before 1000 and certainly before 1450.

Meanwhile, the Nandi, another southern Nilotic group, occupied the whole Rift Valley from 1500 to 1650. Their pastoral way of life was much better adapted to local conditions than any of the other peoples living there. Yet they, too, were swept away from the Great Rift by an Eastern Nilotic group, the Masai. The Masai had improved on the military and the political organization of the Nandi. In less than a full century they occupied the Great Rift. After that, stiff resistance from Bantu groups on the edges of the Rift Valley and the sedentarization of the Kwavi, an offshoot of the Masai, blocked further advances and produced an armed stalemate, which was to last throughout most of the nineteenth century.

Northern Kenya, that part of the Rift Valley and the highlands to the west of the Rift, remained home for different groups of Nilotic nomads. The tragedy of all the nomads in East Africa was to be the very success of their adaptation to the environment in which they lived. For their nomadic ways were to become a major handicap to modernization in our times.

The history of inner Africa is the story of how large numbers of original civilizations grew from Late Stone Age cultures and the common inheritance of the original Bantu civilization. Further growth and development stemmed from internal developments and also from mutual borrowing; these were facilitated by the increase in trade, political growth, conquest, and the more modest practice of intermarriage between groups. These processes led to increasing cultural elaboration, both in the direction of a better adaptation to each particular environment and in the direction of an intellectually more satisfying way of life. Personalities must have played substantial roles in these developments; but the nature of our sources is such that little is known about their impact. Only the fruits of their works are still visible.

As these civilizations emerged, they left a unique legacy for all mankind. Inner Africa has been less affected by the world outside than most of the other civilizations elsewhere on the earth. At the same time the complexity of these ways of life takes them out of the range of the simple societies; there is nothing primitive about them. As Leo Frobenius, the German ethnologist and explorer, said: "They are civilized to the marrow of their bones." Because they grew in relative isolation, the flowering of human ingenuity and creativity that these civilizations and their history represents is a unique thread in the cloth that is the achievement of mankind. And so inner Africa's history teaches man more about himself everywhere.

THE MWINDO EPIC

THE MUSEUM OF PRIMITIVE ART

From the forest peoples of inner Africa have come some of the continent's literary masterpieces, including the Mwindo epic that follows. This work is part of the rich oral tradition of the Nyanga, a Bantu-speaking group that lives in the mountainous rain forest of the former Kivu province in the eastern part of the Democratic Republic of the Congo.

The story was recorded by Professor Daniel Biebuyck, an anthropologist on the faculty at the University of Delaware, who lived and taught in the former Belgian Congo and did field research in its forest zones. He first visited the territory of the Nyanga in 1952, beginning his study among them two years later. In 1956 he spent several weeks in Kisimba, one of the more remote forest areas of the Kivu province, and there was able to transcribe the epic. By that time he had become well acquainted with the Nyanga people and their culture, and had learned that they had a special type of adventure story, known generically as karisi, or epic text, which he had previously heard only in confused or fragmentary form.

In the Kisimba region he visited the village of Bese in a dense rain forest known as Ihimbi. At Bese he met She-karisi Candi Rureke (she-karisi means "maker of an epic text"), a bard who agreed to recite the Mwindo epic for him. For twelve consecutive days the bard narrated, sang, and enacted the many episodes of the tale, while Professor Biebuyck and his aides wrote it down verbatim. However, the narrator stressed to his listeners that the epic was never performed by the Nyanga in immediate sequence within a short span of time, but was told episode by episode at different times. Rureke, who had learned the epic from Kanyangara of Bese, an expert bard, was the only great performer of the epic still alive in 1956.

The population of the Nyanga is about 27,000. They are predominantly trappers, gatherers of wild foods, and cultivators (the plantain is their main crop), but they also hunt and fish. Nyanga chiefs, however, are traditionally prohibited from hunting and trapping. The people of Nyanga observe two forms of wedlock: that between husband and wife, and ritual union in which a woman marries a spirit. In the latter observance the woman dwells apart from her spiritual husband and may have a human lover.

The action of the Mwindo epic takes place in the distant past and is centered in the village of Tubondo in the Ihimbi forest. According to the Nyanga, the universe is divided into four spheres: butu, or "sky"; mwanya, or "atmosphere"; oto, or "earth"; and kwirunga, or "underworld." All are settings for the text.

The hero is called Mwindo, a traditional Nyanga name for a male child who is born after a series of girls. Other important characters are Mwindo's father, Shemwindo, who is the chief of Tubondo, and Shemwindo's sister, Iyangura, who is Mwindo's paternal aunt and the ritual wife of the mythical water serpent Mukiti. Iyangura, whose marriage to Mukiti is not included in the following abridged version of the epic, lives apart from her spouse and wields great power; she is one of Mwindo's principal helpmates.

The narrative begins before the hero's birth, when Shemwindo declares that any of his seven wives who bears him a son shall be killed along with the infant. Thus when Mwindo appears, the midwives are reluctant to reveal his sex; but it is betrayed by a cricket, who in Nyanga legend often divulges secrets and brings ill fortune. Shemwindo unsuccessfully tries to kill his son, but the infant, who can speak and walk at birth and whose most frequent epithet is "Little-one-just-born-he-walked," outwits him. In a last desperate attempt to kill the hero, Shemwindo throws him into a pool, which is part of Mukiti's realm. Mwindo survives and begins a long aquatic journey in search of his aunt Iyangura. His watery road is blocked by crabs and fish, all of whom are Mukiti's allies or enemies. Along the way the hero encounters the water serpent deity Musoka, sister of Mukiti.

After finding Musoka, who is hostile, but never actually in direct conflict with him, Mwindo returns to Tubondo. With the intervention of Nkuba, the divinity of lightning, Mwindo kills all its inhabitants except his father, who escapes; Mwindo then goes in search of him. He begins a lengthy subterranean journey, which he makes alone because everyone else is accustomed only to earthly foods. Entering the underworld through the kikota-fern root, Mwindo travels to the enemy territory of Muisa, a Nyanga god who lives in a desolate underground region where there is no fire. In this bleak land Mwindo encounters Kahindo, Muisa's daughter; Ntumba, the aardvark; and Sheburungu, the supreme deity of fire. He eventually locates his father, who accompanies him on a subterranean journey back to Tubondo, their original starting place.

Finding the village totally destroyed, the hero revives all its inhabitants. A statewide conclave and enthronement rite follow, and Shemwindo acknowledges his errors. Ihimbi is split into two chiefdoms: one ruled by Mwindo, the other by Shemwindo. The final episodes tell of a dragon hunt and a celestial journey. Mwindo overcomes the dreaded dragon Kirimu and is then tested by Nkutu, who takes him on a terrifying journey through extreme heat and cold. During the experience Mwindo become a passive sufferer. He undergoes a catharsis and returns to Tubondo a wiser, better, and more benevolent ruler.

The words in brackets are in the Nyanga text, but add awkwardness to the translation; those in parentheses have been included to help clarify the meaning of the original. The epic was conceived as oral history, and it should be read aloud to gain an appreciation of its original power and beauty.

Long ago there was in a place a chief called Shemwindo. That chief built a village called Tubondo, in the state of Ihimbi. Shemwindo was born with a sister called Iyangura. And in that village of Shemwindo there were seven meeting places of his people. After Shemwindo had married those [his] seven wives, he summoned together all his people. Shemwindo sat down in the middle of them; he made an appeal, saying: "You my wives, the one who will bear a male child among you my seven wives, I will kill him/her; all of you must each time give birth to girls only." Having made this interdiction, he threw himself hurriedly into the houses of the wives, then launched the sperm where his wives were. After a fixed number of days, those [his] seven wives carried pregnancies.

When (many) days had passed, six of his wives pulled through; they gave birth merely to female children. When the preferred-one realized that her companions had already given birth, and that she remained with (her) pregnancy, she kept on complaining: "How terrible this is! It is only I who am persecuted by this pregnancy. What then shall I do?" Where the child was dwelling in the womb of its mother, it meditated to itself in the womb, saying that it could not come out from the underpart of the body of its mother, so that they might not make fun of it saying that it was the child of a woman; neither did it want to come out from the mouth of its mother, so that they might not make fun of it saying that it had been vomited like a bat. When the pregnancy had already begun to be bitter, old midwives, wives of the counselors, arrived there; they arrived there when the preferred-one was already being troubled with (the pains of the) pregnancy. Where the child was dwelling in the womb, it climbed up in the belly, it descended the limb, and it went (and) came out through the medius. The old midwives, seeing

him wailing on the ground, were astonished, they pointed at him asking: "What (kind of) child (is it)?" Some among the old midwives answered: "It's a male child." Where the counselors were sitting together with Shemwindo, they shouted, asking: "What child is born there?" The old midwives who were sitting in the house kept silent. After the birth of the child, the midwives gave him the name Mwindo, because he was the (first) male child who followed only female children in [their] order of birth.

In that house where the child had been born (that day), there was a cricket on the wall. The cricket left the house and went to say to Shemwindo: "You, chief, a male child was born there (from where I came); his name is Mwindo; that is why those who are in that hut there have not answered you." When Shemwindo heard that his preferred-one had given birth to a boy, he took up his spear; he went with it where the child had been born. The moment he prepared to throw it into the birth hut, the child shouted from where it was; it said: "May this spear end up (each time it is being thrown) at the bottom of the house pole; may it never end up where these old midwives are seated here; may it neither arrive at the place where my mother is." Shemwindo threw the spear into the house six times, each time reaching nothing but [at] the pole. When Shemwindo had become exhausted from running back and forth with his spear and had completely failed to kill Mwindo, he spoke to his counselors, saying that they should dig a grave in order to throw Mwindo into it, because he did not want to see a male child. When (the grave) was finished, they went to fetch the child Mwindo; they went to bury him in the grave. Mwindo howled within the grave, saying: "Oh, my father, this is (the death) that you will die, (but) first you will suffer many sorrows." Lo! at his birth, Mwindo was born with a conga-scepter, holding it in his right hand. He was also born with an adze, holding it in his left hand. He was also born with a little bag

of the spirit of Kahombo (female spirit of good fortune), wearing it slung across his back on the left side; in that little bag there was a long rope. Mwindo was born laughing and also speaking.

When the day had ended, those who were sitting outdoors, seeing that where Mwindo had been thrown away [earlier in the day] there was light as though the sun were shining there, went to tell the men (about it) and the (latter) also arrived (there); they saw the place; they could not (bear to) stay a moment "which is long as what?" because the great heat, which was like fire, burned them. When all the people were already asleep, Mwindo got out of the grave; he went to sneak into the house of his mother. As Mwindo was wailing in the house of his mother, Shemwindo began to hear the way in which the child was wailing, he was very much astonished, saying: "This time what was never seen is seen; again a child cries in that house. Has my wife just given birth to another child?" Shemwindo went into the house of his wife, slithering like a snake, without letting his steps be noisy. He questioned his wife, saying: "Where does this child come from again?" His wife replied to him: "This is Mwindo inside here." Where Mwindo was sitting on the ground, he kept silent. Shemwindo, witnessing this marvelous event, left the house without having retorted another word. He went to wake up the counselors. He told them: "What is there (behind me), is what is there; it is astounding." He told them also: "Tomorrow, when the sky will have become day, then you will go to cut a piece from the trunk of a tree; you will carve in it a husk for a drum; you will then put the hide of a *mukaka*-antelope in the river to soften."

When the sky had become day, the people assembled together to see Mwindo in the house of his mother. Mwindo was devoured by the many longing eyes. After they had looked at him, the counselors went to the forest to cut a piece of wood for the husk of the drum. They returned with it to the village. They carved the wood; they hollowed it out so that it became a husk. When the husk was finished, they went again to fetch Mwindo; they carried him; they stuck him into the husk of the drum. Mwindo said: "This time, my father has no mercy; what! a small baby is willingly mal-treated!" The Banashemwindo (follow-ers of Shemwindo) went to get the hide for the drum; they glued it on top of the drum; they covered it (the drum) with it. When Shemwindo had seen how his son had been laid in the drum, he declared to all his people that he wanted two expert divers, swimmers, to go [the next day] and throw this drum into the pool where nothing moves. The swimmers with the drum entered the pool, swimming in the river. When they arrived in the middle of the pool, they asked in a loud voice: "Shall we drop him here?" All those who were sitting on the edge of the river an-swered "Yes," all saying together: "It is there, so that you will not be the cause of his return." That day, when Mwindo was thrown away, earth and heaven joined to-gether because of the heavy rain; it rained for seven days; hailing left the earth no more; that rain brought much famine to Tubondo.

Where the drum was in the water on the sand, it arose all alone to the surface of the water. From Tubondo, from the village where the people dwelt, came a row of maidens; they went to draw water from the river at the wading place. Ar-riving at the river, they saw the drum on the surface of the water, which was turn-ing around there; they said inquiringly to one another: "Companions, we have dazzling apparitions; lo! the drum that was thrown with Mwindo—there it is!" While the maidens still had their at-tention fixed there toward the drum, Mwindo threw sweet words into his mouth; he sang:

I am saying farewell to Shemwindo!
I am saying farewell to Shemwindo!
I shall die, oh! Bira!
My little father threw me into the
    drum!
I shall die, Mwindo!

The counselors abandoned
    Shemwindo;
The counselors will become dried
    leaves. . . .
The counselors have failed (in their)
    counseling! . . .
The little-one is joining Iyangura,
The little-one is joining Iyangura,
Iyangura, the sister of Shemwindo.

When the girls heard the way in which Mwindo was singing in the drum, they climbed up to the village, running and rushing, in disarray. The men, seeing them appear at the outskirts running and rushing, took their spears and went, be-lieving that they were being chased by a wild beast. Seeing the spears, the maidens beseeched their fathers: "Hold it! We are going to bring the news to you of how the drum that you threw into the pool has stayed; it is singing: 'The coun-selors of Shemwindo, the counselors have failed in (their) counseling; the counselors will become dried leaves.'" When Shemwindo heard that, he assem-bled (again) all his people; everybody deserted (the village) for the river carry-ing spears, arrows, and fire (torches).

When Mwindo noticed them waiting in a group on the shore (of the river), he threw sweet words into (his) mouth; he sang:

I am saying farewell to Shemwindo;
I shall die, oh Bira! . . .
What will die and what will be safe
Are going to encounter Iyangura.

When Mwindo had finished singing like that, saying farewell to his father and to all the Banashemwindo, the drum sank into the pool; waves made rings at the surface.

Where Mwindo headed inside the water, he went upstream; he went to the river's source, at Kinkunduri's (crab found at river source), to begin it. When he arrived at Kinkunduri's, he lodged there; he said that he was joining Iyan-gura, his paternal aunt, there, whither she had gone; the news had been given him by Kahungu (hawk). He joined his aunt Iyangura downstream; he sang:

Mungai, get out of my way!

For Ikukuhi shall I go out of the
    way?
You are impotent against Mwindo,
Mwindo is the Little-one just-born-
    he-walked.
I am going to meet Iyangura.
For Kabusa, shall I go out of the
    way?
You are helpless against Mwindo,
For Mwindo is the Little-one-just-
    born-he-walked.
Canta, get out of my way!
Canta, you are impotent against
    Mwindo.
I am going to encounter Iyangura,
    my aunt.
For Mutaka shall I go out of the
    way?
You are helpless against Mwindo!
I am going to meet Iyangura, my
    aunt. . . .

Each time Mwindo arrived in a place where an aquatic animal was, he said that it should get out of the way for him. When Mwindo arrived at Cayo's, he spent the night there; in the morning he went right after awakening; he sang:

For Ntsuka shall I go out of the
    way?
You see that I am going to
    encounter Iyangura.
You see that you are powerless
    against Mwindo.
Mwindo is the Little-one-just-born-
    he-walked. . . .

Musoka, the junior sister of Mukiti, had gone to live upstream from Mukiti:

For Musoka shall I go out of the
    way?
You are powerless against Mwindo
Mwindo is the Little-one-just-born-
    he-has-walked.

When Musoka saw Mwindo arriving at her place, she sent an envoy to Mukiti to say that there was a person there who was in the act of joining Iyangura. Mukiti replied to that envoy that he should tell Musoka that that man should not pass beyond her place; "If not, why would I have placed her there?" That envoy ar-rived at Musoka's; he announced the news of how he had been spoken to by

Mukiti. Musoka kept on forbidding Mwindo like that, without knowing that he was a child of Mukiti's wife, Iyangura. Musoka replied to Mwindo, saying: "Mukiti refuses to let you pass; I here, Musoka, I am placing barriers here; you will not find a trail to pass on." Mwindo answered her, softening his voice: "I, Mwindo, never am I forbidden (to pass on) a trail; I will thrust through there where you are blocking." Mwindo left the water above (him); he dug inside the sand; and he went to appear in between Musoka and Mukiti. After Mwindo had passed Musoka, having broken through the dam of Musoka, he praised himself: "Here I am, the Little-one-just-born-he-walked; one never points a finger at me."

After Mwindo had passed Musoka, he began a journey to go to Mukiti's; he sang:

> In Mukiti's, in Mariba's dwelling place!
> For Mukiti shall I get out of my way?
> You see I am going to encounter Iyangura,
> Iyangura, sister of Shemwindo.
> Mukiti, you are powerless against Mwindo.
> Mwindo is the Little-one-just-born-he-walked.

When Mukiti in his dwelling place heard (this), he moved, asking who had just mentioned his wife. He shook heaven and earth; the whole pool moved. Mwindo on his side said: "This time we shall (get to) know each other today, we with Mukiti." Mwindo pulled himself together; he went to appear at the knot where Mukiti was coiled up. When Mukiti saw him, he said: "This time it is not the one (whom I expected to see); he surpasses (expectation)!" He asked: "Who are you?" Mwindo referred to himself saying that he was Mwindo, the Little-one-just-born-he-walked, child of Iyangura. Mukiti said to Mwindo: "How then?" Mwindo answered him saying that he was going to encounter his paternal aunt Iyangura. Hearing that, Mu-

kiti said to Mwindo: "You are lying; here never anybody passes, who would have crossed over these logs and dried leaves. While Mukiti and Mwindo were still talking to each other like that, maidens went from Iyangura's place to draw water; at Mukiti's place, there it was that the water hole was. As soon as the maidens witnessed the way in which Mwindo constantly mentioned Iyangura saying (she was his) aunt, they ran to Iyangura; (and) said: "Over there, where your husband Mukiti is, there is a little man saying that Mukiti should release him, that he is Mwindo, that he is going to encounter Iyangura, his paternal aunt." When Iyangura heard that news, she said: "Lo! that is my child, let me first go to where he is." Iyangura climbed up the slope; she went to appear at the water hole. As soon as Mwindo in his drum saw his paternal aunt coming to see him, he sang:

> I am suffering much, Mwindo.
> I will die, Mwindo.

He went on singing looking in the direction from which his aunt was coming.

> Aunt Iyangura,
> Mukiti has forbidden me the road.
> I am going to meet Aunt Iyangura,
> I am going to encounter Iyangura,
> Sister of Shemwindo.
> For Mukiti shall I go out of the way? . . .

Aunt Iyangura howled, then she said: "If the sororal nephew of the Banamitandi is in this drum, let it arrive here so that I can see it before me." When the aunt cited the Banamitandi in this way, the

drum refused to move in the direction of Iyangura. His aunt said anew: "If you really are the nephew of the Baniyana, come here before me." When Mwindo heard that, he went singing, in [his] leaving the pool:

> I am going to my Aunt Iyangura,
> Iyangura, sister of Shemwindo.
> Kabarebare and Ntabare-mountain,
> Where the husband of my senior sister sets *byroo*-traps.
> And a girl who is nice is a lady,
> And a nice young man is a *kakoma*-pole (pillar of society). . . .

His aunt seized the drum; her people gave her a knife; she slashed the drum; removing the hide, she saw the multiple rays of the rising sun and the moon. That is the beauty of the child Mwindo. Mwindo got out of the drum, still holding his *conga*-scepter and his axe, together with his little bag in which the rope was. When Kahungu saw Mwindo meeting with his aunt, he went to bring the news to the *mutambo*-elder who had been given to Iyangura to keep watch over her continually. Hearing (the) news, Kasiyembe (guardian of Iyangura) said: "[You] envoy, you go! When you will have arrived at Mwindo's, tell him he should not even try to pass this side; (otherwise) I shall tear out his spinal column; I here am setting up traps, pits and pointed sticks and razors in the ground, so that I shall know where he will step." Seeing that, Katee (the hedgehog) went to appear where Mwindo was (and) told him: "I am going to have a road go by, so that it emerges from the place where you are, and I want to make it come out inside the house of your aunt, at the base of the house pole." Mwindo told his aunt Iyangura: "You, Aunt, you be already on your way home; I shall meet you there; and that Kasiyembe threatening me over there, I shall first meet up with him; if he really has force, I shall deal with him (today)." He also said to his aunt: "Tell him, the one who is threatening me there, that he should prepare himself." Master Spider also emerged from within the pits, (he was) building bridges; he made them come out above the pits; the pits became merely bridges; he said to himself that it was there that Mwindo was going to play. "As far as I, Master Spider, am concerned, Mwindo cannot completely perish, since we are there." Mwindo took the road (made by) Katee; he came out in the house of his aunt. When Kasiyembe saw him, he said: "Mwindo is already over here; now, from where has he emerged?"

When Iyangura saw Mwindo she said to him: "My son, don't eat food yet; come first to this side, so that we may dance (to the rhythm of) the drum." He told his aunt that there he was, that he was going to dance without having eaten food, that he was going to faint with this drum. She replied: "What shall I do then, since the one whom I was given to take care of me is saying you must dance?" Mwindo said: "Oh! Right you are; let me first dance; hunger never kills a man." Mwindo sang; he howled. Mwindo went round about in the middle of the pits; he marched bent over the pits, without even being injured by the razors; he passed and passed everywhere where Kasiyembe had placed traps for him, without injuring himself. He danced; he agitated his *conga*-scepter to and fro, singing:

It is Katee who is crackling of
dried leaves . . .

Iyangura told her son to eat some food. Iyangura gave her son a bovine as a token of hospitality; he/she felled it. After Mwindo had eaten the hospitality gift of the bovine, which his aunt had offered to him, together with the maidens, Kasiyembe, the man of hatred, persisted in trying to kill him, saying: "Is this the boy against whom I shall be impotent?" Kasiyembe implored Nkuba, the lightning-hurler, saying: "You, Nkuba, you will have to come down; may you cut Mwindo into two pieces, in the house here where he is together with all these maidens who are with him here." When Mwindo heard the way in which Kasiyembe threatened

him, over and over again, he told the maidens sitting with him in the house to sit down on one side with him. Then Mwindo said threateningly to Master Nkuba: "You, Nkuba, since you come down, you must come down on one side of the house; don't come down on the side where Mwindo is." Master Nkuba, on hearing the voice of Kasiyembe, descended onto the house where Mwindo was; Mwindo pointed him out, saying: "You too will die the same (death); you are climbing on a hard tree." Master Nkuba came down seven times; he did not come close to the place where he (Mwindo) was; the fire burned on one side; that side became merely ashes.

Mwindo came out of the house together with the maidens; he presented himself (before) the crowd of people; he declared about himself that there he was, the Little-one-just-born-he-walked. He said to his aunt to come close to where he was so that he could speak to her. He told his aunt that within the twinkling of an eye, the mop of hair of Kasiyembe would already be burning. Where Kasiyembe was, (people) were all of a sudden struck (by the fact that) in the mop of hair of Kasiyembe the fire was already flaring up; the tongues (of flame) rose into the air; all the lice and all the vermin that were nestled on his head, all were entirely consumed. The people of Kasiyembe thought about fetching water in the jars in order to extinguish the fire on the head of Kasiyembe. When they arrived at the jars, in arriving there, there was no water left. They went straight to the herbaceous stalks of the plantains; they were (already) dried up. They said: "What then! Spit some saliva on (his) head!" Saliva was lacking among all the people. When they experienced this, they said: "This Kasiyembe is about to die. Go and look for help for him at his Master's; it is at Mukiti's that there is a pool." Arriving there, they found Mukiti with butterflies and flies flitting about him; for him, too, the water had dried up. When his aunt saw that, she went to beg before her son:

"Widen your heart, you my son. Set your heart down; undo my husband together with his *mutambo*-elder, this one Kasiyembe; heal them without harboring further resentment against them." Mwindo woke up Kasiyembe, waving his *conga*-scepter above him; he sang:

He who went to sleep wakes up.
You are impotent against Mwindo,
Mwindo is the Little-one-just-born-he-walked.

"Wake up thanks to my *conga* here of *nderema*-fibers."

Suddenly, Kasiyembe was saved. And the jars, water returned again in them; and the herbaceous stalks of all the plantains, in them again was water; and there where Mukiti was, the water came back again for him; the river was full again. When they saw that feat, they were much astonished, saying: "Lo! Mwindo, he too, is a great man." Kasiyembe gave Mwindo a salute, saying: "Hail! hail! oh! Mwindo." And Mwindo answered, "Yes." Mwindo said to his aunt that tomorrow he would be going to Tubondo to fight with his father. The aunt told him: "Oh! my father, you will be impotent at your father's, in Tubondo; you, (just) yesterday's child, born just a while ago, is it you who will be capable of Tubondo, village with seven meeting places? Iyanguara! I had you taken out from within the drum; as far as I am concerned, I say 'No,' strongly; never again try to go alone; the lonely path is never nice." When Mwindo heard the way in which his aunt was speaking, he refused. The aunt told him: "Do not go to fight with your father; if you go, then I also shall go with you to see how your father will be cutting you into pieces." She went to tell the maidens to pack up her household objects, so as to go with Mwindo, because the lonely path is not nice; it never fails to find something that could kill a man. Mwindo went together with his aunt, together with his servants who were chanting the refrain. Mwindo sang:

I am going over there to Tubondo;
I shall fight over there in Tubondo,

Even though Tubondo has seven
  entries.
We are saying, oh Bira!
Aunt, give me advice
To fight with the people down-
  stream;
They carry spears and shields. . . .

During this journey that Mwindo was making, evening went to find him at his maternal uncles, the Baniyana. He slept there after they had killed a goat of hospitality for him. After he had eaten that goat, Mwindo said to his maternal uncles: "I am going to fight Shemwindo in Tubondo; forge me, you [who are] blacksmiths of large light spears, you my uncles. They dressed him in shoes made entirely of iron and pants of iron; they also forged him an iron shirt and a hat of iron. They told him: "Since you are going to fight your father, may the spears that they will unceasingly hurl at you go striking on this iron (covering) that is on (your) body." After the uncles had finished forging him, they said they would be going with him. In the morning, Mwindo began the journey together with his uncles and his aunt Iyangura, and the servants of his aunt. Mwindo went singing; he howled.

When they arrived in the glen, he said: "Let us spend the night in this village." His aunt howled, she said: "Where will we sleep, here there is no house? Lo! Kiruka-nyambura has arrived, bearer of rain that never ceases." Mwindo looked around, he said that he wanted (to have) houses: (and) the houses built themselves. His aunt shouted saying: "Yes, my father Mwindo, hail for (these) [our]

houses. Lo! Shemwindo has brought forth a hero." When they were there in the glen, Mwindo's aunt said to him: "Oh! my father Mwindo, let us get away; you are powerless against this mass of people who are in Tubondo." Mwindo said that first he would try. Iyangura said to him: "Oh! my father Mwindo, what shall we eat then?" He lifted his eyes to the sky; he said to himself that he first wanted to have all the food that was over there in Tubondo come; so (the food) having joined him, he would go to fight with them. Mwindo sang while transporting the food that was with his father. Mwindo howled, he sang:

The pastes that are in Tubondo,
May the pastes join Mwindo,
Mwindo, the Little-one-just-born-
  he-walked.
The animals that are in Tubondo,
May the animals join Mwindo.
The meats that Shemwindo stores,
May the meats join Mwindo Mboru,
Mwindo, the Little-one-just-born-
  he-walked.
The wood that Shemwindo keeps,
Oh, father, may it join Mwindo
  Mboru,
For Mwindo is the Little-one-just-
  born-he walked.
And the fire that Shemwindo
  possesses,
May the fire also join Mwindo.
And the water that Shemwindo
  possesses,
May the water also join Mwindo
  Mboru.
The jars that are at Shemwindo's
May the jars join Mwindo,
Mwindo, the Little-one-just-born-
  he-walked.
The clothes that are at Shemwindo's,
May the clothes join Mwindo,
Mwindo is going to fight!
The wooden dishes that are in
  Tubondo,
May the wooden dishes also join
  Mwindo,
Oh father! the Little-one-just-born-
  he-has-walked

Hopes to be victorious.
The beds that Shemwindo possesses,
May the beds join Mwindo.
And the wicker plates that
  Shemwindo possesses,
May the wicker plates also join
  Mwindo.
And the salt that Shemwindo
  possesses,
May the salt also join Mwindo,
The Little-one-just-born-he-walked.
It was in this way that Mwindo was
speaking!

And the chickens that Shemwindo
  possesses,
May the chickens also join
  Mwindo. . . .
That which-will-die and that which-
  will-be-saved,
May it join Iyangura here,
Iyangura, sister of Shemwindo.
The goats that are at Shemwindo's,
May the goats join Mwindo.
The cattle that are in Tubondo
May the cattle join Mwindo. . . .
The banana groves that are in
  Tubondo,
May the banana groves join
  Mwindo.
And the tobacco also that is at
  Shemwindo's,
May the tobacco also join
  Mwindo. . . .

Mwindo and his uncles and his aunt and the servants who had arrived with them, the singers and the drummers, when (the latter) opened their eyes—all the things that were in Tubondo at Shemwindo's (had) joined them there where they were. When Mwindo had seen that the things of his father had come to join him, he said that his father (now) remained over there merely as a destitute person. He said to his aunt that he wanted his uncles to go ahead and fight first, and that he, Mwindo, would remain with his aunt for a while here in the vale so that he might first see the way in which his uncles handled their force. They fought on land and in the air, but the people of Tubondo said: "You will not solve the case today."

After a while, Mwindo's uncles were completely wiped out; they died. One of Mwindo's uncles escaped in the middle of the war, being already seriously injured; he fled to Mwindo to report the news to him. Mwindo said to his aunt: "I shall go to find out first the reason why my uncles are all wiped out, and if Shemwindo does not come up face to face with me, then I am not Mwindo. You, aunt, remain with my axe here and my little bag in which there is a rope; and I, Mwindo, am leaving with my *conga* here." When Mwindo arrived in Tubondo, he said to the people of that village that he wanted to dance (to the rhythm of) a drum. The people of that village answered him: "You are helpless against our drums here, you (are a) little fool." The people of that village told him that there was no drum there. To that Mwindo said that the drums would be coming. Mwindo went on speaking in that way with the people of that village, his father being in his compound. Mwindo sang:

He is climbing up here in Tubondo,
He is going to fight with Shemwindo.
While he was singing, he went on enunciating (distinctly): "May what will die and what will be saved join Iyangura."
What will never die but will be saved,
May it, oh father, join Iyangura,
Iyangura, sister of Shemwindo. . . .
Mwindo shouted, saying:
Hatred is in the heart.
My friend, Nkuba, may you be victorious.
I shall fight here in Tubondo,
Even if Tubondo has seven entrances.

Here in Tubondo seven lightning flashes!
I shall fight here in Tubondo.
I want seven lightning flashes right now!
Mwindo reviewed (the causes of) his griefs;
The counselors retreated (before) Shemwindo. . . .
Mwindo raised his eyes into heaven (and) said:
My friend, Nkuba,
Here in Tubondo seven lightning flashes!
While Mwindo was looking up into the sky, he (also) stretched his *conga* toward there. From the sky at Nkuba's things came; there appeared seven lightning flashes; they descended on Tubondo in the village. Tubondo turned into dust, and the dust rose up; all who lived there turned into mere dust. Where Shemwindo was sitting in (his) compound, he exclaimed: "There is no time for lingering here." Where he fled, he went to arrive where there was a *kikoka*-plant. He tore it out; he entered at its root's base. After he had become victorious in Tubondo, Mwindo praised himself in the middle of the village; he said: "This time the one who climbs on me, the one who digs into me while fighting with me, will be wearing himself out in vain." Mwindo went down to where his aunt had remained in the glen. The aunt asked him: "Good news there from where you are coming?" Mwindo answered her that Tubondo was on fire. He also told them: "Now let's go up to Tubondo which is high up; let's get away from here in the glen." They climbed up to Tubondo; they arrived there. Mwindo said that he could not chase his father so long as he had not resuscitated his uncles. He woke them up beating them (with his) *conga* and singing:

He who went to sleep awakes,
My uncle, my mother, wake up.
I have been testing the Baniyana.
My uncle, my mother, forge me!
Shemwindo, you are powerless

against Mwindo,
Mwindo is the Little-one-just-born-he-walked. . . .
Where Shemwindo had fled, he went harming himself running into everything; he went to arrive at Musia's, the place where no one ever clusters around the fire. Mwindo said to his aunt: "You, my aunt, you stay here in the village of your birth, in Tubondo; here is the rope; remain with one end, holding it in your hand, whereas I shall follow my father where he fled to Muisa's; if (one day) you feel that this rope has become still, if it does not move anymore, then pay no more attention to where I have gone; lo! the fire has dwindled; I am dead then." After he had spoken like that, Master Sparrow alit where he was, he told him: "Come here for me to show you the path that your father took and where he entered at the base of the root of the *kikoka*-plant. Mwindo in [his] leaving said farewell to his aunt; he held one end of the rope and the aunt remained holding (the other) end of the rope. When he arrived at the *kikoka*-plant, where his father had entered, he too pulled out the *kikoka*-plant; he passed through; he went to appear at the well. Arriving there, he met Kahindo (female spirit of good fortune), daughter of Muisa. Kahindo embraced him, saying: "This is my welcome, Mwindo." Mwindo in reply said "Yes." She said to him: "Where are you going?" Mwindo answered her that he was going to Muisa's to look for his father. She told him again: "Stop first here where I am. Over there in Muisa's village one never goes through; is it you who will (succeed) in getting through there like that, with all (your) pride?" Kahindo said to Mwindo: "Now you are going to Muisa's. When you will have arrived there, having entered the meeting place, if you see a very big man and tall too, curled up in the ashes near the hearth, it is he who is Muisa; and if he greets you, if he says: 'Blessing (be) with you, my father,' you too will answer, 'Yes, my father'; and when he will have left you a stool, then you will refuse it; you will

tell him: 'No, my father; will the head of a man's father become a stool?' When he will have handed over to you a little gourd of banana beer for you to drink, you will refuse, answering: 'No, my father, even though a person is one's child, is that a reason why he should drink the urine of his father?' After Muisa will have recognized you in that way, he will say to you: 'Blessing, blessing, Mwindo'; and you will answer him: 'And to you blessing, blessing also, father.' When he will have given you paste to eat, you will answer him: 'Even though a person is one's child, is that a reason why he should eat the excrements of his father?' "

After Mwindo had heard Kahindo speaking these useful words to him, he went and climbed up to Muisa's. Muisa, seeing him, greeted him with "Blessing." Mwindo answered, "Yes, my father." Muisa recollected: "Let them give a chair to Mwindo to sit on it." Mwindo answered him: "Not at all, my father, even though a man is a guest, is that a reason for him to sit down on the head of his father?" Muisa also said that he had left a gourd of beer here: "Let me pour you a bit." Mwindo said: "No, my father, even though a man is a guest, is that a reason for him to drink the urine of his father?" Muisa said: "Blessing, blessing, my father." Muisa again said: "Let them prepare some paste for you, oh Mwindo!" Mwindo answered him: "No, my father, even though a man is a guest, is that a reason for him to eat the excrements of his father?" Hearing that, Muisa said to him: "Blessing, blessing, Mwindo. Go and take a rest in the house there of your sister Kahindo." Mwindo went inside. When she saw that Mwindo had entered into the house, she said to herself: "Lo!, Mwindo has hunger." She got up, she went to make some paste, "a little like that," of ashes. After she had stirred it, she brought it to Mwindo in her sacred hut. When Muisa saw Kahindo bringing (the paste) to Mwindo, he dashed quickly toward the house of his daughter; he said to

Mwindo: "Oh, my father Mwindo, tomorrow you will start cultivating a new banana grove for me; may you first cut leaves, then plant the banana trees, then fell the trees; may you then cut the newly grown weeds, then prune the banana trees, then prop them up, then bring ripe bananas. It's after you will have performed all those works that I shall know to give you your father." He also said to him: "When you leave for cultivating, I shall give you a man to observe the way in which you are performing."

When the sky had become daylight, in the morning, Mwindo equipped himself with his billhook; Mwindo went to cultivate. When they arrived in the forest, the man whom Muisa had picked out showed Mwindo a mountain with mango trees on it. Mwindo placed the billhooks on the ground; all by themselves, they laid out the fresh trails. Having finished the trail, they cut the grasses. Having cut the grasses, the banana trees planted themselves; the banana trees having planted themselves, Mwindo sent a bunch of axes down on them; the axes by themselves finished felling the trees. Finishing, he sent a bunch of billhooks down on it (the grove); those billhooks went across the banana grove cutting the newly grown weeds. The companion of Mwindo returned to Muisa. He brought Muisa the news, saying: "This time he there is not (merely) a cultivator; he is fast, a cultivator of marvelous things; he has not touched one iron tool; the iron tools themselves are cultivating—and felling trees and cutting weeds." Having given the news, he returned again where Mwindo was on the fresh banana field. Where Mwindo was, the billhooks having finished cutting their weeds, they now cut gaffs; the gaffs themselves propped up the banana trees. The gaffs having finished sustaining the trees, the banana stems were ripe. The companion ran to bring the news to Muisa. "It is not a man who is there; he has cultivated today; the banana trees already have stems and the bananas already (are)

ripe." Having thus been astonished, Muisa sent his *karemba*-belt of cowries over there; he said to it: "You, my *karemba*, you are going to Mwindo; when you will have seen him, you will have to bend him, then you will have to smash his mouth against the ground." *Karemba*, having heard the way in which it had been instructed by its master, went to the banana grove. When it saw Mwindo, it went to where he was; it fell upon him where he was; it made Mwindo scream; it crushed him; it planted his mouth against the ground. Having seen its master missing all means of getting out, Mwindo's *conga* recalled (its duty); it wagged itself above the head of Mwindo; Mwindo succeeded in sneezing; he raised his eyes upward; he opened his eyes; he raised them; he gazed about a little. After Mwindo had been wedged by Muisa's *karemba*, the rope became still, it did not move any more. Where his aunt had remained in Tubondo, where she had held one end of the rope, she threw herself down saying that lo! her son was dead. She uttered a cry, low and high, imploring the divinities, she said: "It is the one who will escape there who is (my) child." Where Mwindo was, when he lifted up (his) eyes, he sang:

Muisa slaughtered Mwindo,
I shall die, on Bira!
Muisa, you are helpless against
  Mwindo,
Against Mwindo, the Little-one-
  just-born-he-has-walked.

Mwindo, while singing, remembered his aunt: "You there in Tubondo, I had already felt that my rope did not move; but don't suffer from anxiety any more." Mwindo now sent his *conga* to Muisa in the village, saying: "You, my *conga*, when you will have arrived where Muisa is in the village, you will have to smash him with force; you must plant his mouth to the ground; his tongue must penetrate inside the earth; so long as I shall not be back, so long as I shall not have come there into the village, you should not have released him again." The *conga* went whirling around; when it arrived at

Muisa's meeting place, it smashed him; it planted his mouth to the ground; the tongue dug into the earth; breath found no way of coming out. Where Mwindo remained in the banana grove, he prepared a load of green bananas together with ripe bananas. He returned to the village. When he cast his eyes at the meeting place, he saw Muisa—foam had come out of his mouth and nostrils. Kahindo, Muisa's daughter, seeing Mwindo, hurried to the place where he was; she told him: "You are arriving, whereas my father here has already cooled off." Mwindo answered Kahindo that he had come here looking for his father: "Now give me my father here, so that I may go home with him." Kahindo answered him: "Begin first by healing my father, so that I know how to unveil your father. Mwindo sang while awakening Muisa. When Musia had awakened, he said: "You, Mwindo, lo! you also are a man." Muisa also said to Mwindo: "You, child, go as soon as you are awake to extract for me my honey which is in that tree there." Mwindo complained: "This time I am dead once more." When the sky had become day, Mwindo provided himself with his axe; he went ahead into the forest to extract the honey; he also took fire. When he arrived at the base of the tree, he climbed (up into) the tree; he went to arrive at the fascicle where the honey was; he called: "Is this the place?" They answered him: "There it is." Mwindo poked up the fire for it. He struck his axe at the tree.

Where Muisa remained in the village, he said: "Lo! this man will finally extract this honey!" Muisa sent his *karemba*-belt; it went and smashed Mwindo on the tree; it planted his mouth into the trunk of the tree; his breath could not get out; wine and excrements trickled down from him.

Where Mwindo (had) left his *conga* down on the ground, the *conga* realized that lo! its master was dead; it climbed up where he was; it went to beat and beat on the head of Mwindo. Mwindo sneezed; he lifted his eyes and a bit of

breath came out. Mwindo said: "Lo! while I was perched, lo! I was on the verge of death."

In climbing down (from the tree), he implored Nkuba (the lightning divinity), he gazed into the sky: "My friend Nkuba, I am suffering." When Nkuba heard the cry of his friend Mwindo, he came down onto the tree; he cleaved it into pieces. His friend Mwindo went down (but) he did not have a single wound. When he was down with the basket of honey, he went up to Muisa's with the honey. Where Mwindo and Muisa remained, Mwindo told him the truth bluntly. "Give me my father on the shot. Make him come out from where you have hidden him so that I may go with him. You (had) said that when I would have cultivated a field for you, when I would have extracted honey for you, you would then give me my father. I want you to take him out right now; don't let the saliva dry up without having taken him out." When Muisa heard how Mwindo was criticizing him, he twitched his eyes; he said: "This time, this boy makes my belly swell here in my own village."

Having seen that Muisa did not bring his father out, Mwindo beat Muisa on top of his head with his *conga*; Muisa tossed his hoofs up into the air; he stiffened like a *mukusa*-viper. Mwindo said: "Stay like that, you dog." Mwindo went in pursuit of his father, where he had gone to Ntumba's (Ntumba, the aardvark). Mwindo went on singing:

I am searching for Shemwindo
In the place where Shemwindo
    went.
Shemwindo fled into Ntumba's
    dwelling,
Into Muisa's dwelling.
I am searching for Ntumba's
    dwelling.
For Munundu's (Munundu, epithet
    for Ntumba), dwelling.
Ntumba, open for me.
Shemwindo has set a barrier inside
    Munundu's dwelling;
Shemwindo is in flight inside
    Ntumba's dwelling.

I am searching for my father
    Shemwindo
In Ntumba's, in Munundu's
    dwelling.
The sun sets down.
I am searching for Shemwindo;
Shemwindo is in flight inside
    Ntumba's dwelling,
Inside Munundu's.
My little father threw me into the
    drum.
Mwindo implored Nkuba, saying:
My friend Nkuba, may you be
    victorious.
Hatred is in the heart.
My little father, the dearest one,
I am searching for my father in
    Ntumba's dwelling,
In Munundu's. . . .

While Mwindo was still pacing around Ntumba's cave where his father was, and Ntumba from the inside (at first) paid no attention (to him), then Ntumba made a sign to Shemwindo, saying: "You be ready to go; the little male at the door here is strong, and you are witnessing the way in which he is threatening at the entrance of the cave." Shemwindo went to escape to Sheburungu's (creator god Ongo). Where Kahungu dwelt in the sky, he came down; he went to bring the news to Mwindo; he arrived saying: "You know, you Mwindo, that Ntumba has made your father escape; your father had fled to Sheburungu's." Mwindo continued to follow his father, going in search of him all wrapped up in hatred, he went to arrive at the entrance of

Sheburungu's village. He met little children there; they greeted him, saying: "Are you awake, oh Mwindo?" Mwindo answered them: "Yes." They told him: "You, Mwindo don't draw ahead of us; we are hungry; we ask you for food." Mwindo implored his aunt Iyangura to send him food (telling her) that the children of Sheburungu were hungry. Mwindo howled, he said:

Oh! father, where Iyangura
    remained,
Sister of Shemwindo,
I claim seven portions (of food).
You see where Mwindo passed,
I am suffering from hunger.
Aunt Iyangura,
I am claiming meat.

Having implored his aunt, saying that he wanted seven pastes with meat to join him in the place where he was with the children of Sheburungu, when Mwindo looked up, the pastes were already there, having come from his aunt Iyangura. After the food had arrived, Mwindo gave it to the youngsters. When the children had finished eating, Mwindo sent back the wicker plates, singing:

I send back the wicker and wooden
    plates.
Oh! Aunt Iyangura,
I send back the wicker and wooden
    plates.

He proceeded to climb up to Sheburungu's, and the youngsters followed him. He went up to Sheburungu's, singing:

Sheburungu, you,
I am looking for Shemwindo.
Shemwindo gave birth to a hero
In giving birth to the Little-one-
    just-born-he-walked.
Sheburungu,
I am looking for Shemwindo,
My little father, the dearest one.

Sheburungu shouted and said:

Oh Mwindo, let us play wiki (a
    gambling game) together!

And Mwindo shouted, he said:

Oh my father, give me Shemwindo!
My little father threw me into the
    drum;

My little father threw me into the
    river. . . .

After Mwindo had entreated Sheburungu, asking him to give him back his father, Sheburungu said to him: "I cannot give you your father; I am asking that we first play wiki together, so that I may deliver your father to you, so that you may go home with him." Mwindo answered him: "Spread them (the wiki) out on the ground; I will not flee from you; you know the dangers from which I have escaped." After Sheburungu had heard the way in which he was being answered by Mwindo, he went to fetch a mat; he spread it out on the ground; he also went to get the very old wiki-seeds of the isea-tree. Sheburungu wagered: "You, Mwindo, if you beat me, you will carry your father off (with you), and here (are) three bunches of butea-money; if you beat me, you will carry them off." Mwindo wagered three bunches of butea-money. After they had wagered things with each other in that way, Sheburungu was the first to take a handful of wiki-seeds; when he picked them up, with the first take-up, he won Mwindo's butea-money. Mwindo wagered everything and his aunt; Sheburungu again took the seeds; he won all the goods and the people and his aunt from Mwindo. Mwindo remained all alone with his conga, his partner. After Mwindo had been losing all his things and his people, he wagered his conga. When Sheburungu tried to take the seeds, he failed. Mwindo took the seeds; he won on eight; all that Sheburungu had wagered, Mwindo won it back. He won all the things of Sheburungu: people, goats, cattle. Mwindo piled up (things); Sheburungu remained all alone by himself.

Where Kantori and Kahungu remained, they arrived where Mwindo was; they warned him: "You, Mwindo, come quickly; your father wants to flee again." Mwindo abandoned the wiki-game; he headed very quickly to join his father in the banana grove of Sheburungu. Seeing his father, Mwindo inquired of him: "Oh my father, is it

you here?" Shemwindo answered: "Here I am." Mwindo again inquired of his father: "Oh Shemwindo, is it really you?" Shemwindo again answered: "Here I am, you, my son." After Mwindo had seized his father like that, he returned with him; he climbed up with him to Sheburungu's. Mwindo said to Sheburungu: "You, Sheburungu, you have been hiding my father away." Mwindo said further to Sheburungu: "I don't want any of your things that I have won; now keep all your things that I have won; here I am going with my father." Mwindo gave his farewell to Sheburungu and to all his people: "Oh, my father Sheburungu, farewell!" Sheburungu answered: "Yes, you too, Mwindo, go and be strong, along with your father Shemwindo." Mwindo returned singing:

Listen, Ntumba Munundu,
He who went (away) comes back.

Mwindo shook the rope, he reminded his aunt; and where his aunt remained, she had bells attached to the rope. Mwindo sang:

He who went (away) comes back;
You see I am carrying Shemwindo.

Mwindo rushed headlong to Ntumba's cave. Mwindo said to Ntumba: "Why did you hide my father away? Here I am with my father." Mwindo sang:

Ntumba, you are powerless against
    Mwindo,
For Mwindo is the Little-one-just-
    born-he-has-walked.
I am on my way home from this
    point on in Ntumba's house.
Look, I am carrying Shemwindo,
My little father, the dearest-one,
Shemwindo, senior brother of
    Iyangura.
It is Shemwindo, the one who gave
    birth to a hero.
Aunt Iyangura, I am on my way
    back.
Mwindo is the Little-one-just-born-
    he-walked.
I am carrying my little father,
    Shemwindo. . . .

When Mwindo left Ntumba's, together with his father, he went singing, reminding his aunt in Tubondo:

> He who has gone away is back.
> Muisa!
> The sky has become day.
> The rooster cock-a-doodle-dooed,
> And the sparrow pointed him out.
> Mwindo will arrive in the house of
>   Muisa,
> In the house of Nyarire;
> I come from Ntumba's,
> From Munundu's.
> Muisa, you are helpless against
>   Mwindo,
> Since Mwindo is the Little-one-
>   just-born-he-has-walked.
> It is you who are wrong in
>   offending me in vain.
> Look! I am carrying Shemwindo.
> Muisa, you are helpless against
>   Mwindo,
> Since Mwindo is the Little-one-
>   just-born-he-walked.
> Look! I am carrying Shemwindo.
> I am returning to Tubondo,
> Where remained my aunt Iyangura,
> Iyangura, sister of Shemwindo,
> Aunt, birth-giver, Iyangura.
> I shall eat on the wicker and
>   wooden plates
> Only when I shall arrive in Tubondo.

When Mwindo left Ntumba's village with his father Shemwindo, he went headlong into Muisa's house. Kahindo came to Mwindo saying: "You see my father here, his bones fill a basket; what shall I do then? It is befitting that you heal my father; don't leave him like that; wake him up, because he is the chief of all the people." After Kahindo had spoken to Mwindo in that way, Mwindo woke up Muisa singing. While awakening Muisa, he kept on striking him all the time with his *conga*, telling him: "You have offended me in vain; you have tried to be equal to Mwindo, whereas Mwindo is the Little-one-just-born-he-walked, the little one who does not eat terrestrial foods; and the day he was born, he did not drink at the breasts of his mother." After Muisa had resuscitated, Mwindo told him that he had been forged by his uncles, the Baniyana.

"My body is covered with iron only; and you, Muisa, don't you see me?" Muisa asked Mwindo: "You, Mwindo, how were you born? Do you have a medicine that enables your going?" Mwindo unfolded for him the thread of the news of how he was born.

When Mwindo was already as Muisa's, he agitated the rope where his aunt remained in Tubondo; he reminded her. Iyangura said to Mwindo's uncles, the Baniyana, that in the place where Mwindo had gone, he had long ago finished seizing his father, that he was on his way home with him. While returning to Tubondo, Mwindo said farewell to Muisa; he sang:

> You, Muisa,
> You see me already going,
> You, Muisa, taker of others'
>   things.
> Where Aunt Iyangura remains
> In Tubondo,
> He who went away is back.

When Muisa saw Mwindo going, he said to him: "Oh, Mwindo, you my son, it's befitting that you marry my Kahindo here." Mwindo answered him: "I cannot marry here; I shall marry (later) in Tubondo of Shemwindo."

In leaving Muisa's village, Mwindo began the trip; he and his father went home. When Mwindo and Shemwindo arrived at the entrance of Tubondo, those who were in the village, Iyangura and the uncles of Mwindo, swarmed in the village like bees; they went to greet Mwindo and his father at the entrance. Iyangura and the uncles of Mwindo lifted him up into the air; they carried him on their fingertips. When they traversed the village of Tubondo, Mwindo told them to let him down. They put him down in the middle of the village place; they went to take a lot of spearheads, and it is on them that Mwindo sat down—they stood for the *utebe*-stool. Mwindo gave his aunt the news from where he had come and the way in which he had fought, searching for his father. Iyangura gave her son the order: "Since you have arrived with your

father, bring him first into the *iremeso*-hut to let him rest there." In giving hospitality to his father, Mwindo killed for him the goat that never defecates and never urinates; they cooked it, along with rice, for his father. He said to his father: "It is you who were wrong in vain; you made yourself awkward to Mwindo, the Little-one-just-born-he-walked, when you said that you did not want (any) boys, that you wanted girls; Lo! you did not know the strength of the blessing of Mwindo." After Mwindo had given food to his father, Iyangura said to him: "You, my son, shall we go on living always in this desolate village. I, Iyangura, I want you first to save all the people who lived here in this village; when they have resuscitated, it is then only that I shall know to ask our young man, Shemwindo, to tell me some of the news of the ways in which he acted, all the evil that he did against you." Mwindo listened to the order of his aunt to heal those who had died. His uncles, the Baniyana, beat the drum for him while he, Mwindo, was dancing because of the joys of seeing his father. They sang. Aunt shouted and said:

> My father, eternal savior of people.

Mwindo said:

> Oh, father, they tell me to save the
>   people;
> I say: "He who went to sleep
>   wakes up."
> Little Mwindo is the Little-one-
>   just-born-he-walked. . . .

While Mwindo was healing those who died in Tubondo, he continued on in the (following) way: when he arrived at the bone of a man, he beat it with his *conga*

so that the man would then wake up. The resuscitation was as follows:

each one who died in pregnancy resuscitated with her pregnancy;

each one who died in labor resuscitated being in labor;

each one who was preparing paste resuscitated stirring paste;

each one who died defecating resuscitated defecating;

each one who died setting up traps resuscitated trapping;

each one who died copulating resuscitated copulating;

each one who died forging resuscitated forging;

each one who died cultivating resuscitated cultivating;

each one who died while making pots and jars resuscitated shaping;

each one who died carving dishes resuscitated carving;

each one who died quarreling with a partner resuscitated quarreling.

Mwindo stayed in the village for three days resuscitating people; he was dead of weariness. The people and all the houses—each person resuscitated being straight up in his house. Tubondo filled itself again with the people and the goats, the dogs, the cattle, the poultry, the male and the female ewes, the teenage boys and girls, the children and the youngsters, the old males and females; in the middle of all those people (were) the nobles and the counselors and the Pygmies and all the royal initiators; all those also were straight up. All the descent groups that formerly dwelt in Tubondo resuscitated; again they became as they were before, each person who died having things of a certain quantity, resuscitated still having his things. Tubondo again became a big village with seven entrances. When the people were resuscitated, Iyangura began to speak in the middle of the crowd of people, saying: "You, Shemwindo, my brother, in the middle of the whole country of yours, have them prepare much beer and cows and goats; let all the people meet here in Tubondo. Shemwindo uttered a cry,

high and low, to all his people, saying that they should bring beer together.

After a week had passed, all groups within his state swarmed into Tubondo, together with beer and meats. All the people of all the villages of Shemwindo's state pressed together in the assembly. Mwindo dressed himself and became like the anus of a snail (very clean). His aunt Iyangura, she too threw on her clothes, those famous ones of Mukiti's. His father Shemwindo, he too dressed himself from top to bottom: *tuhuhuma*-bark cloths on which (were) red color and castor oil, *ndorera*-fringes, *masia*-hair ornaments. He too became something beautiful. Servants stretched mats out on the ground, there where Mwindo and his father and his aunt would pass. There was sacred silence. Those three radiant stars, Mwindo and his father and his aunt, appeared from inside the house. They marched solemnly. Those who were in the gathering of the assembly gave them the gift of their eyes: there where they appeared, that is where their attention was focused. Mwindo beseeched his friend Nkuba, asking him for three copper chairs. Nkuba made them come down. When they were close to the ground, they remained suspended in the air about five meters from the ground. Mwindo and his father and his aunt climbed up onto the chairs; Iyangura sat down in the middle of both, Shemwindo on the right side and Mwindo on the left side.

When all the men had finished grouping themselves together and had finished becoming silent, Mwindo stood up from his chair; he raised his eyes into the air, he implored Nkuba, saying: "Oh, my friend Nkuba, prevent the sky from falling!" Having spoken like that, he lowered his eyes toward the ground, down upon the mass of people; he lauded them, saying: "Be strong, you chiefs." They approved of it. Then he: "You seniors, be strong." They approved. Mwindo praised the council, holding all the things with which he was born: *conga*, axe, the little bag in which the

rope was; he also held an ancient stick to praise the council. Mwindo made a proclamation: "Among the seven groups that are here in Tubondo, may each group be seated together in a cluster; and the chiefs and the seniors of the other villages, may they also be seated in their (own) cluster." After he had finished speaking like that, the people grouped themselves in an orderly manner, each group in its own cluster. Mwindo also ordered that all his seven mothers be seated in one group but that Nyamwindo, the mother who gave birth to him, should separate herself somewhat from his little mothers. Mwindo also ordered: "Now you, my father, it is your turn. Explain to the chiefs the reason why you have had a grudge against me; if I have taken a portion larger than yours, if I have borne ill will against you because of your goods, if I have snatched them away from you, tell the chiefs the news so that they may understand." Where Shemwindo was sitting, he was flabbergasted: sweat arose from his big toe, climbed up to his testicles, went to arrive at the hair on his head; in his virile impetus Shemwindo got up. Because of the great shame in the eyes of Shemwindo, he did not even praise the chiefs anymore; he spoke while quivering, and a little spitting cough clung to the centipede of his throat, without warning: (all this) caused by the great evil of destruction.

Shemwindo said:

"All you chiefs who are here, I don't deny all the evil that I have done against this, my offspring, my son; indeed, I had passed an interdiction on my wives in the middle of the group of counselors and nobles, stating that I would kill the one among my wives who would give birth to a son, together with her child. After my beloved-one had given birth to a boy, I despised her; my preferred wife became my despised-one. From then on, I always looked at the soles of her feet. In the middle of all this anger, I armed myself with a spear; I threw it into the birth hut six times; I wanted to kill the child with its mother. When I saw that the child was not dead, I made an agreement with the counselors and the nobles; they threw this child away into a grave. When we woke up in the morning, we saw the child already wailing again in its mother's house. When I noticed that, I asked myself in my heart, I said: 'If I continue to fail to kill this child, then it will oust me from my royal chair.' It's only then that I carried him into the drum and that I threw him into the river. Where this child went, I believed that I was harming him, whereas I was only making him strong(er). From there it is that this child's anger stems. From that moment on, my son set out in search of me; he went to take me away in the abyss of evil in which I was involved; he went to seize me at the country's border. I was at that time withered like dried bananas. And it is like that that I arrive here in the village of Tubondo. So may the male progeny be saved, because it has let me see the way in which the sky becomes daylight and has (given me) the joy of witnessing again the warmth of the people and of all the things [of] here in Tubondo."

Iyangura spoke to the men who were sitting in the assembly, reproaching openly their young man here, Shemwindo:

"Here I am, aunt of Mwindo, you chiefs, in your presence. Our young man here, Shemwindo, has married me out to Mukiti. Thanks to my labor and to getting along with him, my husband placed me high up, so that he loved me above all the wives he had married. Suddenly, this child appeared where I lived; Mukiti was then on the verge of killing him because he did not know that he was my child; but his intelligence and his malice saved him. It is from then on that I followed him and followed him to point out to him the way to Shemwindo's. It's there that Mwindo's fights with his father began, because of the anger (caused by) all the evils that his father perpetrated against him. He subdued this village, Tubondo; his father fled. Mwindo went in search of him, saying that his father should not go to die in the leaves.

When he joined him, he seized him; it is that, that Mwindo has made his father return again to this village, Tubondo. So it is that we are in this meeting of the assembly of the chiefs."

After Iyangura had finished speaking, Mwindo also stood up; he praised the assembly, he said:

"As for me, I, Mwindo, man of many feats, the Little-one-just-born-he-walked, I am not holding a grudge against my father; may my father here not be frightened, believing that I am still angry with him; no, I am not angry with my father. What my father did against me and what I did against my father, all that is already over. Now let us examine what is to come, the evil and the good. Now, let us live in harmony in our country, let us care for our people well."

Shemwindo declared that as far as he was concerned, no longer was he chief, that now it was Mwindo who remained in his succession. When Mwindo heard his father's voice, he answered him: "You, father, just sit down on your royal chair; I cannot be chief as long as you are alive." Where the counselors and nobles were seated, they assented to Mwindo; they said to Shemwindo: "Your son did not speak wrongly; divide the country into two parts; let your son take a part and you a part, since, if you were to give away all authority, you would again be immensely jealous of him, and this jealousy could eventually trouble this country." Shemwindo said: "Since you, my counselors and my nobles, come to give this advice, so I am ready to divide the country into two parts: Mwindo a part and I, Shemwindo, a part, because of the fear (you inspire); but in my own name I had wanted to leave the country to Mwindo, and from then on I would always have been eating food after my son Mwindo, because I have felt and do feel much shame in the face of my son and of all the people."

After Shemwindo had spoken like that, he conferred the kingship upon his son: he stripped himself of all the things of kingship which he bore: a dress dyed

red and two red belts; he also gave him *butea watukushi* (string rings) to wear on his arms when he would pile up the *bsebse*-meat, and *butea* (to wear) on the legs; he also gave him a *ncambi*-belt; he also gave him a *kembo*-hat; he also gave him the hide of a white goat. Shemwindo dressed Mwindo (in) all those things while Mwindo was standing up, because a chief is always being dressed in (such) things while standing. The counselors went to fetch the chair imbued with *ukaru*-powder and castor oil; they gave it to Shemwindo; Shemwindo made Mwindo sit on it. Shemwindo handed over to Mwindo the scepter of copper on which there were lamels imbued with *ukaru*-powder and castor oil. He (Shemwindo) handed these things over to him when he was already seated on the chair. When he stood up, his father also handed over to him the wrist protector and the bow; he also gave him the quiver in which there were arrows. Shemwindo also handed Pygmies over to his son; he gave him the *bandirabitambo*-initiators: *mwamihesi* (chief blacksmith), *mushonga* (the cook), *mubei* (the barber), *mushumbiya* (the drummer), *muheri* (the sacrificer), *shemumbo*, counselors, nobles. They dressed him (in) all these things in the guesthouse. After Shemwindo had enthroned his son like that, Mwindo shouted that he now had become famous, that he would not want (to act) as his father had so that only one descent group would remain on earth. "May all the descent groups establish themselves in the country; may boys and girls be born; may there be born deaf and cripples, because a country is never without (some) handicapped-ones." After Shemwindo had dressed his son, he distributed beer and meat for the chiefs who were there; each group took a goat and a cow. They also gave Iyangura one cow for returning to her husband Mukiti. The chiefs and the counselors who were there said: "Let Mwindo remain here in Tubondo and let Shemwindo go to dwell on another mountain." Hearing this, Shemwindo clapped his hands; he was very satisfied. During Mwindo's enthronement, his uncles, the Baniyana, gave him a maiden, and Shamwami also gave him a maiden; Mwindo's father, he too, gave him a maiden called Katobororo and the Pygmies gave him one. After Mwindo had been enthroned, the assembly dispersed: all those who came from somewhere returned there; Shemwindo also took possession of his mountain; he left to his son Tubondo. When Iyangura, aunt of Mwindo, returned to her husband, she anointed Mwindo in the middle of the group saying:

Oh, Mwindo, hail!
Blessing, here, hail!
If your father throws you into the
    grave, hail!
Don't harbor resentment, hail!
May you stand up and make your
    first step, hail!
May you be safe, may you be
    blessed, hail!
And your father and your mother,
    hail!
May you bring forth tall children,
    boys and girls.
Be strong, my father; as for me,
    there is nothing ominous left,
    hail!

When Mwindo took leave of his father, his father also gave him a blessing. Mwindo handed over to his aunt two counselors to accompany her; he also gave her four goats and a return gift of twenty baskets of rice and five little chicken baskets.

While hunting, Mwindo's Pygmies are swallowed by Kirimu the dragon. A sole survivor, Nkurongo, brings Mwindo the news. Mwindo overcomes the Dragon with a song of defiance and with his conga-scepter. Mwindo's conga flies through the air to collect people to carry the monster back to the village. The Dragon is carried to the village, cut up, distributed (with the injunction that every part be eaten); many people are liberated from the monster's belly. Finally, the eyes are roasted and from each, as it bursts in a splatter, come a thousand people. Lightning, who without Mwindo's knowledge had made a blood pact, smells the roasting eyes and decides to put his ally Mwindo to the test.

Where Nkuba resided in the sky it so happened that he had made a blood pact with Dragon. When he inhaled the odor of his friend Dragon, which was passing with the wind, froth dropped from his nose; tears came out his eyes; he said: "What shall I do with this friend here, Mwindo?" He said that he first wanted to make him suffer in order that he would not begin again. Mwindo sang:

Nkuba has just come to take
    Mwindo;
Nkuba came to carry Mwindo away
From the heights of Tubondo,
When he inhaled the smell (of
    roasting).
Mwindo howled, he said:
Eh! Nkuba, you are helpless against
    Mwindo;
Shemwindo brought forth a hero.
Eh! Nkuba, you are helpless against
    Mwindo Mboru.

Mwindo said farewell (to the people), one by one.
Nkuba descended on the spot to take Mwindo. He arrived in Mwindo's village. Nkuba said to Mwindo: "I come to take you, you my friend, since you dared to kill Dragon, whereas Dragon was my friend; so know that you are doing wrong." Hearing this, Mwindo was not afraid of going away with his friend; but his people were stricken with anxiety, thinking that their chief was gone forever. Mwindo sang:

Let us go up to Bisherya [sky] over
    there,
For Nkuba has come to take
    Mwindo.
I am about to climb up to Bisherya
    over there,
For Nkuba has come to take
    Mwindo.

Oh, Nkuba, you are powerless
    against Mwindo,
For Mwindo is the Little-one-just
    born-he-has-walked.
Shemwindo gave birth to a hero;
My friends, you are powerless
    against Mwindo. . . .

Mwindo went on singing like that while Nkuba was climbing up slowly with him into the air, and the people of Mwindo had their attention diverted by (what was happening) above. Nkuba disappeared into the clouds, together with Mwindo; and they arrived at Nkuba's. Nkuba still said to Mwindo: "I have rescued you many times from many dangers, so then you show that you are equal to me." Mwindo arrived there at Nkuba's; he felt there much cold, and the icy wind there was strong. No house! They lived there in mere nomadism, no settling in one spot. Nkuba seized Mwindo; he climbed up with him to Rain. When Rain saw Mwindo, he told him: "You, Mwindo, never accept being criticized; the news about your toughness, your heroism, we surely have heard the news, but over here, there is no room for your heroism." Rain fell upon Mwindo seven and seven times more; he had Hail fall upon him, and he soaked him thoroughly. Mwindo said: "This time I am in trouble in every way." Nkuba lifted Mwindo up again; he had him ramble across Moon's domain. When Moon saw Mwindo, he pointed at him: "This time the news was given us that you were tough, but here in the sky there is no room for your pride." Moon burned Mwindo's hair; Mwindo complained: "Oh, father Shemwindo, bless me, and may my *conga* not get out of my hands." Nkuba lifted Mwindo up again; he went and climbed up with him to the domain of Sun. When Sun saw Mwindo, he harassed him hotly; Mwindo lacked all means (of defense) against Sun; his throat became dry; thirst strangulated him; he asked for water. They said to him: "No, there is never any water; now we advise you to grit your teeth; we advise you to put your heart on your knee." After Sun had made Mwindo sustain these pains, Nkuba lifted Mwindo up; he went and made him arrive in the domain of Star. When Star saw him, he pointed him out; he told him: "The news about you was given us that surely you are very tough; but here there is no room for your heroism." *Kubikubi*-star ordered Rain and Sun (to come). All—Nkuba, Rain, Sun, Star—all those told Mwindo but one single thing: "We have respect for you, just that much; otherwise, you would vanish right here. You, Mwindo, you are ordered to go back; never a day should you kill an animal of the forest or of the village or even an insect like a centipede or like a *ntsine*. If one day we would learn the news that you began again to kill a thing among those that we just forbade, then you will die, then your people would never see you again." They pulled his ears seven times and seven more, saying: "Understand?" And he: "Yes, I have understood." They also said to Mwindo: "It is Nkuba here who is your guardian; if you have done wrong, it is Nkuba who will give the news, and that day he will seize you all at once, without any longer saying farewell to your people.

After Nkuba had made Mwindo ramble everywhere through the sky, they gave him back (the right) of home, saying he was allowed to return. On his return, Mwindo had then finished spending one year in the sky, seeing all the good and all the bad things that are in the sky. Nkuba raised Mwindo up; he returned with him to Tubondo. Mwindo threw sweet words into his mouth; he sang:

Mwindo was already arriving
Where Shemwindo had remained;
Where Shemwindo had remained
Mwindo was already arriving
He who went away returns.
Shemwindo brought forth a hero.
What will die and what will be safe,
Oh my senior sister, may it join
  Mwindo!
My friend Nkuba, be victorious.
Let me go to Tubondo,
To Tubondo, village of my
  mothers.
May I see my mother.
I descend here in Tubondo,
In father's village, my dearest one.
And if, Mwindo, you kill a game,
It is I who have a right to the tail,
In which (normally) father's elder
  brother has a right.

The will says: "Mwindo, if you kill an animal, then you die."

When Nkuba was returning with Mwindo, he went on slowly descending with him; and led him down in the very middle of the village place of Tubondo. When his father Shemwindo saw his son being brought back by Nkuba, he gave Nkuba a reward of a maiden who was dressed with a bracelet of copper of Nkuba; they also gave him the prescribed white fowl. It is there that originated the custom of rendering cult to Nkuba; from then on they always dedicated to him a maiden and her copper ring. After Nkuba had received (his) gift, he returned to his domain in the sky.

After Mwindo had taken rest, he assembled all his people. They arrived. He told them: "I, Mwindo, the Little-one-just-born-he-walked, performer of many wonderful things, I tell you the news from the place from where I have come in the sky. When I arrived in the sky, I met with Rain and Moon and Sun and Kubikubi-Star and Lightning. These five personages forbade me to kill the animals of the forest and of the village, and all the little animals of the forest, of the rivers, and of the village, saying that the day I would dare to touch a thing in order to kill it, that day (the fire) would

be extinguished; then Nkuba would come to take me without my saying farewell to my people, that then the return was lost forever." He also told them: "I have seen in the sky things unseen of which I could not divulge." When they had finished listening to Mwindo's words, those who were there dispersed. Shemwindo's and Nyamwindo's many hairs went, say as "high as that" as the long hairs of an *mpaca*-ghost; and in Tubondo the drums had not sounded anymore; the rooster had not crowed any more. On the day that Mwindo appeared there, his father's and his mother's long hairs were shaved, and the roosters crowed, and that day (all) the drums were being beaten all around.

When Mwindo was in his village, his fame grew and stretched widely. He passed laws to all his people, saying to them:

May you grow many foods and many crops.

May you live in good houses; may you moreover live in a beautiful village.

Don't quarrel with one another.

Don't pursue another's spouse.

Don't mock the invalid passing in the village.

And he who seduces another's wife will be killed!

Accept the chief; fear him; may he also fear you.

May you agree with one another, all together; no enmity in the land nor too much hate.

May you bring forth tall and short children; in so doing you will bring them forth for the chief.

After Mwindo had spoken like that, he went from then on to remain always in his village. He had much fame, and his father and his mother, and his wives and his people! His great fame went through his country; it spread into other countries, and other people from other countries came to pay allegiance to him.

Polychrome mask used by the Yaka people of the Congo (Kinshasa) during initiation rites

THE
BANTU
LEGACY

THE FIRST MIGRANTS

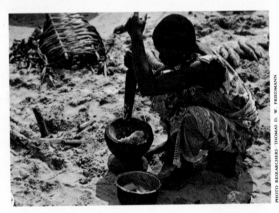

The 2900 mile-long Congo river was the principal highway of the Bantu migrations; its marshy, lakelike segment, known as the Stanley Pool, is pictured above. At left, in a village on the thickly forested Ituri tributary, a woman pounds cassava.

The ancestral homeland of the original Bantu was probably in the Benue valley, along the present-day Nigeria-Cameroon border. At an unknown date (perhaps at the dawn of our era or possibly earlier) groups of Bantu-speaking fishermen—probably only several hundred all told—took their few belongings and headed southward. The easily navigable rivers of the Congo drainage system afforded them quick passage through the rain forests of the Congo Basin, and they soon emerged in a lightly wooded area in what is now northern Katanga. This region would become the nucleus from which Bantu speakers would fan out in all directions.

Stool made by the Luba of the central Congo

PAUL AND RUTH TISHMAN COLLECTION, RAPHO-GUILLUMETTE—MARC AND EVELYNE BERNHEIM

High up in the forest-covered Kigezi mountain range on the Congo border of Uganda, girls perform a ritual dance.

Since the early seventeenth century, the Kuba, Bantu speakers of the Congo (Kinshasa), have been making wooden effigies of their rulers. The one at left portrays Bom Bosh, a great warrior king of the 1650's. Bope Mabinshe, a modern Kuba monarch, is shown opposite at his coronation in 1947. The epitome of Bantu kingship, he, like all Kuba kings, rules by divine right.

The Ituri forest is the home of some 32,000 Mbuti Pygmies, like those pictured at right after a successful hunt.

INTO
THE FOREST

From the forest fringes, waves of Bantu-speaking pioneers moved southward across the Zambezi and eastward to the coast, probably reaching Cape Delgado in the fourth century A.D. There they may have learned to cultivate the banana, Asian yam, and taro, which had been introduced into Africa from southeast Asia. These crops flourish in humid climates, and it is plausible that they were disseminated throughout the rain forests by those Bantu speakers who doubled back and settled in the Congo Basin. The migrants had probably learned to work iron before the Christian era. They were technologically and agriculturally superior to the Neolithic hunters and gatherers—notably the Pygmies—they encountered in their peregrinations, and thus could usually assimilate them without armed conflict.

Bantu-speaking forest dwellers have traditionally lived in small communities. Some forged cosmopolitan kingdoms, like Buganda in modern Uganda. The engraving above of Rubaga, capital of Buganda, was drawn by an eyewitness in 1875. The avenue leads to the royal palace.

STANLEY, *Through the Dark Continent*, 1878

In southern Rhodesia, near Fort Victoria, stands a group of ruins called Zimbabwe, from a local term denoting royal court. Zimbabwe served as the capital of several Bantu kingdoms, such as that of Monomotapa in the fifteenth century. This thirty-four-foot tower dominated the king's residence. Zimbabwe's earliest builders may or may not have been Bantu speakers, but the fine granite surfacing was probably added by them after A.D. 1000.

THE SOUTHWARD WAVE

Those Bantu speakers who gradually moved southward across the Zambezi valley developed enduring civilizations wherever they settled. By A.D. 1300 the southerly migrations had intensified, and peoples from the Bantu heartland (in the Luba kingdom of northern Katanga) had founded such states as Malawi. The Shona and the Thonga nations were developing in Rhodesia and southern Mozambique, and the Sotho and Nguni spread out all over what is now the Republic of South Africa. By this time Bantu speakers had also occupied southern Angola and southwest Africa, and in the eighteenth century the Tswana branch of the Sotho would migrate westward into what is now Botswana. These southern Bantu societies were pastoral—they probably learned cattle-raising techniques at an early date in East Africa. They would also absorb much from the cultures of southern Africa's indigenous inhabitants: the nomadic San hunters and gatherers, and the Hottentots, with whom they often intermarried.

Both the Hottentots and Bantu speakers of southern Africa are pastoralists who live in kraals, which, as shown in the 1822 print at top, are clusters of huts arranged around a cattle corral. The painting above decorates the mud-walled granary of a Rhodesian Bantu group. The warrior at left is a Bantu-speaking Zulu. His ancestors intermarried with the San.

Ekoi (Nigeria)

Lwalwa (Congo, Kinshasa)

Luba (Congo, Kinshasa)

In Africa, as in many areas where people are in close touch with the powers of nature, masks are endowed with supernatural properties and are much more than mere disguises. They conjure up magical forces and are often worn with a costume that covers the entire body. When the masquerader dons his attire, he is transformed into the being he represents, and holds his audience in thrall. The wearing of masks is intimately connected with the dance. They are intrinsic accouterments of funerary rites, where they create a link between the living and the dead; at initiations; and at numerous other festivities.

Kwele (Congo, Brazzaville)

Fang (Gabon)

Kuba (Congo, Kinshasa)

Fang (Gabon)

*Above, Nilotic Turkana girl
of Kenya in everyday clothes*
RAPHO-GUILLUMETTE—MARC AND EVELYNE BERNHEIM

*Right, Luo woman of north-
ern Kenya bedecked in bridewealth of beads, brass rings*
RAPHO-GUILLUMETTE—MARC AND EVELYNE BERNHEIM

*Young Masai warrior, with
characteristic forelock of hair*
ELIOT ELISOFON

*A farmwoman of Kenya
wearing Kikuyu adornments*
RAPHO-GUILLUMETTE—MARC AND EVELYNE BERNHEIM

CATTLE COMPLEX

When groups of Bantu speakers reached East Africa during the first millennium A.D., they found a diversity of peoples—the indigenous Hottentots and Bushmen as well as Nilotic and Cushitic speakers and Persian, Arab, and Indian settlers. Many of the predominantly agricultural Bantu speakers learned cattle-raising techniques from Nilotes and Cushites, and later passed these skills to the Bantu speakers of southern Africa. In some areas, such as the Great Lakes region, Bantu speech finally prevailed.

The Masai are a Nilotic people now living in Kenya and northern Tanzania. Most are nomadic pastoralists, wandering throughout the year, but some have become agriculturalists. They subsist on cereals, meat, milk products, and quantities of fresh blood, which they draw from the necks of their cattle with special arrows. Above, Masai men perform this ritual upon a calf. Below is a view of a Masai settlement in a Tanzanian part of the arid Rift Valley.

PHOTO RESEARCHERS · GEORGE HOLTON

Bamileke dancers of the central Cameroon highlands are pictured at left in the typical long-nosed, high-hatted, beaded masks of the region.

OVERLEAF: *A procession of girls and women from northern Cameroon winds around a man, as hand-clapping male spectators provide the rhythm.*
MICHEL HUET

THE ART OF THE DANCER

The dance, more than any other art form, reflects the ethos of African life. Like oral literature, dance modes have been handed down, with little change, from one generation to another. Styles differ widely from region to region, but throughout the continent dance is always a direct expression of life—its joys and freedoms, its fears and anxieties. Performers are usually masked and brilliantly costumed, but under this patina of unfettered excitement, ritual dancing is taken very seriously. For many African culture groups the masked dance is the means by which they bring the mysterious, magical forces of nature and the supernatural under control. Through movement, a village thanks its guardian spirits or prays for rain and the fecundity of the soil, a hunter asks for success or gives thanks for his kill, a girl woos her lover, or a group celebrates the circumcision of boys emerging from initiation. Leaping, stooping, scuffling, and stomping, the dancer moves to the throbbing of drums, bells, calabashes, chants, and other rhythm makers. At times he seems as free floating as a will-o'-the-wisp or as frenzied as a whirling dervish. Solo dances are rare, as are those involving couples. Generally, several dancers enter the arena together, single file, and they usually move in circular formation.

Costumed as a bird—with a swishing tail and a beak atop his head—a hunter (opposite) *from the village of Pia in northern Cameroon joyously springs into the dusty air. At right is a Luo dancer of Kenya in traditional plumed headgear.*

Os montes claros em affrica

Serra lioa.

Castello damina

Chapter Eight

THE COMING OF THE EUROPEANS

(c. 1440–1700)

by

A. Adu Boahen

AFRICA SOUTH OF THE SAHARA has been known to Europeans since Greco-Roman times, but it was not until the fourth decade of the fifteenth century that they began to arrive in numbers on its shores. The first to come were the Portuguese. They were followed in the 1450's by the Spaniards, who soon after abandoned Africa to explore the Americas; toward the end of the century some English and French adventurers and traders arrived. However, their governments were not to give official backing to such enterprises until the sixteenth and seventeenth centuries. The Dutch were the next to appear on the African scene, and during the last decade of the sixteenth century they effectively challenged the lead enjoyed by the Portuguese. The Danes dropped anchor in 1642, the Swedes in 1647, and the Brandenburgers in 1682.

The reasons for this sudden surge of interest were partly political, partly economic, partly technological. In the first place, no overseas activities could succeed without the patronage and direction of a strong nation-state enjoying stable and peaceful conditions at home, and no such nation-states emerged in Europe until after the end of the fourteenth century; and these continued to be wracked by foreign and civil wars for another hundred years or more.

Portugal was the first European state where conditions were favorable for overseas expansion. It had expelled the Moors in 1262, and a new dynasty, the house of Aviz, had emerged in 1385. The new ruling family drew its support mainly from the towns, and the first of its rulers, John and his wife Philippa, the daughter of John of Gaunt of England, raised a new aristocracy rooted "not in blood and landed estates, but in commercial enterprise." Therefore, unlike most of their contemporaries, the kings of Portugal could count on the support of the aristocracy in any over-

Portuguese map of 1502 depicts with considerable accuracy the shape of West Africa's coast.

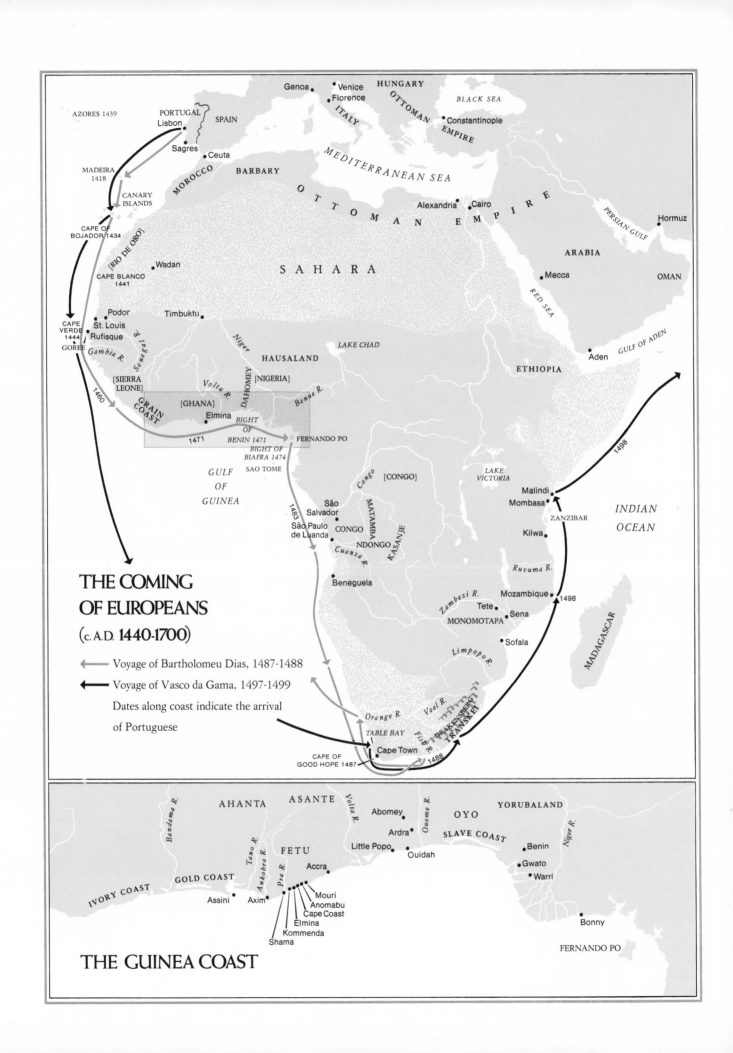

Genoa • • Venice HUNGARY
• Florence OTTOMAN
ITALY BLACK SEA
• Constantinople
EMPIRE

AZORES 1439   PORTUGAL   SPAIN
Lisbon

MEDITERRANEAN SEA

• Sagres   • Ceuta
MADEIRA   MOROCCO   BARBARY
1418   CANARY
ISLANDS
CAPE OF   Alexandria • • Cairo
BOJADOR 1434   O T T O M A N   E M P I R E   PERSIAN GULF
[RIO DE ORO]
• Wadan   • Hormuz
CAPE BLANCO   S A H A R A   ARABIA
1441
Podor   • Mecca   OMAN
St. Louis
CAPE   • Rufisque   • Timbuktu
VERDE   Senegal R.   RED SEA
1444   Gambia R.   Niger   LAKE CHAD   • Aden   GULF OF ADEN
GOREE   HAUSALAND
[SIERRA   ETHIOPIA
LEONE]   Volta R.   [NIGERIA]
1460   GRAIN   DAHOMEY
COAST   [GHANA]   Benue R.
Elmina   BIGHT
1471   OF   FERNANDO PO
BENIN 1471
BIGHT OF
GULF   BIAFRA 1474
OF   SAO TOME
GUINEA   LAKE
VICTORIA   INDIAN
Congo   [CONGO]   Malindi   OCEAN
São   Mombasa
Salvador   MATAMBA   ZANZIBAR
1483   São Paulo   CONGO   Kilwa
de Luanda   NDONGO   KASANJE
Cuanza R.   Ruvuma R.

Mozambique   1498
Zambezi R.   Tete
THE COMING   • Sena
OF EUROPEANS   Beneguela   MONOMOTAPA   MADAGASCAR
• Sofala
(c. A.D. 1440-1700)   Limpopo R.

⟵ Voyage of Bartholomeu Dias, 1487-1488
⟵ Voyage of Vasco da Gama, 1497-1499   Orange R.   Vaal R.   DRAKENSBERG
TRANSKEI
Dates along coast indicate the arrival   TABLE BAY   Fish R.
of Portuguese   CAPE OF   Cape Town   1488
GOOD HOPE 1487

Bandama R.   AHANTA   ASANTE   Volta R.   YORUBALAND
Abomey   OYO
Oueme R.
Ardra   SLAVE COAST
FETU   Little Popo   • Benin
Tano R.   Accra   Ouidah   Niger R.
GOLD COAST   Ankobra R.   • Gwato
IVORY COAST   Axim   Pra R.   Mouri   • Warri
Assini   Anomabu
Cape Coast
Elmina   • Bonny
Kommenda
Shama   FERNANDO PO

THE GUINEA COAST

seas activities. Furthermore, John had five sons, all of whom were anxious to win laurels on the battlefield. The third of them, Henry, later to be called the Navigator, was ready to provide patronage, inspiration, and direction for overseas exploration, especially after 1415, when the Portuguese conquered Ceuta, a Muslim stronghold on the Moroccan side of the Strait of Gibraltar.

It was during this campaign that Prince Henry is said to have had "a vision and a purpose to which he would remain faithful to his death." According to Gomez Eannes de Azurara, the chronicler of his activities, Henry's vision and purpose were to find out what lay beyond the Canary Islands and Cape Bojador, to capture the trans-Saharan trade, to investigate the extent of Muslim power, to convert people to Christianity, and to form an anti-Muslim alliance with any Christian ruler who might be found, especially with Prester John, the legendary ruler of a Christian kingdom thought to be located in the heart of Africa. With the financial and moral support of the Crown, Prince Henry provided the essential impetus to the commencement of overseas adventures, namely patronage, inspiration, and direction.

On his return from Ceuta, Henry settled at Sagres on the southwestern tip of Portugal. There he founded a school of navigation, gathering around him map makers, astronomers, sailors, and shipbuilders, and began the systematic exploration and study of the coast of Africa. Thenceforth, until the seventeenth century, the young and united kingdom of Portugal—under the rule of a new and energetic dynasty, free from attacks from its neighbors as well as from internal struggles, and full of crusading ardor—held the lead in overseas adventuring.

Besides these political conditions, there were also economic and technological reasons for the sudden interest of Europeans in western and southern Africa. Until the fifteenth century Europe did not have much difficulty in obtaining prized commodities from the Orient. Chinese and Persian silks, Indian cloth and emeralds, rubies from Burma, sapphires from Ceylon, and above all, spices, all came by sea, mostly in Venetian, Genoese, and Florentine ships. However, with the occupation of much of the Middle East by the Ottoman Turks in the fifteenth century, not only did the volume of trade decrease but prices of Oriental goods in Europe soared, owing to the prohibitive duties imposed on them. Therefore European consumers began to look for alternative supplies or alternative routes to the East. According to Azurara, Prince Henry was aware of the commercial possibilities of a sea route to the East, and the

Spanish Crown certainly had as one of its cardinal aims the discovery of an overseas route to India and beyond.

Equally strong was the pull exerted by gold. With the steady emergence of nation-states had come the growth of international banking, with many nations beginning to mint gold instead of silver coins. As Europe did not supply any goods to the East in exchange, Europe's reserves of the precious metal were diminishing faster than Hungary and the other continental suppliers could replenish them. It had long been known that the gold that was imported into Europe from Barbary originated in the regions south of the Sahara; but, however strong the economic motivation, Europeans could not have sailed to western and southern Africa until the fifteenth century for the simple reason that it was not technologically feasible.

The types of ships used in western Europe from Roman times until the fourteenth century were the oar-driven galley and the cog. While both were suitable for the calm seas of the Mediterranean, they were helpless in heavy seas and totally unsuitable for long ocean voyages. It was not until the first half of the fifteenth century that, borrowing from the superior technology of Arab sailors, the Portuguese and other western Europeans were able to devise ships capable of undertaking long-distance voyages. The caravel, which had both square sails and fore-and-aft-rigged triangular sails, was able to sail into the wind without the help of oars. This revolutionary development in ship design made possible the great voyages that characterized the fifteenth century.

Furthermore, it was in that same century that most of the problems of navigation were finally solved. By the fifteenth century an experienced navigator could find his latitude and had a good compass and charts to plot his course. It is not surprising that Portugal was the first to begin the systematic exploration of the coast of western and southern Africa, for it was technologically superior and politically more stable than any other European state.

The voyages, under the auspices of the Portuguese kings and Prince Henry the Navigator, began in 1417, and Portuguese explorers reached Madeira in 1418. Cape Bojador was rounded by Gil Eanes in 1434, and in 1441 Nuno Tristão and Antão Gonzalves reached Cape Blanco on the coast of present-day Mauritania; three years later Dinis Dias explored the mouth of the Senegal River and Cape Verde. The mouth of the Gambia River was reached in 1446, and the coast of Sierra Leone was explored in 1460, the year in which the prince died. After a break from 1462 to 1469, due mainly to the fact that King Affonso V of Portugal was engaged in

São Jorge da Mina—Saint George's Mine, as the Portuguese optimistically named their Gold Coast fort—was built in 1482 with labor and materials imported from home. As shown in this engraving, it was a sizable enterprise, housing a garrison of sixty Portuguese soldiers plus African reinforcements. A dozen or more ships, laden with gold and other riches, sailed from this harbor yearly, turning a handsome profit for their owners.
DE BRY, *Small Voyages,* 1604

a crusade against Morocco, the voyages were resumed. The coast of modern Ghana was reached in 1471, the Bights of Benin and Biafra between 1471 and 1474, and the mouth of the Congo in 1483; in December, 1487, Bartholomeu Dias rounded the Cape of Good Hope and sailed as far up the east coast as the Fish River in South Africa. After another pause of ten years an expedition under the command of Vasco da Gama retraced Dias' course, continuing onward along the East African coast as far as Malindi in modern-day Kenya, from which he set sail for India. Thus by the end of the fifteenth century the Portuguese had greatly expanded Europe's geographical knowledge of the world beyond its shores, though it is important to note that with the exception of the interior regions of Angola and Mozambique, this knowledge was to be confined to the coast of Africa until the second half of the eighteenth century.

It is quite evident from the accounts of the Portuguese explorers, particularly those of Alvise da Cadamosto, Pacheco Pereira, Ruy de Pina, and above all, Vasco da Gama, that they were astounded and elated by the complex, even sophisticated, character of the African civilizations they came across, by the extent of political development, and by the wealth and splendor of the courts. They particularly admired the city-states of the East African coast, where a lucrative trade with other Indian Ocean markets had long existed, and the gold and silver mines in the area of modern Ghana, Angola, and Mozambique.

Finally, accounts of the legendary Prester John and his

Christian utopia, as related by Vasco da Gama, must also have filled the hearts of the Church fathers with hope. To quote the explorer: "We were told . . . that Prester John . . . held many cities along the coast, and that the inhabitants of those cities were great merchants and owned big ships. . . . This information, and many other things which we heard, rendered us so happy that we cried with joy, and prayed to God to grant us health, so that we might behold what we so much desired."

Up until 1518, a date that marks the end of the first period of European contact with Africa, the Portuguese were the only Europeans effectively operating in Africa south of the Sahara. Politically, the Portuguese showed interest in colonization, though this interest was confined exclusively to the Atlantic islands off the coast of Africa— the Canaries, Madeira, the Azores, the Cape Verde Islands, São Tomé, and Fernando Po—where they established sugar plantations and vineyards.

On the continent of Africa itself, however, the Portuguese did not attempt any extensive settlement, partly for reasons of climate, but mainly because of the opposition of the Africans themselves. Instead, they erected a number of forts and posts to protect themselves against the African kingdoms as well as other European nations and to serve as collecting centers and depots.

The first and the most impressive of these forts was São Jorge, built in 1482 at Elmina on the coast of modern Ghana; on the same coast were erected during this period forts at

Axim, Shama, and Accra. In 1487, farther north of the Senegal River, the Portuguese established an inland post at the caravan center of Wadan to tap the gold trade across the Sahara; it was abandoned in 1513. They also erected a fort (later named Freetown) on the coast of modern Sierra Leone and another at Gwato, the port of Benin, but soon abandoned both, the latter in 1516.

The very limited nature of the Portuguese colonizing activities in West Africa makes the title "Lord of Guinea," which their king John II assumed in 1486, a particularly empty one. They did not at this time rule any Africans, but engaged in commerce with them. During this first period they also acted as proselytizers. In spite of what some historians say, there is absolutely no doubt that during this first period the Portuguese took the work of converting Africans to the Christian religion very seriously indeed and with the full support and blessing of the pope of the Catholic Church.

The effort began in earnest as soon as the first West African islands were explored; indeed, there were some Franciscan monks aboard the Portuguese ships that anchored at Madeira in 1420 and Cape Verde in 1446. In 1441, when the first shipload of black people was brought to Portugal under circumstances to be discussed below, Prince Henry, as grand master of the Order of Christ, had them baptized. He also selected the most talented man among them to be trained as a missionary, but the African died before repatriation. Again, when in 1458 Henry received reports of the favorable disposition of the rulers of the Wolof kingdom toward Christianity, he promptly dispatched the abbot of Soto de Casa; unfortunately, we do not know the outcome of this mission. By the time of Henry's death in 1460 Christianity had been firmly established on the Portuguese-held islands. Interest in evangelical work continued, and in 1462 Father Alphonsus Bolano was appointed as the missionary, or prefect apostolic, for the whole of Guinea.

Subsequently, when the Portuguese built their castle at Elmina, they also dedicated a church to Saint Anthony; according to the Portuguese chronicler João de Barros, some Africans were converted. It is also recorded that when King John II of Portugal received news of the *oba* of Benin's request for missionaries, he was quick to comply. Not only did the *oba* welcome them and grant permission for a church to be built in Benin but he also "gave his own son and some of his noblemen, the greatest in his kingdom—so that they might become Christians."

Even more spectacular and surprisingly successful were the early Portuguese missionary activities that began in 1484 or 1485, a year or more after the first visit of Diogo Cão. During Cão's second visit the king of the Congo (Kongo), Nzinga Nkuwu, accepted the Christian religion and sent some of his people to Portugal to be educated. He also asked King John for assistance, to which the Portuguese king responded in 1490 by sending three ships with a group of priests, masons, carpenters, and other skilled artisans. This mission was successful, and Nzinga Nkuwu, most of the members of the Congolese royal family, and some of the king's subordinate chiefs were baptized. Nzinga Mvemba, one of the royal family to embrace the religion, was baptized as Affonso and succeeded to the Congo throne in 1507. During his long reign, from 1507 to 1543, Affonso remained a sincere Christian and did initially receive assistance from the Portuguese in his effort to convert his kingdom into a Christian and modernized state. He learned to read and write Portuguese, and he gave every encouragement to the missionaries in their work. He himself supervised the building of a cathedral and other state churches in his capital at Mbanzakongo and saw to the building of schools and churches throughout the kingdom. In 1513 two members of Affonso's family, who were educated in Portugal, headed a Portuguese embassy to the pope. One of them had been baptized with the name of Dom Henrique and was later consecrated as bishop of Utica in Tunis. He returned to the Congo in 1521 as vicar apostolic, and with the assistance of several Congolese who had been ordained priests, he continued the evangelical work in progress. Dom Affonso also established a new court modeled on that of Lisbon, bestowing Portuguese titles of marquis, duke, count, et cetera, on his courtiers and ministers. It looked as if Christianity was taking firm root in the Congo, and that all was set for the conversion of the Congo into the first Christian and Westernized kingdom in western Africa.

Besides their colonizing and missionary activities, the Portuguese also paid a great deal of attention to commerce. And in this field, too, their achievements were not inconsiderable. Portuguese traders literally followed the explorers. The first commodity to be shipped was dried fish, which was obtained from the valuable fishing grounds between Cape Bojador and Rio de Oro, and along various parts of the Guinea coast. Sugar produced from cane grown on the Cape Verde Islands as well as on São Tomé and Fernando Po was the next export, and the output steadily increased throughout the fifteenth century. The traffic in pepper from what became known as the Grain Coast as well as from

Portuguese soldier bearing a match-lock, as portrayed by a Benin artist.

zalves and Tristão and brought to Portugal in 1441. At the time of Prince Henry's death in 1460, five hundred slaves were being exported annually to Portugal and its Atlantic island colonies. By 1500 the slave trade had increased to about six hundred seventy a year, according to Philip Curtin's recent figures. These slaves were obtained mainly from the Senegambia region, the Slave Coast, and the area of the Congo. It was not until 1518 that the first shipment of slaves was sent directly to the New World, an event that can be seen as opening the second phase of Afro-European contact.

At this juncture the Portuguese Crown took complete control of the lucrative commercial contacts that its subjects had developed, making it a capital offense for any Portuguese to go to Guinea without a license. In exchange for gold, fish, sugar, pepper, ivory, and slaves, agents of the king exported to states of western Africa horses, silk items of clothing (imported mainly from the Barbary states and Benin), brassware, beads, handkerchiefs, and wine.

One other accidental but very useful and very lasting by-product of the first phase of the European contact with West Africa was the introduction of a number of food plants from the Americas and the East Indies. From the former the Portuguese brought maize, tobacco, cassava, the sweet potato, the pineapple, and the tomato. From the Indies were introduced oranges, lemons, limes, rice, and sugar cane. The cultivation of these food items, especially maize, the tomato, and rice, spread rapidly throughout western Africa, and there is no doubt that these food crops greatly accelerated the population growth in the coastal regions.

What was the reaction of the Africans to the Europeans during this first phase of their confrontation? Naturally, the Africans found the new arrivals, with their white skin, long hair, and funny-looking ships, profoundly strange. In the beginning trade between the two took the form of dumb barter, or silent trade. However, after a period of fear and distrust, mutual confidence developed, and the Africans began to meet the European ships, and the Europeans to go ashore. It would appear that genuine trouble began only when the Portuguese asked for permission from the African kings to erect permanent fortified posts. João de Barros has left us a detailed account of the negotiations that took place in 1482 between Diego de Azambuja and the representative of the king of Fetu for permission to build a castle on the coast of modern Ghana. Azambuja and his men attended the palaver "smartly dressed but with hidden arms in case of need," while the *caramansa*, the king of Fetu's representative, who was also the chief of that coastal village,

Benin was also sought. Ivory was another prized commodity obtained along the West African coast—especially in Ghana, the region of Little Popo, and the area that was to become known as the Ivory Coast. Other minor exports were wax, hides, amber, and indigo.

By the end of the fifteenth century, however, gold and slaves had superseded all other exports. The first quantity of Ghana coast gold was brought to Portugal by Gonzalves in 1441, and subsequently, so much gold was found in the area that the Portuguese dubbed it the Gold Coast. (This name was later applied to the whole of the British colony, and it was not changed to Ghana until March, 1957, when that colony won its independence from Britain.) By the sixteenth century the monetary value of this export was about one hundred thousand pounds per year (reckoned by the British historian J. D. Fage to be one tenth of the world's supply of gold at the time).

The first batch of slaves consisted of twelve men, who were captured in raids conducted by the explorers Gonturned up with his men in full battle array, "armed after their manner, some with spears and buckles, others with bows and quivers of arrows." After the initial exchange of courtesies, Diego de Azambuja asked for permission to build a storehouse where merchandise could be kept and in which the traders could be housed. He emphasized that that castle could be of advantage to the king "since that same house, and the power of the King [of Portugal] would be there to defend him." Azambuja also expressed the anxiousness of his ruler to convert the chief and his people to Christianity. To this request the *caramansa* replied in words that should be written in letters of gold. Responding courteously to the Portuguese envoy's remark, the *caramansa* is reported to have said:

During that time nothing had astonished him as much as the captain's arrival; on the other ships he had seen ill-dressed and ragged men only, who were content with whatever he gave them in exchange for their goods. This was the aim of their voyages to those parts; all they asked was to be dealt with immediately, since they preferred to return to their country rather than to live abroad. But with him, the captain, it was otherwise. He came with many people, and with much more gold and jewels than there were in these parts where they were found, and moreover with a new request— that he might establish a residence in that land. From this he conjectured . . . that a man as important as he was surely came on great affairs, such as those of God, who made the day and night, about whom he had heard so much, and whose servant his King was. But considering the nature of so important a man as the captain, and also of the gallant people who accompanied him, he perceived that men of such quality must always require things on a lavish scale; and, because the spirit of such a noble people would scarcely endure the poverty and simplicity of that savage land of Guinea, quarrels and passions might arise between them all; he asked him, therefore, to be pleased to depart, and to allow the ships to come in future as they had come in the past, so that there would always be peace and concord between them. Friends who met occasionally remained better friends than if they were neighbors, on account of the nature of the human heart. . . . He did not speak thus to disobey the commands of the king of Portugal, but for the benefit of peace and the trade he desired to

have with those who might come to that port; and also because, with peace between them, his people would be more ready to hear of God, whom he wished them to know. Therefore, since time would reveal these inconveniences, he asked the captain to avoid them by allowing the traffic to continue as it had before.

What words of tact, wisdom, and above all, prophecy! Had the Portuguese listened to them or, alternatively, had they not been allowed to settle or build forts, but carried on their trade from their ships, the course of the European-African confrontation would most probably have been different. However, the *caramansa* and his king allowed themselves to be persuaded by Azambuja to grant permission for the fort on condition that the Portuguese pay rent for the land on which it was built. And as the *caramansa* had predicted, time did reveal the "inconveniences." In fact, shortly after the completion of the fort, Diego de Azambuja burned down the village as punishment for "so many thefts and evil deeds" that the subjects of the *caramansa* were alleged to have committed. However, during this first phase such "reprisals" were very infrequent. The Portuguese by and large remained on good relations with the people of the west coast and treated the African kings as equals and allies rather than subordinates or vassals.

The reception given the first ambassadors from Benin and Wolof, and the early letters exchanged between the kings of Portugal and those of the Congo, bear eloquent testimony of the respect they were accorded. De Barros reported that Prince Bemoym of Wolof, who went to Portugal in 1488, was "treated in every respect as a Sovereign Lord, accustomed to our civilization and not as a barbarous Prince outside the law." In the letters exchanged between the king of the Congo and the king of Portugal between 1512 and 1540, the former referred to the latter as "Most high and powerful prince and king my brother," while the king of Portugal addressed his Congolese counterpart as "Most powerful and excellent king of Manikongo," and as his "friend and brother."

Finally, throughout this period, it was the Africans themselves who dictated the terms of trade, and without their cooperation nothing could be done. It is not surprising that in the 1590's Richard Eden would give the following advice to his English compatriots: "They are a very wary people in their bargaining, and will not lose one sparke of golde of any value. They use weights and measures, and are very circumspect in occupying the same. They that shall have to doe with them, must use them gently; for they will not trafique or bring in any wares, if they be evill used."

There is no doubt that the first phase of European contact with Africa was, from the point of view of the peoples of western Africa and the Congo, both beneficial and promising. Although the trade in slaves had begun, it was relatively small in volume, for the demand was still confined to São Tomé, the Atlantic islands, and the Iberian Peninsula, where it would soon have reached a saturation point. The new food crops that were introduced caught on very rapidly, and two of them, grain and rice, soon became the principal diet of most coastal peoples. The seeds of Christianity were also being sown, and there was every indication that Western education and techniques would soon be firmly established in the Congo and possibly on the coast of Ghana, whence they would spread to other parts of the continent. And throughout, there was an attitude of mutual respect. The first period must have ended, then, on a note of great hope.

Meanwhile, Portuguese policies and activities in Central, South, and East Africa during the first period were quite different from those they pursued in West Africa and the Congo. From the beginning the Portuguese officially ignored the area of western Africa that is modern Angola, though both the Congo kings and the Portuguese living in São Tomé obtained some of their slaves from there. It was not until 1520 that the first official expedition was dispatched to Angola in search of souls and silver. The Portuguese also ignored southern Africa. The reports of the explorers made it clear that there were no prospects there for trade in minerals, spices, and ivory, the commodities then of primary interest to the Portuguese. In fact, it was not until after 1650 that those areas were of any strategic interest to either Portugal or the rest of Europe.

However, along the east coast of central Africa, precisely for strategic considerations—wresting control of the Indian Ocean trade from the Arabs and their Swahili allies—and also because of the great hopes raised by stories of the fabulous gold and silver mines in the African hinterland, the Portuguese Crown did commence activities. As early as 1502 Vasco da Gama returned to East Africa, this time as an invader, compelling the ruler of Kilwa to pay tribute to the Portuguese Crown. He was followed in 1503 by Ruy Ravasco, who sailed along the coast, pillaging and raiding and finally besieging Zanzibar.

Most of the well-established and wealthy states in the region successfully resisted these early attacks, but in 1505 a carefully prepared expedition under the command of Francisco de Almeida was dispatched to subdue the entire East African and Mozambique coast. Sofala yielded after little resistance, and a fort was erected there. Kilwa and Mombasa resisted, but both were captured; a fort was built at Kilwa. Only Malindi, in the north, was friendly to the invaders, and it became one of the two administrative centers from which Portugal controlled the entire coast of Mozambique and East Africa. The other center was the island town of Mozambique in the south, where in 1507 the Portuguese built a fort, a hospital, and administrative buildings. It soon replaced Sofala as the main depot for the Zambezi region and as a revictualing and refitting center for ships bound for India, and the fort at Sofala was abandoned in 1512.

However, apart from isolated journeys, mainly by Antonio Fernandez, the interior parts of the whole of Africa and even some of the coastal areas had still not directly felt the presence of the Europeans. This and every other aspect of the Afro-European confrontation were to undergo revolutionary changes during the second phase from 1518 to 1700, and these changes were by and large to be disastrous to the Africans.

The first and probably the most conspicuous of these changes was the great increase in the number of European nations operating in Africa. The English were the first to encroach on the thitherto exclusive Portuguese preserve. The first English trading voyage to Guinea during this period was undertaken by William Hawkins in 1530. He was followed by Thomas Wyndham in 1553, who traded in Benin late in 1554, and by William Towerson, who made three voyages to West Africa between 1555 and 1557. It is important to note that all these early English traders did not deal in slaves, but in gold, ivory, camwood, wax, and pepper. It was not until 1562 that, with the full support and blessing of the queen of England, John Hawkins (the son of William Hawkins) set off on the first English slave-trading voyage. He made two more voyages: in 1564 and in 1567, selling his captives to planters in the Caribbean.

The French also entered the Guinea trade in 1530, and within a few years their trading and piratic activities had extended as far as the Bight of Benin. It was the Dutch who were the first to successfully challenge the Portuguese monopoly. Entering the Guinea trade for the first time in 1593, soon after their struggle for independence, the Dutch launched systematic attacks on the Portuguese, both in Africa and in the Indian Ocean. Although their attack on Mozambique in 1607 was unsuccessful, by 1610 they had completely destroyed Portuguese naval power in the Indian Ocean. From there they turned their attention to the west

A Dutch legation, sent in 1642 to conclude an alliance with the king of the Congo, discovers that others have preceded it. Here the Congolese Alvaro II, in European boots and with a Christian gold cross at his elbow, receives the disappointed party beneath an imported chandelier.
DOPPER, *Description de l'Afrique*, 1686

coast of Africa. There they soon gained a footing on the coveted golden coast of Ghana. They built a fort at Mouri in 1612, and five years later they also built two forts on Gorée island and established a trading post on the opposite mainland at Rufisque. Finally, between 1637 and 1642, they captured the Portuguese strongholds of Elmina and Axim in Ghana as well as São Tomé and the port of Angola, and they even took Brazil. Although the Portuguese were able to reconquer Angola, São Tomé, and Brazil between 1648 and 1654, they never regained their position on the coast of Ghana. Likewise, the Danes, Swedes, and the Brandenburgers, all focused their attention on coastal Ghana.

The appearance of so many European nations on the African coast touched off a cutthroat rivalry among them. The Dutch, having replaced the Portuguese in the interior regions of Ghana and the Gambia, lost to the English and the French. They then concentrated on the coast of Ghana and on South Africa, which, as will be seen presently, they occupied in 1652. Soon after, the Swedes were eliminated altogether from Africa's shores. It was partly because of this rivalry and partly because of the political divisions on the coast of Africa, and especially that of Ghana, that a great number of European-manned forts and

castles were built on the west coast of Africa.

On the east coast the position of the Portuguese was first challenged from the hinterland when the Zimba invaders, a Central Bantu people, captured Kilwa in 1587 and attacked Mombasa. In the following century the Portuguese also had to face seaborne challenges from the Dutch, the Turks, and the Arabs of Oman on the Arabian Peninsula. At the invitation of the indigenous peoples of the coast, the Oman Arabs invaded Portuguese enclaves in 1652, 1660, 1667, and 1679, and by 1700 had succeeded in expelling them from the area of the East African coast north of the Ruvuma River.

Despite the intensity with which grabs for trade hegemony were purused, no European showed any interest in inland exploration. Traders remained blatantly ignorant of these regions, as dramatically illustrated by the fact that they did not know the direction of the flow of the Niger River until the 1790's or of the location of its mouth until 1830. Scientific curiosity, which had been one of the motives behind Prince Henry and his countrymen, completely lost its thrust during the second period of expansion. Nor did the Europeans show any interest in colonization—not the British, nor the Dutch, nor the Danes, nor the Brandenburgers. Only the French attempted to establish a colony at the mouth of the Senegal River in 1687, but this failed mainly because of the opposition of the king of Cayor. Thus the record of the Europeans in the field of colonization in the second period was nil.

The attempts to introduce Christianity, Western education, and Western technology were also gradually abandoned. The Portuguese did continue their missionary efforts in the sixteenth century, but very haphazardly and halfheartedly. They gave up all interest in missionary work in Benin after 1538. When evangelical activities were resumed in 1657 by the Capuchin Order, they were under the auspices of the *Sacra Congregazione di Propaganda Fide*, founded by the papacy; but the missionaries were soon expelled from Benin for interfering with religious festivals involving human sacrifice. Although the Capuchins sent missions to Benin and Warri in 1663, 1684, 1687, 1691, and 1695, no success attended their efforts, and in 1713 they, too, finally abandoned the attempt.

Christianization was impressed with a similar lack of fervor in the Congo. Whereas both the Portuguese and Affonso, the king of the Congo, had initially taken the work of converting the kingdom into a Westernized Christian state very seriously, the Portuguese seem later to lose interest in this aspect of their activities. For instance, in 1526 Affonso, in a very moving and sincere letter, appealed for "two physicians and two apothecaries and one surgeon, so that they may come with their drug-stores and all the necessary things to stay in our kingdoms." In the same year he wrote to the king, asking him to send neither "merchants nor wares," only "priests and people to teach in schools, and no other goods but wine and flour for the holy sacrament." The Portuguese paid no heed. In 1540 missionary work was resumed with the arrival of three Jesuit priests and a teacher. About two thousand people were baptized within the first four months, three churches were built at Mbanza-kongo, which was now renamed São Salvador, and schools were also established. But these successes were short-lived. In 1552, mainly because of the opposition of the Mani-kongo people and the resident Portuguese community, but partly because even some of the priests took to slave trading, the mission abandoned the Congo. A second mission followed in 1553, but that also failed for the same reason and withdrew in 1555. It would appear that no serious efforts were made again in this field, and by 1700 there was hardly a trace of western education or Christian life in the Congo, excepting the deserted city of São Salvador with its twelve ruined churches.

The English, the Dutch, and the French also made some efforts in the missionary and educational fields, but these initiatives were sporadic, evanescent, and very unproductive. For instance, chaplains who were supposed to administer to the whites as well as the blacks were attached to Dutch stations on the west coast. In 1634 the Dutch actually opened a school for the education of African children at Mouri, but it was soon abandoned. In 1644 they also mooted the idea of establishing a school at the port of Accra, but the scheme was never carried out. Nothing more was heard of Dutch schooling throughout the second half of the century. In 1694 an English mission set up a school at Ghana's Cape Coast, but it was abandoned two years later when its only teacher died. In 1705 a similar attempt failed. The French also made some efforts in the seventeenth century. In 1637 they sent five Capuchins to Assini, another West African port. Subsequently, two young men of the place, Lewis Aniaba (Hannibal) and a man named Roanga, were selected for further training and sent to France in 1687 to be educated. We do not know what happened to Roanga, but Aniaba returned home in 1701 and, upon his arrival, is reported to have done away with his French clothes, his foreign manners, and his Christian faith. The Capuchins, who like the Jesuits lacked the financial resources and manpower to sustain their efforts and were doubtless ill-adjusted to the coastal climate, soon withdrew from Assini, and with this vanished all traces of missionary activities in that area. Although Christianity was flourishing on the Atlantic islands and São Tomé, it had gained no permanent footing anywhere on the mainland.

However, in spite of the many setbacks in the fields of science, missionary work, colonization, and exploration, in this second phase of Afro-European contact (between 1518 and 1700) the Europeans not only stayed on in West Africa but increased their numbers. This was due to one main activity that occupied their attention: trade. Unfortunately for Africa, in this activity they found increasing profit. Indeed, the goods traded became vital to the growing capitalist and industrial economy of western Europe, and the plantation economy of the New World.

As has previously been pointed out, during the first four or even five decades of this second phase of expansion the principal interest of all the European nations involved was in articles such as pepper, gum, wax, ivory, and above all, gold. Had trade been confined to these natural products, there is absolutely no doubt that all would have been well; but in the coastal areas of the Congo, and in areas included in the modern states of Nigeria, Dahomey, Togo, Ghana,

São Salvador, a Portuguese post on Angola's Luege River, was an early collecting point for goods coming from the Congolese interior.

the Gambia, and Senegal, human beings constituted the main export commodity by the end of the sixteenth century. From the end of the seventeenth century to the first four decades of the nineteenth century, the slave trade would completely eclipse all other trade on the entire coast of West Africa and the Congo.

Although the overseas slave trade began as early as 1441, it still had not become the principal objective of the Portuguese even a hundred years later. It was the exploration of the Americas and the West Indies between 1492 and 1504, and the subsequent commencement of mining activities and the establishment of tobacco and sugar plantations there, that brought the slave trade to its full growth. The Europeans, confronted with an acute labor shortage in their attempts to exploit the natural resources of the New World, at first tried to use Indians to work the mines and plantations, but they proved unequal to the task. As one Spaniard reported in 1518: "When Hispaniola [modern Haiti and the Dominican Republic] was discovered, it contained 1,130,000 Indians. Today, their number does not exceed 11,000. And judging by what has happened, there will be none left in three or four years' time unless some remedy is applied." The remedy was indeed found in Africa, and

the first cargo of black slaves was transported from Spain to the Americas in 1501; the second shipment of seventeen slaves followed in 1505. In 1510 the Spanish Crown legalized the sale of white as well as black slaves in the New World. In 1515 the first slave-grown sugar from the Caribbean entered Spain. It was, however, not until 1518 that the first cargo of slaves was shipped directly to the Americas from the west coast of Africa in a Spanish ship. The Portuguese joined in November, 1532, when the *Santo Antonio* transported 201 slaves from the island of São Tomé to Santo Domingo and San Juan. In 1562 the English, represented by John Hawkins, also sent their first cargo of slaves directly to the West Indies. In 1619 a Dutch frigate landed the first twenty Negro slaves on the mainland of North America at Jamestown in Virginia. The Atlantic slave trade had well and truly been inaugurated.

According to Philip Curtin's calculations, the number of slaves that landed in the New World increased from 125,000 between 1501 and 1600 to 1,280,000 between 1601 and 1700 (greatly accelerated in the last quarter of that century by the stepped-up demand for slaves on the North American mainland), and to 6,265,000 between 1701 and 1810. Assuming that about sixteen per cent of them died during

315

African slaves work a Barbados refinery, where sugar cane is turned into sugar, molasses, and rum for the trans-Atlantic triangular trade.
DUTERTRE, *Histoire Generale des Antilles*, 1667

the "middle passage," or sea voyage, Curtin reckons that a total of 11,300,000 slaves were exported from Africa to the New World before slavery ended. (Earlier writers such as W. E. B. Du Bois, Robert R. Kucynski, Roland Oliver, J. D. Fage, and Robert Rotberg have offered estimates of as many as fifteen million forcibly removed from Africa.)

Treated with extreme brutality and inhumanity, all these slaves were used in the New World mainly for the extraction of minerals such as silver and copper and for the raising of sugar, cotton, tobacco, and indigo. It was the ready supply of these commodities that, as Eric Williams has shown in his brilliant study *Capitalism and Slavery*, gave birth to the textile, distilling, sugar-refining, metallurgical, and indirectly, the shipbuilding industries—enterprises on which the economies of the countries of western Europe so heavily depended. And it was some of the simple products of these industries that were exchanged at enormous profits in Africa for the slaves who were sold in the New World for even greater profits. With the rise of the Atlantic slave trade then, the European-African contact developed into a wider European-African-American contact, and as the sole producers of the manufactured goods involved, as the sole sellers of

the slaves in the New World, and as owners of the plantations in the New World, the European nations were obviously the greatest beneficiaries. It is not surprising therefore that all of Europe's leading traders and financiers had interests in one or more sides of the triangle. As the great nineteenth-century British historian L. B. Namier has concluded: "There were comparatively few big merchants in Great Britain in 1761, who in one connection or another, did not trade with the West Indies, and a considerable number of the gentry families had interests in the Sugar Islands, just as vast numbers of Englishmen now hold shares in Asiatic rubber or tea plantations or oil fields." And this was also true of France and Holland; as the French historian G. Gaston-Martin has written: "The founding of industries, private fortunes, public opulence, the rebuilding of towns, the social glories of a new class: great merchants eager for public office that should reflect their economic importance and impatient to be rid of what they called, with careless exaggeration, 'the shame of servitude'; such were the sum of the essential consequences for eighteenth-century France of the African slave trade."

What was the role of the African in all these activities? In

Under the stern direction of their slave trader, a gang of newly arrived captives is lined up for review before a prospective purchaser.

West Africa and to some extent in the Congo, during this period of expansion as in the former period, the Africans themselves were responsible for the production and the supply of all the commodities as well as the slaves involved in the trade. As the Dutch merchant William Bosman correctly pointed out in a letter to his uncle in 1701: "There is no small number of Men in Europe who believe that the Gold Mines are in our Power; that we, like the Spaniards in the West-Indies, have no more to do but to work them by our Slaves. Though you perfectly know we have no manner of access to these Treasures. . . ." Indeed, attempts made by the Dutch themselves in the 1650's and 1690's to prospect for gold along the Ankolora River and in Kommenda in modern Ghana were met with stout local resistance and had to be abandoned.

In the case of the slaves, early forays made by the Portuguese were soon abandoned as a method of acquisition. From about 1500 onward, apart from a few kidnaping attempts made by unscrupulous captains or an occasional adventurer like John Hawkins, it was the Africans themselves who delivered slaves to the Europeans for sale. These slaves were obtained in four principal ways: criminals sold as punishment by their rulers; domestic slaves who were resold; persons obtained from raids upon neighboring states; and prisoners of full-scale wars. It is evident from a recent study of some one hundred seventy-nine freed slaves in Freetown, Sierra Leone, that the principal sources of the slave trade were raids and wars. Similarly, most of the slaves from Ghana, Ouidah, Yorubaland, and Benin were products of war. However, some coastal areas were also ravaged by slave raiders. Likewise in the Congo, the slaves were obtained either as a result of wars or were brought from the inland regions by the *pombeiros*, Afro-Portuguese subtraders who traveled "a hundred and fifty or two hundred leagues up the country to buy or raid for slaves." But throughout West Africa and the Congo it was the ruling aristocracy— the kings and their nobles—who were ultimately responsible for supplying these slaves, for they waged the wars, organized the raids, tried the criminals and debtors, and passed the judgments. The French factor Jean Barbot was correct when he wrote that "the trade in slaves is the business of kings, rich men, and prime merchants."

Why then did African rulers cooperate with the Europeans in this hideous traffic? Before answering this question, it must be pointed out first that some of these rulers did try to stop the slave trade when they realized its disastrous effects. A typical example was Affonso, the king of the Congo. In one of his letters to the king of Portugal in 1526 he complained bitterly:

> . . . we cannot reckon how great the damage is, since the mentioned merchants are taking everyday our natives, sons of the land and the sons of our noblemen and vassals and our relatives, because the thieves and men of bad conscience grab them wishing to have the things and wares of this Kingdom which they are ambitious of; they grab them and get them sold; and so great, Sir, is the corruption and licentiousness that our country is being completely depopulated, and Your Highness should not agree with this or accept it as in Your service. . . . It is our will that in these kingdoms there should not be any trade of slaves nor outlet for them . . .

But no heed was paid to his appeal, and the trade received increasing support from subsequent Congolese kings and the Portuguese authorities. As the Nigerian historian I. A. Akinjogbin has recently shown, another unsuccessful attempt to put a stop to the trade was made by the kings of Dahomey, who extended their sway from the inland town of Abomey to the coast and conquered Ouidah and Ardra. But they also failed and were compelled to join a devil they could not beat.

Alan Ryder, an authority on Benin's history, has also emphasized the *oba*'s "general indifference to the demands and opportunities of the European slave trade" in the early decades of the sixteenth century. Indeed, until the close of the seventeenth century the kings of Benin enforced a total embargo on the export of male slaves.

As European commerce had become increasingly limited to the acquisition of slaves, and as most of the African kings and the members of the aristocracy had by then become addicted to the European goods, especially to spirits, tobacco, guns, and gunpowder, they had no choice but to sell their fellow men to obtain them. From about the middle of the seventeenth century in most areas of West Africa and the Congo the European traders demanded only slaves. C. B. Wadström, who toured many parts of western Africa in the 1780's and made a special study of the slave trade, told England's Privy Council Committee of 1789 that "the Kings of Africa . . . incited by the merchandise shown them, which consists principally of strong liquors, give orders to their military to attack their own villages in the

night. . . ." James Watt, who visited Timbo in Sierra Leone around the same time, reported that he was told by the *almani*'s deputy "with a shocking degree of openness, that the sole object of their wars was to produce slaves, as they could not obtain European goods without slaves, and they could not get slaves without fighting for them."

Cooperation in this shameful business must also, in this author's opinion, have been made easier by the African rulers' ignorance regarding the treatment of slaves on the other side of the Atlantic. Slavery and the slave trade were not European introductions to Africa. Both had existed from time immemorial in many areas in Africa, but a slave in any African society was treated as a human being who could own property, marry, and have children. He lived and was treated as a full member of the household, and very often occupied offices of responsibility. Slavery was a relatively humane institution in Africa and in the Muslim world. It was this humane institution that the African suppliers of slaves must have assumed they were dealing with in the New World. It is this author's feeling that had the kings and chiefs been aware of the enormity of the difference in the status of a slave in their own society and in the society of the New World, they probably would have put up greater and more sustained resistance.

Besides controlling the production and supply of the commodities, the Africans of the coast of West Africa also had a decisive say in the conduct of that trade. Without the permission of the rulers, no European nation could build any fort or trading post, and land rental had to be paid in all cases. In some areas such as Ouidah, Ardra, and later Dahomey, the kings even specified the material that was to be used in the construction of the forts. If the rent was not paid, trade could be stopped. In 1723 the London officials of the Royal African Company wrote to the agent in Sierra Leone: "We are sorry to find there are misunderstandings between you and the Africans. We find it arose from the not paying them the small rent due to them." Furthermore, the Europeans had to pay duties on all imports or give presents before they were allowed to trade. In Ouidah, as Bosman reported: "The first business of one of our Factors . . . is to satisfie the Customs of the King and the great Men, which amount to about 100 Pounds in Guinea value, as the Goods must yield there. After which we have free License to Trade, which is published throughout the whole Land by the Cryer." As the kings and chiefs were traders themselves in many areas, their products and slaves had to be bought first before those of their subjects. Bosman added that "before we can deal with any Person, we are obliged to buy the King's whole stock of Slaves at a set price; which is commonly one third or one fourth higher than ordinary: After which we obtain free leave to deal with all his Subjects of what Rank soever." This was true also in Benin and Bonny. Lastly, the chiefs and leading merchants had a decisive say in fixing the basis of exchange and the prices of commodities, especially of slaves, and this was done after a series of palavers that often dragged on for days, much to the disgust and discomfort of the European traders. Some Africans even set up their own trading concerns and came to gain almost monopolistic control over the trade in their own towns or regions. Typical examples of such merchant-princes of the seventeenth century were John Claesen and John Hennequa of Fetu, John Cabes of Kommenda, John Currantee of Anomabu, and John Konny of Ahanta, all in modern Ghana.

With a view to gaining control of trade, the Europeans encouraged Africans to live around the forts and castles they built. The Europeans furthermore sought treaties giving them exclusive trading rights. However, though many such treaties were exacted, especially by the Dutch and the English, the Africans paid absolutely no heed to their terms and throughout traded with everyone as they chose. Finally, the Europeans resorted to the practice of interfering in local politics, especially in succession disputes, with a view to putting their own nominees on the throne and in other influential positions. The English and the Dutch constantly did this in Kommenda, Aguafo, and Fetu; the Dutch, the French, and the English in Ardra and Ouidah; and the Portuguese in the Congo and Angola. But these methods proved ineffective. Hence, during the second period as in the first, the Africans on the west coast, and to some extent in the Congo, maintained their predominant position and rigidly controlled the trading activities of the Europeans while their states enjoyed complete autonomy.

In Angola, Mozambique, and South Africa, however, the situation was different. Although the people of the Congo and the Portuguese settlers on São Tomé had been unofficially trading for slaves in the region now called Angola in the late fifteenth and the beginning of the sixteenth centuries, it was not until 1520 that the Portuguese dispatched the first official trading mission there. Its leader, Balthasar de Castro, met with failure. Arriving in the kingdom of Ndongo, then a vassal state of the kingdom of the Congo, he was imprisoned by the ruling *ngola*, or king, the title from which the Portuguese formulated the name Angola. Nothing more was done to formalize relations for another

forty years, though trade between São Tomé and the Angola region continued, and it was with the assistance of some of these Portuguese traders that the *ngola* was able to defeat a punitive expedition sent against him by the king of Congo in 1556 and to declare himself independent. Four years later the *ngola* appealed for a Portuguese political, religious, and commercial mission, obviously to prove that he was the equal of his former Congo overlord. Under strong pressure from the Jesuits, who were anxious to start missionary work in that region, the Portuguese Crown dispatched Paulo Dias de Novais and four missionaries; they were to convert the king and his people to Christianity. The 1560 mission was a total failure. They arrived to find that the *ngola* who had issued the invitation was dead, and his successor promptly imprisoned Dias de Novais and one of his Jesuit companions, Father Gouveia. Novais was released five years later, but Gouveia was kept prisoner until his death in 1575. Partly because of the continued imprisonment of the missionary and partly because of the hope of exploiting the silver and copper mines rumored to be in existence in the interior, in 1571 the king of Portugal granted Paulo Dias de Novais a charter for the conquest of Angola and its conversion into a Christian Portuguese colony.

The expedition landed in 1575, and the conquest of Angola and the search for the mines began in 1579. In the following one hundred years and through intermittent wars the Portuguese completed the conquest of Ndongo, or Angola, founded the coastal towns of São Paulo de Luanda and Benguela in 1576 and 1617 respectively, and established a number of fortresses and towns inland. An administrative machinery was also established. The colony was divided into military districts, or *presidios*, ruled by captains who were responsible to the governor of the colony. Each *presidio* was made up of a number of chiefdoms under traditional rulers, on whom the administration imposed a head tax, or *Peca da India*, paid in slaves.

Jesuit missionaries operated in Angola from the time of their first appearance with the 1560 mission. But their number was insignificant, and some of the few soon took on so much trading and political activities that very few converts were won. As late as 1694, according to James Duffy, there were only thirty-six priests actively operating in the whole of the interior, and most of the churches and schools had by then fallen into ruins.

The Portuguese also paid some attention initially to locating the reported silver and copper mines of Angola. In 1604, however, Cambambe, the reputed center of silver mining, was finally reached by Manuel Cerveira Pereira, and a blockhouse was built there. However, no fabulous or even productive mines were found, and with this evaporated all the earlier hopes of mineral wealth. Attention thenceforth was focused essentially on the trade in human beings. According to David Birmingham, by the middle of the seventeenth century as many as ten thousand slaves were being exported annually from Angola, mainly to Brazil.

And what was the reaction of the Africans to all this? Probably nowhere in Africa has an African people put up as stout, spirited, and sustained a resistance to European penetration as in the region of Angola. The opposition existed from the very first Portuguese mission of 1520, when the brave king arrested and imprisoned its leader. Nor did a second mission fare better, and when the Portuguese, bent on conquest, began their invasion in 1579, the *ngola* killed all the thirty or forty European traders in his town and confiscated their goods. He then raised an army and routed a huge force estimated at sixty thousand Congolese and fifty European officers sent to assist Dias. So successful was this resistance that by the time of Dias' death in 1589, he had been able to advance only seventy miles up the Cuanza River. His successors continued the wars, and though they captured hundreds of slaves, by 1600 they had not advanced farther inland.

Only when Ngola Mbandi held the throne from 1617 to 1624 did Angola's will appear to fail, and so the Portuguese were able to conquer the kingdom. The invaders devastated whole areas and even burned the capital city of the kingdom. On his death in 1624, however, Ngola Mbandi was succeeded by his sister Nzinga Mbandi, a woman of extraordinary tact and courage. She was born in 1580 and had been baptized in 1620 or 1621 and given the ridiculous name of Dona Ana de Souza. However, despite her attachments to Portugal, no sooner was she on the throne than she resumed the war against the Portuguese, and she continued fighting till 1636. When she failed to regain Ndongo in this protracted war, Queen Nzinga moved northeastward and conquered the state of Matamba, which she soon developed into a very strong trading kingdom. As soon as the Dutch conquered Luanda in 1641, Queen Nzinga established an alliance with them, and it was a joint force of the queen and the Dutch that attacked and took the last stronghold of the Portuguese at Massangano between 1647 and 1648. But just before the final onslaught a powerful Portuguese fleet under the command of Salvador Correia de Sa entered Luanda and expelled the Dutch, reconquered the Mbundu of Angola, and imposed a humiliating treaty on the Congo, which had also joined the anti-Portuguese co-

alition, Queen Nzinga, however, continued her resistance from her inland headquarters. Anxious to resume the trade, especially in slaves to meet the inexhaustible demand from Brazil and the Spanish colonies, the Portuguese began peace negotiations with the queen. Under the terms of the resulting treaty of friendship between the two in 1656, the Portuguese were compelled to recognize the independence of Matamba, and commercial and friendly relations are said to have been maintained until her death in 1663.

This treaty was not the end of resistance to the Portuguese. In Ndongo itself the new dynasty established by the Portuguese after the withdrawal of Queen Nzinga and her royal household began to kick against the Portuguese. In 1671 the reigning *ngola* actually declared war on the Portuguese in a bid to re-establish Ndongo as a truly independent state. The Portuguese, however, moved in a strong army under Louis Lopes de Sequeira that defeated and killed the dissident ruler. They followed this up by establishing a fort on the site of the royal capital.

Farther inland the successors of Queen Nzinga also revived the struggle against the Portuguese in the 1670's, and in 1680 they attacked and took over the kingdom of Kasanje, an ally of the Portuguese to the east. Once more the Portuguese sent Louis Lopes de Sequeira against them. His first attack was repulsed by Kanini, the king of Matamba, and De Sequeira was killed; only the death of Kanini soon afterward prevented the Africans from following up this victory. Kanini's successor, another queen, reopened peace talks; in her anxiety to resume trade with the Portuguese she signed another, more costly treaty in 1683. In this treaty it was agreed that all slaves that had sought refuge from Portuguese territory were to be sent back, and that the kingdom of Matamba was to pay a war indemnity and was not to trade with any other nation but Portugal.

It is clear then that right from the beginning of the second period almost to its very end the Mbundu people of Angola, led by their rulers, put up stiff and spirited resistance to the Portuguese. Despite the fact that they had lost their Ndongo homeland to the Portuguese, their old dynasty continued to survive under the arrangement, enjoying an antonomous existence in Matamba that would last until the nineteenth century.

Between 1518 and 1700, in the region of Mozambique on the other side of the continent, the same attempts at penetration inland and colonization characterized Portuguese activities. Their drive began in 1530, when they established within the empire of the Shona a trading post, or market, at Sena, about a hundred miles up the Zambezi,

Coastal South Africa's wealth of subtropical flora and fauna was a marvel to visiting Europeans. In this engraving a British amateur naturalist records some of the sights of his travels there in 1746, including a variety of palms, a hyena, tiger, crocodile, and elephant.
CHURCHILL, *Collection of Voyages,* 1746

and a second market at Tete, another one hundred fifty miles farther upriver. But the Portuguese did not make any move to colonize or conquer the reputed gold mines of the interior until 1569, when a huge and well-equipped expedition under the command of Francesco Barreto was sent out. This expedition pushed on to Sena in 1571, and with the approval of the *monomotapa,* as the king of the Shona was known, Barreto launched a series of attacks on one of its rebellious vassal chiefs. (Monomotapa came to be applied to the Shona kingdom as well as its capital.) These attacks failed, and Barreto had to retreat to Sena, where he died shortly thereafter. His successor, Vasco Fernandes Homem, and a small party pushed on to the gold mines, but found

them very disappointing. Because of Homem's discouraging report, coupled with the high rate of mortality, no government expeditions were sent inland again until the first decade of the seventeenth century.

However, it would appear that during the second half of the sixteenth century independent Portuguese traders and adventurers pushed inland in search of gold and trade, and by 1600 a number of them had acquired large land and mining concessions from the local chiefs. After the turn of the century the *monomotapa,* who was facing a series of revolts, again invited the Portuguese government to render aid. In return he made generous concessions of land, and trading and mining rights. In 1629, however, the new *monomotapa,*

Kapararidze, embarked on a policy of driving out all the Portuguese from his empire, and by 1630 only five agents were surviving in the Shona territory and only seven in Manicoland to the south. In retaliation, the Portuguese dispatched a huge army under the command of Diogo da Meneses. This army inflicted a decisive defeat on Kapararidze, who was then executed. A new king, reportedly a Christian, was appointed by the Portuguese, and he was forced to sign a humiliating treaty with them on May 24, 1629. Under its terms the *monomotapa* was to consider himself a vassal of the Portuguese; he was to "make his lands free to the Portuguese" and was to allow complete freedom to Portuguese traders, miners, and missionaries; he was to expel the Arabs, and within a year he was expected to recognize a Portuguese envoy as "Captain of the Gates" at Masapa, the principal Shona market. From then on, more and more Portuguese and Indians living on the coast moved inland to acquire estates, or *prazos*. Many trading posts were also established throughout the gold-bearing regions of Mashonaland. The most important of these were Luanze, Ongoe, Dambarare, and the aforementioned Masapa.

By the 1650's it has been estimated that at Tete there were about forty Portuguese residents and about six hundred Christian Africans and half-castes living in the district. The power of the Portuguese representatives at Masapa had also grown with the years, as is evident from the following account of João Dos Santos, who visited that region at the beginning of the seventeenth century: "The Captain at Masapa has jurisdiction . . . over all the Kaffirs who come to Masapa, and those who live on his lands or within his borders. He has power to give verbal sentence in all cases, and can even comdemn the guilty to be hanged. This authority has been given him by Monomotapa. He serves as agent in all matters between the Portuguese and Monomotapa . . . [and receives] all the duties paid to him by the merchant, Christian or Arab, which are one piece of cloth for every twenty brought into these lands to be sold."

It would appear then that by the middle of the seventeenth century the Portuguese had succeeded in establishing their control over the hinterland of Sofala and Mozambique and the territory of the *monomotapa*. They governed the areas directly under their control through the *prazo* system. The colony was made up of *prazos*, or estates, owned by individual Portuguese. Each *prazo*-holder was ultimately responsible for the people, or *colonos* (freemen), living within his district; but local rule was maintained by headmen, or chiefs, known as *fumos*. The *prazo*-holder appointed and dismissed the *fumos*, dispensed justice, collected tribute,

and could use his *colonos* as guides, carriers, and even soldiers. The armed might of each *prazo*-holder was based on a private force of his own, consisting usually of slaves. The *prazo* system was not abolished until 1832.

In Mozambique the primary interest of the Portuguese was not in slaves, but in gold and ivory. However, as A. J. Willis has pointed out, "it is doubtful whether the government gained more from the gold trade than sufficed to balance the expenditure on forts and warehouses and on official salaries at Sofala and elsewhere." Some missionary efforts were also made in Mozambique in the sixteenth and seventeenth centuries, especially by the Dominican friars; but as late as 1700, as in other parts of mainland Africa, there was hardly a trace of Christian influence anywhere among the Africans, and it can be said that the Portuguese efforts in Mozambique were almost a total failure.

As was the case in Angola, the rulers and people of the eastern interior did not remain indifferent to the encroachment of the Portuguese. The Shona kings of the sixteenth and early seventeenth centuries welcomed them because they needed their help to suppress the numerous revolts with which they were confronted. But as soon as they felt secure, they took up arms against the Portuguese. A trader who visited the interior in 1634 reported that he found the position of the Europeans rather insecure. "The Portuguese," he noted, "have many forts in the empire of Monomotapa. . . . They have to depend chiefly on their flintlocks, which each person keeps ready; for in Kaffir country where trading goes on, rebellions often break out, and then each one's best defense is his gun. . . . The power of the natives is vastly greater than that of the Portuguese in this country." He also noticed the relatively strong position of the Arabs. "Many Arabs," he wrote, "dwell in the empire of Monomotapa. They are opposed to us always and everywhere." As the years rolled on, and as the Portuguese *prazo*-holders grew more arrogant and oppressive, the *monomotapas* and their subjects became more restive. In their helplessness the *monomotapas* appealed to the Changamire rulers of the Rozwi kingdom for help against the Portuguese. In 1693 the Changamire attacked the Portuguese fair at Dambarare and wiped out its residents. Then, after seizing the other posts, they turned against the ruling *monomotapa* and overthrew his kingdom. Thus by 1700 the Portuguese were confined to the Zambezi valley and the immediate hinterland of the coastal areas, the area more or less of modern Mozambique. Politically, economically, and religiously, their adventure in east Central Africa had brought no gains.

On the southern tip of Africa the Portuguese had shown

Dutch flags fly over Commander Simon van der Stel's camp in Namaqualand, a region of the Cape Colony where his Boer party had trekked in search of copper in 1685. Their efforts were rewarded, for they found the mountains "colored from top to bottom with verdigris."

little interest after the late fifteenth-century exploratory visits of Bartholomeu Dias and Vasco da Gama. Meanwhile, by 1610 the Dutch had wrested control of the East Indies from the Portuguese. Failing to capture Mozambique, traditionally the jumping-off point for eastern voyages, they found a more convenient and direct route to the Indies in 1611. This route placed the Cape midway between Europe and the Indies, thus making it of strategic importance in controlling trade. As Dutch, English, and French ships began to stop there, it was obvious that one of these nations would establish a station sooner or later; eventually the Dutch East India Company did so. In April, 1652, it dispatched an expedition of about ninety men under Jan van Riebeeck to the Cape. Van Riebeeck and his men landed at Table Bay in May, 1652, and soon a fort, a hospital, workshops, a mill, houses, and fruit gardens were established. By 1659 the station was flourishing, and each Dutch ship was leaving there victualed with at least a twelve- or fourteen-day supply of carrots, beets, parsnips, turnips, and other sturdy vegetables, plus numbers of live sheep.

The Dutch had no intention of establishing a colony at the Cape. Their decision to found that settlement was precipitated by their need for a refreshment station and by the fear that their deadly enemies, the Portuguese and Spaniards, might otherwise use the Cape as a base for attack. Indeed, Van Riebeeck was given strict instructions to keep the station as small as possible, not to colonize inland, and not to interfere in the affairs of the local people. Lest too much land be acquired, Van Riebeeck ordered planted a hedge enclosing the approximately six thousand acres that he deemed adequate for the task. Less than a decade later the need to raise more cattle as well as crops, and the continued fear of French or English attack, compelled the Dutch East India Company to permit free farmers, or burghers, to migrate there. As a consequence, slaves from Angola and West Africa began to be imported in 1658. By 1679 the number of burghers had increased to two hundred fifty-nine, and by 1680 settlements had been founded as far inland as Stellenbosch. The number of whites at the Cape was further increased after 1688 by the arrival of two hundred Huguenots, who left France following the revocation of the Edict of Nantes. At the close of our second period then, the Dutch revictualing station had developed into a thriving settlement, producing far more grain, cattle, sheep, and provisions than was demanded by Cape Town and passing ships.

Socially, four groups had emerged. The first consisted of black slaves from West Africa and Angola, who by 1700 numbered about seventeen thousand. The second was made up of the company's European employees, who were regarded as temporary residents. The third consisted of the Dutch Boers, or farmers, and Huguenots, who made the

These Hottentot herders, recognizable by their distinctive "peppercorn" hair, high cheekbones, and yellow-brownish complexion, are, with the Bergdama, South Africa's oldest settlers. When this photograph was taken in 1882, the Hottentots were already a disappearing people, many having been decimated by the white man's smallpox, others having been absorbed into the mixed Boer-Malay-Bergdama colored population.

Cape as their permanent home. The fourth was the colored group, who were a product of the miscegenation between the whites and the blacks.

The Boers, numbering about sixteen hundred by 1700, were fanatical adherents of the Calvinist faith. They identified themselves as the chosen people of the Old Testament and regarded the slaves and the blacks as the damned. Thus were formed the racist attitudes that would harden in the eighteenth and nineteenth centuries into the hideous philosophy of apartheid, the philosophy that governs the relations between the Boers and the blacks and colored of South Africa to this very day.

What sort of people did the Europeans find in the region of South Africa on their arrival there in the 1480's and 1490's? Contrary to the contentions of some misguided Boer historians and advocates of apartheid today, South Africa was not unoccupied when the Portuguese and the Dutch arrived there. It is clear from archeological and ethnological evidence as well as from the early accounts of Portuguese sailors that the area was occupied by two principal peoples: the Khoisan-speaking peoples and the Bantu-speaking peoples. The Khoisan group was made up of two principal peoples: the Bushmen and the Hottentots. Both of them had a tawny-yellow skin color, were rather short in stature, and spoke languages with the unique clicking sounds. Although they shared common religious beliefs and practices, they differed in many other respects.

The Bushmen neither practiced agriculture nor kept cattle, but lived in small units of a hundred or so, hunting and gathering wild fruits and tubers. Although they led a wandering life, each unit had a specific territory, which it guarded jealously. The Bushmen had been living in southern and central Africa for thousands of years, though by the time of the Portuguese arrival, they had been forced into the interior part of southern Africa.

Their fellow Khoisan speakers, the Hottentots, were cattle breeders, and though they, too, were nomadic, each group had to have its own home area. They were organized into much larger units than the Bushmen, with each unit made up of a number of related clans under a chief. As cattle owners, the Hottentots recognized wealth and private property. Less widely distributed than the Bushmen, at the time of the Portuguese arrival they occupied southwest Africa, the coastal areas around the Cape of Good Hope, and the eastern coastal strip as far north as Transkei.

The Bantu speakers, consisting of three principal subgroups, were living in the areas mainly to the north of the Orange and Vaal rivers and on the east coast. They were mixed farmers, rearing cattle and cultivating the land. The most numerous of them were the Nguni-speaking peoples— Zulu, Pondo, Tembu, Xhosa—who lived in the fertile and well-watered regions of the east coast. To the west of them were the Central Bantu, or the Sotho-Tswana, peoples, who occupied most of the central plateaus west of the Drakensberg mountains. Farther to the west were the Western Bantu—the Herero and the Ambo. All these Bantu peoples were organized into relatively small kingdoms ruled by chiefs, who were assisted by officials often called *indunas*, or military leaders.

The Bushmen and the Hottentots were the first to come into contact with the Europeans in the 1480's and 1490's; not until 1702 did the Bantu and the Europeans confront each other near the present-day South African town of Somerset East. The Hottentots consistently met the Portuguese with great hostility. They fought with the men of both Bartholomeu Dias and Vasco da Gama. In 1503 the Hottentots attacked and wounded Antonio de Saldanha and his men when they landed at Table Bay. In 1510 they attacked a party led by Francisco de Almeida, the Portuguese viceroy at Gao, and killed sixty of them, including the leader. As a result, the Hottentots earned a reputation as a really fierce and dangerous people, and reports that they were cannibals gained currency in Europe. Indeed, it was not until the favorable reports brought back to Holland by the crew of the *Haarlem*, who lived in Table Bay for a year after having been shipwrecked there in 1647, that the Hottentots' unsavory reputation was perhaps neutralized, thus preparing the way for the establishment of the victualing stations.

It would appear that the Hottentots took more kindly to the Dutch settlers, and they were the main suppliers of meat to the Dutch ships. However, as soon as the Dutch settlers began to expand inland and to occupy the land for farming purposes, both the Hottentots and Bushmen reacted sharply, and the first war between the Hottentots and the Boers broke out in 1658 and lasted two years. Van Riebeeck, having interviewed a Hottentot prisoner, summarized their grievances. They made war on the Dutch, he said, "for no other reason than that they saw that we kept in possession the best lands, and grazed our cattle where they used to do so, and that everywhere with houses and plantations we endeavored to establish ourselves so permanently as if we intended never to leave again, but take permanent possession of this Cape land (which had belonged to them during all the centuries) for our sole use; yea to such an extent that their cattle could not come and drink at this fresh water without going over the corn lands, which we did not like them to do." The Dutch, of course, were not prepared to leave, and a second war broke out in 1673 and continued till 1677. Induced by European commodities, especially tobacco and brandy, and decimated by the white's man's diseases such as smallpox, the remaining Hottentots gave up resistance and began to take on jobs as servants and laborers of the Boers.

The Bushmen, however, proved less susceptible. Unused to the concept of wealth and unattracted by the baubles and liquor introduced by the Europeans, they continued their resistance. They constantly attacked the burghers and killed, maimed, or drove off their cattle, all in defense of their hunting grounds and water holes. With a view to breaking this resistance, the Boers developed the commando system. Organizing themselves into mounted groups and equipped with three days' rations, firearms, and ammunition, which were supplied by the government, they went on periodic hunts for the Bushmen. In this way they steadily exterminated the indigenous population, driving them farther and farther inland to the semidesert areas of the northwest Cape and beyond the Orange River, where they are found to this day. By the middle of the eighteenth century the resistance of the Bushmen had been completely broken.

The Dutch had yet to subdue the third and largest group, the Bantu, and as pointed out already, it was not until the last quarter of the eighteenth century that the Boers, steadily moving eastward, confronted the main body of the Eastern Bantu across the Great Fish River. The result was the Kaffir Wars, which raged throughout the eighteenth and the nineteenth centuries and which in some sense have con-

THE COMING OF THE EUROPEANS

tinued among their descendants to this very day.

By the end of the period under review, there was hardly a coastal region of Africa in which the European nations were not operating. In the case of Angola, South Africa, and Mozambique, they did not confine themselves to trading from their forts and castles as they did in West Africa, but had become colonizers and administrators, thus provoking deadly conflicts with the Africans. It is to the lasting shame of these European nations in general, and to the Portuguese in particular, that they abandoned almost all the activities that would have benefited and improved the lot of the African, at least materially if not spiritually, to concentrate on the most inhuman, the most destructive, sale of man by man.

Politically, Europe's impact on Africa was at best a mixed blessing. In the Congo, Angola, and on the East African coast it led to the weakening and total disintegration of almost all kingdoms that were in existence on their arrival: the kingdom of the Manikongo in the Congo, the Mbundu kingdom in Angola, nearly all the city-states on the east coast of Africa, and above all, the remarkable kingdom of Monomotapa. All these states were the victims of active foreign interference in their internal affairs, coupled with military attack on them by the Portuguese, or by other African invaders, or by both—the Portuguese in Angola, the Rozwi in Monomotapa, the Zimba in Mombasa and Kilwa, and both the Portuguese and the Jaga in the Congo.

The west coast, on the other hand, experienced the rise or rapid expansion of a number of city-states, especially in the Niger delta area, and of no less than four empires—Asante, Dahomey, Oyo, and Benin—which were to dominate West Africa in the eighteenth and the nineteenth centuries. Indeed, many historians are of the opinion that these empires were the product specifically of the Atlantic slave trade, built upon the desire of their rulers to capture slaves for sale. It seems clear to this writer, however, that such an explanation is true only of the states that emerged in the area of the Niger delta, such as Bonny, Opobo, Brass, Cross, and Creek Town, all of which started as trading corporations organized to supply slaves either by war or raids. Significantly, however, not one of them grew into a large kingdom. The empires of Benin, Oyo, Asante, and Dahomey, on the other hand, were not creations of the Atlantic slave trade. As described in Chapter Five, the rise of both Benin and Oyo began long before any European set foot on the coast of Guinea. And though both Asante and Dahomey did commence their development during the second half of the seventeenth century, other motivating factors

are indicated. Dahomey's drive toward the coast was initiated with a view to stopping the slave trade. Asante's rise, as is evident from recent research, was inspired first and foremost by a desire to throw off the tyrannical rule of the kingdom of Denkyra to the south and second to gain control of the trade routes running not only southward to the coast but also northward to Hausaland and the Niger Bend.

It is nevertheless true that the presence of Europeans did affect the growth or expansion of all these empires. Most important, the Europeans brought guns and gunpowder to West Africa, especially after 1640, and there is no doubt that the growth of the four inland states of Oyo, Benin, Asante, and Dahomey was greatly accelerated by the use of these weapons. Additionally, the presence of the Europeans on the coast provided these inland states with a motive to extend their sway down to the coast, thereby trading directly with the Europeans and eliminating the middlemen and their sharp practices. Although these states expanded mostly by waging wars against their weaker neighbors and although most of the captives they took were sold as slaves, it is wrong to see these wars as motivated primarily by the desire to profit from the slave trade. Slaves were only accidental by-products.

The economic effects of the impact of Europe on Africa were even more profound. With the exception of the east coast, the centers of wealth and economic opportunity prior to the arrival of the Europeans were inland. Now trade began to be diverted more and more toward the coastal regions, with the inland states extending themselves to meet the challenge, as we have seen. However, West Africa's ancient trade with the north and the Saharan regions continued, though its volume decreased as the greater part of it, especially the trade in gold, was diverted southward.

The second principal economic effect was that in western and west-central Africa agricultural, hence peaceful, pursuits were neglected, and orderly economic development was ruled out as the slave trade became the principal occupation of the area's rulers. Some historians, including J. D. Fage, have argued to the contrary, saying that the slave trade must "have been a considerable stimulus to the internal economic development in Guinea." But this view is untenable. The sale of slaves simply could not have brought about any internal economic development. On the contrary, by taking away Africans mainly between the ages of fifteen and thirty who could have worked and produced wealth at home, by carting away craftsmen and traditional industrialists, by killing local industries such as the textile industry through the importation of cheap wares and copies, by retarding agricultural development, and by giving to Africans in return for their products only baubles and barrels of liquor, the European trade with Africa in general and the Atlantic slave trade in particular definitely delayed economic development in Africa for well over three hundred years.

It was in the social sphere, however, that the European impact was virtually an unmitigated disaster—in fact, a crime against Africa. The first and obvious effect was the depopulation of Africa. As we have seen, historians are still arguing about the number of slaves that were actually taken out of Africa, from 15 million to Curtin's most recent figure of 9.4 million. Of course, neither figure includes the uncounted numbers of Africans who must have been killed during the raids or in the wars or who died during the march from the inland regions to the coast. But it can be asserted that the total loss of population to Africa as a result of the Atlantic slave trade was something close to 20 million. Some European historians have contended that not only did Africa not suffer far-reaching depopulation, but as J. D. Fage argues, "it may have been preferable for some parts of this area to have exported the equivalent of its natural growth of population rather than to have kept it at home." These views are highly objectionable. Firstly, depopulation in the magnitude of 20 million people—people in the prime of manhood—is very serious and very far-reaching. Secondly, it is nonsensical to talk of overpopulation in sub-Saharan Africa even today, let alone two hundred years ago! And, in any case, given a choice between dying in Africa of hunger or being reduced to chattel and being humiliated, flogged, or worked to death in the New World, this writer, as an African, would have chosen the former!

Beyond the matter of decimating the population, the perpetual raids and wars for slaves must have created an atmosphere of social insecurity, fear, and chaos. The English observer John Atkins wrote in 1721 that on the west coast "they never care to walk even a mile from home without fire arms." Such an atmosphere could not help but impede all orderly social development and retard cultural activities. Indeed, by 1700 the great art and sculpture of the people of Ife, Benin, and Oyo had virtually disappeared. Missionary and educational activities were also halted, partly because of the insecurity and anarchy caused by the inhuman traffic and partly because of the fact that even some of the priests, missionaries, and teachers turned to that traffic themselves. Significantly, it was only after the steady suppression of the slave trade that missionary activities began to take root in Africa.

Furthermore, the slave trade brutalized everyone involved, white as well as black, but especially the traditional African rulers. In their anxiety to obtain people for sale, these rulers abused customary law and practice, fabricated charges of adultery, theft, or treason, and even imposed slavery instead of fines as punishment for petty offenses. In his travels in the northern districts of Sierra Leone in 1822 Alexander Gordon Laing noted that following an investigation into the death of a young girl in a village he visited, the authorities were not able to place blame on anyone. "Had the slave trade existed," he commented, "some unfortunate individual might have been accused and sold into captivity." African religious leaders also abused their offices by turning them into instruments of enslavement. For instance, the Aro people of Iboland, in present-day Nigeria, used their famous oracle Chukwu to enslave thousands of Ibo from the inland regions. There is no doubt that the European presence in general and the slave trade in particular brought about the moral degeneration of many members of the ruling aristocracy.

Another deplorable effect of the trade was the change in the attitude of Europeans toward Africans, or the black race. Once the white man began to buy blacks and to treat them as chattel and beasts of burden, he naturally began to develop an attitude of contempt toward his victims. The feeling of equality and mutual respect that had characterized the first period of Afro-European contact was steadily replaced by one of superiority on the part of the Europeans, an attitude that has not entirely disappeared to this day.

The social impact was not confined to Africa alone, but could be seen in the New World. It was in the United States, South America, and the Caribbean islands that the feeling of white superiority and black inferiority reached extreme proportions, becoming the basis of the present, highly explosive confrontation between blacks and whites.

On balance then, politically, economically, and socially, the European presence and activities in Africa during the second period were virtually an unmitigated disaster for the Africans. By 1700 all the great hopes that had been conjured up during the earlier phase of exploration had turned sour. To borrow Basil Davidson's term, Africa had by then been turned into the "Black Mother," producing slaves solely in the interest of the growing capitalist system in Europe and the New World, and it was to do this for another hundred and fifty years. At the beginning of their contact, sub-Saharan Africa was politically, culturally, and artistically comparable to Europe. By 1700 Europe had leaped forward technologically and socially, but Africa and its black peoples had become paralyzed and impoverished, a tragedy from which they still have not recovered.

RAPE OF THE COAST

SHIPWRECK OFF NATAL

To the historian, the era of slavery offers many ironies. What began with numerous instances of courage and moral fortitude was to end in venality and corruption as exploration gave way to slavery. Typical of the growing hostility of most whites is this highly partisan story of the wreck of the São João, *a Portuguese galleon. The vessel and most aboard it came to a pitiful end after they were shipwrecked off Natal on June 24, 1552. The tragedy was one of the most famous maritime disasters of the period. Contemporary historians bemoaned the fate of the gallant captain, Manoel de Sousa Sepúlveda, and his family and crew, who perished at the hands of the "cruel Kaffirs" of Africa. The following is an abridged version of the tale as it was told to an anonymous chronicler by the boatswain, one of the few survivors of the* São João *ordeal.*

On 13th April, Manoel de Sousa came in sight of the coast of the Cape at thirty-two degrees. . . . [He and his crew] no longer had any other sails than those on the yards after the other equipment of sails had been carried away by a storm they had met with on the Line [the equator], and . . . their present ones were so torn that they were not to be trusted. . . . The violence of the wind and sea would not let them make any reparations and not a man of them could keep his footing. . . . Everything foretold greater hardships; for their sins, nothing availed them. They had not seen land since they left the Cape, but they must have been about fifteen to twenty leagues from it. . . .

Thus Manoel de Sousa was very near land, though helpless. So he asked the opinion of his officers. They all said that

the best manner of saving their lives from death at sea was to wait until they reached ten fathoms, and, when they sounded that depth, drop anchor, and launch the long-boat for them to disembark. They launched a small boat then and there with some men in it to examine the beach and find out which would be their best place to land in. They agreed that, after all had disembarked and come ashore in the long-boat or the smaller boat, such stores and arms as could be fetched should be. . . . Manoel de Sousa could see his galleon would go to the bottom, and that there was no help for it. So he called the master and pilot and told them that the first thing they were to do was to put him ashore with his wife and children, and twenty men to guard them; then they must go and fetch the arms, provisions, and powder out of the ship, and also some cambric cloth, in case there should be some means of purchasing provisions on land. . . .

While they were still in the place to which they had escaped from the galleon, seven or eight Kaffirs leading a cow appeared on a hill. The Christians made them signs to come down, and the captain went to speak to them. When the negroes were fairly cornered they made signs that they wanted iron. Then the captain sent for half a dozen nails and showed them to them, and they were very pleased to see these, and came nearer our men and began to bargain for the price of the cow. Everything had been settled when five Kaffirs appeared on another hill and began to call out to them in their language not to give the cow in exchange for nails. Immediately

the Kaffirs went away, taking the cow with them and not saying a word. And the captain . . . called a council to decide what they should do. And, before they discussed the matter, he spoke to them as follows:

"Gentlemen and friends, you can clearly see the state we are reduced to for our sins. I truly believe that my own alone would have been enough for us to have been submitted to these great privations you see we are undergoing. But Our Lord is pitiful, and He was so merciful to us that He willed that we should not sink to the bottom in that ship, despite the great quantity of water which we had below decks. His will be done, for it is His object to lead us to a Christian country, and may their souls be saved who end their lives in the trials of our quest. . . . I ask one favor of you, not to abandon me or leave me if I cannot travel as fast as the fastest of you because of my wife and children. And may God in His mercy help us all." . . .

They began to move off from the beach (which was at thirty-one degrees) where they had been wrecked, on 7th June [1553]. In the vanguard went André Vaz and his company carrying a banner with a crucifix. Then came Manoel de Sousa with his wife and children, and eighty Portuguese, and slaves; Dona Leonor, the captain's wife, was carried by slaves, in a litter. Immediately behind them followed the master of the galleon with the seamen and the female slaves. Pantaleão de Sá came in the rearguard with the rest of the Portuguese and of the slaves, about two hundred people. Altogether they were about five hundred people, a hundred and eighty of whom were

Portuguese. They proceeded like this for a month, enduring great hardships and great hunger and thirst. All this time they ate nothing but the rice which had been rescued from the galleon and some jungle fruits, for they found no other food in the country, nor any one to sell it to them. So that they went through privations which can neither be believed nor written. . . .

It often happened that these people sold each other a pint pitcher of water for ten crusadoes; and for a cauldron which held two gallons they asked a hundred crusadoes. As this sometimes gave rise to disorders the captain took to sending for a cauldron of it, since the company had no larger vessels, and paying a hundred crusadoes to the man who went to fetch it. The captain then portioned it out with his own hand, and what he took for his wife and children cost him eight and ten crusadoes the pint. . . . For many days they had only had the fruits they found by chance to sustain them, and toasted bones. Often snake-skins were sold in the encampment for fifteen crusadoes. Even when they were dry, they threw them into water and then ate them as they were.

When they went along the beaches they lived on shell-fish or fish thrown up by the sea. In the end they came across a Kaffir, an old man, who was a chief of two villages. He seemed to them a man of merit, and so he was, as can be seen by the welcome he gave them. He told them not to go on any further, but stay with him, and he would supply them as best he could. . . .

They were ready to move on again, but they saw a band of Kaffirs coming. On which they prepared to fight if necessary, thinking the negroes had come to rob them. The band drew near; they began to parley, and the Kaffirs asked our people who they were and what they wanted. Our people replied that they were Christians and that they had been wrecked, and they asked them to guide them to a broad river which lay on ahead. Moreover, if the Kaffirs had provisions, let

them bring them and they should be paid for them. The negroes replied, through a negress who came from Sofala, that if they required supplies they should come with them to a place where their king was, and that he would give them a good welcome. . . .

The Kaffirs' treachery had been planned beforehand and, as soon as they saw that the Portuguese had no weapons, they began to separate them and rob them and take them through the jungle in the groups they had been sorted into. When they reached the appointed places they stripped them, and left them with nothing on them and drove them out, beating them severely. Manoel de Sousa did not go in any of these groups. He, and his wife and children, the pilot André Vaz, and about twenty other people, stayed with the king because they had a great quantity of jewels and precious stones and coins. It is said that what that company brought all that way with it was worth more than a hundred thousand crusadoes. As soon as Manoel de Sousa and his wife and those twenty other people had been separated from the rest they were immediately robbed of all they had brought with them, though the king did not strip them. He told him that he might go away at once in search of his company, for he did not wish to do him any more harm, nor hurt his person or that of his wife. When this happened to Manoel de Sousa he must have seen very clearly what a great mistake he had made in giving up the arms. But he had to do what they told him, for it was not in his power to do otherwise.

The other members of the company, ninety in all, including Pantaleão de Sá, and three other gentlemen, though they had all been separated from each other and robbed and stripped by the Kaffirs to whom they had been apportioned by the king, managed to come together again, little by little, because they were not far from each other. So they started out again together, beaten, despondent, without arms, clothes, or money to buy food with, and without their captain. . . .

By now Dona Leonor was very weak, sad, and disconsolate, because she saw how ill her husband was, and because she found the others were so far off that she thought it impossible ever to join them. To think of it is a thing to break one's heart. As they went along thus the

After Vasco Da Gama's 1497 voyage to India, map makers were able to sketch in Africa's eastern contours, as in this 1508 map.
RADIO TIMES HULTON PICTURE LIBRARY

Kaffirs again came upon the captain, his wife, and the few people who were in their company and stripped them there without leaving anything on them. When they were both left like that, with two very young children with them, they commended themselves finally to the Lord.

Here they say that Dona Leonor would not let herself be stripped, but defended herself with buffets and blows, for she was of a nature to prefer being killed by the Kaffirs to being left naked before all the people. There is no doubt, even, but that her life would have been over if Manoel de Sousa had not begged her to let herself be stripped, reminding her that all were born naked, and, as it was God's will, she should not now refuse to be so, too. One of their great trials was seeing those two little children of theirs there crying and asking for food whilst they, the parents, were unable to help them.

When Dona Leonor was left without clothes she flung herself on the ground immediately and covered herself completely with her hair, which was very long. She made a hole in the sand in which she buried herself up to the waist and never arose from it again. . . .

Truly I do not know who could consider this without great pity and sadness. Here was a most noble woman, the daughter and the wife of very honorable gentlemen, most cruelly and ignominiously used! When the men who were still in their company saw Manoel de Sousa and his wife naked they moved away a little, being ashamed to see their captain and Dona Leonor so. Then she said to André Vaz the pilot: "You see the state we are in and that we cannot go on any further and that we must end our lives here, for our sins. Go on your way, save yourselves, and commend us to God. If you reach India or Portugal at some future time, tell them how you left Manoel de Sousa and myself and our children."

THE VERDANT CAPE

The travelogue of the Venetian explorer Alvise da Cadamosto remains a major source of information on the early European "discovery" of the coast of West Africa. In 1455, traveling in the service of Prince Henry the Navigator of Portugal, Cadamosto sailed southward along that shore as far as the Gambia River. His description of Cape Verde, on the coast between the Senegal and Gambia rivers, and the nearby islands, follows.

This Capo Verde is so called because the first to discover it (who were Portuguese) about a year before I was in these parts found it all green with great trees [mangrove swamps], which remained in leaf throughout the year. For this reason they gave it the name of Capo Verde: just as Capo Bianco, of which we have already spoken, was found entirely sandy and white and was therefore called "Capo Bianco." This Capo Verde is very beauti-

ful and lofty: on the point there are two hillocks. It runs far into the sea, and on the cape and in its vicinity there are many dwellings of negro peasants, huts of straw, close to the sea, and visible to those who pass. These negroes belong to the said Kingdom of Senega.

[Off the cape there are dry patches which extend about half a mile out to sea.] Off it we found three small islands, not very far from the land, uninhabited and covered with tall green trees. Being in need of water, we anchored off one of them [Gorée], which appeared the largest and most fruitful, to ascertain if any springs were to be found there. On landing we found no water, except in one spot where there was a little water, but which was of no use to us. We found many nests on the island, and eggs of various birds [un]known to us. While we remained here we all fished with lines and large hooks and caught a great number of fish: among them shell fish and very large mature dories, weighing from twelve to fifteen pounds each. This was in the month of June.

Thence, the following day, we continued to sail on our voyage, always within sight of land. Beyond Capo Verde there is a gulf inland. All the coast is low, covered with very fine, tall, green trees, which never shed their leaves throughout the year [that is they never wither, as do ours], for new leaves appear before the old fall. These trees come right down to within a bowshot of the beach, so that it appears as though they flourished in the sea—a very beautiful sight. In my opinion, who have sailed to many places in the Levant and in the west, I have never seen a more beautiful coast than this appeared to me—watered by many rivers, and streams of little account, since large vessels cannot enter them.

Running with the wind along this coast, still voyaging southwards, we discovered the mouth of a river, perhaps a bowshot wide, and of no great depth. To this river we gave the name of Rio di Barbazini [the Joal], and thus it is named on the "carta da navigar" of this country

A griot *retelling the stirring history of his people to the accompaniment of a drummer*

made by me. It is distant sixty miles from the Capo Verde. We always navigated this coast and beyond by day, anchoring each evening at a deserted spot in ten or twelve *passa* [two *passa* equal roughly one fathom] of water, and four or five miles from the shore. At dawn we made sail, always stationing one man aloft and two men in the bows of the caravel to watch for breakers which would disclose the presence of shoals.

Sailing thus we reached the mouth of another large river, which appeared to be no smaller than the Rio de Senega. When we saw this fine river [the estuary of the Solum and Jumbas rivers], and the beautiful country, we cast anchor, and debated whether we should send ashore one of our interpreters—for each of our ships had negro interpreters on board brought from Portugal, who had been sold by the lords of Senega to the first Portuguese to discover this land of the Blacks.

These slaves had been made Christians in Portugal, and knew Spanish well: we had had them from their owners on the understanding that for the hire and pay of each we would give one slave to be chosen from all our captives. Each interpreter, also, who secured four slaves for his master was to be given his freedom. Lots were drawn to decide whose interpreter was to go ashore, and it fell to the

Genoese. Whereupon having fitted out his boat, he sent off his man, with orders that the boat was not to be run ashore except in as far as was necessary to land the slave. He was instructed to ascertain the condition of the country, to whom it was subject, and whether gold and other objects of use to us were to be obtained there. Accordingly, when he had landed, and the boat had withdrawn a short distance, he suddenly encountered a great number of negroes who, having observed the ships approaching, had lain in wait with bows and arrows and other weapons to accost any of our men who might land. They conversed for a short while; what he said to them we do not know, but they began furiously to strike at him with their short Moorish swords, and quickly put him to death, those in the boat being unable to succor him.

When we were informed by our men of this, we were left stupefied, realizing that they must be very cruel men to do such a thing to a negro of their own race, and that they might reasonably be expected to treat us much worse. On this account, we set sail, still holding our southerly course within sight of the shore, which appeared to us continually more beautiful, more thickly covered with green trees, and always low, until at length we reached the mouth of the river of Gambra [the Gambia]. Perceiving it was very wide, not less than three or four miles in the narrowest reach, so that our ships could enter in safety, we decided to lie there with the intention of ascertaining on the following day whether this was the country of Gambra, which we so greatly desired to find.

THE GUINEA TRADE

In December, 1460, King Affonso V of Portugal gave one of the Cape Verde Islands, São Tiago, to his brother, Prince Fernando. However, settling it proved difficult, and six years later the king gave his sibling and the Santiagians additional privileges, including trade rights in Guinea. São Tiago soon became the chief center for lucrative commerce with the African mainland. An English translation of the text of Affonso's grant follows.

To all to whom this letter shall come, we make known that prince dom Fernando, my most dear and beloved brother, has sent to inform us that some four years ago he began to populate his island of Santiago, which is opposite Cabo Verde, and that, because it is so remote from our kingdoms, people are unwilling to go to live there, unless they are given very wide privileges and franchises and go at his expense. He, knowing the great profit it would yield us and him, if the island were thus populated, as he wished, in which cause he was ready to go to much personal expense so as to carry it to perfection, and being hopeful of success with God's help, prayed us to be pleased to grant him some privileges for them. We, having seen his petition and having considered it carefully, believe that we may thereby be very well served. And so that we may graciously reward my said brother, we are pleased to command him to be given the following privileges, namely: first, we give and grant him civil and criminal authority over all

A dense cluster of thatch-roofed, mud-walled houses in a southern Senegalese bush village

RAPHO-GUILLUMETTE—MARC AND EVELYNE BERNHEIM

Moors, black and white, free and captive, and over all their descendants, who are in the said island, although they be Christians, and this while our favor continues. This civil and criminal authority, which we thus grant him in the manner stated, is additional to the authority which already before this we gave him in the said island, as is contained in the patent of the said grant which he has from us.

Furthermore, we are pleased to authorize him that henceforward and always the inhabitants of the said island may have and hold license, whenever they wish, to be able to go with ships to trade and to buy in all our trades of the parts of Guiné (save our trade of Arguim [Arguin on the coast of Mauritania], where we do not wish anyone to trade or do anything either in the said trade or in its limits, except him to whom we are pleased to grant license and permission) all the goods, which the said inhabitants of the said island have and desire to carry, except arms and iron tools, ships and their equipment, because our pleasure is that none of these things should be bartered in any manner in the said trades, and we have strictly forbidden this before, under the penalty for such a thing already imposed. . . .

These, our officers, whom we thus appoint there in the said island, shall be ready and diligent to supply clerks to the said shippers, so that each shall carry one, as is required in each ship which goes there, according as is now done in the ships which go from our kingdoms to the said port of Guiné.

The said customs officer or receiver shall thus be ready to collect the said dues, which are to accrue to us from the said ships which are equipped in the said island, as soon as they return from the said ports of Guiné. If the said officers are not ready to collect the said dues and to provide the said clerks, in their absence he may collect and provide who has charge of the government and captaincy of the said island for my said brother, and he shall keep these dues

Nigerian traders, as shown in the Dutch-made Novus Atlas *of 1648, by Willem Blaeu*

NEW YORK PUBLIC LIBRARY, ASTOR LENOX AND TILDEN FOUNDATIONS

himself until we send for them. When this happens, the said governor or captain shall advise us thereof by letter.

These clerks, thus to be supplied, shall be such as are fully competent and suitable for our service, and for their salary they shall receive everything which we have ordered and commanded is to be given to clerks who go from our kingdom to the said parts of Guiné. They shall receive this from the day when the said ship leaves the said island for the said trades till they return to it, and no more.

Furthermore, it is our will and pleasure that, when the amount of our dues has been paid on all the said imported negroes and goods, the said inhabitants of the said island may sell on their own accounts what they have left to all persons, who want and desire them, not only in the said island but in all our kingdoms and abroad; and if they sell in the said island, the buyers shall not have to pay on the said goods, in these kingdoms when they are brought here, either the tenth or any other dues; and if they do not sell them in the said island but wish to bring them to our kingdoms or to carry them to other parts, they may do this, because they are exempt from having to pay us the said dues; and this, provided they carry certificates from our officers, whom we shall thus appoint in the said island, showing that they have already paid our dues. . . .

Furthermore, it is our will and pleas-

ure, in the event hereafter of our farming out the said trades of the parts of Guiné, or a part thereof, that, should we do this, this license, which we thus grant my said brother for the inhabitants of the said island, shall not transgress or stay such a farm, and this shall be thus enacted so that we shall not be reminded of this grant to my said brother.

Furthermore, it is our will and pleasure that henceforward the inhabitants of the said island are always to be freed and exempted from the payment to us in all our kingdoms and lordships of the tenth of all goods which they transport from the said island, not only of goods which are of their own inheritance and gathering, but also of goods which they buy, or secure by exchange, or obtain in any other way.

Likewise, they shall be exempted from the payment to us of the tenth of all goods, which they buy and secure by exchange of other articles of their own in the islands of Canaria, Madeira, Porto Santo and the Açores, and in all the other islands in the ocean sea, and which they bring to our kingdom. This shall be, provided our officers are notified that the said persons are inhabitants of the said island of S. Thiago by report of the captains of the said island.

Therefore, we command all overseers of our exchequer, accountants, treasurers, customs officers and receivers, clerks, magistrates, judges and justices, and other officers and persons whatsoever, to whom this letter shall be shown, and who are cognisant thereof, that henceforward they shall observe and keep it, and cause it to be properly observed and kept, and in the manner stated herein.

Should any desire to disobey this, we command them in no wise to permit it, forasmuch as this is our wish, notwithstanding any doubt or embargo which others may raise or impose. And for its security and our remembrance, we command them to be given this letter, signed by our hand and sealed with our pendent seal. Given in Beja. 12 June 1466. Pedro da Alcaçova made this.

THE CONVERSION OF BEMOYM

In the early years of their involvement in Africa, the Portuguese played the role of ostensibly benevolent outsiders rather than that of oppressors. This excerpt describes the 1488 conversion to Christianity of Bemoym, prince of the Wolof of Guinea, by King John II of Portugal. In contrast to the attitudes that later Europeans would have, no honor was too great for the black king. The account is from the Chronicle of John II, *by Ruy de Pina, a Portuguese historian of the period.*

In this year one thousand four hundred and eighty-eight, while the king [John II] was in Setuvel [Setúbal, near Lisbon], he made a Christian of Bemoym, a negro prince of the kingdom of Gelof [Wolof], which is at the entrance of the Rio de Çanaga [Senegal] in Guinee. . . . Because the said Bemoym was treacherously driven out of his kingdom, he determined to embark on one of the caravels of the trade, which frequent the coast, and to come in person to seek aid, assistance and justice from [John II], who was in Setuvel. Bemoym arrived in Lixboa [Lisbon], accompanied by some negroes of his own royal blood and sons of persons closely related to men of importance. When the king had been informed of their arrival, he commanded that they should come to be entertained at Palmella, where he forthwith commanded his men to make abundant provision for him and to serve him with silver and attendants and every other civility which was proper to his station. Also he commanded all to be given rich and fine clothes to wear, according as the quality and merit of their persons demanded. And when they were in a condition to come to the court, the king sent horses and mules, very well appareled, to them all; and on the day when they were to make their entrance, the king commanded that Bemoym should be received by Dom Francisco Coutinho, the count of Marialva, and with him all the lords and noblemen of the court. . . . Bemoym appeared to be forty years old, and he was a man of great stature, very dark, with a very long beard, limbs all well proportioned and a very gracious presence; and being dressed, he entered the king's rooms, and the king came forward two or three paces from the dais to receive him, raising his cap a little. Then he led him to the dais, where there was a throne; but the king did not sit thereon, and, leaning against it, thus on foot gave ear to him. Then the said Bemoym and all his men threw themselves at his feet to kiss them, and they made a show of taking the earth from under them and, in token of their subjection and his overlordship and of their great respect, threw it over their heads. But the king with much honor and courtesy made him rise, and through negro interpreters, who were already present for this purpose, commanded him to speak. Thereupon, Bemoym with great ease, majesty and considerable gravity made a public speech, which lasted for a long time, and he used such notable words and sentences in support of his case that they did not seem to come from a savage negro but from Prince Grego, educated in Athenas. The substance of his speech was to recount to the king with swift sighs and many tears the tale of his miserable ill-fortune, caused by the treason which had been directed against him in his kingdom. . . . Moreover, he said to him: "Most powerful lord, God knows how, when I heard of thy greatness and thy royal virtues, my spirits were always eager and my eyes desirous to see thee; and I do not know why it was, because the more it pleased me, when I was free and in all my prosperity, the less do my overthrow and exile, by their sad condition, justify my faith and my words; but, it if were thus ordained from above that I should not come and do it so well in other circumstances more favorable to me, since it was ordained for me to see thee, I praise God fervently for my ruin; and this gladness already so satisfies me that I shall not return from this journey discontented." Proceeding further in a word, he said that, if perhaps in reply to his petition for justice and help men

should deny that he was a Christian, even as upon other occasions word had been sent to him by way of an excuse for refusing another similar request, there should now be no doubt or contradiction about it, because he and all his men who were present, among whom there were not wanting men of noble and royal birth, advised at other times by His holy warnings, had come in order that in his kingdoms and at his hands they might at once become Christians. He said that the only sorrow and truly grave anxiety, which they had thereby experienced, arose out of the fact that it seemed that the force of his necessity rather than of his faith had caused him to do it. With these he coupled many other sound reasons touching his purpose. Then the king replied to him in a few words, and devoted great care and much wisdom to everything, expressing great pleasure at their meeting and even more pleasure at his final intention to be a Christian. Therefore he gave him hope in this world of assistance in his cause and of restoration to his kingdom, and in the other that of glory and eternal salvation. Thereupon, he dismissed him, and Bemoym went to speak to the queen and to the prince, before whom he made a short speech, in which with shrewd judgment and very natural dignity he asked them for favor and assistance with the king. The queen and the prince dismissed him, showing him much honor and kindness. Then, on another day, Bemoym came to speak with the king, and, alone and apart, with an interpreter, they both conversed for a long time. Here Bemoym again recounted his affairs with great prudence; and he also replied very wisely and exactly to the questions which the king asked him, and the king remained very satisfied with this. In his honor the king ordered bull-fights and tournaments, and he held fancy-dress balls and dances, and in order that he might see them he gave orders for a chair to be placed at the upper end of the state room opposite the king. Moreover, it was the king's wish that Bemoym, before becoming a Chris-

tian, should first be instructed in matters of the faith; for Bemoym was of the sect of Mafamede in whom he believed, because of his being a neighbor of, and dealer with, the Azanegues, and he had some knowledge of the contents of the Bible. For this reason, theologians and learned men conversed with him and taught and advised him. Then it was decided that he should see and listen to a mass for the king, and this mass was said in pontifical and with great formality and ceremonial in the church of Santa Maria de Todolos Santos. Bemoym with his men and with learned Christians was in the choir, and, at the elevation of the body of Our Lord, when he saw all on their knees with their hands raised in the act of prayer, his hand went up to the cap which he had on his head; and thus, like everybody, with his knees on the ground and his head uncovered, he prayed. Then he said with many indications of truth that the remorse, which he experienced in his heart in that hour, he took as clear proof that this was the only true God of salvation. Then for two days the king proceeded to banquet publicly, for which purpose he put on his robes and he commanded that the house and the table were to be furnished with plate and tapestries, dishes and service, and there were to be minstrels and dances, all in great perfection; for the king was deliberately very particular and exact about ceremonial above all in matters touching his estate. At the second hour of the night of the third day of the month of November, the said Bemoym, and six of the principal persons who had come with him, became Christians in the chamber of the queen, which was decorated for the occasion with elaborate formality. His godfathers were the king, the queen, the prince, the duke, a commissary of the pope who was at the court, and the bishop of Tanger who at that time was the licentiate Calçadilha. Dom Justo, bishop of Cepta, who in pontifical performed the office, baptized them, and Bemoym received the name Dom Joham for love of the king. Moreover, on the seventh day of November, the king dubbed him a knight; and twenty-four of his men were made Christians in the counting-house of the said town. The king gave him a coat-of-arms consisting of a golden cross on a red field surrounded by the escutcheon of the arms of Portugal. On this same day, in a solemn act and speaking as a great lord he rendered obedience and paid homage to the king. Also he sent another submission, written in Latin, to the pope, wherein he gave an account of his case and of his conversion to the faith in words of deep devotion and high praise to the king. The king determined to give him help and assistance, and gave him twenty armed caravels. . . .

CRY OF ALARM

The Portuguese began evangelizing the peoples of the Congo in 1484 or 1485. During the next few years they converted most of the Congolese royal family. One member, Nzinga Mvemba, who was baptized Affonso, came to the throne in 1507. He ruled as manikongo, *or king, until 1543, and was a sincere and diligent Christian. However, by the late 1400's slaves and gold had become Africa's major exports, and King Affonso grew alarmed as he saw his kingdom being depopulated by the Portuguese. He wrote numerous letters of protest to the sovereign of Portugal. The one given here is dated October 18, 1526.*

Moreover, Sir, in our Kingdoms there is another great inconvenience which is of little service to God, and this is that many of our people [*naturaes*], keenly desirous as they are of the wares and things of your Kingdoms, which are brought here by your people, and in order to satisfy their voracious appetite, seize many of our people, freed and exempt men; and very often it happens that they kidnap even noblemen and the sons of noblemen, and our relatives, and take them to be sold to the white men who are in our Kingdoms; and for this purpose they have concealed them; and others are brought during the night so that they might not be recognized.

And as soon as they are taken by the white men they are immediately ironed and branded with fire, and when they are carried to be embarked, if they are caught by our guards' men the whites allege that they have bought them but they cannot say from whom, so that it is our duty to do justice and to restore to the freemen their freedom, but it cannot be done if your subjects feel offended, as they claim to be.

And to avoid such a great evil we passed a law so that any white man living in our Kingdoms and wanting to purchase goods in any way should first inform three of our noblemen and officials of our court whom we rely upon in this matter, and these are Dom Pedro Manipanza and Dom Manuel Manissaba, our chief usher, and Gonçalo Pires our chief freighter, who should investigate if the mentioned goods are captives or free men, and if cleared by them there will be no further doubt nor embargo for them to be taken and embarked. But if the white men do not comply with it they will lose the aforementioned goods. And if we do them this favor and concession it is for the part Your Highness has in it, since we know that it is in your service too that these goods are taken from our Kingdom, otherwise we should not consent to this.

MAKING NEW CHRISTIANS

It did not take the Portuguese long to appreciate the enormous profitability of the slave trade. On the other hand, many individuals and groups, including the Crown, were repelled by commerce in human beings. But, as would be the case elsewhere until the nineteenth century, their repugnance spurred them to justify rather than to cease their evil activities. In 1444 one of the earliest cargoes of African slaves reached the coast of Algarve, Portugal's southernmost province. Henry the Navigator allegedly ordered one of his chroniclers, Gomes Eannes de Azurara, to whitewash the whole episode. As is apparent in the subsequent description of the slave market from Azurara's Chronicle of Guinea, *the historian could not disguise the inhumanity of the spectacle. The best he could do was applaud the Infante's pious intentions.*

On the eighth day of August, 1444, very early in the morning on account of the heat, the mariners began to assemble their lighters and to disembark their captives, according to their orders. Which captives were gathered together in a field, and marvelous it was to see among them some of a rosy whiteness, fair and well made; others less white, verging on grey, others again as black as moles, as various in their complexions as in their shapes. . . . And what heart was so hard as not to be moved to pity by the sight of this multitude, some with bowed heads and tearful countenances, others groaning dolorously and with eyes uplifted towards heaven, as if to implore help from the Father of all mankind; while there were others who covered their faces with their hands and flung themselves down upon the ground, and some again who gave vent to their sorrow in a dirge, after the manner of their country; and although we could not understand the words, well we appreciated the depth of their distress. And now, to aggravate their woe, men came to parcel them out into five distinct lots, to do which they tore the son from his father, the wife from the husband, the brother from his brethren. No tie of blood or comradeship was respected; each was thrown into a place by chance. O irresistible fortune, thou which ridest roughshod over the affairs of this world, bring to the knowledge of these most unhappy folk those ultimate truths from which they may receive consolation! And ye that are charged with this division into lots, deplore so great a misery, and observe how these unhappy ones embrace one another so tightly that it needs no little strength to tear them apart. Such a division indeed, was not to be effected without great trouble, since parents and children, finding themselves in different groups, would run back to each other—mothers clutched up their children and ran away with them, caring not about the blows they received so long as their little ones should not be torn from them. After this toilsome fashion was the task of division accomplished, the work being rendered more difficult by the crowds which flocked from the neighboring towns and villages, neglecting their work, to see this novel sight. And some of these spectators moved to tears, others chattering, they made a tumult which hindered those charged with the business. The Infante (Dom Henry), mounted on a powerful horse, disdained to take his own share, some forty-six souls, but threw it back into the common stock, taking pleasure only in the thought of so many souls being redeemed from perdition. And truly, his hope was not vain, since so soon as they learned the language, with very little trouble, these people became Christians; and I who write this history saw afterwards in the town of Lagos, young men and women, the offspring of these, born in the country, as good and genuine Christians as if they had been descended from the generation first baptized under the dispensation of Christ.

NEGOTIATING FOR CHATTEL

William Bosman, who is quoted below, was the Dutch West India Company's chief factor, or European agent, at Elmina in the late seventeenth century. A factor's right to purchase slaves in a given area was granted by the local black chief in return for "coomey," or customs duty. Bosman's description of Guinean slave dealing, which follows, was given in one of twenty letters he wrote to a friend in Holland. In 1705 these were published in London in English under the title A New and Accurate Description of Guinea.

Most of the Slaves that are offered to us are Prisoners of War, which are sold by the Victors as their Booty.

When these slaves come to *Fida* [in present-day Dahomey], they are put in Prison all together, and when we treat concerning buying them, they are all

brought out together in a large Plain; where by our Chirurgeons, whose Province it is, they are thoroughly examined, even to the smallest Member, and that naked too both Men and Women, without the least Distinction or Modesty. Those which are approved as good are set on one side; and the lame or faulty are set by as *Invalides*, which are here called *Mackrons.* These are such as are above five and thirty Years old, or are maimed in the Arms, Legs, Hands or Feet, have lost a Tooth, are grey-haired or have Films over their eyes; as well as all those which are affected with any Venereal Distemper, or with several other Diseases.

The *Invalides* and the Maimed being thrown out . . . the remainder are numbred, and it is entered who delivered them. In the meanwhile, a burning Iron with the Arms or Name of the Companies, lyes in the Fire; with which ours are marked on the Breast. . . . but we yet take all possible care that they are not burned too hard, especially the Women who are more tender than the Men.

We are seldom long detained in the buying of these Slaves, because their price is established, the Women being . . . cheaper than the Men. . . .

When we have agreed with the Owners of the Slaves, they are returned to their Prison; where from that time forwards they are kept at our charge, cost us twopence a day a Slave; which serves to subsist them, like our Criminals, on Bread and Water: So that to save Charges we send them on Board our Ships with the very first Opportunity; before which their Masters strip them of all they have on their Backs . . . as well Women as Men: In which condition they are obliged to continue, if the Master of the Ship is not so Charitable (which he commonly is) as to bestow something on them to cover their Nakedness.

THE MIDDLE PASSAGE

The ocean crossing from Africa to the Americas was called the middle passage. It was the

most terrifying segment of the slave's journey to bondage; there was no chance of escape, and most of the captives had never before seen the sea. This description of the trans-Atlantic nightmare is from Human Livestock, An Account of the Share of the English-speaking People in the Maintenance and Abolition of Slavery, *published in 1933. The author, British historian Edmund B. d'Auvergne, relied largely on records of testimonies made by slavetraders themselves before parliamentary committees.*

A common type of slaving vessel employed about the middle of the eighteenth century was called a snow, of about 140 tons, square of stern, 57 feet keel, 21 feet beam, 5 feet between decks, 9 feet in the hold. The dimensions of the *Brooks,* a frigate-built ship of 320 tons burthen, without forecastle and pierced for twenty guns were stated by a [British] Government inspector in the year 1786 to be length, 100 feet, beam 25 ft. 4 in., height between decks, 5 feet 8 in. The number of air ports was fourteen. Legally allowed to carry only 450 souls, on leaving the coast of Africa, she carried in addition to her crew of forty-five, 609 slaves (351 men, 127 women, 90 boys, 41 girls). Overcrowding was almost essential to carrying on the slave business. In days of sail, shipmasters could hardly guess the number of trips they might make in a year; and while overcrowding increased the mortality, it might equally result in more survivors to be sold for a profit. In Charles II's time Captain Tallers bought some negroes from another ship which had had them *three months* aboard. They were almost starved and "surfeycatted" [suffocated]. They were fed with little else than musty corn. "There must have been something extraordinary," concludes the letter, "that so many died." The voyage from Guinea to Antigua in the eighteenth century was reckoned at five or six weeks. The longest passage of nine ships reported was fifty days.

Between decks, where it will have been noted a tall man could not stand upright, the human cargo was stowed, males and females in separate compartments. The women were left unfettered. The men were generally kept throughout the voyage chained in pairs, wrist to wrist, ankle to ankle. Those who were left unchained were packed in couples, side by side, like sardines, or spoon-fashion—the head of one against the feet of the other. "They are about as comfortable," one witness told the commission, "as a man might be in his coffin." The slaves, said one captain, often quarreled among themselves —not seldom because one of the pair either could not or would not move when his wretched partner wished to ease himself. One is not surprised to hear that those who went below in the evening apparently in good health were not seldom found dead in the morning; dead and living were often found chained together.

A ship's surgeon says: "Some wet and blowing weather having occasioned the port-holes to be shut and the grating to be covered, fluxes and fevers among the negroes resulted. While they were in this situation, my profession requiring it, I frequently went down among them, till at length their apartments became so extremely hot as to be only sufferable for a very short time. But the excessive heat was not the only thing that rendered their situation intolerable. The deck, that is the floor of their rooms, was so covered with the blood and mucus which had proceeded from them in consequence of the flux, that it resembled a slaughterhouse. It is not in the power of the human imagination to picture a situation more dreadful and disgusting. Numbers of the slaves had fainted, they were carried on deck, where several of them died, and the rest were with difficulty restored. It nearly proved fatal to me also." To these horrors must be added the agonies of sea-sickness, to which most of the wretched creatures must have been subject. Gomer Williams, comparing statistics, finds that out of 7,904 slaves purchased on the Coast, 2,053 died on the Middle Passage. The *Priscilla*, of Liverpool, lost ninety-four out of 350 slaves. On another occasion,

during a gale, fifty slaves perished within eighteen hours.

THE RISE OF GUMBO SMART

Occasionally, through sheer wit or cunning, a slave improved his lot. Following is the success story of Gumbo Smart, who made the best of his enslavement on Bance (now Bunce) Island in the Sierra Leone River. The extract is from the journal of Zachary Macaulay, who was a white colonist living in the region.

June 3, 1797. . . . This Smart I have formerly told you had been a slave on Bance Island. He is a native of the Loko Country which lies three days' journey or more beyond Rokelle [Rokel]. He had been intended for a ship bound for the West Indies, but on the day the slaves were being put on board, he had concealed himself. . . . In the meantime he was employed in boats, and showing much acuteness and fidelity he was retained on the island.

He grew in favor and was at length promoted to be a factor and sent to Rokelle with goods to buy slaves. As this was the key to his native country he had an opportunity of buying numbers of his own Countrymen, none of whom he sent to the Island, but either kept them as domestics, or exchanged them with their friends for slaves of other nations. By this policy he has made himself powerful and independent. So that even Bance Island whose slave he is, stands in awe of him and scarce ventures to press him for the Payment of 150 Slaves which he owes them. His adherents amount to several Hundreds, exclusive of his own family, [which] consists of no less than thirty wives and eighty children alive.

THE CONSUMMATE VILLAINS

One of the more outspoken opponents of slavery was the Reverend John Newton

(1725-1807), an Englishman who before entering the Church had been a dealer in human flesh on Sherbro Island off Sierra Leone and had also captained trans-Atlantic slave brigs. In 1788 he published in London an anti-slave-trade pamphlet, Thoughts upon the African Slave Trade, *which contained this description of the mutually deceptive means by which the trade was conducted.*

Not an article that is capable of diminution or adulteration is delivered genuine or entire. The spirits are lowered by water. False heads are put into the kegs that contain the gunpowder; so that, though the keg appears large, there is no more powder in it, than in a much smaller. The linen and cotton cloths are opened, and two or three yards . . . cut off, not from the end, but out of the middle, where it is not so readily noticed.

The Natives are cheated, in the number, weight, measure, or quality of what they purchase in every possible way. And, by habit and emulation, a marvelous dexterity is acquired in these practices. And thus the Natives, in their turn, in proportion to their commerce with the Europeans, and (I am sorry to add) particularly with the English, become jealous, insidious, and revengeful.

They know with whom they have to deal, and are accordingly prepared. . . . Retaliation on their part furnishes a plea for reprisal on ours. Thus, in one place or another, trade is often suspended, all intercourse cut off, and things are in a state of war; till necessity, either on the ship's part, or on theirs, produces overtures of peace, and dictates the price which the offending party must pay. . . . For, with a few exceptions, the English and Africans, reciprocally, consider each other as consummate villains, who are always watching opportunities to do mischief. In short, we have, I fear too deservedly, a very unfavorable character upon the Coast. When I have charged a Black with unfairness and dishonesty, he has answered, if able to clear himself, with an air of disdain, "What! do you think I am a White Man?". . .

A sixteenth-century Nigerian clay sculpture portrays a fierce Portuguese soldier.

THE INTRUDERS

ARMADADENVNODACVNHÃ

High-pooped Portuguese caravels, like those in the armada above, brought the African coasts within the sphere of European interest. Opposite, a 1493 Portuguese map of Africa locates Prester John's realm along the Upper Nile.

THE EYES OF PORTUGAL

Europeans first touched the sub-Saharan mainland in 1444, when Portuguese explorers under the direction and inspiration of Prince Henry reached the mouth of the Senegal River. What motivated the Navigator were grander designs, among them sheer curiosity to know what his captains would find when they entered southern waters. Technology had made Henry's goal possible: by the early fifteenth century the Portuguese had developed a sailing ship capable of making long ocean voyages. Historic legend abetted the search. Henry sought to discover deep within the uncharted continent the legendary Christian kingdom of Prester John and to enlist his friendly forces in a two-pronged crusade against Islam. Commerical ambitions seem at this stage to have played a relatively minor role. Relations between Europeans and Africans at the start, at least, were auspicious.

338

339

SECURING A FOOTHOLD

Between the Portuguese and Africans the first formal link was trade, a mutually profitable exchange of European textiles and metalware for African pepper, ivory, and gold. To put the thriving commerce on a permanent basis and secure it from European interlopers, the Portuguese built the fortress-depot of São Jorge in 1482 on the coast of present-day Ghana. It was the first of many such Portuguese stations, which would eventually dot the African coast from Senegal to Zanzibar. Close behind the traders came diplomats and missionaries, for in the early days of contact Portugal looked upon a Christianized Africa as a vital ally in its grand design of humbling the Muslim empire. Missionary success was striking in the kingdom of the Congo, whose ruler, baptized Affonso, became an efficient propagator of the faith. By the early decades of the sixteenth century the Congo seemed well on its way to becoming a Westernized Christian realm in the heart of Africa.

An ivory saltcellar at left, from West Africa, combines Portuguese motifs with African craftsmanship. The heavily bearded figure represents a Portuguese official. Below is a French rendering of the huge Portuguese citadel at Mombasa, an Indian Ocean port that the Portuguese seized in 1505. Opposite is a statue of Saint Anthony of Padua made on the Congo coast, where Portugal was most successful in proselytizing.

An enthroned King Affonso of the Congo is depicted here in an audience with the Portuguese envoy. A Christian convert, he asks for missionaries and holy objects.

Upon the advice of the Europeans, Affonso orders his subjects to burn their idols. This and the engraving above are from Théodore de Bry's Petits Voyages, 1598.

BOTH: DE BRY, *Small Voyages*, 1598

341

WONDERS
THAT CEASED

Africa held surprises in abundance for the early European voyagers. First, there were the portents of seemingly unprecedented wealth. "Precious stones were so plentiful," Vasco da Gama was told in Mozambique in 1498, "that there was no need to purchase them as they could be collected in baskets." There were the prospering seaports of East Africa such as Kilwa, "with many fair houses of stones and mortar with many windows after our own fashion, very well arranged in streets." Above all, to Europeans, there was the might and authority of African monarchs. "The King of Wolof can put ten thousand horsemen and one hundred thousand footmen in the field," a Portuguese visitor to Senegal reported in 1505. The great reverence they give to their king filled an English sea captain with awe after he visited the Benin kingdom in 1553. By then, however, the export of slaves to America had begun, and the Africa of wonders would soon cease to exist for Europeans.

THEVET, *Cosmographie Universelle*, 1575

The East African plant opposite was cited in André Thevet's Cosmographie Universelle, 1575, as the source of a miracle cure for snakebite. At right is the sea monster that, he asserted, ruled the Red Sea. Below is an engraving from a 1686 work by Olfert Dopper purporting to record how the natives of Guinea dive for gold.

THEVET, *Cosmographie Universelle*, 1575

DOPPER, *Description de l'Afrique*, 1686

THEVET, *Cosmographie Universelle*, 1575

DE BRY, *Small Voyages*, 1598

The Congolese nobility traveled in litters like that above, according to De Bry's hearsay book on Africa. At left, West Africans defend their village against lions, "scourge of the countryside," as shown in the Cosmographie.

OVERLEAF: The king of Benin sallies from his palace in the company of his retinue in a 1686 French print displaying the pomp of an African ruler.

DOPPER, DESCRIPTION DE L'AFRIQUE, 1686

343

Awaiting shipment to the New World, an African slave sits beneath a heavy forked log, one device used in coffling captives. Below, in a Dahomey appliqué tapestry done in the early eighteenth century, opposing African forces are shown in combat. The work dates from the reign of King Agaja, who, like other inland rulers, was expanding his domain toward the sea in order to deal directly with the Europeans and thus monopolize the local slave trade. At right is a bronze statuette from Benin representing an armed Benin warrior. Regarded with terror by less powerful states, these professionals were the leading procurers of slaves.

A Portuguese force deploys in square defensive lines to hold off Angolan attackers in the Portuguese sketch at left. To secure Angola as a supply base for the Brazilian slave trade, the Portuguese in 1575 sharply reversed their former policies. Setting up a colony at Luanda, they not only waged war against local kingdoms but trained local forces to carry out raids for them, bringing strife and decay to the entire Angolan coast. In time the nearby Congo kingdom was sucked into the maelstrom, and when it eventually rose up against its former friends and fellow Christians, the kingdom was torn apart and destroyed.

THE HIDEOUS TRADE

When Europeans decided to use slave labor in the Americas, they set the seal of doom on vast portions of sub-Saharan Africa. Before the opening of the New World the African slave trade with Europe had been a small and circumscribed evil; some five hundred slaves were sold to the Portuguese each year. Fifty years after the discovery of the Americas the yearly figure climbed to ten thousand. A few decades later the annual figure was doubled again. After 1650 slaves were the main West African commodity that European traders would buy. But it was African rulers themselves who were among the chief suppliers, using their power and position to organize slave hunts for the bustling coastal markets. Even European missionaries neglected their religious duties in order to share in the profits of slavery; and by 1700 Christianity had vanished from tropical Africa. Crippled by the slave hunters' reign of terror, African art and sculpture virtually disappeared from such great centers as Ife and Benin. Luxuries for the profiteers were all that the slave trade brought to Africa, and guns to capture yet more slaves in a widening spiral of greed and ruin.

INTERNATIONAL RIVALRY

Other European nations did not stand idle while Portugal reaped the profits of its African trade monopoly. Avid for Portugal's spoils, they eventually took them by force. Simple thievery was the first method: French and British corsairs would pirate Portuguese ships or pillage Portuguese trade centers in daring, one-shot raids. In 1612, however, the Dutch took a bolder step. They built a fort on the Gold Coast; by 1642 they had ousted the Portuguese from that coveted portion of the coast. As Portuguese control crumbled, the French seized the foreign trade of Senegal and that of the Ivory Coast, and the British took the rest of West Africa's commerce. Nothing, however, was settled. The newcomers were as ready to prey on each other as they had been to prey on the Portuguese. Skirmishing perpetually against one another from massive coastal forts, they added by their bitter competition a further infusion of conflict to the chaos inherent in the slave trade. This the intruders accomplished even before they set foot in the interior.

The figure of a plump-cheeked Portuguese at left adorns an ivory spoon carved in Africa around 1525, when the Portuguese were still the only Europeans that West Africans had encountered. Below is Britain's chief Gold Coast installation at Cape Coast Castle as it looked in 1806. The British Crown won control of the Gold Coast trade in the 1700's, succeeding the Dutch and the Portuguese before them.

OVERLEAF: *Troops of Sir Francis Drake put to flight the defenders of São Tiago, largest of the Cape Verde Islands. Drake stopped to pillage this tropical settlement in 1585 on his way to the Caribbean.*

The arrival of the Dutch on Gabon's shores, as imagined by De Bry, was largely an occasion for rejoicing. Here, a nearly naked king and queen tender a warm welcome to two officers. Depicted in the water color below is the international market town of Xavier in the Guinea kingdom of Juda. From adjacent walled compounds the Portuguese, French, English, and Dutch vied for shares in a lively foreign trade.

Chapter Nine

TIME OF TROUBLES

(c. 1492–1828)

by

John Henrik Clarke

AFRICA'S TIME OF TRAGEDY AND DECLINE started both in Europe and in Africa itself. For more than a thousand years Africans had been bringing into being empire after empire. But the opening of Europe's era of exploration, Africa's own internal strife, and the slave trade turned what had been Africa's golden age into a time of troubles.

The Crusades may be called the beginning of Europe's reawakening. A religious fervor, not unrelated to politics, had stirred Europeans out of their lethargy and their indifference to the larger world. The First Crusade, begun in 1095, was precipitated by the Seljuk Turks, whose persecution of Christians had placed even Constantinople in jeopardy. The Eastern heads of the Church appealed to Pope Urban II for help. At a great Church council in France the pope pointed out that if Constantinople fell to the Turks, Western Europe would soon be overrun. He made an eloquent plea to the kings and princes gathered, and to all Western European Christendom, to rally to the aid of the Christians in the East and to drive the "infidels" from the Holy Land.

This religious crisis gave Europe a semblance of unity; and although it can be said that the Crusades were military and religious failures, they did provide the opportunity to bring new information to Europe. The religious wars also had a profound effect on the political development of Europe. The Western monarchs were able to strengthen their authority and develop a strong central government while many members of their turbulent aristocracies were fighting in the Holy Land.

Contact with the East had a deep and lasting effect on the Crusaders, who belonged to a civilization where culture and learning had almost vanished during the Dark Ages. The princes in their castles and the peasants in their huts were

...low deck on a slaver, as recorded by a member of the British patrol that captured the vessel in 1846

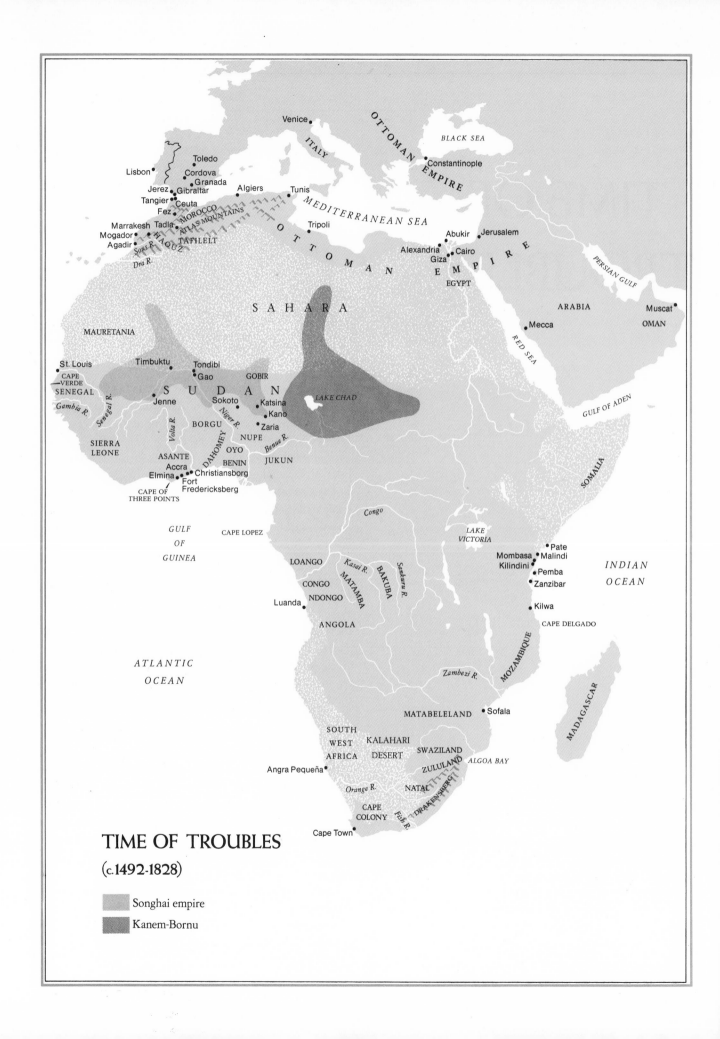

TIME OF TROUBLES

(c. 1492-1828)

Songhai empire

Kanem-Bornu

equally ignorant and uneducated. When they arrived in the East, they soon realized how backward were the people of the West. They marveled at the beautiful cities, the thriving commerce, the busy industries, the art, and the learning. The impetus for exploration was fueled by what the Crusaders met along the way. Ships built to ferry the Crusaders to the Holy Land returned laden with the products of the East. The cargoes of spices, fruits, rich silks, satins, velvets, and other luxury goods had found a ready market. Thus the Crusades brought into being the first attempts to open fresh trade routes to the East. Early in the fifteenth century Europeans, in search of new worlds to conquer and of a food supply to feed the continent's hungry population, began to venture across the seas.

NORTH AFRICA: By 1492 North Africa was confronted with the painful fact of its waning influence in Mediterranean Europe. Spain and Portugal, which had broken the yoke of North African domination, were asserting themselves as powerful, independent nations with colonial aspirations in the lands of their former conquerors. Islam, a great religious and military force in North Africa and the Middle East since the latter part of the seventh century, was now torn apart by internal strife and bickering. The relationship of North Africa to the people of the western Sudan was deteriorating. For hundreds of years this relationship had been good. Africans from the western Sudan had participated in large numbers in the conquest of Spain in the year A.D. 711. These Africans made up the major military force that kept Spain under North African domination, and they participated in that country's intellectual life, as is still reflected in Spain's art, culture, and literature.

In order to understand this neglected aspect of history—the role of Africans in the conquering and ruling of Spain—it is necessary to go back in time to retell, at least briefly, the part that black Africans played in the rise of Islam and in the spread of Islamic influence to Mediterranean Europe.

Hadzrat Bilal ibn Rahab (more often referred to simply as Bilal) was the first high priest of the Islamic empire. After Muhammad himself, it may be said that this great religion began with Bilal, who was an Ethiopian. Bilal is considered to be the Prophet's first African convert. Zayd ibn Harithah, another convert to Muhammad's faith, later became one of the Prophet's foremost generals. Muhammad adopted him as his son and later made him governor of his people, the proud Koreish who lived in what is today Saudi Arabia. Like Bilal, Zayd ibn Harithah was also an Ethiopian. He eventually married into the Prophet's family, the highest

honor possible. Zayd ibn Harithah was killed in battle while leading his men against the armies of the Byzantine empire. The authoritative *Encyclopedia of Islam* has hailed him as one of the first great heroes of Islam.

By the early part of the eighth century the followers of Islam had swept across North Africa and were moving into the western Sudan. Among the Africans' military chiefs who converted to the Islamic faith during the Arab invasion of Morocco was a great general known as Tarik ibn Zayyad. Tarik held the rank of general in the Arab-Moorish armies of Musa ibn Nusayr, the governor of North Africa. Tarik entered into friendly relations with Count Julian, the Christian governor of Ceuta, who was on bad terms with his master, Roderick, the king of Spain. Count Julian urged Tarik to invade Spain. In the meantime, Musa ibn Nusayr learned that the Spanish king was busy in the north of his country in a campaign to put down an uprising of the Basques. Musa decided that time was ripe for an invasion of the Visigothic realm. An African army was recruited and placed under the leadership of Tarik. In 711 the army landed on a Spanish promontory just thirteen miles across the Mediterranean from Ceuta. The place was later named Gebel Tarik, meaning the "Hill of Tarik," or as we now call it, Gibraltar.

Tarik's army captured several Spanish towns near Gibraltar, among them Heraclea. Then he advanced toward Andalusia. King Roderick learned of the invasion and raised an army for defense. The two armies met in battle at a place called Jerez, not far from the Guadalete River. In this battle King Roderick was defeated. Tarik sent for reinforcements from Africa, and with them conquered most of the Iberian Peninsula. Thus began the African domination of Spain. The Gothic kingdom of Spain was laid low by Africans who had been converted to the Islamic faith, not by Arabs.

After consolidating their position in Spain, the Muslims began to establish institutions of research and learning, whose brilliance was felt far beyond Spain's borders. This was an achievement not of the Arabs alone. It was brought into being by a combination of Africans and Arabs, collectively referred to by Europeans as Moors. (The word "Moor" entered the vocabulary of the Europeans meaning "blacks," as in "blackamoor.") The Moors built magnificent cities in Spain. Cordova in the ninth century was much like a modern city, with streets paved and illuminated at night, and sidewalks for pedestrians.

The intellectual achievement of the Africans in Spain outweighs all other things that can be credited to them.

These Islamic Africans re-examined the moral foundations supporting Western civilization. They found that it had been the legacy of the Greeks that had enabled the West to make intellectual progress. This answer created a question: What had gone wrong in Europe—spiritually and intellectually—before and after the decline of the Roman empire? The inquiry led in essence to the following conclusion: By the time Europe's Christian foundation was firmly set, the intellectual means and moral fiber of the people were exceedingly weak, and there existed a deep gulf between faith and reason.

These Muslim Africans in Spain came to this conclusion while trying to bridge a similar gap in relation to their own religion and culture. While Europe was largely ignorant of its Greek legacy, these Africans rediscovered and preserved it. Their assimilation and distribution of that treasure forms one of the most fascinating chapters in the history of man's quest for knowledge.

In the course of their labors the African conquerors of Spain did far more than mere translation. They commented upon and explained the Greeks, gradually erecting upon the Greek foundation an intellectual edifice of their own. While the initial work was done in the Near East, it was greatly elaborated upon by other scholars, mainly in Sicily, Spain, and Morocco.

In the meantime Islam had moved deeper into Africa. The Arabs' language and religion brought together a large number of peoples and cultures that had not previously related one to another. When the second wave of North African merchants reached the western Sudan about the year A.D. 1000, they found flourishing kingdoms that had already been influenced by Islam. The commercial relations they established there lasted for more than five hundred years despite continuing conflict. The Africans south of the Sahara made a rallying cry around Islam and in large numbers began to prey on the nations in West Africa and the Niger River area, accusing the people of not properly observing the faith—Islam. Very often the spread of Islam and trade with North Africa came at the same time. Therefore in the western Sudan the defenders of this religion had both a commercial and a religious motive.

This gave rise to the dynasty of the Almoravids, who derived their name from the Arabic *al-Murabitin*, meaning "members of the ribat," a kind of militarized convent. The Almoravids were started by Ibn Yasin, head of a tough, warlike family from Senegal, across the desert. Puritanical in their approach to Islam, they sought to impose their own interpretation of the faith. After establishing a series of

ribats where the disciples devoted themselves to strict religious practices and military exercises, the Almoravids swept north across the Mauritanian deserts and gained possession of the mountainous regions of Morocco. Ibn Yasin's successor, Yusuf ibn Tashfin, founded the capital at Marrakesh in 1062 and laid siege to Fez in the following year.

The Almoravids succeeded in reuniting Morocco, parts of West Africa, and Islamic Spain. By 1076 they had conquered the ancient empire of Ghana. After ruling this fallen country for ten years, they pulled most of their armies out of Ghana in order to give more support to their coreligionists in Spain. There they were successful in stemming the Christian tide that threatened to engulf all Islamic Spain after the fall of Toledo in 1085.

In the middle of the thirteenth century (about A.D. 1240) another dynasty rose up within the framework of Islam and challenged the rule of the Almoravids in Spain and in Morocco. Its followers are known by the name "Almohads," a Spanish corruption of an Arab word meaning "unitarians." They, too, were a religious and military movement, offering another puritanical interpretation. The conflicts between the Almoravids and the Almohads weakened the Africans' control over Spain. The eventual decline of both dynasties affected all North Africa, the western Sudan, and Mediterranean Europe.

The Almohads did not yield their power easily. They called upon other followers of Islam for support. A vigorous people from the Sahara, known as the Marinids, came to their assistance and eventually usurped the waning power of the Almohads. This dynasty consisted mainly of soldiers and administrators. Abu Yohya (1248–1258) established the Marinid capital at Fez and prepared the ground for another leader, Yaqub al-Mansur, who extended their religious empire into what is now Algeria. The Marinids left their stamp both on Spain and North Africa, where they proved to be some of the greatest builders and patrons of the arts that Morocco had known.

By the end of the fourteenth century southern Europe had gained enough strength—military and otherwise—to challenge their African masters. The constant pressure from Christians in Spain and from the new waves of Arab immigrants from the East created a situation that the Marinids found difficult to handle. By the end of the fifteenth century the Moors had lost all Spain except the kingdom of Granada. The Christians, although they also had their internal disputes, were finally united. The marriage of Ferdinand and Isabella joined the formerly hostile royal houses of Aragon and Castile, and together their forces blockaded the city of

Granada. After eight months the Moorish governor finally surrendered.

This marked the end of an era. Europe had literally been reborn. The Africans who had planted the seeds of progress in southern Europe had not made the best use of the harvest that followed. The progress and excitement that had inspired Europe during the fifteenth century and had carried medieval Europe over into the modern world had brought no progressive changes to North Africa, now rocked with conflict.

In the countries of North Africa, especially in Morocco, political stagnation seemed to be the general rule, and strong men with selfish intent found their opportunity to seize power. They no longer protected the poets and scholars; they left no monuments to embellish the conquered cities. To North Africans the fifteenth century was a time in which Spain was a lost and hated land, a century in which Portugal robbed North Africa of a large part of its western seacoast.

The news in 1492 of Christopher Columbus' discovery of the New World came swiftly to the courts of Fez, Marrakesh, and Cairo, and was no cause for rejoicing. To the marabouts, who were the interpreters of the Islamic world of that day, this event was grave indeed. The same year Granada fell, and Moorish exiles returned to their homes in Morocco without the customary heroes' welcome.

During the early part of the sixteenth century the forces in North Africa were turning two ways. Attempts were made to settle internal differences, and plans to take over the still-rich nations in the western Sudan were formalized. The nations of the western Sudan were comparatively stable, due in part to their lack of firearms and the conflicts that would have resulted.

Portugal's growing control of the northern coast now began to impede commercial progress. This came at a time when the vassals and allies that the Portuguese had among the North African people began to desert them in favor of reawakened nationalism. Most Muslims regarded the Christian Portuguese with hostility and were determined that they should be driven into the sea. To accomplish this, the Muslims needed a leader. The search led them to Abu Abdullah, sheik of the Beni Saadi, a people of Arabian descent who had established themselves in the Dra River region of southern Morocco. Under the leadership of Abu Abdullah, the people of the Sous valley moved against the Portuguese, who had established a port on the Atlantic coast of Morocco at Agadir. Abdullah's power increased, although not all of his wars were successful. In the coastal

strip west of the Atlas Mountains of Morocco he and his two sons established a capital and fought the Portuguese. When Abu Abdullah died in 1518, his sons, as expected, carried on his work. The years of nationalist feeling in North Africa had produced a number of leaders who were able men determined to drive the Portuguese from their land. In 1541 Portuguese power in North Africa began to decline. They lost their stronghold at Agadir, and subsequently, as they became more involved in their Asian colonies, they abandoned other North African territories under their domination.

Meanwhile, in 1549, the Saadian dynasty came to power in Morocco and showed itself to be equal to the job of nation building. The greatest of the Saadian kings was Ahmad al-Mansur, who ruled from 1578 to 1603. He not only defended Morocco from Turkish invasion, strengthening the strategic fortifications of the country and reorganizing it on the Turkish model, but also developed the agriculture of the Sus and Haouz regions and won a favored position for Morocco in the markets of western Europe.

While the reign of Ahmad al-Mansur brought a high degree of security and prosperity to Morocco, it brought tragedy and decline to the nations of the western Sudan, for the Saadians lusted after the gold of the Niger River nations and tried to seize it by force. They were by no means the first Moroccan dynasty to make this national policy; in the eleventh century the Almoravids had financed their northward movement with gold from this region.

After the death of Askia Muhammad in 1528, his great Songhai empire showed signs of having seen its last days of power and glory. Ahmad al-Mansur systematically planned the conquest of the western Sudan, giving his profound attention to this military and administrative heart of West Africa. In the year 1591 an army of some four thousand musketeers under the leadership of a Spanish mercenary officer, Judar Pasha, crossed the Sahara and was on the borders of Songhai before any serious attention was paid to the danger. Songhai's ruler, Askia Ishak II, called up an army that was superior in numbers but armed with traditional weapons. The two armies met on April 12, 1591, at a small town called Tondibi, about fifty miles from the capital city of Gao. In spite of the brave stand made by the army of Songhai, the Moroccan soldiers moved into the country, and the wrack and ruin began.

Ahmad al-Mansur expected great treasures in gold to be sent back to Morocco soon after the conquest. When these treasures were not forthcoming, Ahmad dismissed Judar Pasha and sent another general, Mahmud ibn Zergun, to

Napoleon "the liberator" and local dignitaries observe French soldiers at a Nile reclamation project in a contemporary French print.

Songhai. His orders were to take charge of the army and press onward until he had driven Askia Ishak out of the Sudan and discovered the place where the people were hiding the gold.

The Moroccan invasion of Songhai and other nations of the western Sudan was made all the more tragic because in most cases it was Muslim against Muslim. The invaders from North Africa and their European mercenary troops did not spare anyone—not man, woman, or child. They pitilessly slew the now demoralized citizens who cried out to them: "We are Muslims; we are your brothers in religion." The war brought no honor to either side, and in the years that followed, an appreciation of their intellectual and material contribution to Spain and the other nations of the Mediterranean sphere was lost from the respectful commentary of human history.

While the drama of Morocco and the western Sudan was unfolding, Egypt and other North African nations were encountering a new force. Like the Mameluks before them, this new force came from Turkey, where its dreams of empire had begun to take shape with the conquest of Constantinople in 1453. By 1516 the eastern Mediterranean from Greece through Asia Minor and Syria was under Ottoman rule. By 1517 the reigning Mameluk sultan of Cairo had been publicly executed and replaced by an Ottoman ruler. Algeria was taken in 1518 by Khayr al-Din Barbarossa, who went on to make his reputation as the admiral of Turkey's dreaded corsair fleet. The Barbary Coast states of Tripolitania and Tunis became semi-independent tributaries of the Ottoman empire in the 1550's.

Cultural ties with the Islamic world of northwest Africa and the Middle East continued as before. The Ottoman Turks were content to rule through military oligarchies and to collect taxes, holding the land under a feudal system that invited a steady decline in the prosperity of the people and the fertility of the land. No fresh ideas came in; all business was operated in the interest of the Turks.

It was not until the end of the eighteenth century that a number of influences were combined to rescue Egypt from the decadence of Ottoman rule. First, in 1798, came Napoleon's abortive expedition immediately designed to cut Great Britain's route to the Indian subcontinent. (The French had been considering the idea of seizing Egypt since 1769, when annexation was proposed as compensation for the loss of its American territories.) Napoleon's invasion fleet arrived off Alexandria on July 1. Three weeks later he met the Ottoman forces at Embaba on the left bank of the Nile, just north of Giza. Winning a dramatic victory in the Battle of the Pyramids, Napoleon seemed to have laid France's claim to Egypt. But ten days later Admiral Horatio Nelson located Napoleon's fleet in Abukir Bay, and in the brief Battle of the Nile that followed, gave Napoleon's Egyptian campaign a major setback. (Napoleon would remain in Egypt for another year, his decimated forces suffering further defeats from a variety of diseases and from the Turkish army.) Napoleon returned to France in 1799, leaving Jean-Baptiste Kléber and his lieutenants to oversee the province. They, too, were forced to leave in 1801 when a British expedition of some seventeen thousand men and a Turkish army combined to deliver the final blow.

The United States, as a newborn maritime nation, was confronted with the costly problem of securing safe passage in the Mediterranean for its merchant ships. European states had swallowed pride and capitulated to the tribute demands of the Barbary Coast pirates, but a bumptious America was ready to meet the challenge with arms. Jefferson dispatched a squadron to the shores of Tripoli in 1801; early defeats were followed by Stephen Decatur's daring entry of Tripoli's harbor, where the American frigate Philadelphia *had been impounded. As shown in the print, right, the Yankees chose to burn the ship rather than leave it to the pirates. Strife continued until peace was signed in 1815.*

PEABODY MUSEUM, SALEM, OLDS COLLECTION

Short-lived though the occupation was, the awakening of European interest in the cultural and scientific achievements of ancient Egypt was to have a permanent effect. Napoleon's occupation had included a scientific commission, the Institute of Egypt, which applied itself to studying zoological and botanical curiosities, surveying the land, and exploring the archeological ruins of the ancient Egyptian kingdoms. (At the Delta town of Rashid, called Rosetta by the French, a French engineer stumbled upon a stone showing the multilingual inscription that would lead to the deciphering of Egyptian hieroglyphs.)

Next, Muhammad Ali, an enlightened Turkish soldier who had come to Egypt to expel the French, initiated the modernization of Egypt. Named the Turkish viceroy in Egypt in 1806, he gradually strengthened his power base until, in 1811, he was able to break with the Ottoman empire. The way to Egypt's renaissance was thus opened. Having observed the technological achievements of the French occupation, Muhammad Ali undertook to revolutionize Egypt's agriculture, industry, and army along Western lines. To supply an ever-growing demand for Egyptian cotton, he invited European hydraulic engineers to work with indigenous specialists to revive and improve the land's use of irrigation, and within a few years the Nile Valley was producing two crops per year where one had been the rule. As a further aid to productivity, he nationalized the land, making the peasants all but owners of their fields so long as they paid taxes. The considerable profits realized from these reforms were invested in the military and economic development of the country, for it was one of the tenets of Muhammad Ali's rule that foreign investment capital should be kept out. His remarkable success proved so troublesome to British interests that outside pressures were eventually brought against him. The last years of Muhammad Ali's life showed a considerable slowing down of the modernization process.

THE WESTERN AND CENTRAL SUDAN: The collapse of the western Sudan after the Moroccan invasion of 1591 is one of the saddest events in African history. Security gave way to fear, and violence succeeded tranquillity.

After the fall of Songhai many of their conquered provinces revolted, pillaging and destroying lands to the south and east. Half the kingdom fell prey to anarchy. By 1595 the Moroccans had brought the main parts of the once great empire of Songhai under control. The administrator of the colony, who was appointed by the king of Morocco and served as his representative, took the title of pasha, or governor.

One result of the Moroccan conquest of the western Sudan was the decline of the once-prosperous trans-Saharan trade. The city of Timbuktu, at one time the pride of the western Sudan, was now a ghost of its former self. The Songhai chronicler Abd al-Rahman as-Sadi had once called Timbuktu "an exquisite city, pure, delicious, blessed with luxury and full of life." He boasted that its people had "never been soiled by the worship of idols." Timbuktu, he went on to say, "gradually developed into a trade center. Its greatest days came during the time it was the meeting place for traders from Egypt, the Libyan Desert, the Oases

359

of Tuat, Fez, and the gold lands."

One of the most shameful and far-reaching tragedies of the Moroccan occupation was the attempted destruction of the intellectual life of the nation. The attack on the university of Sankore at Timbuktu and the exiling of its black scholars was an act of inexcusable arrogance. Moroccan troops and their white mercenary leaders literally declared war on all institutions and intellectuals. In 1594 the great scholar Ahmad Baba was exiled to Morocco. He had been the last chancellor at Sankore. Ahmad Baba was the author of more than forty books in Arabic, ranging from Arabic grammar to astronomy. His life is a brilliant example of the range and depth of West African intellectual activity before the colonial era.

With the loss of all its scholars, businessmen, judges, and men of religion, the light of knowledge and education went out in the western Sudan. Moroccan soldiers robbed the houses of valuables, including maps and manuscripts containing the history of the western Sudan. Revolts against the invaders, and the further suppressions that followed, worsened matters, as did internal revolts among the subject people.

The royal family that the Moroccans found on the throne of Songhai was still trying to save the country from the worst aspects of the invaders' wrath. Ishak II had been banished because of his opposition. His brother, Muhammad Gao, became the next *askia*. He pledged allegiance to the sultan of Morocco, but the Moroccans did not completely trust him. Nevertheless, during the great famine of 1592 they were forced to rely heavily on him for their food supplies. Mahmud ibn Zergun, the governor, asked the new *askia* to prove his loyalty by sending the much-needed food to the Moroccan army. This Muhammad Gao did in good faith. He ordered all crops on the Hausa side of the river to be cut and brought to the Moorish camp. Then Pasha Mahmud ibn Zergun chose to test his loyalty again. He asked Muhammad Gao to call the local kings and men of affairs to swear obedience to the sultan of Morocco. This was done, and the assembled men were murdered without warning. Muhammad Gao now knew that none of the Moroccans could be trusted. He continued to go through the motions of being their puppet while passing information to his rebel brother, Askia Nuh.

Nuh had not accepted Moroccan rule. He was an astute leader and fighter. Some of the fragmented army of Songhai rallied around him and helped to keep up continued harassment of the enemy army. The people of Songhai, in defiance of their Moroccan overlords, declared him *askia* and

said that they would obey no other ruler. He was wise enough to avoid giving his enemies a chance to open battle. The hills, swamps, and thick bush of Borgu, a region in northern Nigeria, became his encampment. He attacked the Moroccan outposts at night and withdrew to the forest and the hills. The people of Borgu did not particularly like the army of Songhai, which at a previous time had conquered them; but they united and fought with Askia Nuh because they hated the Moroccans still more, and like the people of Songhai, wanted to drive out the Moroccans.

The pressure and the harassment inflicted by Askia Nuh forced Mahmud ibn Zergun to turn once more to the sultan of Morocco for help. He complained that the tsetse fly was killing his horses and that disease and bad food and water were causing many deaths among his men. The sultan sent more soldiers and supplies and continued to wait for the treasures in gold that he had long expected. At the end of two years Mahmud ibn Zergun had neither large amounts of gold nor news of great success to send to his sultan. He was forced to give up the fight with Askia Nuh for a while, and he returned to Timbuktu.

There he faced more disappointments. The people living in Timbuktu had rebelled against the Moorish guard left to hold the city. The troublesome Tuaregs were raiding the Niger valley again. Ibn Zergun, now an angry and frustrated man, suspected that the educated people were the cause of the rebellions, and he conceived a plan to punish them further.

An announcement was made that all the homes in the town would once again be searched for weapons, except the houses belonging to descendants of a revered local *qadi*, which meant, in effect, the houses of the educated class. Hearing this, the rest of the citizenry took their valuables to the exempted houses for safekeeping. Then the pasha ordered all the holy man's descendants to go to the Great Mosque of Sankore to swear obedience to the sultan of Morocco. Only after the group had gathered at the mosque did they discover the governor's very cunning plan. These men, who had lived in comfort most of their lives, were put in chains and sent together with their wives and children across the desert to Morocco to be sold as slaves. Few of them survived the journey.

Mahmud ibn Zergun derived no benefit from this cruelty. Soon he was once again in trouble with the sultan of Morocco. Out of the vast riches that he had at last obtained from the rape of Timbuktu and other major cities in Songhai, he had sent the sultan only one hundred thousand mithqals of gold. Though this was a large amount, the sultan thought that it should be much larger. In his anger he decided that he could no longer trust Ibn Zergun. After ordering that he be arrested and put to death, the sultan sent another governor.

The news reached Mahmud ibn Zergun before the new governor, Mansur Abdurrahmen, arrived. He left Timbuktu and decided to risk a more honorable fate in the continued fight against his old enemy, Askia Nuh. Mahmud ibn Zergun met his death in the city of Zaria, located in present-day northern Nigeria.

Over the years Moroccan pashas were either poisoned or forced to leave the Sudan after failing to bring the area under control. The first contingent of invaders from Morocco who were still in the Sudan chose to elect their own officers. Some had married into the local population and had local loyalties. Some had fought fiercely among themselves over the control of what was left of Songhai. (In certain ways this condition would still prevail when the French arrived in this area during the latter part of the nineteenth century.)

Intermarriage between the local Africans and the Moroccan invaders produced, in another generation, a large number of Africans bent on the pursuit of power alone. Fights over who would inherit their fathers' land and power lasted for well over a hundred years; they wrecked or retarded the progress of most of the nations in inner West Africa and the central Sudan. Still, old nations were reorganized, and new nations were born in the midst of this recurring conflict. We should look, at least briefly, at some of these nations and how they survived Africa's time of troubles.

A number of states began to emerge in the area that is present-day Nigeria. Some of the former colonies of Songhai began to consolidate their territories and form new states. In parts of the central Sudan a degree of safety and security was re-established by people who moved away from the area of Moroccan domination. Some of the internal trade routes of the sub-Sahara not specifically connected with North Africa were reopened.

Among the new states that emerged before and during the Moroccan occupation of the western Sudan, Kanem-Bornu is outstanding. This state had the strength and leadership that was needed to preserve its independence from the Moroccans. Perhaps the greatest of the Bornu kings was Mai Idris Alooma, who reigned from 1570 to 1602 and was a contemporary of Queen Elizabeth of England. Although the slave trade had already started, the central Sudan would not feel its full effect until much later. The Hausa states had already reached a high level of pros-

perity and cultural development. The Yoruba, the Ibo, and the people of Nupe, Borgu, and Jukun were also developing powerful state structures.

At the close of the eighteenth century the two most powerful states in Hausaland were Gobir in the northwest and Bornu in the northeast. The Jukun kingdom had ceased to be a menace, but Nupe retained its independence, though much weakend. Some of the Hausa states were nominally independent, but still under some strong influence from Bornu. This was the political situation on the eve of the nineteenth-century Fulani wars, which would resolve some of the old problems and create new ones.

Meanwhile, the effects of the coastal slave trade had reached the states of inner West Africa while the area was still trying to recover from the Moroccan invasions. With the aid of firearms, the Europeans and their corrupted African partners pushed the slave trade farther into the interior. When the conflicts between rival West African states did not produce enough prisoners of war to be sold into slavery, new conflicts were created. As a result, a number of states collapsed. This first occurred along the coast in such once-powerful states as Benin, Dahomey, and Asante; within a hundred years the pressure of the slave trade was felt in the interior, diverting energies from the development of politics, the arts, and culture to a preoccupation with slaving wars and wanton destruction. Africans who had lived in peace with their neighbors for hundreds of years now became suspicious and started wars to capture their neighbors, for fear their neighbors would capture them.

With the opening up of the New World, and the vast plantation systems that followed, very often the slave-hungry Portuguese literally put a gun in an African's hand and pointed another one at his stomach, saying, in effect, "Either you capture a slave for me or you become one." And thus Africans were caught in one of the most tragic binds in history. Other Africans went into the slave trade because they were corrupt, having developed a liking for European liquor, clothes, guns, and other foreign goods.

Apart from the physical destructiveness and social dislocations that the Europeans inflicted on African societies, the absence of political unity exposed some of the small and poorly organized African communities to the ravages of their more powerful neighbors. Entire communities were fragmented and driven from their original homes. Those African people who did not have strong leadership attached themselves to one of the larger and stronger nation-states for protection. Sometimes the attached people were reduced to vassals; sometimes they were sold as slaves; sometimes they were totally integrated into the larger society, enjoying all benefits, responsibilities, and privileges of that society.

The slave trade had projected the Africans into a cross-fire the like of which no one had ever before encountered. On the economic side the slave trade had damaged the production of goods and the creation of wealth in Africa. The market towns in many cases went out of existence. The most valuable African resource, human labor, was forced into slavery and sent to the New World. Those African craftsmen who had escaped slavery could not compete economically with European manufacturers. As a result, African art and craftsmanship deteriorated and in some cases had to be abandoned.

The long period of slavery had completely undermined all elements of culture and growth in Africa. In some cases the evidence of the achievements of medieval times had been destroyed. At Timbuktu the once-great university of Sankore was now a fallen heap of bricks, stone, and mud. There was no one alive who could remember Ahmad Baba.

Near the end of the eighteenth century, when the era of slavery was drawing to a close, Islam reasserted itself in the western Sudan, and several jihads, or holy wars, were set in motion. The most noted of these was led by Usman Dan Fodio of northern Nigeria's Fulani. The real nature of Usman Dan Fodio's jihad is still in debate. To understand this war it is necessary that we know more about the Fulani people and their evolving role in the Sudan.

At the time when England and other European powers were attempting to end the slave trade and start the colonial system, the Fulani movement burst upon northern Nigeria like a thunder clap, setting in motion a long chain of events that is still reverberating.

The Fulani were a pastoral people living in scattered clusters from the Atlantic margin of the Sudan in the Senegal valley to the Adamawa plateau in Cameroon. They generally lived without opposition on the fringes of agricultural societies, taking those lands that were relatively poor for crop cultivation. Their origins are usually traced to the Senegal valley, where, it is thought, they long ago mixed with Berber nomads who had been driven south from Morocco in the eleventh century. This theory would account for the remarkable physical diversity found among the Fulani, who range in complexion from the light skin of a large number of North Africans to the darker complexion and more Negroid physical features of most of the people of western Africa. Prospering, the Fulani began to expand eastward from the Senegal basin, marrying with still other peoples along the way, leaving large settled populations in Futa

Toro, Futa Jallon, Kita, Macina, Liptako, Sokoto, Bauchi, and Adamawa. Their search for new grazing land for their large herds of cattle was combined with a search for new areas to convert to Islam.

A careful examination of the events leading up to the jihad shows that the movement was purely religious at first, owing much to the inspiration of Islam. It would develop, according to some interpreters, into a national and political movement of the Fulani people seeking domination over peasants and traders. Usman Dan Fodio became the great national leader, taking the title of Sarkin Musulmi (meaning "commander of the faithful"), which is still borne by his descendants. He was born in the Hausa state of Gobir in 1754, and in his youth became known as a strict Muslim teacher, continually traveling to the countries of northern Nigeria to exhort the people to a more conscientious performance in their religious duties. This eventually brought him into conflict with the young *sarkin* of Gobir, one of his former pupils, who was also a leader of a northern Nigerian movement that did not strictly impose Islam upon all his subjects. Disciples and adherents flocked to both men. The younger man hoped to defeat Dan Fodio's movement before it could gain a foothold in the large cities. The *sarkin* of Gobir attacked the town of Degel, where Usman Dan Fodio was living. Not being prepared to fight at this time, Dan Fodio fled to the city of Gudu, where he was joined by others who believed in his cause. The *sarkin* of Gobir, who had pursued him, was defeated on June 21, 1804, at Tabkin Kwotto on the shores of Lake Tobin. This battle began the Fulani wars.

The Lake Tobin outbreak also stirred up other opponents of the Fulani. Some of the Hausa kings attacked the followers of Usman Dan Fodio and were met with a widespread Fulani uprising, led by the trusted generals of Dan Fodio. Each general had a flag personally given to him by his leader. These flag bearers took over most of northern Nigeria and claimed the land for their respective families. (The descendants of these generals are even today considered the rightful bearers of power in northern Nigeria.) Very quickly they swept through Hausaland. In 1804 the city of Zaria was taken, followed in 1805 by Katsina and Kano. Before the *shehu* met any formidable opposition, the great trading cities of northern Nigeria had fallen. Not until Dan Fodio's forces reached Bornu did a national leader, Al-Kanemi, successfully resist Fulani advances. The Fulani army was able to take only the border country. The rest of Bornu maintained its independence. By 1810 the jihad was almost over. Usman Dan Fodio had established his rule over more than one hundred thousand square miles and was recognized as sovereign by five million people. He died in 1817 and was buried in the city of Sokoto.

In many ways the ground had been prepared for Usman Dan Fodio before he was born. The Niger River states had been torn with internal strife since the early part of the eighteenth century. The Oyo empire had long been in decline before the jihad. The warning signs began to appear during the period of Bashorun Gaha (1754–1774). During this time the Egba people revolted and were not brought back into the fold of the empire. As the Oyo army became a mere shadow of its former self, other peoples broke away from Oyo domination. Eight years before the jihad the collapse of the empire was already noticeable; the jihad merely accentuated it.

This jihad was the last flowering of African military prowess in the central Sudan before the British and the French took over. It had its glorious aspect and its tragedy, too. Before the war was over, some Muslims were attacking other Muslims. By attacking Bornu, an ancient Islamic state with its roots in the tenth century, the men of the Fulani jihad made it apparent that political ambition as well as religious zeal drove them. The state of Bornu had scrupulously observed the tenets of Islam, and as its ruler Shaykh al-Amin protested, there was no justification for the Fulani to attack. But, as in all revolutions, separate resentments and grievances found their opportunity. In 1812 Dan Fodio retired in triumph, dividing his huge empire between his brother, Abdullah, who received the lands east of Sokoto, and his son, Muhammad Belo, who was given the capital at Sokoto and the remaining Hausa states. As the nineteenth century progressed, threats to Fulani power developed. Some of the original inspiration of the movement faded away, and no further conquests by the Fulani were attempted. The forest and the tsetse fly were obstacles to the kind of cavalry warfare that had made the Fulani warriors famous and feared. Yet the kings and emirs retained their positions, ruling strongly until they were challenged at the very end of the nineteenth century by another invading power: the British.

THE WEST COAST: During the latter half of the fifteenth century Spanish ships began to interfere with the Portuguese slave trade. This caused the Portuguese to build a cluster of forts along the west coast of Africa to protect their interests. The first and most famous of these forts was at Elmina, in what is present-day Ghana. Gold was the currency of the day, and this naturally attracted the Portu-

guese. They had landed in this part of Africa early in the year 1482. The leader of the expedition, Diego de Azambuja, wasted no time in asking to see the country's reigning king, Nana Kwamena Ansa. The Portuguese offered friendship; but Nana Kwamena Ansa was slow in accepting their offers and in showing that he believed their promises. However, he still did not gain enough time to rally the support of his people and allies. Azambuja's expeditionary force set to work fortifying the area.

Europe's Reformation and the subsequent conversion of England and Holland to Protestantism in the sixteenth century also had repercussions in Africa. Protestant kings no longer felt bound to obey the authority of the pope. Owners of ships in these countries felt free to enter the slave trade in areas that the pope had assigned to the Portuguese and the Spaniards in 1493. Francis I of France voiced his celebrated protest: "The sun shines for me as for others. I should very much like to see the clause in Adam's will that excludes me from a share of the World." The king of Denmark refused to accept the pope's ruling as far as the East Indies was concerned. Sir William Cecil, the famous Elizabethan statesman, denied the pope's right to "give and take kingdoms to whomsoever he pleased."

The years of rivalry among European nations over their place in the African sun had started. At the close of the sixteenth century France had no colonies. Henry IV wished to develop trade with the new lands in America and Africa, including, of course, the slave trade, but his minister of state, the Duc de Sully, who represented large groups of rural interests, did not share the expansionist desires of his monarch. It was not until after the noted Cardinal Richelieu came to power in 1624 that the French began to trade in slaves. Richelieu and Louis XIII approved of the early plans, and the Saint Christopher Company was founded in 1626 to exploit the tobacco and wood found on the Caribbean island of this name. The French also occupied Tortuga and parts of Saint Domingue. In Africa they took over an area stretching from the mouth of the Senegal River to the Bight of Benin and started trading with peoples living along the Gambia River. By virtue of licenses issued on June 24, 1633, the French traders of Dieppe and Rouen obtained "permission to trade in Senegal, Cape Verde, and other places." In 1640 a stockade was constructed on an island at the mouth of the Senegal River, marking the founding of the settlement of St. Louis. The concession for Cape Lopez was accorded the Maloe Company of Guinea, as it was called. This was the first French challenge to the power and territories of the Portuguese; the effort would soon peter out because of the lack of French resources or interest.

By the beginning of Louis XIV's reign in 1643 only a few private traders sustained the original effort poorly, taking no more than a few hundred slaves a year, as the demand was still small. There was no regular commercial traffic between France, its small West African holdings, and the developing colonies in the Caribbean islands. From Cape Verde to the Congo the whole remaining coast of West Africa was in the hands of governments hostile to France or in competition with it commercially.

Of the European nations competing for a place in Africa, France had shown the least astuteness. This condition changed rapidly when it began to understand the importance of the slave trade in the intensive exploitation of their New World colonies. In 1664 Jean-Baptiste Colbert, Louis XIV's minister of finance, officially organized the trade for France. Soon the French caught up with the other European nations in West Africa, becoming at least their equal in competition.

The British, for their part, came late and furious into the slave trade. Captain John Hawkins and his "good ship Jesus" inaugurated the venture with the approval of Queen Elizabeth, who invested some of her personal fortune in underwriting it. The year of this first English slave-trading expedition was 1562. This was a buccaneering expedition that was meant to challenge the papal decree giving Portugal and Spain exclusive rights in Africa. After the establishment of the British colonies in the West Indies and the introduction of the sugar industry, the British participation in the slave trade became widespread and better organized, with various corporations being formed in England for that purpose. King Charles II and King James II held stock in some of these companies.

After the French and the British entered the slave trade, the Portuguese outposts were threatened. For a hundred years the Portuguese had been moving down the west coast of Africa, looking for new lands to conquer and new slave-trading areas. They made their first appearance in the Congo as early as 1482. The people of the Congo did not oppose the Portuguese at this time. The Congolese were a secure people, with years of well-organized government behind them.

Manikongo Nzinga (also known as a Nkuwu) welcomed them to his domain. Diogo Cão, the captain of this expedition, had broken the long isolation of the Congo, but the significance of this act eluded him. He sailed a little farther before going ashore. Months later, after returning to Lis-

bon, he told the king of Portugal about the Congo discovery. Thenceforth nothing was spared in the effort to make the Congo a Christian nation.

All the converts did not stay in the new religion. After having been converted to Catholicism and baptized in 1491, old King Nzinga gradually returned to the religion of his ancestors; but before his death in 1506 he designated as his successor his son, who had been converted under the name Affonso. Once on the throne, Affonso turned out to be a great king, and the kingdom of the Congo entered active international life. However, this good relationship between the kingdom of the Congo and the Portuguese did not last. By the end of the reign of Dom Affonso, extortion, alcoholism, and the slave trade were rampant in the Congo.

In 1590 another *manikongo* started a campaign to expel the Portuguese from the Congo. He made use of the known rivalry between European powers, pretending to put his country under the tutelage of the Holy See. Then he encouraged the arrival in the Congo of the Dutch, who were beginning at the time to acquire a foothold in Africa. The Portuguese were forced to abandon the Congo, and they turned their attention to the region of Angola, which offered them a more favorable field in which to further their commercial ambitions.

Early in the seventeenth century other areas in the Congo showed new life and new creative efforts in state building. One of the most remarkable of these states was the kingdom of Kuba of the Bantu-speaking Shongo people. Situated between the Kasai and Sankuru rivers, it is perhaps the most ancient of the Congolese kingdoms. Among the kingdoms in Central Africa only the Shongo culture kept its records and transmitted them almost intact to modern researchers. Oral tradition preserves what appears to be an accurate list of more than one hundred and twenty Kuba kings, the earliest of whom lived in the fifth century A.D.

In the Congo, where the technology of iron smelting has ancient origins, weaponry is often as beautiful as it is deadly. The artfully curved device opposite is a Congolese throwing knife, its several flat blades subtly balanced for hurling at quarry as much as fifty yards away. Also shown (below and right) are an execution sabre, two elaborately decorated ceremonial swords, and another throwing knife.

GALERIE KAMER

GALERIE KAMER, COLLECTION OF MR. AND MRS. ALLAN GERDAU

GALERIE KAMER, COLLECTION OF MRS. ELINE ROSENFELD

GALERIE KAMER, COLLECTION OF MR. AND MRS. HERBERT PRASHKER

Oral history relates that their greatest king was Shomba. The years of his reign, from 1600 to 1620, were really the golden age of the Kuba kingdom. He had the originality and humanity to abolish the use of weapons, especially the famous throwing of knives that had earned his people the epithet "the lightning people." It was also he who was the first to have a sculptor of his court execute his portrait statue. We also know from oral tradition that King Bakama Bomanchala saw an eclipse at noon on March 30, 1680, and that King Mbope Mobinji, who lived to be very old, saw the comet of 1843 and was the first Kuba to come in contact with Europeans in 1884, when Hermann von Wissmann's expedition passed through.

In the meantime, while this picture of order and culture was being revealed in one part of the Congo, more troubles were developing wherever the Europeans were involved. The contest between the Netherlands and Portugal for control of the kingdom of the Congo continued throughout the entire seventeenth century. After the Dutch captured Luanda in 1641, thereby briefly supplanting the Portuguese on the western shore of Africa, a new diplomatic current was established between the Dutch and the king of the Congo. The latter sent ambassadors to Brazil and Amsterdam and asked the prince of Orange for help against the Portuguese. On the other hand, a Dutch delegation was received at the Congolese court with ceremonial splendor reportedly equal to anything that the visitors had seen in the courts of Europe.

The Dutch intrusion did not make the Portuguese give up their desire to re-enter the Congo. In a few years the Portuguese recovered their lost positions and some of their military power. In the sixteenth century they had been driven by greed for imaginary gold mines. This greed was now more rampant among them, though they still had no proof of the mines' existence. They embarked on open warfare against the king, Dom Antonio, and defeated him in

the battle of Mpila in 1665. A search of the country did not reveal any gold mines. After this they left the Congo and devoted the next one hundred years to completing the conquest of Angola.

In David Birmingham's book, *The Portuguese Conquest of Angola*, we are told: "The first incentive to the Portuguese to conquer a colony in Angola was the hope of acquiring lands suitable for European settlement similar to those which were being settled in Brazil. Another reason was the Portuguese expectation of finding mineral wealth in Angola, which led them to conquer the site of supposed silver mines."

The failure to find the mineral wealth in Angola made the Portuguese double their efforts in the slave trade. Their most stubborn and colorful opposition as they entered the final phase of the conquest of Angola came from a queen who was a great head of state and a military leader. The important facts about her life have been extracted from a biography by the American historian Roy A. Glasgow.

Nzinga's story begins in 1583, when one of the most extraordinary and romantic figures in African history was born. She was the sister of the then-reigning king of Ndongo, Ngola Mbandi. Nzinga was one of a long line of African women freedom-fighters that dates back to the reign of Queen Hatshepsut in Egypt, fifteen hundred years before the birth of Christ. Nzinga belonged to the Jaga people. The Jaga were an extremely militant group and became more so when Queen Nzinga took over their leadership.

Nzinga's ancestry goes back to the end of the fifteenth century when her great-great-grandfather, the king of Matamba, conquered neighboring Ndongo and gave it to his son, Ngola Kiluanju, as an appendage to the other territory held by the Jaga. Nzinga stated that she was descended "from the kings who had reigned over the whole state before it was split into two parts." She based her claim to rule over the entire region upon her ancestral connections.

365

Queen Nzinga's relations with the Portuguese were from the outset marked with conflict. When she went to Luanda, headquarters of the Portuguese in Angola, to negotiate with the governor, he refused her a chair, a courtesy due one of equal rank. Seemingly undaunted, she is said to have sat down, as shown in this old engraving. Never one to be inhibited by rules, Nzinga circumvented local prohibitions against female sovereigns. She dressed as a male chief and surrounded herself with an entourage of concubines, young men also in disguise.

G. WEIDENFELD AND NICHOLSON

In 1623, at the age of forty-one, Nzinga became queen of Ndongo—even while her right to the throne was being questioned under the law. The supporters of her late brother had not wasted any time before stirring up dissension against her. She began at once to strengthen her position of power. One of her first acts was the strengthening of the traditional laws that ensured the cultural integrity of the Jaga people. She also forbade her subjects to call her queen, preferring to be called king; and when she led her army in battle, she dressed in men's clothing.

Nzinga never accepted the Portuguese conquest of her country and was always on the military offensive. As part of her excellent strategy against the invaders, she formed an alliance with the Dutch, intending to use them to defeat the Portuguese slave trade. At her request she was given a militia of Dutch soldiers. The officer commanding this detachment in 1646 described her as "a cunning and prudent virago so much addicted to the use of arms that she hardly uses other exercise, and withal so generously valiant that she never hurt a Portuguese after quarter was given and commanded all her slaves and soldiers the like."

She believed that after defeating the Portuguese it would be easy to surprise the Dutch and expel them from her country. Consequently, she maintained a good relationship with the Dutch and waited for the appropriate time to move against them. Her ambition extended beyond the task of freeing her country from European control. In addition to being queen of Ndongo, she envisioned commanding a great western empire stretching from Matamba in the east to the Atlantic Ocean in the west. To this end she was an astute agitator-propagandist, easily summoning large groups of her fellow countrymen to hear her. In convincing her people of the evil effects of the Portuguese, she would single out slaves and slave-soldiers who were under Portuguese control and direct intensive political and patriotic messages in their direction, appealing to their pride as Africans. She offered them land and freedom. This resulted in a serious security problem for the Portuguese, with thousands of these slave-soldiers deserting to join her forces. Politically far-sighted, competent, self-sacrificing, and devoted to the resistance movement, she attempted to draw many kings and heads of families to her cause in order that they in turn might recruit their people for her revolution against the Portuguese.

Nzinga's most enduring weapon was her personality. She was astute and successful in consolidating power. She was particularly good at preserving her position by ruthlessly dealing with her foes and graciously rewarding her friends. She possessed both masculine hardness and personal charm, depending on the need and the occasion.

The Portuguese now suspected that they were not going to win her over to their side by peaceful means. The priests were disappointed because they had seemingly lost the battle to convert her to Catholicism. However, in her campaign to drive the Portuguese out of Angola she suffered a series of setbacks in 1645 and 1646. Her sister was taken as a prisoner of war and thrown into the river. Nzinga began to weigh the merits of her own god, Tem-Bon-Dumba, against the god of the Portuguese. Was it possible, she asked, that the Catholic god was stronger? A number of other questions arose for which there was no satisfactory answer. She had heard the Jesuits say that the Christian god was a just person and an enemy of all suffering. Why then did he assist the invaders of her country? Why were the Portuguese building forts in her country without her consent? With these questions still unresolved, she decided to join this religion and test its strength in her favor. For the remainder of her life she used Christianity or put it aside, depending on her needs.

In 1659 she signed a treaty with the Portuguese that brought her no feeling of triumph. However, time would reveal that her part of the treaty had been based upon political and military realities, for she was now faced with overwhelming odds and superior weaponry. She had fought the Portuguese for most of her adult life. She was more than seventy-five years old now, and some of her faithful assistants and followers were dead or had given up the long fight.

On December 17, 1663, this great African woman died,

marking the end of one epoch and the beginning of another. With her passing, the planting of the Cross and the occupation of the interior of South West Africa had begun. The massive expansion of the Portuguese slave trade followed.

As stated earlier, the British opened the last phase of the slave trade in West Africa. When Captain John Hawkins organized the manpower and ships for this aspect of England's worldwide expansion, the structure and administration of this inhuman business were permanently changed. Spheres of influence were established among slave traders, guaranteeing one another's rights to conduct business in certain areas of West Africa without interference. In a word, the business was put on a business basis. Because of his success, Captain Hawkins is often referred to as "the man who stole a continent."

It took the British nearly a hundred years to drive the Portuguese and other lesser powers out of West Africa. In 1701 the "Most Christian King of France," Louis XIV, and "His Catholic Majesty," Philip V of Spain, signed an agreement conceding to the Guinea Company a monopoly on the introduction of black slaves into the Spanish West Indies. This agreement lasted ten years, ending in 1712. Its objective was to procure reciprocal profits to both the Catholic king of Spain and the very Christian sovereign of France, who derived considerable revenues from the trade through a head tax levied against the slave merchants for each captive delivered. The Guinea Company pledged to introduce an increased number of slaves from all parts of sub-Saharan Africa, with the exception of Elmina and Cape Verde, the latter still under Portuguese control.

The War of Spanish Succession (1701–1714) radically changed this and other schemes for expansion in Africa. As a consequence of a protracted series of battles on the European continent, French domination of Europe was ended, parts of the Spanish empire were parceled out to a number of claimants, and Britain's supremacy of the seas established. The Peace of Utrecht, which followed, was an attempt to set guidelines for the peaceful expansion of overseas empires, one of several European treaties that decided the destiny of Africa without African participation.

One of its acts, the infamous Asiento Treaty signed on March 26, 1713, granted the British government a monopoly on the importation of slaves to Spain's remaining American empire for a term of thirty years (1713–1743). His British Majesty, no less illustrious than the French and Spanish majesties, pledged through the agency of the South Sea Company to introduce 144,000 slaves of both sexes at

With east coast citadels like Fort Jesus, built at Mombasa in 1593, the Portuguese sought to supplant Arab spiritual and economic influence.
JAMES KIRKMAN

the rate of 4,800 annually. The conditions of the contract, with few exceptions, were the same as those previously made with France. In every possible way the British got the best of the deal. The Anglo-Spanish contract was later altered to permit importation of a still larger number of slaves annually, and at a higher price per head than originally negotiated. For the rest of the eighteenth century, the British would maintain leadership in this hideous business.

By the end of the eighteenth century, however, the slave trade had run its course and was a declining institution. But the Africans had no cause for rejoicing. The British, who led the fight to abolish chattel slavery, became the major architects for the establishment of the colonial system, another form of slavery.

EAST AFRICA: When the Portuguese explorers arrived along the east coast of Africa, they found the shore from Sofala (in present-day Mozambique) to Somalia occupied by a chain of Arab-Swahili settlements, strongly Africanized by centuries of contact with the Bantu-speaking people. They traded with the Africans who brought gold and ivory from the hinterland. They were at first cautious about their interest in slaves. The Portuguese almost at once identified Sofala with the gold-rich biblical Land of Ophir. They built a fortress along this coast in 1505 with the intent of monopolizing trade. In order to accomplish this, the Portuguese first tried to bypass the Arabs and the large number of Swahili-speaking people and deal directly with the Africans. Fortunately for the Portuguese, their arrival in East

Africa occurred during a time when intertribal rivalries prevailed. Some of the great city-states along the coast were in decline. A number of the powerful trading families were torn apart by internal disputes. Later, when the first strategy proved inadequate, the Portuguese took full advantage of this lack of unity to gain a greater measure of control. They supported the sultans of Malindi against the more powerful rulers of Mombasa in the sixteenth century, and in the next century they helped the princes of Faza, another of the coastal city-states, against their Pate (Patta) neighbors.

The main effect of the Portuguese on East Africa was destructive and negative. They built forts, churches, and homes for themselves, while literally declaring war on all local institutions. But they could not govern the coast after the East Africans had turned against them. The traditional rulers still controlled the city-states, and it was largely a matter of political expediency that some of them acknowledged the sovereignty of the Portuguese. The external Muslim powers such as the Turks and the Oman Arabs did not even go that far, as will be shown later.

What can be said of the Portuguese can also be said, with varying degree, of all East Africa's invaders. East Africa, more than any other part of Africa, was preyed upon by one invader after the other for well over one thousand years. All these invaders took more from East Africa than they gave. The modern history of East Africa is the history of a people trying to recover from the aftereffects of invaders and build or rebuild indigenous institutions.

At the beginning of the eighteenth century Portuguese pressure was lessened, but not out of any benevolence. The Portuguese were in serious trouble in other areas of the world, and they did not have the forces that were necessary to maintain their old power connections in East Africa. The divide-and-rule tactics that had worked so well for them in the early years of their expansion were no longer dependable. Some of their puppets now had power ambitions of their own. In Asia their presence was being seriously challenged. In the New World the original settlers of Brazil were questioning the authority of the mother country while still demanding more slaves. To the Portuguese, East Africa was only one part of their global design. They extracted both gold and slaves from the coastal states and did not try to occupy all of them. For a number of years Mombasa Island, off the coast of modern-day Kenya, was their major stronghold in East Africa, along with neighboring Fort Jesus.

The relative security the Portuguese had known along the east coast was first upset in 1649 by the emergence of

the Oman leader, Nasir ibn Murshid, who had a navy strong enough to challenge the Portuguese at sea. The Mombasa Chronicle records that the inhabitants of that city made an appeal to Sultan ibn Seif, who became ruler of Oman in 1649. In 1652 vessels from the sultan's fleet raided Zanzibar, one hundred fifty miles south; a number of Portuguese settlers, including several Augustinian Fathers, were killed. As a result of a poorly planned expedition, the following year the queen of Zanzibar was driven off the island by the sultan's forces, who joined with dissident locals. A Portuguese official who was responsible for the defense of the island claimed that he rescued four hundred Christians and saved them from being captured by the Arabs.

For the next forty years the revolts against Portuguese rule continued, mainly in the city-states. The city of Pate was in a state of perpetual revolt. In the punitive expeditions against this city the Portuguese had the assistance of some East African communities that felt threatened by the strength and military prowess of a small and powerful trading city-state like Pate. The king of Faza, who ruled another microkingdom on the island, considered the ruling family of Pate to be his hereditary foe. In 1687 a former king of Pate crossed the Indian Ocean to the Portuguese colony of Goa and offered many concessions in exchange for assistance in his attempt to regain his throne. His most attractive offer was to allow the Portuguese to erect a church at Pate and convert Muslims and pagans without hindrance.

When this king returned to Pate, escorted by a squadron of Portuguese ships, he found that an Arab fleet from the Persian seaport of Muscat had anticipated his action and was ready to forestall him and his allies. The greater damage to the king's pride was in the discovery that his former subjects had turned against him. The Portuguese were not strong enough to fight the Arabs nor could they protect the king. There was no choice for them but to take refuge in Mombasa. For the remainder of the seventeenth century the Portuguese in East Africa would have no rest from conflict; their African allies would fare no better.

On the island of Pemba a state of rebellion kept the Portuguese from making strategic use of the land and the people. In about 1679 a distant faction of the royal family drove out the reigning queen. Like the king of Pate, she took refuge in 1687 in the Portuguese colony of Goa. While there, she became a Christian, an act that destroyed the chance that she would effectively be restored to power in her island kingdom. Nevertheless, the exiled queen continued to speak for the people of Pemba, and the Portuguese listened and indulged themselves. They were slow to realize that the aging queen no longer had power. In an act of desperation, partly in gratitude for refuge she had received, she willed her kingdom to the Portuguese. They were never able to claim this inheritance. In 1694 the island was still in a state of rebellion. The viceroy of India reported the matter to Lisbon, where the decision was made to give up the plan to reduce the Pemba people to submission.

Two years later, in 1696, the Arabs took full advantage of this and other conflicts along the east coast. A fleet from Oman arrived in Kilindini, the chief port of Mombasa, and wasted no time in laying siege to Fort Jesus, where a large number of local inhabitants, including many who were unfriendly to the Arabs, had taken refuge. Among the refugees was Bwana Daud ibn Bwana Shaykh, whose father had been driven from power by the people of Pate in 1686. The struggle lasted nearly three years. The Portuguese sent ships from Goa and Mozambique in support of the Africans, but were not able to lift the siege. Plague and disease reduced the defending forces until they could no longer continue the resistance. Before the Portuguese conceded defeat, the queen of Zanzibar made one last unsuccessful attempt to run the blockade and send supplies to the fort. The garrison became so weak that African women were taking their turn as sentries. With the fall of Mombasa, the Portuguese had lost all of their holding stations north of Cape Delgado. Faza had been abandoned in 1688, when the Arabs of Muscat took possession of Pate Island. Zanzibar had also been taken by the Arabs. Zanzibar's queen, Fatima, who had been loyal to the Portuguese, was deported to Muscat; but she was allowed to return after ten years of exile. Sometime before 1710 the Arabs, in search of materials with which to build a small fort, had partly dismantled the Augustinian church on the island. All evidence of the once-obvious Portuguese presence was destroyed.

The Africans now were trapped in a bind between the Arabs and the Portuguese. They would not extricate themselves for another hundred years. When the Portuguese retreated from Mombasa, some of them went to their Indian colony at Goa, and others went to their southeast African colony at Mozambique. The Arabs at Mombasa acted unwisely, as if the Portuguese threat was over forever. Large numbers of Africans who disliked both Portuguese and Arab rule would attempt to get rid of the Arabs at Mombasa now that the Portuguese had been driven out. The opportunity came quite unexpectedly.

In 1727 Ahmad ibn Said, the Oman governor of Mombasa, set out on a pilgrimage to Mecca and left his deputy,

Nasser ibn Abdullah al-Mazrui, in charge. He then began to treat the garrison of soldiers at Mombasa with severity. Grievance over this matter developed into open revolt. The rebels made Ibn Abdullah al-Mazrui a prisoner and took over Fort Jesus. Immediately they began to seek support from the local inhabitants. They, like the mutineers, feared the governor, Ahmad ibn Said, and knew that he could get support from the Arab states. The rebels hoped to organize the local inhabitants in their favor before the governor returned. But a member of the Malindi family persuaded the people not to support this rebellion. They in turn demanded that the rebels surrender the fort. This demand was rejected. The conflict that followed is called a war, but it was really an internal dispute. Without a large supply of arms, the rebels were limited in what they could do. Knowing that Fort Jesus was more or less impregnable, they made no attempt to attack it. They found targets within their limitations and took possession of several walled towns and some outlying forts at Kilindini. The local population had grown accustomed to conflicts and reverses in power struggles, but was somewhat confused over this turn of events. For the rebels, fortune turned temporarily in their favor. The rulers of Oman became involved in civil disorders at home on the Arabian Peninsula and could not send support to the Arabs at Mombasa. The rebels now had the opportunity to set up an independent state, and would have, except for the intervention of the Portuguese, who had partly recovered from their defeat on the island.

The Portuguese found their opportunity when a special emissary was sent by the king of Pate to Goa to obtain Portuguese help in expelling the Oman Arabs from Pate. An agreement was drawn up between the emissary and the Portuguese viceroy at Goa. The main parts of this treaty were: no Portuguese subject, Christian or otherwise, could be compelled to become a Muslim; all previous Christians who had been compelled to become Muslims should have the right to return to the Roman Catholic Church, if they desired to do so. On the other hand, the Inquisition was not to function in the land.

When the Portuguese reached Pate early in 1728, some resistance was offered from one faction, but they eventually surrendered, knowing that they could expect no support from Oman at this time. The Portuguese took full advantage of the unrest at Mombasa and similar dissensions in the island of Pate farther to the north. Both Pate and Mombasa were regained with very little fighting. At Mombasa Shaykh ibn Ahmad al-Malindi at once disclaimed all relations with the rebels. The Arab governor, having little stomach for warfare, quickly surrendered. The Portuguese had promised that he and his men would be given ships to return to Oman.

In celebration of this event the Portuguese entered what was still left of the church of the Augustinian convent and conducted High Mass before a roughly made wooden cross. An Augustinian Father preached on this occasion from the text in Isaiah LXVI: 10: "Rejoice ye with Jerusalem, and be glad with her, all ye that love her: rejoice for joy with her, all ye that mourn for her." Inside the church the Fathers found a chest containing church ornaments; it had been left unharmed for more than thirty years. The chapel of the Misericordia was also found undamaged.

The Portuguese became more confident when the king of Zanzibar came to Mombasa to make submission to the governor. A party of Portuguese soldiers and civil servants was sent to Zanzibar to establish a "factory," or in more precise language, the slave trade.

In their short-lived triumph the Portuguese had overlooked issues relating to their return. They had not been invited back by the populace at large, nor did a large number welcome them. They had been asked back as arbitrators of an internal dispute, mainly involving the rulers of Mombasa, Pate, Zanzibar, and related territories.

In spite of the comparative ease with which the Portuguese seemed to have regained their lost possession, trouble between the Portuguese and the inhabitants was soon to develop. Treaties were barely signed before they were broken. On August 29, 1728, a new treaty was made with Pate. The Portuguese, with unwarranted confidence, made new demands and tried to revise some old ones. They insisted on the payment of tribute and took for themselves a large share of the island's revenue. The African faction that had invited the Portuguese to help them against the Arabs was now having second thoughts. Friction developed between the king of Pate and the Portuguese commander. Eventually, the Portuguese garrison found itself in a state of siege with no local allies. After being reduced to the verge of starvation, the Portuguese were willing to forgo all previous agreements and return to Goa. Also, the Portuguese garrison at Mombasa was expelled and their flag lowered at Fort Jesus for the last time.

Portuguese conduct had destroyed whatever good will had been previously built up among the people in East Africa. The Portuguese were completely intolerant of the Muslims. According to the Mombasa Chronicle: "They flung stones at the people while they were at their prayers;

and they used to turn the people out of their houses and take possession of them; and take their wives to themselves."

The loss of Fort Jesus and other Portuguese settlements left the Oman Arabs militarily in charge of the east coast of Africa and the large slave-trading island of Zanzibar. Fort Jesus was handed over to an Oman garrison, and Muhammad ibn Said al-Maamri was installed as governor. After the final withdrawal of the Portuguese from Mombasa, we hear no more of Christianity and Christians in East Africa for a century. An uneasy partnership developed between the Portuguese and the Arabs. The big Portuguese colony of Brazil was calling for more slaves than the Portuguese could furnish, and the Arabs filled the breach as suppliers.

The East African trade, in a formal sense, can trace its roots no further than the first half of the eighteenth century, and the early Portuguese chronicles make only passing mention of the slave trade. Much more important were the gold and ivory traded to Arabia and India. It was in search of these products that the Portuguese invaders had come in the sixteenth and seventeenth centuries. But the Arabs had dealt in human chattel since the twelfth century. Not only along the coast of Kenya and Tanzania but also in Mozambique and Zimbabwe did they deal in slaves. The great trading center at Zanzibar had about one hundred years of active commercial slave trading before the European powers entered the area.

Near the end of the eighteenth century other European powers, principally Great Britain, began to make themselves felt along the east coast of Africa. They would in the next fifty years wage a successful war on the East African slave trade and, subsequently, install the European colonial system.

SOUTH AND SOUTHWEST AFRICA: In the year 1652, when Oliver Cromwell was proclaiming his creed of "liberty and conscience," and American seekers of religious freedom were cautiously penetrating the American continent in search of new lands, a band of thirty white settlers (employees of the powerful Dutch East India Company under the leadership of Jan van Riebeeck) came ashore below the three-thousand-five-hundred-foot shadow of Table Mountain to establish the Cape Colony at the southernmost tip of the horn of Africa. Although this did not mark the first appearance of European people in southern Africa, it was the first sustained attempt to form a permanent white settlement. This was the beginning of South Africa's

After Europeans and Americans ended the slave trade, Great Britain brought its influence to bear in order to halt the much older traffic in humans along Africa's east coast. The island of Zanzibar, seen below in a view of the 1850's, was the principal center of that trade. In 1840 it had become the capital of Sayyid Said, sultan of the Persian Gulf state of Oman, who ruled the Swahili ports from Somalia to Mozambique and extended Islamic influences inland as far as the Congo. Said built up Zanzibar's famed clove trade, sought Indian investors, and encouraged Arab merchants to venture in search of ivory and slaves to work on the clove plantations. Following those ancient routes by which Africans from the inland had brought goods to the coast, traders like Tippu Tib (left), an Afro-Arab who had been born in Zanzibar, pressed beyond Lake Tanganyika to the central Congo, and with their firearms, established hegemony over large numbers of Bantu-speaking peoples. Said's successors were weaker than he, and his dominions along the coast were gradually divided among Italy, Great Britain, and Germany. In 1890 the British proclaimed a protectorate over Zanzibar and in 1897 officially put an end to slaving activities.

"Troubled Years." Contestants for control of the area would soon be the Dutch, the British, the Hottentots, the Bushmen, and the Bantu-speaking peoples.

Although the Portuguese had landed on the Cape before the arrival of the Dutch, they had not established a trading station. There were many reasons for this. The coast was a stormy one, and there were no settled tribes with whom they could barter for slaves. Almost a hundred and fifty years elapsed before the Dutch decided to set up a station, and only after they had wrested a large part of Europe's Indian Ocean shipping business from the Portuguese.

The stated intent of Van Riebeeck was to start a refueling

station for the ships of the Dutch East India Company on their way to and from the East. His band of settlers absorbed a handful of Huguenot refugees who had arrived ahead of them, and after 1667 started importing slaves from Malaya and other Asian countries. The first African people they encountered were the Hottentots, or more properly, the Khoikhoi people. (The term Khoisan is anthropologists' construct, meant to include both the Khoikhoi and the San, or Bushmen.) A king of the Hottentots, Autshumayo, led them in the first futile attempt in 1659 to stop Van Riebeeck and his company from seizing the best pasture lands in the Cape Peninsula. Thus the nationalist struggle in South Africa had its beginning in this little-known rebellion. King Autshumayo's people were enslaved and deprived of their cattle. The Bushmen were hunted like game. To keep from being destroyed, they retreated into the Kalahari Desert, where they still live. The basic historic conflict in South Africa—the struggle between different national entities to control the land—had been set in motion.

The first European settlers took on some of the habits and traits of the Africans that they had practically destroyed. These Boers, or farmers, acquired large herds of cattle, mainly from Africans whom they had defeated. They became nomadic, land-hungry "white Africans," hunters without human regard for the indigenous people of South Africa.

The settlement grew with infusions of slaves from the east, Mozambique, Angola, and the addition of still more Huguenots and Dutchmen. While the women of the Khoikhoi and the San were sexually used and abused by the white settlers, the Dutch East India Company for a number of years countenanced, and even encouraged, legal marriages between the white settlers and their Asian slaves. They were building the ethnic buffer between themselves and the blacks; this group was to become known as the "Cape Coloreds." In present-day South Africa they number more than a million. The dangerous doctrine of white superiority had already been developed by the Boers (later called Afrikaners), but they did not at this time see that the sanctioned marriages between themselves and their Asian slaves were in contradiction to this concept.

Many of the Boers who made up the first large white settlement in southern Africa were political and religious malcontents before leaving their homes in the Netherlands. Their outlook on life was based on strict Lutheranism and Calvinism, the aftermath of the bitter struggle to preserve the newly established Protestant faith against the powerful attacks of the resurgent Catholic Church.

The Boers had neither security nor peace during their first one hundred years in South Africa. The Khoikhoi people, who were friendly to them when they first arrived, soon began to look upon them as invaders and land grabbers. They saw their land being fenced off and white men with guns protecting the land that the whites had claimed for settlements. The Khoikhoi considered the land to be inalienable and sacred, a part of nature for common use. Continued encroachment on their land caused this friendly and peaceful people to take up arms.

The Khoikhoi fought three major wars to regain the vast grazing lands of South Africa. Between 1786 and 1795 over two thousand five hundred Hottentots were killed and six hundred captured. Those taken prisoner, mainly women and children, were enslaved by the farmers. None of the adult males submitted to the enemy; they fought to the bitter end. Their courage, even in the face of overwhelming odds, was phenomenal. These early wars of resistance have in most cases been lost from the official history of southern Africa.

The lack of labor to tend the vegetables and fruit gardens of the Dutch hampered the work of European settlement. The Khoikhoi could not see the necessity of exchanging their freedom for money when they had the land. The importation of slaves to do the hard work became the next logical step. As for the Boers, the status of being Christian and master was becoming confused in their minds with their being white. Color consciousness helped them to erase the knowledge that all men were human.

The real dynamics of the black-white struggle in South Africa did not reach profound and tragic proportions until after the British occupation of the Cape in 1795. The British pushed the Boers, the Boers pushed the Zulu, and the Zulu pushed back. But this is, of course, an oversimplification. The story of this clashing of powerful forces and the struggle to control South Africa is complicated and protracted. In the meantime, other forces, issues, peoples, and nations were evolving in southern Africa.

South West Africa is a little known, though important, part of southern Africa. This country and its people were late in coming into the mainstream of southern African history. In some ways this was fortunate. During the early period of European expansion South West Africa was not an area desired for large-scale European settlement or slave trade. A number of ethnic groups, but chiefly the Herero, a pastoral people, and the Ambo (Ovamba), an agricultural people, developed small nations within the region.

The Portuguese, led by Diogo Cão, made a brief appearance in South West Africa in 1484, leaving a lonely cross to mark the occasion. John II of Portugal had sent them to explore that area of the coast which until that time had remained for the Europeans a land of fable and mystery. This was eight years before Christopher Columbus and his sailors set foot on the islands of the New World. The landscape that the Portuguese beheld was not encouraging and did not cause them to prolong their stay. There were seemingly endless high sand dunes along the dreary desert coastline, known to later seamen as the Coast of Dead Ships. Two years later Bartholomeu Dias, a Portuguese adventurer, brought an expedition to these shores aboard a little fifty-ton ship. He landed at a narrow southwest bay, which he named Angra Pequeña (today, Lüderitz).

In the next few centuries this part of Africa remained free of any conflict relating to European expansion. The few Europeans who ventured into this large and thinly populated land did not at first make any claim. In 1738 a secret overland expedition was organized by William Van Wyk and other Boer farmers in an attempt to establish trade with the people in this area. The leader of the expedition was surprised to find that another white man, Pieter de Bruyan, had arrived ahead of his party. Bruyan was probably the first white man to set foot in the interior of South West Africa. In 1762 Jacobus Coetsee, an elephant hunter, crossed the Orange River and heard reports of great herds of cattle possessed by the Herero people. Rumors of copper in the interior drew several expeditions to South West Africa during the middle of the eighteenth century. The governor of the Cape, Simon van der Stel, sent an expedition to find the mouth of the Orange River. Men returned from South West Africa with wild stories about long-haired blacks who wore linen clothes. A later expedition, in 1762, also sent out by a Cape governor, found none of these mythical people.

In 1795 the British proclaimed ownership of the South West African coast and declared that only British ships were permitted to hunt whales and seals offshore. This was an empty claim because the British did not have the manpower to patrol this vast area. The full weight and reality of European colonial oppression did not reach South West Africa until the latter part of the nineteenth century. During the period of the partition of Africa in the 1880's, the heavy hand of German colonialism would take over this part of Africa.

Meanwhile, in South Africa the Zulu began to be a force to reckon with. In his book *The Bantu Past and Present* (1920), the South African writer S. M. Molema argues that these Bantu-speaking people have been migrating in and out of southern Africa for more than ten thousand years. South African archeologists discovered in 1970 a mining complex in Swaziland that is reportedly forty-three thousand years old. This opens up still other matters for further investigation (for example, what has been considered to be the youngest part of Africa for human habitation may yet prove to be one of the oldest parts).

In the Nigerian magazine *Tarikh*, November, 1965, J. D. Omer-Cooper presents one of the numerous new appraisals of the Zulu people and the impact of Chaka (Shaka) on South Africa. He tells us, in essence, that the eastern coastland of South Africa, known as Zululand and Natal, is one of the most attractive places for human settlement in all Africa. This is the area where the Zulu people first settled after migrating to southern Africa.

The Zulu were mixed farmers, with cattle as their chief possession. They did not begin to make their mark on the history of South Africa until early in the nineteenth century. Before this time they gave allegiance to the king of the Mtetwa people. Then in 1786 a son was born to the reigning king of the Zulu, Senzangakona. The child's name was Chaka. In his lifetime his impact on southern Africa would be profound, dramatic, and to a degree, tragic. This warrior-nationalist was literally the father of the Zulu nation. He fought to consolidate the blacks of South Africa in order to save them from white enslavement. He was not understood then, and he is not completely understood now. Chaka and his people stood astride the history of South Africa for the entire nineteenth century. For this period the history of this troubled land is essentially the story of the rise and fall of the Zulu people.

Chaka's early years were not easy, and he had to fight for a place among his people. Except for his mother, Nandi, the favorite wife of King Senzangakona, Chaka might have been lost from Zulu history. Nandi was the daughter of the king of the Langeni people and a woman of great influence among the Zulu.

When Chaka was a year old, Nandi took him to her parents' house to be weaned, as was the custom among the Zulu. Chaka was a restless boy who did not get along well with anyone except his mother. It is said that when his father offered him the lion-skin covering that is worn by older Zulu boys to symbolize their future status as warriors, he refused it and behaved disgracefully. This angered his father because he had high hopes for Chaka, his first-born son, and he naturally expected Chaka to grow up and become king after him.

At last Chaka found a friend, probably through the efforts

of his mother. Dingiswayo of the Mtetwa people saw that this troublesome young man had fine qualities. He presented him with the young warrior's lion skin that he had refused to accept from his father years before. Chaka became a soldier in Dingiswayo's army and soon earned the name "Dingiswayo's Hero."

Who was this man whom Chaka was willing to follow? He, too, had had trouble at home with his father. As he grew toward manhood, the Mtetwa prince found that his father, the great King Jobe, suspected him of treachery. The chief thought his elder son was going to rebel and usurp his power. The bitter feud caused the son to be driven into exile, where he remained until his father died. His years of his journeying away from his people earned him the name "Dingiswayo," meaning "The Wanderer."

When the news reached him that Jobe was dead, he sent word that he was coming back to be king. He at once began to teach the Mtetwa to fight a new way. He had lived in the Cape Colony and learned much about European methods of training men for warfare. He had seen firearms and had learned how to use them. Chaka had his first taste of success in battle in Dingiswayo's army.

Chaka had outgrown his brooding and rebellious disposition. In 1816 Senzangakona died, and Dingiswayo helped Chaka become king of the Zulu. The two men—one king of the populous Mtetwa people, the other king of the smaller Zulu people—were friends, and their warriors fought together. But about two years later Dingiswayo was captured by one of his rivals and was put to death. Then the Mtetwa people, who already knew Chaka as one of their leaders in battle, placed themselves and their great army under the Zulu king and took the Zulu name. This was the beginning of the greatness of the Zulu empire, the foundation of their war machine, and the real power of Chaka.

The famous king Moshoeshoe, then trying to build up the Basuto nation, kept Chaka out of his country only by sending the warrior a message declaring that he recognized no other king but Chaka. Mzilikazi, who had been one of Chaka's best commanders, grew sick of the slaughter of other Bantu-speaking people and deserted the Zulu army, taking over fifteen thousand men with him. He went across the Drakensberg mountains and established a new nation called Matabeleland.

Still Chaka's war machine rolled on. He united by conquest the scattered thrones of numerous smaller kingdoms and incorporated their survivors into the Zulu nation. Four years after he started his first campaign, Chaka had conquered a territory larger than France. The loot and indem-

nities of war had made his people wealthy. He was at the peak of his military prowess, and all his known enemies had been killed or conquered. His magnificent army, one hundred thousand strong, was still ready and restless for more battle, and there were no battles to be fought. Chaka's rigid methods of army training had made the Zulu among the finest soldiers in the world. The whites in South Africa at that time thought it best to be on friendly terms with him.

Chaka's military movement was called the *mfecane*, meaning "the crushing." It was a process of social, political, and military organization and change that was largely internal to African society. In southern Africa this movement was created mainly out of the efforts of several Bantu-speaking peoples who were attempting to establish their status and their salvation. The Zulu were fighting their way up from vassalage. Once this was accomplished, they began to bring other people under their rule. In some respects this movement can be compared to the jihad in northern Nigeria during the early part of the nineteenth century, though it was not a religious movement.

The power of Chaka began to decline in 1827, after the death of his mother. He led the Zulu in mourning for her and seemed not to be able to come out of mourning and lead them again in battle. Chaka became melancholy, constantly pinching his hands in self-reproach. Anyone who did not show grief became repugnant to him. He seemed to have lost all interest in governing his people and his empire. Many self-seekers were quick to take advantage of this. Those Zulu who had silently hated Chaka's terror for years grew openly rebellious.

In 1828, a year after the death of Chaka's mother, his two half brothers, Dingane and Mhlangana, crept into his hut and stabbed him to death. This event shook the Zulu, but the empire did not fall until many years later.

During the last moments of Chaka's life he is reported to have said to Dingane, who was to succeed him: "It is your hope that by killing me you will become kings when I am dead. But you are deluded; it will not be so, for the white man will come and you will be his slave. What have I done to you? Oh, children of my father."

After Chaka's death the Boers began their trek into the hinterland, looking for more land away from the English, who had taxed and restricted them severely. This inland push of the Boers once more set the Zulu in motion. Dingane, now king, led the fight against the encroachment on Zululand. This phase of the struggle for control of South Africa would continue until Dingane was defeated in the Battle of Blood River in December, 1839.

CONTINENT IN TURMOIL

Bakongo maternity figure
THE MUSEUM OF PRIMITIVE ART

"THE UNIQUE PEARL"

The Moroccan invasion and conquest of the Songhai empire in 1591 marks the onset of a tragic epoch in West African history. The northerners made their headquarters at Timbuktu, until then the intellectual center of the entire region. The Moroccans pillaged the city and arrested its leading scholars, sending them and their families across the desert to Marrakesh. Among these learned exiles, all of whom made the trans-Saharan trek in chains, was Ahmad Baba, a distinguished historian attached to the renowned Sankore mosque. The following account of Ahmad Baba's years in Morocco was originally written in French by Félix Du Bois, a scholar who visited the Sudan in the late 1800's.

Among the exiles was a learned doctor, Ahmed Baba by name, born in 1556 at Arawan.... In spite of his youth, he enjoyed a considerable reputation in Timbuctoo at the time of the Moorish conquest, and his brethren gave him the title of "The Unique Pearl of his Time." His renown increased in Morocco and became universal, spreading from Marrakesh to Bougie, Tunis, and even to Tripoli. The Arabs of the north called this [African] "very learned and very magnanimous," and his jailers found him "a fount of erudition." At the request of the Moorish scholars the doors of his prison were opened a year after his arrival (1596). All the believers were greatly pleased with his release, and he was conducted in triumph from his prison to the principal mosque of Marrakesh. A great many of the learned men urged him to open a course of instruction. His first thought was to refuse, but overcome by their persistence he accepted a post in the

Mosque of the Kerifs and taught rhetoric, law, and theology. An extraordinary number of pupils attended his lectures, and questions of the gravest importance were submitted to him by the magistracy, his decision always being treated as final. With a modesty worthy of his learning, he said concerning these decisions: "I carefully examined from every point of view the questions asked me, and having little confidence in my own judgment I entreated the assistance of God, and the Lord graciously enlightened me."

The ancient histories of Morocco relate many other interesting details, and the author of the *Bedzl el Mouasaha* reports the following utterance of Ahmed Baba: "Of all my friends I had the fewest books, and yet when your soldiers despoiled me they took 1600 volumes." The *Nozhel el Hadj* gives the following instance of the courage and pride of the [African] sheik: "After he was set at liberty Ahmed Baba presented himself at the palace of El Mansour, and the sultan gave audience to him from behind a curtain. 'God has declared in the Koran,' said the sheik, 'that no human being can communicate with Him hidden behind a veil. If it is your wish to speak to me, come forth from behind that curtain.' When El Mansour raised the curtain and approached him, Ahmed Baba continued, 'What need had you to sack my house, steal my books, and put me into chains to bring me to Morocco? By means of those chains I fell from my camel and broke my leg.' 'We wished to establish unity in the Mussulman world,' replied the sultan, 'and since you were one of the most distinguished representatives of Islam in your country,

we expected your submission to be followed by that of your fellow-citizens.' 'If that is so, why did you not seek to establish this unity amongst the Turks of Tlemcen and other places nearer to you?' 'Because the Prophet says, Leave the Turks in peace so long as they do not interfere with thee.' 'That was true at one time,' responded Ahmed Baba, 'but since then Iba Abbas has said, Leave not the Turks in peace even though they should not interfere with thee.' El Mansour, being unable to reply to this, put an end to the audience."

Although apparently free, Ahmed Baba was detained in Morocco for twelve years; the sultan had only released him on that condition, fearing the effect of his influence on his fellow-citizens. It was not until after the death of El Mansour that permission was obtained from his son for the learned man to return to the Sudan. Ahmed Baba then set out for the country to which he had so ardently desired to return, and of which he never spoke without tears in his eyes. The following verses were written by him in his exile:—

"O thou who goest to Gao, turn aside from thy path to breathe my name in Timbuctoo. Bear thither the greeting of an exile who sighs for the soil on which his friends and family reside. Console my near and dear ones for the deaths of their lords, who have been entombed."

The principal marabouts of Marrakesh formed him a guard of honor at his departure, and, at the moment of farewell, one of them seized Ahmed Baba by the hand and saluted him with the following sura from the holy book: "Certainly he who has made the Koran for thee shall

lead thee back to thy point of departure"
—a customary address to a traveler in
wishing him a safe return. On hearing
these words, the sheik abruptly withdrew
his hand, exclaiming, "May God never
bring me back to this meeting, nor make
me return to this country!"

He reached Timbuctoo in safety, and
died in 1627.

THE RAPE OF GUINEA

*British participation in the trans-Atlantic
slave trade was inaugurated in the 1560's by
John Hawkins, the shrewd, unscrupulous son
of William Hawkins. He had already made
several trips to the Canary Islands before he
embarked on his three triangular voyages
(1562, 1564, and 1567) between England,
the Guinea coast, and the West Indies. Accounts of these triumphs were included in
Richard Hakluyt's* Voyages, *which was first
published in three volumes in 1598–1600.
Hakluyt was a discriminating editor who depended mostly on firsthand information. He
reports that while in the Canaries, Hawkins
was "assured that Negros were very good
Marchandise in Hispaniola and that the
store of Negros might easily be had upon the
Guinea coast." Below is an extract from
Hakluyt's narrative of Hawkins' second
Africa-Caribbean voyage, which began at
Plymouth on October 18, 1564. The islands
from which the raids were made are probably
in the Bijagós Islands off Portuguese Guinea.*

Sir John Hawkins, slave trader

The 8 of December wee ankered by a
small island called Alcatrarsa, wherein
at our going a shore, we found nothing
but sea-birds, as we call them Ganets,
but by the Portugals, called Alcatrarses,
who for that cause gave the said Island
the same name. Herein halfe of our boates
were laden with yong and olde fowle,
who not being used to the sight of men,
flew so about us that we stroke them
down with poles. In this place the two
shippes riding, the two Barkes, with their
boates, went into an Island of the Sapies,
called La Formio, to see if they could
take any of them, and there landed to the
number of 80 in armour, and espying
certaine made to them, but they fled in
such order into the woods, that it booted
them not to follow: so going on their
way forward till they came to a river,
which they could not passe over, they
espied on the otherside two men, who
with their bowes and arrowes shot ter-
ribly at them. Whereupon we discharged
certaine harquebuzes to them againe, but
the ignorant people wayed it not, because they knewe not the danger thereof:
but used a marveilous crying in their
fight with leaping and turning their
tayles, that it was most strange to see,
and gave us great pleasure to beholde
them. At the last, one being hurt with a
harquebuz upon the thigh, looked upon
his wound and wist [knew] not howe it
came, because hee could not see the
pellet. Here Master Hawkins perceiving
no good to be done amongst them, because we could not finde their townes,
and also not knowing how to goe into
Rio grande, for want of a Pilote, which
was the very occasion of our comming
thither: and finding so many sholes,
feared with our great ships to goe in, and
therefore departed on our pretended way
to the Idols.

The 10 of December, we had a Northeast winde, with raine and storme, which
weather continued two dayes together,
was the occasion that the Salomon, and
Tygre loste our companie; for whereas
the Jesus, and pinnesse ankered at one
of the Islands called Sambula, the twelfth
day, the Salomon and Tygre came not
thither till the 14. In this Island we stayed
certain daies, going every day on shore,
to take the Inhabitants, with burning and
spoiling their townes, who before were
Sapies, and were conquered by the
Samboses, Inhabitants beyond Sierra
Leona. These Samboses had inhabited
there three yeres before our comming
thither, and in so short space have so
planted the ground, that they had great
plentie of Mil, Rise, Rootes, Pompions,
Pullin, goates, of small frye dried, every
house full of the Countrey fruite planted
by Gods providence, as Palmito trees,
fruites like dates, and sundry other in no
place in all that Countrey so aboundantly,
whereby they lived more deliciously than
other. These inhabitants have diverse of
the Sapies, which they tooke in the warres
as their slaves, whome onely they kept to
till the ground, in that they neither have
the knowledge thereof, nor yet will
worke themselves, of whome wee tooke
many in that place, but of the Samboses
none at all, for they fled into the maine.
All the Samboses have white teeth as we
have, farre unlike to the Sapies which doe
inhabite about Rio grande, for their teeth
are all filed, which they doe for a braverie,
to set out themselves, and doe jagge their
flesh, both legges, armes, and bodies, as
workemanlike, as a Jerkinmaker with us
pinketh a jerkin. These Sapies be more
civill than the Samboses: for whereas
the Samboses live most by the spoile of
their enemies, both in taking their
victuals, and eating them also. The Sapies
do not eate mans flesh, unlesse in the
warre they be driven by necessitie there-
unto, which they have not used but by
the example of the Samboses, but live
onely with fruites, and cattell, whereof
they have great store.

THE ROYAL ADVENTURERS

*The English were anxious to begin their ex-
ploitation of Africa, as were all Europeans. In the mid-seventeenth century a group
of courtier-adventurers suggested to King*

Charles II that he charter a company "for the purpose of sending an expedition to the Gambia to dig for gold." The result was the Company of the Royal Adventurers into Africa, which thrived from 1600 to 1672 and which was succeeded by the Royal African Company. The extract below is from a history of the enterprise, written in 1919 by George F. Zook, an American educator. This passage points up the organized, commercial aspects of slaving.

On December 18, 1660, the king, who was pleased with the adventurers for having "undertaken so hopeful an enterprise," granted them a charter under the name of "The Company of the Royal Adventurers into Africa."

By this charter the Royal Adventurers received the land and the adjacent islands on the west coast of Africa from Cape Blanco to the Cape of Good Hope, for a period of one thousand years. . . . The king himself reserved the privilege of becoming an adventurer at any time and to invest an amount of money not exceeding one-sixteenth of the company's stock.

Furthermore, it was provided that the king "shall have, take and receive two third parts of all the gold mines which shall be seized possessed and wrought in the parts and places aforesaid, we . . . paying and bearing two third parts of all the charges incident to the working and transporting of the said gold." The company was to have the other third and bear the remainder of the expense. That this provision was not a matter of mere form, as in so many of the royal charters, is evident from the stimulus which had led to the formation of the company. Indeed in one part of the charter the purpose of the company is presented as "the setting forward and furthering of the trade intended (redwood, hides, elephants' teeth) in the parts aforesaid and the encouragement of the undertakers in discovering the golden mines and setting of plantations there." The trade in slaves was not mentioned in the charter. . . .

The Company of Royal Adventurers . . . received its charter December 18, 1660. In the same month, Captain Robert Holmes sailed from England in command of the five royal ships which composed the first expedition. In March, 1661, he arrived at Cape Verde where he at once informed the Dutch commander that he had orders from Charles II to warn all persons of whatsoever nation that the right of trade and navigation from Cape Verde to the Cape of Good Hope belonged exclusively to the king of England. Holmes ordered the Dutch to vacate their forts and to abandon the coast within six or seven months. Thereupon he seized the island of Boa Vista, one of the Cape Verde group claimed by the Dutch since 1621. Later he sent a frigate into the mouth of the Gambia. . . .

The early trade of the English to the coast of Africa was very largely in exchange for products which could be sold in England. Among these may be mentioned elephants' teeth, wax, malaguetta and gold. . . . The hope of discovering gold mines was the principal cause of the first expedition sent to Africa by the Royal Adventurers in December, 1660. When this scheme to mine gold was abandoned the company's agents traded for gold which was brought down from the interior or washed out by the slow and laborious toil of the natives. The other African products, especially elephants' teeth, were brought to London where they sold quite readily for very good prices.

Although this direct trade between England and Africa was never neglected, the slave trade with the English colonies in the West Indies was destined to absorb the company's attention because the supply of indentured servants was never great enough to meet the needs of the rapidly growing sugar and indigo plantations. From the planters point of view, moreover, slaves had numerous advantages over white servants as plantation laborers. Slaves and their children after them were chattel property for life. The danger of rebellion was very small because often the slaves could not even converse with one another, since they were likely to be from different parts of Africa and therefore to speak a different dialect. Finally, neither the original outlay for slaves nor the cost of feeding and clothing them was great, and therefore slaves were regarded as more economical than indentured servants. Moreover, there was much to be said against encouraging the lower classes of England to come to the plantations, where they often engaged in disturbances of one kind and another. . . . Not only did the company supply the planters with slaves, their greatest necessity, but in exchange for these it took sugar and other plantation products which it carried to England. It was natural that the company should endeavor to make a success of its business. . . .

Sir Thomas Modyford, speaker of the assembly [of Barbadoes], also became the agent for the Royal Adventurers in Barbadoes. Modyford was very enthusiastic about the company's prospects for a profitable trade in Negroes with the Spanish colonies. The people of Barbadoes neither shared Modyford's enthusiasm for this trade nor for the company's monopoly because they believed that thereby the price of slaves was considerably increased. On December 18, 1662, the council and assembly of Barbadoes resolved to ask the king for a free trade to Africa or to be assured that the factors of the Royal Company would sell their slaves for the same price as other merchants. Very shortly, the duke of York, the company's governor, informed Governor Willoughby that the company had made arrangements to provide Barbadoes and the Caribbee Islands with 3,000 slaves per annum and that the needs of the islands would be attended to as conditions changed. Moreover, the company pledged itself to see that all Negroes imported into the island should be sold by lots, as had been the custom, at the average rate of seventeen pounds per head or for commodities of the island rated at that price. The duke of York also requested Governor Willoughby to ascertain if possible how many Negroes were desired by the planters at that rate, and to see that any planters who wished to become members of the company should be given an opportunity to do so. . . .

The monopoly of supplying the colonies with slaves, conferred upon the Company of Royal Adventurers, was most cordially hated on account of the great degree of dependence placed upon slave labor in the plantations. As a result of this conflict of interests the planters early resorted to numerous devices such as the laws for the protection of debtors, to embarrass the company in the exercise of its monopoly. Since the company had received its exclusive privileges by a charter from the crown the English planters in the West Indies soon found that their troubles with the Company of Royal Adventurers brought them also into direct conflict with the king. In this way the planters enjoyed the distinction of being among the first to begin the opposition which later, in the Great Revolution [the Glorious Revolution of 1688], resulted in the overthrow of James II and the royal prerogative.

THE FULANI JIHAD

Historians have long debated the causes and nature of the Fulani jihad, or holy war, that swept across the central Sudan in the early nineteenth century. The war has been viewed as a political revolution in which the Fulani overthrew the tenuous Muslim aristocracy of Hausaland and extended their power over much of the central Sudan, and as a revival movement intent on bringing the region a more austere type of Islam. Certainly both these factors must now be accounted in understanding the jihad, which began in 1804. Its leader was Usman Dan Fodio, a fanatical Muslim who became chief of the Fulani empire. The selection below presents Usman Dan Fodio's personal explanation of the origins of the revolution. It was probably written in 1811, when most of his objectives had been realized and he was about to retire.

I declare, and God the Accomplisher is my witness, that Ahmad Baba ibn Ahmad ibn Al-Hajj laid down in his book, *Exposition and Information about the kinds of Sudanese Captives*, that Bornu, Kano, Katsena, Songhay, and part of Zagzag [Zaria] were Muslim countries, but the whole of the country to the west was a country of the Unbelievers. If someone asks—of what use is this inquiry into the mode of government of the people mentioned in the passage?—I reply, "May God and you, reader, put the information to good use." The people are Muslim except the Afanu [the Hausa]. I do not know from whence these latter come, and never heard. To the west of Hausa all the people are Unbelievers. According to our author, Islam was accepted by some kings and others of these parts in his time. Every learned man judges according to the knowledge of his age. Conditions change with the times, and the cure changes with the disease. It is well known that in our time Islam has become widespread in the land of Hausa among other than kings. The Kings are Unbelievers and nothing else. If they are believers in Islam, why are they idolators, refusing to follow in the way of God, and raising the flag of earthly power above the flag of Islam?

All this is Unbelief, according to the general opinion.

The government of a country is the government of its King without question. If the King is a Muslim, his land is Muslim; if he is an Unbeliever, his land is a land of Unbelievers. In these circumstances it is lawful for anyone to leave it for another country. There is no dispute that the Hausa Kings worshiped many places of idols, and trees, and rocks, and sacrificed to them. This constitutes Unbelief, according to the general opinion.

This view of mine rests on the weight of authority, but does not deny the existence of some Muslims here and there. We cannot judge from exceptions specially chosen:—

> "You should prefer the usual to the unusual; for the usual and common is what we want to elucidate."

The above description was applicable to the condition of the Hausa peoples as we found them, before the *jihad*. Since then we have fought them and put them to flight, and killed some, and driven others from this land by the power of God (Exalted be He).

We have appointed Muslim Governors over the land, and it has become a land of Islam, without doubt. Praise be to God. . . .

To explain our flight from Gobir and the reasons of our holy war with the Hausa Sultans.

I declare, and God the Accomplisher is my witness, that the work of my brother Abdullah on this subject is sufficient. I said to him on a day: "Write for us the reasons for our flight from Gobir and our holy war with the Hausa Sultans, to be our apology to whoever reads the book, if he serve God." He answered that he would write, and wrote:—

. . . Know that our Sheikh, Uthman ibn Muhammad Amir al-Mu'minin (May God prolong his life in his service) came forth to call all persons, wherever they might be, to the Faith, and to expound to all whom he could reach their duty to God, and noble endeavor, trying to clear away their doubts concerning God, to deliver them from the doom to come and to save them, to keep alive the doctrines of Islam and to banish wickedness.

Many people received his teaching, and helped him, till his fame spread abroad. There were learned men, his contemporaries, who disputed and denied his mission.

In the beginning he did not address himself to the kings. After a time his people grew and became famous, till they were known in Hausaland as "*The People*." Men kept leaving their countries and coming to him. Of the ruling classes some repented, and came to him with all they possessed, leaving their Sultans. Then the Sultans became angry, till there ensued between them and their chiefs the war we remember. Matters did not rest there.

The Sheikh said: "I will not interfere between anyone and his chief; I will not be a cause of parting." He strove to avert a quarrel. But the trouble grew and grew. The Sultans kept sending protests to their people. The rupture became open between the Sheikh and them. They saw the growing numbers of his following and the hold that Islam had gained. Its growing strength made them furious, and devils among Jinns and men urged them on, saying: "If you do not disperse this concourse of people, your power will be gone; they will destroy your country, by causing all the people to leave you and go to them."

The Sultan of Gobir sent to us plotting our destruction, as we discovered. This showed us the true meaning of his words and deeds. But God averted from us his evil design. He told us, what we know, namely, that they only wished to kill us. So we returned to our abode. The Sultan of Gobir attacked the Sheikh's people; they fled, for they were afraid. The Gobir army followed them and captured some and slew others, seizing children and women, and selling them in our midst.

This made us greatly afraid. The Sultan of Gobir ordered the Sheikh to leave the country with his children and wives and relatives, but to take no one else with him, and disperse his people. The Sheikh replied: "I will not disperse my people, but I will go away with any who wish to come with me. Let those who wish to remain, remain."

So we fled from their land in the year 1218 A.H. on the 10th of Dhu'l-qa'da [February 23, 1804] to a place outside Gobir territory.

The Muslims all fled, following us. Many of them joined us with their people and property; some brought nothing but their people; some came with no following at all.

The Sultan of Gobir ordered his Chiefs to seize the goods of all who fled or prevent them leaving.

They seized much property of the Muslims, and killed some of them.

Then he ordered those of the Chiefs nearest to us on the east to keep on killing our people, and plundering, and imprisoning.

The people suffered sorely.

We went to the Sheikh and said: "Truly this matter has become intolerable; recourse must be had to arms. There can be no doubt that the situation demands a prince to manage our affairs, for Muslims should be without order or government."

Then we did homage to the Sheikh, as is directed by the Qur'an and Sunna in such circumstances, and made him the leader of the Holy War.

We rose to ward off attack. Self-defense and defense of dependents and possessions is a righteous act, according to received opinion.

FULANI WISDOM

According to the Fulani, who speak a Nigritic language, "a Fulani will lie but not make a lying proverb." The following collection of adages was compiled by C.E.J. Whitting.

A dark night brings fear but man still more.

However little you think of the elephant, you will not say it will not fill a pot.

The ant-eater's grief is not the monkey's.

Whoever cooks the food of malice, remnants will stick to his pocket.

Alive he was insufficient, dead he is missed.

An enemy slaughters, a friend distributes.

If you want to hear the news of the heart ask the face.

They know the calabash is useful but they make a spoon.

If a knife is lacking, a strip of bark will cut.

It is not his deserts that a man gets but his destiny.

If death encircles the mortar, it wants not the mortar but the pounder.

Fair words, evil deeds.

Hate you your buttocks never so much, you sit on them perforce.

He who rides the horse of greed at a gallop will pull it up at the door of shame.

He who has no authority will not have ceremonial drums.

Six things cannot be trusted, a prince, a river, a knife, a woman, string and darkness.

Concentration brings near the distant camp.

Guile excels strength.

Be the town never so far, there is another beyond it.

A porcupine will not mind needle grass.

KUBA LAW

The kingdom of the Kuba, home of about seventy-five thousand Bantu speakers, is flanked by the Kasai, Sankuru, and Lulua rivers in the former Kasai province of the Congo (Kinshasa). Comprised of several chiefdoms, it is ruled by the centrally located Bushoong chiefdom, whose head is automatically the king of all the Kuba. The king and chiefs hold their offices by divine right and are the only persons who have power over life and death. The Kuba do not use precedents or compare cases to deduce analogies; their legal process is based on equity and the power of Kuba political authorities— the chiefs and the king. The following discussion of Kuba procedural law is by Dr. Jan Vansina, the author of this volume's chapter on inner Africa and professor of history at the University of Wisconsin. The court cere-

monial and formula he describes date back to about A.D. 1650 *and were used until* 1892, *the beginning of the colonial era in Kuba-land. Since then there have been some minor changes, but on the local level Kuba law remains as outlined in the following essay.*

A case is introduced by one of the disputing parties. He brings his complaint to any judge in the capital, who directs him to a competent judge. The party deposits a payment of 700 cowries for the formal lodging of the complaint. Through informal consultation the judge then forms a panel. In cases where a public authority has been flouted, the responsible political official, a village headman, for instance, lodges the complaint. When the day of hearing is set, usually a few days after reception of the complaint, the judges send somebody to notify the defendant. The messenger may be the child of one of the judges or *nyim shapdy*, a special messenger. The messengers must be well treated in the villages, for courts can hold villages in contempt. The courts of appeal have their own means of summoning the defendant: baang [the appeals court that oversees marriage cases] sends the *iyol abaang;* kikaam [appeals court for debtors] and the supreme court have the summons announced on the main square of the capital by the town crier. Anybody who meets the accused is under obligation to notify him. When an accused person refuses to answer the summons, he is fined and arrested either by his covillagers or by slaves of the king or the chief, who form the police force. He is then bound and put in the stocks at the jail in the kikaam's compound. The stocks are used only for preventive detention of this sort. Any person may arrest any other *in flagrante delicto*, a fact that often leads to fights. A wise man notifies the two village policemen who exist in every village.

Before the session of the court opens, the accused pays 700 cowries to the panel, and the 1,400 cowries of both parties is divided among the judges. This

Wooden drum of the Kuba
THE MUSEUM OF PRIMITIVE ART

amount constitutes their salary. Both parties, one after the other, then tell the facts, the plaintiff being the first speaker. At this stage they may be interrupted only by judges or spectators who want to elucidate one or another detail. Eyewitnesses or character witnesses are then called in and are cross-examined by the judges, who also cross-examine the parties. Usually the statements of the parties and the testimony of the witnesses elicit the facts to the satisfaction of the judges. The latter, in any event, have a general knowledge of the facts, having heard about the matter through gossip at the capital or through inquiries made beforehand by the provincial chief. Sometimes, however, the facts are not clear and there are no witnesses. The accused may then propose to swear an oath (*ndokl*). He says that he is innocent, invokes the Creator God as a witness, and steps over a leopard skin, the symbol of political authority. If he lies, he should die on the spot. But the oath is rarely used, for it is believed that the Creator punishes those who swear for trifles. I believe that the judges feel that swearing an oath is taking the matter out of court. A milder oath also exists, but it is considered no more than an emphatic form of speech.

After the evidence is heard and the facts are elicited to the satisfaction of the judges, they withdraw to deliberate. They must reach a unanimous verdict. After doing so, they emerge and proceed to the announcement of the verdict, which is introduced by the following formula:

The king doesn't walk with a bow the

collecting of conflicts, the verdicts of the cases.

The black genette eats the white termites

Be not afraid of the grass the genette carries

The old animal of the councilors of the supreme court

when he proceeds to decide cases, he doesn't like protests.

Above the thieves, the leopard of the witches

the spoon of the porridge

is the instrument which probes the depths of the fire.

It dawns at the chasm which begets the hills

at the world which begets the living.

The river of trade bears the weak ones.

It becomes daylight at Mbeky Butwiim

at Makum maNyaang

at the king who stares intently at the verdicts

at Mboom Kol Mishumn.

The formula means:

The king is in court to

settle the conflicts.

The king destroys the criminals

the innocents must not be afraid.

The king in the supreme court does not stand for protests against the verdicts.

Despite the thieves, the king can find the culprits.

It dawns at the king's who creates the world

who creates all the living beings.

The king protects the weak.

It dawns at the famous capitals

at the king's capital when he holds his court.

The formula is given in full because it is typical of Kuba thought. It emphasizes that the court holds its authority from the king, and that the king has authority by virtue of divine kingship. It reminds the guilty parties that justice will find them out, and the innocent parties that they are protected by the king. It reminds all that verdicts should not be questioned. It expresses the Kuba philosophy of law, and stresses that fundamentally the law has equity. It is guaranteed by the powers of the king, but the equity of the king himself is guaranteed by the supreme court.

SONG OF THE SPIRITS

The divine powers of Kuba kings are emphasized in the "songs of the spirits," which were composed by the women of the king's harem in praise of the souls of deceased rulers. They were sung each month at the appearance of the new moon and have the quality of a dirge. This example, recorded by Jan Vansina, salutes the spirit of Mbope Kyeen, who ruled from 1900 to 1902. Mboong was the name of the first Kuba king, hence it is often used to designate his successors. Mbope Kyeen's death, so soon after his coronation, makes his aged grandmother, Mabiinc, weep.

Mboong has donned the coronation
    costumes
Come admire him!
And those in the streets will tell the
    news.
King Mboong, the thread which sews
    the peoples of the king;
He is the thread who unites the provinces.
Mbope, son of Kyeen speaks:
  I am not envious, I am the God who
    created trees and plains!
The woman Mabiinc of the twin spirits,
    she who nursed the king's mother
    speaks:
  "I am truly the resident of the royal
    quarter, I am from that august place.
The dancing mask Mashingady weeps
    for pity.
The woman of his heart, I come from the
    village of Mulek, I come from the
    royal quarter; I Mbaawoot daughter
    of Pish, daughter of Pash must don
    the wrapper of mourning, the dress
    of funeral white."

ANIMAL LYRICS

Ncok is a lighthearted genre of Kuba poetry recited in song, often to the accompaniment of a dance. Three examples collected by Dr. Vansina in 1953 follow. The first refers to

an ancient Kuba myth in which the sun vanishes forever. The hero gives the Bushoong, the Kuba ruling group, a rooster. The cock's cry awakens the sun and chases away the moon, which has been called by the cuckoos.

The rooster sings during the night
The cuckoos have provoked the rising of
    the moon
The rooster sang his cry
The rooster the Bushoong have taken.

The crocodile is dying in the water
The crocodile has become deaf
The huge crocodile has become blind.

The land of the goat, we are trampling it
The heaven of God, we touch it with the
    hand
I will go to the village of the dead, borne
    on the arms of men.
One day in the future, during the heat
The day of my death, don't bury me
at the foot of the *ngum* tree
I fear its spines;
at the foot of the tree *buncweemy*
I fear the drops of water;
One day in the future, bury me
on the main square near the tree *bushaang*
I want to hear the beat of the drumming
    and the rattles of the dancers!

NDABA, A MAN OF AFFAIRS

Praise poems are an integral part of the social life of the Zulu, who belong to the Nguni cluster of Bantu speakers. Today there are over two million Zulu inhabiting Zululand and Natal in the Republic of South Africa. This Zulu praise song is dedicated to Ndaba, an eighteenth-century chief who was probably the grandson or great-grandson of Zulu, legendary founder of the core clan of Zulu people. His name means "man of affairs." Sonani means "What wrong did we do?" The Mababela, Gabela, and Gcabashe are Zulu ancestors. Ndaba lives "with his shield on his knees," as he is always ready to fight.

Ndaba son of Sonani, they say "What
    wrong did he do?",
Since the people are living with their
    herds

Belonging to Mababela's people of the
    Gabela clan.
He who hunted the forests until they
    murmured,
Until eventually they cried "Enough!
    Isn't it?",
Today there is so much game
That they snip off a titbit of a duiker for
    him.
Who when he lay down was the size of
    rivers,
Who when he got up was the size of
    mountains.
    Precious little amulet of our people, of
      Gcabashe's people,
That continually lives in a towering rage,
With his shields on his knees,
Watching over the herds of those who
    meditate evil
Against Mababela's people of the Gabela
    clan.

CHAKA'S RECEPTION

Henry Francis Fynn, an Englishman, was one of the few white men to be intimately acquainted with Chaka (Shaka), "Father of the Zulu." In 1819 Fynn journeyed to Cape Town, where he became a partner in the Farewell Trading Company. He traveled in the area, and in 1824 went to Natal with the first group of white settlers. He soon learned that Natal was virtually the private property of Chaka and determined to visit the Zulu warrior-king. Negotiations ensued, but Chaka stalled the arrival of Fynn and his party in order to prepare an impressive reception for them. In July, 1824, the coveted invitation finally came. The following account of Fynn's first meeting with Chaka is from his diary, an invaluable source for Africanists.

The distance from the port to Shaka's residence was 200 miles. Our progress was exceedingly slow, each day's journey being arranged by Mbikwana [one of Shaka's aides]. We afterwards found out that he had not taken us by a direct route, but to kraals of minor chiefs and some of the barracks of Shaka's regiments. Cattle-slaughtering occurred sometimes twice and thrice a day. Numbers of Zulu joined our column in order to relieve Mbikwana's people of their burdens. We were struck with astonishment at the order and discipline maintained in the country through which we traveled. The regimental kraals, especially the upper parts thereof, also the kraals of chiefs, showed that cleanliness was a prevailing custom and this not only inside their huts, but outside, for there were considerable spaces where neither dirt nor ashes were to be seen. . . .

Messengers passed three or four times a day between Shaka and Mbikwana, the former enquiring about our progress and doubtless directing how we should proceed so as to fall in with his own preparations for our reception. . . . While encamped that night we saw much commotion going on in our neighborhood. Troops of cattle were being driven in advance; regiments were passing near by and on distant hills, interspersed with regiments of girls, decorated in beads and brass with regimental uniformity, carrying on their heads large pitchers of native beer, milk and cooked food. . . .

The following morning . . . we arrived at a ridge from which we beheld an extensive and very picturesque basin before us, with a river running through it, called the Umfolozi.

We were requested to make a stand under a large euphorbia tree, from whence, about a mile before us, we saw the residence of Shaka, viz: a native kraal nearly two miles in circumference. . . .

On entering the great cattle kraal we found drawn up within it about 80,000 natives in their war attire. Mbikwana requested me to gallop within the circle, and immediately on my starting to do so one general shout broke forth from the whole mass, all pointing at me with their sticks. I was asked to gallop round the circle two or three times in the midst of tremendous shouting of the words, *"UJojo wokhalo!"* (the sharp or active finch of the ridge). Mr. Farewell and I were then led by Mbikwana to the head of the kraal, where the masses of the people were considerably denser than else-

where. The whole force remained stationary, as, indeed, it had been since the commencement of the reception.

Mbikwana, standing in our midst, addressed some unseen individual in a long speech. . . .

While the speech was being made I caught sight of an individual in the background whom I concluded to be Shaka, and, turning to Farewell, pointed out and said: "Farewell, there is Shaka." This was sufficiently audible for him to hear and perceive that I had recognized him. . . .

Elephant tusks were then brought forward. One was laid before Farewell and another before me. Shaka then raised the stick in his hand and after striking with it right and left, the whole mass broke from their position and formed up into regiments. Portions of each of these rushed to the river and the surrounding hills, while the remainder, forming themselves into a circle, commenced dancing with Shaka in their midst.

It was a most exciting scene, surprising to us, who could not have imagined that a nation termed "savages" could be so disciplined and kept in order.

Regiments of girls, headed by officers of their own sex, then entered the center of the arena to the number of 8,000–10,000, each holding a slight staff in her hand. They joined in the dance, which continued for about two hours. . . .

The King came up to us and told us not to be afraid of his people, who were now coming up to us in small divisions, each division driving cattle before it. The men were singing and dancing and whilst so doing advancing and receding even as one sees the surf do on a seashore. The whole country, as far as our sight could reach, was covered with numbers of people and droves of cattle. The cattle had been assorted according to their color. . . . After exhibiting their cattle for two hours, they drew together in a circle, and sang and danced to their war song. Then the people returned to the cattle, again exhibiting them as before, and, at intervals, dancing and singing. The women

now entered the kraal, each having a long thin stick in the right hand, and moving it in time to the song. They had not been dancing many minutes, when they had to make way for the ladies of the seraglio, besides about 150 others, who were called sisters. These danced in parties of eight, arranged in fours, each party wearing different colored beads, which were crossed from the shoulders to the knees. Each wore a head-dress of black feathers, and four brass collars, fitting closely to the neck. When the King joined in the dance, he was accompanied by the men. This dance lasted half an hour. The order observed and the precision of every movement was interpreted to us by his interpreter, Hlambamanzi. He desired to know from us if ever we had seen such order in any other state, assured us that he was the greatest king in existence, that his people were as numerous as the stars, and that his cattle were innumerable. . . . The following morning we were requested to mount our horses and proceed to the King's quarters. We found him sitting under a tree in the upper end of the kraal decorating himself and surrounded by about 200 people. A servant was kneeling by his side holding a shield above him to keep off the glare of the sun. Round his forehead he wore a turban of otter skin with a feather of a crane erect in front, fully two feet long, and a wreath of scarlet feathers, formerly worn, only, by men of high rank. Ear ornaments made from dried sugar cane, carved round the edges, with white ends, and an inch in diameter, were let into the lobes of the ears, which had been cut to admit them. From shoulder to shoulder, he wore bunches, five inches in length, of the skins of monkeys and genets, twisted like the tails of these animals. These hung half down the body. Round the ring on the head, were a dozen tastefully arranged bunches of the loury feathers, neatly tied to thorns which were stuck into the hair. Round his arms were white ox-tail tufts, cut down the middle so as to allow the hair to hang about the arm, to the number of four for each arm. Round the waist, there was a kilt or petticoat, made of skins of monkeys and genets, and twisted as before described, having small tassels round the top. The kilt reached to the knees, below which were white ox-tails fitted to the legs so as to hang down to the ankles. He had a white shield with a single black spot, and one assegai. . . .

Two oxen were slaughtered for us. After dinner we prepared to retire, but messengers from Shaka requested us to go to him, with Jacob the interpreter. I was then led into the seraglio, where I found him seated in a carved wooden chair and surrounded by about 400 girls, two or three chiefs and two servants in attendance.

My name Fynn had been converted into Sofili by the people in general; by this, after desiring me to sit in front of him, he several times accosted me in the course of the following dialogue:

"I hear you have come from umGeorge, is it so? Is he as great a king as I am?"

Fynn: "Yes; King George is one of the greatest kings in the world." . . .

Shaka: "Have you medicine by you?"

Fynn: "Yes."

Shaka: "Then cure me, or I will have you sent to umGeorge to have you killed."

Fynn: "What is the matter with you?"

Shaka: "That is your business to find out."

Fynn: "Stand up and let me see your person."

Shaka: "Why should I stand up?"

Fynn: "That I may see if I can find out what ails you."

Shaka stood up but evidently disliked my approaching him closely. A number of girls held up lighted torches. I looked about his person and, after reflecting on the great activity he had shown during the day, was satisfied he had not much the matter with him. I, however, observed numerous black marks on his loins where native doctors had scarified him, and at once said he had pains in his loins. He held his hand before his mouth in astonishment, upon which my wisdom

was applauded by all present. Shaka then strictly charged me not to give medicine to his dogs, and, after a few commonplace questions in which he showed good humor, I was permitted to retire for the night. . . .

He sent the next day requesting me to follow him.

On my arrival he desired me to look at and then to count a large drove of oxen I had not before seen. I did so, making the number 5,654. When I announced the result the crowd that was present burst out laughing asking how it was possible for me to count so many, seeing I had not counted up to ten on my fingers. They at once concluded I had not counted them. . . .

Shaka went on to speak of the gifts of nature, or, as they term it, *uMvelinqangi*. He said that the first forefathers of the Europeans had bestowed on us many gifts by giving us all the knowledge of arts and manufactures, yet they had kept from us the greatest of all gifts, such as a good black skin, for this does not necessitate the wearing of clothes to hide the white skin, which was not pleasant to the eye. He well knew that for a black skin we would give all we were worth in the way of our arts and manufactures. He then asked what use was made of the hides of cattle slaughtered in our country. When I told him they were made into shoes and other articles, which, however, I could not explain so as to make him understand, he exclaimed that that was another proof of the unkindness of our forefathers, for they had obliged us to make use of hides to protect our feet, but as such protection was unnecessary in their case their forefathers revealed to them that hides should be used for making more handsome and serviceable articles, namely shields. This changed the conversation to the superiority of their arms; these he endeavored to show in various ways were more advantageous than our muskets. The shield, he argued, if dipped into water previous to an attack, would be sufficient to ward off the effect of a ball fired when they were at a distance.

THE BRAVE AND MAGIC LAND

The Zulu cultural tradition has been recently enriched by the poems, plays, stories, and essays of the late Herbert Dhlomo, a Zulu poet. His masterpiece which was first published in 1941, is Valley of a Thousand Hills, *a poem extolling the heroes and wonders of his Natal homeland. Its prologue follows.*

On your dear fame, proud offspring here
    I stand!
Sweet names of a sweet strand!

O charms of my dear fatherland!
Blest spots! I long to see them all!
Where men of yore, great Shaka's band,
Sang wrought and fell! To me they call!

Great scenes of old—like magic wand!—
Of heroes wise and strange feats done,
Where men of might, like ocean sand,
Mocked seas of life . . . and wrought
    for fun!

Born sealed with immortality,
Hymned Shaka, god of war-writ fame,
Homeric feats attained, and we
Plumed Trojan Black Bulls, claim a
    name!

For Shaka, now our Jove, more than
Sung classic names achieved. His name
More than vain demagogue boasts can,
Or ever will, has brought us fame.

And those whom we in pride adore,
Moshoeshoe, Hintsa, Khama's strain . . .
Hannibal, Aggrey—these and many
    more
With gleaming names, deck Shaka's
    train.

Out of the living past they haunt me still!
And voices mute forever speak to me!
My eyes with tears, my thoughts with
    visions, fill!
I see them all, but see not where they be!

These men and places call to me!
They speak out of Eternity!
I see, I feel, I live it all!
I rise! and yield before the call!

Held captive in a net, a slave sits on the Congo shore waiting to be sold and shipped.

THE RISE
OF RACISM

Emblems of African Spain: above, "stalactite" ceiling embellishing the splendid Granadan citadel of Alhambra, built after 1248 by the last Muslim dynasty in Spain; right, the four-foot-tall "Alhambra Vase," finest extant example of blue pottery made under Moorish patronage.

NO TEARS
FOR THE MOORS

It is a bitter irony of history that when Europeans first impinged upon Africa, the European spirit was dominated by a surging religious fanaticism. "Reduce to perpetual slavery their persons, domains, and possessions" was the official Church policy toward the "infidels," and no one heeded the call more fiercely than the Catholic rulers of Spain, whose zeal had been tempered in the long struggle against the Moors. The Christian reconquest of Spain did not, however, bring peace between Cross and Crescent; viewing its long struggle as part of a global holy war, Spain soon launched a counteroffensive against the Moors in North Africa. Nor did European religious zeal moderate after the Protestant Reformation in the mid-sixteenth century. Indeed, it intensified. In the continuing conflicts among the aggressive, self-righteous believers—Catholic, Protestant, and Muslim, each wed to a "universal" faith—Africa's diverse animist faiths would be the victims.

The end of Moorish rule is recorded in a
Spanish bas-relief retable above. It shows
a richly garbed Muhammad XI, or Boabdil, as the Spanish called him, filing
out of the Alhambra en route to surrender
to the Catholic monarchs, Ferdinand and
Isabella. Muhammad's demise had been
brought on by a civil war between him
and his uncle, in which it had been Spanish strategy to support Muhammad just
long enough to see his rival destroyed. No
sooner had Muhammad taken Granada
than the Crown demanded he withdraw,
and unable to enlist the aid of Muslim
rulers in Africa, he retired in 1492.

The Count of Barcelona, an eleventh-century knight, is
shown stabbing a Moor in a medieval manuscript painting.

387

The girl at left belongs to the Sokoto Fulani of northern Nigeria. The Fulani rose to power in the early nineteenth century in scattered regions of the western Sudan, revolutionizing once again a flagging Muslim culture. Below, the Dogon of Mali hold a funeral. Although Muslim dress is evident, the dance itself is part of the Dogon's animist tradition, in which the vital force of the deceased is passed to a descendant.

LOSS OF THE PAST

With Portugal occupying a number of strategic cities in the western Maghreb, Spain holding most of the ports of the central coast, and Turkey pressing from the east, North Africa seemed in the sixteenth century to have surrendered its future to alien rulers. The Turks would long continue to hold their gains as far west as Tunisia, making the southern Mediterranean littoral a haven for Barbary pirates. Morocco, however, met its foreign-borne adversity by spawning the vital Saadian dynasty. One of its sultans, Ahmad al-Mansur, expelled the Portuguese at the battle of Alcazar in 1578. Encouraged by this victory, Morocco's "Victorious One" sent a force across the Sahara, defeated the armies of the Songhai empire, and inaugurated a policy of plunder and destruction there, reducing such centers of learning as Timbuktu to impoverished villages and leaving a commercial civilization in ruins.

Within the shadows of the great brick mosque of Sankore (above) once lived more than a hundred Muslim teaching clerics. The Koranic schools they ran, the extensive libraries they accumulated, went to make up a kind of university quarter for Timbuktu. Below is a reconstruction of the old mosque at Jenne, a rival intellectual center. Said to equal Mecca in architectural magnificence, it was destroyed in 1830 by Seku Ahmadu, Muslim zealot and leader of a Fulani jihad, as punishment for the moral corruption that he judged had infected the citizens.

DU BOIS, Timbuctoo the Mysterious, 1896

KOLB, *The Present State of the Cape of Good Hope*, 1731

COLOR AND SLAVERY

The heavier the slave traffic grew and the more dehumanized its victims became in the years after 1650, the more avidly did Europeans search for ways to justify themselves. The theory that the African was an "infidel" could only suffice for a time, for if the chattel became a Christian, where was the justification then? More useful was the premise upon which the Dutch in the Cape Colony defended slavery. Dark-skinned people, it was said, are the sons of Ham. Since Noah had condemned Ham to serve his brothers, clearly the whites were only fulfilling a biblical curse. From deep within such pseudo-Christian rationalizations, certain deadly equations began to emerge (for example, the African stood outside all justice, human and divine). Later these notions would be replaced by equally destructive misapplications of "science." The new ethnological concept of "race" led to classifying peoples as superior and inferior, and even Darwin's theory of the survival of the fittest was bent to prove their argument.

CLARKSON, *History of the Abolition of the African Slave Trade*, 1808

Opposite, a well-dressed Boer imperiously instructs a Hottentot slave in a sketch made by a Dutch scientist who visited the Cape Colony in 1705. Right, the whipping of a bound slave on a plantation near Rio de Janeiro was depicted by a French visitor to Brazil in 1834. Below, a diagram of the hold of a nineteenth-century slave ship showed how to load the maximum number of humans.

DEBRET, *Voyages Pittoresques et Historiques au Brésil 1816–1831, 1834*

The annual yam harvest festival of the Asante (above) was seen and sketched by Thomas Bowdich, leader of an 1817 British mission to the West African kingdom. The umbrellas belong to the vassals of the Asante king, who is seated beneath the red canopy in the center panel. At the festival, an elaborate affair of state, chiefs and captains accused of some crime were tried and punished. "I never felt so grateful for being born in a civilized country," was Bowdich's smug response to the scene. At right, "messengers of the sacred forest" dance during initiation rites in a Toma village. These Mande people live near the Liberia-Guinea border.

392

PEOPLES OF "DARKNESS"

Rationalizing the slave trade eventually required Europeans to turn a self-blinded eye toward African life itself. If Africans were accursed and inferior, so the implicit argument ran, then they *could not* have produced anything that was not inherently inferior and accursed. Europeans in general held the view that slavery in the New World was better than "savage barbarism" in Africa. The relatively objective reports of the early explorers now gave way to a kind of perpetual propaganda. Although Europeans had been negotiating with rulers of African states and kingdoms since the earliest days of contact in the fifteenth century, the famed nineteenth-century naturalist Louis Agassiz could declare, with all the authority of "science," that Africans "never originated a regular organization among themselves." Agassiz's logic was the prevailing logic: political organization was a recognized human achievement; therefore Africans had no political organization. To the moralistic, what was different in Africa would appear simply as "repugnant"; to the less censorious, what was different would appear as "colorful" or "quaint" or "childlike." The unfamiliar could not be worthy of respect, of being seen on its own terms.

Wood carvings, once dismissed simply as naive, enliven a door of a palace built for Gezo (1818–1858) in Abomey, capital of the ancient kingdom of Dahomey.

British brigantines are careened for repairs at a Guinea river village. The sketch, penciled around 1850, was made by one of the officers.

WHITE MAN'S AFRICA

European outposts on the African coast remained for the most part insecure toeholds until the nineteenth century. They depended entirely on the sufferance of local rulers, whose favors had to be won with gifts and bribes, including that commodity that creates its own demand: alcohol. "You send your boat on Shore," a trader explained in 1789, "to acquaint the Alkaide, or Mayor, of the Town of your arrival; he . . . receives from you Anchorage-money, Ten Gallons of Liquor for the King. . . ." A hundred years earlier a Frenchman already noted the prominence of alcohol in the African trade: "The French commonly compose their cargo . . . of brandy mostly, white and red wine, *ros solis*, firelocks, muskets, flints. . . ." Firearms and firewater, these symbolized European civilization and culture in Africa for three centuries and more.

OVERLEAF: *The capital of the kingdom of Loango on the Congo coast and a slave-trading base when this fanciful view was done in* 1732.

ASTLEY, *Collection of Voyages,* 1732

REFERENCES.

A. Kings Palace ....
B. Womens Palace ....
C. Cryers Steeple ....
D. Royal Wine House ....
E. Royal Banqueting House .....
F. Publick Audience Place ....
G. Kings Garden ....
H. Queens Garden ....
I. a Mokisso ....
K. Another ....
L. the Broad way Where those found
   Guilty by the Imbondo drink, are dragged
   and Executed.

The CIT

OANGO

The Zulu soldiers above perform a pre-battle ceremony in 1879, the year of their last struggle against the British. The kraal at right is the traditional settlement of the cattle-raising Zulu and other Bantu peoples. Below is a portrait of Chaka, the Zulu's military and political hero. He holds the traditional Zulu assagai, which earlier warriors had thrown at their enemies. In line with Chaka's new mode of warfare, the spear would later be shortened for deadly hand-to-hand combat.

STIRRINGS OF PATRIOTISM

His name was Chaka and he was born in the late eighteenth century to a chief of the Zulu, an insignificant clan within a loose grouping of Bantu people living in Natal. By the time he reached manhood, Boers and Bantu farther south had already fought several wars, and Chaka saw with the clarity of genius that the old clan ways were no longer adequate. He set about to forge a new kind of Bantu nation: a nation whose warriors were replaced by a standing army drilled to fight in close formation; a nation in which the tribal chiefs gave way to generals chosen for their ability; a nation centrally organized and ruled by Chaka himself. Before his death in 1828 the little Zulu clan had absorbed through combat a host of smaller states and had raised an aggressive state, which was ready to fight the Boer and the British on equal terms. A cruel nation, it was the product of a cruel time and of one man's extraordinary response to its challenge.

Opposite a woman of Zululand, a segregated territory in Natal, South Af

Chapter Ten

WARS OF RESISTANCE

(c. 1800–1900)

by

Stanlake Samkange

OPPOSITION TO THE SLAVE TRADE had by 1800 gained numerous spokesmen in Africa, Europe, America, and other parts of the world. It will be remembered that in 1526 Affonso, king of the Bakongo along the Congo, told King John III of Portugal: "It is our will that in these kingdoms there should not be any trade in slaves nor market for slaves." In 1724 King Agaja of Dahomey informed the British government that he wanted to stop the export of people from his country. A Swedish traveler visiting Africa in 1789 reported that the *almany*, or ruler, of Futa Toro in northern Senegal, had passed a law forbidding the transportation of slaves through his territories and declared that all the riches in the world would not make him change his mind.

In Europe Frenchmen could cite a royal declaration of 1571, forbidding the importation of slaves into France, and a legal dictum of 1607, not only confirming the freedom of all people in the kingdom but also declaring all slaves to be free as soon as they set foot on French soil and became baptized. In England the reform movement began with Lord Mansfield's judgment of 1772, which declared that common law did not recognize the status of slave; in the United States as many as sixty thousand black men had managed to gain their freedom, and many more had taken up arms for freedom in the Caribbean.

There were several reasons for this attitude. Decent men everywhere had become surfeited with the bestial cruelties perpetrated in the interests of the slave trade. Furthermore, the Industrial Revolution was creating a need for a different kind of labor. Slave traders found themselves less and less influential in political circles because of an organized movement for the abolition of the slave trade.

A strong argument for a new policy was that legitimate

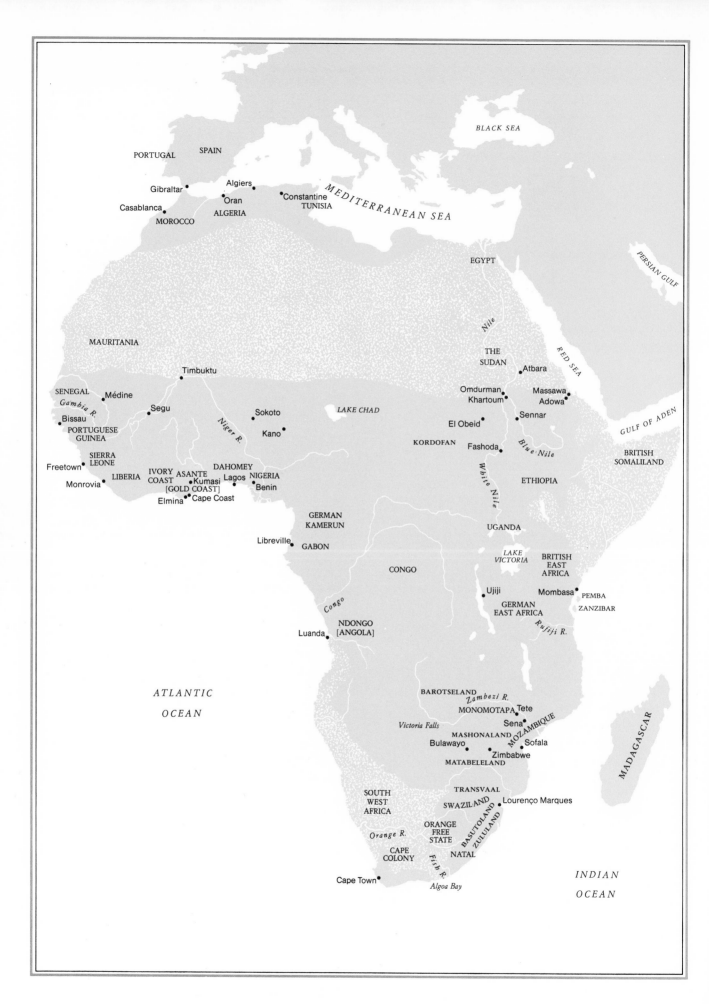

PORTUGAL   SPAIN

BLACK SEA

Gibraltar   Algiers
Casablanca   Oran   Constantine
MOROCCO   ALGERIA   TUNISIA

MEDITERRANEAN SEA

PERSIAN GULF

EGYPT

MAURITANIA

Nile

THE
SUDAN   Atbara   *RED SEA*

Timbuktu   Omdurman   Massawa
Khartoum   Adowa
SENEGAL   Médine
Gambia R.   Segu   Sokoto   LAKE CHAD   Sennar   *GULF OF ADEN*
Bissau   El Obeid
PORTUGUESE   Kano   KORDOFAN   Fashoda   *Blue Nile*   BRITISH
GUINEA   *Niger R.*   SOMALILAND

SIERRA   DAHOMEY   ETHIOPIA
LEONE   IVORY   ASANTE   NIGERIA
Freetown   COAST   Kumasi   Lagos
LIBERIA   [GOLD COAST]   Benin   *White Nile*
Monrovia   Elmina   Cape Coast

GERMAN   UGANDA
KAMERUN

Libreville   GABON   *LAKE*
VICTORIA   BRITISH
EAST
CONGO   AFRICA

Ujiji   Mombasa
Congo   PEMBA
GERMAN   ZANZIBAR
EAST
NDONGO   AFRICA   *Rufiji R.*
Luanda   [ANGOLA]

ATLANTIC

OCEAN

BAROTSELAND   *Zambezi R.*
MONOMOTAPA   Tete
Victoria Falls   Sena   *MOZAMBIQUE*
MASHONALAND
Bulawayo   Sofala
Zimbabwe
MATABELELAND

TRANSVAAL
SOUTH   SWAZILAND   Lourenço Marques
WEST
AFRICA   ORANGE
FREE   *Orange R.*   STATE   NATAL
CAPE
COLONY   *Fish R.*

Cape Town   *Algoa Bay*

MADAGASCAR

INDIAN

OCEAN

trade with Africa in manufactured goods and other merchandise could profitably take the place of slave trade. European industrialists also began to look to Africa for primary products in their own manufacturing enterprises (for example, palm oil used in making soap). Thus Africa became an important potential market and source of raw materials. Before long there was bitter rivalry among European powers for this market and its primary products. So taken were Europeans by this idea that they supported three schemes to repatriate freed slaves to Africa in order that they would become a nucleus for such trade.

Following Justice Mansfield's decision, fifteen thousand destitute black people were set free in England. Abolitionists, among whom was an African and former slave, Olaudah Equiano, later renamed Gustavus Vassa, supported a scheme to repatriate these "Black Poor," as they were called. The Black Poor from England were joined by other black people from Canada, where promises of land made to black soldiers had not been fulfilled, and by blacks—the Maroons—from the West Indies. This movement resulted in the founding of Sierra Leone in 1787.

Another scheme originated in the United States, where the Back-to-Africa movement was supported by wealthy Afro-Americans like Paul Cuffee, who on his own financed voyages of black people returning to Africa. Other prominent white and black Americans sponsored the American Society for Colonizing the Free People of Color (more commonly the American Colonization Society), which led to the founding of Liberia in 1822. A third such settlement was Libreville in Gabon, founded in 1849 under French auspices as a settlement for former slaves.

Europe's contact with Africa through the slave trade resulted in its becoming richer from the wealth generated by the slave labor of the millions upon millions of Africans who crossed the seas in chains. Africa, on the other hand, was impoverished by the loss of its manpower and material wealth. Internecine warfare, engendered by the slave trade, weakened or destroyed its once-proud armies. Its village industries disappeared. Only weakness and disunity remained.

European powers needed to know more about Africa—its geography, natural resources, and people—to trade effectively or stake their claims with any degree of accuracy. So, travelers and explorers, backed by organizations of varied interests and motives, went into the interior of Africa to augment the scanty and sketchy knowledge of the coast that had been provided by sailors and traders. Mungo Park, David Livingstone, Henry M. Stanley, Richard Burton, Heinrich Barth, John Speke, René Caillié, Paul Soleillet,

and many others made remarkable journeys and "discoveries." As feats of endurance, these journeys *are* truly remarkable; but perhaps even more remarkable are their inflated claims, for how does one discover, as Livingstone is said to have done, something like the Victoria Falls, which millions and millions of other people have known for generations by the name Mosi Oa Tunya, meaning "smoke that thunders?"

The journeys had another merit to Europeans. They portrayed Africa as virgin land for the planting of Christianity (and some would give the word "planting" the meaning it has in detective stories). So, European missionaries went to Africa to preach the gospel. They wore out soles saving souls and found themselves not only agents of life through death but of peace through war, accord through discord, education through Westernization, civilization through dehumanization, construction through destruction. Europeans were soon persuaded that only by waging ruthless wars of conquest or pacification (as such wars are euphemistically called) could peace reign in Africa. Only through discord—inherent in the injection of Christianity and rejection of traditional African ideas of god—could accord be achieved. Only through keeping Africans ignorant of the good in their culture and of the greatness in their history by teaching them Western values and the superiority of Europeans could they be educated. Only through the abandonment of a culture based on humanistic family and tribal ties, responsibilities, and sanctions, and the imposition of a dehumanizing, individualistic, and materialistic culture, could Africans be civilized. Only through the total destruction of African ideas, values, and mores could a new Africa be built.

The possession of colonies in Africa was regarded by European powers as a means of acquiring national prestige, mollifying wounded national pride, and keeping the balance of power in Europe even. Indeed, it is essential to study European politics of this period in order to understand why certain countries in Africa became colonies of certain powers in Europe and why boundary lines were often drawn in such an arbitrary manner as to put people of identical ethnic backgrounds into different states or lump together people who had no natural political affinity in one state. Some of these boundaries, drawn in the nineteenth century and dictated primarily by events in Europe, are a source of friction even today; indeed, many of Africa's present major problems can be traced to decisions made in Europe at this time.

Actual colonization was, as a rule, undertaken not by

governments but by syndicates and chartered companies because they were better suited for the task. The legal fiction under which such companies operated was that they were not representatives of the governments from whom they derived their charters. Their actions therefore did not necessarily have the agreement and sanction of their governments. This fiction enabled chartered companies to rush in where governments feared to tread. They were financed privately, at no cost to the taxpayer; so, according to the fiction, governments could not scrutinize and control minute details of the companies' operations. In actual fact governments could and did interfere with chartered companies. It suited governments, however, to appear powerless against them because chartered companies were useful tools. They could conveniently be repudiated when they failed to pull off a particularly audacious and reckless plot like the 1895 Jameson Raid, by which British fortune hunters sought to displace the Boer government of the Transvaal in South Africa. On the other hand, territory in which a company operated was invariably taken over by a European power and turned into a protectorate, colony, or overseas province, when convenient.

Often protectorates were proclaimed and colonies carved on the map of Africa on the basis of fraudulent treaties and bogus purchases of land from unsuspecting African rulers. There were also poorly demarcated spheres of influence in which a single European power sought to exercise exclusive trading rights. The cupidity, intrigue, cutthroat competition, and rivalry that characterized the activities of some unscrupulous agents of syndicates and chartered companies generated much friction, hatred, and animosity not only among Africans but also among the nations that licensed them. To bring about some sort of order, the Berlin West African Conference of 1884–1885 was called to lay down ground rules governing the staking of claims and carving of colonies in Africa.

Conferees, which included all the major powers in Europe, plus the USA and the Ottoman empire, decided that any power wishing to claim a colony or protectorate in any part of Africa should formally notify the other signatories and back its claim with demonstrable effective authority in the area concerned. Contrary to British wishes, there was to be freedom of navigation along the Niger and Congo rivers. In spite of the conference's decision requiring the effective occupation of an area before a claim could be recognized, most claims to colonies in Africa continued to be, in fact, based on concessions and treaties of very doubtful and questionable validity. The impressive point, however, is

that European powers agreed to base their partition of Africa on a set of rules acceptable to them all, and thus avoided coming to blows.

With this accord in Europe, the age of colonialism began in Africa. Europeans no longer took Africans into slavery in far-off places, but took possession of the land itself. Whereas in 1880 more than ninety per cent of the continent of Africa was ruled by Africans, by 1900, a mere twenty years later, only a tiny fraction—Ethiopia and Liberia—was ruled by Africans.

What was Africa's response to the Berlin conspiracy of 1884–1885? Was there also concerted action to meet the European threat to Africa? It is safe to say that Africans in general knew little about Europe and even less about Berlin. The days when radio, television, and jumbo jets would facilitate the formation of an Organization of African Unity were still far away. Yet, in spite of the social dislocations, in spite of the weakness of African armies, in spite of the inability of African rulers to consult, plan, and agree on a common strategy, the Africans continued to resist. They stood up and fought. Uncoordinated and inadequately armed though they were, Africans took up arms all over the continent. Let us look at these wars more closely. Let us scrutinize, one by one, the attempts of each European power to colonize Africa and see how Africans reacted.

Portugal was the first European power that tried to colonize Africa. It was the first to be resisted. When in 1556 a vassal of the king of the Congo, the *ngola* of Ndongo (or Angola), expected to be attacked by his overlord, he appealed to the Portuguese king for help. The Portuguese king responded by sending an expedition under the command of Paulo Dias de Novais, a grandson of the explorer Bartholomeu Dias. By the time the expedition arrived in Ndongo, however, the people had already fought and defeated the Congo army sent against them and declared their independence. Furthermore, the *ngola* who had requested Portugal's help had died. Succeeding him on the throne was Ngola Mbandi, who received Dias with great politeness, but compelled him to assist the Ndongo army in several local wars in which the Portuguese were not interested.

Paulo Dias was eventually allowed to return to Portugal, after which Sebastião, the king of Portugal, decided to undertake the military conquest of the Ndongo kingdom. Ndongo was divided into two colonies: one part, bounded in the west by the Atlantic, in the north by the Congo, and in the south by the Cuanza River, was to belong to the king; the other area, south of the Cuanza, was to belong to

Portuguese interest in Africa's east coast kept pace with its thriving Indian Ocean spice trade. This engraving, purportedly showing the stylish manner in which the wives of Portuguese traders were carried about in Kilwa, was published in Jan van Linschoten's Itinerario, 1596; it is hearsay information the author gathered while in the colony of Goa, India. He noted that Kilwa "was inhabited by Mahometans, and they are all most white [reflecting the mixed African-Arab population], apparelled in silk, and clothes of cotton wooll."

LINSCHOTEN, Itinerario, 1596

Paulo Dias and his descendants. Dias was to govern the king's as well as his own portion.

Dias returned to Angola in 1574 with the title "Conqueror, Colonizer, and Governor General of Angola." He took with him seven ships carrying seven hundred men. It was four years before the first skirmish with Africans took place. By that time Africans no doubt knew what the Portuguese were up to. In 1578 they engaged a detachment of eighty Portuguese soldiers, killed twenty, took the rest prisoner, and freed them only after they had been ransomed. Having been warned that Dias was advancing with a strong army to fight him, Ngola Mbandi condemned to death the Portuguese traders at his court, confiscated their goods, and enticed the Portuguese soldiers into combat in the interior. There he massacred five hundred of them and then attacked their fort at Nzele, thirty miles from their principal port at Luanda.

It was not until 1580 that Dias was able to march against Ngola Mbandi once more. This time he first raided several independent African kingdoms, recruiting their men to fight on his side against the army of the *ngola*. Meanwhile, another Congo force was marching against Mbandi. The *ngola* was able to drive off this second threat, but when he met Dias at Massangano, his fatigued army was defeated. However, the Portuguese had not yet won conclusively. One of their detachments, comprising at least a hundred men, was not long after completely routed by another African chief. At his death in 1589, fifteen years after he had

set out as "Conquerer, Colonizer, and Governor General of Angola," Paulo Dias had not conquered, colonized, or governed the people of Angola.

Portuguese activity as slavers and would-be colonizers appears to have solidified African resistance, for in 1590 the *ngola* entered into an alliance with his former enemy, the king of the Congo, and with other neighboring kingdoms. That year the African alliance defeated a Portuguese expedition, forcing it to retreat with heavy losses to Massangano. In 1594 another African force, under the command of chief Kafuche Kambara, ambushed and massacred a Portuguese force at Kissama. As long as the alliance held, the Portuguese made no progress toward colonizing Angola. But the alliance broke up about 1600, and the Portuguese gained the advantage.

In 1612 the *ngola* of Ndongo sent his sister Nzinga Mbandi to Luanda to negotiate a peace treaty with the Portuguese. When the Portuguese governor of Luanda would not give her a chair, she called forth one of her attendants, instructed him to get down on his hands and knees, and sat on him. Although the Portuguese agreed to recognize Ndongo as an independent kingdom, they reneged on other agreements. When sometime later the *ngola* died and was succeeded by Nzinga, who immediately renounced Christianity, the Portuguese sought to depose her and install a puppet. War broke out. Nzinga organized another African alliance, and for over thirty years, until her death in 1663, she valiantly warred against the Portuguese.

WARS OF RESISTANCE

When the Dutch captured Luanda in 1641, the Portuguese found themselves fighting on two fronts. In 1643 two hundred of their soldiers were captured by an African force, and an army sent to retrieve them was routed. Before his death Ngola Kanini of Matamba defeated a Portuguese army at Katole. Long after, in 1872, another war of resistance to the Portuguese broke out in the Dembo region northwest of Luanda.

Farther south a similar history unfolded. The Mbundu kingdoms of Huambo, Tchiyaka, Bailundo, Ndulu, Bié, and Kakonda resisted Portuguese slavers and colonizers. As early as 1660 Kapango, king of Tchiyaka, prevented the advance of a Portuguese expedition into the interior. In 1718 an African alliance inspired by Kapango's example attacked a Portuguese fortress at Kakonda, forcing them to withdraw from that area. In 1896 Numa, king of Bailundo, died while leading an attack on a Portuguese fort, and in 1902 his successor, Mutu-ya-Kevela, led another attack in an attempt to recover land occupied by Europeans.

In the kingdom of Huíla, Africans launched a series of ten wars, the Nano Wars, resisting Portuguese rule throughout the greater part of the nineteenth century. In the Humbe kingdom there was an uprising against the Portuguese in 1858 that resulted in a temporary withdrawal of the Portuguese from that kingdom. Resistance continued intermittently until the turn of the century, when a Portuguese army was massacred. In 1904 another Portuguese army was ambushed, and three hundred of its soldiers were killed. Resistance in Humbe continued until 1915. Between 1874 and 1916 the Congo region in the north fought eight wars against the Portuguese. In the 1950's resistance to Portuguese colonialism in Angola broke out again and continues to this day.

Along the Atlantic coast of West Africa, in the region now known as Portuguese Guinea, the indigenous peoples also challenged the foreign presence as early as 1679. In that year the African chiefs of Mata and Mompataz unsuccessfully resisted Portuguese domination of the region around the Cacheu estuary. In 1697 the Papel people under Chief Incinhate and the Mandingos again took up arms against Portuguese rule and tried to expel them from the settlement at Farim. These wars persisted throughout the eighteenth century, compelling the Portuguese to maintain a military force for the protection of the European population. In 1753 the Papel people, led by Chief Palance, interfered with Portuguese attempts to rebuild their fort in Bissau, killing nine men.

In 1824, 1842, 1844, and 1846 there were further Papel uprisings against Portuguese rule in Bissau. The last one was supported by the Mandingos, who again attacked Farim. Africans attacked Geba in 1865, assassinated the governor of Bissau in 1871, and massacred a Portuguese military force near Bolor River in 1879.

That same year the Portuguese separated the governance of Guinea from the Cape Verde Islands, creating two colonies. This new policy was aimed at undermining African resistance to its rule through the encouragement of intertribal rivalry. This time-honored colonialist device paid dividends when in 1880 one of the Fulani peoples under Mamadu Paté attacked a Portuguese military post at Buba. Their example was followed a year later by Chief Bacar Guidali of Forrea. One hundred Portuguese soldiers, supported by hundreds of Mandingos, Fula-Preto (another Fulani group), and Beafada marched against the insurgents in 1881. The Portuguese failed to subdue Bacar Guidali, but succeeded in turning Mamadu Paté against him, with the result that Bacar Guidali was defeated by his former ally on behalf of the Portuguese.

In 1882 the Portuguese fought the Beafada at Jabada, and in the following year they attacked the Balanta. In 1884 a Portuguese military force that had been sent to Kakonda was ambushed by Felupe, and its gunboat seized. Two years later another Portuguese army was forced to retreat to Bijante after suffering heavy casualties. The policy of divide and rule stood the Portuguese in good stead, however, when they were challenged in 1886 by Musa Molo. Leading the Fula-Preto, this Fulani chieftain succeeded in taking large areas around Buba and south of the Gambia River. He harassed the Portuguese at Geba and cut communications between that settlement and Bissau by attacking river boats and supply trains. However, the Fula-Preto were forced to desist and retreat when four thousand Fulani and hundreds of Mandingos and Beafada came to Portugal's assistance.

In 1889 the Portuguese were compelled once more to take the field against the Fula-Preto, Mandingos, and Beafada, and the following year they devastated many villages in a four-month campaign against Moli Boia, while Mamadu Paté and Musa Molo resumed their attacks on Buba and Farim. Throughout 1891 and 1892 the Portuguese in Bissau were in a state of siege. In April, 1891, Africans destroyed a Portuguese force at Intim and killed forty-seven Portuguese officers and men near Bissau in May, 1891.

In December, 1893, over three thousand Papel and Balanta tribesmen attacked a Portuguese fortress at Pijiguiti. Later they attacked Bissau. In response, the Portuguese conducted two military operations: one against the Man-jaco and the other against the Balanta and Mandingos. The Portuguese had as allies more than three thousand Africans under the combined command of Mamadu Paté and the Beafada chief of Cuor, Infali Sonco. But these allies later turned against the Portuguese, causing them to retreat with heavy casualties.

By 1901 the Portuguese were in a position to resume military operations. In 1904 an expedition against the Manjaco in the Farim district met with disaster when more than four hundred Portuguese soldiers were killed. Infali Sonco, leader of the Beafada, harassed the Portuguese on the Geba River, successfully preventing any commercial intercourse between Bissau on the estuary and Bafatá upriver. The Felupe at Varela, the Balanta at Gole, and the Papel people near Bissau continued their resistance. In 1907 the Portuguese were compelled to mount a major military campaign against African resistance to their rule, plundering and burning many villages. The Papel responded by attacking Bissau. Near the end of the year the Portuguese were ravaging Balanta villages in Gole; the Africans retaliated by attacking the Portuguese military post. The Balanta were driven off after Abdul Injai, a Fulani, joined the Portuguese against them.

In 1912 the Portuguese appointed João Teixeira Pinto commander of forces in Guinea. In March, 1913, with Abdul Injai and several hundred Africans on his side, Pinto was attacked by the Balanta and Mandingos. By June he had occupied Mansoade and Mansaba. From January to April, 1914, Pinto campaigned against the Papel and Manjaco peoples in the Cacheu region. From May to July he marched against the Balanta in Mansoa, and sought revenge against the Papel, who had earlier attacked Bissau, killing eighty-eight Portuguese. Abdul Injai was rewarded for his services to the Portuguese with appointment as chief of Oio, but before long he turned against the Portuguese, who were compelled to mount a campaign against him. The insurgent was exiled from the country.

This was not the end of African resistance to Portuguese colonialism in Guinea. In March, 1917, a state of siege was declared in the Bijajós archipelago, and in July troops were sent to Nhambalam. In 1918 troops were sent to Baiote. There was trouble at Canhabague in 1925; at Bissau in 1931; and again in Canhabague in 1936. Resistance continues to this day.

In Mozambique (or Portuguese East Africa), the colonial government was never without its challengers. In July, 1572, Francesco Barreto set out from Sena to conquer the kingdom of Monomotapa. Barreto commanded an army of eight hundred Europeans and two thousand Africans. Along the Ruwenya River, toward Mount Fura, the Portuguese expedition came across the main village of the Mongaze people. They fired a few rounds and dispossessed the people of their village. For three days they remained in the village, experiencing only minor attempts on the part of the Mongaze to regain their homes.

At dawn on the fourth day, however, Francesco de Sousa reported that there came "like a great dust storm with loud clamor, the Mongaze army: Some sixteen thousand men with great intrepidity and noise of drums." The army was led by a doctor carrying spells in a gourd to assure victory. A cloud of arrows and spears flew toward the Portuguese, who responded with a volley of musketry and a barrage of cannonballs. The doctor and four thousand Mongaze men were killed. The Portuguese lost forty men in the battle.

Although Barreto and his army were decimated by fever before they got to Zimbabwe, Monomotapa's capital, news of their victory over the Mongaze impressed the kingdom's ruler. Chisa Mharu Nogomo, who had problems with his vassals, decided to come to terms with the Portuguese and secure his position on the throne. In 1575 Vasco Fernandes Homem, taking another route, led an expedition of four hundred twelve Portuguese soldiers to Zimbabwe. He met only minor resistance. On the throne of Monomotapa now sat Gatsi Rusere, who honored his predecessor's agreement with the Portuguese. However, Gatsi Rusere was succeeded by Nyambo Kapararidze, who was openly hostile to the Portuguese and forced them to retire. Africans were, once more, resisting foreign domination. His army was defeated by the Portuguese in 1628, and Kapararidze's nephew, Mavura Mhande, who was friendly to the Portuguese, was installed as ruler.

At his death another puppet was appointed; but in 1693 one of his vassals, Changamire, raised an insurrection and routed the *monomotapa*'s army. Changamire then attacked and destroyed a number of Portuguese settlements, including Dambarare. This ended Portuguese political influence beyond the borders of Mozambique.

The Portuguese position in East Africa was once again seriously shaken in the nineteenth century when Nyande, or Joaquin José da Cruz, a half-caste, organized an insurgent force and established inland headquarters at Massangena in the southern region of Mozambique. In 1853 his son Bonga destroyed the colonial post at Tete, and a Portuguese expedition, sent some sixteen years later to regain control of the area, only resulted in Bonga's gaining a still larger territory. When Bonga died in 1885, his brother succeeded him, but was captured three years later.

The Shangana, a Nguni people, also challenged the Portuguese in Mozambique. At the port city of Lourenço Marques near the southern frontier the followers of Soshangana besieged the Portuguese fortress and massacred its garrison. The Shangana also attacked Inhambane in 1834 and Sofala in 1836. They overran Portuguese *prazos*, or estates, south of the Zambezi and occupied Sena. When Soshangana died, however, there were two claimants to his throne. Mahueva, the legitimate successor, was, like his father, opposed to the Portuguese. He lost to Mzila, who maintained official relations with the Portuguese while continuing to demand tribute from them and to raid their settlements. Mzila was succeeded by Gungunyana. He cooperated with both the Portuguese and the British, whose South Africa Company, under the direction of Cecil Rhodes, was eyeing the southern portion of Mozambique.

Wars of resistance also broke out in the eastern Sudan. This ancient land of Kush had in 1805 come under Turko-Egyptian rule. Although the Sudan remained under the official administration of the Egyptian khedive, it came increasingly under the influence and control of the British government.

In 1882 the Anglo-Egyptian consortium suffered a major upset when a Sudanese spiritual leader, Muhammad Ahmad, declared himself the Mahdi, or messiah, and urged his countrymen to rise against the forces of evil. Muhammad Ahmad called for no less than a holy war against the Egyptian government. Before long the holy war became for the Sudanese people a war of liberation from colonialism, injustice, and economic exploitation.

The British government had strived to avoid active involvement. Its efforts were, however, doomed to failure since the Egyptian government was virtually its puppet, obliged to accept British advice on all matters of importance in exchange for British military protection. Thus it was only a matter of time before Queen Victoria's agents were actively involved in suppressing Sudanese resistance. To the Sudanese Africans, however, the issue remained always simple and crystal clear; resistance was seen as a duty inspired and sanctioned by their religion. Its success was believed to be ordained by Allah and assured through the appearance among them of the expected Mahdi.

Soon after Muhammad Ahmad had declared himself the Mahdi, the Egyptian government sent the assistant governor general of the Sudan, Muhammad Bey Abu al-Saud, to talk him into abandoning his claim. When this failed, the

government dispatched two companies of regular troops to Aba Island in the Nile, where Muhammed Ahmad and about two hundred of his supporters, including members of the militant dervish sect, were gathered.

Muhammad Ahmad offered his followers the choice of either freely joining him in his holy war or returning to their homes. His followers unanimously swore allegiance to his cause and leadership, whereupon he armed them with swords, spears, and sticks. Then, while awaiting the arrival of the army, he trained them in the rudiments of defense and attack.

One night during the fasting month of Ramadan, while Muhammad Ahmad and his followers were performing their prayers, news reached him that the Nile steamer carrying government troops sent to capture him had arrived in the neighboring city of El Fashashuyah.

The government soldiers disembarked on Aba Island at 3 A.M. and, ignoring instructions to send the local *qadi* to parley with the Mahdi, marched straight to the village. Meeting a villager, they asked him to point out the Mahdi's house. The villager said he did not know. There followed an altercation during which one of the soldiers fired a gun, whereupon the Mahdi's followers, armed only with their primitive weapons, fell upon the soldiers, killing one hundred twenty-six of them, including six officers. The rest of the soldiers ran away and took refuge aboard the steamer that had brought them. The following day, the twelfth of August, 1881, the Mahdi's dervishes completely defeated the government force at the battle of Aba, giving the Mahdi his first great victory.

Emulating the Prophet's flight to Medina, the Mahdi left Aba Island, scene of his first victory, and trekked westward with his followers to Qadir Mountain in the Nuba hills of Kordofan. This was territory inhabited by people who had never completely submitted to government authority.

Hoping that local jealousies and dissension would disintegrate the Mahdi's movement, causing it to collapse of itself, the government decided to take no further military action against the Mahdi. But Rashid, the governor of Fashoda (modern Kodok in southeast Sudan), ignoring instructions, set out against the Mahdi with three hundred fifty soldiers, seventy irregulars, and one thousand Shilluk tribesmen under the leadership of their chief, Kaikun Bey. Rashid's plan was to surprise the Mahdi, so he compelled his men to march long hours; utterly exhausting them. But the Mahdi was not to be taken by surprise. A Qadir chief warned him by lighting large fires on top of a mountain, and a Kinanah woman walked the whole night to report that she had seen the soldiers. It was Rashid who was surprised. The Mahdi laid an ambush for him and completely annihilated Rashid's exhausted force. Only a few Shilluk escaped to tell the tale. The Mahdi had won another great victory, and rumors crediting him with invincibility and the ability to turn bullets into water were related in the Sudan. New adherents flocked to the Mahdi's lair at Qadir.

A new governor general was appointed to the Sudan. While awaiting his arrival, however, the acting governor general, a German known as Geigler Pasha, grossly underrated the Mahdi's strength. He reversed the wait-and-see policy of his predecessor and decided to restore law and order in the Sudan by striking the Mahdi's stronghold with a force of some three thousand five hundred men under the command of Yusuf Pasha al-Shallali.

Geigler Pasha also sent Yusuf Agha al-Malik with fifty soldiers and some officers to the eastern bank of the Blue Nile, where Sherif Ahmad Taha, who claimed to be a descendant of the Prophet, was about to declare his allegiance to the Mahdi. Al-Malik met with disaster. All his officers and most of his soldiers were slain. When he saw that all was lost, rather than be disgraced, Al-Malik calmly sat on his sheepskin and ordered his slave to kill him. On May 4, 1882, Geigler ordered another attack on Sherif Ahmad Taha. Sherif Ahmad Taha was once more victorious, killing two hundred ten officers and men. Reinforced by Awad al-Karim's Shukria tribesmen, Geigler again attacked Sherif Ahmad Taha the following day and completely defeated him.

Meanwhile, the government force sent to Qadir under the command of Al-Shallali traveled via Fashoda, making a long halt at Funqur, where Taifarah, a local chief, reneged on an earlier agreement with the Mahdi and handed over the latter's spies to Al-Shallali. The spies were cruelly and slowly put to death by having their limbs severed, one after another, before a crowd of spectators. But the fortitude with which they met their death, uttering defiance to the executioners and professing a profound conviction in the divine mission of the Mahdi, demoralized the troops. They concluded that the Mahdi must really have supernatural powers if he could make men face death as these spies had done. On June 6, 1882, Al-Shallali's force arrived in the vicinity of the Qadir, fatigued and morally depressed. They hardly had strength to construct a *zaribah* (a thorny enclosure) before falling asleep. At dawn the Mahdi's men attacked and annihilated them in spite of a heroic stand. The wife of one of the slain leaders of the government forces gallantly beat the war drum to rally her husband's

troops. The Mahdi had scored another brilliant victory, and again rumor had it that supernatural forces were working in concert with him. It was said that a mysterious fire had consumed the bodies of the soldiers and had left the Mahdi's name clearly written on eggshells and the leaves of trees.

When the new governor general, Abd al-Qadir Pasha, took his appointment, he first made overtures of peace to the Mahdi. Failing in this, he plotted to assassinate the Madhi by sending him a gift of poisoned dates purportedly from an adherent, dispatching a parcel containing dynamite, and hiring two men to murder him. When these attempts failed also, Al-Qadir directed the mufti, Sudan's chief judge of Muslim law, and other learned men to engage in a propaganda war against the Mahdi, while soldiers to fight him were being recruited and trained.

The Mahdi was also changing his course. He decided to abandon the purely defensive policy he had hitherto pursued. In the two months after the annihilation of Al-Shallali's expedition, he sent troops to attack government garrisons in Kordofan. One by one these fell and were occupied by the Mahdi's men; only Kordofan's provincial capital at El Obeid and the nearby city of Bara remained. In August, 1882, the Mahdi's troops began their march against El Obeid, and in September, 1882, the Mahdi sent messengers to the garrison, urging it to surrender. Authorities of El Obeid arrested the messengers and hanged them. As a result, many citizens went over to the Mahdi.

Thirty thousand warriors then rushed El Obeid, as Father Joseph Ohrwalder, who spent ten years as a captive in the Mahdi's camp, described in his memoirs:

> The first ditch was soon crossed, and then the Mahdists spread out and completely encircled the town; masses of wild fanatics rolled like waves through the deserted streets; they did not advance through these alone, but hurrying on from house to house, wall to wall, and yard to yard, they reached the ditch of the Mudirieh, and like a torrent suddenly let loose, regardless of every obstacle, with wild shouts they dashed across it and up the ramparts, from which the din of a thousand rifles and the booming of the guns suddenly burst forth; but these wild hordes, utterly fearless of death, cared neither for the deadly Remington nor the thunder of the guns, and still swept forward in ever-increasing numbers.
>
> The poor garrison, utterly powerless to resist such an assault, ran to the tops of the houses and

kept up an incessant fire on the masses, which now formed such a crowd that they could scarcely move —indeed the barrels of the rifles from the rapidity of the fire became almost red-hot; and soon the streets and open spaces became literally choked with the bodies of those who had fallen. . . . It was impossible not to admire the reckless bravery of these fanatics who, dancing and shouting, rushed up to the very muzzles of the rifles with nothing but the knotty stick in their hands, only to fall dead one over the other. Numbers of them carried large bundles of Dhurra stalks, which they threw into the ditch, hoping to fill it up and then cross over.

The Mahdi lost about ten thousand men and decided to change his tactics. He surrounded El Obeid and Bara. Before long the besieged inhabitants were short of food and plagued by disease. A government relief expedition under Ali Bey Lufti was attacked and completely destroyed by the Mahdi's men. Over 1,127 of its men were killed. Bara surrendered on the fifth and El Obeid on the seventeenth of January, 1883. Large stores of military equipment, rifles, guns, and ammunition fell into the Mahdi's hands.

A new governor general, Ala al-Din, was appointed, and a new army under the command of William Hicks, a British officer, was sent to reconquer El Obeid. The Mahdi let his army—7,000 infantry, 500 cavalry, 400 *bashbazuks*, or mounted Turkish irregulars, with 10 mounted guns, 100 cuirassiers, 2,000 camp followers, and 5,500 transport camels—wear itself out marching. The insurgents cut its line of retreat, constantly harassed it as it came nearer, and then in November, 1883, attacked and overwhelmed it.

It was at this point that the British government, believing that the Sudan could not be held against the Mahdi, exerted pressure on the Egyptian government to abandon it and evacuate the capital at Khartoum. In response to public demand, the British government also returned General Charles George "Chinese" Gordon, Britain's hero of campaigns in China and Anglo-Egyptian North Africa and former governor of the Sudan. He was instructed to ascertain the best means of evacuating Egyptian forces from the Sudan. Instead, Gordon tried to hold Khartoum against the Mahdi. The Mahdi delayed attacking the city in the hope that it would surrender without bloodshed.

When in the fall of 1884 a British relief column under the command of Sir Herbert Stewart started for Khartoum, the Mahdi was compelled to take action. He dispatched a strong force to meet Stewart's troops and prepared to assault the capital. Near the Abu Tlaih wells, where the relief column had camped for the night, they encountered the Mahdi forces. Early the following morning the Mahdi forces opened fire on the British force as breakfast was being served. Stewart decided to take the offensive and ordered the column to march in square formation. As it marched, the column was subjected to heavy fire and frequently came to a halt in order to enable the rear to catch up. At one such halt Stewart's men were amazed to see a large mounted force of the Mahdi's men emerge from a nearby ravine in which they had been hiding and advance upon them in close formation. In spite of accurate fire from the relief column's Martini-Henry rifles, the Mahdi's army advanced to within eighty yards; then the fire began to take its toll and dead bodies fell one upon another in huge piles. Those still alive veered to the right and attacked the rear of the column, penetrating the square at several points. Sir Charles Wilson, who took over command of the column when Sir Herbert Stewart was wounded, later wrote:

> I remember thinking, by Jove, they will be into the square! and almost the next moment I saw a fine old Shaikh on horse back plant his banner in the center of the square, behind the camels. He was at once shot down falling on his banner. He turned out to be Musa, Amir of Dighaim Arabs, from Kurdufan. I had noticed him in the advance, with his banner in one hand and a book of prayers in the other, and never saw anything finer. The old man never swerved to the right or left, and never ceased chanting his prayers until he had planted his banner in our square. If any man deserved a place in the Moslem paradise he did.

The relief column closed the gaps and killed all who had penetrated the square. The rest of the Mahdi's forces retreated. The British column made it to the river near Metemma, where its wounded and most of its able-bodied men were left in fortified positions while Wilson, with British and African troops, embarked in late January, 1885, on steamers for Khartoum. Khartoum, which had been under siege for over a year by a force of up to one hundred thousand men, was beginning to show the strain. There was famine and disease in the town. The low water level of the Nile at the time of the year made breaching the town's fortifications possible. The Mahdi tried to persuade General Gordon to surrender, even offering him a safe-conduct to the British column. Gordon was defiant and determined to fight.

On January 26 the Mahdi forces launched their attack on Khartoum. The fortifications yielded in the first assault

Mahdist power was finally broken at Omdurman in 1898, when Sir Horatio Herbert Kitchener (right) and his Anglo-Egyptian army devastated the Sudanese army with its ranks of sword-brandishing dervishes (above).

and great slaughter followed. General Gordon was killed and Khartoum captured. The fall of Khartoum had a profound effect in England. Queen Victoria told her ministers that earlier action by them might have prevented the catastrophe and saved many precious lives. After this, it became a matter of Britain's national honor to suppress the Mahdiyya, the Mahdi's resistance movement.

However, on June 22, 1895, the Mahdi died. At his death his resistance movement had liberated from foreign rule most of Muslim Sudan. He was succeeded by Abdullahi, Khalifa al-Mahdi. But the new leader's position was shaky, for he could not cope with the military might of England. In 1897 at the battle of Atbara (some two hundred miles downriver from Khartoum) and in 1898 at Omdurman (opposite Khartoum) British and Egyptian regiments under Sir Horatio Herbert Kitchener finally shattered the Khalifa al-Mahdi's power. The Khalifa himself lost his life on the field of battle at Om Dubreikat on November 25, 1899. Despite the Sudan's prolonged bid for independence, the Anglo-Egyptian Sudan had come into existence.

Resistance continued. Among the Dinka people living between the White Nile and the Sobat River there was strong opposition to the new order. In 1904 the British were compelled to send an expedition against the Nyima tribes of the western Bahr-el-Ghazal. In 1908 a Halawi tribesman in Sennar declared himself to be Jesus Christ come to expel Europeans from the Sudan. He was hanged

by the British. And during 1911 and 1912 two expeditions were sent against the Annak on the Sobat River.

Between 1899 and 1904, and again between 1908 and 1910, Muhammad ibn Abdallah, sometimes called quite wrongly the Mad Mullah, organized resistance to colonial rule in British Somaliland, that portion of the Horn which Britain had administered as a protectorate since 1884. An army of seven thousand men, raised at a cost of over two million pounds, was sent against him. After more than one disaster had befallen British troops, however, it was decided to leave the interior of British Somaliland alone and to confine British occupation to the coastal towns along the Gulf of Aden.

South of Anglo-Egyptian Sudan, in the territory of modern-day Uganda, Mwanga, the *kabaka*, or king, of Buganda, and Kabarenga, the king of Bunyoro, responded in 1898 to the rivalries of Europe's empire builders by attempting to massacre British officers and missionaries. For over a year the British were kept at bay until Captain John Evatt and a detachment of Sikh soldiers from British India captured the African kings in 1899.

In Zanzibar, where in 1890 the sultanate had been placed under British protection and the administration of the islands of Zanzibar and Pemba conducted by English ministers, a palace revolt occurred in 1896 on the occasion of the death of Sultan Hamid ibn Thwain. It was really a premature outbreak of resistance to British occupation.

Along that part of the East African coast under German "protection"—roughly the area later designated as Tanganyika—between the Tana and Odzi rivers, African resistance to foreign rule resulted in a British naval expedition under Admiral Edmund Fremantle being sent to the area in 1890. Southwest of Mombasa Sir Arthur Hardinge was compelled, on assuming control of British East Africa, to fight a long war of skirmishes, ambushes, and raids of resistance until 1896. Kikuyu warriors attacked British settlers and big game hunters in Kenya.

In southern Africa the earliest resistance to European encroachment on African land rights was in 1659, when Hottentot clans that had always grazed their cattle in the Cape Peninsula were ordered by the Dutch to keep away. Although there was plenty of grazing land to which they could have taken their cattle, they insisted on their right to graze their cattle where they liked. So, the first Hottentot-Dutch war broke out. The Hottentots avoided a pitched battle, and the Europeans were unable to surprise any sizable body of them or inflict large number of casualties.

The second Hottentot-Dutch war was sparked in 1673 by the Europeans' destruction of too much game on land under the Hottentot king Gonnema. Although Hottentot tribes hostile to him joined the Dutch, Gonnema and his people held on in the mountains until both sides desired peace.

In 1779 the Dutch fought their first war against the Bantu-speaking Xhosa, who resisted attempts to remove them from lands west of the Great Fish River. Ten years later the Xhosa reoccupied large areas west of this river. The Dutch tried to expel them, and so the second Xhosa-Dutch war was fought. As the Xhosa proved more than able to hold their own, the Dutch finally agreed to make peace with them.

In 1795 the Cape came under British rule. Four years later Ndlambe, who had been Xhosa regent during the minority of his nephew Gaika, was forced to hand over power to the younger man. Ndlambe escaped, crossed the Great Fish River, and immediately won the allegiance of most clans between the Great Fish and the Kowie rivers. White people in these areas took their cattle and fled. In a few days Ndlambe was master of the entire Zuurveld east of the Sunday River.

Ndlambe's forces attacked a British party on its way to Algoa Bay, under the command of General John Ormsby Vandeleur. The Europeans beat them off and then fell back to form a camp so that an approaching patrol of twenty men could join them. But the Xhosa surrounded the patrol and killed all but four of its members. Then they turned to the camp, rushing it with spear shafts broken so short that they could be used as assagais for stabbing. The charges were met with such a volley of musket balls and grapeshot that the Xhosa were forced to retire. General Vandeleur made it to Algoa Bay, sent some of his soldiers back to Cape Town by sea, and ordered burgher commandos to expel the Xhosa. Some Hottentots joined the Xhosa and overran the area. Twenty-nine white people were killed. Once more Africans had resisted attempts by Europeans to run them off their land.

In 1811 a strong body of European soldiers and a Hottentot regiment was sent to force Ndlambe and his men to abandon the lands they occupied. In a parley with Major Jacob Cuyler, Ndlambe told him, stamping his foot on the ground: "This country is mine; I won it in war, and intend to keep it." Then, shaking an assagai with one hand, he raised a horn to his mouth and signaled his forces, concealed in the thicket, whereupon three hundred men rushed on the British party, which escaped solely because of the fleetness of their horses. Soon after this, the *landdrost*, meaning governor, of Graaff-Reinet, and eight farmers were killed by the Xhosa. In 1812 six Hottentot units, with European soldiers in the rear, attacked the Xhosa and succeeded in forcing them northeast across the Great Fish River.

This was by no means the end of Ndlambe. Several chiefs, including an influential seer named Makana, defected from Gaika and joined him. In the ensuing war between the uncle and nephew, Gaika lost and appealed to the white men for help. Believing Ndlambe to be a much more determined and dangerous enemy, Lord Charles Somerset, governor of the Cape Colony, in 1818 sent European troops to fight side by side with Gaika's men against Ndlambe, who was believed to have eighteen thousand men under arms. Ndlambe's men took shelter in the dense thickets, but their villages were destroyed and twenty-three thousand of their cattle taken.

When the British soldiers withdrew, Ndlambe fell on Gaika and put him to flight. Then he attacked Europeans between the Great Fish and Sunday rivers. A burgher force was called out, but before it could take the field, the British settlement at Grahamstown was attacked on April 22, 1819, by ten thousand warriors led by Ndlambe's ally, Makana.

It was three months later that a strong army of colonists succeeded in driving Ndlambe's warriors northeastward to the Kei River, slaughtering many and burning their kraals, or villages. Makana gave himself up so that his friends could be spared. He was imprisoned on Robben Island off Cape Town, where he died three years later while trying to escape. As a buffer against further trouble, the colonial government placed Gaika's people between the Cape Colony and Ndlambe. Ndlambe died and his sons quarreled for the throne. Gaika also died, leaving Sandile, then a child, as heir; Makoma, his half brother, was named regent. Ndlambe's sons allied themselves with Makoma to win his support.

When in 1834 European soldiers near Fort Beaufort wounded a Xhosa chief and took cattle belonging to Tyali, another of Gaika's sons, the Xhosa regarded this act as a declaration of war. About twenty thousand warriors rushed into the Cape Colony, seized all the cattle east of the Sunday River, burned houses, and killed every white man they found. Knowing that a white commando force would follow, they herded the cattle across the Kei River to the territory of another Xhosa king, Hintsa, before retiring to their mountain strongholds. Hintsa, seeking to avoid further trouble with the Europeans, agreed to give up the cattle, but was treacherously shot dead by a colonist while en route to carry out the terms. Kreli, his son, succeeded him; he undertook to restore the cattle and concluded a peace treaty with the Europeans, but African resistance was by no means over.

In 1846 a Xhosa man accused of stealing an axe at Fort Beaufort was arrested by white constables. While being taken to a magistrate's court for trial, his compatriots swooped down on the police patrol, overpowering it. They killed a Hottentot policeman and released the prisoner. The Europeans applied to Sandile for extradition of the alleged offenders. Sandile ignored the request. Thus began the War of the Axe. A military force was then ordered to occupy Sandile's kraal. A very long wagon train carrying provisions, tents, baggage, and ammunition followed the military force. Xhosa warriors ambushed the wagon train and captured it. The military force was compelled to retreat. Xhosa warriors then took the field and in the area surrounding the town of Vitenhage burned Europeans' houses, killed all Europeans who could not escape, and seized the cattle. The Tembu people joined the Xhosa and devastated European settlements north of Winterberg. Another wagon train, on its way from Grahamstown to a frontier garrison with supplies of food and ammunition, was ambushed, and the supplies fell into Xhosa hands. It was a long time before the colonists could organize themselves and induce Sandile to submit to their rule.

In 1850 war broke out again. Sir Harry Smith, then gov-

ernor of the Cape, received several reports that the Xhosa were preparing for war. He called a meeting of African chiefs and kings, but the most important figure, Sandile, did not show up. Sir Harry Smith then ordered Sandile, who was known to be in the forests at the headwaters of the Keiskama River, to be arrested. On their way to arrest the Xhosa king, the European troops were attacked by warriors at Boomah. Twenty-three Europeans were killed and many wounded. A few hours later, in another part of the country, a patrol of fifteen European soldiers was completely wiped out by Sandile's warriors, and on Christmas day of that year Xhosa warriors surprised European settlements near Auckland and Woburn, killing forty-six men and burning down houses. European settlements along the frontier districts were devastated once more. Again, the Tembu tribe joined the uprising, and even the Hottentot regiments under colonial arms deserted the Europeans and joined their fellow Africans. This became the longest and, to Europeans, the most costly war in South Africa. The steamship *Birkenhead*, proceeding from Ireland and carrying among its passengers four hundred reinforcements, struck a rock off Danger Point, a few miles beyond the Cape of Good Hope. Women, children, and the sick were put into boats; but the soldiers perished in the shark-infested sea.

Not until their food supplies began to run low did Africans pretend to submit to European rule and hostilities ended, but resistance to European colonialism remained in their hearts and minds. To some of them it became such an obsession that it led to a terrible tragedy. In May, 1856, a girl named Nongqause returned from drawing water at a little stream not far from her village and said she had seen men who differed greatly in appearance from the men she was accustomed to see there. Umhlakaza, her uncle, went to the stream and found the strangers where his niece had indicated. The strangers told Umhlakaza to return home, perform certain rituals, sacrifice an ox to the spirits of the dead, and then return to them on the fourth day.

Since there was in their appearance something that commanded obedience, Umhlakaza did as he had been told and returned to the stream on the fourth day. The strange people were there as before, and to his astonishment he recognized among them his brother, who had been dead for many years. It was then he learned that the strange men were the eternal enemies of white men who had come from battlefields beyond the sea; they would with their invincible power assist the Xhosa in driving the Europeans from the land. He, Umhlakaza, was to be the medium between the kings and chiefs of the land and the strange men. Their first message to the kings, chiefs, and people was to abandon the practice of witchcraft and to kill fat cattle and eat them. One of the kings of the land, Kreli, son of Hintsa, received the message with joy and immediately commanded that the spirits be obeyed throughout his land, and the best cattle be killed and eaten. King Sandile hesitated.

Nongqause again went to the river, and in the presence of a multitude of people, strange unearthly sounds beneath her feet were heard. All averred that they were voices of the spirits holding council over the affairs of men. People were ordered to slay and eat more cattle, and more cattle, and more cattle.

King Sandile joined the believers when his brother told him that he had himself seen and conversed with the spirits of two of his father's dead councilors and that they had commanded Sandile to kill his cattle or perish.

Umhlakaza then communicated the final message of the spirits: when not a single animal out of all their herds was left alive, when not a single grain remained in their granaries, supplications would be complete, and the Xhosa would be worthy of the aid of a spirit host. Then, on a certain day, two blood-red suns would fall and crush to dust the bones of every white man in the land, together with his allies the Fingo, a Zulu subtribe that had consistently supported the white settlers, and every one who opposed the will of the spirits or disobeyed their commands.

Myriad cattle, more beautiful than anyone had ever seen, would issue from the earth and cover pastures far and wide. Large fields of millet, maize, pumpkins, and monkeynuts, ripe and ready for the pot, would appear. The ancient heroes of the Xhosa, the great, brave, and wise ones long since departed, would rise again to feast and dance with the faithful. Trouble, sickness, and old age would disappear, and youth, beauty, peace, and happiness would reign forever. Thus spoke Umhlakaza, spokesman of the spirits.

There were some who thought the real aim of the spirits was to throw the full force and might of all Xhosa, fully armed and desperate for food, on the whites in the Cape Colony. Most, however, took what Umhlakaza said as the literal description of what was to happen. Great kraals were built for the expected cattle, and enormous gourds prepared to contain their milk. Huge granaries were erected to hold the marvelous millet, maize, pumpkins, and monkeynuts.

When the appointed day dawned and there were no blood-red suns over the eastern hills, or the heavens falling to crush white men and their Fingo allies, or myriad beautiful cattle, or large fields of millet, maize, pumpkins, and

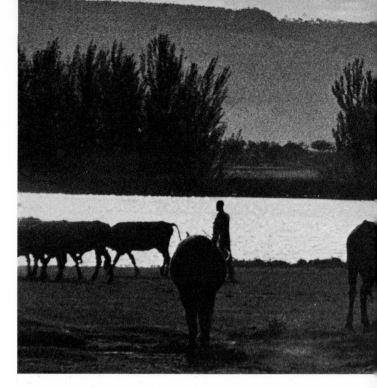

Atop a 5,000-foot plateau of the Drakensberg range, Basuto herdsmen water their cattle. An amalgam of Sotho and Tswana peoples, the Basuto settled in the relative security of these mountains during Chaka's rampages. When the Boers began to move in, King Moshoeshoe was driven to accept British "protectorship"; it lasted until 1966, when the Basuto set up the autonomous kingdom of Lesotho.
MAGNUM—ERNST HAAS

monkeynuts, or a resurrection of the heroes of the race; misery and death stalked the land. Over thirty thousand Africans died of starvation.

Ironically, the tragic events did much to reduce, for a time, the Xhosa's ability to resist white rule. It was not until February, 1878, twenty-two years later, that five thousand Xhosa, the combined forces of Kreli and Sandile, were able once more to take the field against the white man at Kentani. Several months later Sandile was killed in another action. After his death his people surrendered to the British. Kreli was driven across the Bashee River and spent the rest of his life in a segregated location at Elliotdale. Thus ended, for a time, African wars of resistance in the Cape Colony.

In Basutoland, which is today independent Lesotho entirely surrounded by South Africa, a different course of resistance was followed in the early nineteenth century. The genius behind it was a Sotho king, the great Moshoeshoe (also known as Moshesh). While he was joining together diverse African societies into a single nation of Basuto people, King Moshoeshoe was compelled to resist European encroachment. With his own position among the various tribes far from secure, he could not risk defeat or a prolonged war with the British. Giving in to European demands was, nevertheless, out of the question; so, he resorted to both fighting and diplomacy.

In 1851 Cape governor Sir Harry Smith sent Major Henry Warden with a force of one hundred and sixty-two professional soldiers, one hundred and twenty armed farmers, and fifteen hundred Africans against Chief Molitsane, a vassal of Moshoeshoe. Major Warden's force was drawn into a trap at Viervoet and crushed. Many Boers in the neighboring Orange River Sovereignty saved their skins by promising not to take part in hostilities against the Basuto. Moshoeshoe kept his word not to molest the neutrals, but sought out pro-British farmers and plundered them mercilessly.

It was not until December, 1852, that Sir George Cathcart, who had replaced Sir Harry Smith as governor at the Cape, brought together a well-equipped force of two thousand infantry, five hundred cavalry, and some artillerymen with two field guns, hoping that such a force would intimidate Moshoeshoe into acceding to the demands without fighting. The British governor ordered King Moshoeshoe to comply with certain conditions and deliver, within three days, ten thousand head of cattle and one thousand horses.

Moshoeshoe preferred not to fight, but his people chose to go to war rather than part with so many of their cattle and horses. Moshoeshoe decided to compromise by sending three thousand five hundred head of cattle. He hoped for the best and prepared for the worst by assembling his warriors at a new capital and stronghold at Thaba Bosigo. The compromise was not acceptable to the British, so Sir George Cathcart and his force entered Basutoland.

On Berea Mountain Moshoeshoe left a large herd of cattle, which appeared easy to capture, and with this decoy drew half the British forces into an ambush. Although this deployment seized about four thousand cattle, they suffered heavy losses. The other half of the force, personally led by Sir George, was routed by six thousand Basuto horsemen, some of whom were armed with guns. The British retreated.

Although Moshoeshoe had carried the day, he instructed the Reverend Eugene Casalis, a missionary in his realm, to write what has been called "the most politic document that has ever been penned in South Africa." The communiqué, dated Thaba Bosigo, Midnight, 20th December, 1852, began: "Your Excellency,—This day you have fought against my people, and taken much cattle. As the object for which you have come is to have a compensation for the Boers, I beg you will be satisfied with what you have taken. I entreat peace from you—you have shown your power—you have chastised—let it be enough I pray you; and let me no longer be considered an enemy to the Queen. I will try all I can to keep my people in order for the future. Your humble servant, Moshoeshoe." Sir George Cathcart grasped this opportunity to extricate himself with honor from an awkward situation. He announced he was satisfied with the number of cattle captured and considered his obligations fulfilled. He returned to the Cape.

Burghers in the Orange River Sovereignty elected as president Josias Hoffman, a farmer who was a very close friend of Moshoeshoe. In 1855 the Boers deposed him because they felt by electing a friend of the Basuto king they had conceded more to Moshoeshoe than was consistent with the dignity of an independent state. Jacobus Nicolas Boshof became their next president.

Dingane, who succeeded Chaka as king of the Zulu, showed none of his half brother's political skill. Rather, he devoted his energies to his two passions—eating and dancing. These engravings of the ruler in dancing and ordinary clothes are from Journey to the Zoolu Country, *by Allen Francis Gardiner, a nineteenth-century English missionary who tried to convert Dingane to Christianity.*
OLD HOUSE MUSEUM, DURBAN

Moshoeshoe began harassing them with a view to recovering land lost by some of the tribes who were now his vassals. In 1858 the Boers decided to invade Basutoland and thus carry the war into Moshoeshoe's territory. The Basuto king let the Boers fight their way to the very gates of Thaba Bosigo, where they learned that swarms of Basuto horsemen were at that very moment ravaging their farms back home. Since it was impossible to take Moshoeshoe's mountain stronghold by storm, and they had not the means to lay siege, they abandoned the battle and hurried home, leaving Moshoeshoe master of his land once more. Sir George Grey, who had become Cape governor in 1854, was asked to mediate, and he awarded the Basuto king most of the land he wanted.

Meanwhile, in Zululand in the northern corridor between the Indian Ocean coast of South Africa and the Drakensberg range, political units capable of military resistance to the colonial government were forming. When Chaka, the founder of the Zulu nation, was assassinated in 1828, he predicted the advent of white rule in southern Africa. Dingane, his successor, however, had to deal with the problem. Events were precipitated by the Great Trek, the migration of great numbers of Boer cattlemen into the interior and away from British rule. One such group was led by Pieter Retief. Retief approached Dingane at Umgungundhlovu, his capital, and asked for land to settle his party. Dingane indicated his willingness to consider making a grant of land to Retief if in exchange the Boers would retrieve cattle that had been taken by Sikonyela, one of Dingane's rivals. Retief retrieved the cattle without bloodshed and, accompanied by sixty-five other white men and about thirty Hottentots, waited on Dingane to make the grant of land.

Instead, Dingane gave the order, "*Bulalani abathakati!* (Kill the wizards!)" and Retief's party was massacred to a man.

Dingane then sent soldiers to wipe out the rest of Retief's group, temporarily settled at Weenen, the "place of weeping," as the Dutch subsequently named it. Two hundred eighty-two white men, women, and children and fifty African servants perished that day. Fortunately for the white people, one man escaped; he was able to ride and warn other groups so that when the Zulu army arrived, they were already in a laager, their wagons drawn up in a defensive circle for the night.

Pieter Uys, Hendrick Potgieter, Gert Maritz, and some English leaders then assembled an army of three hundred forty-seven men to fight the Zulu. The English were to attack from one side, while Potgieter and Uys attacked from the other. Maritz was to stay and protect the camp. In April, 1838, after a five-day march, the Boers sighted a Zulu army and attacked it impetuously. The Zulu skillfully drew them into a planned ambuscade between two parallel ranges of hills. Retreating into the narrowest part of the gorge, the Boers found themselves surrounded. They were so hemmed in that they could not, as was their usual strategy, fall back rapidly after firing, load again, and charge. The Boers turned back, directed their fire upon a mass of Zulu, cleared a path, rushed through, and escaped, although not without leaving behind many dead and some of their horses, baggage, and spare ammunition. Among the dead were Pieter Uys and his fifteen-year-old son.

The English contingent left the port of Natal with fifteen hundred Africans, four hundred of whom were armed with muskets. On April 17, 1838, some miles south of the Tugela River, they came upon a Zulu regiment. The regiment pretended to take flight; they even left food cooking on fires and a number of assagais and shields lying about. The English contingent pursued with all speed, crossed the Tugela, and took possession of a Zulu kraal on the northern bank before it realized it had been drawn into the horns of a Zulu army, seven thousand strong.

Three times the English contingent beat back the Zulu regiments that furiously charged upon it. Zulu reinforcements arrived. Another rush was made. This time the English contingent was cut in two. One half tried to escape by a path along a steep bank of the Tugela. A Zulu regiment cut off its retreat, but four Englishmen and five hundred Africans escaped.

The other half was completely surrounded. A young Zulu regiment was selected to charge, while the veterans watched from a hill. Whole masses of young Zulu went down before the withering fire, but still they came and came again, until all the Englishmen and over a thousand of their African allies lay dead on the battlefield.

During the winter Dingane sent an army to attack various white groups. The white people, however, were now careful to avoid being lured out of their laagers by any stratagem. In December, 1838, Andries Pretorius assembled a force of four hundred sixty-four men and a sufficient number of wagons to form a laager every night. This army vowed that if God gave it victory, it would build a church and set apart an annual thanksgiving day to commemorate the victory. Pretorious sent word to Dingane, offering to enter into peace negotiations if Dingane restored the property of the white people killed by the Zulu. Dingane's reply was to send an army of ten thousand men. The impi, or army, attacked Pretorius' camp at dawn and for hours sent waves of Zulu warriors charging upon it; thousands were felled by the white man's gunfire. When at length the Zulu withdrew, thousands upon thousands of men lay dead, and a stream that flowed near the field of battle was colored with blood. (From that day this stream has been known as Blood River, and December 16 has been officially celebrated as the Day of the Covenant in South Africa.) Pretorious went on to Umgungundhlovu and found that Dingane had set it on fire and fled. His commando force returned with five thousand cattle.

In September, 1839, Mpande, a half brother of Dingane, conspired to seize the throne. This divided the Zulu nation in two. Mpande's supporters sought white people's support against Dingane. Dingane sent Tambusa, his trusted *induna*, or chief, to negotiate with the white people. But the Boers, bent on avenging Retief's death, arrested Tambusa and

executed him and his party.

The combined force of Boers under the command of Pretorius and Mpande's impi under Nongalaza defeated Dingane, who fled north toward the Swazi border, where he was later assassinated. Mpande became king of the Zulu and a vassal of the Boers. With great bravery and loss of life Africans in Zululand had resisted European encroachment, but had succumbed in defeat when internal quarrels divided them in fratricidal strife.

As soon as Mpande was king, he became lethargic both mentally and physically. He grew grossly fat and discipline in his army declined. His two sons, Mbulazi and Cetshwayo, however, were energetic and brilliant men. It became clear that, as no two bulls can remain in one kraal, these two princes could not both live in Zululand. In December, 1856, civil war broke out, and the two princes led opposing forces into battle. The result was a complete victory for the handsome Cetshwayo, who became from that day the real ruler of the Zulu, even though his father lived until 1872. Mbulazi was never heard of again. His followers—men, women, and children—were put to death.

Under Cetshwayo, discipline in the Zulu army was restored, and the Zulu fighting machine became formidable, as it had been in Chaka's time. This was felt by neighboring European settlements, who began to fear for their safety. In 1878 the British governor, Sir Bartle Frere, collected a military force in Natal and sent an ultimatum to Cetshwayo, calling upon the Zulu king to disband his army. Cetshwayo ignored the ultimatum. An army of British soldiers, colonists, and Africans loyal to the colonial government under the command of Lord Frederick Chelmsford entered Zululand in three divisions.

The first division proceeded toward the Buffalo River. One column camped at the foot of Isandlwana Hill. On January 22, 1879, Lord Chelmsford and a small party left camp to attack kraals several miles away. At noon that day the remaining camp suddenly found itself enclosed within the horns of a Zulu impi. Seven hundred British soldiers, over one hundred and thirty colonists, and hundreds of their African allies were killed. Lord Chelmsford's party heard of the disaster in the afternoon, marched back to spend the night among the corpses of their comrades, and the next day returned to Port Natal.

A Zulu impi, under the command of another of Cetshwayo's brothers, Dabulamanzi, attacked a column guarding a depot of provisions at Rock Drift about 5 P.M. on the day of the Zulu victory at Isandhlwana. The one hundred thirty soldiers at the depot had been warned of the attack and formed a laager. Waves of Zulu warriors continued to besiege the depot until dawn, when they retired, leaving seventeen enemy dead and hundreds of their brave comrades killed.

Meanwhile, the division commanded by Colonel Charles Pearson crossed the Tugela River and marched toward Ulundi, where the three divisions intended to unite. A Zulu impi, about five thousand strong, attacked Pearson's column, consisting of two thousand Europeans and an equal force of African allies, at Inyezane and inflicted heavy losses. When he learned of the disaster of Isandhlwana, Colonel Pearson sent most of the remaining cavalry and Africans back to Natal, and with a smaller force fortified a Norwegian mission station near Eshowe, where he remained until reinforcements from England arrived.

The third division, consisting of one thousand seven hundred British soldiers, fifty Boer farmers, and four hundred Africans under Brigadier General Evelyn Wood, fortified a post at Kambula and made frequent sallies on Zulu villages. At Hlobane ninety-six of the column were surrounded by an impi and killed.

When news of the British defeat at Isandhlwana reached England, nine thousand soldiers—cavalry and infantry—with large quantities of munitions and provisions, were sent out. Among the soldiers was Louis Bonaparte, heir to Napoleon III's throne, who lost his life in Zululand while with a reconnoitering party that was surprised by the Zulu. His companions abandoned him and rode away when he was unable to mount his horse. He was stabbed to death.

Cetshwayo's army was eventually defeated by a British force at Ulundi. The Zulu king went into hiding, and for a long time no one could be induced to say where he was. At length one man, threatened with death, revealed the name of a small village where Cetshwayo was found and taken prisoner. In captivity, the Zulu king conducted himself with such dignity that in 1883, after visiting England, he was allowed to return to his throne. In his absence a rival named Sikepu had arisen and won the allegiance of many Zulu. There was civil war. Cetshwayo died and was succeeded by his son, Dinizulu. The war continued, but Dinizulu secured the assistance of Europeans in exchange for land in the Vryheid district in northern Natal. Dinizulu won, but before long fell out with the Europeans and began to resist their rule. In 1889 he was arrested and exiled to the island of St. Helena, and Zululand was put under European rule.

In the area now included in Southern Rhodesia, the Bantu-speaking Mashona also resisted foreign occupation of their country. Europeans entered Mashonaland in 1890. The Mashona, under the impression that the invaders were mere transients interested in trade, were advised by their *midzimu*, or spirit mediums, not to resist, but to trade with them amicably. However, under the auspices of Cecil Rhodes' British South Africa Company, the Europeans began to carve for themselves large farms, and mine gold, eject Africans from what they called their property, impress young men into labor gangs, and abuse African women. When, in short, they gave every indication that they had come to stay, Mashona resistance began to simmer.

In 1893 the British South Africa Company also treacherously invaded Matabeleland, a neighboring kingdom whose capital was near present-day Bulawayo. Six thousand Matabele warriors were on a military expedition across the Zambezi when the white men invaded their land in three columns.

The Matabele king, Lobengula, was informed that the *indunas* he had sent to the Cape at the request of the governor had been murdered by white men at Macloutsie. Lobengula was mad with rage and regarded this act as the most despicable treachery. His *indunas* had been sent on an errand of peace, their safety guaranteed by the high commissioner, yet the white men had turned around and murdered his men. "The white men," he declared, "are the fathers of liars." Ordering his army to take up arms, he appeared before them daubed with paint and carrying an assagai. Before thousands of his warriors Lobengula drove the spear into the earth, signaling war. In response the warriors gave the royal salute, "*Bayete! Bayete! Bayete! Uyi Zulu!*", leaping high and striking their shields, causing such a din as to make the whole earth shake. In the excitement few noticed that the King's assagai broke as it hit the earth—a bad omen.

Although Lobengula's best regiments had been recalled from Barotseland, most of them had contracted smallpox in the north and had been isolated in special kraals so that the disease would not spread. Thus the Matabele army was not at full strength when it went to meet the European invaders.

Several regiments went out to meet the foe. They were prevented by fog from making contact with the enemy in the thick Somabula forests. Consequently, the Matabele met the invaders on the plains of the Shangani, where conditions favored the white men and their guns. Leander Starr Jameson, who was to gain dubious fame as the leader of the Jameson Raid two years later, was with this force. A. J. de Roos, a Hollander who also fought on the side of the invaders, wrote of the Shangani encounter:

It was full moon, the Matabele had marched all night and were well informed of our movements. Near the laager they waited for the dawn to attack. Their tactics nearly succeeded.

If the Makalangas, who were sleeping outside the laager, had not immediately given the alarm, we would all have gone where the woodbine twineth and the wangdoodtle uttereth its mournful song.

It was still too dark to take in the whole situation, but the surrounding veld was absolutely black with Matabele. On one side the impi was so closely massed that they resembled a stretch of burnt grass in the half light.

However, as dawn approached, the situation changed. De Roos went on to say that the Matabele were so close that it was impossible to miss; he continues: "The maxims and other guns began to speak and within a quarter of an hour one could see that it was all up with them. The sun rose and the surrounding country was strewn with dead and wounded. I estimate that a few thousand Matabele must have taken part in the fight."

Major Forbes pressed on to Bulawayo, the Matabele capital, but on November 18, as the invaders were about to make camp, the Matabele attacked again. De Roos described the battle:

This was also a surprise attack. Most of the men were occupied in preparing their food, when suddenly shots were heard from the horse pickets. The Matabele nearly captured our horses, and draught animals, and this calamity was averted only by the resolute boldness of few Colonials [Cape Colony Africans] who did not retire nor hesitate, but fired as rapidly as possible at the charging enemy. They, were soon reinforced from the laager. Within half an hour the enemy were in full retreat. Here also the maxims did their deadly work. A thousand Matabele must have fallen before they retreated. A sortie was made to pursue the retreating enemy. A few wounded Matabele were brought into the laager, but they were killed, when the laager broke up and the column trekked on. I say killed. I know what I am saying, for I saw it myself—without trial or hearing. If there is any question of a "blot" anywhere—here is one. No prisoners of war were made at that time. I don't know what the English parson, who taught us to sing: "Onward Christian Soldiers," had to say about it.

Then this Christian army, which slaughtered prisoners of war, marched on to Bulawayo. On November 4, they were met by two traders, who told them that King Lobengula had abandoned his town, after instructing an *induna* to see to the safety of the two white men. When the invaders were close, the *induna* told the traders, "I have carried out my king's instructions and must go now, for your people are not far, and they will kill me. If any harm comes to you, it will be from your own people, not mine." Then he set fire to the royal kraal and disappeared. The imperial force arrived in Bulawayo on November 15.

In Bulawayo, De Roos tells us: "The first thing we did was to hold a thanksgiving service, which was conducted by the English Bishop. The subject of his sermon was that we had been led by the hand of God through all those dangers, to the greater glory of His Name, and His Kingdom and the extension of the glorious Empire. 'Onward, Christian Soldiers,' was sung again, for we had not yet captured Lobengula, with his cattle, diamonds, and gold."

Jameson asked Lobengula to return to Bulawayo, promising him safety and friendly treatment, but threatening pursuit if he refused. The king replied that he was prepared to come, but wanted to know what had happened to the *indunas* he had sent on a peace mission to the white men. Finding no satisfactory answer, Lobengula set off in the direction of the Shangani River, with the British in pursuit.

After he had crossed the Shangani, Lobengula told his men: "Matabele! The white men will never cease following us whilst we have gold in our possession; for gold is what they prize above all things. Collect now my gold, and you, and you [indicating two *indunas*], carry it back to the white men. Tell them they have beaten my regiments, killed my people, burnt my kraals, captured my cattle, and that I want peace." Two *indunas* carried the gold to the white soldiers. The gold was taken by two troopers, and the message ignored.

Matabeleland was placed under white rule, but on March 24, 1896, a white man was killed in the Mzingwane district, and an uprising, very ably described by Terence Ranger in *Revolt in Southern Rhodesia 1896–7*, had begun. From Mzingwane the uprising spread to large parts of Matabeleland and Mashonaland. Prominent among the leaders of the uprising was the Mashona priest Mkwati. His communications network coordinated moves throughout the area as, for once, the Mashona and Ndebele peoples acted in unison. When the uprising in Mashonaland eventually ended, ten per cent of the white population in the country had been killed, "a staggeringly high figure," which, Lewis Gann has noted, was "infinitely greater than the proportion of casualties suffered by white colonists in the Algerian national rising or the Mau Mau in Kenya in the twentieth century."

In West Africa the indigenous peoples also struggled to hold their birthright. In the Gambia in 1891 France recognized Britain's claims to both banks of the Gambia River as far as the sea. Soon after this, there was friction between the French and the Mandingos and Fulani. As a result, a chief named Fodi Kabba was exiled to Médine (in present-day Mali), from where he directed a movement against the British. It took a combined British and French military operation in 1901 to destroy Fodi Kabba's movement.

In 1893 another Gambian chief, Fodi Silah, inflicted heavy losses on a British punitive expedition sent against him. He was, however, eventually driven into French-claimed territory, where he died.

In Sierra Leone the indigenous peoples rose against the British in 1898. They massacred white people, including American missionaries, in their opposition to the "hut tax," a tax charged against every dwelling. The British were compelled to mount an expedition, under Sir Francis de Winton, against them.

In the territory of modern Ghana, the Asante in 1807 attacked and destroyed a British fort at Anomabu and the Dutch fort of Kormantin, and besieged the Cape Coast Castle. They held the area until 1824, when the governor of Sierra Leone, Sir Charles Macarthy, landed at Cape Coast Castle while on a tour of inspection. Impetuously he embarked on a war with the Asante. He was defeated and committed suicide. It took the British imperial government three years to contain the Asante.

Between 1871 and 1872 the Dutch turned over their possessions on the Gold Coast to the British in exchange for certain British claims in Sumatra. The transfer of territory involved the latter in another war with the Asante. The Asante king put forty thousand men in the field. The British allied themselves with the Fante, providing the Africans with British weapons. They were badly defeated twice, before the Asante assaulted the British at Elmina. In 1873 Sir Garnet Wolseley, with a strong force of British soldiers, contingents of West Indian regiments, British seamen and marines, joined Sir John Glover, who commanded Hausa levies, in attacking and burning Kumasi, the Asante capital.

In 1895 another war broke out. The British captured Kumasi and demanded an indemnity of 357,000 pounds in gold. When this was not paid the *asantehene*, or king, the queen mother, and important chiefs were exiled to the Seychelles in the Indian Ocean. The British looted the

A local chief's version of the Asante kings' Golden Stool.
ELIOT ELISOFON

Asante palace and dynamited sacred trees and altars.

To add insult to injury, in 1900 the governor of the Gold Coast, Sir Frederick Hodgson, demanded the surrender of the Golden Stool so that he could sit on it. Not even the *asantehene* himself sits on the Golden Stool, which is believed to hold the soul of the Asante nation; rather, the stool is placed on its side, atop a stool of its own. To defend themselves against this sacrilege the Asante revolted and besieged the governor and his wife in Kumasi from, appropriately, April Fool's Day to June 23, 1900, when, with a force of six hundred Hausa soldiers and British officers, Hodgson fought his way through Asante warriors to the Gold Coast colony. Later, Colonel James Willcocks arrived from Nigeria with several hundred Yoruba and Hausa troops; these were joined by other African and Indian troops from British Central Africa and officers from England. When the British force eventually advanced on Kumasi in July, it numbered three thousand five hundred officers and men and thousands of African allies from regions hostile to the Asante.

In Nigeria the British were compelled in 1851 to mount a naval expedition against Kosoko, the king of Lagos. They expelled the king, putting his cousin on the throne. The British met more resistance, however, from Jaja, who had risen from slavery to become a formidable merchant prince of the Niger delta, capable of putting in the field a large force of fighting men. Jaja jealously guarded his independence, and when threatened, engaged the British with armed forces. He was defeated and removed to the West Indies.

Another Nigerian potentate who resisted the British was the king of Benin. In January, 1897, he massacred an ostensibly peaceful British expedition under the command of J. R. Phillips, the acting consul general. The *oba* was subsequently exiled, and a number of his chiefs executed. Yet another resistance flared up in 1899, when a punitive British expedition was sent to Benin.

Between 1900 and 1910 several wars were fought to subdue the Aro, an Ibo people in the northeastern part of the Niger delta. The Fulani kingdom of Nupe also fought wars of resistance to British rule. Colonel T. L. N. Moreland, with a force of eight hundred African soldiers and British officers, equipped with artillery and maxim guns, was compelled in 1902–1903 to fight not only in Nupe but also in Bornu, Kano, and Sokoto.

French interest in West Africa was stimulated by René Caillié, who in 1827 traveled up the Niger to Timbuktu and across the Sahara to Morocco. At this time the Fulani conqueror, Al Hajj Umar, dominated this area. He blocked Caillié's route and threatened French settlements on the Senegal River. In 1854 General Louis Faidherbe was appointed governor general of Senegal, and he conducted skirmishes against African tribes resisting French rule north of the river. He annexed the Wuli country and built a fort at the river port of Médine. Umar sent an army of twenty thousand men against him.

In 1864 a French expedition under Lieutenant Abdon Mage reached Segu, but was detained for two years by Umar's nephew and successor, Ahmadu ibn Tindani (Ahmadu Seku), who also resisted French forces under General Gustave Borgnis-Desbordes, Colonel Louis Archinard, and other officers.

In 1890 the Tukolor Fulani of Takrur and the Macina Fulani under Ahmadu Abdulei (Ahmadu Cheiku) fought a war of resistance against the French, and the following year a Mandingo king, Samori Touré, also led his people in resisting white rule. In the years 1885 and 1886 the French undertook a campaign against him, but the king's dogged resistance turned it into a seven years' war. In 1894 and 1895 Colonel P. L. Monteil led an unsuccessful military expedition against Samori. Monteil was recalled by the French government; but in 1898 Samori was taken prisoner and exiled to Gabon. Similarly, in Dahomey, King Behanzin fiercely resisted French rule from 1891 to 1893, when he was captured and exiled to the West Indies. Unrest existed as well in other parts of French-held Africa: near Timbuktu in 1894; in the Ivory Coast in 1900; in Mauritania in 1908 and 1909.

In Algeria Abd al-Kader inflicted defeat after defeat on the French between 1835 and 1837. Only after the French had suffered great losses did they send in an army sufficient to rout the guerilla leader. Forced to retire to Morocco, he again attacked the French with a large army. The bey of Constantine, who ruled over much of eastern Algeria, repulsed French assaults for many years until his stronghold

In 1830 the French "swore by their blood" that they seized Algeria only to destroy its piratical oppressors. But by 1845, when this patriotic poster was issued, French colons were in control of its destiny.
GIRAUDON

finally fell to the enemy in 1847. In 1863 the Kabylia Berbers rose in resistance to French rule, and to the south of Oran there was another uprising under Bu Amama. In Tunisia in 1882 there were uprisings against the French and the bey's government, which had placed the country under French control. A French expedition, led by Paul Flatters, was massacred by the Tuaregs in the Sahara in 1881. In Morocco Europeans were killed, and Casablanca was sacked by Africans in 1907. In response, France sent fifteen thousand troops, who fought sporadically until 1911.

In the Congo the sultan of Bagirmi, who had been induced to accept French protection, was forced to flee, together with the French resident, from the army of Robah Zobeir, sultan of Bornu. It was not until after two years' fighting, in which the French suffered many defeats, that Zobeir was slain. His sons and successors continued the struggle until 1902. To the northeast of Bagirmi, the Wadai ruler attacked French outposts on the Chari River in 1904, thereby opening a war that did not end till 1911.

Relations with the Portuguese, the British, and the French pale before the record left by the Belgians. Few episodes in the history of colonialism in Africa can surpass the

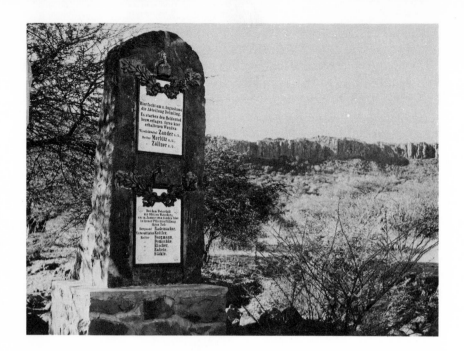

The German encroachment on South West Africa was met with fierce rebellion in the Herero uprising of 1904–1906. Equipped with obsolete rifles and little ammunition, the Herero were no match for the quick-firing Krupp gun used by the Germans. By the end of the war these embattled Africans had been reduced from 80,000 cattle-rich nomads to 15,000 starving fugitives. This memorial, near Waterberg, commemorates ten of the Germans who died in the war.

revolting brutality and sordid crimes committed in the name of Leopold, king of the Belgians, on Africans in the Congo. The imposition of Belgian rule is the most miserable chapter of a miserable story.

In less than twenty years after the first Belgian attack, an African population that had been estimated at between twenty and thirty million was reduced to eight million. Fighting became endemic in the Congo. Belgian officials ordered that recalcitrant villagers be punished by having the hands and sexual organs of males cut off and brought to them for check and tally. In 1892 Belgians were attacked and massacred all over the upper Congo. In 1895, as a result of the murder by the Belgians of Gongo Lutete, chief of the Manyema, there was an uprising at Luluabourg, and another in 1897.

Meanwhile, back on the east coast, the German East Africa Company obtained from the sultan of Zanzibar a fifty-year lease on his mainland territory extending from the Ruvuma River to the Umba River. Over sixty German officials were sent to administer the region. On August 21, 1888, disturbances broke out. A month later the Germans hardly held any post in the interior. Not only Germans but all Europeans suffered. It took a thousand Sudanese troops, two hundred German sailors, and sixty German officers over eighteen months to put down the uprising.

In 1891 the Wahehe, a warlike people on the Rufiji River, rose against German rule and fought a war that lasted until 1893. In 1905, however, other African tribes between northern Nyasaland (present-day Malawi) and the Kilwa coast rose against the Germans. German officials, male and female missionaries, planters, and traders were killed. It took the Germans nearly a year and a half to subdue the Africans, using not only Masai and Sudanese Africans but also New

Guinea, Papuan, and Melanesian troops to fight for them.

In German Kamerun (or Cameroon), cruelties committed between 1887 and 1896 resulted in a mutiny of African soldiers. In 1904 and 1905 African groups rose against German rule and were suppressed after much fighting.

In South West Africa the Hottentot leader Hendrik Witbooi led his people in several victories against the Germans, who were eventually persuaded to sign a treaty of peace. In 1903 another group of Hottentots—the Bondelswarts living north of the Orange River—took up arms against the Germans and fought them for four years before being exterminated. While this war was in progress, Bantu-speaking Herero tribes also rose up against Germans. Led by Samuel Maherero, they attacked and killed every white man in sight, burning their houses until they were defeated in the Waterberg Mountains in 1904. Maherero escaped to British territory, where he died while organizing further resistance to the Germans.

Resistance erupted again in the following year, when under Witbooi and his successor Jacob Marengo the Hottentots took up arms. Sixty German settlers in the southeast were killed. By 1908, when the troubles finally came to an end, the Germans in South West Africa had lost five thousand soldiers and settlers, and spent over fifteen million pounds trying to hold on there.

The Italians also entered Africa in the last quarter of the nineteenth century. Italy had for a very long time cast an envious eye over what it called Abyssinia (Ethiopia, as it is known today). In 1873 Italy purchased the small coaling station of Assab on the Red Sea. After the downfall of Egypt, Italy occupied the neighboring port of Massawa and other areas in the region of Eritrea, and so came to loggerheads with Emperor Yohannes IV of Ethiopia.

The Italians had already occupied Sahiti, an inland town formerly under the Egyptians, when the Ethiopian general Ras Alulu moved against them with ten thousand men. An Italian army of four hundred fifty men was completely destroyed. In 1895, when Emperor Menelik sat on the Ethiopian throne, the Italians tried again. First they made secret treaties with one of the vassal kings of Ethiopia—Ras Mangasha of Tigre. Menelik had reason to doubt the loyalty of Ras Mangasha of Tigre, his rival for the emperorship of Ethiopia. In 1891 Ras Mangasha had made a treaty with the Italians: in return for their support, he undertook to detach Tigre from the Ethiopian empire. This the Italians did, though they were still bound by the Treaty of Wichale to support Menelik.

Ras Mangasha, tiring of an alliance that proved to be meaningless, threw in his lot with Menelik in 1895. He ignored Italian general Baratieri's order to disband, and the Italians, being short of men and funds, did nothing about it. Baratieri went to Rome and succeeded in obtaining money and supplies. He, nevertheless, underestimated the strength of Menelik's troops and counted on some vassal kings rising against the emperor. This did not happen. In September, 1895, Menelik had issued a proclamation about the foreign menace, which raised a wave of genuine patriotism among his subjects. All his vassals came to his side.

The Italians staked the reputation of their army on the Ethiopian campaign. Having decided upon a surprise attack on Adowa, the capital of Tigre, Baratieri chose for his attack Sunday, March 1, 1896, a feast day in the Ethiopian Church, with the hope that Ethiopian soldiers would have gone to worship at the holy city of Axum. It never occurred to him that Menelik could move so many troops so quickly from one distant point to another. Nor did he know that Menelik had for some years been importing arms and ammunition. Over and above all, he had faulty and inaccurate maps of Ethiopia.

On the night of February 29 (it was leap year) an Italian force of 14,500 in three columns advanced toward Adowa. Its objective was to occupy three hills commanding the plain. Rain slowed the march. One column, which was to encamp on a hill called Chidan Meret, had far outdistanced the two other Italian detachments. When they encamped at daybreak, there was no sign of the rest of the army, which should have been on its right. Runners, sent to reconnoiter, never returned. The commander's African guides reported that the maps were wrong and that the hill they were on was not Chidan Meret. He seriously considered

whether to rely on the map or on his African informants. He decided to rely on his map. The Ethiopians attacked, outmaneuvering and overwhelming the Italian force. A detachment of African troops under Italian command fought well, but could not do anything against a determined Ethiopian attack. Finally, they broke and ran, forcing the Italian officers to surrender. The Ethiopians then cut off the other two Italian columns. Over 8,000 Italians and some 4,000 of their African troops were killed. Fugitives not taken prisoner were harried in the gorges, which were their only way back to Eritrea. Had Menelik not ordered all his troops back into camp on the evening of the battle, his cavalry could have cut off the few passes available to the retreating army and exterminated the entire Italian force. The ignominy of this defeat was never to be forgotten in Italy.

From the evidence presented throughout this chapter, it is abundantly clear that the vast majority of Africans responded bravely to the Berlin conspiracy. The European invader enjoyed the advantage of superior weaponry. In all other aspects of the conflict—in generalship, strategy, and battle tactics—it is clear Africans more than held their own against graduates of the best military academies of Europe. It could be said that in these encounters Africans, armed usually only with spears, displayed greater valor than Europeans firing guns from a safe distance. As a king of the Ndebele once observed: a gun is a weapon that must have been invented by a coward.

What, then, turned the scales in favor of Europeans? It was the assistance they received from a small number of African collaborators, who acted as soldiers, carriers, informants, and food suppliers. Without internal division, then, Europeans would never have been able to win the wars of resistance against them.

Even today in Rhodesia, South West Africa, South Africa, Angola, and Mozambique, where armed opposition to white rule is taking place, the success of the white man in suppressing this resistance is due in no small measure to the extent and manner in which he has been able to use Africans as soldiers, secret agents, and intelligence gatherers. Perhaps this part of our history illustrates the point of the Zulu saying: "*Isitha somunthu nguye uqhobo lwake.* (The enemy of an African is he, himself.)" There can be no doubt, however, that these early wars were a source of great inspiration and spiritual strength to the generation of Africans whose destiny it was to carry on the fight against European colonialism and, from the late 1950's on through the 1960's, eradicate it from most of the soil of Africa.

SPEARS AND MAXIM GUNS

A LOYAL SUBJECT'S PLAINT

For England's "Black Poor," as its African freedmen were called in the late eighteenth century, the idea of returning to Africa and founding a colony in Sierra Leone was extremely appealing. A committee was set up to oversee such a project, and in November, 1786, Olaudah Equiano, an Ibo and a former slave, was appointed Commissary for Stores for the Black Poor Going to Sierra Leone. In 1756, when he was ten or eleven, Equiano had been captured by raiders in eastern Nigeria. He eventually was taken to Virginia, where he was bought by a British naval officer, who renamed him Gustavus Vassa. After adventures in England, the Mediterranean, and Canada, Equiano purchased his freedom in 1766. He returned to England, where he became active as an abolitionist. His description of his role in the settlement of the Black Poor follows. It comes from his autobiography, The Interesting Narrative of the Life of Olaudah, *written following his dismissal from the post of commissary. Equiano spent the rest of his life traveling through Britain, lecturing on abolition and publicizing his best-selling book.*

On my return to London in August I was very agreeably surprised to find that the benevolence of government had adopted the plan of some philanthropic individuals to send the Africans from hence to their native quarter; and that some vessels were then engaged to carry them to Sierra Leone; an act which redounded to the honor of all concerned in its promotion, and filled me with prayers and much rejoicing. There was then in the city a select committee of gentlemen for the black poor, to some of whom I had the honor of being known; and, as soon as they heard of my arrival they

sent for me to the committee. When I came there they informed me of the intention of government; and as they seemed to think me qualified to superintend part of the undertaking, they asked me to go with the black poor to Africa. I pointed out to them many objections to my going; and particularly I expressed some difficulties on the account of the slave dealers, as I would certainly oppose their traffic in the human species by every means in my power. However these objections were over-ruled by the gentlemen of the committee, who prevailed on me to go, and recommended me to the honorable Commissioners of his Majesty's Navy as a proper person to act as commissary for government in the intended expedition; and they accordingly appointed me in November 1786 to that office, and gave me sufficient power to act for the government in the capacity of commissary, having received my warrant and the following order.

By the principal Officers and Commissioners of his Majesty's Navy:
Whereas you were directed, by our warrant of the 4th of last month, to receive into your charge from Mr. Irving the surplus provisions remaining of what was provided for the voyage, as well as the provisions for the support of the black poor, after the landing at Sierra Leone, with the clothing, tools, and all other articles provided at government's expense; and as the provisions were laid in at the rate of two months for the voyage, and for four months after the landing, but the number embarked being so much less than was expected, whereby there may be a considerable surplus of

provisions, clothing, etc. These are, in addition to former orders, to direct and require you to appropriate or dispose of such surplus to the best advantage you can for the benefit of government, keeping and rendering to us a faithful account of what you do herein. And for your guidance in preventing any white persons going, who are not intended to have the indulgence of being carried thither, we send you herewith a list of those recommended by the Committee for the black poor as proper persons to be permitted to embark, and acquaint you that you are not to suffer any others to go who do not produce a certificate from the committee for the black poor, of their having their permission for it. . . .

I proceeded immediately to the execution of my duty on board the vessels destined for the voyage, where I continued till the March following.

During my continuance in the employment of government, I was struck with the flagrant abuses committed by the agent, and endeavored to remedy them, but without effect. One instance, among many which I could produce, may serve as a specimen. Government had ordered to be provided all necessaries (slops, as they are called, included) for 750 persons; however, not being able to muster more than 426, I was ordered to send the superfluous slops, etc. to the king's stores at Portsmouth; but, when I demanded them for that purpose from the agent, it appeared they had never been bought, though paid for by government. But that was not all, government were not the only objects of peculation; these poor people suffered infinitely more; their accommodations were most wretched; many of them wanted beds, and many more clothing and other necessaries. For the truth of this, and much more, I do not seek credit from my own assertion. I appeal to the testimony of Capt. Thompson, of the *Nautilus*, who convoyed us, to whom I applied in February 1787 for a remedy, when I had remonstrated to the agent in vain, and even brought him to be a witness of the injustice and oppression I complained of. I appeal also to a letter written by these wretched people, so early as the beginning of the preceding January, and published in the *Morning Herald* of the 4th of that month, signed by twenty of their chiefs.

I could not silently suffer government to be thus cheated, and my countrymen plundered and oppressed, and even left destitute of the necessaries for almost their existence. I therefore informed the Commissioners of the Navy of the agent's proceedings; but my dismission was soon after procured, by means of a gentleman in the city, whom the agent, conscious of his peculation, had deceived by letter, and whom, moreover, empowered the same agent to receive on board, at the government's expense, a number of persons as passengers, contrary to the orders I received. By this I suffered a considerable loss in my property: however, the commissioners were satisfied with my conduct, and wrote to Capt. Thompson, expressing their approbation of it.

Thus provided, they proceeded on their voyage; and at last, worn out by treatment, perhaps not the most mild, and wasted by sickness, brought on by want of medicine, clothes, bedding, etc. they reached Sierra Leone just at the commencement of the rains. At that season of the year it is impossible to cultivate the lands; their provisions therefore were exhausted before they could derive any benefit from agriculture; and it is not surprising that many . . . whose constitutions are very tender, and who had been cooped up in ships from

October to June, and accommodated in the manner I have mentioned, should be so wasted by their confinement as not long to survive it.

Thus ended my part of the long-talked-of expedition to Sierra Leone; an expedition which, however unfortunate in the event, was humane and politic in its design, nor was its failure owing to government: everything was done on their part; but there was evidently sufficient mismanagement attending the conduct and execution of it to defeat its success.

I should not have been so ample in my account of this transaction, had not the share I bore in it been made the subject of partial animadversion, and even my dismission from my employment thought worthy of being made by some a matter of public triumph. The motives which might influence any person to descend to a petty contest with an obscure African, and to seek gratification by his depression, perhaps it is not proper here to inquire into or relate, even if its detection were necessary to my vindication; but I thank Heaven it is not. I wish to stand by my own integrity, and not to shelter myself under the impropriety of another; and I trust the behavior of the Commissioners of the Navy to me entitle me to make this assertion; for after I had been dismissed, March 24, I drew up a memorial thus:

To the Right Honorable the Lords Commissioners of his Majesty's Treasury: The Memorial and Petition of GUSTAVUS VASSA a black Man, late Commissary to the black Poor going to AFRICA. Humbly Sheweth,

That your Lordships' memorialist was, by the Honorable the Commissioners of his Majesty's Navy, on the 4th of December last, appointed to the above employment by warrant from that board;

That he accordingly proceeded to the execution of his duty on board of the *Vernon*, being one of the ships appointed to proceed to Africa with the above poor;

That your memorialist, to his great grief and astonishment, received a letter of dismission from the Honorable Commissioners of the Navy, by your Lordships' orders;

That, conscious of having acted with the most perfect fidelity and the greatest assiduity in discharging the trust reposed in him, he is altogether at a loss to conceive the reasons of your Lordships' having altered the favorable opinion you were pleased to conceive of him, sensible that your Lordships' would not proceed to so severe a measure without some apparent good cause; he therefore has every reason to believe that his conduct has been grossly misrepresented to your Lordships; and he is the more confirmed in his opinion, because, by opposing measures of others concerned in the same expedition, which tended to defeat your Lordships' humane intentions, and to put the government to a very considerable additional expense, he created a number of enemies, whose misrepresentations, he has too much reason to believe, laid the foundation of his dismission. Unsupported by friends, and unaided by the advantages of a liberal education, he can only hope for redress from the justice of his cause, in addition to the mortification of having been removed from his employment, and the advantage which he reasonably might have expected to have derived therefrom. He has had the misfortune to have sunk a considerable part of his little property in fitting himself out, and in other expenses arising out of his situation, an account of which he here annexes. Your memorialist will not trouble your Lordships with a vindication of any part of his conduct, because he knows not of what crimes he is accused; he, however, earnestly entreats that you will be pleased to direct an inquiry into his behavior during the time he acted in the public service; and, if it be found that his dismission arose from false representations; he is confident that in your Lordships' justice he shall find redress.

Your petitioner therefore humbly

prays that your Lordships will take his case into consideration, and that you will be pleased to order payment of the above referred-to account, amounting to £32 4s. and also the wages intended, which is most humbly submitted.

London, May 12, 1787.

The above petition was delivered into the hands of their Lordships, who were kind enough, in the space of some few months afterwards, without hearing, to order me £50 sterling—that is, £18 wages for the time (upwards of four months) I acted a faithful part in their service. Certainly the sum is more than a free negro would have had in the western colonies!!!

XHOSA FREEDOM FIGHTERS

In the late eighteenth century there appeared among the Xhosa a spiritual leader and warrior named Makana, whose self-proclaimed religious mission was to annihilate all white men and to bring back to life all the Africans and cattle they had killed. In the spring of 1819, provoked by numerous attacks by the whites, he led his army across the Great Fish River into the Cape Colony. The Xhosa were repulsed; by the following summer the British had driven them back across the Fish and as far as the Kei River, slaughtering and burning as they went. Makana went personally to the British camp, hoping that his own surrender would restore peace to the country. He was sentenced to life imprisonment on Robben Island. A few days later a group of his people approached his captors, offering themselves and other prominent Xhosa in exchange for Makana's release. One of them delivered the following speech, recorded by a British officer attending the parley. The British would neither make peace nor free the prophet, who died in 1820 while attempting to escape from the island.

The war, British chiefs, is an unjust one. You are striving to extirpate a people whom you forced to take up arms. When our fathers and the fathers of the Boers first settled in the Suurveld [an area west of the Fish River], they dwelt together in peace. Their flocks grazed on the same hills: there herdsmen smoked together out of the same pipes; they were brothers . . . until the herds of the Xhosas increased so as to make the hearts of the Boers sore. What those covetous men could not get from our fathers for old buttons, they took by force. Our fathers were *men*; they loved their cattle; their wives and children lived upon milk; they fought for their property. They began to hate the colonists who coveted their all, and aimed at their destruction.

Now, their kraals and our fathers' kraals were separate. The Boers made commandos on our fathers. Our fathers drove them out of the Suurveld; and we dwelt there because we had conquered it. There we were circumcised; there we married wives; and there our children were born. The white men hated us, but could not drive us away. When there was war we plundered you. When there was peace some of our bad people stole; but our chiefs forbade it. Your treacherous friend, Gaika [the Xhosa chief who was an ally of the British] always had peace with you; yet, when his people stole, he shared in the plunder. Have your patrols ever found cattle taken in time of peace, runaway slaves or deserters, in the kraals of our chiefs? Have they ever gone into Gaika's country without finding such cattle, such slaves, such deserters, in Gaika's kraals? But he was your friend; and you wished to possess the Suurveld. You came at last like locusts [in attack of 1818]. We stood; we could do no more. You said, "Go over the Fish River . . . that is all we want." We yielded and came here.

We lived in peace. Some of our bad people stole, perhaps; but the nation was quiet . . . the chiefs were quiet. Gaika stole . . . his chiefs stole . . . his people stole. You sent him copper; you sent him beads; you sent him horses, on which he rode to steal more. To us you sent only commandos.

We quarreled with Gaika about grass . . . no business of yours. You sent a commando . . . you took our last cow . . . you left only a few calves, which died for want, along with our children. You gave half of what you took to Gaika; half you kept yourselves. Without milk . . . our corn destroyed . . . we saw our wives and children perish . . . we saw that we must ourselves perish, we followed, therefore, the tracks of our cattle into the Colony. We plundered and we fought for our lives. We found you weak; we destroyed your soldiers. We saw that we were strong; we attacked your headquarters, Grahamstown: . . . and if we had succeeded, our right was good, for you began the war. We failed . . . and you are here.

We wish for peace; we wish to rest in our huts; we wish to get milk for our children; our wives wish to till the land. But your troops cover the plains, and swarm in the thickets, where they cannot distinguish the man from the woman and shoot all.

You want us to submit to Gaika. That man's face is fair to you, but his heart is false. Leave him to himself. Make peace with us. Let him fight for himself. . . . and *we* shall not call on you for help. Set Makana at liberty; and Islambi, Dushani, Kongo and the rest will come to make peace with you at any time we fix. But if you will still make war, you may indeed kill the last man of us . . . but Gaika shall not rule over the followers of those who think him a woman."

THE ZULU ARMY

The following selection is by Colonel G. Hamilton-Browne, a member of Britain's "Noble 24th." It describes the training of the Zulu army. The passage below is from A Lost Legionary in South Africa (1879).

As soon as a youth was ten years old he might be inspanned to carry the swag of his father, uncle or elder brother on the war-path; which would consist of a sleeping-mat, water-calabash, cooking-pot, docha-pipe, a few pounds of dried meat or mealies and perhaps a spare assagai and knob-stick. When he reached the age of fourteen or fifteen he would be drafted with other boys of his own age to the nearest military kraal where he would have to do fatigue duties, herd and milk cattle, fetch firewood, etc., at the same time being taught how to use his arms, how to fence with sticks, military drill and dances. During this period of his training, provided he wanted to eat, he had to skirmish around and find or steal the materials for his meal as the only provision for his sustenance, made by the kraal commandant, were a number of the wildest cows, drawn from the royal herd entrusted to the care of the regiment, and these unruly animals the recruit boys had to run down, hold and milk before they dined. This was very rough training and a boy had to be soundly constituted to survive the ordeal of his initiation into military life. As soon as a lad was old enough to be considered fit for active service he might be drafted into a regiment, or if there were enough boys fit for the purpose they might be all formed into a new regiment, each sub-tribe forming its own company, while warriors of repute were selected by the king to officer it. A Zulu regiment numbered from three to six thousand men and had its own kraal at which the men on duty lived, and a newly-formed regiment would have to build its own barracks, break up ground for cultivation, and when this was done it would receive a name from the king and be considered a unit of the royal army. . . .

A warrior's war outfit consisted of a shield made out of dried ox-hide, oval in shape, about 2 feet 6 inches wide and long enough for the owner to look over, when he held it by the middle of the strengthening stick that ran up it length-ways. His offensive arms consisted of from two to three assagais, one of which would be the stabbing assagai (*bogwan*) that had a blade of at least a foot to 18 inches long fixed to a strong shaft of wood about 2 feet in length. This weapon . . . was never thrown but only used in

hand-to-hand combat, while the others, if carried, being much lighter might be thrown, though the Zulu warrior was not encouraged to throw his assagai but was taught to rush in, defend himself with his shield and stab home with his bogwan. He also carried a knobkerry and a plain stick both made of hard wood. His food, carried for him by a boy, consisted of a small bag of dried meat and grain, but as all the kraals, on the line of march, had to contribute to the maintenance of the king's troops very little food was carried on an expedition. A force equipped, as above, could easily march 30 miles a day and put up a big fight at the end of their journey or if necessary cover 50 miles a day and continue to do so for weeks at a stretch, so that an army opposed to them must always be on the alert as no cavalry could keep pace with them over rough and broken country. Their favorite time to attack was the early morning, their plan being to surprise and envelop their enemy, when they would rush in and kill everything with the exception of the girls and cattle.

The Zulu discipline was very strict, disobedience or neglect of duty being punished by death; in fact death was the only penalty served out and the guilty one might not only bring death to himself but to all his family and friends; so it behoved a Zulu soldier to obey and obey smartly. He showed no mercy, he expected none, and when ordered on active service he well knew he must conquer or die for certain disgrace and death, probably torture, awaited a beaten army. A Zulu soldier . . . had to put in six months out of the year, under arms, at his military kraal; the balance of the year he might go home but was always liable to be called out at any moment, not only in case of war, for his regiment might be required to do duty at the royal kraal, also at certain feasts the majority of the army would be mobilized, before the king, for the purpose of showing off their capabilities in drill and dancing. At such times petitions might be presented to the sable potentate, who also took the

opportunity of rewarding or punishing those brought before him. The most frequent petition was for permission to marry and at times the king would allow aspirants to holy wedlock to prove their right to be considered . . . in the following way: A wild and savage bull would be turned loose into a large enclosed space and a dozen love-lorn young men sent in to kill it with no weapons except their bare hands; should they succeed . . . the king granted their request. . . .

The Zulu march was usually conducted in single file, the companies moving in parallel lines, while each regiment would take its own line for the objective point, and on reaching that point, or rather some given spot a few miles short of it, the leading files of each petty column would halt and the rear close up, until each company formed a dense mass of men in a ring formation, as the Zulu was quite incompetent to form or advance in line.

The regiments having converged together the chief *induna* (General) would give his orders for the attack and the regiments be formed up to carry them out. In case it should be a laager, camp or village to be stormed, the youngest regiments would be placed on the flanks whose first duty was to surround and completely envelop the enemy, thereby preventing the escape of any fugitives and these men were called the horns of the army. The main body, called the chest of the army, never moved until the flankers had taken up their positions. Then a combined attack would be made but always the junior regiments were first engaged.

The Zulu well understood the utility of a flank attack and should the position of the enemy be so extended or their numbers be so great that the Zulus could not surround them they would still try to out-flank them, but all attacks, whether frontal or flanking, were first made by the youngest regiments and should these be beaten back then the more matured and veteran soldiers moved forward to do the work. The oldest veterans formed the reserve which encouraged the fighting line and killed any combatant who turned tail.

The Zulus had no field ambulances, so after a fight the wounded were examined by their *indunas* and if found to be unable to march or to be otherwise seriously hurt were put to death, usually by drowning, provided a river was close at hand, otherwise he was put out of his misery by his nearest relation. . . . The Zulus were very superstitious, being great believers in omens, witchcraft, divinations and bone-throwing and also believed that the moon exercised great power for good and evil and that at certain phases of the luminary it was lucky or most unlucky to undertake any important act especially that of war.

The numerical strength of the Zulu army has always been disputed but I am of the opinion that it must have been near sixty thousand men at the declaration of the war and these men, trained as they were and as mobile as monkeys, were not an enemy to be sneezed at, much less to be treated lightly.

Young Xhosa boys play a stick game, in imitation of traditional methods of warfare.
MAGNUM—ERNST HAAS

ZULU WISDOM

Iqhawe lifel' ebuqhaweni, *or "the hero dies in heroism," was a popular Zulu proverb in the days when warfare was the order of the day and men prayed that they would die in battle fighting valorously for their king. Below is a collection of other Zulu wise sayings.*

A man is not stabbed with one spear.
(A man worthy of the name should not fall down with the first thrust of the spear.)

Even where there is no cock day dawns.
(No one is indispensable.)

He who installs a king never rules with him.
(Kings have short memories, and tend to forget the people who helped them in the days when they were not kings.)

He cries with one eye.
(He pretends to be sorry when he is not.)

The mouth is the shield to protect oneself.
(It is by means of one's mouth that one defends oneself.)

The sheep has killed an elephant.
(The impossible has happened.)

The bite of the black mamba cannot be cured.
(Used to describe a deadly thing for which attempts at cure are almost useless)

There is no frog that does not peep out of its pool.
(Everyone will take a chance in the hope that he will succeed.)

No buffalo was ever beaten by its calf.
(Old people are usually far more experienced than the young.)

Days are things which want to be provided for.
(One has to make proper provision for the bad days.)

One does not follow a snake into its hole.
(It is not wise to take unnecessary risks.)

There is no mountain without a grave.
(Death is everywhere. There is no way of running away from it.)

He holds the spear by the blade.
(A person who has been bragging gives himself away by doing a foolish thing.)

A king is a king because of people.
(A king is no king if he has no followers.)

When the big bird dies, the eggs rot.
(A man's family collapses when he dies.)

AN OFFER OF SAFE CONDUCT

In 1881 Muhammad Ahmad, a Muslim ascetic from the Sudan, declared himself the Mahdi, or messiah, of his country. He proclaimed a jihad and enlisted the support of tens of thousands of followers, who fought brutally and fanatically to free the Sudan from Anglo-Egyptian control. Success followed success as the Mahdists mowed down their enemies. Finally, in January, 1884, England sent out one of its ablest generals, Charles George Gordon, a former governor of the Sudan. Ignoring his instructions to evacuate the Egyptians from the Sudan, Gordon determined to defeat the Mahdi. He stubbornly remained at Khartoum. The following March the Mahdists besieged the city. Wishing to take it without bloodshed, their leader urged the British general to surrender. To this end he wrote Gordon several letters, the last of which appears below. But Gordon stood firm, and on January 26, 1885, the Sudanese breached Khartoum's defenses, taking it amid frightful slaughter. Gordon was pierced with several spears, and his head was sent to the victorious Mahdi.

In the name of God the merciful, the compassionate.
Praise be to God the kind guardian.
May God's blessings and peace be upon our Lord Mohammed and his household.
Greetings.
From: The Servant dependent upon God,

Mohammed el-Mahdi Ibn Abdallahi To: Gordon Pasha, may God protect him from every evil He did not will.

If God wills your happiness and you accept our advice and enter into our security and guarantee—that is what we wish. If, however, you would rather rejoin the English we will send you to them.

Having seen what you have seen, how long are you going to disbelieve us? We have been told by God's Apostle, may God's blessings and peace be upon him, of the imminent destruction of all those in Khartoum, save those who believe and surrender: them God will save. We do not wish you to perish with those doomed to perish because we have frequently heard good of you. Yet often as we have written to you about your regeneration and felicity, you have not returned to us an answer that will lead to your good, as we hear from those who come to us from your place. However, we have not yet despaired of your regeneration and felicity, and because of the virtue we hear is in you we will write you a single text from God's book in the hope that by it God will facilitate your regeneration since he has made us the doorway to his mercy and guidance. For this reason we have repeatedly written to you urging you to return to your own country where your virtue will achieve the highest honor. In order that you should not abandon hope of God's mercy I say to you that God has said "Kill not thyself for God is merciful to thee." Peace be upon you. 25th Rabi' Awwal, 1302 [January 12, 1885].

It was reported to me in the reply you sent us that you had said that the English wished to ransom you alone from us for £20,000. We know that people say many bad things about us which are not in us, in order that those shall be misled whom God has condemned to perdition. The falsehood of these allegations can only be known to those who meet us. As for you, if you accept our advice you will be thereby blessed; but if you wish to rejoin the English we will send you to

them without claiming a farthing. Peace be upon you.

ETHIOPIAN RESISTANCE

Another dedicated opponent of European encroachment was Menelik II, emperor of Ethiopia from 1889 to 1913. The following letter, from this sovereign to the Khalifa who was the Mahdi's successor, reveals the Ethiopian's determination to strengthen his alliance with the Sudan. Both nations faced the threat of French and British territorial expansion.

This is to inform you that the Europeans who are present round the White Nile with the English have come out from both the east and the west, and intended to enter between my country and yours and to separate and divide us. And I, when I heard of their plan, dispatched an expedition, sending detachments in five directions. The group [of Europeans] who are near are the English and the French, who are located in the direction from which the Belgians came. And do you remember when I sent to you Kantiba Jiru, you wrote to me by him that you have men in the direction from which the Belgians came?; and I ordered the chiefs of [my] troops that if they met with them, they were to parley with them and explain [my] intention. And now I have ordered my troops to advance towards the White Nile. And perhaps [if] you heard the news from merchants or from others you might misunderstand my action, [so now] I have written to you so that you would understand the object [of this expedition].

And you look to yourself, and do not let the Europeans enter between us. Be strong, lest if the Europeans enter our midst a great disaster befall us and our children have no rest. And if one of the Europeans comes to you as a traveler, do your utmost to send him away in peace; and do not listen to rumors against me. All my intention is to increase my friendship with you, and that our countries may be protected from [their] enemies.

IN PRAISE OF FOLLY

Gabriel Hanotaux (1853–1944), a French statesman and historian who twice served as his country's foreign minister, wrote this eulogy of French colonialism in 1896. His chauvinistic, superior attitude toward Africa is typical of the period and his station in life. Hanotaux earnestly believed, as he wrote in 1909, that "the nineteenth century has bequeathed to the twentieth century the colonial achievement. Of its first efforts, we see only the most noble results; the spectacle of mounting progress . . . permits us to hope that the future will surpass our dreams."

I know of nothing more heartening than the spectacle of the struggle waged for a century by the sons of civilized Europe against the enigmatic sphinx that guards the mystery of Africa. . . .

What . . . is this strange vocation . . . that from early life fixes the destiny of those who are to become heroes of this odyssey?

François Levaillant . . . was seized from infancy with a passionate taste for natural history. . . . He left for the Cape of Good Hope, and in 1780 began his fine explorations of South Africa.

René Caillié, son of a baker of Deux-Sèvres, orphan and apprentice shoemaker, read *The History of Robinson Crusoe* and *l'Histoire des Voyages* when he was twelve. Later, the sight of African maps —broad and blank—awakened a gleam of curiosity in him. . . . In 1816, with sixty francs in his pocket, he embarked at Rochefort for Senegal, . . . and going barefoot through the desert, he plunged himself into the exploration of everything not known on the African continent.

[Heinrich] Barth was a scholar and a professor. . . . After several preliminary archeological excursions, he left for "the places that were Carthage" . . . and then, beginning with the year 1850, he plunged into the Sahara and the Sudan, where he would pass the better years of his life.

[Sir Richard] Burton was an officer in the Indian army, philologist, and expert in oriental languages. . . . On a wager, he disguised himself, joined a Muslim pilgrimage, and visited the holy cities of Arabia. In 1857 he set himself another daring plan: to discover the sources of the Nile. With [John] Speke, another reckless officer, he realized the impossible and the great lakes were discovered.

The best of all, [David] Livingstone, . . . was of a Scottish family in which integrity was heredity. . . . Religious sentiments infused his life. . . . When he had received his doctorate in medicine and had finished his theological studies, he left for Africa and debarked at the Cape in 1840.

Scholar, missionary, army officer, vagabond, adventurer, not one of these men was motivated by a spirit of gain. They were driven to act by a strong and courageous passion, an overflow of life, and a thirst to give of themselves. There is not a businessman among them. . . .

The role of France in the exploration of Africa has been considerable. . . . It is curiosity and the attraction of the strange that sets the French traveler in motion. But in the more recent years, [exploration] has taken on a systematic and practical character owing, in large part, to the intervention of the state. The Department of Scientific Missions plays a preponderant role in these matters. . . .

In the course of one century, three great feats of French initiative have left a decisive mark on the evolution of the African continent: the occupation of Egypt by Bonaparte, the conquest of Algeria, and the construction of the Suez Canal.

The Egyptian campaign was not only a brilliant military operation but it left in the country the seeds of organization and of civilization. . . . Under the influence of the French, who come and go from Marseille to Alexandria, Egypt has developed, enriched, and enlarged itself. . . .

The conquest of Algeria has been the second gash in the border of states that

Islam spread out along the coast of the Mediterranean. The country has been occupied and colonized. . . . The question of the Sahara has been approached practically and scientifically. . . .

[Thanks to the Suez Canal] the Mediterranean has recovered all at once the importance that the discovery of the Cape of Good Hope had seized from it. At the same time, the general commerce of the world has again taken up its traditional route. East Africa, from the Red Sea to Madagascar, has suddenly been drawn closer to Europe and placed in immediate contact with civilization. . . . Today the other coast of Africa is a few weeks from Marseille, two steps from Alexandria. . . .

Compared to these considerable undertakings, the works of French exploration seem a small thing, and yet, how extensive and varied they are! . . .

We come now to 1889. . . . The French Committee for Africa was founded; the administration of the colonies was directed by a spirit at once practical and vigorous; diplomats lay hold of their often neglected interests; French traders banded together; the flower of our youth, and above all, of our military youth, offered themselves, a smile on their lips; it was not just the native auxiliaries who contributed their discipline, their endurance, their indefatigable courage. . . . The definitive joining of all our continental colonies by a system of simultaneous exploration was decided upon.

Binger left from Senegal and, crossing the country of the Kong, arrived at the Ivory Coast, after having fallen in with Treich-Laplene. . . . Monteil, leaving from Saint-Louis, penetrated the Niger basin and traversed its entire length, reaching Sokoto, Bornu, and Lake Chad. From there he returned to France by way of Tripoli, accomplishing in the desert the most complete and daring trip that had been achieved up to that time.

Mizon went up the Benue [River] and again plunged deeply into Adamawa. After vicissitudes without number he

rejoined Brazza himself, whose brilliant campaign on the Sanga [River] was not only an exploration but a veritable taking of possession. . . .

And ever since then, there has been a constant new assault against the African sphinx, from which daily is wrenched another of its mysteries. . . .

In short, the end is attained. The symbolic event of this combined march was the meeting of Mizon and Brazza on leaving Adamawa, the one coming from the Niger and the other from the Congo; departing from such distant points, they connected with each other without a precise, prearranged meeting place, carried along, so to speak, by the common purpose that drew the one to the other.

Thus a thin ribbon of routes has tied together across the continent, the French colonies that had been separated by chance exploration and occupation. . . .

The merit of our explorers is enhanced still further by the methods employed. They were unusually peaceful, gentle to the natives, tolerant of ignorance, prejudice, and hostile dispositions. . . .

The savage campaigns of the navigators of the sixteenth century, the thirst for gold, the hunting of the Negroes, all the passions and all the violences excited by a cupidity without bridle and without future, have only produced ruin and devastation throughout.

The poor inferior races; do they merit such harsh treatment?

The modern explorers have judged otherwise. In the second half of the nineteenth century their achievement has been ennobled by its peaceful glory. It has at the same time placed the fundamentals of modern African politics on the firm bases of peace, humanity, and unselfishness.

But only useless trails, hastily covered over again with brush, would have been left on the face of the black continent if national expansion and political sanctions had not supported the efforts of the explorers and stamped Africa with the European imprint par excellence—

organization.

"Exploration has prepared the way for the partition of Africa": arms and diplomacy have achieved it.

"NAPOLEON OF THE SUDAN"

Samori Touré, who created the Mandingo empire and opposed French colonialism for many years, was born in the 1830's in what is now southwestern Guinea. At that time the Mandingos were divided into many warring states; some were populated by animists; others had a distinctly Muslim culture. As a youth Samori was probably a pagan and a trader, but he soon gained renown as a warrior. By about 1870 he had become a Muslim and had assumed the title of almami, *or leader of the faithful. He had also begun his conquest of the Mandingo chieftaincies. Within sixteen years his empire became one of the largest political units in the western Sudan, covering 115,000 square miles. It was bounded by the Tukolor empire in the northwest, the state of Futa Jallon in the west, the kingdom of Sikasso in the east, and the forest fringes of Liberia and Sierra Leone to the south. By this time, however, Samori had also begun to clash with French colonial aspirations. Forced to retreat between 1894 and 1898, he moved his empire eastward, but to no avail. The French captured him and overran his state. The following analysis of Samori's achievements is by the French scholar Yves Person, chairman of the history department at Dakar University.*

Without doubt, Samori Turé is one of the most impressive figures of pre-colonial Africa. He is one on whom the young nationalists of post-colonial Africa have placed great stress. To protect his great achievement—the African empire he had built up in the years from 1870 to 1887—Samori fought the French with skill and determination for fifteen years. However, the efforts Samori had to make in seeking to halt French military imperialism were so great that they led to the dissolution of his empire. . . .

Beginning in 1878, Samori organized the conquered territories of the north into military governments. The empire was thus divided into large regions which were occupied and governed by autonomous armies supported by tribute payments. There were never more than five of these autonomous territories and they were all located on the perimeter of the empire. . . .

The entire empire rested on the shoulders of one man who had proved himself by his exceptional ability and who never ceased to reiterate that God had clearly designated him to secure order in the human world. Following the animistic tradition, Samori surrounded himself with a group of friends and relatives. This assembly finally became institutionalized as a council whose decisions Samori always seemed to accept even when he did not completely agree with them. What was remarkable and rather revolutionary was that the council members soon took on specialized tasks resembling ministerial functions—the secretariat, the treasury, justice, religion, and relations with the Europeans. The nonspecialists acted as inspectors and oversaw the various regional governments. . . .

Although Samori's return to the religion of his ancestors has never been questioned, it must be recalled that he started his career by defending his animist "uncles" against the Muslims. But beyond the territorial limits of this loyalty, Samori had fraternized with the Muslim inhabitants of the commercial centers. When he stated that "a woman alone should be able to travel as far as Kempu" (Freetown), he was indicating the kind of order that he intended to establish. Finding this most attractive to their way of life, all the *dyula* [Muslim Mandingo traders] from the traveling salesmen to the big merchants pledged him their loyalty and even served him as spies and propaganda agents.

The empire was thus dependent upon the massive loyalty of the traders to the imperial organization and upon a strong sense of personal loyalty to Samori which was inspired by his exceptional personality. . . . Fearing that the empire would crumble after his death, Samori sought a unifying force capable of cementing together the disparate elements he had assembled through military strength. It was only natural that he would turn toward Islam, because in it he saw the only available culture of any worth and the only available system of universal values. This former trader seems to have been most influenced both by his rivals, the Tukolor, and by his friends of Futa Dyalon, whose frontier he had reached in 1878. . . .

From 1889 on, the ravaged empire was reconstructed on the basis of personal loyalty to Samori, and all efforts were united in the common cause of war against the French. . . .

Until 1881, during the time that his expansion to the north was advancing smoothly, Samori does not seem to have paid much attention to the European menace. He and the dyula tradesmen viewed the Europeans as a not very populous race of educated people who lived on small islands in the middle of the ocean and whose sole business was trade with the African coast. Similarly, the French in Senegal and the British in Sierra Leone, although they had heard vague reports about the conqueror, paid little attention to him.

In 1878 the French began consciously to occupy West Africa. It was their plan to advance from the upper Senegal River to Bamako on the Niger River. Thus they would pass through the Tukolor empire. Samori, who lacked the prestige of al-hajj Omar, the former leader of the Tukolor, and who seemed to be active far to the south of their planned area of penetration, apparently did not worry the new conquerors. . . .

Because the French had to have peace on the Niger, they lost their desired initiative against Samori.

[In March, 1886, Samori signed the treaty of Kényèba-Kura with the French. The agreement] was more concerned with peace and commerce than with the establishment of a French Protectorate. This pleased Samori, especially since he was then able to reopen trade in horses and firearms with the territory under French control. Although he had to forgo all rights to the lands north of the Niger and Tenkiso rivers, the Burè and the Manding in Kangaba were included on the condition that he would station no troops there. Samori showed his confidence in his new allies by entrusting to them his favorite son, Dyaulé-Karamogho. . . .

The treaty had raised a great cry in Paris. . . . [The] terms for peace were considered too lenient by the colonial party. The Ministry of Foreign Affairs demanded nothing less than a Protectorate which would both integrate Samori's lands into the French system and demonstrate to other nations the extent of France's hegemony in Africa. . . .

Samori did not expect any help from new allies, but he did expect the French to observe a benevolent neutrality . . . .

When Samori protested against frontier incidents, he was so sharply rebuffed that he believed he had no choice but to cede all the left bank of the Niger in order to gain time, not realizing that this would cut him off from Sierra Leone. Samori, therefore, signed the Treaty of Nyako on 21 February 1889, and Archinard made arrangements to meet him at Siguiri for formal ratification of the alliance. . . .

Then, in May 1889, Samori denounced the treaty and sent it back to Siguiri. This reversal ruined Archinard's dream of hemming in Sierra Leone and expanding along the Niger. . . .

Colonial historiography has helped to spread the legend that the rupture between Samori and the French began with the rejection of the Treaty of Nyako in 1889. This is not so. The Almami considered that his alliance with the French which dated from the Treaty of Kényèba-Kura in 1886 was still in effect, and a serious study of the events on the frontiers proves that civil, if not cordial, relations reigned until 1891 between the commanders of the French and Samorian forces. . . .

During 1896 Samori showed a strange lack of energy. It is evident that he was looking for a temporary solution and ways to prolong his respite and that he had given up the grand designs of the dyula revolution [by which is meant his Islamization of the Mandingo Empire]. This revolution was of no concern to the Senufo and other Voltaic people who now populated his new domains. Therefore, he was content to exact tribute to support his army. The army had been greatly reduced in size . . . but it had retained its cache of modern arms and the number of soldiers who had been trained in the European style grew every day.

Having been driven back again into the thick forest of the Dan mountains, Samori was surprised, on 29 September [1898] at Géulè (Guelémou) by French reconnaissance troops. These troops had crossed the devasted zone in the west while the Almami had been waiting for an attack from Touba. Thus Samori finally fell into enemy hands. Realizing that his position was hopeless Samori had earlier offered to give himself up on condition that he could live at Sanankoro as a private person. But his actual capture made French concessions unnecessary.

Because he had been deprived of capturing Samori, Trentinian was very harsh toward him. He solemnly notified the Almami at Kayes on 22 December that he would be deported to Gabon. The old man, believing that his earlier negotiations were still valid, felt that he had been tricked and attempted to commit suicide before embarking from Saint-Louis. Samori died of bronchial pneumonia on 2 June 1900, on the small island of Ndjolé in the middle of the Ogooué River in Gabon.

To his adversaries and the writers of colonial history, Samori was, despite his courage and loyalty, a slave merchant and a bloody tyrant—the very personification of evil. To young African leaders, he became one of the great heroes of the anticolonial struggle.

Neither of these two visions of the man is entirely accurate, but the second is closer to reality. Samori was essentially a man of battle and the builder of a state. His work answered the needs of a society in the midst of grave crisis. Events forced him to place himself in the path of the French colonizers. He then wasted most of his ability and strength in the continuous battle against them, even though that had not been his original purpose in assuming power. In fact, from the day on which his struggle against the French absorbed most of his time, the positive aspects of his work began to degenerate.

As a son of the Konyan, his first desire had been to save his own animistic society by regenerating it so that he could undertake the risks of the dyula revolution. But this was possible only through military means, and he soon began to make use of his tactical abilities and strategic genius, both of which were praised by the French. His superiority was manifested in 1885 in his struggle with Combes, and he was only deprived of the ultimate victory by the crushing technical superiority of his adversaries. The same tactical ability is seen in his politics. His policy was to accomplish his objectives through negotiation—not to use force unless all other means failed—but once compelled, he fought with the greatest obstinacy. . . .

It is clear that the action of Samori, in spite of its revolutionary aspect, belonged to the traditions of his society. His conservatism, however, surprises us—for example, his scrupulous respect for the established local chiefs and other notables. It is, therefore, quite difficult to see him as the forerunner of modern nationalism. On the other hand, it is evident that his uprooting and moving of large populations might have been, without his realizing it, the prelude to the upheavals of the colonial era.

His work was condemned to failure because, in spite of all his energy and clairvoyance, he could not make up for his people's technical backwardness.

"Invincible" Algiers falls to the French in 1830, a prelude to Europe's partition of Africa.

TIDE
OF
CONQUEST

A romanticized rendering of English and African partnership, following the Congress of Vienna's condemnation of the slave trade in 1815

In 1839, off Cuba, fifty-two African slaves, led by Cinquè (above), mutinied aboard the Amistad. *The vessel reached the shores of Long Island, where the Africans, who had been illegally captured and sold to Cuban planters, won their freedom.*

NEW HAVEN COLONY HISTORICAL SOCIETY

THE END OF SLAVERY

The eighteenth century—Europe's self-proclaimed age of enlightenment—was also the heyday of the Atlantic slave trade. European nations themselves had little use for slaves, but their Caribbean possessions absorbed all the Africans who had survived the rigors of the middle passage. Under the whip they raised the sugar cane, tobacco, and cotton; these were sold in Europe, providing huge profits for a burgeoning class of colonial tycoons. However, as the new century approached, political and economic interests began to turn slowly but irrevocably toward abolition. The revolutionary egalitarianism emanating from France sparked Negro and mulatto uprisings in the French colony of Saint Domingue, which in 1804 became the independent black-ruled Republic of Haiti. In England, where the first signs of the Industrial Revolution were manifesting themselves, the economy was becoming less dependent on the importation of "king sugar" and more reliant on the exportation of manufactured goods. At the same time, amid a gathering tide of humanitarian liberalism, abolitionists were growing more vocal on both sides of the Atlantic. Sierra Leone and Liberia were founded in 1787 and 1822, respectively, as havens for free Negroes. In 1792 Denmark outlawed the slave trade, the first nation to do so. Britain followed suit in 1807, and for the next half century it maintained a naval force in West African waters to discourage the trade. Parliament banned slavery in 1833, but it would take the United States another thirty years and a civil war before its slaves would be emancipated. In Cuba and Brazil most of the enslaved would not win freedom until the 1880's.

The plight of human bondage is shown on the plaque of an English emancipation society.

JOSIAH WEDGWOOD AND SONS

In 1791, having failed to win from the French assembly civil rights and freedom for Haiti's blacks and mulattos, patriot Vincent Ogé returned home, as depicted in the print at right. He led an abortive rebellion and was executed for treason. Resistance leader Toussaint L'Ouverture (below) unified Haiti and improved life on the island before he was imprisoned by the French in 1802.

Below, American-born black president's mansion in Monrovia, Liberia, about 1840.

Although Africa's white explorers made extravagant claims regarding their exploits, they surmounted many genuine physical dangers, as above.

THE EXPLORERS

"The map of the interior regions [of Africa] is still a great white spot on which the geographer . . . has traced out with an uncertain hand a few names of unexplored rivers and doubtful nations." So wrote the founders of the African Association, established by a group of Englishmen in 1788, primarily to open up Africa's uncharted waterways. The main impetus behind the first phase of exploration, which dealt mostly with West Africa, was a well-meaning desire to discourage the slave trade through the introduction of "legitimate commerce" and Christianity. But by the 1850's disinterested probing had given way to exploitation. Most expeditions were now government financed. With the help of African guides, white explorers were "discovering" the natural wonders long known to Africans and were renaming them after European dignitaries and sites. David Livingstone, who went to South Africa in 1841 as a missionary, was blazing a trail across the continent as "Her Majesty's Consul for Inner and Undiscovered Africa." Like many of his fellow discoverers, he was the conscious agent of a government bent on conquest through exploration.

A resolute Henry M. Stanley poses with his solemn, young gunbearer.

Dixon Denham, explorer of the central Sudan, pursues a giraffe.

John Speke, who "found" the Nile's source, runs from some Somali.

David Livingstone is shown here reading the Bible to his guides. The engraving was done from details given by Stanley, who found the ailing missionary-doctor at Ujiji on Lake Tanganyika in 1871. At Murchison Falls (right), twenty-two miles east of Lake Albert, the Victoria Nile plummets over cleft rocks into a misty gorge. Samuel Baker named them in 1864 for Roderick Murchison, president of the Royal Geographical Society.

NO ROOM FOR THE AFRICANS

During the nineteenth century, when Muslim Africa was torn by jihads, largely against European dominators, the Bantu speakers were waging wars of resistance in southern Africa. For centuries the Bantu had been free to expand, notably in the fertile plains between the Drakensberg range and the Indian Ocean. After the 1770's their movements were impeded by the encroachment of Boers and English settlers. The Bantu fought back under great leaders such as Makana, Chaka, and Moshoeshoe, but in vain. By the mid-nineteenth century the white man was master. The discovery in 1867 of diamond deposits near what is now the city of Kimberley prompted the rise of a new class: a black proletariat, who were the virtual serfs of white industrialists. In 1891 a Lagos editor lamented: "A forcible possession of our land has taken the place of a forcible possession of our persons."

This engraving, from an 1848 issue of the Illustrated London News, *shows a group of Boer Trekkers coaxing their wagon train through the mountain country of the Xhosa.*
Illustrated London News, 1848–MANSELL COLLECTION

Armed only with traditional weapons, Xhosa fighters, like the lance bearer above, were the first Bantu speakers to clash with the Boers and the British of the Cape Colony.

Under the Mahdi, Sudanese warriors, like the hero at right, defeated Anglo-Egyptian forces at Khartoum in 1885; enraged, the British crushed them at Omdurman in 1898.

The Zulu below are descendants of the fierce warriors who under Chaka's leadership forged the Zulu nation and controlled much of southern Africa until the 1880's.

Germany formally entered the Scramble at the Berlin West Africa Conference when Bismarck declared protectorates over four African territories: Togoland, Kamerun, South West Africa, and East Africa. Tanganyika (now Tanzania) was to be a resettlement area for the empire's surplus population, but, as elsewhere, the Germans had first to contend with native opposition. Not until they had defeated the

coastal Swahili did the task of holding this huge area become eased. Thereafter, the urban Swahili were brought into the colonial adminis-tration as policemen, clerks, translators, and soldiers, and made to function as the shock troops for Germany's penetration of the hinterland. In the painting above, by a Swahili artist, uniformed African mercenaries under white officers clash with ill-equipped inland people.

General Louis Faidherbe, architect of France's West African empire

African recruits, like the instructor and infantrymen below, swelled the ranks of the French colonial army. The Foreign Legion, several of whose veterans appear at left, was another vital arm of French imperialism.

Abd al-Kader, bedecked with honorary medals at right, led Algeria's indigenous population in a jihad against the "infidel" French. Proud even in defeat, he hands over his scimitar to the Duc d'Aumale, governor general of Algeria, in the print opposite.

THE GALLIC THRUST

France, anxious to restore its waning prestige, attacked Algiers in 1830. The city fell easily, but the Muslim Arabs and Berbers of the mountain fastnesses and desert fringes, who regarded the Christian French with hatred, rose in opposition. Under the leadership of Abd al-Kader, the son of a Muslim holy man, they waged a heroic war of resistance. By 1840 Al-Kader had molded the petty Berber chieftaincies of the Algerian interior into the most substantial polity the region had known for centuries. However, his empire soon conflicted with French dreams of glory. In 1847 he was forced to capitulate and was exiled to Syria. The Arab and Berber masses were a defeated people, whose land would be confiscated by the tens of thousands of European *colons* who flocked there. France tightened its grip on Senegal, which then comprised St. Louis, Gorée island, and several riverine posts. At the conclusion of Louis Faidherbe's governorship in 1865, France controlled most of the Senegal River, a springboard from which to build its West African empire.

Ethiopian Emperor Menelik II (left), who ruled from 1889 to 1913, was a reforming monarch, whose 1896 victory over the Italians at Adowa won him international respect. The Ethiopian painting opposite depicts scenes of this battle. Menelik's empress, who is popularly believed to have participated, carries a parasol as she rides on horseback into the fray. Saint George intercedes at top; in the center two Italians are emasculated.

Below, African scouts in English service set fire to an Asante village in the war of 1873–1874.

THE WHITE MAN'S GREED

Throughout the nineteenth century the white man's greed propelled him deeper and deeper into Africa. Much of the continent was deemed climatically unsuitable for European settlement, but the lure of its raw materials proved irresistible. Some nations, such as Italy, were drawn by a thirst for glory. In 1896, on the eve of the battle of Adowa, its premier sent a dispatch to General Baratieri in Ethiopia: "We are ready for any sacrifice in order to save the honor of the army and the prestige of the Monarch." Italy's sacrifice was indeed great, for it lost over 7,500 men, and stalwart Ethiopia retained its cherished independence.

445

DEFEAT
AND SUBMISSION

In 1892, after defining their respective zones of influence on the Gold and Ivory Coasts, France and Britain resumed their subjugation of the hinterland. That year the French finally occupied Abomey, and in 1898, after over sixteen years of guerilla opposition, they conquered Samori Touré's Mandingo empire. Meanwhile, the British were pursuing their drive against the Asante and preventing any alliance between their king, Prempeh, and Samori. In 1896 they occupied Kumasi, Prempeh's capital, humiliating and deporting him. Furthermore, in 1900 they demanded surrender of the Golden Stool, believed to contain the nation's spirit. This sacrilege provoked many months of warfare before England could make Asante a colony.

RADIO TIMES HULTON PICTURE LIBRARY

Above, King Prempeh and the queen mother submit to the British at Kumasi in 1896. Below, French troops prepare to exile Samori Touré, the proud man in the foreground. Opposite, Behanzin of Abomey sits for a royal portrait before his deportation in 1894.

H. ROGER VIOLLET

Chapter Eleven

UNDER COLONIAL RULE

(c. 1884–1957)

by

George Shepperson

FROM THE WEST AFRICAN CONFERENCE OF BERLIN of 1884–1885 to the independence of Ghana in 1957 the history of Africa is one of terrifying complexity. The former set the stage for the partition of the continent among the powers of Europe in little more than ten years; the latter touched off the emergence of the new, modern Africa of independent states, also largely within a decade. To employ the adjective "terrifying" in this colonial context is not merely to evoke a sensationally journalistic element that was never far from the surface throughout this intricate story; nor is it a confession of the historian's failure to cope with a diverse mass of detail that often defies analysis and generalization.

There was, to be sure, a genuine touch of terror about relations between white and black in Africa during this three quarters of a century. It revealed itself in the obvious horrors of the European presence in Africa, such as Joseph Conrad witnessed during his journey into the Belgian Congo in 1890 and which he was to transmute into the terrifying tale, *Heart of Darkness*. It was to be seen in atrocity and counteratrocity in the many conflicts between European and African, such as the Maji Maji Rising in southern Tanzania against the Germans in 1905, which resulted in the death of some one hundred twenty thousand Africans. But this terror manifested itself, above all, in the harnessing of almost the whole of Africa, through the hectic period of the so-called Scramble for Africa.

Indeed, the leitmotiv of much of the history of Africa in this three quarters of a century is war; not the localized, so-called tribal wars of old Africa, of which Europeans spoke so disparagingly and often inaccurately when they were flush with the confidence of the virtues of their own civilization, but major wars, mainly of European origin. Five such wars provided a challenge and evoked a response from

...nch officers survey a captured farmhouse, ruined during their "pacification" of Morocco about 1910.

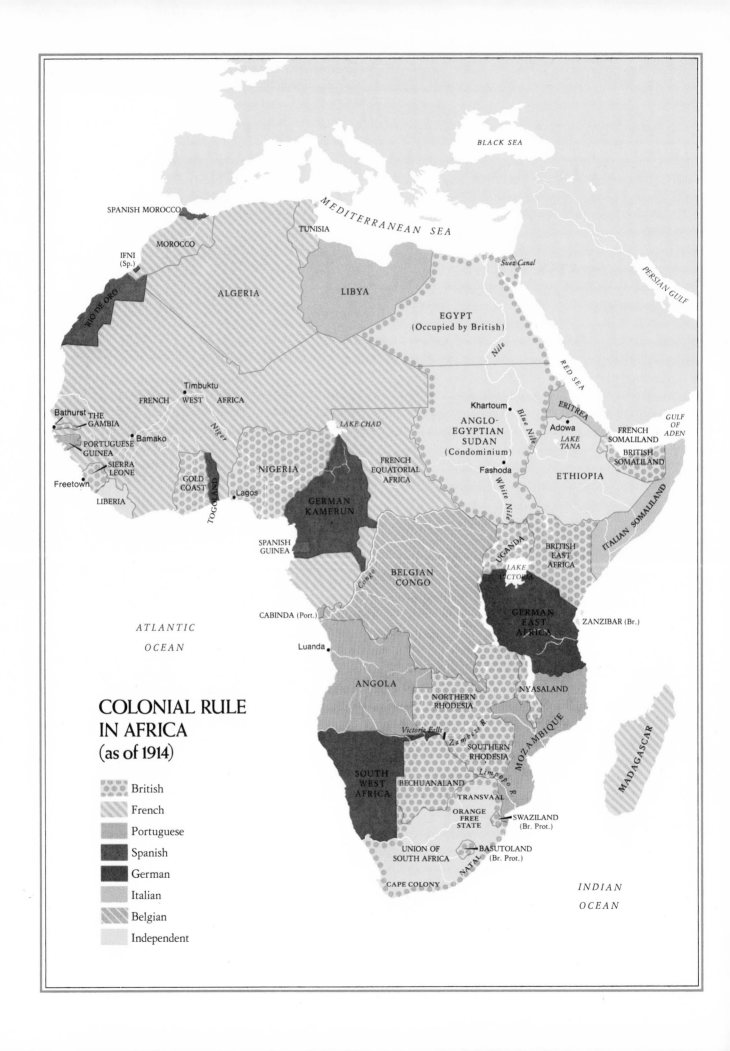

BLACK SEA

MEDITERRANEAN SEA

SPANISH MOROCCO

MOROCCO

TUNISIA

IFNI (Sp.)

RIO DE ORO

ALGERIA

LIBYA

EGYPT (Occupied by British)

Suez Canal

PERSIAN GULF

Nile

RED SEA

FRENCH WEST AFRICA

Timbuktu

Bathurst

THE GAMBIA

Bamako

Niger

LAKE CHAD

Khartoum

Blue Nile

ERITREA

GULF OF ADEN

ANGLO-EGYPTIAN SUDAN (Condominium)

Adowa

LAKE TANA

FRENCH SOMALILAND

PORTUGUESE GUINEA

SIERRA LEONE

NIGERIA

FRENCH EQUATORIAL AFRICA

Fashoda

ETHIOPIA

BRITISH SOMALILAND

Freetown

GOLD COAST

TOGOLAND

Lagos

GERMAN KAMERUN

White Nile

LIBERIA

SPANISH GUINEA

UGANDA

BRITISH EAST AFRICA

ITALIAN SOMALILAND

BELGIAN CONGO

LAKE VICTORIA

CABINDA (Port.)

Congo

GERMAN EAST AFRICA

ZANZIBAR (Br.)

ATLANTIC OCEAN

Luanda

ANGOLA

NYASALAND

NORTHERN RHODESIA

COLONIAL RULE IN AFRICA (as of 1914)

Victoria Falls

Zambezi R.

SOUTHERN RHODESIA

MOZAMBIQUE

Limpopo R.

MADAGASCAR

SOUTH WEST AFRICA

BECHUANALAND

TRANSVAAL

SWAZILAND (Br. Prot.)

ORANGE FREE STATE

BASUTOLAND (Br. Prot.)

British

UNION OF SOUTH AFRICA

French

NATAL

Portuguese

CAPE COLONY

INDIAN OCEAN

Spanish

German

Italian

Belgian

Independent

the people of Africa, whether they came from the sophisticated Islamic societies of the north, from the subsistence economies of central Africa, or from the countries of southern Africa that had experienced European penetration from the fifteenth century onward. These wars were the Franco-Prussian War, 1870–1871 (although it precedes the period discussed in this chapter, it must be noted because its role in the rearrangement of the European state system in the late nineteenth century was an important factor behind the partition of Africa); the war between the British and the Boers in South Africa, 1899–1902; the First World War, 1914–1918; the Italian invasion of Ethiopia, 1935–1936; and the Second World War, 1939–1945. They span the period of the rise and decline of European power in Africa. They pose the perennial questions in an African context: Is war entirely destructive? Is there not also a constructive element in it? They provide a convenient periodization for the complex history of Africa in the age of European colonial rule.

When the architect of the modern German state, Chancellor Otto von Bismarck, declared, "My map of Africa lies in Europe," he indicated, in his circuitous manner, the background to the conference he convened at Berlin from November 15, 1884, to February 25, 1885, to decide the fate of Africa. This West African Conference of Berlin, at which fourteen European countries and the United States of America were represented, is commonly looked upon as the starting point of the Scramble for Africa (*The Times* newspaper of London, indeed, had popularized this phrase in a leading article only two months before the conference began). Yet its roots lay in the previous fifteen years of European history—in particular, in the war between France and Prussia that led to the loss by France of the region of Alsace-Lorraine and to the proclamation of the German empire at Versailles in 1871. A humiliated France faced a new Germany, powerful but not completely convinced of its security. In the decade and a half that followed, Bismarck, the master diplomat, wanted to divert France's ambitions from the recovery of its lost provinces. The best way of doing this was to involve France in rivalries with other European states for overseas territories, especially in Africa.

The old empires of Portugal and Britain and the emerging new empires of Italy and Belgium were, of necessity, involved in the attempt to keep the balance of power in Germany's hands. To political drives were harnessed powerful economic forces: the emergence of industrially based economies throughout Europe, which sought new markets, areas for capital investment, and sources of raw materials overseas. Africa was a convenient field into which this political and economic imbroglio of Europe could extend itself. Although Africa's interior by the 1880's had been charted in considerable outline by European explorers, those parts that were in doubt provided excellent sources of controversy for the powers of Europe, especially Germany, France, and Britain. The extension of European rivalries to another chessboard sometimes had the effect of dissipating them, but more often of exacerbating them. The countries and people of Africa were hardly consulted in the matter, although, as recent historical researches have demonstrated, political and economic forces inside Africa had much to do with deciding where the main thrusts of the powers of Europe into Africa should be directed.

In particular, British and French rivalry in northern Africa converged on Egypt and its hinterland, in the early 1880's under the tenuous rule of the Ottoman empire. The British intervention in and occupation of Egypt in 1881–1882 coincided with the start of the Mahdiyya in the Sudan. The Mahdiyya began with the proclamation by Muhammad Ahmad, son of a boat builder near Khartoum, that he was the Mahdi, the messiah of Islam, who would cast out socioreligious corruption and restore the faith in all its pristine purity. At the same time, but at the other end of Africa, Britain, defeated by rebellious Boers at Majuba Hill on February 27, 1881, was forced to give up its control over the Transvaal. At both ends of Africa, therefore, as well as on the west and east coasts, European rivalries, under the influence of local African problems, were reaching a point of no return.

Bismarck's convening of the Berlin Conference had, no doubt, more than enough of the characteristically Machiavellian motivations of the Iron Chancellor. But his ostensible motive—and that of the powers represented at the conference—was to prevent a European war, and this was serious enough. Much that happened around the conference table at Berlin and in backroom bargaining in those thirteen weeks in 1884–1885 undoubtedly made more certain the Scramble for African territory and concessions by the powers of Europe. It could be argued that it prevented a European war in the mid-1880's, but only at the expense of partitioning and Balkanizing Africa and, ultimately, of ensuring the emergence of a major European war.

It must also not be forgotten that the Berlin Conference indicated a growing American interest in Africa. Some historians would claim that the creation of the so-called conventional basin of the Congo (by which the relatively free sphere of trade was extended beyond the geographical Congo

Meeting at the Berlin residence of Chancellor Otto von Bismarck in 1884, the foreign ministers of fourteen European powers and the United States established ground rules for the future exploitation of the "dark continent." Africans were not invited or made privy to their decisions.
CULVER

Basin to include the east coast between the boundaries of what is now southern Somalia and northern Mozambique) owed something to the East African commercial interests of the United States. Its representatives at the conference, by their emphasis on America's interests on the East African coast, ensured that these factors would not be overlooked. But the American Senate, under isolationist influences, did not ratify the General Act, as the resultant treaty was known; and United States' interests in the partition of Africa and the subsequent erection of modern types of colonial administration took the unofficial but nonetheless frequently influential forms of trade and investment, especially in the minerals of southern Africa and the Congo.

It was, indeed, the personal empire of King Leopold II of Belgium that profited most notably from the Berlin Conference. Its General Act led to Leopold's recognition as sovereign head of the Congo Free State, although the checking of British and Portuguese expansion in West and East Africa, French gains in West Africa, and the triumph of Bismarckian diplomacy were also important results. The cunning and avaricious Belgian king took every advantage through his own tortuous brand of diplomacy of the requirements of the conference that claims to colonies and protectorates on any part of the African coast line should be formally notified to the other powers that took part in the Berlin Conference and that such claims must be backed by

an effective degree of authority. The calling at Brussels in 1890 of a second international conference on Africa to regularize and humanize the partition was used by Leopold to make a breach in the free-trade provisions of the Berlin Conference to the advantage of his Congo possession. By the mid-1890's the Congo Independent State, a vast area eighty times the size of Belgium, was a reality under the absentee regime of King Leopold.

The Congo Independent State included not only some of the most isolated, culturally traditional peoples of Africa but also the potentially rich rubber territory and wealthy copper country of Katanga. Others besides Leopold had their eyes on this fabulous region where for nearly forty years a Nyamwezi trader, Msiri, had been ruler, presiding from his capital at Bunkeya over a highly profitable commercial network that stretched from Luanda in the west to Zanzibar in the east.

Leopold's most powerful rival for the lordship of Katanga was Cecil Rhodes, the British mining magnate whose British South Africa Company had received a royal charter in 1889. Rhodes wanted Katanga as part of his mining empire in southern and central Africa; and he realized also that the area could be made into a main link in his dream of a "Cape-to-Cairo" corridor of British power, spanning the continent from south to north. Katanga at this time was an element in Rhodes' subsidization of British rule in Nyasa-

The Congo Free State, conceived as a "neutral" zone to be run by an international association in the interests of bringing science, civilization, and Christianity to the indigens, received the Berlin Conference's blessings. Belgium's King Leopold (left) soon took control, reaping fabulous personal profits through the sale of land and development rights. Scandalously little was reinvested in schools like that shown above.

land (modern Malawi), over which a British protectorate was defined and declared between 1891 and 1893. (It was known as British Central Africa between 1893 and 1907.) The territory, in Rhodes' opinion, could have become a useful link in a trade route from Katanga to the coast of East Africa. But the Belgian king outmaneuvered him; in 1891 one of Leopold's mercenaries shot Msiri, and the modern exploitation of Katanga's riches was started.

Seven years before, Leopold had been about to take into his service in the Congo the mystically minded British soldier of fortune Charles George Gordon, who had served the Ottoman empire between 1874 and 1880 in the Egyptian equatorial provinces and the Sudan. The rise of the Mahdiyya, however, had complicated British policy, particularly as a result of the rapid extension of Mahdist power in the Sudan during the next three years. Gordon was thus persuaded by the British government, which had made itself responsible for the administration of Egypt and its dependencies, to postpone his engagement with Leopold and to go out to Khartoum to evacuate the Turko-Egyptian garrisons that were threatened by Mahdist advances. A year later, on January 26, 1885, while Bismarck and the powers of Europe were attempting to settle the fate of Africa on paper in Berlin, the killing of Gordon by Mahdist forces in Khartoum demonstrated that the people directly involved were determined to have some say in Africa's future.

Shortly after the capture of Khartoum, the Mahdi died. Abdullahi, his general, followed him to power, and was known as the Khalifa, from the Arabic word meaning "successor." He established a strong secular administration that lasted thirteen years. Had the European partition of Africa not taken place, the government of the Mahdiyya in the Sudan, under the Khalifa's rule, might have continued much longer. But British fear of the threat to their strategic interests in Egypt brought an end to the Mahdiyya's rule. In 1896 an Anglo-Egyptian army under Lord Horatio Herbert Kitchener, the British commander, advanced into the Sudan, and in 1898 defeated the Mahdist forces at Omdurman. About twenty thousand Sudanese lost their lives.

Kitchener's services to the British empire in Africa did not end with the defeat of the Mahdiyya. He hastened two hundred miles to the south, with a large army, to the Sudanese city of Fashoda (now Kodok), where Commandant Jean-Baptiste Marchand had taken up a position with a force of French-African soldiers. France and Britain were poised on the brink of a war that seemed likely to be something much larger than a localized conflict in the Sudan. After several months the French gave way; and the so-called Fashoda incident of 1898 was solved in Britain's favor. The détente also signaled the closing of a protracted period of Anglo-French rivalry, especially in Uganda, where English

Despite steadfast opposition from Britain, the French completed the rebuilding and extension of the pharaonic canal across the hundred-mile Isthmus of Suez in 1869. The genius behind this feat of engineering and financing was Ferdinand de Lesseps (right), who in gaining the Egyptian viceroy's cooperation was insured a huge human labor force. But work went painfully slowly until 1864, when English and American protests against this new slavery embarrassed the French into devising steam-run machinery, including dredgers like those above.

Protestant and French Roman Catholic missionaries had been the chief protagonists, largely in Britain's favor. The British government's fear that the headwaters of the Nile would pass into foreign control and that this, in its turn, would jeopardize Britain's suzerainty over Egypt and the Suez Canal was, if only for a moment, greatly diminished.

The same could not be said at this time for the Italians, who two years earlier had received the most resounding defeat that any European power experienced in Africa during the Scramble. In 1896 Italy had seemed in a strong position vis-à-vis Ethiopia, an ancient Christian state that, in spite of a distinctly centralizing process, from the middle of the nineteenth century onward suffered from the problems of maintaining control over a difficult terrain and from traditional border warfare with its African neighbors. To avenge a border defeat in 1887 by Ethiopian troops, the Mahdists invaded western Ethiopia, and in battle with them in 1889 the Ethiopian emperor Yohannes IV was killed.

Meanwhile, the Italians had been gaining: they held a substantial section of the Red Sea coast bordering on Ethiopia; and from 1886 had shared in the divisions of the sultan of Zanzibar's possessions on the mainland of East Africa by claiming a large portion of the Somali coast adjacent to eastern Ethiopia. Yohannes IV's successor, Menelik II, signed with the Italians on May 2, 1889, the Treaty of Wichale (Ucciali), by which he surrendered some of Ethio-

pia's northern territory; the area was organized the following year by the Italians as the colony of Eritrea.

Menelik believed that this was the last concession he would have to make to the Italians and that the treaty gave him international recognition. Italy, however, used its interpretation of the treaty to notify the other Berlin Conference participants that it claimed a protectorate over Ethiopia. Protesting to the European governments, Menelik abrogated the whole treaty in 1893. Italy invaded Ethiopia two years later in an attempt to compel Menelik to accept its protectorate. But by this time he had strengthened Ethiopian political unity and had managed to acquire a larger number of firearms. At Adowa, on March 1, 1896, an Ethiopian army of over 80,000 men, outnumbering the Italian forces by about four to one, inflicted a heavy defeat on them: about 6,000 dead, 1,500 wounded, and 3,000 prisoners of war.

Italy was forced to admit that the Treaty of Wichale was void and that Ethiopia was a sovereign and independent state. This gave Menelik the opportunity to return to his mission of extending the boundaries of his kingdom to the south—enlarging them to such an extent that it has been said that he, too, was a participant in the Scramble for Africa. As one of the first occasions in modern times when a non-European army had inflicted a major defeat on a European-led force, the Ethiopian victory also gave heart to Africans all over the continent at a moment when so many of them were losing their ancestral lands and prestige to the might of the white man.

The victory at Adowa in 1896 became an element in what many whites toward the end of the nineteenth century were coming to call "Ethiopianism," by which they meant the Africans' political and religious reaction to European conquest, anticipating pan-Africanism. Many white men at this time, particularly in southern Africa, were fearful that a "Black Peril" would sweep them out of the continent. They believed that this challenge to their supremacy was manifesting itself, to begin with, in the reorganization of African churches, which were breaking away from European tutelage and putting themselves under independent African control. These bodies often called themselves Ethiopian churches, not because they claimed any affiliation with the ancient Coptic Christian Church of Ethiopia but because, in the King James version of the Bible, Black Africa, following the Greek, was called Ethiopia.

The first so-called Ethiopian Church was established in South Africa by black separatist Wesleyans four years before the battle at Adowa. After 1896, therefore, the "Ethiopianism" of the often politically conscious separatist Churches in southern Africa could take pride in the successful militancy of the territorial Ethiopians as well as in their own "Ethiopian" religious self-assertion. The white men, for their part, feared that the day of white domination was coming to an end. Even before the Scramble for Africa drew to a close and Europeans got ready to consolidate and administer their hastily acquired possessions, both the proto-nationalism of the Ethiopian Church leaders and the real nationalism, bloodied in battle, of Menelik and his followers were forces to be reckoned with. Within little more than half a century they would grow into a movement that would oust Europeans from the political control of the greater part of Africa.

But to this trend there was one great exception, the other nationalism that was growing in southern Africa, the nationalism of the Afrikaners, or as the British and others called them, the Boers. The defeat of the British at Majuba Hill in 1881 did not stop what seemed to the Afrikaners to be a relentless determination on the part of Great Britain to drive on until it had swallowed up the whole of South Africa. The Afrikaners' isolated, agrarian way of life, bolstered by a devout, if often too rigidly inspired, biblical culture, was at odds with the cosmopolitan capitalism that the discovery of gold in the Witwatersrand in 1886 had encouraged in the Boer's South African Republic (as the Transvaal was then called). The British were in an ideal position to profit from these discoveries. Unlike the Boers, they were a people who were accustomed to the intricacies and intrigues of international capitalism; and in the person of Cecil Rhodes they had a financier and a leader who had the capital, knowledge, ruthlessness, and luck to take every advantage of the gold strikes in the southern Transvaal.

Also bolstering the position of British adventurers and speculators in the Transvaal was the establishment, the previous year, of a British protectorate over Bechuanaland (modern Botswana). Lord Salisbury, the British prime minister, had grabbed this arid territory between German South West Africa and the Transvaal in order to gain access not only to the Boer Republic but also to the territories to the north, where many, including Rhodes, believed that a second Witwatersrand, ripe for plundering, was to be found.

Rhodes' British South Africa Company in 1890 pushed its pioneer column of white settlers into the lands north of the Limpopo River. Within six years Rhodesia was created. The great Ndebele chief, Lobengula, died after the defeat of his army in 1893. The Ndebele and the Mashona, angry at the loss of their lands and cattle to the victorious white settlers, made a last effort at resistance in 1896, but gave way to superior fire power.

To many Afrikaners in the Transvaal it must have seemed that Rhodes and his English-speaking followers were all around them, particularly when, from 1890 to 1896, he became the prime minister of the Cape Colony. Rhodes' ideal of a union of all white men south of the Zambezi did not appeal to the majority of the Boers who, although they had ingrained ideas of white supremacy, preferred to live there on their own terms. The Boer president of the South African Republic, Paulus Kruger, and his people angered British immigrants into the Transvaal by taxing them heavily and by making it difficult for them to get the vote.

Rhodes was incensed. With the foreknowledge of the imperialist-minded British Colonial Secretary Joseph Chamberlain and other powerful figures in Britain and South Africa, he supported a sudden invasion of the Transvaal from Bechuanaland in 1895 under the leadership of his lieutenant, Dr. Leander Starr Jameson. The Jameson Raid was a fiasco, easily stopped by the Boers. Rhodes fell from power in the Cape Colony, and while the Fashoda incident was in progress in 1898 far to the north, Britain and the Boers stood at the brink of war.

By 1898, however, the Scramble for the greater part of Africa was largely complete. The French had taken the lion's share of territory, particularly in the north, the Sahara

BROWN BROTHERS

Paulus Kruger (right) devoted his life to the cause of Afrikaner resistance. Elected president of the South African Republic in 1883, he led his state inexorably toward the Boer War, which began in October, 1899. Initial Afrikaner successes were reversed within two months, when British reinforcements landed. Despite the stubborn defense waged by the Boer commandos (at left), Kruger's capital at Pretoria fell the following June. A peace accord was signed in May, 1902.

CULVER

regions, and West Africa. In 1894 Timbuktu fell to them, and in 1896 Say (in the western portion of the modern Niger Republic). And, two years later, their advance down the Niger succeeded in defeating and exiling Samori, the Muslim Mandingo leader whose determined resistance to the French had made him the hero of many African peoples in the huge area between the basin of the Upper Volta and the Niger sources. But Britain was not without compensations in West Africa. Sir George Goldie's Royal Niger Company, which was chartered in 1885, helped to push British power into the Nigerian hinterland; and from its existing coastal possessions, especially in the northward thrust against the Asante of the Gold Coast, Great Britain extended an already sizable empire.

Germany, meanwhile, taking advantage of the bargaining positions obtained by Bismarck, emerged from the Scramble with a sizable empire. It spread-eagled across Africa, from Togo and Kamerun in West Africa, through the extensive possessions of German South West Africa (which, by its closeness to the Transvaal and the obvious sympathy of the Germans to Afrikaner nationalism, was a constant source of worry to the British at this time) to German East Africa. German East Africa's common borders with what later became the British colonies of Kenya and Uganda were defined in a series of agreements in 1890. By this same treaty British claims to Zanzibar were also recognized. A year later Britain and Portugal agreed on their Nyasaland and Rhodesian borders; and Portugal, in spite of evident internal weaknesses, succeeded in maintaining

its claim to substantial segments of the vast territories in western and eastern Africa, which, with little effective government in the hinterland, it had insisted on calling its own for three centuries.

It seems hardly accidental, then, that in 1898, at this final stage of the European partition, the Anglo-French writer Hilaire Belloc published *The Modern Traveller*, a satire on the Scramble, a kind of epic poem in reverse, in a sequence of caustic couplets of which the best known are those famous lines that sum up both the confidence and the basic insecurity of the Scramblers:

Whatever happens we have got
The Maxim Gun, and they have not.

The limitations of the Maxim Gun, however, had been demonstrated in the Jameson Raid. A semiautomatic weapon that could create havoc amongst the close formations of Ndebele warriors, and whose praises could be sung by the English officer Frederick Lugard for the "moral effect" of its "long-distance shooting" and its "apparent ubiquity" in the conquest of Uganda, had proved ineffective against the Afrikaners. These skillful sharpshooters did not offer the same kind of target, for they fought a largely guerilla resistance, utilizing every nook and cranny of the land in which they were born. It was this dogged nationalism, harnessed to an almost inborn skill with horse and rifle, that enabled them to stand against the might of the British empire in the Boer War of 1899-1902. The consequences of this war for Africa were profound.

The conflict was precipitated by the deliberate attempts

of Sir Alfred Milner, the British high commissioner in South Africa, to incite the South African Republic to war. The Transvaalers were supported by their fellow Afrikaners in the Orange Free State. Indeed, modern Afrikaner nationalism was consolidated in the fight against Britain. The protracted war led to British reprisals against the Boers, particularly the burning of their farms and the herding of their women and children into concentration camps. The Boers surrendered their independence in the Peace of Vereeniging of May 31, 1902. But, in an attempt to conciliate them, the British bestowed on the Afrikaners in the Transvaal and the Orange Free State the right to decide whether or not the vote should be given to the indigenous Africans. In accordance with their white supremacist traditions, the Boers decided in the negative; and an opportunity was lost to bring about peaceful political change among the nonwhites of South Africa. This British compromise with Boer attitudes continued, helped by former Afrikaner leaders such as Jan Christiaan Smuts and Louis Botha, who were prepared to meet the British more than halfway in order to preserve essential Boer interests. When the four South African provinces united in 1910, it was clear that the block to African political advancement, which had been established at Vereeniging, was to be maintained and, indeed, extended. The Union Act of 1910, while preserving the franchise for qualified Africans at the Cape, ensured that they would have no political rights in the former Boer republics and in Natal. And it also stipulated that not even in the Cape, in spite of all its liberal traditions, should an African be able to stand for Parliament. The Afrikaners may have lost the Boer War on the battlefield, but like the Southerners of the Confederacy in America, they appear to have won it in the council chamber.

A further consequence of the Boer War was that it showed once again how African issues and European diplomacy intertwined and stretched almost to breaking point. This had been seen in an event that was a minor cause of the Boer War and a manifestation of acute tensions in Anglo-German relations: the dispatch of a telegram on June 3, 1896, from Kaiser Wilhelm of Germany to President Kruger congratulating him on his success in suppressing the Jameson Raid. Looking back on the Boer War, behind the scenes as well as at the overt pattern of assistance and sympathy that was given to the combatants, it is possible to see it as a kind of rehearsal for the First World War.

Out of the Boer War came the stimulus to the first important analysis of that imperialism of which the Scramble for Africa had been a leading but not an isolated example.

Jan Smuts, prime minister of South Africa, regarded the racial problem as an "intolerable burden" to be deferred for future solution.
BROWN BROTHERS

In the year of the Treaty of Vereeniging, the English author John A. Hobson produced his seminal work, *Imperialism: A Study*. Nikolai Lenin, the ideologist for many of the responses of today's Third World to European colonialism, acknowledged the importance of Hobson's book for his own influential *Imperialism: The Highest Stage of Capitalism* (1917). Hobson spent the summer and autumn of 1899 in South Africa, and he used his experiences and his meditations on them not only for a book entitled *The War in South Africa* (1900) but also for his masterpiece, *Imperialism*. Recent scholars have been critical of Hobson's economic interpretation of the Anglo-Boer conflict, but no student of the colonial age in Africa can afford to neglect it.

Many Africans could not avoid noticing that the Boer War was a major breach in white unity in Africa; but most of them were in no position to take advantage of this for the advancement of their own emerging nationalist movements. They could, however, draw from it conclusions that were often highly embarrassing for the colonial powers. As one African nationalist could later write: "We reason that if the British Government were so generous with the Dutch, will they not also see to it that we of British Africa have just peace and educational treatment, such as the good missionary pioneers assured us of and which we still confidently look for?"

This was the voice of an African who was prepared to reason with his colonial masters. And, to be sure, this was largely the spirit of the first pan-African conference at which thirty-one delegates, mainly from America and the

The French Foreign Legion, composed largely of European volunteers, was established in 1831 for the purpose of pacifying Algeria. With Saharan forts like that shown, it developed into a fierce instrument for the maintenance of order throughout France's restive African empire.

West Indies, met in London in July, 1900, to discuss the many problems that confronted men of African descent everywhere as the new century opened. One issue that concerned the delegates was the conflict that had broken out between 1896 and 1898 in Sierra Leone; there, the British, consolidating their rule and imposing relatively heavy taxes on African dwellings, stung many Africans into resistance. Their opposition was stamped out, often with brutality (the systematic razing of African villages was one method). And the delegates to the first pan-African conference protested to Queen Victoria against the treatment of nonwhites in South Africa and Rhodesia. Their feelings were summed up in an "Address to the Nations of the World" that was drafted by the Afro-American scholar W.E.B. Du Bois, in which he first made his famous prophetic statement: "The problem of the twentieth century is the problem of the color line."

Elsewhere in Africa, while the Boer War was being fought, the colonial powers were stamping out much of the old-style resistance to the imposition of their new order. In 1900 the French defeated and killed Rabih, an Arab soldier from the Sudan. He had conquered Bagirmi and much of eastern Bornu, where he had established a slave-raiding state and defied French power in West Africa. By this victory, which came after a long and fierce series of campaigns, the French united their West African and equatorial empires.

From 1898 to 1900, in bitter warfare, the British eradicated the last Asante resistance to their rule in the Gold Coast. And having halted by 1898 Banyoro attempts to stop their expansion in Uganda, they made the Uganda Agreement of 1900. As a not uncommon consequence of European rule in Africa, the settlement favored one group of Africans (in this instance, the Baganda) over another, thereby setting in motion a train of future difficulties for European and African alike. And, although the British had defeated the Mahdiyya in the Sudan, another Mahdi declared himself in British Somaliland in 1899. During the next two decades he would gain virtual control over much of greater Somalia. To the colonialists, he was the Mad Mullah; to his countrymen, he was Said Muhammad and a national hero.

By the end of the period of the Boer War, however, the development of modern communications and economies based on Western models in Europe's colonial possessions —a notable example was the Kenya-Uganda railway—presaged the end of much of the old African order, which had neither the resources nor the communications to match the accomplishments of new conquerors. Although Morocco and Tripolitania were independent at the start of the twentieth century, by the outbreak of World War I in 1914 most of Morocco had been swallowed up by France, with a small portion going to Spain, and Tripolitania passed under Italian domination. Only the Afro-American state of Liberia and proud Ethiopia remained independent.

The characteristic patterns of European colonial administration were established in Africa in the two decades before the First World War: Portuguese "assimilation"; German rational but ruthless "scientific" development; French attempts to create an African elite closely tied to the metropolitan culture; Belgian barefaced exploitation (at least until an international outcry against Leopold II's methods forced the Belgian nation in 1908 to assume direct responsibility for the Congo); and British pragmatism, drawing upon three centuries of British experience of ruling India, respecting—too often overpaternalistically—the local African cultures and their traditional rulers. The combination, and the conflict, of principle and expediency was best seen in Africa in the British method of indirect rule through traditional chiefs and potentates, of which the outstanding example was the fusion of northern and southern Nigeria in 1914 into a viable but volatile state under the watchful eye of its first governor general, the high priest of indirect rule, Sir Frederick Lugard.

Road, rails, reading, writing, modern medicine, technology, Christianity, and commerce pushed relentlessly into Africa in these years. On both sides of the Sahara many Africans were won over to the charms of the European way of life. It was, to be sure, essential for the colonial powers to win them over because they could not administer their vast territories without the assistance of literate Africans accustomed to the white man's ways and wishes. Nevertheless, many Africans remained unconvinced of the desirability of the new European order. The Maji Maji Rising in German East Africa in 1905 was an outstanding example of this. In German South West Africa the resistance of the Herero and other African peoples from 1904 to 1906 led to the destruction of the Herero in the course of German reprisals. In Angola in 1913 there were extensive risings against Portuguese rule. In the French island of Madagascar the Malagasy people continued their resistance to the rule of the French and their African allies. The last Zulu revolt against the white man in South Africa took place in 1906. A complex web of the resistance of Islamic peoples was spun across North Africa; this embarrassed France, Italy, and Spain. And, in the British-occupied countries of Egypt and the Sudan, the situation was by no means settled, as discontent matured during the First World War, and revolt against the British broke out in Egypt between 1919 and 1920. As if not to be outdone by men of darker skins, a group of pro-German Boers who had still not made their peace with Great Britain revolted in South Africa in 1913.

The First World War rearranged the formal pattern of European colonialism in Africa. Parts of Germany's Togoland and Kamerun were divided between Britain and France, and Germany's East African possessions were split between Britain (receiving Tanganyika) and Belgium (re-

Western education, with its potential for stirring discontent, was dispensed sparingly during the colonial era. Students, like those above attending Gordon Memorial College (founded in 1904 and the forerunner of the University of Khartoum), were being trained to serve their various European overlords. But many were also becoming nationalists, members of an elite who sought to borrow Western ideas and technology and apply them to an independent Africa.

ceiving Ruanda-Urundi). World War I also dragged thousands of Africans into a major international conflict against their own choice, dashing the hopes raised by the Berlin Act of 1885. The signatories had then agreed that in time of war among European powers the African territories would be neutralized and African people spared from the kind of modern conflict, of which there had been a foretaste in the Franco-Prussian War.

Although many Germans in East Africa feared that the coming of war into their colony would touch off another African revolt akin to the terrible Maji Maji Rising, the commander of their forces, General Paul von Lettow-Vorbeck, was determined to fight the British in order to embarrass their war effort in Europe. For four years, with remarkable skill, his army resisted combined British and West, East, and South African forces. And Lettow-Vorbeck himself was still fighting when the news of the German capitulation in Europe reached him in 1918. Throughout the East African campaign the armies relied largely on African porters for their communications, as motorized transport was not suited to the difficult terrain. Many of these porters, especially those from Nyasaland and Kenya, went through considerable hardships, and both they, and later their sons, became increasingly critical of the Europeans. The grievances of the African military carriers of the First World War, indeed, were an important factor in the subsequent emergence of African nationalism.

It was curious, however, that the dispersal of the larger part of the West's armies on the European continent between 1914 and 1918 was not made the occasion for a widespread intensification of African resistance to European rule. Certainly, in northern Africa, where an Islamic power, Turkey, was at war with Britain, France, and Italy, the opportunity was taken to embarrass them; particularly troublesome was the Sanusiyya brotherhood, which accepted Turkish support in its own nationalist drive to wrest Libya from the Italian colonial rule. But in tropical Africa resistance was the exception rather than the rule. Many Africans seemed stunned by the sight of fighting among white men, who had come into their countries under the banner of the Prince of Peace. As one Christian missionary witness put it: "They can't understand the war, and ask such questions as: 'Why have the Christian countries gone to war? Have the evil spirits got into the hearts of Kings?'"

In West and East Africa, apart from small disturbances—some of which were more the continuation of traditional grievances than a direct response to the war—the outstanding African militant reaction to it was the rising against the British in Nyasaland led by the pastor of an independent African Baptist Church, John Chilembwe, who had been educated in the United States at Virginia Theological Seminary in Lynchburg, Virginia. Even Chilembwe's rising in 1915 was as much, if not more, the result of grievances against harsh practices by Europeans, particularly planters, in Nyasaland as it was the consequence of the coming of the 1914 war; and it was put down quickly with few casualties on either side. Nevertheless, Chilembwe protested against the war in no uncertain terms: "Let the rich men, bankers, titled men, storekeepers, farmers and landlords go to war and get shot. Instead the poor Africans who have nothing to own in this present world, who in death leave only a long line of widows and orphans in utter want and distress are invited to die for a cause which is not theirs." Chilembwe's movement, moreover, represented something of a break with the traditional, tribal revolts against European rule in Africa; and it stands out not only as an indication of the disturbing effect of the 1914–1918 World War on Africans but also as a foretaste of the new type of African discontent. The point, indeed, was driven home in Norman Leys' *Kenya*, published in 1924. In one of the first important books to emerge from World War I, Leys predicted that nationalist movements would increasingly disturb the continent unless Europeans took the opportunity to reform their colonial rule and to live up to the promises implicit in their Christian and democratic ideologies.

The employment of African troops in European armies, whether as labor battalions, as with South Africa, or as combatants, as in the case of the French Senegalese soldiers,

opened the eyes of many Africans to the contradiction between European principle and practice. And many of the two hundred thousand Afro-American soldiers who fought in Europe during the First World War experienced similar disillusion. The ground, indeed, was being prepared for a pan-African approach to the problems of peoples of African descent everywhere.

Leadership was not lacking. There was the fiery Jamaican Marcus Garvey, who had taken his Universal Negro Improvement Association and African Communities League to the United States in 1916; the scholarly Afro-American W.E.B. Du Bois, who had played an important part in the first pan-African conference of 1900; and Blaise Diagne, Senegalese member of the French Chamber of Deputies in Paris, who was given special responsibility by the French during the World War for the recruitment of black soldiers. Diagne's position in France contrasted strikingly with the situation in British Africa, where it was unthinkable that a black man should become a member of a European legislative assembly.

When Du Bois was sent to Europe in 1919 by the National Association for the Advancement of Colored People of the United States to inquire into the grievances of black American troops, it was the influential Blaise Diagne who obtained permission for a second pan-African conference to be held that year in Paris. The congress continued, in the new circumstances of the postwar world, the criticisms of European colonial rule that had been launched by the 1900 conference. And although, like the earlier gathering, it did not ask for African political independence, it insisted that "the natives of Africa must have the right to participate in the Government as fast as their development permits." Du Bois later claimed that the 1919 congress influenced the League of Nations in its mandates system, by which the Allied Powers planned to parcel out the enemy colonial territories among themselves. However, a few other advanced thinkers hoped for a more fundamental approach to the African problem than the League's mandates system: nothing less than a descrambling of Africa. Du Bois favored the establishment of a genuine system of international trusteeships for African underdeveloped countries in which a part would also be played by peoples of African descent settled in other continents.

The following year Garvey's organization arranged in New York a massive thirty-one-day convention at which Marcus Garvey was elected Provisional President of Africa. It was a grandiloquent and unrealistic title; but it indicated his power over many disillusioned blacks in America (some of whom hoped to participate in Garvey's schemes for the settlement of "Negroes" from the New World in Africa). It reveals now, with the insights of recent historical research, that the influence of the Universal Negro Improvement Association, with its defiant assertion of black nationality and its unashamed adherence to black cultural virtues, was greater than has been commonly realized. The 1920 Garveyite convention issued a "Declaration of Rights of the Negro Peoples of the World." It was a moving appeal for a place in the sun for the black man; and it illustrates the attraction of Garveyism, with its perfervid belief in the "African personality," for men of African descent all over the world. It was not accidental that Kwame Nkrumah, the first president of an independent Ghana, declared that during his student period in the United States in the 1930's and 1940's the philosophy and opinions of Marcus Garvey influenced him more than anything else.

Both wings of the pan-African movement, the Garveyite and the Du Bois, suffered not only from factionalism and the feud between their leaders but also from the opposition of Blaise Diagne. In 1921 he refused to condemn French colonial policy, claiming that of all the powers France alone gave constitutional and social equality to its African citizens. With declining support but a nonetheless determined stance, Du Bois and Garvey continued their opposition to European imperialism in Africa in a sequence of Pan-African and Universal Negro Improvement Association conferences and other activities up until the eve of the Second World War.

By 1939, however, a new generation of African politicians indicated that the leadership of nationalism was moving firmly into the hands of native-born organizers and ideologists. But the acceleration of nationalism immediately after the First World War is even more remarkable. To be sure, this indigenous movement started well before the 1914–1918 war, as the life of the talented African bishop of the Niger Delta pastorate, James Johnson, illustrates. Johnson lived from 1836 to 1917, and his pro-African activities and attitudes anticipated much subsequent Africanism, although he was influenced entirely by a West African environment.

Another foretaste of Africanism was provided by the meetings of the National Congress of British West Africa in 1920, 1923, 1925, and 1929 at Accra, Freetown, Bathurst, and Lagos respectively. And, although French colonial administration imposed tight controls on political activities in its overseas possessions, African students in Paris developed a series of militant groups. In this they were often influenced by Marxist thought. The death in 1934 of the paternalist and pro-French Blaise Diagne and the emergence among French-speaking Africans of the pro-black philosophy and poetry of Negritude (a literary movement stressing the importance of black, African values) were also spurs to their growth.

In Kenya opposition to the white settlers' appropriation of land and to their oppressive labor policy led, as early as 1922, to the formation of the East African Association, under Kikuyu leadership. Jomo Kenyatta, who went to Britain in the 1930's to agitate on behalf of East Africans, especially the Kikuyu people, became involved in the association. He wrote that its members were driven underground, where they developed methods of conspiratorial organization: "Forbidden to hold meetings, the members divided into groups of three and four, kept in touch with each other secretly, and continued their work of protest and organization. The Africans of Kenya had their Maquis long before Hitler appeared on the European scene." These words display both the spirit and the techniques that a generation later continued in the so-called Mau Mau insurrection, which erupted in Kenya in 1951.

Similarly, the spirit that was displayed in the Egyptian revolt against the British in 1919 and 1920 forced from the colonial government a measure of independence for Egypt in 1922; and in 1936 the Anglo-Egyptian treaty stipulated that British troops were to be confined to the Suez Canal zone. All over Africa, under the stimulus of the economic depression of the 1930's and the democratic and counter-democratic currents then moving with increasing momentum around the world, organizations demanding social and economic justice and greater autonomy were springing up with a frequency often bewildering to all concerned, rulers and ruled.

In South Africa, despite—and, indeed, because of—the increasing restrictions placed on the movement and freedom of expression of nonwhites, attempts were made at political and economic organization. The South African Native National Congress, founded in 1912, was the first congress movement of its kind in Africa. And in 1919, under the leadership of a migrant worker from Nyasaland, Clements Kadalie, the Industrial and Commercial Workers Union of Africa was started. It grew to a membership of two hundred thousand; and by 1926 it had achieved a degree of militancy rare among African workers at that time. But white men in South Africa sprang to the defense of their own "supremacy" system. In 1934 Generals Jan Christiaan Smuts and James Hertzog formed the United Party, which was to remain in power until 1948. It was then superseded by the still more segregationist Afrikaner National Party, which legislated for outright apartheid. Yet the tendency toward apartheid in South Africa was apparent at least as early as 1936, when the United Party introduced the Natives Representation Act. This legislation swept away the limited multiracial democracy whereby qualified non-Europeans had been able to register as voters on the common roll with whites in the Cape Province. By the mid-1930's, therefore, the leadership of African political movements for greater independence and democracy was clearly passing from South Africa and was moving north. Meanwhile, men such as Nnamdi Azikiwe of Nigeria and Léopold Senghor of Senegal, who were to play leading parts in the securing of independence after the Second World War, were sharpening their wits for the struggle by obtaining an education overseas in Europe and America.

The mid-1930's were for African nationalists, at home and abroad, dark days. Ethiopia, the oldest independent African state, with its ancient history and Christian culture, was invaded and conquered by Italy, then under the brash and brutal Fascist order of Benito Mussolini. Even before the coming of the xenophobic leader, Italy had never been reconciled to its defeat at Adowa in 1896. But it was in no position to take revenge until its war with the Sanusiyya in Libya, which lasted from 1912 to 1931, was at an end. On the eve of the Italian invasion Ethiopia had just received its first modern constitution. The charter anticipated the increasing modernization of the country at the hands of its own people, assisted but not dominated by foreign advisers. Its architect was Haile Selassie (formerly Ras Taffari Makonnen), who had also brought Ethiopia into the League of Nations in 1923. He had shown his independent spirit when he denounced Britain and Italy before the League. Without consulting Ethiopia, the two powers had decided to support each other in plans to construct a dam at Lake Tana and a railway from Eritrea to Italian Somaliland. In 1928 Haile Selassie signed a treaty of friendship with Italy. It proved of no avail.

As early as 1933 the Italians had decided to conquer Ethiopia. An excuse for invasion was found in a border incident at Walwal in December, 1934; and on October 2, 1935, the Italian armies crossed into Ethiopian territory. The Ethiopians experienced the full onslaught of modern weapons, from aerial bombardment to the spraying of poisonous gas over soldiers and civilians alike. Haile Selassie appealed to the League of Nations for action against the Italians; and in a historic speech at its headquarters at Geneva on June 30, 1936, three months after the

decisive battle in which the Italians had defeated his army, he asked: "Are the States going to set up a terrible precedent of bowing before force?"

An Italian empire of Eritrea, Somaliland, and, finally, Ethiopia had been created, but nearly forty years after the Scramble for Africa and at a period when most other European powers were reforming their colonial policies and, on paper at least, looking forward to ultimate African independence. Winston S. Churchill, in the first volume of his history of *The Second World War*, commented trenchantly that Mussolini's Ethiopian adventure "belonged to those dark ages when white men felt themselves entitled to conquer yellow, brown, black or red men, and subjugate them by their superior strength and weapons." He went on to describe how Mussolini's show of force had deceived the British government, which might otherwise have stopped him: "Mussolini's bluff succeeded, and an important spectator [Adolph Hitler] drew far-reaching conclusions from the fact." The Second World War, it might be said, really began in Africa.

The Italian conquest of Ethiopia further undermined the confidence of countless Africans in the promises and practices of white men. In London an association called the International African Friends of Abyssinia was formed, the forerunner of the more widely based International African Service Bureau, which began in 1937; this, in turn, prepared the way for the Fifth Pan-African Congress, held in Manchester, England, in 1945. The Italian war on Ethiopia, indeed, brought together black men from many different countries and conditions in a fierce crescendo of criticism of white rule in Africa; it precipitated much of the spirit and some of the structure of the African nationalism that was to triumph after the Second World War. And in the destruction of Mussolini's short-lived empire in East Africa in 1941 not only Ethiopian guerrillas but also other African soldiers played their part.

In the three years before the outbreak of the Second World War, the European powers were recovering from the worst ravages of the economic depression of the 1930's. Their African possessions had suffered with them, especially in those territories in which a start had been made on the export of modern primary products. The mining of the potentially rich copper belt of Northern Rhodesia (now Zambia), which had got off to a splendid start in the early 1920's, and the valuable copper production of the Belgian Congo, were hit almost as drastically as those countries with subsistence economies and little export trade, such as Nyasaland and Tanganyika. Even in the more heavily capitalized white settler areas such as Algeria, Kenya, and Southern Rhodesia (which had voted in 1922 for responsible government under Britain, rather than for incorporation in the Union of South Africa) were hard hit.

The colonial governments could do little to remedy the situation until, on the eve of the Second World War and partly as a consequence of it, prosperity began to return to the metropolitan countries. In the interim, nationalism was sharpened not only among Africans but also among white settlers. Many Southern and Northern Rhodesians at this time were critical of the influence of the British South Africa Company over their economic life. A modest proposal by the French Popular Front government in 1936 to admit Algeria's Muslims to the political rights of French citizens was bitterly opposed by whites. And throughout British-ruled East and Central Africa European settlers fought for closer union between their territories in order to ensure white domination of them. Indeed, the beginnings of the ill-fated Federation of Rhodesia and Nyasaland (1953–1963) may be seen at a 1936 conference at Victoria Falls, when white representatives met to discuss the amalgamation of Southern and Northern Rhodesia.

It was paradoxical, but the outbreak of the Second World War united many black and white nationalists in Africa (if only for the duration of the campaigns) against Fascism, Nazism, and Japanese imperialism. The French in Africa, however, were divided between the supporters of the Vichy government and of General Charles de Gaulle's Free French Forces as France's metropolitan dissensions were exported to its African colonies. The black governor of Chad, Félix Eboué, unlike many white Frenchmen in Africa, supported the Free French Resistance to Germany. He became governor general of the whole of French Equatorial Africa, which by 1943 was in the Gaullist camp. Eventually, French West Africa and Madagascar also went over to the Gaullist side. But the squabbles, intrigues, and dissensions among white Frenchmen during the Second World War reduced their prestige in the eyes of their subjects all over Africa.

A similar process was at work elsewhere in Africa. Although the British had no Vichy-style problems, and many white British fought as comrades-in-arms with Africans in the African and Burmese campaigns, their prestige was also lowered, particularly when their African soldiers witnessed the force of Asian nationalism against their white masters. "General China," as one of the leaders of the insurgents during the Mau Mau emergency in Kenya in the 1950's called himself, is not untypical in dating his political awakening to his war service with the British army in Burma.

Decked out in pith helmet, pince-nez, umbrella, and briefcase, a tourist sets out to "discover" Uganda; Africans tote his valises.
LIBRARY OF CONGRESS

The process of disillusion and political awakening among Africans under colonialism, which the First World War had intensified and the Italian-Ethiopian conflict of 1935–1936 had further increased, was completed during the Second World War.

The generation of Africans who had benefitted from the educational policies of the Europeans, particularly of Britain and France, in the interwar years were anxious for political independence. The five years of the Second World War brought forward the date when this could become possible by weakening the colonial powers and by holding before the eyes of African nationalists and their followers a sequence of democratic promises, from the Atlantic Charter of 1941 to the Charter of the United Nations in 1945.

Unfortunately, the colonial powers had not extended education much beyond the relatively small circles of privileged Africans. Yet this, in its turn, was to sharpen the Africans' appetite for independence all over the continent, whether they had received European-style education or not. The nature of the education given to the subject peoples was different according to the nationality of the colonial power bestowing it. France, by its emphasis on metropolitan-style education, provided exclusively in French, aimed at the creation of an elite of black Frenchmen and produced in them a deep attachment to Parisian norms.

The division between French-speaking and English-

Matadi, typical of centers that grew under the aegis of foreign investments, is the main port of Congo (Kinshasa). Located about one hundred miles upriver from the Atlantic coast, Matadi is also a rail head; it handles a large percentage of the Congo's imports and exports, which are chiefly coffee, cacao, palm products, rice, cotton, copal, and minerals. Good facilities, such as warehouses and cranes, expedite its growing commercial operations.

speaking Africa, which had begun well before 1939, was not diminished during the Second World War. African independence was to come within little more than a decade and a half after the end of the war; but it was to be an independence that was to follow largely the state boundaries the European nations who partitioned Africa had scored across it and the European systems of values and loyalties.

Yet only a month after the surrender of the Japanese at the end of the war, the last pan-African conference to be held outside Africa was convened at Manchester, England, from October 15 to 19, 1945. There were over a hundred delegates, primarily from Africa and the Caribbean. They came predominantly from the English-speaking world; there were, apparently, no representatives from French-speaking Africa, although French translations of the main resolutions were provided. Whether this was the result of poor planning and finances in the immediate postwar situation, or of problems of communication, or of deeper political realities is a matter for research and speculation.

Du Bois, the doyen of pan-Africanism, was present at the 1945 congress; but its control and planning were in the hands of younger men—especially Kwame Nkrumah, Jomo Kenyatta, and George Padmore of Trinidad—most of whom were destined within the next two decades to play leading parts in bringing their countries to independence. The spirit of the conference was one of young men in a hurry, and it matched the mood of the ending of the war. It went further than previous congresses in demanding "for black Africa autonomy and independence"; it spoke out against "a false aristocracy and a discredited Imperialism"; and in its condemnation of "the rule of private wealth and industry for private profit alone," it came close to the concept of African socialism that was to be adopted by many political parties on the achievement of independence.

The 1945 Pan-African Congress was a symbol of the rapid and intense achievement of independence throughout most of colonial Africa. The following year eight hundred delegates from the colonies of French West Africa and French Equatorial Africa met at Bamako (located in what is today Mali) and formed the *Rassemblement Démocratique Africain.* Although it revealed and represented differences between French-speaking African leaders (especially Léopold Senghor of Senegal, Félix Houphouët-Boigny of the Ivory Coast, and Sékou Touré of Guinea) and asserted a characteristic attachment to French ideals, it manifested a growing spirit of impatience at the slow pace of political advancement in French Africa.

In 1946 the first modern political party was founded in Madagascar, with independence as its objective; the island was shaken by a violent rebellion, which, it has been claimed, took forty thousand Malagasy lives. Until the outbreak of the Mau Mau insurrection in Kenya in 1951, however, the course of independence in the British tropical African territories was relatively peaceful. Also in 1951, under social revolutionary pressures, tension mounted in Egypt, whose government abrogated the 1936 treaty with Britain, by which British troops were permitted to remain in the Suez Canal zone. On July 23, 1952, a group of young army officers, led by Colonel Abdel Nasser, seized power; and four years later he nationalized the Suez Canal, forcing Britain to withdraw its troops. Britain and France, assisted by newly formed Israel, attacked Egypt, but were compelled to withdraw under international pressure. The coup represented the destruction of the old imperialist pattern in Egypt and the beginning of the end of the European colonial epoch in northern Africa. In 1956 the Egyptians agreed to British proposals for the independence of the Sudan. It was the first formal break in the chain of British colonial power in Africa; and this was emphasized when the Sudan voted to become a republic and not to remain within the British Commonwealth of Nations.

The achievement of independence by the Gold Coast, together with the British Trust territory of Togoland under the name of the old African state of Ghana, in March, 1957, made a much greater impact on aspiring African nationalisms than did the achievement of self-government in the Sudan. In the leader of its Convention People's Party and its first prime minister, Kwame Nkrumah, it possessed a dramatic and dramatizing leader who passionately believed: "Freedom for the Gold Coast will be the fountain of inspiration from which other African colonial territories can draw when the time comes for them to strike for their freedom." That time was very close at hand. Throughout British, French, and Belgian Africa the ensuing transfer of power took place at a speed that rivaled the partition in the nineteenth century. As was often said at the time, the Scramble for Africa had become the Scram from Africa. Only white South Africa, Rhodesia, and the Portuguese colonies continued to confront the new Africa of the future with little visible change.

At the threshold of independence for the greater part of colonial Africa, the leaders and the led of the emerging new states could look back over three quarters of a century of European political domination and ask what it had all been worth. A similar question had been posed toward the end of the Scramble by the young Winston Churchill after his service with the British forces that defeated the Mahdiyya in the Sudan. Writing in his book *The River War* in 1899, Churchill questioned acutely the relation of means to ends in the imperialist process. Though he was convinced that progress had been made, he observed that it was achieved at great cost to both sides, the dominators and the dominated: "The inevitable gap between conquest and dominion becomes filled with the figures of the greedy trader, the inopportune missionary, the ambitious soldier, and the lying speculator, who disquiet the minds of the conquered and excite the sordid appetites of the conquerors. And as the eye of thought rests on these sinister features, it hardly seems possible for us to believe that any fair prospect is approached by so foul a path." Before he asked this mordant question, however, Churchill had indicated the less negative aims of imperialism, which, as he analyzed it, were: "To give peace to warring tribes, to administer justice where all was violence, to strike the chains off the slave, to draw richness from the soil, to plant the earliest seeds of commerce and learning, to increase in

whole peoples their capacities for pleasure and diminish their chances for pain." Churchill undoubtedly exaggerated here the underdevelopment of the complex and differentiated cultures of Africa on the eve of imperialism. Nevertheless, even the harshest critic of its role in Africa between 1885 and 1947 would find it difficult to deny that the European presence in Africa during this period had some advantages for the indigenous inhabitants.

Perhaps the colonialists' greatest service was the extension of scientific medicine in Africa, although this was counterbalanced, as a result of improvement in communications, by the spread of new diseases such as sleeping sickness and influenza, causing thousands of deaths. Europe left Africa Balkanized, with the pan-African dreams of political unity far from realization. It could be argued that Europe had reduced considerably the number of separate sovereignties in Africa, but at the expense of overriding old national boundaries and of splitting up once-complete cultures bound together by intimate ties of language, land, and religion.

Modern industry and the promises of an ever-developing science and technology had been thrust into an increasingly wider area of Africa, but, as in Europe, it was introduced with all the attendant disadvantages of a series of severe cultural shocks. And the colonial powers had introduced into their African possessions, often unconsciously and unintentionally, ideas of democracy, socialism, and nationalism that could be employed not only against Africa's own ancient and variegated ways of life but also against European control of the continent. Discontent was inevitable, whether in the form of the older, "tribal" types of reaction and resistance to the white man's rule or in the newer nationalist movements.

Indeed, as the British imperialist Frederick Lugard put it, speaking of the African peoples whom he and other European conquerors had uprooted from their ancient and well-tried ways of life: "Their very discontent is a measure of their progress." But progress, as in Europe where the concept originated, was purchased in Africa at a steep price. Well might Aimé Césaire, the poet of Negritude, cry out in 1939 when that supreme manifestation of the consequences of European progress, the Second World War, was imminent:

Eia pour ceux qui n'ont jamais rien inventé
pour ceux qui n'ont jamais rien exploré
pour ceux qui n'ont jamais rien dompté . . . .
("Hurrah for those who have never invented anything
for those who have never explored anything
for those who have never conquered anything . . . .")

AFRICA REAFFIRMED

Figures pounding manioc atop a Congo comb

MUSEE ROYAL DE L'AFRIQUE CENTRALE, TERVUREN, BELGIUM

NEGRITUDE DEFINED

It was a group of Paris-exiled poets who in the early nineteen thirties evolved the formal concept of Negritude, by which they sought to affirm the validity of their ancestral culture. These first exponents of Negritude came from many countries, but they shared a commonality of race, colonial experience, and the French language. Léopold Sédar Senghor, a Senegalese poet who was to become his country's president in 1960, was its chief theoretician and most militant communicant. As in the excerpt that immediately follows, he has argued that Negritude is not only a means toward revitalizing the arts but a key to the meaning of the black man's existence (others have defined Negritude in terms of a political instrument against colonial domination). Two of Senghor's poems are also given below. "Black Woman" symbolically relates to his motherland; "For Khalam" is a somber allusion to his strife-torn land. The khalam mentioned is a stringed instrument, the tama a small tam-tam, and the dyali a musician.

Negritude is the whole of the values of civilization—cultural, economic, social, political—which characterize the black peoples, more exactly, the Negro-African world. It is essentially *instinctive reason*, which pervades all these values. It is reason of the impressions, reason that is "seized." It is expressed by the emotions through an abandonment of self and a complete identification with the object; through the myth of the archetype of the collective soul, and the *myth primordial* accorded to the cosmos. In other terms, the sense of communion, the gift of imagination, the gift of rhythm—these are the traits of Negritude, that we find like an indelible seal on all the works and activities of the black man.

BLACK WOMAN

Nude woman, black woman,
Clothed in your color which is life, your
    form which is beauty!
I grew in your shadow, the sweetness of
    your hands bandaged my eyes,
And here in the heart of summer and of
    noon, I discover you, promised land
    from the height of a burnt mountain,
And your beauty strikes my heart, like
    the lightning of an eagle.

Nude woman, dark woman,
Ripe fruit of the dark flesh, somber
    ecstasies of black wine, mouth that
    causes my mouth to sing;
Savanna of pure horizons, savanna
    trembling under the fervent caresses
    of the East wind,
Carved tom-tom, tense tom-tom, grum-
    bling under the fingers of the con-
    queror,
Your low contralto voice is the song of
    the lover.

Nude woman, dark woman,
Oil unwrinkled by winds, oil smooth on
    athletes' thighs, on the thighs of the
    princes of Mali,
Gazelle with heavenly joints, the pearls
    are stars on the night of your skin,
Delightful play of the spirit, image of
    red gold on your flaming skin
In the shadow of your hair, my anguish
    is relieved by the nearby suns of
    your eyes.

Nude woman, black woman,
I sing your passing beauty, fixing your
    form in eternity
Before a jealous fate turns you to ashes
    to feed the roots of life.

FOR KHALAM

Is it surprising my dear if my melody has
    become somber
If I have laid aside the smooth reed for
    the *khalam* and *tama*
And the green smell of the ricefields for
    the grumbling of the drums?

Listen to the menace of the old men—
    diviners, cannonade of wrath of
    God.
Ah! perhaps tomorrow the crimson
    voice of your *dyali* will cease
    forever.
That is the reason my rhythm has grown
    so urgent my fingers bleed on my
    khalam.

Perhaps tomorrow my dear I shall fall on
    our unappeased soil
Full of regret for your setting eyes,
    and the drumming of the mortars
    through the mist, back home.
And in the dusk you will be full of regret
    for the burning voice that sang once
    of your dark beauty.

And we shall bathe my dear in an ambi-
    ence of Africa.
Furniture from Guinea and Congo,
    heavy and polished, somber and
    serene.
On the walls, pure primordial masks
    distant and yet present.
Stools of honor for hereditary guests, for
    the Princes of the High Lands.
Wild perfumes, thick mats of silence
Cushions of shade and leisure, the noise
    of a wellspring of peace.
Classic words. In the distance, antiph-
    onal singing like the cloths of the
    Sudan.

And then, friendly lamp, your kindness
   to soothe the obsession of this
   ambience
White black and red, oh red as the soil
   of Africa.

THE JOY OF BLACKNESS

Aimé Césaire, born on the island of Martinique in 1913, came to Paris as a student in 1928. Eleven years later he published what was to be his most famous poem, "Cahier d'un Retour au Pays Natal (Memorandum on My Martinique)." Césaire is considered the outstanding poet of the Negritude movement. "Cahier," from which this excerpt is taken, has been called by the French critic-poet André Breton the greatest lyrical monument of the twentieth century.

For beauty is Black
and wisdom Black
for endurance is Black
and courage Black
for patience is Black
and irony Black
for charm is Black
and magic Black
for love is Black
and hip swinging Black
for dance is Black
and rhythm Black
for art is Black
and movement Black
for laughter is Black
for joy is Black
for peace is Black
for life is Black

SPACE THAT ONCE WAS MINE

The poet Léon Damas was born in French Guiana in 1912. During a period of study in Paris he became a part of the Negritude movement. The tone of his poetry ranges from irony, directed at his subjection to Western mores, to a deep-seated anger at the results of colonialism. This work, entitled "Limbe," is taken from a collection of Damas' poems entitled Pigments, *published in Paris in 1937.*

Will they ever know this rancor in my
   heart?

From beneath suspicion's eye that
   opened all too late.
they have robbed me of the space that
   once was mine
tradition
days
life
song
rhythm
effort
pathway
water
cabin
the gray, fertilized land
wisdom
words
palavers
the aged
cadence
hands
measure
hands
footbeats
soil

SPLENDIDLY ALONE

David Diop's legacy to the literature of Negritude is a slim volume of seventeen poems, Coups de Pilon (Pounding). *Diop was born in Bordeaux in 1927 of African parents and lived for a while in West Africa. He was killed in an air crash over Dakar in 1960; with him went a quantity of unpublished manuscripts. Despite Diop's profound hatred of colonialism, his work is typically tempered with optimism, as in this poem.*

Africa my Africa
Africa of proud warriors on ancestral
   savannahs
Africa that my grandmother sings
On the bank of her distant river
I have never known you
But my face is full of your blood
Your beautiful black blood which waters
   the wide fields.
The blood of your sweat
The sweat of your work
The work of your slavery
The slavery of your children
Africa tell me Africa

Is this really you this back which is bent
And breaks under the load of insult
This back trembling with red weals
Which says yes to the whip on the hot
   roads of noon

Then gravely a voice replies to me
Impetuous son that tree robust and
   young
That tree over there
Splendidly alone amidst white and faded
   flowers
That is Africa your Africa which grows
Grows patiently obstinately
And whose fruit little by little learn
The bitter taste of liberty.

AFRICA AT THE CENTER

The young William Edward Burghardt Du Bois wrote in his diary in 1893: "Be the truth what it may, I shall seek it on the pure assumption that it is worth seeking—and Heaven nor Hell, God nor Devil shall turn me from my purpose till I die." Until his death seventy years later, at the age of ninety-five, the man was true to his word. W.E.B. Du Bois was born in Great Barrington, Massachusetts, in 1868. After receiving his doctoral degree from Harvard University in 1895, he taught for several years; but in 1905 he became involved in the Niagara movement, which led to the founding of the National Association for the Advancement of Colored People and to the scholar's emergence as an Afro-American leader. A prolific writer and editor, he is also considered to be the father of the pan-African movement and an outstanding spokesman for African nationalism. Du Bois published more than a dozen books in the black studies area, including Black Reconstruction, *and wrote uncounted speeches and articles in the cause of reawakening African consciousness. The following excerpt is from an essay that appeared in the* Atlantic Monthly *in May, 1915. In it Du Bois cites European rivalries in Africa as the chief cause of World War I.*

Nearly every human empire that has arisen in the world, material and spiritual, has found some of its greatest crises on this continent of Africa, from Greece to

Great Britain. As [the German classical historian Theodor] Mommsen says, "It was through Africa that Christianity became the religion of the world." In Africa the last flood of Germanic invasions spent itself within hearing of the last gasp of Byzantium, and it was again through Africa that Islam came to play its great role of conqueror and civilizer....

So much for the past; and now, today. . . . The methods by which this continent has been stolen have been contemptible and dishonest beyond expression. Lying treaties, rivers of rum, murder, assassination, mutilation, rape and torture have marked the progress of Englishman, German, Frenchman, and Belgian on the Dark Continent. . . .

It all began, singularly enough, like the present war, with Belgium. Many of us remember Stanley's great solution of the puzzle of Central Africa when he traced the mighty Congo sixteen hundred miles from Nyangwe to the sea. Suddenly the world knew that here lay the key to the riches of Central Africa. It stirred uneasily, but Leopold of Belgium was first on his feet, and the result was the Congo Free State—God save the mark! . . .

Thus the world began to invest in color prejudice. The "color line" began to pay dividends. For indeed, while the exploration of the valley of the Congo was the occasion of the scramble for Africa, the cause lay deeper. The Franco-Prussian War turned the eyes of those who sought power and dominion away from Europe. . . .

With the waning of the possibility of the big fortune, gathered by starvation wage and boundless exploitation of one's weaker and poorer fellows at home, arose more magnificently the dream of exploitation abroad. . . .

It is no longer simply the merchant prince, or the aristocratic monopoly, or even the employing class, that is exploiting the world: it is the nation, a new democratic nation composed of united capital and labor. . . .

Such nations it is that rule the modern

Dr. Du Bois at a Paris conference in 1949
UPI

world. Their national bond is no mere sentimental patriotism, loyalty, or ancestor-worship. It is increased wealth, power, and luxury for all classes on a scale the world never saw before. . . .

Whence comes this new wealth and on what does its accumulation depend? It comes primarily from the darker nations of the world—Asia and Africa, South and Central America, the West Indies and the islands of the South Seas. . . .

Thus, more and more, the imperialists have concentrated on Africa.

The greater the concentration the more deadly the rivalry. From Fashoda to Agadir, repeatedly the spark has been applied to the European magazine and a general conflagration narrowly averted. We speak of the Balkans as the storm center of Europe and the cause of war, but this is mere habit. The Balkans are convenient for occasions, but the ownership of materials and men in the darker world is the real prize that is setting the nations of Europe at each other's throats today.

The present world war is, then, the result of jealousies engendered by the recent rise of armed national associations of labor and capital whose aim is the exploitation of the wealth of the world mainly outside the European circle of nations. These associations, grown jealous and suspicious at the division of the spoils of trade-empire, are fighting to enlarge their respective shares; they look for expansion, not in Europe but in Asia, and particularly in Africa. "We want no

inch of French territory," said Germany to England, but Germany was "unable to give" similar assurances as to France in Africa. . . .

What, then, are we to do, who desire peace and the civilization of all men? . . . How can love of humanity appeal as a motive to nations whose love of luxury is built on the inhuman exploitation of human beings, and who, especially in recent years, have been taught to regard these human beings as inhuman? . . .

What the primitive peoples of Africa and the world need and must have if war is to be abolished is perfectly clear:

First: land. Today Africa is being enslaved by the theft of her land and natural resources. . . .

Secondly: we must train native races in modern civilization. . . .

Lastly, the principle of home rule must extend to groups, nations, and races. . . .

We are calling for European concord today; but at the utmost European concord will mean satisfaction with, or acquiescence in, a given division of the spoils of world dominion. . . . From this will arise three perpetual dangers of war. First, renewed jealousy at any division of colonies or spheres of influence. . . .

Secondly: war will come from the revolutionary revolt of the lowest workers. . . . Finally, the colored peoples will not always submit passively to foreign domination. To some this is a lightly tossed truism. When a people deserve liberty they fight for it and get it, say such philosophers; thus making war a regular, necessary step to liberty. Colored people are familiar with this complacent judgment. They endure the contemptuous treatment meted out by whites to those not "strong" enough to be free. These nations and races, composing as they do a vast majority of humanity, are going to endure this treatment just as long as they must and not a moment longer. Then they are going to fight and the War of the Color Line will outdo in savage inhumanity any war this world has yet seen. For colored folk have much to remember and they will not forget.

But is this inevitable? Must we sit helpless before this awful prospect? . . .

Steadfast faith in humanity must come. The domination of one people by another without the other's consent, be the subject people black or white, must stop. The doctrine of forcible economic expansion over subject peoples must go. . . .

Twenty centuries before Christ a great cloud swept over sea and settled on Africa, darkening and well-nigh blotting out the culture of the land of Egypt. For half a thousand years it rested there until a black woman, Queen Nefertari, "the most venerated figure in Egyptian history," rose to the throne of the Pharaohs and redeemed the world and her people. Twenty centuries after Christ, black Africa, prostrate, raped, and shamed, lies at the feet of the conquering Philistines of Europe. Beyond the awful sea a black woman is weeping and waiting with her sons on her breast. What shall the end be? The world-old and fearful things, war and wealth, murder and luxury? Or shall it be a new thing—a new peace and new democracy of all races: a great humanity of equal men? *"Semper novi quid ex Africa!"*

THE LION OF JUDAH

In 1930 Ethiopia's regent, Ras Taffari Makonnen, became emperor and assumed the title of Haile Selassie I (meaning in Amharic "the power of the Trinity"). Five years later his rule was brutally challenged by Italian invasion. Numerous attempts to arouse the conscience of world leaders were climaxed in 1938 by an urgent last plea he placed before the League of Nations, to which Ethiopia belonged. Betrayed by the other members, Haile Selassie was forced into exile until 1941, when, with British help, he was restored to power. Since that time numerous internal revolts have shaken, but not unseated, the durable monarch, and small but progressive changes in his administration are discernible. Portions of his speech before the League follow.

Ethiopia, the victim of an inexcusable

Haile Selassie recording a radio appeal
ACME

aggression, had placed her confidence in the signature of the States Members of the League. . . . Since 1935 Ethiopia has with pain noted successive abandonments of signatures that had been appended to the Covenant. Many Powers threatened with aggression and feeling their weakness have abandoned Ethiopia. . . .

Article 10 of the Covenant requires Members to undertake to respect and maintain as against all external aggression the territorial integrity and political independence of each Member. Nevertheless, non-recognition of a conquest by aggression is the least onerous obligation in observing Article 10, since it involves merely a passive attitude. It does not call upon States Members to make any national sacrifice, nor does it lead them to incur any risk of war or reprisals. . . .

To-day, we have the brutal abandonment of this principle, which is contemplated and which even seems to be called for by the powerful British Empire. . . .

I, as legitimate Emperor of Ethiopia, on behalf of my martyred people, address to the nations of the world the most energetic protest. In order to lessen the flagrant violation of the Covenant, the suggestion made to-day to the Council invokes the situation in actual fact in Ethiopia at the present time. But if it were true—and it is not so—that the invader has broken the resistance of my people, even if in fact he occupied and effectively exercised his administration

over the territory of my empire—which is not the case—even in those circumstances the proposal submitted to the Council should be set aside without hesitation. Did not the world hail as one of the most important marks of progress in international law . . . the refusal to grant juridical recognition to the effects of aggression?

As legitimate sovereign of the Ethiopian people, I would invoke this principle, for I have incumbent on me the duty to defend the political independence of the Ethiopian people, the territorial integrity of Ethiopia, and at the same time the life, the property and the liberty of each of those individuals and each of those religious or civil institutions which go to make up the Ethiopian people. . . .

Millions of men and women throughout the world are to-day anxiously following the deliberations of the League of Nations. They know that this is the tragic hour in which the destiny of the League is to be determined. Being responsible for ensuring respect for the principles of international justice, is the League of Nations about to end its own existence by tearing up, with its own hands, the Covenant which constitutes its sole reason for existence? The magnificent edifice that has just been reared for the triumph of peace through law, is this henceforth to become an altar reared to the cult of force, a market-place in which the independence of peoples becomes the subject of trafficking, a tomb in which international morality is to be buried? . . .

In order to break down the resistance of my people, its refusal to abandon that independence which it had enjoyed for more than thirty centuries, the Italian authorities are counting upon propaganda with the object of demoralizing the people, and in this they make great play with the abandonment of Ethiopia by the League of Nations. . . .

International law absolutely prohibits the belligerent making any annexation and it prohibits any Power that is foreign to the conflict from recognizing the occupant as the legal sovereign. Thus the *de facto* situation does strengthen and supplement the provisions of the Covenant and of the Pact of Paris, which in the most categorical way prohibit *de jure* recognition of annexation, for that would be recognizing the conquest of territory by force. . . .

The distinguished representative of Great Britain has just put the question very clearly. He said there are at present two ideals in conflict, the ideal of devotion to a lofty aim, and the ideal of ensuring peace as a practical measure. He asserted that it is often difficult to reconcile what is ideally just with what is possible in practice. He asserted that it is the essential mission of the League to maintain peace. Yes, the League has as its essential object the maintenance of peace. But there are different ways to maintain peace; there is the maintenance of peace through right, and there is peace at any cost. Ethiopia firmly believes that the League of Nations has no freedom of choice in this matter. It would be committing suicide if after having been created to maintain peace through right it were to abandon that principle and adopt instead the principle of peace at any price, even the price of the immolation of a State Member at the feet of its aggressor.

THE WEAVER OF DREAMS

Marcus Aurelius Garvey came to the United States from Jamaica about 1916. According to a re-evaluation of black history, his back-to-Africa movement is a relevant link in the development of Afro-American history and the growing recognition of African kinship. Two million followers joined Garvey's organization, stirred to wild enthusiasm by his infectious exhortations and his dream of an African homeland free from the oppressions of a biased society. Claude McKay, Jamaica-born poet and novelist, product of the Harlem renaissance of literature in the nineteen twenties and thirties, has captured the flamboyant character of the man and the temper of his times in the following excerpt from Harlem: Negro Metropolis, *published in 1940.*

Garvey en route to a U.N.I.A. rally, 1921
UPI

There has never been a Negro leader like Garvey. None ever enjoyed a fraction of his universal popularity. He winged his way into the firmament of the white world holding aloft a black star and exhorting the Negro people to gaze upon and follow it. His aspiration to reach dizzy heights and dazzle the vision of the Negro world does not remain monumental, like the rugged path of the pioneer or of the hard, calculating, practical builder. But it survives in the memory like the spectacular swath of an unforgettable comet. . . .

In 1917 Garvey organized in Harlem the Universal Negro Improvement Association. He had as a nucleus an intelligent group of men who belonged to a long established History Club, which specialized in the Negro people's ancient past. Auspiciously Garvey started off on a lecture tour, which covered a majority of the States that had a considerable Negro population. He was warmly welcomed and received large contributions of money. . . .

Africa for the Africans! Renaissance of the Negro Race! Back to Africa! A Black Star Line! These were the slogans Garvey broadcast in a thousand different ways to move the mind of the Negro people. There was magic in his method. It worked miraculously. The Negro masses acclaimed the new leader. The black belts clamored to hear his voice and competed with one another for his lectures. Money poured in for subscriptions to the *Negro World,* money that

would help establish the Black Star Line and set in motion the Redemption of Africa. Garvey struck African Redemption medals. A bronze cross was bestowed upon subscribers of from $50 to $100, a silver cross for subscribers of from $100 to $500 and a gold cross for donors of $500 to $1000.

Now, after many vicissitudes, Garvey was successfully launched on his career of world leadership of the Negroes. . . .

Girding for a supreme war effort, America had little time to devote to the growing problems of its large Negro minority. Harassed in the South and rebuffed in the North, the southern Negroes eagerly swallowed the sayings and the projects of Garvey.

Marcus Garvey became the mouthpiece of these southern and West Indian migrants to the northern centers of industry. Whether they worked in Jersey or Pennsylvania, Connecticut or Massachusetts, Harlem was their Mecca. They gave Garvey all the money he needed to institute his programme. . . .

Just a few months after the founding of his organization, Garvey was involved in disputes with his most prominent officials. . . . Early in 1919 he was nearly assassinated by one George Tyler, who shot him three times in the arms and leg. He was saved by his secretary, Miss Amy Ashwood, who threw herself between him and his antagonist. . . .

The attempt on Garvey's life, besides his arrest sky-rocketed his stock. He incorporated the Black Star Line, capitalized at ten million dollars. . . . "Up, you mighty race!" cried Garvey. And the race rose up. Garvey spoke and the Negro masses were transformed. "Negro, Black, and Africa," the magic words repeated again and again made Negroes delirious with ecstasy. Wherever Garvey led they were ready to follow. He was the modern Moses, the black savior. His message reached Negroes everywhere. From the plantation of the deep South, they hearkened to his voice, in the islands of the Caribbean they were moved as never before, now that the voice of Marcus Garvey was broadcast from New York. Across the Atlantic, in the heart of the Congo, Negroes talked of the black Messiah. . . .

In the latter part of 1919 . . . Marcus Garvey announced that the Black Star Line had acquired its first boat. . . .

There was a wild invasion of Harlem by Negroes from every black quarter of America. Hordes of disciples came with more dollars to buy more shares. The boat was moored at the pier with its all-Negro crew. And the common people gladly paid half a dollar to go aboard and look over the miracle. . . .

Now, in this first boat of the Black Star Line, owned by the Universal Negro Improvement Association, they saw something different. They saw themselves sailing without making any apology for being passengers. It was their own ship, a Negro ship. It was their money that had bought it. But it had required a black leader to show them how they could do it.

That night Liberty Hall was jammed with Negroes. Hundreds could not get in and the sidewalks overflowed with spectators between Lenox Avenue and Seventh Avenue. Marcus Garvey transformed the great audience into a waving, shouting, frenzied host as he cried: "Up, you mighty race, you can accomplish what you will." . . .

In 1920 Marcus Garvey staged the first Universal Negro Convention in Harlem. . . .

Delegates arrived from Africa, Brazil, Colombia, Panama and other Central American countries, and from the islands of the West Indies. Every State of the Union was represented. Harlem blinked at the dazzling splendor of that wonderful parade. Garvey wore a magnificent uniform of purple, green and black, and a plumed hat. He stood in his car and saluted the cheering crowds. . . .

The following evening, Garvey packed Madison Square Garden with his followers and admirers. In a long speech he exhorted the Negroes to unite and work for the redemption of Africa. . . .

Garvey's invasion of the South, the acclamation of the Black Belts and the attitude of the Southern whites presented a puzzle to northern Negro intellectuals. Garvey had announced previously that he was going South to talk to his own people and that the white man should leave him alone.

Now many Northern blacks and whites had been manhandled and run out of the South for attempting to hold peaceful meetings with colored people! . . .

In Louisiana and Alabama, notably, Garvey succeeded in holding some extremely boisterous and enthusiastic meetings and getting away without a scratch. Of course, he had his way of doing it. He employed a special technique. He thundered, "Africa for the Africans," and shouted at the white South in a semi-religious harangue, "Let my people go!" . . .

Meanwhile, the Federal government had undertaken an investigation of Garvey. In January, 1922, he was arrested on a charge of using the mails to defraud. . . . The charge was that Garvey had used the mails to solicit funds for a Black Star Line which was not established. He was released on bail of $2500. . . .

For the balance of the year he remained unmolested, and organized in Harlem one of his grandest conventions. From every State in the union, from the West Indies, from Central and South America, from Europe and Africa, an inspiring deputation of delegates converged upon Harlem. It was the greatest swarm since Garvey started his movement. They brought gifts to Garvey: special contributions to defend his case, sums for African Redemption and thousands of subscriptions to reorganize the Black Star Line. . . . To the tremendous tributes he responded as befitted a grand potentate. The ribbons and braids of his gleaming satin robe were richer than ever, his plumes were as long as the leaves of the Guinea grass and as white as snow; seated in his car as upon a throne, he received the ovations and salutes of Harlem. . . .

A delegation consisting of three members of the Universal Negro organization was dispatched to Liberia. . . .

The Black Star Line was reorganized as the Black Cross, and the *General Goethals*, a boat of over four thousand tons, was purchased from the government. The first members of the colony were scheduled to sail in 1924. But trouble broke in Liberia. It was said that the Garvey party there was using the world-wide influence of the Universal Negro Organization to overthrow the government. . . .

The August, 1924, convention of the Universal Negro and Black Cross was designed as a monster farewell party to the Negroes who were to leave for Liberia in the fall. . . . Those who were chosen to go were religiously regarded as angels of the New Heaven, Marcus Garvey's promised land, the Negro Zion.

The Archbishop of the African Orthodox Church, the Right Reverend C. A. McGuire, in his robes of state, pronounced a blessing upon the convention, said a special prayer for Marcus Garvey and the Universal Negroes who were the first to have elected to return to Africa. . . .

But in the midst of the thirty-day convention, the Liberian government issued a statement repudiating the Universal Negro organization, and refusing to recognize its advance delegates. . . .

However, if Marcus Garvey felt his movement betrayed by the American-Liberian aristocracy, he and his following were inspirited and uplifted by a significant event. That year the Prince Kogo Honeou Tovalou of Dahomey made his first voyage to America. Prince Kogo, as a royal native potentate, was honored with a picturesque reception at Liberty Hall, where all the colors of God's fertile imagination were assembled in his honor. He made a speech full of praise for the work of the Universal Negro Association and saluted Marcus Garvey as the leader of the Negro people of the world. . . .

And above all there was Garvey's Universal Negro propaganda. Its repercussion in Africa was greater than the American Back-to-Africa devotees realized. In the interior of West Africa legends arose of an African who had been lost in America, but would return to save his people. . . .

Enemies black and white were constantly badgering Garvey and reminding the authorities of his menacing existence. His appeal slowly dragged along its course. . . . Finally, in 1925, the appeal was rejected by the United States Supreme Court. In February, 1925, Marcus Garvey entered Atlanta Federal Penitentiary to serve a five-year term. . . .

But in prison he was perhaps as powerful as he was when free. His message to his followers appeared every week on the front page of the *Negro World*. Often it read like an epistle of one of the Apostles. While he was on trial, the prosecuting attorney referred to him as "The Tiger." . . . The Garvey people delighted in the phrase and . . . they fought hard to free Garvey. His lawyer released a memorandum showing that the chief count upon which Garvey was convicted was untenable. Petitions were sent to the President of the United States. The jury that convicted him came out with a statement in favor of his release. Metropolitan newspapers, such as the *Daily News*, which has a large circulation in Harlem, demanded that Garvey be pardoned. He was turned loose in November, 1927, and deported to Jamaica. . . .

Marcus Garvey's influence over Aframericans, native Africans and people of African descent everywhere was vast. Whether that influence was positive or pervasive and indirect, Negroes of all classes were stirred to a finer feeling of racial consciousness. . . .

The "Black Tiger" and "President-General" of the Negro World, Marcus Garvey, died in London on June 10, 1940. At the time of his death he still was revered as their greatest leader by the American Negro masses.

"STRIKE A BLOW AND DIE"

John Chilembwe, who led an abortive revolt against British coffee and tobacco planters in Nyasaland in 1915, had prepared for his role of African nationalist leader under the aegis of British Protestantism. His mentor, evangelist-egalitarian Joseph Booth, advocated the formation of a separate African Christian Union, which would incorporate local religious practices within its Christian framework. He took Chilembwe to the United States for further training, but encounters there with militant Afro-Americans led the young man to break with Booth. Returning to Nyasaland in 1901, Chilembwe established the Providence Industrial Mission and began to speak against the oppressive colonial system. Just what motivated Chilembwe to take up arms against the British and face almost certain death has been widely debated. It is estimated that a black army, numbering somewhere between two hundred and nine hundred men, was involved. British losses were slight, and Chilembwe was shortly ambushed and killed. However, George Mwase, a Tonga and compatriot of Chilembwe, later wrote A Dialogue of Nyasaland, *in which he gave an account of what he observed.*

When the army gathered on Saturday morning on the 23rd January 1915 [John Chilembwe gave instructions to his army]. After a long debate, he prayed to Almighty God. Then he delivered his speech as follows:

"You are all patriots as you sit. Patriots mean[s] to die for Amor Patria. This very night you are to go and strike the blow and then die. I do not say that you are going to win the war at all. You have no weapons (guns?) with you and you are not at all trained military men even. One great thing you must remember is that Omnia Vincet Amor so for love [of] your own country and country men, I now encourage you to go and strike a blow bravely and die.

"This is only way to show the whiteman, that the treatment they are treating our men and women was most bad and we have determined to strike a first and a last blow, and then all die by the heavy storm of the whitemen's army. The whitemen will then think, after we are dead, that the treatment they are treating our people is almost (most) bad, and they might change to the better for our peo-ple. After we are dead and buried. This blows means 'non sibi sed patria.' ['Not for oneself, but for one's country.']

"You must not think that with that blow, you are going to defeat whitemen and then become Kings of your own country, no. If one of you has such an idea in his head, 'God forbid,' he must throw such idea now, before it grows bigger in his head, for it will lead him astray. I am also warning strongly against seizing property from anybody, does not matter what or where. If among you there is a lecher, such a man must not go with you. You are Patriots and not Lechers. Where you are going to find money, goods and other kind of wealth, does not matter what, do not touch such for 'Amor Patria' sake. But where ever your hand is going to lay on any kind of a weapon, take that, for it will help you in your struggle for the 'Amor Patria.' Another order I want you to remember, is about women and young children, do not, in any way, do anything to them, treat them as innocents, what you are to do with them is to bring them over peacefully, and afterwards send them back to the Boma. Women must be carried on Machilla if some will be available. If some of the whitemen will be killed during the assault, one or two of the important men bring the head or heads over, leave the body alone."

He repeated saying "Be of good courage, and strike the blow and die for the 'Amor Patria,' and not with intention to win and become Kings of your own." He bade them "God's speed." At last he prayed again and said "Deusvobiscum." ["God be with you."]

So the army scattered that day for their food. This was the morning of Saturday the 23rd January. The army then gathered themselves, at the evening, and they were divided as I have already said on the front page (earlier). I have also to mention that there were also some members of this army in Zomba Township, but they all shrinked and diminished, and they did not appear for help; although the arrangement was that.

TOWARD POSITIVE ACTION

Gamal Abdel Nasser entered the public political arena in July, 1953, when his Free Officers movement staged a coup d'état, deposing King Farouk and with him Egypt's bankrupt monarchical system. Nasser's cadre was drawn largely from the frustrated lower middle classes; it was committed to a broad reordering of society, including radical agrarian reform. The Free Officers also sought to strengthen Egypt's military establishment and the international Arab League, of which it was the leader. Nasser held a number of posts in the new government, becoming president both of Egypt in 1956 and of the United Arab Republic (Egypt and Syria) from 1958 to 1970. The following excerpt is taken from Nasser's Philosophy of the Revolution *(1953), the manifesto of his master plan for Egypt, Africa, and the Arab world.*

What is it we want to do? And which is the way to it?

There is no doubt we all dream of Egypt free and strong. No Egyptian would ever differ with another about that. As for the way to liberation and strength, that is the most intricate problem in our lives. . . .

Ever since I was at the head of demonstrations in Al Nahda School [Nasser's secondary school], I have clamored for complete independence; others repeated my cries; but these were in vain.

They were blown away by the winds and became faint echoes that do not move mountains or smash rocks. Later "positive action" meant in my opinion that all leaders of Egypt should unite on one thing. Rebellious cheering crowds passed our leaders' homes one by one demanding, in the name of the youth of Egypt, that they should unite on one thing. It was a tragedy to my faith that the one thing they united on was the Treaty of 1936 [an Anglo-Egyptian treaty reducing Britain's military occupation in Egypt to a zone bordering the Suez Canal].

Then came the second World War and the events that preceded it. Both inflamed our youth and spread fire to its innermost feelings. We, the whole generation, began to move towards violence. I confess, and I hope the Attorney-General will not incriminate me on account of this confession, that political assassinations blazed in my inflamed mind during that period as the only positive action from which we could not escape, if we were to save the future of our country. . . .

I thought of assassinating the ex-King and those of his men who tampered with our sacred traditions. In this I was not alone. When I sat with others our thoughts passed from thinking to planning. Many a design did I draw up those days. Many a night did I lie awake preparing the means for the expected positive action. . . .

I remember one night in particular which was decisive in directing my thoughts and my dreams along that channel. We had prepared everything necessary for action. We selected one, whom we found essential to put out of the way. We studied the circumstances of the life of this individual, and made the plot in detail. This plot was to shoot him as he returned home at night. We organized a squad of assault which would shoot him, another to guard this first and a third to organize the plan of getting away to safety after the plot had been fully carried out.

The appointed night came and I went out myself with the squad of execution. Everything went to plan as we imagined.

The scene was empty, as we had expected. The squads lay in the hiding places fixed for them. The person whom we wanted to get out of the way came and bullets were fired at him. The squad of execution withdrew, covered in its retreat by the guards, and the operation of getting away began. I started my motor car and dashed away from the scene of the positive action we planned. Cries, wailings and moans suddenly rang in my ears. The wailing of a woman, the voice of a scared child and the continuous feverish appeals for help assailed my ears. I was steeped in my rebellious set of emotions as my car rushed me along. I then became conscious of something strange; the sounds I heard were still tearing my ears, as well as the cries, wails and moans and the feverish appeals for help. I was then away from the scene, further than sound could reach. Nevertheless I felt all these beginning to haunt and chase me.

I got home, threw myself on the bed, my mind in a fever, my heart and conscience incessantly boiling. The cries, moans and wails and the appeals for help still rang in my ears. All night long I could not sleep. I lay on my bed in darkness, lighting one cigarette after another, wandering away with my rebellious thoughts which were driven away by the sounds that haunted me. "Was I right?" I asked myself. With conviction I answered, "My motives were patriotic." "Was this an unavoidable means?" I again asked myself. In doubt I replied: "What could we have done otherwise? Is it possible that the future of our country could change by getting rid of this one individual or another? Is not the question far deeper than this?" In bewilderment I would say to myself: "I almost feel that the question is deeper. We dream of the glory of a nation. Which is more important? That some one should pass away who should pass away or that someone should come who should come."

As I mention this I see rays of light gradually filtering through these crowded sensations. "What is important," I would say to myself, "is that someone should come who should come. We are dreaming of the glory of a nation: A glory that must be built up." As I tossed on my bed in a room full of smoke and charged with emotions, I found myself asking: "And then?" "And what then?", a mysterious voice called out. . . .

The principal question is to find out the positive action. Since then we began to think of something more deeply rooted, more serious and more far-reaching. We began to draw the preliminary lines of the vision that was realized in the night of July 23rd, namely a revolution springing from the very heart of the people, charged with its aspirations and pur-

473

suing completely the steps it had previously taken along its destined path. . . .

Fate has so willed that we should be on the crossroads of the world. Often have we been the road which invaders took and a prey to adventurers. In certain circumstances we found it impossible to explain the factors latent in the soul of our nation without due consideration of these circumstances.

In my opinion we cannot overlook the history of Egypt under the Pharaohs or the reaction between the Greek spirit and ours, the Roman invasion, and Muslim conquest and the waves of Arab migrations that followed.

I believe we should pause for a time and examine the circumstances we went through in the Middle Ages; for it is these that got us up to the stage we are in today.

If the Crusades were the dawn of a renaissance in Europe they were also the commencement of the dark ages in our country. Our nation has borne the brunt of the Crusades. They left it exhausted, poverty-stricken and destitute.

Often, when I go back to turning the pages of our history, I feel sorrow tearing my soul as I consider the period when a tyrannical feudalism was formed, a feudalism which had no other object save sucking the blood of life out of our veins and sapping from these veins the remnants of any feeling of power and of dignity. It left in the depth of our souls an effect that we have to struggle long to overcome.

European society passed through the stages of its evolution in an orderly manner. It crossed the bridge between the Renaissance at the end of the Middle Ages and the Nineteenth Century step by step. . . . In our case everything was sudden. European countries eyed us covetously and regarded us as a crossroad to their colonies in the East and the South.

Torrents of ideas and opinions burst upon us which we were, at that stage of our evolution, incapable of assimilating. Our spirits were still in the Thirteenth Century though the symptoms of the

Nineteenth and Twentieth Centuries infiltrated in their various aspects. Our minds were trying to catch up the advancing caravan of humanity. . . .

I believe, without paying any compliment to people's emotions, that our nation has realized a miracle. Any nation, exposed to the same conditions as our country, could be easily lost. It could be swept away by the torrents that fell upon it. But it stood firm in the violent earthquake.

It is true we nearly lost our equilibrium in some circumstances; but generally we did not fall to the ground. As I consider one normal Egyptian family out of the thousands that live in the capital, I find the following: the father, for example, is a turbaned "fellah" from the heart of the country; the mother a lady descended from Turkish stock; the sons of the family are at a school adopting the English system; the daughters the French. All this lies between the Thirteenth century and the outward appearances of the Twentieth.

As I see this I feel within me I can comprehend the bewilderment and the confusion that assail us. Then I say to myself. "This society will crystalize; its component parts will hold together; it will form a homogeneous entity; but this necessitates that we should strain our nerves during the period of transition."

Such are, then, the roots from which sprang our conditions of today. Such are the sources from which our crisis flows. If I add to these social origins the circumstances for which we expelled [King] Farouk and for which we wish to liberate our country from every foreign soldier; if we add all these together, we shall discover the wide sphere in which we labor and which is exposed, from every side, to the winds, to the violent storm that raged in its corners, to flashing lightning and roaring thunder.

Therefore, one may ask, "Which is the way? and what is our role in it?"

The way is that which leads to economic and political freedom.

Many people come to me and exclaim,

"You have angered everybody." To which explanation I always reply, "It is not people's anger that influences the situation. The question should be: Was what aroused their anger for the good of the country or for the interest of whom?" I realize we have upset big land-owners; but was it possible not to upset them and yet behold some of us owning thousands of acres, while others do not own the plot of land wherein they are buried after their death?

I realize we have aroused the wrath of old politicians; but was it possible not to do so and yet behold our country a victim to their passions, their corruption and their struggle for the spoils of office?

I realize we have angered many government officials; but without this was it possible to spend more than half the budget on officials' salaries and yet allot, as we have done, forty million pounds for productive projects? What would have happened if we had opened the coffers of the treasury of the state, as they had done, and distributed their contents among officials and let come what may thereafter. The year that ensued would have found the Government unable to pay the salaries of officials.

How easy it would have been to satisfy all those malcontents! But what is the price that our country would pay out of its hopes and its future for that satisfaction? . . .

When I attempt to analyze the components of our power I cannot help but point out three principal forces of power which should be the first to be taken into account.

The first source is that we are a group of neighboring peoples joined together with such spiritual and material bonds as can ever join any group of peoples. Our peoples have traits, components and civilization, in whose atmosphere the three sacred and heavenly creeds have originated. This cannot be altogether ignored in any effort at reconstructing a stable world in which peace prevails.

As for the second source it is our territory itself and the position it has on the map of the world, that important strategic situation which can be rightly considered the meeting-place, the cross-road and the military corridor of the world.

The third source is petroleum which is the vital nerve of civilization, without which all its means cannot possibly exist whether huge works for production, modes of communication by land, sea and air, weapons of war whether they are planes flying above the clouds or submarines submerged under layers of water. All these, without petroleum would become mere pieces of iron, rusty, motionless and lifeless. . . .

Such is the first circle in which we must revolve and attempt to move in as much as we possibly can. It is the Arab circle.

If we direct our attention after that to the second circle, the circle of the continent of Africa, I would say, without exaggeration, that we cannot, in any way, stand aside, even if we wish to, away from the sanguinary and dreadful struggle now raging in the heart of Africa between five million whites and two hundred million Africans.

We cannot do so for one principal and clear reason, namely that we are in Africa. The people of Africa will continue to look up to us, who guard the northern gate of the continent and who are its connecting link with the world outside. We cannot, under any condition, relinquish our responsibility in helping, in every way possible, in diffusing the light and civilization into the farthest parts of that virgin jungle.

There is another important reason. The Nile is the artery of life of our country. It draws its supply of water from the heart of the continent.

There remains the Sudan, our beloved brother, whose boundaries extend deeply into Africa and which is a neighbor to all the sensitive spots in the center of the continent.

It is a certain fact that Africa at present is the scene of an exciting ebullition. White man, who represents several European countries, is trying again to reparti-

tion the continent. We cannot stand aside in face of what is taking place in Africa on the assumption that it does not concern or effect us.

The third circle now remains; the circle that goes beyond continents and oceans and to which I referred, as the circle of our brethren in faith who turn with us, whatever part of the world they are in, towards the same Kibla [direction in prayer] in Mecca and whose pious lips whisper reverently the same prayers. . . .

As I stood in front of the Kaaba and felt my sentiments wandering with every part of the world where Islam had extended I found myself exclaiming, "Our idea of the pilgrimage should change. Going to the Kaaba should never be a passport to heaven, after a lengthy life. Neither should it be a simple effort to buy indulgences after an eventful life. The pilgrimage should be a great political power. The press of the world should resort to and follow its news; not as a series of rituals and traditions which are done to amuse and entertain readers, but as a regular political congress wherein the leaders of Muslim states, their public men, their pioneers in every field of knowledge, their writers, their leading industrialists, merchants and youth draw up in this universal Islamic Parliament the main lines of policy for their countries and their cooperation together until they meet again. They should meet reverently, strong, free from greed but active, submissive to the Lord, but powerful against their difficulties and their enemies, dreaming of a new life, firm believers that they have a place under the sun which they should occupy for life."

THE AVENGERS

James T. Ngugi, today a young man in his early thirties, was born in Kenya. While growing up he watched his people, the Kikuyu, struggle to gain a voice in the colonial government. Under men like Jomo Kenyatta, the Kenya Africa Union (K.A.U.) worked for peaceful reform, but in 1952 dissatisfaction over their failure to gain ground exploded

into the Mau Mau resistance. Influenced by these events, Ngugi devoted himself to the cause of African justice and African destiny; his writings are a testimony to the valor and hope of his people. Although Weep Not, Child, *excerpted here, was written as a novel, the experiences of Njoroge, the protagonist, closely parallel the author's own life in Kenya.*

Everyone knew that Jomo would win. . . . If he lost, then the black people of Kenya had lost. . . .

At school a little argument ensued. It was begun by Karanja. . . . He said, "Jomo is bound to win. Europeans fear him."

"No. He can't win. My father said so last night."

"Your father is a homeguard," another boy retorted. . . .

"The homeguards with their white masters. They are as bad as Mau Mau."

"No. Mau Mau is not bad. The Freedom boys are fighting against the white settlers. It is bad to fight for one's land? Tell me that."

"But they cut black men's throats."

"Those killed are the traitors! Black white settlers."

"What's Mau Mau?" Njoroge asked. He had never known what it was and his curiosity overcame his fear of being thought ignorant.

Karanja, who had just joined the group, said, "It is a secret Kiama. You 'drink' oath. You become a member. The Kiama has its own soldiers who are fighting for the land. Kimathi is the leader."

"Not Jomo?" a small boy with one bad eye asked.

"I don't know," Karanja continued. "But father says that Kimathi is the leader of the Freedom Army and Jomo is the leader of K.A.U. I like K.A.U. and fear Mau Mau."

"But they are all the same? Fighting for the freedom of the black people." This was said by a tall but weak boy. Then with a distant look in his eyes, "I would like to fight in the forest."

All eyes were turned to him. He seemed to have said a very profound thing. Or

Summarily tried and convicted, a leader of the Mau Mau revolt is led off to execution.
MAGNUM · GEORGE RODGER

seemed to have put in words what most of them felt. . . .

"Hurrah and victory for the black folk!"

"Hurrah and victory for Jomo—" . . .

The bell went, the group dispersed. They rushed back for their evening classes. . . .

Mr. Howlands sat in the office with his left elbow on the table with the palm of the hand supporting his head. . . . He gazed out through the small open glass window with a strained expression. . . .

He stood and walked across the office, wrapped in thought. . . . The present that had made him a D.O. reflected a past from which he had tried to run away. . . . It was no good calling on the name of God for he, Howlands, did not believe in God. There was only one god for him—and that was the farm he had created, the land he had tamed. And who were these

Mau Mau who were now claiming that land, his god? Ha, ha! He could have laughed at the whole ludicrous idea, but for the fact that they had forced him into the other life, the life he had tried to avoid. He had been called upon to take up a temporary appointment as a District Officer. . . . If Mau Mau claimed the only thing he believed in, they would see! . . . Who were black men and Mau Mau anyway, he asked for the thousandth time? Mere savages! A nice word—savages. . . . The strike which had made him lose Ngotho and now brought about the emergency had forced him to think, to move out of his shell. But they all would pay for this! . . .

He looked at his watch. . . . He was expecting the Chief. Mr. Howlands despised Jacobo because he was a savage. . . .

There was a knock at the door. Jacobo, gun in hand, came in. He removed his hat and folded it respectfully. There was a big grin which Howlands hated. He had known him for quite a long time. Jacobo had occasionally come to him for advice. . . . In turn Jacobo had helped him to recruit labor and gave him advice on how to get hard work from them. However all this had been a part of the farm. Duty had now thrown them together and he could now see Jacobo in a new light.

"Sit down, Jacobo."

"Thank you, sir."

"What did you want to see me for?"

"Well, sir, it's a long affair."

"Make it short."

"Yes, sir. As I was telling you the other day, I keep an eye on everybody in the village. Now this man Ngotho, as you know, is a bad man. . . . He has taken many oaths." It looked as if Howlands was not attending, so Jacobo paused for a while. Then he beamed. "You know, he is the one who led the strike."

"I know," Howlands cut in. "What has he done?" . . .

You know this man has sons. These sons of his had been away from the village for quite a long time. I think they

are bringing trouble in the village. . . . I am very suspicious about Boro, the eldest son. . . .

"Yes! yes! What have they done?"

"I, well, sir, nothing, but you see these people work in secret. I was just thinking that we should sort of remove them from the village . . . send them to one of the detention camps. . . . Their detention would make it easier to keep an eye on this Ngotho because as I was telling you he may be the real leader of Mau Mau."

"All right. Just keep an eye on the sons. Arrest them for anything, curfew, tax, you know what."

"Yes sir." . . .

"All right. You can go." . . .

Ngotho and his family sat in Nyokabi's hut. These days people sat late only in families. Two were missing from the family group. Kamau was in the African market. He preferred staying and even sleeping there. He felt it safer that way. Boro was not in. He would probably be late. They sat in darkness. Lights had to be put out early. And they spoke in whispers, although they did not speak much. . . . They knew the dark night would be long. Boro and Kori kept their beds in Njeri's hut. Her hut was a few yards away from Nyokabi's. Njeri and Kori waited for Boro to turn up but when he failed they rose up to go. Perhaps Boro would come later in the night or he could sleep wherever he was. Who would dare to go home on such a night, and there being curfew order for everyone to be in by six o'clock? They went out. . . . All of a sudden there was a shout that split the night—

"*Halt!*"

Njoroge trembled. He would not go to the door where his father and mother stood looking at whatever was happening outside. . . . His father came back from the door and sat heavily on the stool he had quickly vacated when he had heard the order for Njeri, his wife, and Kori, his son, to stop. Nyokabi later came in. . . .

"They have taken them away," Nyokabi sobbed. Njoroge felt as if there were some invisible dark shapes in the hut. . . .

Mr. Howlands felt a certain gratifying pleasure. The machine he had set in motion was working. The blacks were destroying the blacks. They would destroy themselves to the end. What did it matter with him if the blacks in the forest destroyed a whole village? . . . Let them destroy themselves. Let them fight against each other. The few who remained would be satisfied with the land the white man had preserved for them. . . . He looked up at Chief Jacobo. A wicked smile lit his face. The desire to kick the Chief was uppermost in his mind. The Chief was grinning.

"Are you sure it's Boro who is leading the gang?"

"Well, one can't be quite sure, but—"

"What?"

"This man, as you are aware, is known to be dangerous. I told you so when you and I talked together before he ran away. Well, I think, I mean there are rumors that he probably comes home . . . but even if this is not the case, Ngotho surely knows his son's hiding-place."

"Haven't you planted men to watch Ngotho's movements and report on them?" . . .

"I have, sir, but there's something else. I didn't, you know, want to tell you, but a few days ago I received this note in an envelope dropped at my door." The Chief fumbled in the inner pockets of his coat and took out a hand-written note which he handed to the curious Howlands.

STOP YOUR MURDEROUS ACTIVITIES. OR ELSE WE SHALL COME FOR YOUR HEAD. THIS IS OUR LAST WARNING.

"Why! Have you received more?"

"Yes—two. But—"

"What did you do with them, you fool?" Mr. Howlands was furious. He stood up. Jacobo moved a few steps back to the door. Howlands could never understand such ignorance. To receive two notes of warning and keep quiet! After a time he cooled down. . . .

It was a cold Monday morning. Njoroge had gone through the first two terms and now was in the third. . . . Njoroge woke up as usual, said his prayers and prepared himself for the morning parade. . . .

The first class was English. Njoroge loved English literature.

"Why, you look happy today," a boy teased him.

"But I'm always happy," he said.

"Not when we're doing maths," another boy put in.

They laughed. Njoroge's laughter rang in the class. The first boy who had spoken said, "See, see how he's laughing. He is happy because this is an English class."

"Do you want me to cry?" Njoroge asked. He felt buoyant.

"No. It's only that my mother tells me that a man should not be too happy in the morning. It's an ill-omen. . . ."

Njoroge was in the middle of answering a question when the headmaster came to the door. . . .

His heart beat hard. He did not know what the headmaster could have to say to him. A black car stood outside the office. But it was only when Njoroge entered the office and saw two police officers that he knew that the car outside had something to do with him. Njoroge's heart pounded with fear. . . .

But when Njoroge went to the car he realized that the headmaster had not given him a clue as to what his family had done. His words of comfort had only served to increase Njoroge's torment.

He would never forget his experience in the post. That particular homeguard post was popularly known as the House of Pain. The day following his arrival in the post he was called in to a small room. Two European officers were present. One had a red beard.

"What's your name?" the red beard asked, while the grey eyes looked at him ferociously.

"Njo-ro-ge."

"How old are you?"

"I think 19 or thereabouts."

"Sema affande!" one of the homeguards outside the small room shouted.

"Affande."

"Have you taken the Oath?" . . .

"No affendi."

"How many have you taken?"

"I said none affendi!"

The blow was swift. It blinded him so he saw darkness. . . .

"Have you taken the Oath?"

"I-am-a-school-boy-affendi," he said, automatically lifting his hands to the face.

"How many Oaths have you taken?"

"None, sir."

Another blow. Tears rolled down his cheeks in spite of himself. He remembered the serenity of his school. It was a lost paradise.

"Do you know Boro?"

"He's my—brother—"

"Where is he?"

"I—don't—know—"

Njoroge lay on the dusty floor. The face of the grey eyes had turned red. He never once spoke except to call him Bloody Mau Mau. A few seconds later Njoroge was taken out by the two homeguards at the door. He was senseless. He was covered with blood where the hobnailed shoes of the grey eyes had done their work. . . .

They had not finished with him. He was in the room the next day. . . . His body had swollen all over. But the worst thing for him was the fact he was still in the dark about all this affair.

"You are Njoroge?"

"Yees."

"Have you taken Oath?" All eyes turned to him. Njoroge hesitated for a moment. He noticed that Mr. Howlands was also present. The grey eyes took the momentary hesitation and said, "Mark, you tell us the truth. If you tell the truth, we shall let you go." The pain in his body came and asked him to say *Yes*. But he instinctively said *No* withdrawing a few steps to the door. Nobody touched him.

"Who murdered Jacobo?" Mr. Howlands asked for the first time. For a time, Njoroge was shaken all over. He thought he was going to be sick.

"Murdered?" he hoarsely whispered in utter unbelief. . . .

The white men closely watched him.

"Yes. Murdered."

"By whom?"

"You'll tell us that."

"Me, Sir? But—" . . .

Mr. Howlands rose and came to Njoroge. He was terrible to look at. He said, "I'll show you." He held Njoroge's private parts with a pair of pincers and started to press tentatively.

"You'll be castrated like your father."

Njoroge screamed.

"Tell us. Who really sent you to collect information in Jacobo's house about . . ?"

Njoroge could not hear: the pain was so bad. . . . And whenever he asked a question, he pressed harder.

"You know your father says he murdered Jacobo."

He still screamed. Mr. Howlands watched him. Then he saw the boy raise his eyes and arms as if in supplication before he became limp and collapsed on the ground. Mr. Howlands looked down on the boy and then at the officers and walked out. The red beard and the grey eyes laughed derisively.

Njoroge was not touched again and when he became well a few days later, he and his two mothers were released.

The hut in which he had been put was dark. Ngotho could not tell day or night. For him, darkness and light were the same thing and time was a succession of nothingness. . . .

The awareness that he had failed his children had always shadowed him. Even before this calamity befell him, life for him had become meaningless, divorced as he had been from what he valued.

In spite of his pain, however, he never regretted the death of Jacobo. . . . This was an act of divine justice. For a day or two he had walked upright only later to hear that his son Kamau was arrested in connection with the murder. For a day and a half, he had remained irresolute. . . . But Ngotho could never tell where he had found courage to walk into the

D.O.'s office and admit that he had killed Jacobo. It was a confession that had shocked the whole village.

And Ngotho had now for days been tortured in all manner of ways, yet would tell nothing beyond the fact that he had killed Jacobo.

Mr. Howlands had, as was the usual practice with government agents and white men, taken the law into his own hands. He was determined to elicit all the information from the man. So he had Ngotho beaten from day to day. . . .

Ngotho, who had worked for him and had thwarted his will, would not now escape from him. For Ngotho had become for him a symbol of evil that now stood in his path. . . .

But Ngotho had stuck to his story. . . .

Ngotho struggled to one side and for the first time opened his eyes. Nyokabi and Njeri quickly moved nearer the bed. Ngotho's eyes roamed around the hut. They rested on each of the women in turn, Njeri first. He opened his mouth as if to speak. Instead a round tear rolled down his face. He wanted to rub it away. But as he could not lift his hand, he let the tear run down unchecked. . . . Ngotho turned his eyes and rested them on Njoroge. He seemed to struggle with his memory. He then made an effort to speak.

"You are here. . . ."

"Yes, father."

This rekindled hope in Njoroge. He felt a cold security when he saw that his father was still in command.

This was Ngotho's first speech since they moved him from the homeguard post, four days before. Njoroge was long to remember the day. Ngotho had to be supported by a man at either side. His face had been deformed by small wounds and scars. His nose was cleft into two and his legs could only be dragged. For four days now his mouth and eyes had remained shut.

"You come from school—"

"Yes, father."

"To see me—"

"Yes." He lied.

"Did they beat you there?"

"No, father."

"Then—you—come to laugh at me. To laugh at your own father. I'll go home, don't worry."

"Don't say that, father. We owe you everything." . . .

Ngotho went on, "Your brothers are all away?"

"They'll come back, father."

"Ha! At my death. To bury me. Where's Kamau?"

Njoroge hesitated. Ngotho continued, "Perhaps they'll kill him. Didn't they take him to the homeguard post? . . . Now, don't ask, Did I kill Jacobo? Did I shoot him? I don't know. A man doesn't know when he kills. I judged him a long time ago and executed him. Ha! Let him come again. . . ."

Ngotho rambled on. All the time his eyes were fixed on Njoroge.

"I am glad you are acquiring learning. Get all of it. They dare not touch you. . . . Who's knocking at the door? I know. It's Mr. Howlands. He wants to get at my heart. . . ."

Ngotho's laughter was cold. It left something tight and tense in the air. By now darkness had crept into the hut. Nyokabi lit the lantern as if to fight it away. Grotesque shadows mocked her as they flitted on the walls. What was a man's life if he could be reduced to this? And Njoroge thought: Could this be the father he had secretly adored and feared? Njoroge's mind reeled. The world had turned upside down. Ngotho was speaking. Except for his laughter, his words were surprisingly clear.

"Boro went away. He found me out— a useless father. But I always knew that they would change him. He didn't know me when he came. . . . You see. . . ."

Njoroge turned his head. He was aware of another presence in the room. Boro was standing at the door. Nobody has seen him enter. His hair was long and unkempt. Njoroge instinctively shrank from him. Boro went nearer, falteringly, as if he would turn away from the light. The women remained rooted to their place. They saw Boro kneel by the bed where Ngotho lay. And at once, long before Boro began to speak, the truth came to Njoroge. He could only hold his breath.

Ngotho could not at first recognize Boro. He seemed to hesitate. Then his eyes seemed to come alive again.

"Forgive me, father—I didn't know—oh, I thought—" Boro turned his head.

The words came out flatly, falteringly. "It's nothing. Ha, ha, ha! You too have come back—to laugh at me? . . . No. Ha! I meant only good for you all. I didn't want you to go away—"

"I had to fight."

"Oh, there—Now—Don't you ever go away again."

"I can't stay. I can't." Boro cried in a hollow voice. A change came over Ngotho. For a time he looked like the man he had been, firm, commanding—the center of his household.

"You must."

"No, father. Just forgive me."

Ngotho exerted himself and sat up in bed. He lifted his hand with an effort and put it on Boro's head. Boro looked like a child.

"All right. Fight well. Turn your eyes to Murungu and Ruriri. Peace to you all —Ha! What? Njoroge look . . . look—to —your—moth—"

His eyes were still aglow as he sank back into the bed. For a moment there was silence in the hut. Then Boro stood up and whispered, "I should have come earlier. . . ."

He ran quickly out, away from the light into the night. It was only when they turned their eyes to Ngotho that they knew that he too would never return. Nobody cried.

THE WAGES OF JEALOUSY

Birago Diop, born in 1906 in Dakar, Senegal, was trained as a veterinary surgeon and has since served the government of Upper Volta in that capacity. In addition, Diop has achieved distinction as a poet and storyteller, preserving in his work the ancient traditions of the folk tale, though adding his own personal embellishments. The following excerpt is taken from a short story entitled "Mamelles." In it Diop purports to pass on information, given him by an African sage, on the origin of the Mamelles hills, "two humps on the Cape Verde peninsula, the last bits of African soil that the sun contemplates lingeringly each evening before sinking into the big sea."

Where wives are concerned, two is not a good number. Anyone who wants to avoid frequent quarrels, cries, reproaches, and spiteful insinuations, needs either three wives or one, but not two. Two wives in the same home always have with them a third companion who is not only good for nothing but also proves to be the worst of counselors. This companion is Envy with a voice as sharp and bitter as tamarind juice.

Envious, Momar's first wife Khary certainly was. She could have filled ten calabashes with her jealously and thrown them in a well, and still have ten times ten goatskins full in the depths of her evil heart. It is true that Khary probably had no great reason to be too happy about her fate, for she was a hunchback. Oh! hers was an infinitesimal little hump that a well-starched blouse or a wide-pleated boubou could easily hide. But Khary imagined that all eyes were riveted on her hump.

She could still hear ringing in her ears the cries: "Khary-the-hunchback! Khary-the-hunchback!" and the mockery of her playmates when as a little girl she went around, like the others, bare to the waist. Every few minutes her playmates would ask to hold the baby that she carried on her back. Enraged, she would chase them, and woe betide anyone who fell into her clutches! Khary would scratch her, tear out her hair and snatch off her ear-rings. . . .

As she matured, Khary's disposition had not improved, quite the contrary; it had soured like milk stepped over by a genie. And now it was Momar who suffered from the wretched humor of his hunchback wife. When he went to the fields, he had to carry along his own meal. Khary was unwilling to leave the house, for fear of mocking glances, nor would she help her husband with the farming.

Tired of working all day without getting a hot meal until dark, Momar had decided to take a second wife and had wed Koumba. At the sight of her husband's new wife, Khary should have become the best of spouses, the most loving of wives. That was what Momar had naively expected—but nothing of the sort happened.

And yet, Koumba, too, was a hunchback. Her hump really exceeded the bounds of normality. But in spite of her hump, Koumba was gay, sweet, and lovable.

Back in the days when she used to play, bare-breasted, and they poked fun at little Koumba-the-hunchback by asking to hold the baby she had on her back, she would answer, laughing louder than the others: "I hardly think he would go to you. He doesn't even want to come down and nurse."

Later, on meeting adults, Koumba, who knew them to be less mocking, perhaps, but more wicked than children, had not changed her disposition. In her husband's home she remained the same as ever. Considering Khary as a big sister, she tried hard to please her. She did all the heavy housework, sifted the grain, and pounded the millet. Each day she took Momar his meal and helped him with his work in the fields.

Khary was no happier for that, far from it. More than before she was sour and embittered, seeing that Koumba didn't seem to mind being a hunchback. Envy is so gluttonous that it feeds on any food. So Momar lived half-happily between his two wives, both humpbacked, but one, gracious, kind, and amiable, the other mean, grumbling, and ill-disposed.

Often, to help her husband for a long period, Koumba would carry to the fields the meal prepared the evening before or at daybreak. When, after digging and weeding since morning, they saw their shadows crouch beneath them seeking refuge from the sun, Momar and Koumba would stop work. Then Koumba would heat the rice or the stew and share it with her husband. Later they would lie in the shade of the tamarind tree that stood in the middle of the field. Instead of sleeping like Momar, Koumba would stroke his head and perhaps daydream of women with perfect forms.

Of all trees, the tamarind is the one that provides the thickest shade. Through its foliage, which the sun rarely penetrates, one can sometimes catch a glimpse of the stars—in broad daylight. That is why the tamarind is the tree most frequented by spirits, good or bad, calm or dissatisfied.

Many madmen, who were sane on leaving their village or their hut in the morning, scream and sing in the evening. In the middle of the day they have passed beneath a tamarind tree, where they have seen what should not have been seen, beings from another realm, spirits whom they had offended by their words or deeds.

There are women, weeping, laughing, yelling, and singing in the villages, who have gone crazy because they poured on the ground boiling water from a pot and burned spirits who were passing by or resting in the courtyard. These spirits had then waited for them in the shade of a tamarind tree and had touched their brain.

Neither Momar nor Koumba had ever offended or injured the spirits by word or deed. So they could rest in the shade of the tamarind without fearing the visit or vengeance of the wicked spirits.

While Momar was sleeping that day, Koumba, sewing near by, thought she heard a voice in the tamarind tree calling her name. Lifting her head, she saw, on the first branch of the tree, an old, a very old woman whose long hair, whiter than unspun cotton, covered her back.

"Are you at peace, Koumba?" the old woman asked.

"At peace, thank you, Grandmother," Koumba answered.

"Koumba, I know how good-hearted and deserving you have been ever since you were first able to tell right from left. I want to do you a great favor. On Friday under the full moon on N'Guew Hill, the girl-spirits will dance. When the tom-toms are beating furiously, and the dance becomes most animated, and when one dancer hurries to replace another dancer, you will come closer and say to the girl-spirit next to you 'Here, hold the baby I have on my back; it's my turn to dance'." . . .

In the village, those who stayed up latest had already turned over once or twice when Koumba left her hut and started out toward N'Guew Hill.

From afar she heard the irrepressible tom-toms and rhythmic hand-clapping. . . . Koumba drew nearer and clapped her hands to the astounding rhythm of the tom-tom and the frantic whirlwind of dancers as one gave way to another.

One, two, three . . . ten of them had twirled and twirled, with boubous and pagnes flying. Then Koumba, offering her hump to her neighbor on the left, said; "Here, hold my baby; it's my turn to dance."

The girl-spirit took the hump and Koumba ran away. She did not stop running till she was back in her hut, which she entered just as the first cock crowed....

Koumba no longer had her hump. Her finely plaited hair fell down over her long, thin gazelle-like neck. As he left his first wife's hut in the morning, Momar saw Koumba and thought he was still dreaming; he rubbed his eyes several times. Koumba told him what had happened.

Khary's saliva turned to gall in her mouth when she saw Koumba drawing water from the well. Khary's eyes became bloodshot; when she opened her mouth, it was as dry as clay awaiting the first rains. But no sound came forth, and she fell in a faint. Momar and Koumba picked her up and carried her back to the hut. . . .

When Khary recovered from the suffocation of the jealousy rising from her stomach to her throat, Koumba, still friendly, told her how she had lost her hump and indicated how Khary, too, might get rid of hers.

Impatiently Khary awaited the next Friday with a full moon; she thought it would never come. Dragging around all day long, the sun no longer seemed in a hurry to return home, and night lingered long before leaving its hut to lead its herd of stars to pasture.

Finally, the Friday arrived, as everything eventually does. Khary couldn't eat a mouthful that evening. She made Koumba repeat the old woman's advice and instructions. Then she heard all the noises of early nightfall diminish and vanish; she listened as the sounds of later night were born and grew. When the earth was cold she started out toward N'Guew Hill where the girl-spirits were dancing. . . .

Khary approached, clapped her hands as her husband's second wife had advised; then, after one, three, ten girl-spirits had entered the circle twirling and left it gasping for breath, she said to her neighbor; "Here, hold my child; it's my turn to dance."

"Oh! No you don't!" the girl-spirit snapped. "It's my turn. Here, hold this one that was handed to me a whole month ago and that no one has come to claim!"

With this, the girl-spirit stuck on Khary's back the hump that Koumba had entrusted to her. The first cock crowed that very instant, the girl-spirits disappeared, and Khary remained alone on N'Guew Hill, alone with her two humps.

Lifting her skirts, she began to run straight ahead. She ran by night, she ran by day, she ran so far and so fast that she reached the sea and jumped in. But she didn't disappear completely. The sea was unwilling to swallow her whole.

So it's the two humps of Khary-Khougue that overhang the point at Cape Verde. It is them that the last rays of the sun light up on the soil of Africa. It's the two humps of Khary that have become the Mamelles.

Somewhere in western Uganda, a priest hears the confession of a parishioner.

A PLACE
IN THE SUN

Bay of Tangier, a water color from Delacroix's Moroccan sketchbook

THE LURE OF AFRICA

Napoleon's Egyptian campaign of 1798–1801 excited widespread interest in the ancient land of the pharaohs. The French army of invasion was accompanied by a team of scholars whose studies inaugurated the new science of Egyptology. With them also was the artist Baron Dominique Denon, whose sketches and paintings created a mania for pharaonic décor. Suddenly, Egyptian-inspired motifs proliferated in the decorative arts—on turbans and tombstones, as crocodile couches and sphinx sofas. Baudelaire dreamed of a "burning Africa," and affluent Europeans "wintered" in Egypt and the Maghreb. In 1832 Eugène Delacroix sketched his impressions of Morocco and Algiers and wrote that the streets of Tangier "assassinate you with reality." Beyond beckoned even more romantic places like the Gold Coast and Madagascar, known mainly through reports of far-ranging merchants.

482

A Denon sketch applied to one of the plates in Napoleon's Sèvres service

Former American president Ulysses S. Grant (seated on a rock in the foreground) and party, posing at the Giza pyramids in the late 1870's

Above, British troops fight from behind a redoubt at Honey Vest Kloot during the Boer War. Cecil Rhodes (below), "roughing it" in the field while his forces put down one of the last native revolts in Rhodesia, the Matabele Rebellion of 1896.

South Africa's industrialization was based on diamonds, first unearthed in 1866. The availability of these gem stones, and of gold, attracted settlers and capital, with which South Africa developed such other enterprises and mineral resources as asbestos, coal, and copper. The Premier Mine near Pretoria (shown at left in a 1927 photograph) is the largest diamond mine in the world. In 1905 it yielded the huge 3,106-carat Cullinan Diamond. At right, gold miners work a vein at Johannesburg's Crown Mine, located in the gold-rich Witwatersrand area.

CECIL RHODES' DREAM

The discovery in the mid-nineteenth century of southern Africa's wealth in diamonds and gold precipitated that region's industrial boom. Railroads and telegraph lines were built to connect the coast with the bountiful resources of the interior. Among the numerous prospectors who went out in the 1870's was Cecil Rhodes, who would eventually control all the diamond mines of southern Africa. Like many other English imperialists, he dreamed of an Africa "all British from the Cape to Cairo." He was prepared to use his millions, ruthlessly if need be, to implement the vision. In 1885 Rhodes persuaded Parliament to annex the land corridor of Bechuanaland as a "Suez Canal to the north." The next year extensive gold deposits were discovered in the Transvaal, spurring his government's determination to add a united South Africa to its expanding empire. Rhodes' British South Africa Company, which received a royal charter in 1889, became the agency for his conquest of what are now Rhodesia and Zambia. Uganda was "protected" by the Crown in 1894, and the Sudan secured by Lord Kitchener in 1898. Britain's victory in the Boer War of 1899–1902 gave it control of all South Africa. Only German-ruled Tanganyika now obstructed its African corridor.

Through the exploitation of labor gangs, like that above, the railway system of southern Africa expanded rapidly. Between 1860 and 1910 tracks were laid from the Cape as far north as Elizabethville in the Congo.

Many startling incongruities appeared as white colonialists attempted to impose their manners and life styles on Africans. Left, the black policemen of Natal, South Africa, have borrowed all the trappings of European gendarmes, including whistles, caps, and shining brass buttons, but their feet are bare. The Durban rickshaw boys below have decked themselves in traditional headgear to attract fares. And, in East Africa, a colonial gentleman (opposite below) clears a hurdle on a tamed zebra.

The British advocated indirect rule in Africa; the French favored more direct control of their possessions. But both in their behavior sought the affectations of Europe's gentry. The English enjoyed their sports and garden parties. The 1947 photograph (opposite) of a Kenya master of the hunt could have been taken in England were it not for the black estate-hands. And the Moulin Rouge girl and her Foreign Legionnaire "beau" (right) are not in gay Paris, but in Sidi-bel-Abbes, Algeria, long the Legion's headquarters.

H. ROGER VIOLLET

THE COLONIAL SCENE

Aloof, self-satisfied, and patriotic, the English colonialists, who were generally from the upper middle class, took a little bit of England with them wherever they went in their vast empire. Parasoled and pomaded, they always remained unmistakably British—"Just We Our Noble Selves," as Kipling put it. They enjoyed their colonial existence, with its endless round of teas and tennis, but failed to grasp the aspirations of the "natives," whom they considered primitive and uncivilized. However, the Africans would rise up against their exploiters. Charles Domingo, an uneducated black from Nyasaland (now Malawi), expressed the whispers of his continent in 1911: "There is too much failure among all Europeans in Nyasaland. The three combined bodies—Missionaries, Government and Companies or gainers of money—do form the same rule to look upon the native with mockery eyes … They are altogether too cheaty, too thefty, too mockery. Instead of 'Give,' they say 'Take away from.'"

LIBRARY OF CONGRESS

487

Wedding of Manuel Kisende, pastor-teacher
at Mataba, Quessua District, Angola.

Missionary John Brastrup pulls a tooth, Belgian Congo.

Bishop Moore and native Chiefs Wembo Nyama.

Dr. Sheffrey and native assistant in laboratory of Methodist Hospital Wembo Nyama, Belgian Congo.

Sewing in the Methodist School Nyadiri, So. Rhodesia.

Group of Pathfinder Scouts, Nyadiri School. So. Rhodesia

Close-up of a witch doctor. Ganta, Liberia

TOWARD A NEW ORDER

Mussolini's conquest of Ethiopia in 1936 enraged Africans all over the continent, adding fuel to the fire of nationalistic sentiments that had been intensifying since World War I. Many Africans had emerged from the Great War yearning for democracy and Wilsonian self-determination. By the 1920's colonial revenues were, for the first time, beginning to show modest profits, and metropolitan governments started to develop medical, educational, agricultural, and veterinary services in their dependencies. Soon a slowly expanding school system was producing Africa's first professionals, a bourgeois class equipped for leadership and participation in government. They watched, horrified, as France stamped out Berber resistance in Morocco and colonial forces subdued local uprisings. They aimed not at the restoration of the precolonial order, but were determined to develop the political and social institutions introduced from Europe. In this spirit they welcomed the establishment of African, or "Ethiopian", churches and launched West Africa's first popular press. European and traditional authorities looked contemptuously at this new elite, calling its members "trousered blacks." But these "handfuls of examination-bred students" would mold Africa's future.

The Foreign Legionnaires (opposite) were part of the joint French and Spanish military force that in 1926 finally "pacified" Abd al-Karim and his Berbers in Morocco's Rif mountains. Above, Italian troops prepare to leave for the Ethiopian front in 1935.

President Gamal Abdel Nasser (right) of the United Arab Republic is greeted by cheering throngs at the Cairo railroad station on his return from a foreign mission. He masterminded the army coup that in 1952 ousted Egypt's King Farouk. Within two years Nasser had established himself as head of state, thus becoming his country's first native-born ruler in over two thousand years. Nasser's seizure of power signaled the beginning of the end of European rule in North Africa. Dashiki-clad Kwame Nkrumah (above) waves to crowds in Accra on Independence Day, March 6, 1957, when the Gold Coast became Ghana. Long a leader of the pan-African movement, Nkrumah, like Nasser, helped create Africa's new order.

FREEDOM NOW

Between the end of World War II and the early 1960's African nationalism intensified. The colonial powers were no longer invincible bastions of strength. Two new super powers, the United States and Soviet Russia, shared the limelight of world domination. Both courted the favor of Africa's emergent states, now part of the nonaligned Third World. For the first time Africans possessed a modicum of political maneuverability. They were also becoming more conscious than ever of the potential of black solidarity in a white world. It was in this atmosphere that Kwame Nkrumah of the Gold Coast agitated for his people's independence, which was won without bloodshed in 1957. In Kenya freedom came in 1963, but only after the violent Mau Mau terror of the 1950's. By this time cries of *uhuru*—Swahili for "freedom"—were reverberating throughout Africa.

Jomo "Burning Spear" Kenyatta, the idolized leader of Kenya's Kikuyu people, is pictured above after his arrest by the British in 1952. Charged with directing the Mau Mau terrorists, he was detained until 1961. Kenyatta then led the fight for independence, becoming prime minister of the new state of Kenya in 1963. OVERLEAF: *A member of the banned Mau Mau society is captured.*

Chapter Twelve

AFRICA FOR THE AFRICANS

by

Immanuel Wallerstein

MARCH 6, 1957, was an important, symbolic date in the history of modern Africa. It was the day on which Ghana (formerly the colony of the Gold Coast) became independent, the first Black African state to do so in the twentieth century.

Ghana was not, however, the first autonomous state on the continent. Ethiopia had been independent throughout its history except for a very brief period from 1935 to 1941. Liberia had been founded as a free republic in 1847. Egypt had been independent since 1922. The Union of South Africa had become a self-governing state in 1910 (though under the domination of a white minority).

In addition, a number of states of Arab North Africa had become independent in the six years preceding 1957. Libya had been granted independence in 1951; Tunisia and Morocco in 1956. The Anglo-Egyptian Sudan had become the Republic of the Sudan on January 1, 1956.

Although the Sudan might legitimately be considered by many to be part of Black Africa, it was, nonetheless, Ghana's independence that in the eyes of Africa and of the world represented the dawning of a new era. The countries of the whole world sent representatives to the festivities. Princess Alexandra represented Queen Elizabeth; President Habib Bourguiba of Tunisia came in person. The United States sent its then vice president, Richard M. Nixon.

The independence of Ghana as the "first" independence had a psychological impact on the rest of Africa that far outweighed the importance of this relatively small African state. It meant that for Africans and for others a transfer of power to an all-black independent government was a realizable alternative to the continuance of colonial rule in one guise or another.

The effect could be seen in many places. In nearby Nigeria political leaders of the three regions, into which the

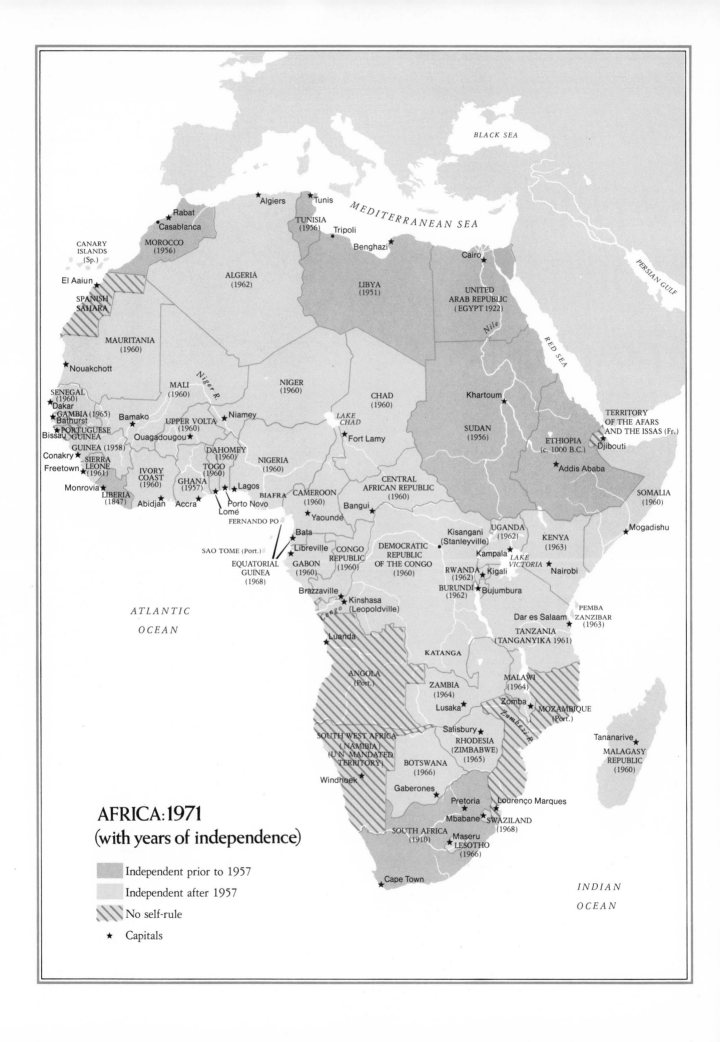

BLACK SEA

MEDITERRANEAN SEA

PERSIAN GULF

★ Algiers   ★ Tunis

Rabat ●
Casablanca   TUNISIA
(1956)   ● Tripoli

MOROCCO
(1956)   Benghazi ●

CANARY
ISLANDS
(Sp.)

ALGERIÁ
(1962)

LIBYA
(1951)

Cairo ●
★

UNITED
ARAB REPUBLIC
(EGYPT 1922)

El Aaiun ★

SPANISH
SAHARA

MAURITANIA
(1960)

Nile

RED SEA

Nouakchott ★

MALI
(1960)

Niger R.

NIGER
(1960)

CHAD
(1960)

Khartoum ●

TERRITORY
OF THE AFARS
AND THE ISSAS (Fr.)

SENEGAL
(1960)
★ Dakar
★ GAMBIA (1965)
Bathurst
Bissau PORTUGUESE
GUINEA (1958)

Bamako ★

Niamey ★

SUDAN
(1956)

ETHIOPIA
(c. 1000 B.C.)

Djibouti ★

UPPER VOLTA
(1960)
Ouagadougou ★

LAKE
CHAD

Fort Lamy ★

Conakry ●
★ SIERRA
Freetown LEONE
(1961)

GUINEA
(1958)

IVORY
COAST
(1960)

DAHOMEY
(1960)

GHANA
(1957)

Addis Ababa ★

Monrovia ★
LIBERIA
(1847)

Abidjan ★

TOGO
(1960)

Accra ★

Lagos ★

NIGERIA
(1960)

Porto Novo
Lomé

BIAFRA

CENTRAL
AFRICAN REPUBLIC
(1960)

SOMALIA
(1960)

CAMEROON
(1960)

Mogadishu ★

FERNANDO PO

★ Yaoundé

Bangui ★

SAO TOME (Port.)

Bata ★

Libreville ★

EQUATORIAL
GUINEA
(1968)

GABON
(1960)

CONGO
REPUBLIC
(1960)

DEMOCRATIC
REPUBLIC
OF THE CONGO
(1960)

Kisangani
(Stanleyville) ●

UGANDA
(1962)

Kampala ★

KENYA
(1963)

RWANDA
(1962)

Kigali ★

LAKE
VICTORIA

Nairobi ★

BURUNDI
(1962)

Bujumbura ★

Brazzaville ★

ATLANTIC

OCEAN

Congo

★ Kinshasa
(Leopoldville)

PEMBA
ZANZIBAR
(1963)

Dar es Salaam ★

Luanda ★

KATANGA

TANZANIA
(TANGANYIKA 1961)

ANGOLA
(Port.)

ZAMBIA
(1964)

MALAWI
(1964)

Zomba ★

MOZAMBIQUE
(Port.)

Lusaka ★

Zambezi R.

SOUTH WEST AFRICA
(NAMIBIA)
(U N MANDATED
TERRITORY)

Salisbury ★
RHODESIA
(ZIMBABWE)
(1965)

Tananarive ★

MALAGASY
REPUBLIC
(1960)

BOTSWANA
(1966)

Windhoek ★

Gaberones ★

Pretoria
★

Lourenço Marques ★

AFRICA: 1971
(with years of independence)

Mbabane ★ SWAZILAND
(1968)

Maseru ★
LESOTHO
(1966)

SOUTH AFRICA
(1910)

Independent prior to 1957

Independent after 1957

No self-rule

★ Capitals

Cape Town ★

INDIAN

OCEAN

country was divided, buried their differences the following month and agreed to work together to achieve independence. In French Black Africa the main political movement, the *Rassemblement Démocratique Africain* (RDA), had always eschewed independence as a specific political goal. In October of 1957, however, at the Third Interterritorial Congress of the RDA at Bamako, capital of Mali, the RDA proclaimed that all African states had "the right to independence." In East and Central Africa leaders of nationalist movements rejected "multiracial" formulas—by which the black African, white, and Asian communities were to be separately represented in the legislature—and indicated their intention to strive for independence on the basis of one man, one vote, and majority rule.

Ghana's independence affected the white settler-dominated areas of southern Africa as well. The inconceivable —the governance by blacks of an independent state—had become conceivable. At the conferences of the Commonwealth's British prime ministers, the white prime minister of South Africa found as his peer and colleague the black prime minister of Ghana. The sense of the ongoing revolution was felt throughout the white world—in Africa, in the United States, and in the colonial metropoles of the United Kingdom, France, and Belgium.

Ghana saw its role not merely as a symbol of the new possibilities. The government of Ghana immediately began to pursue an active policy of pan-Africanism, of support for the struggle for independence and majority rule in other African countries. One of the first objectives was to convene a Conference of Independent African States (CIAS), which took place in Accra, Ghana's capital, in April, 1958. *All* independent states on the African continent, even white-dominated South Africa, were invited to the initial preparatory committee meeting. South Africa demanded as a condition of its attendance that an invitation be extended to the various colonial powers. When Ghana rejected this condition, South Africa declined to come. This was the first and last time the white government of South Africa was to be invited to a pan-African conference.

Eight states came to the CIAS meeting in Accra: Ethiopia, Ghana, Liberia, Libya, Morocco, Sudan, Tunisia, and the United Arab Republic. Without the Arab-African states, there would hardly have been a meeting. A crucial turning point in the history of pan-Africanism had been reached; pan-African meetings would thereafter include the whole continent, not just "black" areas. The geopolitical concept that had seemed immutable during the colonial era, that of two Africas—one north of the Sahara and the other south

of the Sahara—was all but banished from the vocabulary and the minds of those living on the continent.

Delegates at the first meeting of the CIAS made two decisions of great importance. They decided to give the liberation of still-dependent territories priority in their political efforts. Specifically, they voted to support the Algerian *Front de Libération Nationale* (FLN), leading what was at that time Africa's most significant war of independence. The support was very concrete. The independent African states undertook to send diplomatic missions to potentially sympathetic governments in Scandinavia, Central America, and South America to encourage support for the FLN as the legitimate representative of the Algerian people. Their ultimate goal was to enlist votes for United Nations resolutions, calling on France to negotiate with the FLN and grant independence to Algeria. Indeed, the United Nations was a central focus of African independent states' early politico-diplomatic activity.

The second major decision of the CIAS meeting was to establish permanent consultative machinery in the form of regular meetings in New York of its ambassadors to the United Nations. Thus was formed the so-called African Group, which would play an increasingly important role at the United Nations in the years to come.

Ghana's pan-Africanist thrust did not stop at the convening of the CIAS. Later that same year, in December, 1958, Ghana's Africa Bureau, an agency of Ghana's government to promote pan-African ideas, arranged the first meeting of a new group, the All-African Peoples' Conference (AAPC). The invitees represented were not states but movements— political parties and trade unions—coming not only from independent Africa but also from the states of colonial and white settler-controlled Africa.

The atmosphere of the AAPC was more lively and more militant than that of the CIAS, which had represented governments. Also, from a pan-African point of view, it represented a far larger cross section of the continent's peoples and ideologies. It was at this meeting of the AAPC that the creation of the Commonwealth of Free African States, an all-African governmental structure, was first recognized as an objective of pan-Africanism. It was at this meeting, too, that "tribalism" was denounced as a barrier to African progress.

On colonial issues the AAPC called for the recognition of the Provisional Government of the Algerian Republic (known by its French initials as the GPRA), a structure that had been created by the FLN after the April CIAS meeting. The meeting also called for special efforts to secure

After 1957, fashionable Ghanaians and other Africans expressed their delight in freedom by wearing Nkrumah-emblazoned clothing.

fed upon itself and was to a large degree self-fulfilling.

Events all over the continent reflected this movement. In North Africa the continuing strain of the Algerian war led to a French internal crisis of major proportions in early 1958, which brought Charles de Gaulle back to power. Although many of the forces supporting De Gaulle were motivated by a desire to halt or slow down the decolonization of French Africa, particularly of Algeria, De Gaulle's accession to power nonetheless set in train a series of events that would bring about within four years independence for virtually all of French Africa, even Algeria.

At first, however, the French sought at all costs to keep Algeria. To consolidate his power, De Gaulle submitted a new constitution to a referendum throughout the French Union. The constitution provided for increased powers to the president and increased political rights for French overseas territories, not, however, including Algeria. For voters in France itself, the issue of the referendum was seen to be the structure of the French government. In Algeria a vote in favor of the new constitution was interpreted as a vote to keep Algeria French.

In the rest of French Africa, however, the referendum took on another meaning. This was because, as a concession to growing nationalist sentiment, De Gaulle had written into the proposed laws a new autonomous status for the Black African states. De Gaulle actually went to France's Black African territories to seek support for his referendum. There, egged on by nationalist stirrings, he went one step further. He said he would interpret a "no" vote in any African territory as a rejection of the status of autonomy and a withdrawal from the new French community. "Yes" would mean autonomy; "no" would mean independence.

The states of French Black Africa were faced with an important political choice. Very few political parties decided to seek a "no" vote, and only one of these succeeded in pulling it off: the ruling party of Guinea, affiliated with the RDA, called for a "no" vote and received almost unanimous backing. After the vote the new president of Guinea, Sékou Touré, extended the hand of friendship to France, but President De Gaulle, reacting in pique, abruptly withdrew all French assistance, personnel, and equipment (even some telephone lines) in an attempt to punish and isolate the rebellious state.

As a response to this attempt by France to stifle Guinea's impact on other French African states, Ghana and Guinea announced on November 23, 1958, their union. Although, structurally, the Ghana-Guinea Union amounted to little more than a financial loan by Ghana to Guinea,

UN-supervised elections in French Cameroun *before* independence in order to foil what were considered to be French attempts to install a puppet regime rather than one led by the most militant nationalist organization, the *Union des Populations du Cameroun.* This concern with the Cameroun situation caused the African Group to seek and obtain a special convening of the UN General Assembly in February, 1969, solely to deal with Cameroun. However, in what was to be the first of many frustrations encountered by the African states in attempting to use the UN machinery to achieve difficult political goals, the African Group was unable to secure the UN-supervised elections they sought.

Nonetheless, the years from 1958 to 1960 were years of tremendous forward movement for African nationalism and pan-Africanism. The independence of Ghana, followed by the two Accra conferences of 1958—the CIAS and the AAPC—created a sense of dynamism and optimism that and the establishment of some joint political committees; psychologically and politically it meant much more. The Ghana-Guinea Union was the first real bridging of the linguistic gap that European colonialism had created in Africa.

Meanwhile, the struggle for independence was escalating throughout Africa. As already noted, Algeria's FLN responded to De Gaulle's return to power by creating the Provisional Government, or GPRA. The determination to gain independence without compromise was reinforced. In East and Central Africa, inspired by the CIAS meeting at which they had been observers, the leaders of the nationalist movements of the various British colonies created the Pan-African Freedom Movement for East Central Africa (PAFMECA) on September 17, 1958. The object of PAFMECA was to coordinate the political efforts of the different parties in order to secure a rapid transfer of power.

In French Black Africa De Gaulle's moves against Guinea were of no avail. Guinea, sustained initially by African and east European assistance, maintained its equilibrium and joined the UN, where it promptly became the most vigorous and radical spokesman of African liberation. Guinea's example spread. By 1960 President De Gaulle was forced to accede by negotiation with the other states within the French community to the very independence that he had been punishing Guinea for achieving. The British agreed to grant Nigeria its independence in 1960. Somalia, an Italian trust territory, had long been scheduled to get independence the same year. In the Belgian Congo, thought to be an impervious stronghold of eternal colonial rule, riots broke out in Leopoldville in January, 1959, a few weeks following the All-African Peoples' Conference, to which Congolese nationalist leaders had gone. Suddenly the dike broke. The Belgians began to talk of decolonization, and one short year later, on June 30, 1960, they agreed to give the Congo its freedom.

Even in the citadel of white-settler ideology—South Africa—events took on a new face. In February, 1960, Prime Minister Harold Macmillan visited South Africa, where he addressed Parliament. This was the famous speech in which he said: "The wind of change is blowing through [Africa], and whether we like it or not this growth of national consciousness is a political fact. We must all accept it as a fact, and our national policies must take account of it."

The very next month was a month of crisis. An African demonstration at Sharpeville was gunned down by the police, and by March 30 a state of emergency had been declared. (By the end of the year South Africa's white electorate had voted to become a republic. The British govern-

ment deemed that this meant that South Africa had to reapply for membership to the Commonwealth. At first South Africa did so, but in March, 1961, Prime Minister Hendrik Verwoerd withdrew South Africa's application to stay in the Commonwealth as a republic in the face of almost certain refusal.)

Nineteen hundred sixty, often called the Year of Africa, was a year in which much formal political change was occurring on the continent of Africa in the direction of African liberation. Despite this, 1960 was also the year of the first of a series of major setbacks for African liberation. It was the year of the first Congo crisis. On June 30 the Congo became independent. Within one week the Congolese army, the *Force Publique*, had rebelled—largely against the Belgian officers still in command and against the Congolese government, which countenanced this situation. In the confusion that followed, mineral-rich Katanga, under provincial president Moise Tshombe, seceded, and Belgian troops invaded the Congo, ostensibly to protect Belgian lives in areas controlled by the central government. The Belgians, however, actually landed in Katanga. The Congolese government appealed to the UN for troops, which were sent, the contingents coming in part from African countries. The UN troops went to all parts of the Congo except Katanga, where Belgian troops provided a de facto defense shield for the secessionist province. The UN command rather hindered attempts by the Congolese army, partially back under the control of the government, to restore the authority of the central government in Katanga.

Throughout July and August public order continued to be uncertain in the Congo, and the political strains between the two main central government factions—the one led by Prime Minister Patrice Lumumba and the other by President Joseph Kasavubu—worsened steadily. A special meeting of the foreign ministers of the CIAS in Leopoldville in August solved nothing.

In early September Kasavubu dismissed Lumumba in a move of dubious constitutional validity. Lumumba challenged the legality of this action. The army, under Colonel Joseph Mobutu, who had ousted his superior officer, announced neutrality, closed Parliament, and then claimed power itself in conjunction with Kasavubu. The UN command also claimed neutrality, but acted in a way that many observers felt supported Kasavubu.

African independent states, including those with troops in the Congo, split over the question of whether Kasavubu or Lumumba represented the legal central government. Outside Africa, Western powers generally supported Kasa-

Dr. Hendrik Verwoerd (above), South Africa's prime minister from 1958 to 1966, was the chief architect of apartheid. Under this policy the white minority pursues a separate, privileged life, as in the game of bowls at left. Black protest is crushed, as in the scene opposite at Sharpeville in 1960, where the police killed sixty-seven African demonstrators.

vubu. The Soviet Union supported Lumumba. Meanwhile, Katanga's secession continued.

Beneath the welter of detail and the purely legal-constitutional issues of the Congo crisis lay a fundamental political issue that divided Africa, then and ever since. On the one side were those Africans who felt that the achievement of state sovereignty for African states was merely a minor step in a more basic and revolutionary thrust for African liberation. They drew a series of conclusions from this premise. They felt that political independence was not secure as long as other African states were colonized; hence very active support should be given to the remaining anticolonial struggles in southern Africa. They felt that most African states were too small to be politically viable; hence steps toward meaningful African unity had to begin rapidly. They felt that political independence would not bring true independence unless it was coupled with economic independence; hence states should reject "neocolonial" links to their former colonial power and other Western capitalist states. (The third All-African Peoples' Conference, in 1961, denounced as manifestations of neocolonialism: puppet governments; regrouping of states in federations linked to overseas powers; deliberate fragmentation

by the creation of artificial political entities; economic interference in a variety of guises, including direct monetary dependence; and the maintenance of foreign military and/or research bases.) They felt, further, that African states should be "nonaligned" internationally, which meant, in their view, cultivation of new diplomatic, political, economic, and cultural ties with the Communist world in order to reduce the primacy of ties with the Western world, and gain a new balance. Finally, they felt that economic development required rapid industrialization and the establishment of socialist modes of organization of the economy.

African political theorists of the opposing view worked on a quite different premise: that Africa, being weak, required assistance from the Western world in order to make economic progress, and that such assistance required a political quid pro quo. They placed less emphasis on the liberation of southern Africa (though they lent verbal support). They thought African political federation to be a utopian goal, and talked of loose forms of economic cooperation. Far from wanting to break economic ties with the West, they wished to reinforce and expand them. Their version of "nonalignment" was limited to a reluctance to form *formal* political alignment with the West. They were highly suspicious of Communist motives. While sometimes utilizing the term "socialist" to describe their objectives, this group sought to keep African economies open and welcoming to Western capital.

In the immediate Congo crisis the first group supported Lumumba, and the second Kasavubu. In the parallel debate over what kind of action the UN should take on the continuing Algerian war of independence, the first group unequivocally supported the GPRA, the second group sought to be more conciliatory toward France.

This split was soon to take institutional form. In October, 1960, President Félix Houphouët-Boigny of the Ivory Coast invited the states that formerly made up French Black Africa, plus the Malagasy (Malgache) Republic on the Island of Madagascar, to come together in Abidjan to discuss a common position on the Congo and Algerian issues. Soon thereafter this group of states became the *Union Africaine et Malgache* (UAM), otherwise known as the Brazzaville Group. This group supported Joseph Kasavubu. In January, 1961, a countergroup was formed. The so-called Casablanca Group included Ghana, Guinea, Mali, Morocco, the United Arab Republic, and Algeria's GPRA. This group supported Lumumba and, of course, the GPRA.

The states of East and Central Africa were placed in a delicate position by this split among African independent states. The nationalist movements of seven states had created PAFMECA. Three of the PAFMECA states bordered the Congo. All were under British rule, and they were hopeful of achieving independence within the foreseeable future. For the time being they supported Patrice Lumumba.

Lumumba himself fell into the hands of the Kasavubu government and in January, 1961, was turned over to the Katanga authorities, who murdered him. The Lumumbists set up their rival central government in Stanleyville. Lumumba became a martyr to revolutionary Africa.

The Congo turmoil had a direct impact on neighboring Angola, which became the first Portuguese territory to experience armed rebellion. On February 4, 1961, there was an uprising in Luanda, the capital, led by the *Movimento Popular para Libertação da Angola* (MPLA), and on March 15 rural guerrilla warfare started in the northern province adjoining the Congo, led by the *União das Populações da Angola* (UPA). The MPLA-UPA split paralleled the Lumumba-Kasavubu and Casablanca-Brazzaville splits, and alliances were made accordingly.

Some attempts were made to heal this inter-African split.

AFRICA FOR THE AFRICANS

Some African states belonged neither to the Brazzaville nor the Casablanca groups. In May, 1961, a meeting of all independent states was convened in Monrovia, Liberia. At the last minute the Casablanca powers declined to come. The resulting organization, which called itself the Inter-African and Malagasy Organization (IAMO), or Monrovia Group, was nothing but an enlarged Brazzaville Group.

The attempt to reunify inter-African political structures was premature. In 1962, however, two events occurred that would make such reunification more plausible. One was the Evian Accords, so named because the agreement was reached in the French city of Evian, which led to the independence of Algeria in July, 1962. The second was a temporary internal reconciliation in the Congo. In August, 1961, the two claimants to central power in the Congo— the Kasavubu forces in Leopoldville and the Lumumbists in Stanleyville—agreed to a united government under Cyrille Adoula as prime minister. The UN command strongly supported this new regime and, after two false starts, sent in troops to Katanga in December, 1962, and finally put down the secession. Congolese sovereignty was thus re-established.

The two immediate thorns to African unity being removed—differences concerning the Congo and Algeria— and an international détente between the United States and the Soviet Union seemingly established, the moment was ripe for new attempts at unity.

But just as independent African states were about to shelve their differences and join together in an Organization of African Unity (OAU), the first of a series of coups began when President Sylvanus Olympio of Togo was assassinated by army elements on January 13, 1963. Once again, this "first" was not a real first. Egypt's monarchy had been overthrown by a coup in 1952; in November, 1958, the army overthrew the government of the Sudan and remained in power until October, 1964. However, the Togo coup was the first since the large spate of nations had achieved their separate independences in 1960 and the first marked by an assassination of the top political leader.

Olympio's assassination profoundly shocked the governments of all African states. Many were reluctant to recognize the new regime, and they split anew over the Togo recognition issue. The lines drawn were unexpected. Among the most hostile to recognition were Guinea (of the Casablanca Group) and the Ivory Coast (of the Brazzaville Group). On the other hand, Togo's two neighbors, Ghana (a Casablanca power) and Dahomey (a Brazzaville power), were inclined to work with the new government. Although the Togo recognition issue would not be solved in time for

Frantz Fanon (above), born in Martinique but caught up in Algeria's liberation, became in his brief life a romantic hero of decolonization and a polemicist for the Third World. With Algerian independence achieved, rebel leader and later premier Ahmed Ben Bella (opposite) returns home in 1962.
ALGERIAN MINISTRY OF INFORMATION

MAGNUM—MARC RIBOUD

the founding meeting of the Organization of African Unity in May of 1963, and hence Togo was not invited to that meeting, the new government was eventually recognized by all African states, indeed by all states throughout the world. A clear precedent for further coups was set. De facto control would lead to recognition and full participation in inter-African activities.

Between 1963 and 1971 seventeen African states have known successful coups d'état, a few of them several times. In addition, there have been abortive coups in many other states. Although the circumstances vary from case to case, there seem to be two main patterns among the coups, those arising in the Casablanca-type states, sometimes called the revolutionary states, and those in the Monrovia-type states, sometimes called the moderates.

All African states, of whatever bent, have faced some basic dilemmas after independence. The state machinery has been very weak. The bureaucracy has been insufficient in size and effectiveness; nonetheless, government administration has absorbed too large a part of the states' budgets. The budgets of these regimes have steadily expanded under the pressure of demands of the urban middle class and of the workers, both rural and urban. The latter class has

504

placed particular pressure on expansion of schooling and job-earning opportunities, while the former has pressed for uneconomic expenditures that have provided them with greater facilities and perquisites. These expenditures have been compounded by the "corruption" that has been a widespread feature of the regimes.

However, almost nowhere has governmental income risen to match increased governmental expenditures—partly because of widespread tax evasion, partly because of political resistance to higher taxation by urban wage earners and foreign investors. The only exceptions are some mineral-producing countries, the high demand for whose products has placed them in a relatively better international bargaining position. In any case, the results have been very simple: governments have suffered a steadily increasing budgetary gap.

The Monrovia-type powers have tried to handle this difficulty by maintaining a relatively open economy, and hence continuing close economic involvement in the international economic networks of their former colonial overlords, perhaps supplemented by new links to the United States and West Germany. As unemployment increased because of the swelling numbers of educated individuals who could

not be absorbed into a more slowly developing economy, and Western powers became more reluctant to compensate for budget deficits, governments often attempted mild austerity programs. This tended to alienate the cadres against whom they were directed—the new elite in particular— while irritating the unemployed by the mildness of the measures.

In the tight employment situation of such countries, "tribalism" (that is, giving particularistic preference to others coming from the same "tribe" or ethnic group) became a natural corollary of self-protection. This often led to outbreaks of violence, which were increasingly met by political or military repression. Often the outcome was a coup.

To the extent that rivalry among Western powers was important in a particular country, coup leaders may have received the support and encouragement of a power displeased by the former regime. Togo in 1963 is a case in point. The immediate precipitant to the coup was Olympio's austerity program. In furtherance of this program, he refused to employ in the Togo army individual Togolese released from service in the French army. Since many of these persons came from the Kabre people, and many of the noncommissioned officers and privates of the Togo army were also Kabre, the Kabre precipitated a coup. It was not without relevance that France had been very displeased with the Olympio regime because he had opened the country to United States and German economic involvement and had refused to join the Brazzaville Group (despite the fact that Togo was a member of the Monrovia Group). The government that succeeded Olympio's regime developed closer ties with France and joined the Brazzaville Group.

So-called radical regimes were faced with somewhat different dilemmas. (The first of these governments was not to fall until 1965.) These regimes invested more in job opportunities and had tighter monetary and import controls, which meant less luxury expenditures. They had therefore less unemployment and, consequently, less "tribalism." But the bureaucrats, the armies, and the political classes were increasingly unhappy about the constraints on their style of life. There was also growing displeasure among the Western powers, both because of their foreign policy and because of the difficulties caused to Western firms and their employees. In some of these states the accumulation of enemies came to be too much for the regime, and a coup ensued.

In May of 1963, at Addis Ababa, Ethiopia, the division of African states came to an end with the creation of the Organization of African Unity (OAU). It momentarily renewed the optimistic atmosphere so prevalent in early 1960. The divisions of Casablanca and Monrovia seemed surmounted, and the assassination of Olympio was not allowed to undo this new drive for unity. Beneath the euphoria of the founding of the OAU could be discerned the crumbling of internal stability of the independent African states. Yet it was euphoria nonetheless.

Furthermore, unity was based on an unstable compromise between the member states. The Monrovia powers got the kind of loose confederal structure they wanted for the OAU (rather than the United States of Africa some had called for). In addition, they got a promise from the Casablanca states that they would cease giving political support to opposition elements in the Monrovia states. In return, the OAU was officially committed to nonalignment. And most important, all African states were obligated to contribute material aid to the African Liberation Committee (ALC), a body established under the OAU. The function of the ALC was to organize and channel financial, political, and military assistance to liberation movements in the remaining colonies, principally in southern Africa.

Almost immediately the OAU discovered a knotty problem. Most inter-African organizations disbanded in its

TIME INC.—RALPH CRANE

favor, including the Casablanca and Monrovia groups and PAFMECSA, which consisted of the earlier Pan-African Movement of East and Central Africa, or PAFMECA, begun in 1958 but expanded in 1962 to include southern African parties. But the Brazzaville powers, or UAM, refused to dissolve. They insisted they were a regional organization permitted within the framework of OAU. They did, however, as a gesture, eliminate their office at the UN to indicate they had no political function, and in 1964 they went further and changed the name of the organization so as to emphasize the primarily economic character of the association. It now became the *Union Africaine et Malgache de Coopération Economique* (UAMCE). Some UAM states, notably the Ivory Coast, were unhappy with this shift and declined to participate in the UAMCE. The spirit of OAU primacy appeared to be gaining ground.

The pace of African liberation also quickened again, and the British timetable for granting independence to its former colonies in East and West Africa was advanced. Kenya, once the great white-settler state of East Africa, became independent under majority rule in 1963. The British broke up the Central African Federation (of the Rhodesias and Nyasaland), which African nationalists had persistently opposed since 1953, and Malawi and Zambia became independent in 1964. There was hope that Southern Rhodesia would follow the path of Kenya.

But the compromise of the OAU was, as stated above, very unstable. By December, 1963, the internal compromise of the Congo had broken down and the ex-Lumumbists established the *Conseil National de Libération* (CNL), with headquarters in neighboring Brazzaville (a more radical

Throughout Africa, modern technology is attacking age-old agricultural problems. The UAR's Soviet-backed Aswan Dam, shown opposite during construction, was completed in 1970. It will control floods and irrigate 1,300,000 acres of previously arid land, but at the same time it prevents silt from reaching the Delta, where farmers are now forced to buy synthetic fertilizers. By the 1960's Rhodesia's tea industry was competing successfully on the world market. As at right, Africans pluck the young tea shoots for processing.

regime had been installed there after a coup the previous July). Guerrilla warfare broke out in the Congo (Kinshasa). In June, 1964, the last United Nations' troops were scheduled to be withdrawn from the Congo. President Kasavubu, fearing the strength of the CNL forces, appointed the former Katanga secessionist leader Moise Tshombe as prime minister. Tshombe returned to the Congo from exile in Angola with his white, mercenary-led ex-Katanga forces.

Civil war broke out again in the Congo, and the OAU sought to put out the fire. It appointed a special committee under the chairmanship of President Jomo Kenyatta of Kenya. As the situation deteriorated, concern focused on the fact that the CNL forces held hostage a group of whites in Stanleyville, attempting to use these hostages to force central government troops to halt their march on the CNL-held city. In the midst of negotiations under the aegis of the OAU committee, Belgian paratroopers with United States logistical aid (consisting of large US air transport planes) invaded Stanleyville. They liberated most of the hostages, an act that had the effect of militarily ending the civil war in favor of the central government. Half the members of the OAU introduced a resolution calling upon the Security Council at the United Nations to condemn Belgian and United States aggression. In the resultant declaration, much weaker than they had hoped, the UN merely "deplored" the intervention and "encouraged" the OAU to continue its efforts toward resolving the Congo split.

Soon thereafter the Ivory Coast took the lead in recreating the Brazzaville group in a political form. The UAMCE was replaced by the *Organisation Commune Africaine et Malgache* (OCAM). Several members of OCAM began a campaign against the holding of the next OAU meeting in Accra, Ghana, on the grounds that the government of Ghana was involved in active subversion against OAU states, notably Niger. The compromise of the OAU was cracking further.

In the summer of 1965 the OCAM admitted the Congo (Kinshasa) to membership, thus giving moral sanction to Tshombe's government. In Algeria Ahmed Ben Bella was overthrown. Whatever this overthrow involved in terms of internal politics, on the African scene Ben Bella was known as a strong advocate of maximum aid to the liberation movements of southern Africa.

In 1960 the accumulated impact of ten years of struggle in Africa had led to a feeling—both among the African nationalists and the white settlers—that southern Africa was likely to follow the path of the rest of Africa: independence under governments with majority rule. There were small signs in the period from 1960 to 1962 that the Portuguese in their several African colonies and the white regimes of Southern Rhodesia and even South Africa were thinking of making some accommodations to the pressure.

However, the first Congo crisis marked the beginning of the end of what one African leader called "the downward sweep of African liberation," referring to the geographical thrust. The white redoubt of southern Africa stiffened. By the time of the second Congo crisis, there was no longer any doubt that the white rulers would resist to the very end.

When the African Liberation Committee came into existence in 1963, they decided on a strategy of liberation that involved the support of guerrilla warfare in Portuguese Africa. (Fighting had begun in Angola in 1961 and in Portuguese Guinea in 1962. It would break out in Mozambique in 1964.) The eventual use of force was also slated for South Africa. However, the liberation of South West Africa was sought through the International Court of Justice. In 1960 Ethiopia and Liberia, as the only African states then recognized by the World Court, had begun litigation against the Union of South Africa, which, they charged, had violated the League of Nations mandate in South West Africa. The issue was still pending, and the ALC hoped for a favorable decision, which it could use as a political weapon. In the case of Southern Rhodesia the ALC was banking on the assumption that the British would arrange things as they did in Kenya, if only sufficient pressure were put on them by the independent African states who were members of the Commonwealth. This optimism regarding the efficacy of political means for South West Africa and Southern Rhodesia turned out to be seriously misplaced.

The cause of liberation of southern Africa received a series of major blows in 1965 and 1966. The Accra meeting of the OAU was seriously divided, and some members boycotted it. On November 11, 1965, the whites of Southern Rhodesia issued a unilateral declaration of independence of a state they named Rhodesia. The British refused to send troops to put down the rebellion. The OAU was unable to muster any military riposte. Although it voted to respond with a political answer—the breaking of diplomatic ties with Great Britain because of its failure to quell the white revolt—only ten African states actually carried out the resolution.

In January, 1966, Nigeria had a coup, which was at first greeted enthusiastically by the population. However, it led to great internal difficulties in Nigeria, which would force Africa's most populous country to turn inward for several years, unable to devote much attention to the liberation of southern Africa. In February, 1966, Kwame Nkrumah's regime in Ghana was overthrown, thus removing from the OAU one of the dynamic centers of activity on liberation questions. And in July, 1966, the World Court unexpectedly ruled that the complainants against South Africa in the South West Africa case had no legal right to bring suit. The last doorway of peaceful change seemed to have been closed.

The years from 1960 to 1966 can be seen as a shift in Africa from easy optimism to the realization of deep resistance to further change, especially in southern Africa. New tactics were going to have to be developed to meet this new and more difficult struggle. During this very same period there was a parallel shift among black Americans. The optimism of 1960, the period of the great sit-ins that would lead to the Civil Rights Acts of 1964 and 1965, came to be

After a bitter childhood and a prison term, Malcolm X found his course among the American Black Muslims. Expelled in 1964, he formed the more militant Organization of Afro-American Unity.
WIDE WORLD

displaced by the realization of great resistance to change. Malcolm X was the prophet of this new awareness, and his address to the OAU meeting in Cairo in 1964 marked the first significant attempt in the postindependence era to link the African and Afro-American struggles.

Nineteen hundred sixty-four also was the year of the Watts riots in Los Angeles, the signal of the great frustration of blacks in urban centers. It was the year that the Mississippi Freedom Democratic Party did not receive recognition at the National Convention of the Democratic Party. In 1965 Malcolm X was assassinated, and in 1966 the Black movement took new directions. A more militant leadership took over the most militant student group, the Student Nonviolent Coordinating Committee (SNCC), and the new leader, Stokely Carmichael, proclaimed the slogan "Black Power." In Lowndes County, Alabama, the Black Panther Party came into existence. This shift in Black America involved the beginning of a new kind of interest in Africa, a directly political interest. The fruits of this new interest, however, were not to be seen immediately.

In the years from 1966 to 1970 the questions of inter-African structures moved to the background of African affairs. In southern Africa it was a time of reorganization and retrenchment for the liberation movements, which sought to find new ways of cracking the strong resistance of the white redoubt. In independent Africa it was a time of considerable instability, in which the case of the Nigerian civil war is especially notable and important.

In October, 1965, nationalist movements from Portuguese Africa met together in Dar es Salaam. It was the third conference of the *Conferência das Organisações Nacionalistas das Colonias Portuguesas* (CONCP), which grouped the radical independence movements of Guinea (PAIGC), Angola (MPLA), and Mozambique (FRELIMO). This loose federation of liberation parties, first formed in 1965, took stock of the situation in Africa and of the setbacks to liberation and African unity. They decided, in the light of what they found, to reinforce their links and plan a coordinated politico-military strategy of the only three areas in colonial Africa then conducting active guerrilla warfare.

Nineteen hundred sixty-six was a year of dilatory activity on Rhodesia. The British, who had refused to use troops against the illegal actions of the white settler government, proposed, instead, a United Nations boycott. Most countries, of course, supported the boycott, but not South Africa or Portugal. Since these two countries controlled the borders of Rhodesia and the outlets for the railway system, their noncooperation made the boycott ineffective. That same year Great Britain made the so-called NIBMAR pledge, NIBMAR standing for "no independence before majority rule." This meant that they would not negotiate any agreement with Rhodesia that would provide for British recognition of Rhodesian independence *before* the majority of the population—that is, the Africans—had the suffrage. White Rhodesians simply held tight, and no agreement was ever negotiated, nor was the white Rhodesian government overthrown. The settlers seemed to have won their gamble for the moment.

In April, 1967, there was an abortive attempt to revive the Casablanca alliance. A so-called Little African Summit was held in Cairo, bringing together the leaders of Algeria, Guinea, the United Arab Republic, and two non-Casablanca powers—Tanzania and Mauritania. The major purpose of the meeting was to discuss ways and means of using force to oust the regime in Rhodesia. Unfortunately, however, the participants did not appear to have uncovered any effective ones.

In May the United Nations General Assembly reacted to the World Court nondecision on South West Africa by ordering that the United Nations assume direct administration of South West Africa, now to be called Namibia. Since, however, no armed force was to be used to oust South Africa from de facto control of the territory of Namibia, the reso-

lution was as politically efficacious as was the UN boycott of Rhodesia.

At this point in time the white southern African governments faced a Black African belt of three countries that spanned the continent: Tanzania, Zambia, and the Congo (Kinshasa). Tanzania was the headquarters of the ALC and offered active support to African liberation movements. Zambia was equally militant in its support, if slightly more prudent. Its prudence derived from a geographical necessity. Zambia is landlocked, and historically its outlet to the sea was largely via Rhodesia and Mozambique. Until it could obtain alternate routes to the sea, it had to cooperate to a limited extent on economic matters with Rhodesia. Zambia was very anxious to get out from under this yoke and had begun the process of constructing a new rail line through Tanzania to the sea.

The Congo (Kinshasa) saw a shift of government in late 1965. Tshombe was removed from power. Soon thereafter Joseph Mobutu staged a military coup and seized control. Although Mobutu represented in pan-African terms a centrist and pro-American position, Tshombe had represented a viewpoint of active cooperation with white settlers. Mobutu's government was willing to give support to anti-Portuguese forces, although they preferred the UPA in Angola (the MPLA was the Angolan group backed by Tanzania and Zambia). Under the circumstances, the governments of Tanzania and Zambia saw Mobutu's regime as a great improvement over Tshombe's, and they moved to create closer links with it.

In 1967 some white mercenary soldiers still in the Congo (Kinshasa), some remaining Belgian settlers, and some remnants of Tshombe's old Katanga forces tried to arrange a pro-Tshombe coup d'état. Thus the third Congo crisis began. This time, however, the fight was between Mobutu and Tshombe, since the United States gave assistance to Mobutu, and the Casablanca-type groups also gave tacit support to Mobutu, who defeated the mercenaries and solidified his control.

The failure of the mercenary-led coup was a rebuff to the South African counteroffensive against the liberation movements. Another setback was the announcement in August by the outlawed African National Congress (ANC) of South Africa and the outlawed Zimbabwe African People's Union (ZAPU) of Rhodesia of a joint military agreement and of their first common guerrilla action in Wankie in Rhodesia.

The riposte of the White government to joint ANC-ZAPU action was the announcement on September 10 by Prime Minister Ian Smith of Rhodesia that he had invited the cooperation of the South African police in "anti-terrorist operations." That very same day the South African government announced a great diplomatic and political achievement. It revealed its first exchange of diplomatic relations with an independent Black African state, Malawi. South Africa offered Malawi economic and technical assistance. In the years to follow, South Africa would seek to enter into more and more such arrangements—with Lesotho, Botswana, Swaziland, Malagasy Republic, and Mauritius—with the intent to both undermine the support of independent African states for the liberation movements and to develop a new economic network of outlets for its own burgeoning industries.

The South African counteroffensive pushed the liberation movements into closer cooperation. In September, 1968, the three members of the federation of liberation parties in Portuguese Africa (CONCP), plus ZAPU and ANC, plus the South West Africa Peoples' Organization (SWAPO), issued a joint statement to the Algiers meeting of the Organization of African Unity. These six organizations were cooperating quite closely. In January, 1969, they met together in Khartoum (Sudan) under the aegis of an International Conference in Support of the Liberation Movements of the Portuguese Colonies and Southern Africa. In February, 1969, the leader of FRELIMO, Dr. Eduardo Mondlane, was assassinated by the Portuguese, which would lead to an internal political crisis in the Mozambique liberation movement.

In April, 1969, the Fifth Summit Conference of East and Central Africa States, meeting in Zambia, issued the so-called Lusaka Manifesto on southern Africa, restating their belief in the equality of men and calling for the reordering of southern Africa to achieve such liberation. It was a moderate statement in view of the events that provoked it, but was given no response by these states except the proclamation in March, 1970, by the white settler regime that Rhodesia would be a republic. In June, 1970, the Sixth Summit Conference of East and Central African States declared that by rejecting the Lusaka Manifesto, Portugal and South Africa had closed the door to the possibility of a peaceful settlement. No progress had been achieved.

This same period (1966 to 1970) saw the acting out of the great Nigerian drama. The first coup in January, 1966, was followed by a second coup in July, 1966, in which army elements coming from northern Nigeria played a large role. In the turmoil that surrounded the second coup, there were riots and murders of persons coming from eastern Nigeria (mainly Ibo) living in northern Nigeria. Nigeria was faced

with a typical legacy of the colonial era in which one segment of the population—in this instance the Ibo—had secured greater access to education and hence to bureaucratic positions than many other segments. As typically happens, this more educated sector then began to monopolize bureaucratic and clerical positions in an educationally backward region—in Nigeria's case, the north. As independence came, the educationally backward region began to regard the monopoly of skilled positions in the hands of "outsiders" as oppressive and hateful. In the turmoil of the coup, this resentment led to bloody riots.

The easterners retreated from the hostile north to their own region and began to talk of secession. The issue was complicated by the fact that the Eastern Region was the focus of recently discovered oil, and the Eastern Region came to feel that it in turn was being economically exploited by the rest of Nigeria.

New formulas for governing Nigeria that would reconcile the conflicting interests were sought. In May, 1967, they ended in a breakdown of negotiations. The federal government implemented its twelve-state proposal, eliminating the four existing administrative regions of Nigeria and replacing them by twelve states. From the federal government's point of view this would strengthen the center and eliminate the foci of secession. From eastern Nigeria's point of view this would break up the Eastern Region into three states and weaken them politically. The leaders of the Eastern Region seceded and proclaimed themselves the Republic of Biafra. The central government immediately sought to restore national unity by military means.

At the September, 1967, meeting of the OAU in Kinshasa, the OAU established a consultative commission to help restore peace in Nigeria, carefully refraining from defining the situation as an interstate conflict. This consultative commission functioned throughout the Nigerian civil war with limited effect.

The first nation to recognize Biafra and break the solid African opposition to secession was Tanzania. Tanzania's action, on April 13, 1968, was followed by Zambia's; then came the Ivory Coast and Gabon. Elsewhere in the world no other state was to recognize Biafra, except Haiti. But many outside forces were sympathetic to Biafra. Indeed, the Nigerian civil war was to produce strange bedfellows. Biafra received various kinds of political and economic support, overtly or covertly, from France, Portugal, South Africa, Israel, and Communist China. Some say the American Central Intelligence Agency also gave support. Biafra also received strong support from the Vatican and from various

Nigeria, a polity created under British rule, holds in uneasy union large numbers of Hausa, Yoruba, and Ibo peoples, as well as several smaller societies. The federation was shattered by two coups in 1966, leading to the secession of the Ibo-dominated Eastern Region. The self-proclaimed Republic of Biafra was invaded by federal troops, and in the thirty-month-long civil war that ensued, mass starvation became one of the government's chief weapons. A generation of damaged children, like this refugee, is its tragic legacy.

Protestant relief agencies. The Nigerian federal government received military assistance from Great Britain, the Soviet Union, and the United Arab Republic, and formal support from the US government. Within Africa, Nigeria was supported strongly not only by the majority of states but by the liberation movements of southern Africa.

Ultimately, all initiatives for a peaceful settlement failed. The federal government, however, triumphed on the battlefield, and the secession ended in January, 1970. It was followed by a prompt and reasonably effective policy of reconciliation pursued by the federal government.

Elsewhere in independent Africa there were no civil wars to match that of Nigeria. But political instability remained the norm. In Ghana the overthrow of Kwame Nkrumah's regime led to several years of army rule, which was replaced by a civilian government in 1969, in which the forces historically opposed to the Nkrumah regime assumed the leadership. Ghana's partner in the Casablanca Group, Mali, also saw its regime overthrown by an army coup in November, 1968. The only one of the Casablanca Group regimes in West Africa to survive was Guinea; it was menaced by an abortive Portuguese-led invasion in early 1971, but the commandos were rebuffed.

In the center of Africa we have already described the political evolution of the belt of states opposed to the white domination of South Africa. The most important event in other states in the region occurred in the Congo (Brazzaville), where the radical regime emerging from the 1963 coup survived various attempts to overthrow it or modify its character. In 1968 the regime took a further turn to the left, proclaiming itself a Marxist state. This outlook led to hostile relations with the Congo (Kinshasa), considered an American puppet, and sympathetic ties with the socialist block, especially China and Cuba. The Congo (Brazzaville) never-

theless maintained close links with France and membership in OCAM, the majority of whose member states were former French colonies.

While the OAU was finding itself in great internal difficulties, OCAM was strengthening itself as an organization. Although it lost Mauritania in 1965, it had been able over the years to add to the original Brazzaville Group Togo, Rwanda, the Congo (Kinshasa), and Mauritius, thus embracing most of French-speaking Africa except North Africa.

In 1969 there was a sudden spurt of radicalization in northeast Africa. There were coups in the Sudan (May), Libya (September), and Somalia (October). In all cases military regimes came to power. In all cases the regimes were more anti-Western than their predecessors had been, and they talked of substantive social change at home. The Sudan and Libya moved toward a close alliance with the UAR on the Arab and African scene. About this time Uganda also moved leftward, but this was reversed by a military coup in early 1971. Britain's Conservative government resumed arms shipments to South Africa in defiance of a United Nations ban and over the vigorous protests of the African members of the Commonwealth.

In summary, the years from 1966 to 1971 were years of political uncertainty and relative stagnation for Africa. The liberation movements of southern Africa worked very hard to survive; they succeeded, but did not advance much. Nigeria, Africa's largest country, survived a bloody civil war and was trying to catch its breath. Elsewhere the balance sheet was about even.

The decade from 1960 to 1970 had started high and ended lower. It was the decade to come, 1970–1980, that would probably more clearly indicate how and to what degree Africa would move forward to political liberation and economic development.

THE THIRD WORLD

Cadet corps parading during Ghanaian celebrations
MAGNUM–IAN BERRY

THE MOTION OF DESTINY

The argument for independence for the Gold Coast was eloquently articulated by Kwame Nkrumah, who placed a motion to that purpose before its House of Assembly on July 10, 1953. Four years later the Gold Coast became the first British colony south of the Sahara to achieve independence, with Nkrumah as prime minister of the new republic, renamed Ghana. Following are extracts from that historic speech, since known reverently as "The Motion of Destiny."

The right of a people to decide their own destiny, to make their way in freedom, is not to be measured by the yardstick of color or degree of social development. It is an inalienable right of peoples which they are powerless to exercise when forces, stronger than they themselves, by whatever means, for whatever reasons, take this right away from them. If there is to be a criterion of a people's preparedness for self-government, then I say it is their readiness to assume the responsibilities of ruling themselves. For who but a people themselves can say then they are prepared? . . .

There is no conflict that I can see between our claim and the professed policy of all parties and governments of the United Kingdom. We have here in our country a stable society. Our economy is healthy, as good as any for a country of our size. In many respects, we are very much better off than many Sovereign States. And our potentialities are large. Our people are fundamentally homogeneous, nor are we plagued with religious and tribal problems. And, above all, we have hardly any color bar. In fact, the whole democratic tradition of our so-

ciety precludes the *herrenvolk* doctrine. The remnants of this doctrine are now an anachronism in our midst, and their days are numbered.

We have traveled long distances from the days when our fathers came under alien subjugation to the present time. We stand now at the threshold of self-government and do not waver. The paths have been tortuous, and fraught with peril, but the positive and tactical action we have adopted is leading us to the New Jerusalem, the golden city of our hearts desire! . . .

Today, more than ever before, Britain needs more "autonomous communities freely associated." For freely associated communities make better friends than those associated by subjugation. We see today how much easier and friendlier are the bonds between Great Britain and her former dependencies of India, Pakistan and Ceylon. So much of the bitterness that poisoned the relations between these former colonies and the Unied Kingdom has been absolved by the healing power of a better feeling so that a new friendship has been cemented in the free association of autonomous communities. . . .

In the very early days of the Christian era, long before England had assumed any importance, long even before her people had united into a nation, our ancestors had attained a great empire, which lasted until the eleventh century, when it fell before the attacks of the Moors of the North. At its height that empire stretched from Timbuktu to Bamako, and even as far as the Atlantic. . . .

Thus may we take pride in the name of Ghana, not out of romanticism, but as an inspiration for the future. It is right

and proper that we should know about our past. For just as the future moves from the present, so the present has emerged from the past. Nor need we be ashamed of our past. There was much in it of glory. What our ancestors achieved in the context of their contemporary society gives us confidence that we can create, out of that past, a glorious future, not in terms of war and military pomp, but in terms of social progress and of peace. For we repudiate war and violence. Our battles shall be against the old ideas that keep men trammeled in their own greed; against the crass stupidities that breed hatred, fear and inhumanity. The heroes of our future will be those who can lead our people out of the stifling fog of disintegration through serfdom, into the valley of light where purpose, endeavor and determination will create that brotherhood which Christ proclaimed two thousand years ago, and about which so much is said, but so little done. . . . And so today we recall the birth of the Ashanti [Asante] nation through Okomfo Anokye and Osei Tutu and the symbolism entrenched in the Golden Stool; the valiant wars against the British, the banishment of Nana Prempeh the First to the Seychelles; the temporary disintegration of the nation and its subsequent reunification. And so we come to the Bond of 1844. Following trade with the early merchant adventurers who came to the Gold Coast, the first formal association of Britain with our country was effected by the famous Bond of 1844, which accorded Britain trading rights in the country. But from these humble beginnings of trade and friendship, Britain assumed political control of this country. But our inalienable right remains . . . as my friend, George Padmore, puts it in *The Gold Coast Revolution:* "When the Gold Coast Africans demand self-government today they are, in consequence, merely asserting their birthright which they never really surrendered to the British who, disregarding their treaty obligations of 1844, gradually usurped full sovereignty over the country."

Then the Fanti Confederation: The earliest manifestation of Gold Coast nationalism occurred in 1868 when Fanti Chiefs attempted to form the Fanti Confederation in order to defend themselves against the might of Ashanti and the incipient political encroachments of British merchants. It was also a union of the coastal states for mutual economic and social development. This was declared a dangerous conspiracy with the consequent arrest of its leaders.

Then the Aborigines Rights Protection Society was the next nationalist movement to be formed with its excellent aims and objects, and by putting up their titanic fight for which we cannot be sufficiently grateful, formed an unforgettable bastion for the defense of our God-given land and thus preserved our inherent right to freedom. Such men as Mensah-Sarbah, Atta Ahuma, Sey and Woode have played their role in this great fight.

Next came the National Congress of British West Africa. The end of the first Great War brought its strains and stresses and the echoes of the allied slogan, "We fight for freedom" did not pass unheeded in the ears of Casely-Hayford, Hutton-Mills and other national stalwarts who were some of the moving spirits of the National Congress of British West Africa. But the machinations of imperialism did not take long to smother the dreams of the people concerned, but today their aims and objects are being more than gratified with the appointment of African judges and other improvements in our national life.

As with the case of the National Congress of British West Africa, the United Gold Coast Convention was organized at the end of the Second World War to give expression to the people's desire for better conditions. The British Government, seeing the threat to its security here, arrested six members of the Convention and detained them for several weeks until the Watson Commission came. The stand taken by the Trades Union Congress, the Farmers, Students and Women of the country provides one of the most epic stories in our national struggle.

In June 1949, the Convention People's Party with its uncompromising principles led the awakened masses to effectively demand their long lost heritage. And today the country moves steadily forward to its proud goal. . . .

According to the motto of the valiant *Accra Evening News*—"We prefer self-government with danger to servitude in tranquillity." Doubtless we shall make mistakes as have all other nations. We are human beings and hence fallible. But we can try also to learn from the mistakes of others so that we may avoid the deepest pitfalls into which they have fallen. Moreover, the mistakes we may make will be our own mistakes, and it will be our responsibility to put them right. As long as we are ruled by others we shall lay our mistakes at their door, and our sense of responsibility will remain dulled. Freedom brings responsibilities and our experience can be enriched only by the acceptance of these responsibilities. . . .

Honorable Members, you are called, here and now, as a result of the relentless tide of history, by Nemesis as it were, to a sacred charge, for you hold the destiny of our country in your hands. The eyes and ears of the world are upon you; yea, our oppressed brothers throughout this vast continent of Africa and the New World are looking to you with desperate hope, as an inspiration to continue their grim fight against cruelties which we in this corner of Africa have never known! Cruelties which are a disgrace to humanity and to civilization, which the white man has set himself to teach us. At this time, history is being made; a colonial people in Africa has put forward the first definite claim for independence. An African colonial people proclaim that they are ready to assume the stature of free men and to prove to the world that they are worthy of the trust.

I know that you will not fail those who are listening for the mandate that you will give to your Representative Ministers. For we are ripe for freedom, and our people will not be denied. They are conscious that the right is theirs, and they know that freedom is not something that one people can bestow on another as a gift. They claim it as their own and none can keep it from them.

And while yet we are making our claim for self-government I want to emphasize that self-government is not an end in itself. It is a means to an end, to the building of the good life to the benefit of all, regardless of tribe, creed, color or station in life. Our aim is to make this country a worthy place for all its citizens, a country that will be a shining light throughout the whole continent of Africa, giving inspiration far beyond its frontiers. And this we can do by dedicating ourselves to unselfish service to humanity. We must learn from the mistakes of others so that we may, in so far as we can, avoid a repetition of those tragedies which have overtaken other human societies. . . .

To Britain this is the supreme testing moment in her African relations. When we turn our eyes to the sorry events in South, Central and East Africa, when we hear the dismal news about Kenya and Central African Federation, we are cheered by the more cordial relationship that exists between us and Britain. We are now asking her to allow that relationship to ripen into golden bonds of freedom, equality and fraternity, by complying without delay to our request for self-government. . . .

The self-government which we demand, therefore, is the means by which we shall create the climate in which our people can develop their attributes and express their potentialities to the full. As long as we remain subject to an alien power, too much of our energies is diverted from constructive enterprise. Oppressive forces breed frustration. Imperialism and colonialism are a twofold evil. This theme is expressed in the truism that "no nation which oppresses another can itself be free." Thus we see that this evil not only wounds the people which is subject, but the dominant nations pay the price in a warping of their finer sensibilities through arrogance and greed. Imperialism and colonialism are a barrier to true friendship.

LIBERTY AND FRATERNITY

In the wake of World War II, among the most influential politicians in French West Africa was Félix Houphouët-Boigny, president of the Ivory Coast since 1960. His is the most prosperous of the former French territories in Africa; his has been the strongest African voice in Paris, where he served as minister in a succession of French cabinets; his has been the most powerful political organization in West Africa (the Rassemblement Démocratique Africain), *which before independence extended into most French-African territories. Houphouët-Boigny was at one time considered to be a radical and a Communist, but is now regarded as the most conservative of West Africa's leaders, a product of the so-called elite class of Africans whose political and economic prosperity was established during the colonial period. In the following article, Houphouët-Boigny acknowledges his long love affair with France, and argues for maintaining close economic and cultural ties despite political independence.*

I am a man of the African soil, having lived constantly in the midst of our rural Negro masses, sharing their joys and their sorrows, and making their great hope of liberty my own. For ten consecutive years, they have elected me to represent them in the French Parliament. I am the leader of the most powerful African political movement—a movement which continues to this very day to denounce the abuses and errors of colonialism, and to call untiringly for justice

Houphouët-Boigny, president of Ivory Coast
UPI

and equality. For these reasons, I think I have the right to consider myself the authentic spokesman of the millions of African men and women who have chosen, in preference to the type of independence just acquired by the neighboring state of Ghana, a Franco-African community founded on liberty, equality and fraternity.

In considering where the real interests of the colored peoples of the French territories in Africa lie, we do not begin with a blank slate. The relations which prevail between Frenchmen of the mother country and Frenchmen of Africa already exist in an historical complex of events lived in common, in which good and bad memories mingle. . . . I will therefore examine only the present state of relations within the French Union, as they have evolved during the past ten years.

As a preliminary, we must remove the aura which the concept of independence holds in our imaginations. Why do we not demand independence? To answer this question, I can only ask another: What is independence? Industrial and technical revolutions are making peoples more and more dependent on one another. . . . Indeed, who doubts that close and sustained economic relations are essential to a country which wants to raise its standard of living? What countries are self-sufficient? Not even the United States. Indeed, the countries of Europe in the Coal and Steel Community, in Euratom and in the Common Market

are prepared to relinquish a part of their sovereignty, that is to say, a part of their national independence. Why, if not to bring about, by association and mutual aid, a more fully elaborated form of civilization which is more advantageous for their peoples and which transcends a nationalism that is too cramped, too dogmatic and by now out of date? . . .

I am a native of a territory whose development has scarcely begun. Between 1939 and 1955 the tonnage handled by the port of Abidjan in the Ivory Coast went from 231,250 tons to 930,000 tons. The population has increased tenfold in the space of a few years and this rate shows no sign of diminishing. The Ivory Coast could not, by itself, find the means of providing the investment monies needed to cope with this heavy and continuing expansion. For many more years —10? 20? 50?—it will require enough capital aid to allow its inhabitants to make up for the heavy handicaps which nature imposes on tropical countries. . . .

The Investment Fund for the Economic and Social Development of the Overseas Territories (F.I.D.E.S.) was created in 1946 to centralize and coordinate, with the cooperation of the Central Fund for France Overseas, a major program of internal development. In the space of ten years, more than 600 billion francs of government funds have been devoted to territories whose area is 9,000,-000 square kilometers but whose population does not exceed 30,000,000. . . .

The fact is that the manner in which money is given can be a guarantee of continuity and stability. Perhaps we will on occasion find some creditor, public or private, capable of loaning, if not of giving, the billions necessary for the industrial, technical and social development of the African territories. But what guarantee would we have that this aid would be forthcoming year after year? How could we control the allocation of the loans offered? For what would we be asked in exchange?

We know what France asks of us—to share in her institutions and to share in them as equals. The right of citizenship has been granted without restriction to all the inhabitants of the French Union, and all the electors, whatever their origin, are gathered in a single college. At one stroke universal suffrage has been instituted everywhere—a privilege that not even the state of Ghana nor British Nigeria has yet dared extend to the tribal regions of the interior. No racial or religious discrimination prohibits any activity, public or private. Opportunities are legally the same for all, and if inequalities exist they arise from circumstances or local conditions which the authorities are making every effort to eliminate.

Thus the democratic institutions of republican France have little by little been established in the overseas territories. During the past several months, free elections throughout French Africa have enabled the people to choose those who would direct communal, urban, rural or territorial institutions. As a result, Africans are now in a position to exercise their responsibilities and to assert their political personality. Municipal councils exercise sovereign power over local affairs. Territorial assemblies are endowed with broad deliberative powers allowing them to adopt autonomous laws distinct from legislation which applies to the mother country. They have an executive responsible to them, to whom is entrusted the direction of territorial affairs with the exception of foreign relations, defense and security, which remain in the hands of the central power. It is in some degree self-government, but it maintains essential links with the Republic, and is not without analogy to the federal structure of the United States of America.

What makes it certainly unique, however, among various relationships that have existed in modern times between a mother country and its dependencies is the participation of overseas populations in the central government of the Republic. There are, in the National Assembly and in the Council of the Republic, Ne-

gro deputies and senators, elected in the same way as their colleagues of the mother country. The fusion has succeeded so well, mutual courtesy and comprehension have developed so naturally, that no one in France finds it remarkable any longer that the third-ranking dignitary of the Republic, the President of the Senate, is a Negro—Mr. Monnerville. It will seem then just as unremarkable that other colored people have for several years played a part in the Government, and that I myself was able to represent France in the United Nations at the time of the debates on Togo. . . .

Since the French Union is dynamic, our evolution continues on the national level, and other ties are contemplated in a constitutional reform now being prepared and soon to be debated in the French Parliament. We took part in the preparations for this debate, maintaining as our guiding principle the idea of a federal community, freely joining the peoples of French language and culture. The specific terms by which the principle will be expressed must now be decided by French legislators—black and white.

Naturally, we cannot help but compare our own evolution with the experiment which Great Britain has just undertaken in granting independence to the state of Ghana. Actually, the terms of agreement do not differ greatly, although we have not asked for the type of independence which Mr. Nkrumah has just obtained. After much reflection, bearing in mind the highest interest of this Africa which we dearly love, the human relations existing between French and African, and the imperative of this century —the interdependence of nations—from which no power can claim to escape, we have preferred to try a different experiment, more difficult perhaps, but unique of its kind and unknown until now in the long history of nations—that of a community of peoples, equal and fraternal. . . .

Today, no nation, however powerful, can pretend to impose its absolute will on another for long. By doing so, it

would irremediably compromise its own future as a great nation. France knows this. Its own best interests no less than its sensitivity to human values and the absence of any racist feelings among its people have led it voluntarily to renounce force as an instrument of policy in Black Africa and to seek new political arrangements with us, actively and sincerely. . . .

The presence of the French in Africa is the result of military conquests or of peaceful penetrations which go back to the end of the last century. France has suppressed slavery wherever it existed and has put an end to the quarrels which set different ethnic groups against one another; it has given its education to the African masses and its culture to an elite; it has instituted sanitary and medical improvements without precedent. In French ranks, in turn, we have poured out our blood on the battlefields for the defense of liberty, and we have won a place in the history of France and of the free world. We do not want to abandon this recent heritage by trying to go back to our origins. . . . It is important that the Franco-African community—egalitarian, humane and fraternal—appear to all nations not only as an example to be emulated but also as an element of international stability on which a sure future can be built.

In our view, that community is an act of faith in this future and also an act of human solidarity. It enables us to bring our stone to the world edifice without losing either our national identity or the French citizenship which we have earned and acquired worthily. And it constitutes a home we wish to keep, as in the definition which Robert Frost gave of it:

"Home is the place where, when
you have to go there,
They have to take you in."

AFRICA'S COMMON MARKET

In response to the urgent need for a radical revision of France's relationship with its overseas territories, Charles de Gaulle dissolved the Union Française *in 1958, "offering" its territories the choice of entering a quasi-federal "community," with France as director of all foreign and economic affairs, or of becoming fully independent. Initially, all the countries agreed to continue their Paris association save Guinea, whose people responded to the French referendum with a "no" vote. In this they were led by Sékou Touré, who has been president, prime minister, and chairman of Guinea's only political party since independence. In the following article, published in 1962, Touré presents his program for cooperation within the African community.*

Guinea's president, Sékou Touré, at the UN
UPI

We of course know that the world today is interdependent, and Africa, which cannot live in isolation, does not intend to remain at the margin of this modern world. She thinks she is entitled to benefit from the experience of other nations as well as from the fruits of her own efforts. In turn, she must contribute actively to the creation of a world society in which each nation, while retaining its own personality, will be considered on an equal footing with the others and will, like them, take on its proper share of international responsibilities. . . .

Colonialism's greatest misdeed was to have tried to strip us of our responsibility in conducting our own affairs and convince us that our civilization was nothing less than savagery, thus giving us complexes which led to our being branded as irresponsible and lacking in self-confidence. Our greatest victory, then, will not be the one we are winning over colonialism by securing independence but the victory over ourselves by freeing ourselves from the complexes of colonialism, proudly expressing Africa's authentic values and thoroughly identifying ourselves with them. Thus the African peoples will become fully conscious of their equality with other peoples.

The colonial powers had assimilated each of their colonies into their own economy. . . . We know that we must rebuild Africa. To win and proclaim a nation's independence but keep its old structures is to plow a field but not sow it with grain for a harvest. Africa's political

independence is a means which must be used to create and develop the new African economy. Our continent possesses tremendous reserves of raw materials and they, together with its potential sources of power, give it excellent conditions for industrialization. . . .

African unity is no more a goal in itself than was independence. It simply is a means of development, a force of inter-African cooperation. It is indispensable because of the unjust nature of the relationship between the underdeveloped African nations and the economically strong nations. The equality of this relationship must be improved in order to overcome the social inequalities and differentiations in the present levels of development throughout the world. The highly developed nations have economic relations among themselves either of cooperation or of competition. But their relations with the undeveloped nations are those of exploitation, of economic domination. The direct colonial exploitation of former days is being succeeded by exploitation by international monopolies, and this has a tendency to become permanent. Paradoxically, it is the underdeveloped nations, exporting raw materials and crude products, which contribute an important share of the costs and the social improvements from which workers in the fully developed countries benefit. . . .

The mere fact that there are cries of alarm about the production of coffee,

cacao or peanuts, while there is silence about the products for which the demand is increasingly active but whose prices remain stable, such as diamonds, gold, oil, radioactive ores, zinc and copper, illustrates the mercantile nature of the economic relations between the highly developed nations and the nations producing raw materials. . . .

Here, as in other realms, the interests of the African peoples are one, and the awareness of this unity is rapidly becoming more and more explicit. The African nations are realizing that in order to solve their urgent social problems they must speed up the transformation of their trade economy; and if this is to be done through industrialization, it cannot be done within the limits of our national micro-economies. But unconditional integration into a multi-national market consisting of highly developed and underdeveloped nations negates the possibility of industrial development in advance; it could only be the association of horse and rider. If they are to complement each other economically, the development of all associated nations must be carried out according to their united needs and common interests. . . . The leaders of the European Economic Community seem not to be aware of all this, at least as far as Africa is concerned, and make no secret of their desire to achieve a political community of Europe which cannot be reconciled with Africa's desire for political independence; Africa remains as grimly hostile as ever to the division of Africa which began with the Congress of Berlin in 1885.

The unity so much desired by all Africans will not be achieved around any one man or any one nation, but around a concrete program, however minimal. The rules of the union must favor and reinforce generally accepted concepts: equality of all nations, large or small; fraternal solidarity in their relationships; the common use of certain resources; and respect for the character and institutions of each state. Not only must there be no interference in the internal affairs of any state by another, but each must help to solve the other's problems. If we do not rapidly achieve such a framework of solidarity, permitting the peaceful evolution of our countries, we risk seeing the cold war enter Africa and divide the African states into antagonistic forces and blocs, jeopardizing their whole future in common.

The evolution of our countries in peace and harmony requires a high degree of cooperation. We have always thought that Africa should be considered like the human body: when a finger is cut off, the whole body suffers. The growing awareness that we all share the same future must make us increase our efforts for this cooperation, for solidarity and active and conscious African participation in world progress. . . .

Some have claimed to see political antagonisms in the formation of various African groupings. Actually these were the first concrete manifestations of unity, and were inspired by human and historical necessity. Skepticism notwithstanding, this tendency toward unity will increase. Political choices which do not correspond to the needs and aspirations of our peoples—and it is important that this be understood—will inevitably fail.

As for what face a united Africa will wear, whatever the choices she makes in her orientation, it will not be turned either against the East or against the West. It will be above all and essentially directed toward the emancipation and progress of Africa and her peoples. In our struggle for freedom there is no room for negative choices, but only for positive thought and constructive action. What will be destroyed or defeated in this struggle are those things that historical necessities, human needs and the forces of progress consign to destruction and oblivion.

To attempt to interpret Africa's behavior in capitalist or Communist terms is to neglect the fundamental fact that Africa's present condition corresponds neither to the given facts of capitalism nor to those . . . of Communism.

Africa's way is the way of peaceful revolution, in which the morality of an action counts much more than its form and conditions. That some believe socialism corresponds best to the aims of the African revolution, while others suppose it is preferable, despite the lack of national capital, to espouse capitalist principles—these considerations will not in the last analysis prevent our peoples from deciding their own fate. It is they who are called on to make the sacrifices and the creative efforts necessary to ensure Africa's development. Their awareness is sufficiently keen to enable them to choose the way they want to go. . . .

African neutralism, then, is not shameful indifference, a sort of political demobilization. On the contrary, it is the expression of a lively faith in a happy future for mankind. It is something active, a participating force, an active agent in the struggle for the achievement of a world society—emancipated, fraternal and united. Let us hope that the highly developed nations and peoples can understand this historical movement in its universal significance, and that they will take full part in it, in the conscious desire to help build a free and prosperous Africa in a world of peace and brotherhood.

FAREWELL WITHOUT TEARS

Patrice Lumumba, once a postal clerk, rose from obscurity to take control of the Mouvement National Congolais *and become first prime minister of the Democratic Republic of the Congo. In a letter to his wife, written in French in January, 1961, shortly before his assassination by rival forces, this controversial personage muses on the cruel course of history.*

I am writing these words not knowing whether they will reach you, when they will reach you, and whether I shall still be alive when you read them. All through my struggle for the independence of my country, I have never doubted for a single instant the final triumph of the sacred cause to which my companions and I

have devoted all our lives. But what we wished for our country, its right to an honorable life, to unstained dignity, to independence without restrictions, was never desired by the Belgian imperialists and their Western allies, who found direct and indirect support, both deliberate and unintentional, amongst certain high officials of the United Nations, that organization in which we placed all our trust when we called on its assistance.

They have corrupted some of our compatriots and bribed others. They have helped to distort the truth and bring our independence into dishonor. How could I speak otherwise? Dead or alive, free or in prison by order of the imperialists, it is not I myself who count. It is the Congo, it is our poor people for whom independence has been transformed into a cage from beyond whose confines the outside world looks on us, sometimes with kindly sympathy, but at other times with joy and pleasure. But my faith will remain unshakeable. I know and I feel in my heart that sooner or later my people will rid themselves of all their enemies, both internal and external, and that they will rise as one man to say No to the degradation and shame of colonialism, and regain their dignity in the clear light of the sun.

We are not alone. Africa, Asia and the free liberated people from all corners of the world will always be found at the side of the millions of Congolese who will not abandon the struggle until the day when there are no longer any colonialists and their mercenaries in our country. As to my children, whom I leave and whom I may never see again, I should like them to be told that it is for them, as it is for every Congolese, to accomplish the sacred task of reconstructing our independence and our sovereignty: for without dignity there is no liberty, without justice there is no dignity, and without independence there are no free men.

Neither brutality, nor cruelty nor torture will ever bring me to ask for mercy, for I prefer to die with my head unbowed, my faith unshakeable and with profound

Deposed Prime Minister Lumumba in 1960
UPI

trust in the destiny of my country, rather than live under subjection and disregarding sacred principles. History will one day have its say, but it will not be the history that is taught in Brussels, Paris, Washington or in the United Nations, but the history which will be taught in the countries freed from imperialism and its puppets. Africa will write her own history, and to the north and south of the Sahara, it will be a glorious and dignified history.

Do not weep for me, my dear wife. I know that my country, which is suffering so much, will know how to defend its independence and its liberty. Long live the Congo! Long live Africa!

FREEDOM

The political consciousness of the sixties in Africa permeated almost every part of society. Excerpted below is a prize-winning essay submitted in a student competition that was conducted in 1962 *by the Uganda-based magazine* Transition. *The author, Bertha Lomayani, attended a girls school in Tanganyika, which had become independent in* 1961.

Whenever I see the word "freedom" my mind spreads widely like a flood on a flat land. I begin to think of various things with which it is connected and I have come to conclude that freedom should be given to any creature lacking

it. All living creatures need a certain amount of freedom. Even a small child in its first week and unable to talk will cry if it is uncomfortable. I am a Masai by tribe and from my experience I have seen babies who are forbidden to have the automatic freedom: freedom of breathing.

My mothers, the Masai women, carry their children on their backs, covering them all over including the face and head. The material used is animal skins soaked in animal fat which has a distasteful smell. Under this condition the baby can't breath properly, so it suffocates. It feels uncomfortable and begins to cry and dance up and down. If the mother ignores this the baby will start scratching, pinching and beating the mother's back. The mother then becomes angry and releases the baby and carries it in her hands . . . .

Traditionally, Masai women cover their babies because they believe that if a baby is exposed when still young, the sight of men may cause a serious disease and it may die of it, or at least the baby must receive a serious shock. If the older ones who can speak are covered, they will shout: "*Yeyo taboluoki,*" meaning "Mammy—uncover me." The mother may hesitate to uncover the child, thinking she is protecting it, but seeing that the child can bite, scratch and repeat the same words, she uncovers it.

Among the creatures who lack freedom are the people ruled by another country. Under British trusteeship, Tanganyikans still ate food, wore clothes, grew and sold things and performed all other physical functions, but they could not hold responsible jobs or posts because they were thought unable to hold any responsibility. It is clear that the British never beat the natives, but they were still uncomfortable spiritually: there was something torturing their minds, when they thought that they were forbidden to establish ownership over what is theirs—their land. This put a pressure in their minds and the older, thoughtful people in the nation thought so deeply and were

so depressed that either they had to take action or, in the extreme cases, they went mad.

Eight years ago a politician appeared: Dr. Julius Nyerere, who started expressing the spiritual discomfort boldly and started TANU, a party which fought for freedom. Just as a Masai woman hesitates to uncover her child, so the governing power hesitates to free the dominated, saying that it is not ready for responsibility. But when will it be ready? The Masai woman says her baby is not ready for exposure yet, but when will it learn to breathe?

CONTINENTAL INTEGRITY

Inter-African political behavior is governed by the Charter of the Organization of African Unity (OAU), founded and agreed upon by thirty-two independent African states at Addis Ababa, Ethiopia, in 1963. *The charter and the union represent a practical attempt on the part of African leadership to effect pan-Africanism in matters economical, political, and cultural. Included below are the charter's prologue of purpose and introductory articles.*

We, the Heads of African States and Governments assembled in the City of Addis Ababa, Ethiopia;
CONVINCED that it is the inalienable right of all people to control their own destiny;
CONSCIOUS of the fact that freedom, equality, justice and dignity are essential objectives for the achievement of the legitimate aspirations of the African peoples;
CONSCIOUS of our responsibility to harness the natural and human resources of our continent for the total advancement of our peoples in spheres of human endeavor;
INSPIRED by a common determination to promote understanding among our peoples and co-operation among our States in response to the aspirations of our peoples for brotherhood and solidarity, in a larger unity transcending ethnic and national differences;

CONVINCED that, in order to translate this determination into a dynamic force in the cause of human progress, conditions for peace and security must be established and maintained;

DETERMINED to safeguard and consolidate the hard-won independence as well as the sovereignty and territorial integrity of our States, and to fight against neo-colonialism in all its forms;

DEDICATED to the general progress of Africa;

PERSUADED that the Charter of the United Nations and the Universal Declaration of Human Rights, to the principles of which we reaffirm our adherence, provide a solid foundation for peaceful and positive co-operation among States;

DESIROUS that all African States should henceforth unite so that the welfare and well-being of their peoples can be assured;

RESOLVED to reinforce the links between our states by establishing and strengthening common institutions;

HAVE agreed to the present Charter.

ESTABLISHMENT

1. The High Contracting Parties do by the present Charter establish an Organization to be known as the ORGANIZATION OF AFRICAN UNITY.

2. The Organization shall include the Continental African States, Madagascar and other Islands surrounding Africa.

PURPOSES

1. The Organization shall have the following purposes:

a. to promote the unity and solidarity of the African States;

b. to co-ordinate and intensify their co-operation and efforts to achieve a better life for the peoples of Africa;

c. to defend their sovereignty, their territorial integrity and independence;

d. to eradicate all forms of colonialism from Africa; and

e. to promote international co-operation, having due regard to the Charter of the United Nations and the Universal Declaration of Human Rights.

2. To these ends, the Member States shall co-ordinate and harmonize their general policies, especially in the following fields:

a. political and diplomatic co-operation;

b. economic co-operation, including transport and communications;

c. educational and cultural co-operation;

d. health, sanitation, and nutritional co-operation;

e. scientific and technical co-operation; and

f. co-operation for defense and security.

PRINCIPLES

The Member States, in pursuit of the purposes stated in Article II, solemnly affirm and declare their adherence to the following principles:

1. the sovereign equality of all Member States;

2. non-interference in the internal affairs of States;

3. respect for the sovereignty and territorial integrity of each State and for its inalienable right to independent existence;

4. peaceful settlement of disputes by negotiation, mediation, conciliation or arbitration;

5. unreserved condemnation, in all its forms, of political assassination as well as of subversive activities on the part of neighboring States or any other State;

6. absolute dedication to the total emancipation of the African territories which are still dependent;

7. affirmation of a policy of non-alignment with regard to all blocs.

PURSUIT OF HAPPINESS

The following lecture, by the late Dunduzu K. Chisiza, former parliamentary secretary to Malawi's ministry of finance, is an assessment of the African personality. His remarks were delivered before the Economic Symposium, held at the town of Blantyre in 1962.

Unlike Easterners who are given to meditation or Westerners who have an inquisitive turn of mind we of Africa, belonging neither to the East nor to the West, are fundamentally observers, penetrating observers, relying more on intuition than on the process of reasoning.

Our field is not that of spiritualism which is the domain of the East nor that of science and technology which is the hobby-horse of the West, but that of human relations. This is where we excel and where we shall set an example for the rest of the world. . . .

With us, life has always meant the pursuit of happiness rather than the pursuit of Beauty or Truth. We pursue happiness by suppressing isolationism, individualism, negative emotions, and tension, on the one hand; and by laying emphasis on a communal way of life, by encouraging positive emotions and habitual relaxation, and by restraining our desires on the other. . . .

Our attitude to religion has more often than not been determined by our habitual desire for change. We adhere to a religious faith only so long as it is the only faith we know. If some other faith comes our way we do not insulate ourselves against its influence. . . . That we behave in this way is no indication that we are fickle; rather it is an indication of the fact that in each one of the religious faiths which we encounter there is an element of divine truth whose fascination we fail to resist. And this is as it should be for religion is one. Iqbal has told us: "There is only one religion but there are many versions of it." . . .

In Africa, we believe in strong family relations. We have been urged by well meaning foreigners to break these ties for one reason or another. No advice could be more dangerous to the fabric of our society. Charity begins at home. So does love of our fellow human beings. . . .

How can a person who has no real affection for his brothers or sisters have any love for a poor Congolese or Chinese peasant? When we talk about international peace, understanding and goodwill, we are actually talking about international love. But universal love does not grow from nothing; its root is family love and unless this root is there it cannot grow. The unification of mankind ultimately depends on the cultivation of family love. . . .

Love for communal activities is another feature of our outlook. Look at any African game or pastime and you notice right away that its performance calls for more than one person. Our dances are *party* dances demanding drummers, singers and dancers. Game hunting is done in *parties*. (Even those Africans who own guns cannot abandon the habit of taking some friends along with them when going out for a hunt!) The telling of fables and stories with us calls for a *group* of boys and girls not just one or two. Draw-net fishing is done by a *group* of people. Fishing with hooks is also done in *canoe parties* of two, three or four; each canoe taking at least two people. The preparation of fields, the weeding, the sowing of seeds, the harvesting, the pounding of grains—all these activities are done in parties of either men or women. . . .

Such an outlook can only emanate from genuine love for each other—an unconscious love which has existed in our society since time immemorial. . . . Foreign missionaries should come to Africa not so much to teach love to the indigenous people but to see living examples of selfless love manifested in the African way of life.

We are also famous for our sense of humor and dislike for melancholy. Gloom on the face of an African is a sure sign that the wearer of that expression has been to a "school" of some kind where he might have got it into his head that joy and melancholy can be bed fellows in his heart. Otherwise our conception of life precludes, as far as possible, the accommodation of dejection. . . .

Even if there are real causes for sorrow somehow our people manage to make molehills of these and mountains of the causes for happiness. . . . Our society stifles malice, revenge and hate with the result that we are free from these cankers. Were we disposed to avenge the wrongs that have been meted out to us by foreigners down through the ages the course of human events would have taken a different turn altogether. . . . But God spared us all that. As a result we tolerate on our soil even neurotic crowds of foreigners who could not be tolerated in their own countries; we waste love on foreign elements which are inveterately selfish, individualistic and ungrateful. Above all, we do not look forward to a day when we shall have nefarious schemes against any race.

Among those who have studied Africa closely we have a reputation for taking delight in generosity, kindness and forgiveness. It has been said, with great truth, by some foreigners that few Africans will ever get rich "for the simple reason that the African tends to be too generous." Well, we do not want to be rich at the cost of being mean! Our society hinges on the practice of "mutual aid and co-operation" whose corrollary is generosity. When our chiefs, kings and emperors gave out acres and acres of land to foreigners they weren't prompted by bribes or stupidity but by this self-same relishable habit of generosity. . . .

Nor is the scope of our kindness limited to our own race. Many are the days when we have preserved the life of one foreigner or another. Times without number we've gone out of our way to hunt for water, eggs, milk, chicken, fish, meat, fruits, vegetables, etc., for a choosy stranger. We've carried literally thousands of foreigners on our heads and shoulders; we've washed their clothes; we've reared their children; we've looked after their homes; we've stood by their sides in peril; we've defended them in times of war; we've given them land . . . we've given them our all. But all the gratitude we get for all that is ridicule, contempt, ill-treatment and the belief on their part that God created us to be "hewers of wood and drawers of water." No. God knows our kindness does not stem from a feeling of inferiority. God knows we are not kind because we are fools, but because he had it that we should be kindness drunk and not pride drunk.

And yet, in spite of all this ingratitude, we are still capable of forgiving and forgetting. We are in a position to do this because in our society forgiveness is the rule rather than the exception. . . .

Another outstanding characteristic of our outlook is our love for music, dance and rhythm. Our throats are deep with music, our legs full of dance while our bodies tremor with rhythm. The proper sub-title for Africa should have been "Land of music, dance and rhythm." This three pronged phenomenon is indeed the spice of our life. We sing while we hoe. We sing while we paddle our canoes. Our mourning is in the form of dirges. We sing as we pound food grains in mortars. We sing in bereavement just as on festive occasions. Our fables always include a singing part. We sing to while away the monotonous hours of travel. We sing to the strains of our musical instruments. The pulses of our drums evoke in us song responses. We sing under moonlit nights. We sing under the canopy of the blue sky. Gramophone record music entrances us not because it's foreign or something out of the way, but just because it's music. With us music, as also dance and rhythm, is a relishable obsession.

We have war dances, victory dances, stag dances, remedial dances, marriage dances, dances for women only, mixed dances, dances for the initiated only, dances for the youth—but all indulged in with ecstatic abandon. We nod our heads, rock our necks, tilt our heads and pause. We shake our shoulders, throw them back and forth, bounce breasts and halt to intone our thanks to Him who ordained that we be alive. We rhythmically hefty shake our rear ends, our tummies duck and peer, our legs quick march, slow march, tap dribble, quiver and tremble while our feet perform feats. "Dance!" What a world of emotions that word calls forth in us!

But dance and music by themselves are crude art, rough hewn and devoid of sublimity. So to these we unconsciously add rhythm for a blend that possesses both charm and grace. Rhythm is our second nature.

There is rhythm in the winnowing and pounding of grains, there is rhythm in the gait of our women folk; there is highly developed rhythm in coition, there is rhythm in the groan of a sick person, there is complex rhythm in the milking of a cow, there is rhythm in pulling a drawnet to the shore, there is rhythm that beggars description in the beats of our tom-toms, there is rhythm that defies analysis in "marimba," there is rhythm in almost everything we do.

Finally, we have a strong dislike for imposing our beliefs on other people. British people established themselves in their erstwhile and present day dependencies with the self-assuredness of angels. They believed with puritanical fervor—that the British way is the God-vouchsafed way of doing things. Their way of living is what mankind was destined to evolve up to; their ideas the gospel truth; their beliefs the paragons of man's triumph over "superstition." No other way—least of all the colonial people's way—could measure up to it still less be better than it. So they believed there was nothing for them to learn from their colonial subjects while the colonial indigenes had to be recast into the British mould of life, thought and belief.

That mode of thinking was all very well for purposes of empire building. To rule a people successfully you've got to drill it into their heads that you are in every way superior to them and that, therefore, it is the right thing for them to be under you. . . .

If persisted in, this attitude of finality, superiority and self-deception can only promote hate and racial discord. When other peoples do not assert themselves it isn't that they haven't got something to be proud of, something that they believe

is unrivaled, but just that they haven't got the same vulgarity of throwing their weight about and imposing themselves and their beliefs on other people. They are willing to live and let live. Further they have the sense of knowing that the part of a listener and an open mind are the "open sesame" to the fortune of knowledge and wisdom. There is a great deal that foreigners, here as well as abroad, have to learn from the colonial peoples.

THE MANIPULATORS

Yambo Ouologuem has described Bound to Violence *as "a fresco, an epic, a legend and a novel." The work, published in France in 1968, chronicles in barely fictional form the brutal sequence of Africa's oppressors—black and white, animist, Muslim, and Christian. In the following excerpt, the Saif of Nakem—symbolizing the state—sets forth his cynical philosophy of men and government.*

"You mustn't imagine," [Saif] went on, clucking softly, "that the sun will never shine again. We are wanderers in disaster, that's a fact; but we fall, we are humble, we gargle with poison from the bloody cup of violence, the chipped glass of values; we are sick, degraded; but that's because the world *is* odd. Steeped in the strangest sediments ever churned by God in His chaotic blessing! I am quite capable of judging Him, and in so loud a voice that Satan would think he was listening to a jubilant angel nearby."

Then in a falsetto:

"You see, my friend, in Nakem we have a tale. Of men and their madness Destiny said: '*I must forgive them, mankind is so young.*' And it waited. And it's still waiting. Like patience on a monument. Isn't that delightful? But suddenly the unforeseen! The rules are thrown headlong: 'What broke down?' The whole human machine, the boiler was ready to burst and it burst. But Destiny is right there, and Destiny always forgives. Its pardon is signed by a cabinet minister: read and approved, place, date, and seal. That's

what we call a reprieve; when it expires, mankind in its arch way starts all over again; and Destiny never wearies of forgiving, by proxy. How could it weary? If it did, would it not know Tedium, the empty consciousness of a time without content? The tedious innocence of one who has never sinned! But we are sinners. And God forgives. Out of constraint. Or out of love, perhaps." . . .

"Man is in history, and history is in politics. Politics is cleavage. No solidarity is possible. Nor purity."

"The essential is to despair of purity and to believe one is right to despair. Love is nothing else. Politics does not know the goal but forges a pretext of a goal. Regimes collapse because their politicians don't know how to handle the forge."

"But their awkwardness is unavoidable, because politics is seldom honestly expressed, or rather, politics does not lend itself to honest expression."

A PARADOX

Albert John Luthuli, a Zulu chief, was deposed by the South African government in 1951. He was, nevertheless, deeply committed to an interracial solution to his country's future, and as president-general of the African National Congress, the oldest nonwhite political organization on the continent, he continued to work for reform. Luthuli was placed in detention on his farm in 1959, but when he was awarded the Nobel Peace Prize for his efforts to bring much-needed peace between the races of his homeland, the government reluctantly permitted him to travel to Scandinavia to receive the prize. Following are excerpts from his address, made in Oslo in December, 1961. Luthuli died at his farm in 1967.

It is not necessary for me to speak at length about South Africa. It is a museum piece in our time, a hangover from the dark past of mankind, a relic of an age which everywhere else is dead or dying. Here the cult of race superiority and of white supremacy is worshiped like a god. . . . Thus it is that the golden age of

Africa's independence is also the dark age of South Africa's decline and retrogression. . . .

To remain neutal, in a situation where the laws of the land virtually criticized God for having created men of color, was the sort of thing I could not, as a Christian, tolerate. . . . How great is the paradox and how much greater the honor that an award in support of peace and the brotherhood of man should come to one who is a citizen of a country where the brotherhood of man is an illegal doctrine.

Outlawed, banned, censured, proscribed, and prohibited; where to work, talk, or campaign for the realization in fact and deed of the brotherhood of man, is hazardous, punished with banishment or confinement without trial or imprisonment; where effective democratic channels to peaceful settlement of the race problem have never existed these 300 years, and where white minority power rests on the most heavily armed and equipped military machine in Africa.

JUSTICE FOR NAMIBIA

In 1960, following the Sharpeville massacre in South Africa, all black African parties were banned. Five years later this decree was extended to include South West Africa, which is administered as a protectorate by the Republic of South Africa. (The United Nations charges that the present government operates illegally and that the area should be administered as the UN Trust Territory of Namibia.) Among the blacks caught in the dispute is Herman Toivo Ja Toivo, an Ovambo and an active nationalist. His South West African People's Organization was banned in 1963, and he was imprisoned under the Terrorism Act. Excerpts from his defense before the Pretoria court follow.

We find ourselves here in a foreign country, convicted under laws made by people whom we have always considered as foreigners. We find ourselves tried by a judge who is not our countryman and who has not shared our background. . . .

You, my Lord, decided that you had the right to try us, because your Parliament gave you that right. That ruling has not and could not have changed our feelings. We are Namibians and not South Africans. We do not now, and will not in the future recognize your right to govern us; to make laws for us in which we had no say; to treat our country as if it were your property and us as if you were our masters. We have always regarded South Africa as an intruder in our country. This is how we have always felt and this is how we feel now, and it is on this basis that we have faced this trial. . . .

We are far away from our homes; not a single member of our families has come to visit us, never mind be present at our trial. The Pretoria jail, the police headquarters at Compol, where we were interrogated and where statements were extracted from us, and this Court are all we have seen of Pretoria. We have been cut off from our people and the world. We all wondered whether the head-men would have repeated some of their lies if our people had been present in Court to hear them.

The South African government has again shown its strength by detaining us for as long as it pleased; keeping some of us in solitary confinement for three hundred to four hundred days and bringing us to its capitol to try us. It has shown its strength by passing an act especially for us, and having it made retrospective. It has even chosen an ugly name to call us by. One's own are called patriots, or at least rebels; your opponents are called Terrorists. . . .

It suits the government of South Africa to say that it is ruling South West Africa with the consent of its people. This is not true. Our organization, S.W.A.P.O., is the largest political organization in South West Africa. We consider ourselves a political party. We know that whites do not think of blacks as politicians—only as agitators. Many of our people, through no fault of their own, have had no education at all. This does not mean that they do not know what they want. A man does not have to be formally educated to know that he wants to live with his family where he wants to live, and not where an official chooses to tell him to live; to move about freely and not require a pass; to earn a decent wage; to be free to work for the person of his choice for as long as he wants; and finally, to be ruled by the people that he wants to be ruled by, and not those who rule him because they have more guns than he has. . . .

Those of us who have some education, together with our uneducated brethren, have always struggled to get freedom. The idea of our freedom is not liked by South Africa. . . .

Your government, my Lord, undertook a very special responsibility when it was awarded the mandate over us after the first world war. It assumed a sacred trust to guide us toward independence and to prepare us to take our place among the nations of the world. South Africa has abused that trust because of its belief in racial supremacy (that white people have been chosen by God to rule the world) and apartheid. We believe that for fifty years South Africa has failed to promote the development of our people. Where are our trained men? The wealth of our country has been used to train your people for leadership, and the sacred duty of preparing the indigenous people to take their place among the nations of the world has been ignored. . . .

Nineteen hundred sixty-three for us was to be the year of our freedom. From 1960 it looked as if South Africa could not oppose the world forever. The world is important to us. In the same way as all laughed in Court when they heard that an old man tried to bring down a helicopter with a bow and arrow, we laughed when South Africa said that it would oppose the world. We knew that the world was divided, but as time went on it at least agreed that South Africa had no right to rule us.

I do not claim that it is easy for men of different races to live at peace with one another. I myself had no experience of this in my youth, and at first it surprised me that men of different races could live together in peace. . . . Separation is said to be a natural process. But why, then, is it imposed by force and why then is it that whites have the superiority?

Head-men are used to oppress us. This is not the first time that foreigners have tried to rule indirectly—we know that only those who are prepared to do what their masters tell them become head-men. Most of those who had some feeling for their people and who wanted independence have been intimidated into accepting the policy from above. Their guns and sticks are used to make people say they support them. . . .

Your Lordship emphasized in your judgment the fact that our arms came from communist countries, and also that words commonly used by communists were to be found in our documents. But my Lord, in the documents produced by the State there is another type of language. It appears even more often than the former. Many documents finish up with an appeal to the Almighty to guide us in our struggle for freedom. It is the wish of the South African government that we should be discredited in the Western world. That is why it calls our struggle a communist plot; but this will not be believed by the world. The world knows that we are not interested in ideologies. We feel that the world as a whole has a special responsibility towards us. This is because the land of our fathers was handed over to South Africa by a world body. It is a divided world, but it is a matter of hope for us that it at least agrees about one thing—that we are entitled to freedom and justice. . . .

We are sure that the world's efforts to help us in our plight will continue, whatever South Africans may call us.

That is why we claim independence for South West Africa. We do not expect that independence will end our troubles, but we do believe that our people are entitled—as are all peoples—to rule themselves. It is not really a question of whether South Africa treats us well or badly, but that South West Africa is

our country and we wish to be our own masters.

There are some who will say that they are sympathetic with our aims, but that they condemn violence. I would answer that I am not by nature a man of violence and I believe that violence is a sin against God and my fellow men. S.W.A.P.O. itself was a nonviolent organization, but the South African government is not truly interested in whether opposition is violent or nonviolent. It does not wish to hear any opposition to apartheid. Since 1963, S.W.A.P.O. meetings have been banned. It is true that it is the Tribal Authorities who have done so, but they work with the South African government, which has never lifted a finger in favor of political freedom. We have found ourselves voteless in our own country and deprived of the right to meet and state our own political opinions. . . .

I have spent my life working in S.W.A.P.O., which is an ordinary political party like any other. Suddenly we in S.W.A.P.O. found that a war situation had arisen and that our colleagues and South Africa were facing each other on the field of battle. Although I had not been responsible for organizing my people militarily, and although I believed we were unwise to fight the might of South Africa while we were so weak, I could not refuse to help them when the time came. . . .

But some of your countrymen, when called to battle to defend civilization, resorted to sabotage against their own fatherland. I volunteered to face German bullets, and as a guard of military installations, both in South West Africa and the Republic, was prepared to be the victim of their sabotage. Today they are our masters and are considered the heroes, and I am called the coward.

When I consider my country, I am proud that my countrymen have taken up arms for their people and I believe that anyone who calls himself a man would not despise them. . . .

Even though I did not agree that people should go into the bush, I could not

refuse to help them when I knew that they were hungry. I even passed on the request for dynamite. It was not an easy decision. Another man might have been able to say "I will have nothing to do with that sort of thing." I was not, and I could not remain a spectator in the struggle of my people for their freedom.

I am a loyal Namibian and I could not betray my people to their enemies. I admit that I decided to assist those who had taken up arms. I know that the struggle will be long and bitter. I also know that my people will wage that struggle, whatever the cost. . . .

We believe that South Africa has a choice—either to live at peace with us or to subdue us by force. If you choose to crush us and impose your will on us then you not only betray your trust, but you will live in security for only so long as your power is greater than ours. No South African will live at peace in South West Africa, for each will know that his security is based on force and that without force he will face rejection by the people of South West Africa.

My co-accused and I have suffered. We are not looking forward to our imprisonment. We do not, however, feel that our efforts and sacrifice have been wasted. We believe that human suffering has its effect even on those who impose it. We hope that what has happened will persuade the whites of South Africa that we and the world may be right and they may be wrong. Only when white South Africans realize this and act on it, will it be possible for us to stop our struggle for freedom and justice in the land of our birth.

THE CHOICE TO COMPETE

Dennis Brutus has been hailed as the poet laureate of South Africa. An ardent campaigner for racial justice, he was shot and wounded by the South African police in 1963 and subsequently jailed for eighteen months for attempting to leave the country to attend the International Olympic Committee at Baden.

Let not this plunder be misconstrued
This is the body's expression of need—
Poor wordless body in its fumbling way
Exposing heart's-hunger by raiding and
    hurt;

Secret recesses of lonely desire
Gnaw at the vitals of spirit and mind
When shards of existence display eager
    blades
To menace and savage the pilgriming
    self:

Bruised through your flesh and all-
    aching my arms
Believe me, my lovely, I too reel from
    our pain—
Plucking from you these agonized gifts
Bares only my tenderness-hungering
    need.

FROM THE GRIM PLACE

*Arthur Nortje, a South African poet now
a resident in Canada, won the first Mbari
Poetry Prize (Nigeria) in 1963. His work
conveys the black man's anguish in his land.*

The sergeant laughs with strong teeth
    his jackboots nestle under the
    springbok horns
Those bayonets are silent,
the spear of the nation gone to the
    ground.
Warriors prowl in the stars of their
    dungeons.
I've seen the nebulae of a man's eyes
squirm with pain, he sang his life
through cosmic volleys. They call it
genital therapy, the blond bosses.

Why is there no more news?
Bluetits scuffle in the eaves of England,
an easy summer shimmers on the
    water.
Fields of peace, I lie here
in the music of your gaze
so beautiful we seem no strangers.
Curling smoke, a white butt is
brother to my lips and fingers.
You watch the ash on grass blades gently
    crumble.

Your hands are small as roses,
they cancel memory.
Once going down to the sea through the
    mountains
my limbs felt freedom in the glide of air:
over the bridge at the window I found
speech an impossible cry.
Under the fatal shadows spun down the
    chasm
my heart squirmed in the throat of
    snaking water.
I have since forgotten what they call the
    place.

EXIT

*Harold Head, a black South African jour-
nalist forced into political exile in 1964, relates in this excerpt from a forthcoming autobiography some of his last thoughts as he left
his homeland and made his way to freedom.*

It was my second day in Pukwane. I had
left Cape Town four days ago, and everything so far had gone according to plan.
Time was important and had to be measured in terms of the minute hand. My
flight had begun with six days between
myself and the South Africa-Bechuanaland border and I had, on arrival in
Pukwane, already used four days along
the route.

The Bechuanaland border was two
miles away, but I did not realize it. I
had arrived under cover of darkness.
Learning, in fact, that I was on the
threshold of freedom, I strongly felt
that it was not worth the risk after having passed unnoticed across a thousand-
mile sea of trepidation, possible appre-
hension, or death as a result of resisting
arrest. Reports were still rife of persons
apprehended or shot on the Bechuanaland border.

Time was important. I was required by
law to report my presence to the police
every Monday morning under the Suppression of Communism Act. (This law
has precious little to do with the pre-
vention of Communism in the country,
but is merely used to suppress all out-

spoken opposition to apartheid, whether
inspired by socialism, capitalism, religious principles, a sense of justice, or just
plain human feeling.) I had acquiesced
to this form of repression and human
deprivation for two weeks. The third
time I reported was my last. Obliquely,
but not unobtrusively, I decided to pit
black agility against the surveillance of
the government's Special Branch and
cross the Kalahari Desert.

Just living in South Africa requires
guts and the coolness of a call girl.
Otherwise, one unconsciously reconciles
one's sensibilities to the situation and
remains a being without growth. One
becomes a still-life victim, forced to
apologize or explain his own existence, a
subhuman creature, sometimes indifferent or frustrated, always conditioned.
And it is this conditioning that gives
strength.

I, myself, had forsaken the South African way of life when I reported on the
one persistent reality of black humanity,
the South African War. As is the case
now, I then wrote out of impulse and a
sense of duty. I gave up teaching to become a journalist because of my inability
to reconcile myself to the structure of
life in South Africa. Short-lived was my
youth. I was part of the struggle before
I was twenty.

Many South Africans have long re-
signed themselves to accept segregation
and the other deformities and infirmities
that make up the politics of that guilty
land. But there are others: those who
will not allow themselves to be governed
by the sickness of someone's political
aberrations.

When I was served with the banning
order, my sword of combat and my
shield of protection were taken from
me. I was supposed not to write for pub-
lication anymore. I was supposed not to
speak—or breathe, because the "liberal"
Establishment press, which I had tried to
use as a vehicle, still obeyed the laws of
the land.

Whether these ruminations of life in
South Africa were considered during my

last hours in apartheidland is uncertain to me now, but in my mind's eye the land I walked through remains crystal clear. The air was tranquil, the women gently going about their tasks of cleaning their modest huts, sweeping the surrounding yards, or making the perpetual trip to the communal fresh-water well to replenish their daily household needs. Viewing this vestige of the old life, I waited for the propitious moment to enter a life of freedom.

The men for their part were involved in a varied number of activities, from working in the fields to tending livestock—mainly for white farmers. They seemed to justify their existence by tinkering on pots or pans or on fences and flat rooftops.

As most sparsely sufficient South African villages must, Pukwane's future balanced on the precipice of frustrating uncertainty, its people wondering whether the illegal activity known as "the government" was really going to declare their tiny homeland a "whites-only" area, as rumored. Consequently, Pukwane had by this time produced a large number of men who measured time and their daily existence in terms only of waiting for the guillotine to cut off the next birthright. They had seen, and some had read, of the power of "the government" elsewhere in the country. And by 1964 the Verwoerd regime had demonstrated quite clearly its invincibility in dealing with the underground resistance movement: this repression had a paralyzing effect on the people who retained only the hope that some day the spirits of Mzilikazi, Cetshewayo, or Chaka would be unleashed to restore them to human dignity. So they waited.

Teko's father was my contact in Pukwane. He was away on a trip to a nearby town when I arrived. Due to South Africa's Sabotage Act, I refrained from letting his wife know the real reason for my sudden presence. As the custom of African women is not to question men, I was accepted and made to feel at home as I waited for the man of the house.

I had told Teko's mother that I was a scoutmaster on my way to meet a patrol in nearby Lichtenberg the following day —*the day*. This story had also been told to a black priest and his daughter in the town where I had spent the night before. I hated myself for not being able to take them into my confidence, but would have hated myself even more had I done so. There are hundreds of innocent persons in South Africa's gaols today who were put away simply because they were taken into the confidence of those entertaining the thought of political freedom.

Four hours later I was greeted by a tall, well-built man nearing fifty, anxious to hear of his student son in one of Cape Town's high schools.

Teko's father had been an activist in the labor movement in the early thirties and forties, but after minor failures of schemes that he had considered important for the liberation of his people, he had ceased being active. His faith was now in what he called the young men of the movement. His time was spent in farming and the operation of one of the local village stores. He was glad that I had not told anyone of my plans. We then made arrangements when I would cross an unmanned fence along the South Africa-Bechuanaland border.

Teko's father and I were still discussing strategy, possible ploys to use to cross the border, when suddenly a light delivery van roared up his driveway. Such vans are common forms of transport used by the South African police. We were together in the guest hut, which had only one door and one window. Instinctively, I jumped up from my bench and dived through the window, managing to catch a glimpse of Teko's father hurriedly trying to hide my knapsack under the bed in the room.

It was pitch dark outside, but for a strong beam of light streaking across the stillness, the van. My immediate reaction on now finding myself in the yard was to climb on top of the hut's downward sloping thatch roof, but it proved too hard and steep to grasp. Without pon-

dering the possibility further, I moved silently into the unknown night on all fours. Thirty yards farther I found myself stumbling into a goat pen! Afraid of the goats being startled and disclosing my whereabouts, I cast my faith to the darkness and lay silently on my stomach. I had made my dash for safety without a coat, and after ten minutes in the goat pen began to feel the cruel frost of the night seeping relentlessly into my skin. It was winter.

Half an hour later the van drove off. I returned to the guest house an hour later, however, even though I could hear Teko's father calling after me as soon as the van was out of hearing distance. I had to be sure.

Thus, this improbable, fateful day dawned. The movement of the minute hand of my pocket watch filled me with intense anxiety. It was Friday—three days away from the morning when I would be expected to keep intact the laws of the land by reporting my presence. I tried not to be engaged in negative thoughts or fear or the knowledge that I was leaving the country forever. But in the forefront of my mind was the very real possibility that I could be ambushed, shot on sight, just as I stood on the threshold of freedom. And so I left my fate in Teko's father's hands. And I concentrated on a show of outward calm, following him as he casually went outside to do his daily chores.

Strangely coming to consciousness, I found myself looking at four boys, aged between five and eight, cheerfully milking some goats. The sight reminded me of a chilly and affectionate memory of an incident the previous night.

Coming out of my reveries, I continued to watch the playfulness of the boys with the goats. It was perhaps the last genuine pleasure I have felt since leaving South Africa.

Soon my silent watching focused only on the goats. I felt a kinship with them and fancied a similarity between their lives and those of the people of South Africa. Of all domesticated animals, goats live on the barest minimum. Still they are expected to produce, contribute —justify their being around.

My romance with the goats was distracted by a gentle tap on my thigh. Looking down I found the youngest of the boys standing in front of me, offering me a drink of goat's milk. There was no longer need for me to check the minute hand of my pocket watch. The time had come. In acknowledgment of our camaraderie and brotherhood we smiled at each other as I took a swig of the hot, sweet milk.

Feeling good, I walked back to the hut where I had spent my last night, oblivious to the shrill iciness in the air.

MY FIRST WEDDING

Amos Tutuola was born in Nigeria in 1920. *After six years of elementary education he became a blacksmith, and later a messenger for the Nigerian government's labor department. He published the first of several works of fiction in* 1952, The Palm Wine Drinkard. *As in later writings, Tutuola makes Yoruba myth and legend the basis of his whimsical, picaresque tales. The following story is taken from his second novel,* My Life in the Bush of the Ghosts (1954). *It follows the hero from his escape—during a slave raid—to the bush, through which he travels for twenty-four years. In this episode he marries a local ghostess, is baptized, and reluctantly moves on.*

Before the wedding day was reached my friend had chosen one of the most fearful ghosts for me as my "best man" who was always speaking evil words, even he was punished in the fire of hell more than fifty years for these evil talks and cruelties, but was still growing rapidly in bad habits, then he was expelled from hell to the "Bush of Ghosts" to remain there until the judgment day as he was unable to change his evil habits at all. When the wedding day arrived all the ghosts and ghostesses of this town, together with the father of the lady whom I wanted to marry, my friend and his mother, my best man and myself went to the church at about ten o'clock, but it

was the ghosts' clock said so. When we reached their church I saw that the Reverend who preached or performed the wedding ceremony was the "Devil." But as he was preaching he reached the point that I should tell them my name which is an earthly person's name and when they heard the name the whole of them in that church exclaimed at the same time . . . "Ah! you will be baptized in this church again before you will marry this lady."

When I heard so from them I agreed, not knowing that Revd. Devil was going to baptize me with fire and hot water as they were baptizing for themselves there. When I was baptized on that day, I was crying loudly so that a person who is at a distance of two miles would not listen before hearing my voice, and within a few minutes every part of my body was scratched by this hot water and fire, but before Revd. Devil could finish the baptism I regretted it. Then I told him to let me go away from their church and I do not want to marry again because I could not bear to be baptized with fire and hot water any longer, but when all of them heard so, they shouted, "Since you have entered this church you are to be baptized with fire and hot water before you will go out of the church, willing or not you ought to wait and complete the baptism." But when I heard so from them again, I exclaimed with a terrible voice that . . . "I will die in their church." So all of them exclaimed again that . . . "you may die if you like, nobody knows you here."

But as ghosts do not know the place or time which is possible to ask questions, so at this stage one of them got up from the seat and asked me . . . "By the way, how did you manage to enter into the 'Bush of Ghosts,' the bush which is on the second side of the world between the heaven and earth and which is strictly banned to every earthly person to be entered, and again you have the privilege to marry in this bush as well?" So as these ghosts have no arrangements for anything at the right time and right

place, then I answered that I was too young to know which is "bad" and "good" before I mistakenly entered this bush and since that time or year I am trying my best to find out the right way back to my home town until I reached the town of "burglary-ghosts" from where I came with my friend to this town. After I explained as above, then the questioner stood up again and asked me whether I could show them my friend whom I followed to that town. Of course as my friend was faithful, before I could say anything, he and his mother whom we came to visit got up at the same time and said that I am living with a burglar-ghost in the town of the burglar-ghosts. But when my friend and his mother confirmed all that I said and as all the rest of the ghosts are respecting all the burglar-ghosts most because they were supplying them the earthly properties, so they overlooked my offense, then Revd. Devil continued the baptism with hot water and fire.

After the baptism, then the same Revd. Devil preached again for a few minutes, while "Traitor" read the lesson. All the members of this church were "evil-doers." They sang the song of evils with evils' melodious tune, then "Judas" closed the service.

Even "Evil of evils," who was the ruler of all the evils, and who was always seeking evils about, evil-joking, evil-walking, evil-playing, evil-laughing, evil-talking, evil-dressing, evil-moving, worshiping evils in the church of evils and living in the evil-house with his evil family, everything he does is evil, attended the service too, but he was late before he arrived and when he shook hands with me on that day, I was shocked as if I touch a "live electric wire," but my friend was signaling to me with his eyes not to shake hands with him to avoid the shock but I did not understand.

Having finished the marriage service, all of us went to my in-laws' house where everybody was served with a variety of food and all kinds of ghosts' drinks. After that all the ghost and ghostess dancers started to dance. Also all the terrible-creatures sent their representatives as "Skulls," "Long-white creatures," "Invincible and invisible Pawn" or "Give and take" who fought and won the Red people in the Red-town for the "Palm-Wine drinker," "Mountain-creatures," "Spirit of prey" whose eyes flood of light suffocated Palm-Wine Drinker's wife and also the "hungry-creature" who swallowed Palm-Wine Drinker together with his wife when returning from Deads'-town came and saluted my wife's father and they were served immediately they arrived. But at last "Skull" who came from "Skull family's town" reported "Spirit of prey" to my wife's father who was chief secretary to all the terrible and curious creatures in all dangerous bushes, that the spirit of prey stole his meat which the skull put at the edge of the plate in which both were eating as both were served together with one plate, because plates were not sufficient to serve each of them with a plate. But before my wife's father who was their chief secretary could have a chance to come and settle the matter for them, both of them started to fight fiercely so that all the ghosts and all the other representatives came nearer and surrounded them, clapping hands on them in such a way that if one of these fighters surrenders or gives up it would be very shameful to him.

Some of these scene-lookers were clapping, and an old Ape, who was a slave and inherited by my wife's father from his first generation since uncountable years, was beating a big tree under which both these terrible creatures were fighting as a drum which had a very large sound. But as this old slave ape was beating the tree as a drum in such a way that all the scene-lookers who stood round them could not bear the lofty sound of the tree which was beaten as a drum and wait or stand still in one place, so all the ghosts, evils, terrible creatures, my friend, my wife and her father and myself started to dance at the same time. But as I was intoxicated by

the strong drinks which I drank on that day, so I mistakenly smashed a small ghost to death who came from the "9th town of ghosts" to enjoy the merriment of the marriage with us as I was staggering about.

At last I was summoned to the court of evil for wilfully killing a small ghost, but as a little mistake is a serious offense as well as big offense in the "Bush of Ghosts," so the "Evil judge" judged the case at one o'clock of the judgment day and luckily I was freed by a kind lawyer whose mother was the native of the "Bottomless Ravine's town," the town which belongs to only "triplet ghosts and ghostesses." But if it was not for this incognito lawyer who was very kind to me without knowing him elsewhere I would be imprisoned for fifty years as this is the shortest years for a slightest offense.

After I freed the case then I returned to my in-laws' town and lived there with my wife for a period of about three months and some days before I remembered my mother and brother again, because I did not remember them again when I married the lady. So one morning, I told the father of my wife that I want to leave this town for another one, but I did not tell him frankly that I want to continue to find the way to my home town which I left since I was seven years old. So I told him that I should leave with his daughter who was my wife, he allowed me to go or to leave, but disallowed his daughter to go with me. Of course, when I thought over within myself that however an earthly person might love ghosts, ghosts could not like him heartily in any respect, then I alone left his town in the evening after I went round the town and bade good-bye to the prominent ghosts.

POLICY TOWARD AFRICA

Dr. Elliott P. Skinner, professor of anthropology at Columbia University, served as United States ambassador to Upper Volta from 1966 to 1969. The following article is

excerpted from a policy statement made before a congressional committee in March, 1970.

America can no longer afford an African policy predicated on European primacy in that continent. It can also no longer hide behind a smokescreen of pious words and platitudinous hopes for Africa while doing as little as possible. We must not permit Europeans to provide the guidelines for our policy toward Africa, nor must we continue to protect the short-term interests of racist minorities there. America must develop a realistic policy toward Africa based upon its own ethos, its own national character, its own history and its position in the contemporary world. Failure to do so may have grave implications not only for Africa, but also for the United States during this decade.

America was diplomatically and psychologically unprepared for Africa's entrance upon the world scene in the late 1950's. As a matter of fact, our policy toward Africa during the 1950's was based on the prior consideration that: "All of the so-called colonial powers represented on the continent of Africa are our friends and allies in the worldwide contest between the Free and Communist worlds." Nevertheless, this did not stop Africa's drive for independence and to combat the expected Soviet efforts, President Eisenhower sent Mr. Richard M. Nixon to take part in Ghana's independence celebration as well as to report on the other independent African states.

Mr. Nixon clearly recognized that America needed a new policy toward Africa. He declared: "The leaders and peoples of the countries I visited in Africa have many things in common. They cherish their independence which most of them have only recently acquired, and are determined to protect it against any form of foreign domination. They rightfully expect recognition from us and others of their dignity and equality as individuals and peoples in the family of nations. They want economic progress

for their undeveloped economies. . . .
There must be a corresponding realization throughout the executive branches of the Government, throughout the Congress and throughout the nation, of the growing importance of Africa to the future of the United States and the Free World and the necessity of assigning higher priority to our relations with that area."

There was the usual cant in this statement, for during the remaining years of the Eisenhower administration the United States followed France's lead with respect to both Algeria and Guinea. The more forward-looking Kennedy administration still recognized Belgium's primacy in the Congo, and did not seriously urge the Portuguese to decolonize Angola, Guinea-Bissau, and Mozambique. We refused to sanction South Africa for its odious policy of apartheid, and followed the British Lion to a stalemate on H.M.S. Tiger, and only reluctantly left Salisbury in order not to embarass the new toothless King of the Beasts. The United States muddled through the Nigerian crisis, faithfully following the lead of Great Britain whose "traditional primacy" in that nation-state we took for granted. And even when the Federal government won the war we insulted its gallant leaders by declaring that we were consulting with France, of all countries, to provide aid to the Biafrans.

Africa's travail during the 1960's was largely due to the difficulties of decolonization, and the trauma of building new institutions to cope with a rapidly changing world. The European-derived political systems have not worked well in Africa, but there is still no evidence that the military regimes in power will persist. Indeed, the political pattern suitable for contemporary African societies has probably not yet emerged, and the process by which it comes into being may well be long and hard. Africa has also not yet decolonized its social systems. Middle-men and stranger groups have come under attack as the societies try to institute freer mobility. There have been grave personal

injustices, and this has led to social strife and civil wars. These may well continue until cross-cutting interests in the African societies outweigh parochial ones. Conditions similar to those in the United States, whereby a man from Massachusetts or California could represent New York in this House, may be long in coming. The Africans have also not yet decolonized their economic institutions—normally the most difficult of all institutions to gain control of. Most of their resources are still in expatriate hands, and most African states are still members of foreign-run specie zones. The economic effect is that the Africans cannot freely trade across their borders without contravening trade relations with their ex-Metropoles, nor can they protect their fragile economies from the vicissitudes of the world economies. French Finance Minister, Giscard d'Estaing did not consult nor notify a single African state before devaluating the franc, even though the Africans were to be hurt materially as well as psychologically this action.

America's economic policy toward Africa has always been predicated upon European primacy and has not greatly helped the Africans to deal with their developmental problems. In the 1950's we were willing to play "only a cooperative role with the administering power." Indeed, we primarily wished to "assure the development of mutually advantageous economic relations between Europe and Africa in the interest of contributing to the restoration of a sound European economy and of furthering the aspirations of the African peoples." Our Marshall Aid was expected to help Europe, and the Europeans were left to deal with Africa. In 1957, Mr. Nixon, an economic nationalist, recognized the dilemma of the colonial economic ties between Africa and Europe and recommended that "We should encourage the continuance of these special ties where they are considered mutually advantageous by the states concerned." The difficulty with this recommendation is

that the horse and its rider normally have different views about what is mutually beneficial, but only the rider can speak. Nevertheless, we have maintained the naive or perhaps moral position that since the Europeans profitted most from their African colonies, they should bear the burden of African reconstruction. This, indeed, was the thrust of the (General Lucius D.) Clay's report to President Kennedy in 1963, in which he recommended that the African states should seek aid essentially from their former masters to help with their development; that the very limited U.S. grant programs already in Africa be reduced; that new grant projects be discouraged; and that loans be provided only after severe screening. The General felt that America was "trying to do too much for too many too soon" but the fact remains that the Africans were not the ones favored by America's attention.

American economic aid to Africa has always been inferior to that given to the other continents and, as to be expected, designed to be secondary and supplementary to that of the former colonial powers. . . .

Not only has the United States aid to Africa been relatively small, but it has always been distributed to a small group of countries. . . .

Indeed, many Africans and Africanists believe that apart from a few technical assistance programs and Cold-War related loans, U.S. aid to Africa has not been motivated by developmental objectives. . . . The result is that many of our projects failed. . . .

If we are to continue to have diplomatic relations with African states, a well-thought-out aid program is necessary, because at this point in time, African foreign relations are conceived in terms of economic development. Failure to understand this is to jeopardize the other aspects of our relations with the African states. . . .

America is too great a nation to surrender to expediency. Let us develop a realistic policy for Africa during the 1970's.

The sun sets over Tanzania today as at the dawn of history.

RECOMMENDED READING

Arkell, Anthony J., *A History of the Sudan from Earliest Time to 1821*, N.Y., Oxford Univ. Press, 1961.

Boahen A. Adu, *Topics in West African History*, London, Longmans, Green and Co. Ltd., 1966.

Bovill, Edward W. and Robin Hallett, *The Golden Trade of the Moors*, London, Oxford Univ. Press, 1968. Also paperback.

Cartney, Wilfred and Martin Kilson, *The Africa Reader: Colonial Africa; The Africa Reader: Independent Africa*, N.Y., Random House, 1970. Also paperback.

Clark, J. Desmond, *The Prehistory of Africa*, N.Y., Praeger Publishers, Inc., 1970. Also paperback.

Collins, R. O. and R. L. Tignor, *Egypt and the Sudan*, Englewood Cliffs, N.J., Prentice-Hall, Inc., 1967. Also paperback.

Crowder, Michael, *West Africa under Colonial Rule*, Evanston, Northwestern Univ. Press, 1968.

Curtin, Philip D., *The Image of Africa: British Ideas and Action, 1780–1850*. Madison, The Univ. of Wisconsin Press, 1964.

Davidson, Basil, *Africa, History of a Continent*, London, Weidenfeld & Nicolson, 1966.
Black Mother: The Years of the African Slave Trade, Boston, Little, Brown and Company, 1961.
East and Central Africa to the Late Nineteenth Century, London, Longmans, Green and Co. Ltd., 1967. Paperback.

Duffy, James, *Portugal in Africa*, Cambridge, Harvard Univ. Press, 1962.

Fage, J. D., *An Atlas of African History*, N.Y., St. Martin's Press, 1958.

A Geography of Africa, R. Mansell Prothero, ed., N.Y., Frederick A. Praeger, 1969.

Hallett, Robin, *Africa to 1875*, Ann Arbor, The Univ. of Michigan Press, 1970.

Herskovits, Melville J., *The Human Factor in Changing Africa*, N.Y., Random House, 1958. Also paperback, Vintage.

July, Robert W., *A History of the African People*, N.Y., Charles Scribner's Sons, 1970. Also paperback.

Leiris, Michel and Jacqueline Delange, *African Art*, trans. by Michael Ross, N.Y., Western Publishing Co., Inc., 1968.

Marlowe, John, *History of Modern Egypt and Anglo-European Relations, 1800–1956*, 2nd ed., Hamden, Conn., 1966.

The Middle Age of African History, Roland Oliver, ed. London, Oxford Univ. Press, 1967. Also paperback.

Morris, Donald R., *The Washing of the Spears, The Rise and Fall of the Zulu Nation*, N.Y., Simon and Schuster, 1965. Also paperback.

Murdock, George Peter, *Africa: Its People and Their Culture*, N.Y., McGraw Hill Book Company, 1959.

Nickerson, Jane Soames, *A Short History of North Africa*, N.Y., Biblo and Tannen Booksellers and Publishers, Inc., 1968. Copyright © 1961 by the Devin-Adair Company.

Oliver, Roland and J. D. Fage, *A Short History of Africa*, Baltimore, Penguin Books, Inc., 1962. Paperback.

The Oxford History of South Africa, Monica Wilson and Leonard Thompson, eds., N.Y. and Oxford, Oxford Univ. Press, 1969.

Pankhurst, Richard, *An Introduction to the Economic History of Ethiopia, from Early Times to 1800*. Essex, Eng., Lalibela House, 1961.

Protest and Power in Black Africa, Robert I. Rotberg and Ali A. Mazrui, eds., N.Y., Oxford Univ. Press, 1970.

Reuters Guide to the New Africans, London, Paul Hamlyn Ltd., 1967.

Roux, Edward, *Time Longer Than Rope, A History of the Black Man's Struggle for Freedom in South Africa*, Madison, The Univ. of Wisconsin Press, 1964.

Samkange, Stanlake, *On Trial for My Country*, London, Heinemann Education Books Ltd., 1966. Paperback.

Shepperson, George and Thomas Price, *Independent African: John Chilembwe and the Origin, Setting and Significance of the Nyasaland Native Rising of 1915*, Chicago, Aldine Publishing Company, 1958.

Shinnie, Margaret, *Ancient African Kingdoms*, N.Y., St. Martin's Press, 1966.

Shinne, P.L., *Meroe: The Civilization of the Sudan*, N.Y., Praeger Publishers, Inc., 1966.

Skinner, Elliott P., *The Mossi of the Upper Volta: The Political Development of a Sudanese People*, Stanford, Calif., Stanford Univ. Press, 1964.

Snowden, Frank M., Jr., *Blacks in Antiquity: Ethiopians in the Greco-Roman Experience*, Cambridge, Harvard Univ. Press, 1970.

Survey of North Africa, The Magreb, 2nd ed., Nevill Barbour, ed., London, Oxford Univ. Press, 1962.

Tarikh, Journal of African History, Ibadan, Nigeria; N.Y., Humanities Press.

A Thousand Years of West African History, J. Ade Ajayi and Ian Espie, eds., N.Y., Humanities Press, 1969.

Vansina, Jan, *Kingdom of the Savanna*, Madison, The Univ. of Wisconsin Press, 1966. Paperback.

Walker, Eric. A., *A History of Southern Africa*, London, Longmans, Green and Co. Ltd., 1968.

Wallerstein, Immanuel, *Africa: The Politics of Independence*, N.Y., Random House, 1961. Paperback.
Africa: The Politics of Unity, N.Y., Random House, 1967. Paperback.

Webster, J. B. and A. A. Boahen, *History of West Africa: The Revolutionary Years—1815 to Independence*, N.Y., Praeger Publishers, Inc., 1967. Paperback.

West African Kingdoms in the Nineteenth Century, Daryll Fords and P. M. Kaberry, eds., London, Oxford Univ. Press, 1967.

Wilson, John A., *The Culture of Ancient Egypt*, Chicago, The Univ. of Chicago Press, 1951. Paperback.

Zamani: A Survey of East African History, B. A. Ogot and J. A. Kiernan, eds., N.Y., Humanities Press, 1969. Paperback.

ACKNOWLEDGMENTS

The editors gratefully acknowledge the valuable editorial assistance of Douglas Tunstell, Geneva; Urszula Slupik, Paris; Christine Sutherland, London; Audre Proctor. They are also grateful to the following individuals and institutions for providing pictorial material and supplying information:

African American Institute
Harry Stein

African Bibliographic Center
Dan Matthews

I. A. Akinjogbin, University of Ife, Nigeria

Army Museum, London

Marc and Evelyne Bernheim

Bibliothèque Nationale
Estampes
Manuscrits
Service Photographique
Documentation Française

BOAC Library, London

British Museum

William D. Carlebach

Dr. Gwendolyn Carter, Northwestern University

Geoffrey Clement

Columbia University
Graham Irwin
Dr. Hollis Lynch

Eliot Elisofon

Victor Englebert

Dr. Brian Fagan, University of California

Freedomway's Magazine
Ernest Kaiser

André Held, Lausanne

Horniman Museum and Library, London

John H. A. Jewel, Mombasa

Mburumba Kerina, Department of African Studies, Brooklyn College

Library Company of Philadelphia

Library of Congress
Virginia Daiker
Dr. Samie Michel Zoghby

Dr. Richard A. Long, Center for African and African American Studies, Atlanta University

Mansell Collection, London

Mr. and Mrs. Jan Mitchell

Metropolitan Museum of Art
Susan Valenstein
Kent Weeks

Kasimierz Michalowski, Warsaw

Richard Moore

Hon. Joseph Murumbi, Nairobi

Musée d'Ethnographie de Neuchatel

Musée de l'Homme, Paris
Georges Sirot

Musée Royal de l'Afrique Centrale, Tervuren, Belgium

Museum für Volkerkunde, Hamburg
Dr. Wilhelm Seidensticker

Museum of Primitive Art

National Maritime Museum,
Greenwich, Eng.

New York Public Library
 Miss Elizabeth Roth
 Oriental Division
 Rare Book Division
 Schomberg Collection
 Spencer Collection

Pitt Rivers Museum, Oxford, Eng.

Staff College, Cambridge, Eng.

Time Inc.
 Vassilia Moore

Constance Turnbull, Nairobi

United Methodist Church Board of
Missions
 Theodora Cameses

Dr. I. William Zartman, New York
University

Maps by Herbert Borst,
Francis & Shaw Inc.

Index by Edmée Busch

PERMISSIONS

SEEKING MAN'S ORIGINS: page 36 from *Légendes Africaines*, by Tchicaya U Tam'si. Editions Seghers, Paris. Translation by Kaari Ward. #37 from *The Origin of Life and Death (African Creations Myths)*, edited by Ulli Beier. Copyright © 1966. Reprinted by permission of Heinemann Educational Books Ltd., London. #38 "Man's Noble Pedigree" from *The Descent of Man*, by Charles Darwin, in The Modern Library, Random House, Inc./ "Emerging Man" from "The Origin of Man," by C. Loring Brace, in *Natural History*, January, 1970. Reprinted by permission of the American Museum of Natural History, New York. #41 from *Finding the Missing Link*, by Robert Broom. Copyright © 1950. Reprinted by permission of C.A. Watts & Co. Ltd., London. #42 from *Adam's Ancestors: The Evolution of Man and His Culture*, by Louis S. Leakey. Reprinted by permission of Harper & Row, New York, Methuen & Co. Ltd., London, and Doctor Louis S. Leakey. #43 from *The Rock Art of South Africa*, by A. R. Willcox. Copyright © 1963. Reprinted by permission of Thomas Nelson & Sons (South Africa) Ltd., Johannesburg. #44 from *Preliminary Report of OvaTjimba Groups*, by H.R. MacCalman and B.J. Grobbelaar. Copyright © 1965. Reprinted by permission of the State Museum, Windhoek, South West Africa. #45 "Bushman's Prayer," from *Ants Will Not Eat Your Fingers: A Selection of Traditional African Poems*, edited by Leonard W. Doob and translated by Viktor Lebzelter. Copyright © 1966. Reprinted by permission of Walker & Co., New York./ "Hunters of Modern Africa," from *The Oxford History of South Africa, South Africa to 1870*, vol. I, edited by Monica Wilson and Leonard Thompson. Copyright © 1970. Reprinted by permission of The Clarendon Press, Oxford. #47 "Tracking Father Elephant" "Death of a Hunter" from *Primitive Song*, translated by C.M. Bowra. Copyright © 1962 by C.M.

Bowra. Reprinted by permission of The World Publishing Company, New York, and Weidenfeld Ltd., London.

OF MEN AND MYTHS: page 66 from *The Geography of Strabo*, vol. VIII, edited by T.E. Page, E. Capps, and W.H.D. Rouse and translated by Horace Leonard Jones. The Loeb Classical Library. Reprinted by permission of Harvard University Press. #67 "Hymn to the Nile" from *A Comparative Study of the Literature of Egypt, Palestine and Mesopotamia*, edited by T. Eric Peet. Reprinted by permission of The Clarendon Press, Oxford./ "Memphis, the Fair One" from "Love Song" in *The Glory of Egypt*, by Samivel and Audrain. Reprinted by permission of Vanguard Press, Inc., New York, and Thames and Hudson, London./ "King Zoser's Magician" from *Imhotep, the Vizier and Physician of King Zoser*, by Jamieson B. Hurry. Copyright © 1928. Reprinted by permission of The Clarendon Press, Oxford. #69 "The Silent Man" from *Ancient Egyptian Religion*, by Henri Frankfort. Copyright © 1948. Reprinted by permission of Columbia University Press, New York./ "The Amarna Heresy" from *Literature of the Ancient Egyptians*, by Adolph Erman. Reprinted by permission of Methuen & Co. Ltd., London. #71 "Egyptian Way of Death" from *The Great Travelers*, vol. I, edited by Milton Rugoff. Copyright © 1960. Reprinted by permission of Simon and Schuster./ "Song of the Harper" from *Egypt: The Home of the Occult Sciences*, edited by T. Gerald Garry. John Bale, Sons & Danielson Ltd., London. #72 "Pepi's Legions" #73 "The Queen's Peace" #74 "In Search of Peace" #76–77 "King of Pure Mountain" from *Ancient Near Eastern Texts Relating to the Old Testament*, 3rd ed., with Supplement, edited by James B. Pritchard. Copyright © 1969. Reprinted by permission of Princeton University Press. #72 "The Broken Reed" from *Egypt of the Pharaohs, and Introduction*, by Sir Alan Gardiner. Copyright © 1961. Reprinted by permission of The Clarendon Press, Oxford. #73 "The Fabled Land of Punt" #75 "The Kushite Takeover" from *Ancient Record of Egypt Historical Documents from the Earliest Times to the Persian Conquest*, vols. II, IV, by James Breasted. The University of Chicago Press. #77 from *The Natural History of Pliny*, translated by John Bostock and H.T. Riley. Henry G. Bohn, Covent Garden, England. #78 from *Kebra Negast (The Glory of Kings)*, translated by Mrs. John Van Vorst. Funk & Wagnalls. #79 "Shoppers Guide to Axum" adapted from *Travellers in Ethiopia*, edited by Richard Pankhurst. Copyright © 1965. Reprinted by permission of Oxford University Press in Three Crowns Books. #80 from *A History of the Sudan*, by A.J. Arkell. The Athlone Press of the University of London. (Abstracted from *A Survey of Nubian Origins*, by L.P. Kirwan, from *Sudan Notes and Records*, vol. 20, Khartoum, the Sudan.)

BETWEEN SEA AND SAND: page 118 from *Ritual and Belief in Morocco*, by Edward Westermarck. Copyright © 1926. Reprinted by permission of Macmillan, Basingstoke, England. #119 "The Tongue" from *Contes et légendes populaires du Maroc*, compiled by Doctoress Legey. Editions Ernest Le Roux et de Pine, Paris. Translation by Iris Eaton./ "Hannibal's Oath" #121 "Arbiter of Destiny" from *The Histories*, by Polybius, translated by Evelyn S. Shuckburgh. Indiana University Press. #119 "Rule in Carthage" from *Politics*, by Aristotle, in *Oxford Translation of Aristotle*, edited by W.D. Ross. Reprinted by permission of The Clarendon Press, Oxford. #121 "The Wealth of Carthage" from *Carthage*, by B.H. Warmington. Copyright © 1960. Reprinted by permission of Praeger Publishers, Inc., New York, and Robert Hale & Co., London. #121 "Unwelcome Miracle" #122 "Up from Poverty" from *Tunisia*, by Claude Roy and Paul Legab.

Published 1961. Reprinted by permission of Delpire Editeur, Paris. Translation by Deirdre Butler. #121 "Tacfarinas' Revolt" from *The Complete Works of Tacitus*, translated by Alfred John Church and William Jackson Brodribb. Copyright © 1942. Reprinted by permission of Random House, Inc. #122 "A Paternal Scolding" "Caracalla's Edict" from *An Economic Survey of Ancient Rome*, vol. II, by Allan Chester Johnson. Copyright © 1936. Reprinted by permission of Johns Hopkins Press. #123 from *The Life of the North Africans as Revealed in the Sermons of Saint Augustine*, by Sister Marie Madeleine Getty, M.A. of the Sisters of the Presentation of Mary, St. Hyacinth, Quebec. Copyright © 1931. Reprinted by permission of The Catholic University of America Press. #124 "Justinian's Africa" from *Secret History*, by Procopius, translated by Richard Atwater. The University of Michigan Press. #124 "The First Hermit" #127 "The Desert Fathers" from *The Desert Fathers*, by Saint Jerome, translated by Helen Waddell. Copyright © 1936. Reprinted by permission of The University of Michigan Press and Constable & Co. Ltd., London. #126 "Saint Anthony of Egypt" from *A History of Christianity: Readings in the History of the Early and Medieval Church*, edited by Ray C. Petry. Copyright © 1962. Reprinted by permission of Prentice-Hall, Inc., Englewood Cliffs, New Jersey./ "God's 'Saucy Servants'" from *A Source Book of Ancient Church History*, by Joseph Cullen Ayer. Reprinted by permission of Charles Scribner's Sons. #128 from *Ecclesiastical History of John, Bishop of Ephesus*, translated by Richard Payne Smith. University Press, Oxford.

IN THE NAME OF ALLAH: page 150 "God's Messenger" #151 "The First Muezzin" adapted from "The Life of Muhammad" in *Sirat Rasul Allah*, by Ibn Ishaq, translated by Alfred Guillaume. Copyright © 1955. Reprinted by permission of Oxford University Press, Pakistan. #151 "The Word of God" #152 "The First Revelation" "The City" from *The Meaning of the Glorious Koran*, by Mohammed Marmakude Picthall. Reprinted by permission of George Allen & Unwin Ltd., London. #152 "Antar the Lion" from "The Romance of Antar" in *Anthology of Islamic Literature*, selected, edited, and introduced by James Kritzeck. Copyright © 1964. Reprinted by permission of Holt, Rinehart and Winston, Inc. #153 "Antar Poet" from "Mu Allakt" in *Arabic Literature*, 2nd ed., by Sir H.A.R. Gibb. Copyright © 1963. Reprinted by permission of The Clarendon Press, Oxford. #153 "Muslim Battle Code" #155 "How to Get Rich Quickly" #156 "Instruction of Children" #157 "What to Wear to Mecca" from *The Muqaddimah, An Introduction to History*, by Ibn Khaldun, translated by Franz Rosenthal. Bollingen Series XLIII. Copyright © 1958 and 1967. Reprinted by permission of Princeton University Press. Footnotes not used. #153 "Tarik the Moor" from *The Moors in Spain*, by Stanley Lane-Poole. #155 "A Pope's Letter" from the unpublished thesis on medieval Africa by Dr. Samir Zoghby, the Library of Congress. Translation by Kaari Ward. #157 "Ibn Yasin's Jihad" from *The Encyclopedia of Islam*. Published by E.J. Brill Ltd., London. #159 from "Book of Roger" #161 "Mogadishu in 1331" from "Les voyages d'Ibn Batoutah" both in *East African Coast*, edited by G.S.P. Freeman-Grenville. Copyright © 1962. Reprinted by permission of The Clarendon Press, Oxford. #160 "The Land of the Zanj" "The Gold of Sofala" from *The Medieval History of the Coast of Tanganyika with Special Reference to Recent Archaeological Discoveries*. Copyright © 1962 by G.S.P. Freeman-Grenville. Published by Oxford University Press, London. #163 "A Giraffe for the Emperor" #164 "China Looks at Africa" from lectures given

at the University of London by J.J. I. Duyvendak, professor of Chinese, Leyden University. Copyright © 1949 Arthur Probsthain, London. #164 "The Pillar of Zion" from *A History of Ethiopia, Nubia, and Abyssinia*, by Sir. W.E.A. Budge. Copyright © 1928. Reprinted by permission of Methuen and Co. Ltd., London. #166 from *The Stories of Abu Zeid the Hilali*, translated by J.R. Patterson. Copyright © 1930. Reprinted by permission of Routledge & Kegan Paul Ltd., London. #168 from *Wit and Wisdom in Morocco*, by Edward Westermarck. Reprinted by permission of Routledge & Kegan Paul Ltd., London.

THE GOLDEN IMPERATIVE: page 200 from *Légendes Africaines*, by Tchicaya U. Tam'si. Editions Seghers, Paris. Translation by Mary Elizabeth Wise. #201 from *Sundiata: An Epic of Old Mali*, by D.T. Niane. Copyright © 1965. Reprinted by permission of Longman Group Ltd., Harlow, England. #203 from *Olodumare, God in Yoruba Belief*, by E. Bolaji Idowu. Copyright © 1963 by E. Bolaji Idowu. Reprinted by permission of Longman Group, Ltd., Harlow, England. #205 from *Hausa Folklore Customs, and Proverbs: Part IV Arts How Benin Figures Are Made*, collected and transliterated, with English translation by R. Sutherland Rattray. Oxford University Press, London. #206 "A Child Is . . ." #208 "Yoruba Praise Song *(Oriki Oshun)*" "Yoruba Riddles" from *Black Orpheus, Yoruba Poetry*, compiled and translated by Ulli Beier. Longmans of Nigeria, Ltd./ "The Illustrious Metal" from *West African Explorers*, edited by C. Howard. Copyright © 1955. Reprinted by permission of Oxford University Press, London. #207 "Yoruba Proverbs" from *Wit and Wisdom from West Africa*, compiled by Richard F. Burton. Reprinted by permission of the Negro Universities Press. / "Scuffles Often Occur" from *The Content and Form of Yoruba Ijala*, by S.A. Babalola. Copyright © 1966. Reprinted by permission of The Clarendon Press, Oxford.

MERCHANTS AND POTENTATES: page 232 from the unpublished thesis on medieval Africa, by Dr. Samir Zoghby, the Library of Congress. #233 from *The Voyages of Cadamosto and Other Documents on Western Africa*, second series, no. LXXX, edited and translated by Gerald Crone. Copyright © 1937. Reprinted by permission of Cambridge University Press on behalf of The Hakluyt Society, London. #234 "Umme Jilma" #235 "Kanem at Its Height" from *Nigerian Perspectives*, compiled by Thomas Hodgkin and translated by H.R. Palmer. Copyright © 1960. The Government Printer, Lagos, Nigeria. #235 "Song of the Bornu Slaves" from "Song of the Slaves in the Desert" in *The Languages and Peoples of Bornu Being a Collection of the Writings of P.A. Benton*. Frank Cass & Co. Ltd., London. #235 "A Most Excellent Prince" from *History of the First Twelve Years of the Reign of Mai Idris Alooma of Bornu*, by Ahmed ibn Fartua, translated from the Arabic, with introduction and notes by H.R. Palmer. The Government Printer, Lagos, Nigeria. #238 "The Yerima's Praise Song" #239 "Star of the Morning" from *Kanuri Songs*, translated by J.R. Patterson. The Government Printer, Lagos, Nigeria. #240 from "Old Kanuri Capitals," by A.D. Bivar and P.L. Shinnie, in *Journal of African History*, vol. III, 1962, No. 1. Reprinted by permission of Cambridge University Press, New York. #241 "Sarki the Snake" #245 "The Two Rogues" from *A Selection of Hausa Stories*, compiled and translated by H.A.S. Johnston. Copyright © 1966. Reprinted by permission of The Clarendon Press, Oxford. #242 "Barbushe the Hunter" #244 "Yaji's Revenge" "The Islamization of Kano" from "The Kano Chronicle" in *Sudanese Memoirs*, translated by H.R. Palmer. Frank Cass & Co. Ltd., London. #245 "An Epistle on Kingship" from "The Obligation of Princes," by Sheikh Muhammad al Maghili of Tlemcen, in *The Bornu Sahara and Sudan*, by Sir Richmond Palmer. John Murray, London. #247 "Wilde Woodie Hausaland" from *The Seventh Booke of the Historie of Africa*, by Leo Africanus. The Hakluyt Society, London./"Bortorimi and the Spider" from *Hausa Superstitions and Customs*, by Major A.J.N. Tremearne. John Bale, Sons & Danielson Ltd., London. #248 from *Hausa and Fulani Proverbs*, compiled and edited by C.E.J. Whitting. Copyright © 1940. Reprinted by permission of Gregg International Publishers Ltd., Farnborough, England.

THE MWINDO EPIC: abbreviated from *The Mwindo Epic*, edited and translated by Daniel P. Biebuyck and Kahombo C. Mateene. Copyright © 1969. Originally published by The University of California Press; reprinted by permission of The Regents of the University of California and Daniel P. Biebuyck.

RAPE OF THE COAST: page 328 from Everyman's Library Edition of *Portuguese Voyages, 1498–1663*, edited by Charles David Ley. Copyright © 1947. Reprinted by permission of E.P. Dutton & Co., Inc., New York, and J.M. Dent & Sons Ltd., London. #330 from *The Voyages of Cadamosto and Other Documents on Western Africa*, second series, no. LXXX, edited and translated by Gerald Crone. Copyright © 1937. Reprinted by permission of Cambridge University Press on behalf of The Hakluyt Society, London. #331 "The Guinea Trade" #332 "The Conversion of Bemoym" from *Europeans in West Africa 1450–1560*, translated and edited by John William Blake. Copyright © 1942. Reprinted by permission of Cambridge University Press on behalf of The Hakluyt Society, London. #334 "Cry of Alarm" from *The African Past*, edited by Basil Davidson. Copyright © 1964 by Basil Davidson. Grosset & Dunlap. Reprinted by permission of Basil Davidson. #334 "Making New Christians" #335 "The Middle Passage" from *Human Livestock*, by Edmund B. d'Auvergne. Grayson and Grayson, London. #335 "Negotiating for Chattel" adapted from *West African Explorers*, edited by C. Howard. Copyright © 1955. Reprinted by permission of Oxford University Press, London. #336 "The Rise of Gumbo Smart" "The Consummate Villains" from *Sierra Leone Inheritance*, by Christopher Fyfe, edited by G.S. Graham. West African Graphic Co. Ltd., London.

CONTINENT IN TURMOIL: page 376 from *Timbuctoo the Mysterious*, by Félix du Bois. Longmans Green and Co., London. #377 "The Rape of Guinea" from *The Portable Hakluyt's Voyages*, edited by Irwin R. Blacker. The Viking Press, Inc./"The Royal Adventurers" from "The Company of the Royal Adventurers of England Trading into Africa, 1660–1672," by George F. Zook, in *Journal of Negro History*, vol. 5, April, 1919. Copyright The Association for the Study of Negro Life and History, Inc. Reprinted by permission of said Journal. #379 from *Nigerian Perspectives*, compiled by Thomas Hodgkin. Copyright © 1960. The Government Printer, Lagos, Nigeria. #380 from "Fulani Wisdom" in *Hausa and Fulani Proverbs*, compiled and edited by C.E.J. Whitting. Copyright © 1940. Reprinted by permission of Gregg International Publishers Ltd., Farnborough, England. #380 "Kuba Law" from *African Law, Adaptation and Development*, edited by Hilda and Leo Kuper. Copyright © 1965. Originally published by The University of California Press; reprinted by permission of The Regents of the University of California. #382 "Songs of the Spirits" "Animal Lyrics," from the unpublished collection of Dr. Jan Vansina. #382 "Ndaba, a Man of Affairs" from *Izibongo: Zulu Praise Poems*, collected by James Stuart, translated by Daniel Malcolm, edited by Trevor Cope. Copyright ©

1968. Reprinted by permission of The Clarendon Press, Oxford. #382 "Chaka's Receptions" from *The Diary of Henry Francis Fynn*. Copyright © 1950. Reprinted by permission of Shuter & Shooter (Pty.) Ltd., Pietermaritzburg, Natal, South Africa. #384 from "Prologue" to *Valley of a Thousand Hills*, by H.I.E. Dhlomo. Copyright © 1941. Reprinted by permission of Knox Printing Company (Pty.) Ltd., Durban, Natal, South Africa.

SPEARS AND MAXIM GUNS: page 424 from *Equiano's Travels*, abridged and edited by Paul Edwards. Copyright © 1967 by Paul Edwards. Reprinted by permission of Praeger Publishers, Inc., New York, and Heinemann Educational Books Ltd., London. #26 "Xhosa Freedom Fighter" from *Time Longer Than Rope*, by Edward Roux. Copyright © 1964 by The Regents of The University of Wisconsin. Reprinted by permission of The University of Wisconsin Press./"The Zulu Army" from *A Lost Legionary in South Africa*, by Colonel G. Hamilton-Browne. T. Werner Laurie, London. #428 "Zulu Wisdom" from *Zulu Proverbs*, rev. edition by C.L.S. Nyembezi. (pages 54, 60, 62, 69, 72, 116, 124, 135, 152, 193, 177, 159, 197, 228, 116.) Reprinted by permission of Witwatersrand University Press, 1963, Johannesburg, South Africa. #428 "An Offer of Safe Conduct" from *Sudan Notes and Records*, vol. 24, 1941. Khartoum, the Sudan. #429 "Ethiopian Resistance" from "The Foreign Policy of the Negus Menelik 1896–1898," by G.N. Sanderson, in the *Journal of African History*, vol. 5, 1964. Reprinted by permission of Cambridge University Press./"In Praise of Folly" from *La Partage de l'Afrique: Fachoda*, by Gabriel Hanotaux. Ernest Falmmarion, Editeur, Paris. Translation by Mary Elizabeth Wise. #431 from *Protest and Power in Black Africa*, edited by Robert I. Rotberg and Ali A. Mazuri. Copyright © 1970. Reprinted by permission of Oxford University Press, New York.

AFRICA REAFFIRMED: page 466 "Negritude Defined" from *Léopold Sedar Senghor and the Politics of Negritude*, by Irving Leonard Markovitz. Copyright © 1969 Irving Markovitz. Reprinted by permission of Atheneum Publishers, Inc., New York, and Heinemann Educational Books Ltd., London/"Black Woman" from *African Poetry for Schools and Colleges*, edited by O.R. Dathorne. Copyright © Ulli Beier. Macmillan, London./"For Khalam" from *Selected Poems of Léopold Sedar Senghor*, translated and edited by Clive Wake and John Reed. Copyright © 1964. Reprinted by permission of Atheneum Publishers, Inc., New York, and Oxford University Press, London. #467 "The Joy of Blackness" "Space That Once Was Mine" ("Limbe") from *Whispers from a Continent*, translated by Wilfred Cartey. Copyright © 1969. Reprinted by permission of Vintage Books, Random House, Inc., New York, and Heinemann Educational Books Ltd., London/"Splendidly Alone." The poem "Africa (Afrique)" from *Coups de Pilon*, by David Diop. Copyright © 1956. Reprinted by permission of Présence Africaine, Paris. #467 "Africa at the Center" from "The African Roots of War" in *W.E.B. DuBois Speaks: Speeches and Addresses 1891–1919*. Reprinted by permission of Pathfinder Press, Inc. #469 from speech made by Haile Selassie to the League of Nations, 1938. #470 from "Marcus Aurelius Garvey" in *Harlem: Negro Metropolis*. Copyright © 1940 by E.P. Dutton. Reprinted by permission of Harcourt Brace Jovanovich, Inc. #472 from *Strike a Blow and Die*, by George S. Mwase, edited by Robert I. Rotberg. Copyright © 1967 Robert I. Rotberg. Reprinted by permission of Harvard University Press. #473 from *The Philosophy of the Revolution*, by Gamal Abdel Nasser. Copyright © 1959. Reprinted by permission of Smith, Keynes

& Marshall, Inc., Buffalo, New York. #475 from *Weep Not, Child*, by James Ngugi. Copyright © 1964 James Ngugi. #1969 the Macmillan Company. Reprinted by permission of the Macmillan Company, New York, and Heinemann Educational Books Ltd., London. #479 from *Black Orpheus, Yoruba Poetry*, compiled and translated by Ulli Beier. Longmans of Nigeria Ltd.

IN THE THIRD WORLD: page 512 from speech by Dr. Kwame Nkrumah on July 10, 1953, in *Ghana: The Autobiography of Kwame Nkrumah*. Thomas Nelson. #514 "Liberty, Equality, Fraternity" from "Black Africa and the French Union," by Félix Houphouët-Boigny. #515 "Africa's Common Market" from "Africa's Future and the World," by Sékou Touré, in *Africa: A Foreign Affairs Reader*, edited by Philip Quigg. Copyright © 1964 Council on Foreign Relations, Inc. Reprinted by permission of Praeger Publishers, Inc., New York. (Frost quote from "The Death of the Hired Man" from *The Poetry of Robert Frost*, edited by Edward Connery Lathem. Copyright © 1930, 1939, © 1969 by Holt, Rinehart and Winston, Inc. Copyright © 1958 by Robert Frost. Copyright © 1967 by Lesley Frost Ballantine. Reprinted by permission of Holt, Rinehart and Winston, Inc.) #517 from *Congo, My Country*, by Patrice Lumumba. Copyright © 1962 Graham Heath, England. Reprinted by permission of Praeger Publishers, Inc., New York, and Pall Mall Press Ltd., London. #518 essay: "Freedom," by Bertha Lomayani, from *Transition*, October, 1962, Kampala, Uganda./"Continental Integrity" from the Charter of the Organization of African Unity. #519 from speech made before Economic Symposium in Blantyre in 1962, in *The New African*, Columbia University Press. #521 "The Manipulators" from Chapter IV: "Dawn" in *Bound to Violence*, by Yambo Ouologuem, translated by Ralph Manheim. Copyright © 1968 Editions du Seuil, © 1971 Harcourt Brace Jovanovich, Inc., and Martin, Secker & Warburg, Ltd. Reprinted by permission of Harcourt Brace Jovanovich, Inc., New York, and Martin Secker & Warburg Ltd., London. #521 "A Paradox" from the acceptance speech for Nobel Peace Prize made in Oslo, December, 1961, in *The African Nationalist: Luthuli Speaks*, Bantam Books. #522 from the defense of Herman Toivo Ja Toivo before Pretoria court, 1963, in *The African Reader: Independent Africa*, Random House Vintage. #523 "Dennis Brutus" from *Sirens, Knuckles, Boots*. Copyright © 1963 Dennis Brutus. Published by Mbari Publications, Idaban, Nigeria. Reprinted by permission of Dennis Brutus. Also in *African Writings Today*, Penguin Books Ltd., Harmonsworth, England. #524 "From the Grim Place," poem by K.A. Nortje "At Rest from the Grim Place" from *Modern Poetry from Africa*, edited by Gerald Moore and Ulli Beier. Copyright © 1963 Penguin African Library. #524 original, unpublished work by Harold Head, New York. #526 from *My Life in the Bush of Ghosts*, by Amos Tutuola. Reprinted by permission of Grove Press, Inc., New York, and Faber and Faber Ltd., London. All Rights Reserved. #527 from *Policy Toward Africa for 1970*, a speech by Dr. Elliott Skinner before The House Subcommittee on Africa, March, 1970.

TEXT: page 101 Thucydides quote from *History of the Peloponnesian War*, Book I, Chapter IV, Nos. 104 and 109, by Thucydides, translated by Richard Crawley. Everyman's Library Edition. Reprinted by permission of E.P. Dutton & Co., Inc., and J.M. Dent & Sons Ltd., London. #102 Herodotus quote from *The Histories*, by Herodotus, translated by Aubrey de Selincourt. Copyright © 1954 Aubrey de Selincourt. Reprinted by permission of Penguin Classics, Harmondsworth, England. #104 Juvenal quote from *The 16 Satires*, by Juvenal, trans-

lated by Peter Greer. Copyright © 1967 Peter Greer. Reprinted by permission of Penguin Classics, Harmondsworth, England. #108 Sallust quote from *Jugurthine War*, by Sallust, translated by S.A. Handford. Copyright © 1953 S.A. Handford. Reprinted by permission of Penguin Classics, Harmondsworth, England. #112 Strabo quote from *The Geography of Strabo*, edited by T.E. Page, E. Capps, and W.H.D. Rouse and translated by Horace Leonard Jones. The Loeb Classical Library. Reprinted by permission of Harvard University Press. #179 #182 Ibn Battuta quotes from *Studies on the Civilization of Islam*, by Hamilton A.R. Gibb. Copyright © 1962 Hamilton A.R. Gibb. Reprinted by permission of Beacon Press, Boston. #183 Leo Africanus quote #188 Sultan Mansur quote both from *The Golden Trade of the Moors*, by E.V. Bovill Copyright © 1968. Reprinted by permission of Oxford University Press, London. #189 #191 Pacheco Pereira quotes from *Arabs*, by E.C. Hodgkin. The Modern World Volume 10. Copyright © 1966. Reprinted by permission of Oxford University Press, London. #310 João de Barros quote from *Pageant of Ghana*, by Freda Wolfson. Copyright © 1958. Reprinted by permission of Cambridge University Press, New York, on behalf of the Hakylut Society. Published by Oxford University Press, London. #318 Affonso letter from *The African Past*, edited by Basil Davidson. Copyright © 1964 Basil Davidson. Published by Grosset & Dunlap. Reprinted by permission of Basil Davidson. #409 Father Ohrwalder quote #410 Sir Charles Wilson quote both from *The Independent Sudan*, by Mekki Shebeika. Copyright © 1959. Reprinted by permission of Robert Speller & Sons, New York. #462 Winston Churchill quote from *The Second World War: The Gathering Storm*, by Winston S. Churchill. Copyright © 1945. Reprinted by permission of Houghton Mifflin Company, Boston, and Cassell & Co., London. #465 Aimé Césaire quote from *Cahier d'un Retour au Pays Natal*, by Aimé Césaire. Copyright © 1956. Published by Présence Africaine, Paris.

INDEX

Page numbers in italics refer to captions.

A GROUP PEOPLE, 51, 55
ABA ISLAND, 408
ABBASIDS, 143, 222
ABD AL-KADER, 421, *443*, 443.
ABD AL-KARIM, 491
ABD AL-QADIR PASHA, 409
ABD AL-RAHMAN AS-SADI, *Tarikh as-Sudan*, 186, 359–60 (excerpt)
ABD AR-RAHMAN AS-SUYUTI, 181
ABDA, 185
ABDUL INJAI, 407
ABDULLAH, 363
ABDULLAHI, KHALIFA AL-MAHDI, 411, 429, *429 (quoted)*, 453
ABDULLAHI BURJA, 227
ABIDJAN, 503
ABOMEY, 318, 393, 446
ABRAHA, 139
ABU ABDULLAH, 357
ABU BAKR, 183
ABU BEKR, 158–59 (excerpt)
ABU SALIH THE ARMENIAN, 230
ABU YOHYA, 356
ABU ZEID, 166–68 (excerpt)
ABYDOS, 53
ABYSSINIA *see* ETHIOPIA
ACACUS CAVES, 32
ACCRA, 189, 309, 461, 499–500, 501, 507, 508
ACHEULIAN CULTURE, 26, 27
ADAL, 142
ADAMAWA EASTERN GROUP (lang.), 263, 266

ADANSI, 190
ADDIS ABABA, 506
ADEL, 230
ADEN, GULF OF, 55, 143, 411
THE ADMONITIONS OF THE PROPHET IPUWER, 55 (excerpt)
ADOULA, CYRILLE, 504
ADOWA, battle of, 423, 445, 454, 455, 462
ADRAR DES IFORAS (Mali), 180, 220–21
ADRAR MASSIF (Mauritania), 148, 149
ADULIS, 63, 79, 137; in Periplus of the Erythrean Sea, 80 (excerpt)
ADZE AND HAND ADZE, 29, 31
AEGYPTOPITHECUS ZEUXIS (ape), 21
AFFONSO V, KING OF PORTUGAL, 307–308, 331–32 (quoted)
AFFONSO (NZINGA MVEMBA), 309, 314, 318, 340, 341, 364; letter to John III, 401 (excerpt); on slave trade, 334 (quoted)
AFiLAS, 64, 139
"AFRICA" (AFRICA ROMANA), 108–15 passim, 128, 132
AFRICA PROCONSULARIS, 113, 128
AFRICAN ASSOCIATION, 436
AFRICAN COMMUNITIES LEAGUE, 460
AFRICAN LIBERATION COMMITTEE (ALC), 506, 507–508, 509
AFRICAN NATIONAL CONGRESS (ANC), 461, 509, 510, 521
AFRIKANERS see BOERS
AFRO-ASIATIC LANGUAGES, 99
AFRO-MEDITERRANEAN TYPE, 28, 32, 52
AGADES, 137, 175, 180
AGADIR, 357
AGAJA, 346, 401
AGASSIZ, LOUIS, 393
AGONA, 190
AGRICULTURE, 30, 49, 63, 65, 180, 266; "Africa," 109, 110–11, 132; Bantu, 30, 44, 45, 263, 264, 265, 266, 268, 269, 272, 293, 325; Berbers, 32, 106, 107, 108, 110; Carthage, 104, 107; Egypt, 30, 49, 51, 52, 59, 65, 82, 83, 110; Ethiopia, 32, 65; foods introduced from Americas and East Indies, 7, 310; foods introduced from Asia, 7; hunting lands encroached on, 44, 45; prehistory, 30, 31, 32, 49, 51, 52; Sudan, 52, 65, 185, 186, 213, 219–20; see also livestock; water control and conservation
AGUAFO, 190, 319
AHAGGAR MOUNTAINS, 220, 233
AHANTA, 319
AHMAD AL-MANSUR see MANSUR, AL-
AHMAD BABA, 360, 363; Du Bois on, 376–77
AHMAD IBN FARTUA, History of the First Ten Years of Mai Idris Alooma, 219 (excerpt), 224, 231 (excerpt), 236–38 (excerpt)
AHMAD IBN SAID, 370
AHMADU ABDULEI (AHMADU CHEIKU), 421
AHMADU IBN TINDANI (AHMADU SEKU), 388, 421
AHMOSE I, 58, 59
AIR, 219
AJJER, 233
AKAN, 177, 183, 188, 189, 190, 229; Marees on, 188 (quoted); see also Aguafo; Fante; Fetu
AKHENATEN (AMENHOTEP IV), 58, 59, 69–70
AKINJOGBIN, I. A., 318
AL-. For Arabic personal names beginning with this article or its variants, see the following word.
AL-KAWKAW see GAO
ALA AL-DIN, 410
ALABASTER, 51, 57, 58
ALCAZAR, battle of, 388
ALEXANDER THE GREAT, 62, 101, 107
ALEXANDRA, PRINCESS, 497
ALEXANDRIA, 62, 63, 67, 107, 234; Caracalla's edict, 122 (excerpt); Eastern Orthodox Church, 63, 112, 114, 141
ALFONSO X, KING OF CASTILE AND LEON, Cantigas, 154
ALGERIA, 97, 99, 106, 107; French, 420, 421, 421, 432, 443, 443, 457, 463; independence struggle (Front de Libération Na-

tionale and GPRA), 499–500, 501; 503, 504; Marinids, 356; Ottoman empire, 358; prehistory, 26, 28, 32, 33; as republic, 504, 504, 507, 509; Vandals, 115; see also Barbary Coast; Berbers; Mauretania; Numidia
ALGIERS, 145, 432, 510
ALGOA BAY, 270, 412
ALI B. AL-HASAN, 144
ALI BEY LUFTI, 410
ALL-AFRICAN PEOPLES' CONFERENCE (AAPC) (1958), 499, 500, 501; 1961, 502
ALMEIDA, FRANCISCO DE, 312, 325
ALMOHADS, 146, 159, 356
ALMORAVIDS, 146, 148, 149, 179, 186, 356, 357; Encyclopedia of Islam on, 157–59 (excerpt); in Spain, 146, 159, 356
ALODIA, 114–15, 128, 230, 231, 250
ALVARO II, 313
AMALFI, 155
AMANTARI, 62, 63
AMARA DUNQAS, 231
AMARNA, 59, 70
AMBER TRADE, 143, 310
AMBO (OVAMBA), 325, 373; see also Bantu
AMDA SEYON, 164–66
AMENEMHET, 56
AMENEMHET III, 58
AMENHOTEP IV see AKHENATEN
AMERICAN SOCIETY FOR COLONIZING THE FREE PEOPLE OF COLOR (AMERICAN COLONIZATION SOCIETY), 403
AMERICAS, 314, 315, 327; foods introduced to Africa, 310; mining, 315, 316; slave trade, 312, 315–18, 316, 317, 320, 327, 335–36 (excerpt), 342, 346, 347, 361, 362, 391, 435; sugar, 315, 316; tobacco, 315, 316, 434
AMISTAD (ship), 434
AMON, 64; temple, Karnak, 74, 75
AMON-RE, 73, 101, 108; temple, Thebes, 74, 108; see also Zeus
AMSAKA, 236
AMULETS, 53, 73, 107, 108
ANASTHASIUS, SAINT, 126 (quoted)
ANCESTOR WORSHIP, 37, 47, 206 (excerpt), 263, 267, 268, 270
ANECDOTA see SECRET HISTORY
ANGLO-EGYPTIAN SUDAN, 459, 485; Mahdiyya, 408–11, 411, 428, 428–29 (excerpt), 439, 451, 453, 454, 458; see also Sudan (republic)
ANGOLA, 264, 265, 268, 269, 294, 308, 312, 326, 373, 395; Dutch, 313, 366; Portuguese, 8, 312, 313, 315, 319–20, 326, 347, 364, 365, 366, 366–67, 404–405, 406, 423, 459; resistance by Movimento Popular para Libertação da Angola (MPLA) and União das Populações da Angola (UPA), 503, 507, 509, 510; slave trade, 312, 319, 320, 323; trade, 319, 320; see also Ndongo
ANGRA PEQUENA see LUDERITZ
ANIMALS, 19, 20; domestication of, 30, 31, 180; mimed in dance, 44, 46, 47; as sacrifice, 57, 61, 64, 107, 118, 243, 269; trade, 59, 63, 73, 91, 106, 112, 132, 140, 155, 185, 234, 235, 310; see also hides and skins; hunting; livestock
ANIMISM, 29, 30, 44, 53, 73, 107, 108, 118–19, 149, 160, 181, 182, 186, 187, 190, 234, 263, 267, 296, 301, 388
ANJOUAN-JOHANNA, Al-Idrisi on, 159–60 (quoted)
ANKOLE, 272
ANKOLORA RIVER, 317
ANNAK, 411
ANNALS, by Tacitus, 122 (excerpt)
ANOMABU, 191, 319, 420
ANTAR, exploits in Sirat Antar, 152–53 (excerpt); odes, 153 (excerpt)
ANTELOPE, 20, 29
ANTHONY, SAINT, Saint Anasthasius on, 126 (quoted); Saint Jerome on, 125 (quoted)
ANTHONY OF PADUA, SAINT, 340
ANTHROPOLATRY, 107
ANTIOCHUS III, 104, 119
ANTONIO ("MARQUIS OF NIGRITIA"), 390
ANTONIO, DOM, 365
ANUBIS, 54

ANZIR, AL- see NASIR, AL-
APE, dryopithecines, 21–22; pithecanthropines, 40, 41; Pongidae (pongids), 21, 22, 41; trade, 73; see also australopithecines; chimpanzee; gorilla; hominids
APEDEMEK, 62
APIS, 109
APOPI, 58
AQIB, AL-, 184 (excerpt)
ARAB LEAGUE, 473
ARABIC (lang.), 99, 130, 141, 146
ARABS, 63, 130, 137, 139, 145, 146, 166; in Mozambique, 322, 368; and Portuguese, 312, 313, 369, 370; slave trade, 371, 372; trade, 137, 141–45, 155–56, 161–64, 170, 270, 312, 371, 372; see also Islam
ARAGON, 146
ARAWAN, 187
ARCHEOLOGY, 19, 21
ARCHERS, 60, 61, 103, 115, 184, 229
ARCHINARD, COL. LOUIS, 421
ARCHITECTURE, Axum, 63; Berbers, 121; Carthage, 108; Egypt, 49, 54–55, 59, 71, 75, 85, 108; Ethiopia, 126, 135; Islamic, 143, 147, 170, 175, 181, 185, 211, 388; Kanem-Bornu, 225, 230, 240–41; Nubia, 57, 60, 61, 62, 63, 95, 95, 112, 220, 230; see also building construction
B-GROUP PEOPLE, 51
BAAL, 101, 107; see also Sarapis; Saturn
BABALOLA, S. A., 208 (quoted)
BABOON, 26, 39
BACAR GUIDALI, 406
BADARI, 30, 51
BAFATA, 407
BAGANDA, 458
BAGAUDU, 242, 243
BAGIRMI, 421, 458
BAHR-EL-GHAZAL, 411
BAHUTU, 271
BAILUNDO, 406
BAIOTE, 407
BAKEL, 148
BAKER, SAMUEL, 437
BAKONGO, 376
BAKRI, AL-, 118; on Ghana, quoted, 181–82, 183–84, 185; on Kumbi Saleh, 179 (quoted)
BAL, 183
BALANTA, 406, 407
BALEARIC ISLANDS, 101
BALLANA, 64
BAMAKO, 464, 499
BAMBARA, 200
BAMILEKE, 301
BANADIR, 142, 144
BANANAS, 32, 160, 264, 268, 272–73, 293
BANDIA, 266
BANGWEULU SWAMP, 30
BANI MASUFA see MASUFA
BANTU (people), 44, 141, 261, 263–73, 290, 293, 294, 324, 325, 372, 438; agriculture, 30, 45, 263, 264, 265, 266, 268, 269, 272, 293, 325; art and sculpture, 263, 266, 267, 268, 269, 293, 295, 296; and Boers, 325–26, 373, 375, 412, 416, 417, 438, 439; and British, 398, 398, 401, 412, 413, 416–17, 417–18, 426, 426 (excerpt), 438, 439; and Bushmen, 30, 45; cattle complex, 263, 264, 269, 273, 294, 299, 325; divine kingship, 267, 293; divinities and religious beliefs, 47, 263, 267, 268, 269, 270, 273, 274; dwellings, 295, 398; fabrics and textiles, 263, 266, 268; fishing and hunting, 261, 263, 265, 266, 290; government, 267, 268, 269; hereditary kingship, 269; and Hottentots, 412; ironwork and metalwork, 264–68 passim, 272, 293; marriage customs, 269, 274; myth and legend, 267, 270, 273, 274, 275–88 (excerpt); pottery, 263, 265, 267, 268, 272; territorial kingship, 266, 267; trade, 144–45, 265–70 passim, 272; see also separate listings under individual groups and peoples
BANTU (lang.), 261, 263–64, 265, 272, 273, 299; "Chimbelazi," 143; Proto-Bantu A and Proto-Bantu B, 265
THE BANTU PAST AND PRESENT, by Molema, 374
BANYORO, 458
BARA, 409, 410

ARDRA, 318, 319
ARIANISM, 114, 115
ARISTOTLE, Politics, 119–21 (excerpt)
ARKAMI (ERGAMENES), 62
ARO, 327, 421
ARROW, 28, 29, 30, 31, 34–35, 43, 44, 45, 46, 61, 184, 185, 188; see also archers
ARROW POINT AND ARROWHEAD, 29, 31, 43–44, 51, 61
ARTAXERXES, 101
ARUSSI, 411
ASANTE, 188, 189, 190, 326, 361, 392; and British, 392, 420, 445, 446, 456, 458; gold, 200, 208, 213; Golden Stool, 420, 420, 446; see also British West Africa; Gold Coast
ASBESTOS, 485
ASEBU, 189, 190
ASHIR, 145
ASIA, Egypt invaded, 55, 57, 58, 83; foods introduced to Africa, 7; prehistory, 22, 26, 27, 30, 31, 49, 52, 180; trade, 51, 52
ASIENTO TREATY, 367
ASKIA, 184, 185, 187; Kitab al-Fattash, 186 (excerpt); see also Songhai
ASKIA DAUD, 187
ASKIA ISHAK II, 357, 358, 360
ASKIA MUHAMMAD GAO, 360
ASKIA MUHAMMAD THE GREAT, 179, 180, 183, 184, 185, 187, 210, 226, 227, 357; pilgrimage to Mecca, 181, 185
ASKIA NUH, 360, 361
ASPALTA, 76–77
ASS, 31, 233
ASSINI, 190, 314
ASSYRIA, 60, 62
ASTAR, 63
ASWAN (SYENE), 29, 51, 58, 66
ASWAN DAM, 507
ASYUT, 58, 234
ATBARA, 411
ATBARA RIVER, 60, 61, 66
ATEN, 59, 69; Hymn to Aten, 70
ATERIAN CULTURE, 29
ATHENS, 101
ATLANTIC CHARTER, 463
ATKINS, JOHN, 327 (quoted)
ATLANTIC OCEAN, legends about, 102
ATLAS MOUNTAINS, 97, 99, 130, 149, 175
AUGUSTINE, SAINT, 114, 123; sermons, 123–24 (excerpt)
AUGUSTINIANS, 369, 371
AUGUSTUS, 110, 132
AUCKLAND, 413
AUMALE, DUC D', 443
AUSTRALOPITHECINES, 22, 23, 24, 25, 40
AUSTRALOPITHECUS, 22, 25, 39
AUSTRALOPITHECUS AFRICANUS, 23, 24
AUSTRALOPITHECUS BOISEI, 23
AUSTRALOPITHECUS ROBUSTUS, 23, 24; Broom on, 41–42 (quoted)

AUTSHUMAYO, 373
AUVERGNE, EDMUND B., Human Livestock . . . , 335–36 (excerpt)
AVARIS (TANIS), 58, 60, 74
AVIZ, 305
AVONGARA, 266
AWAD AL-KARIM, 409
AWDAGHAST, 232, 233
AXE AND HAND AXE, 26, 27, 29, 31, 32, 59, 143, 265
AXIM, 188, 309, 313
AXUM, 63–64, 65, 78, 95, 112, 137, 139, 141, 142, 423; Cathedral of St. Mary of Zion, 134; Christianity, 63, 112, 134; described in Periplus of the Erythrean Sea, 80 (excerpt); and Nubia, 64, 80, 95, 112, 137; steles, 63, 94; trade, 63, 80, 95, 112, 137; and Yemen, 63, 64, 137
AZAMBUJA, DIEGO DE, 190, 310–11, 363
AZANIAN COAST, 145
AZIKIWE, NNAMDI, 462
AZORES, 308
AZURARA, GOMEZ EANNES DE, 307; Chronicle of Guinea, 334–35 (excerpt)

BARATIERI, GEN. ORESTE, 423, 445
BARAWA see BRAVA
BARBADOS, 316
BARBARY ("LIBYA"), 96–115, 388; see also Berbers; Carthage
BARBARY COAST, 310; Ottoman empire, 357, 358; and United States, 359
BARBOT, JEAN, 189, 317 (quoted)
BARBUSHE, in Kano Chronicle, 242–43 (excerpt), 244
BARCA, 101
BARINGO, LAKE, 23
BARK CLOTH, 107, 263
BARLEY, 30, 31, 32, 51, 65, 83
BAROTSELAND, 418
BARRETO, FRANCESCO, 321, 407
BARROS, JOAO DE, De Asia, 161 (excerpt); on Kilwa and Sofala quoted, 142, 145, 160–61; on Portuguese conversions, 309; on Portuguese fortifications, 310–11, 311 (quoted); on Prince of Wolof, 311 (quoted)
BARTER, 62, 91, 102, 253
BARTH, HEINRICH, 229, 403, 429
BASHEE RIVER, 414
BASHORUN GAHA, 363
BASKETRY, 30, 51, 61, 265, 272
BASUTO AND BASUTOLAND, 375, 414; Boers, 415–16; British, 414, 414–16; see also Lesotho
BATHURST, 461
BATTLE OF THE NILE, 358
BATTLE OF THE PYRAMIDS, 358
BATWA, 30, 271
BAUCHI, 362
BAUDELAIRE, CHARLES, 482
BAULE, 213
BAYAGIDDA, 227; in legend (as Abuyazidu), 241–42 (excerpt)
BAYNES MOUNTAINS, 30, 44
BEAFADA, 406, 407
BECHUANALAND, British, 455, 485; see also Botswana
BEDJA see BEJA
BEGHO, 148, 188
BEHER, 63
BEIER, ULLI, Yoruba translations, 206 (excerpt), 208 (excerpt)
BEJA (BEDJA), 99, 141
BEHANZIN, 421, 446
BELGIAN CONGO (CONGO FREE STATE), 421–22, 452–53, 453, 459; independence and war, 501–502, 503, 504, 506–507, 509; mining, 8, 452, 462; see also Congo (Brazzaville); Congo (Kinshasa); Katanga
BELGIUM, and Africa, 451, 452, 459, 465, 499
BELISARIUS, 124
BELLOC, HILLAIRE, The Modern Traveller, 456
BEMOYM, 311; Ruy de Pina on, 332–34 (quoted)
BEN BELLA, AHMAD, 504, 507
BENGA, 183
BENGHAZI see EUESPERIDES
BENGUELA, 319
BENI HILAL see HILALI
BENI SAADI, 357, 388
BENI SULAIM, 166
BENIN, 177, 188–92 passim, 309, 314, 326, 343, 361; art and sculpture, 65, 177, 189, 192, 193, 194–95, 197, 205, 205, 215, 310, 327, 346, 347; British, 312, 342, 420; divine kingship, 191, 192; Pereira on, 189 (quoted), 191 (quoted); Portuguese, 309, 310, 311, 314; slave trade, 189, 317, 318, 319, 326, 346; trade, 189, 190, 309–10, 312, 319, 326
BENIN, BIGHT OF, 188, 308, 312, 363
BENIN RIVER, 214–15
BENUE RIVER, 189
BENUE VALLEY, 219, 290
BERBER (lang.), 99, 130, 145
BERBERA, 142
BERBERS ("LIBYANS"), 32, 99–100, 104–108, 115, 118, 119, 121, 122–23 (excerpt), 130, 179, 219, 362; agriculture and livestock, 32, 106, 107, 108, 110; and Arabs, 130, 145, 146; burial customs, 107, 118, 149; and Carthage, 102, 103, 106–107;

clothing, 107, 130, 223, 252, 253; demonology, 107, 118; divine kingship, 106; divinities and religious beliefs, 101, 107, 108, 109, 114, 118–19, 137, 145, 146, 149, 175; and French, 421, 443, 491; hereditary kingship, 105, 106, 233; languages, 99, 107, 130, 145, 146; Lebu, 100, 105, 130; Masmuda, 146; metalwork, 107, 149; myth and legend, 119 (excerpt); pottery, 106, 107, 110; and Roman empire, 106–11 passim, 113; Sanhaja, 146, 148, 158, 186; serfs and slaves, 104, 106, 108, 109; taxation, 103, 106, 108, 109, 110; trade, 106, 107, 180, Ursifan, 118; utensils, 106, 107; Westermarck on, 118–19 (quoted); see also Barbary; Kharijites; Maghreb; Tuareg
BERGDAMA, 269–70, 324
BERLIN WEST AFRICAN CONFERENCE (1884–1885), 404, 423, 440–41, 449, 451–52, 452, 453, 454, 459
BIAFRA, BIGHT OF, 308
BIAFRA, REPUBLIC OF, 510–11, 511
BIBLE, 61, 455
BIE, 406
BIEBUYCK, DANIEL, 274
BIERCE, AMBROSE, 41
BIJAGOS ISLANDS, 377 (excerpt), 407
BIJANTE, 406
BILAL (HADZRAT BILAL IBN RABAH), 151, 355
BILMA, 219, 221, 223
BIRAM, 227
BIRDS AND FOWL, 31, 43, 117, 118, 139, 147, 243
BIRKENHEAD (ship), 413
BIRMINGHAM, DAVID, 320; The Portuguese Conquest of Angola, 365 (excerpt)
BIRNI N'GAZARAGAMU, 225, 240, 241
BISMARCK, OTTO VON, 440, 451, 452, 452, 453, 456
BISSAU, 406, 407
BIVAU, A. D. H., 220; on Kanem-Bornu, 240–41 (quoted)
BLACK RECONSTRUCTION, by Du Bois, 467
BLACK VOLTA, 148
BLADES, as tools, 28, 29, 30, 31
BLAEU, WILLEM, Novus Atlas, 332
BLANCO, CAPE, 307
BLEMMYES, 64, 112
BLOOD RIVER, battle of, 375, 417
BLUE NILE, 66, 217, 219, 231
BLYDEN, EDWARD, 8 (quoted)
BOABDIL see MUHAMMAD XI
BOATS AND SHIPS, 53, 91; canoes, 189, 215, 233, 261, 263, 265, 266; Carthage (Punic), 102, 104; dhows, 143, 171; Egypt, 52–53, 74, 90, 91; European, 307, 394; navigation, 51, 62, 91, 99, 103, 307; Phoenician, 132; shipbuilding in Americas, 316
BOBO-DIOULASSO, 188
BODY DECORATION AND ORNAMENTATION, 43, 51, 197, 220, 255
BOER WAR (1899–1902), 451, 456, 456–57, 458, 484, 485
BOERS (AFRIKANERS), 324, 373, 375, 459; and Bantu (Xhosa, Zulu), 325–26, 373, 375, 412, 416, 417, 438, 438, 439; Basutoland, 415–16; and British, 373, 375, 404, 451, 455; and Bushmen, 325, 373; Cape Colony, 323, 323–24, 371, 372–73, 383, 390, 391, 412, 439; Great Trek, 416; and Hottentots, 325, 373, 412; Orange River Sovereignty and Orange Free State, 415, 457; South Africa, Republic of, 374; South West Africa, 374; Transvaal, 404, 451, 455, 456
BOJADOR, CAPE, 307, 309
BOLANO, FATHER ALPHONSUS, 309
BOLOR RIVER, 406
BOM BOSH, 293
BON, CAPE, Diodorus Siculus on, 121 (quoted)
BONAPARTE, LOUIS, 418
BONDELSWARTS, 422
BONDUKU, 148
BONE see HIPPO REGIUS
BONE TOOLS, IMPLEMENTS, AND UTENSILS, 25, 28, 29, 30, 43, 45, 51
BONGA, 407–408

BONIFACIUS, 114
BONNY, 319, 326
BONO, 188
BONO-MANSO, 190
BOOK OF ROGER see KITAB RUJAR
BOOK OF WAYS AND PROVINCES, by Ibn Hawqal, 179 (excerpt)
BOOKS, trade in, 155, 185, 186
BOOMAH, 413
BOOTH, JOSEPH, 472
BORGNIS-DESBORDES, GEN. GUSTAVE, 421
BORGU, 360, 361
BORNU, 217, 224–31 passim, 234, 235–36, 238, 242, 256, 361, 362, 363, 421, 458; cavalry and royal bodyguard, 225, 226, 226, 229, 236; kingship, 224, 226, 227, 229–30, 236, 239, 250; slaves, 226, 229, 235 (excerpt), 239; see also Kanem-Bornu; Kanuri
BORORO, 220
BOSHOF, JACOBUS NICOLAS, 415
BOSMAN, WILLIAM, New and Accurate Description of the Coast of Guinea, 188–89; excerpts, 206–207, 317, 318–19, 325
BOTSWANA, 294, 510; see also Bechuanaland; Commonwealth of Nations
BOUNA, 188
BOUND TO VIOLENCE, by Ouologuem, 520 (excerpt)
BOURGUIBA, HABIB, 497
BOVADIGLIA, PIETRO, 228
BOW, 28, 29, 30, 34–35, 43, 44, 45, 184, 185, 188, 226; see also archers
BOWDICH, THOMAS, 392
BRACE, LORING C., 38–41 (quoted)
BRANDENBURGERS, 305, 313–14
BRASS (metal), 155, 189, 298, 310
BRASS (state), 326
BRAVA (BARAWA), 142, 144, 160
BRAZIL, 313, 320, 365, 369; slave trade, 320, 347, 369, 391, 434
BRAZZAVILLE, 506–507
BRAZZAVILLE GROUP, 503, 504, 506, 507; see also MONROVIA GROUP; UNION AFRICAINE ET MALGACHE DE COOPERATION
BRETON, ANDRE, 467
BREVIE, JULES, 149
BRITISH CENTRAL AFRICA see NYASALAND
BRITISH EAST AFRICA, 372, 411, 412, 463, 501, 506; see also Kenya; Tanganyika; Uganda; Zanzibar
BRITISH SOMALILAND, 411, 458
BRITISH SOUTH AFRICA COMPANY, 408, 418, 452, 455, 463
BRITISH WEST AFRICA, 312, 348, 349, 367, 452, 456, 461, 506; see also Asante; Cameroon; the Gambia; Gold Coast
BRONZE, lost-wax casting, 65, 191, 192, 195, 205–206 (excerpt); sculpture, 65, 101, 189, 191, 192, 193, 193, 194–95, 197, 205, 205, 215, 310, 346; tools and utensils, 61, 64, 65, 107
BROOM, ROBERT, 22, 41–42 (quoted)
BRUCE, JAMES, 219 (quoted)
BRUSSELS, 452
BRUTUS, DENNIS, 523, 524 (quoted)
BRUYAN, PIETER DE, 374
BRY, THEODORE DE, Petits Voyages, 341, 343, 349
BU AMAMA, 421
BUBA, 407
BUDGE, SIR WALLACE ERNEST ALFRED, Ethiopian Royal Chronicles translated, 165–66 (excerpt)
BUDONGO FOREST, 25
BUFFALO, 20
BUGANDA, 272–73, 293, 411
BUHEN, 55, 93, 93
BUILDING CONSTRUCTION, brick and clay, 52, 62, 108, 181, 186, 220, 225, 226, 229, 230, 240, 241, 256; grass, reeds, thatch, 32, 53, 186, 241, 256; salt, 233, 252; stone, 54, 62, 108, 110, 145, 167, 230, 270; stucco, 108; wattle and daub, 270; wood, 32, 54, 226, 263, 270
BULALA, 225, 235, 238, 241
BULAWAYO, 418, 419

BUNKEYA, 452
BUNYORO, 272, 411
BURIAL AND FUNERARY CUSTOMS, 63, 94, 103, 107, 118, 119, 149, 296, 388; Egypt and Nubia, 54–55, 57, 61, 62, 64, 71 (excerpt), 87, 112; prehistory, 27, 29, 32; sacrifice of animals, 57, 61, 64; sacrifice of humans, 64; see also pyramids
BURMA, 307
BURTON, RICHARD, 403, 429–30; Yoruba proverbs, 207 (quoted)
BURUNDI, 271, 273; see also German East Africa; Ruanda-Urundi
BUSH (lang.), 32, 324
BUSHLAND see SAVANNA
BUSHMEN (SAN), 21, 29–30, 31, 32, 44, 45, 46, 47, 269, 270, 271, 294, 295, 299, 324–25, 372, 373; and Bantu, 30, 44, 45; and Boers, 325, 373; divinities and religious beliefs, 45, 47, 270; myth and legend, 44, 47, 270; rock art, 32, 33, 33, 43–44 (excerpt), 270
BUSHOONG, 380, 382
BYBLOS, 55, 58, 74
BYZANTINE CHURCH, 63, 65, 114; see also Coptic Church; Eastern Orthodox Church
BYZANTINE EMPIRE, 64, 100, 112, 115, 124 (excerpt), 132, 139, 234, 355

C-GROUP PEOPLE, 51, 57
CABES, JOHN, 319
CACAO, 464
CACHEU RIVER, 406, 407
CADAMOSTO, ALVISE DA, 190, 308, 330, 330–31 (quoted)
CAELESTIS, 107; see also Isis; Tanit
CAESAR, JULIUS, 110
CAILLIE, RENE, 211, 403, 421, 429
CAIRO, 223, 233, 235, 357, 508
CALABASH, 43, 207, 208, 301
CALVINISM, 324, 373
CAMBAMBE, 319–20
CAMBYSES, 62, 101
CAMEL, 100, 111–12, 180, 213, 217, 232, 233, 234, 236, 252–53, 252
CAMEROON, 266, 267, 301; British, 459; French (Cameroun), 459, 499–500; German (Kamerun), 422, 440, 456, 459; Monrovia Group, 504, 505, 506
CAMWOOD, 266, 312
CANAAN, 87
CANADA, 403
CANARY ISLANDS, 308
CANDACE, 61
CANHABAGUE, 407
CANOES see BOATS AND SHIPS
CANTIGAS, by Alfonso X, 154
CAO, DIOGO, 309, 364, 373–74
CAPE COAST (CAPE COAST CASTLE), 188, 314, 348, 420
CAPE COLONY (CAPE PROVINCE), 373, 457, 462; Boers, 323, 323–24, 371, 372–73, 383, 390, 391, 412, 439; British, 412–14, 439, 455; see also Basutoland; South Africa, Republic of; South Africa, Union of
CAPE TOWN, 323
CAPE VERDE ISLANDS, 307, 308, 309, 367, 406; Cadamosto on, 330–31 (quoted)
CAPITALISM AND SLAVERY, by Williams, 316
CAPUCHINS, 309
CARACALLA, 111, 122 (quoted)
CARBON DATING see RADIOCARBON DATING
CARBUNCLE (precious stone), 103, 106
CARIBBEAN AND WEST INDIES, 315, 316, 327, 434; British, 316, 316, 364, 420; cotton, 316, 434; Dutch West India Company, 188; French, 363, 364; pan-African conference (1900), 457–58; slave trade, 312, 315, 316, 316 (excerpt), 367, 377, 401, 403, 434, 435; Spanish, 367; sugar, 315, 316, 316, 363, 434; tobacco, 315, 316, 434; see also Americas
CARMEL, MOUNT, 27
CARMICHAEL, STOKELY, 508

CARTHAGE, 65, 100–108 *passim*, *105*, 110, 114, 115, *120*; Aristotle on, 119–21 *(quoted)*; Herodotus on, 101 *(quoted)*, 102 *(quoted)*; and Roman empire, 101, 103, 104–105, 107, 108, 110, 119; trade, 102–103, 104, 107–108, 119, 180; *see also* "Africa"
CASABLANCA, 421
CASABLANCA GROUP, 503, 504, 506, 509, 511
CASALIS, REV. EUGENE, 415
CASSAVA, 268, *290*, 310
CASSIN, 71
CASTRO, BALTHASAR DE, 319
CATHCART, SIR GEORGE, 415
CATTLE, 31, 33, 45, 51, 57, 59, 60, 61, 185, 219, *220*, 231, 234, 255, 272, 325, 412; cattle complex, 263, 264, 269, *271*, 273, 294, 299, 299, 325, 374; domestication of, 31–32; oxen and bullock as transportation, 100, 112, 180, 213, 233; as sacrifice, 57, 61, 269
CAVE, as burial site, 32; as dwelling, 27, 42, 46, 221; prehistory 22, 23, 27, 32, 42
CAVE ART *see* ROCK ART
CAYOR, 314
CECIL, SIR WILLIAM, 363
CEDAR, 51, 52–53, 71, 74, 91
CENTRAL AFRICA, BRITISH *see* NYASALAND
CENTRAL AFRICAN REPUBLIC, 266, 267; Brazzaville Group, 503, 504, 506, 507; *see also* French Equatorial Africa
CERAMICS *see* POTTERY AND CERAMICS
CEREMONIAL OBJECTS, 53, 59, 64, 77, *84*, 87, *91*, 106, 108, 183, *208*, 213, *236*, *365*, *392*, *420*, 420, 446; *see also* masks
CEREAL *see* GRAINS AND CEREALS
CERVEIRA PEREIRA, MANUEL, 319–20
CESAIRE, AIME, 465 *(quoted)*, 467; "*Cahier d'un Retour au Pays Natal,*" 467 *(excerpt)*
CETSHWAYO, 417, 418
CEUTA, 145, 307
CEYLON, 307
CHAD, *244, 255, 256*; Brazzaville Group, 503, 504, 506, 507; *see also* French Equatorial Africa
CHAD, LAKE, 25, 99, 180, 217, 219, 220, 221, *222*, 225, 256, 266
CHAKA (SHAKA), 374–75, 375 *(quoted)*, *398*, 398, 414, 416, 438, *439;* Fynn on, 382–84 *(quoted)*
CHAMBERLAIN, JOSEPH, 455
CANGAMIRE, 322, 407
CHARI RIVER, 266, 421
CHARIOT, 58, *60*, 90, 103, *130*, 180, 221
CHARLES II, KING OF GREAT BRITAIN AND IRELAND, 364, 377–78
CHELMSFORD, LORD FREDERICK, 417
CHENG HO, 163, 164
CHEOPS, 85
CHEPHREN, 85
CHILEMBWE, JOHN, 460 *(excerpt)*, 472; Mwase on, 472 *(quoted)*
CHIMPANZEE, 21, 22, 24–25, 41
CHINA, 26, 163–64, 170, *171*, 307
CHINA, COMMUNIST, 510, 511
CHISA MHARU NOGOMO, 407
CHISIZA, DUNDUZU K., 519–21 *(quoted)*
CHOPPER, 23, 25, 44
CHRISTIANITY, 8, 63, 64, 65, 95, 97, 112, 113–14, 115, 134, 223, 230, 233, 356, 436, 459, 460; Arianism, 114, 115; Axum, 63, 112, 134; Berbers, 114; Byzantine Church, 63, 65, 114; Covenants, 139; Crusades, 141, 353, 355; Donatists, 113–14, 115, 123; Egypt, 63, 64, 114, 134; Ethiopia *see* ETHIOPIA; ETHIOPIAN CHURCHES, 455, 491; Isiac rituals, 109; Islam, jihads, 140–41, 157, 386, 438 *(see also* Fulani, jihad; Mahdiyya); Islam replacing, 80, 124, 134, 140–41, 173; Jesus and the Virgin Mary, 109, *135;* Melchites, 114; missionaries, 309, 312, 314, 319, 322, 327, 332, 334, 340, 347, 364, 367, 369, 370, 371, *390*, 390, 403, 411, 418, 420, 422, 453, 454, 487; Monophysites, 114, 115, 134; Nubia, 65, 80, 114, 115, 128 *(excerpt)*, 134, 170, 230–31; Portuguese seek alliance against Islam,

307, 308, 338, 340; relief work, 510–11; and slave trade, 314, 327, *390*, 390; *see also* Coptic Church; Eastern Orthodox Church; Protestants; Roman Catholic Church
CHRONICLE OF GUINEA, by Azurara, 334–35 *(excerpt)*
CHRONICLE OF JOHN II, by Ruy de Pina, 332–34 *(excerpt)*
CHRONICLE OF THE ZANJ *(KITAB AL-ZANUJ)*, 143
CHUKWU, 327
CHURCHILL, WINSTON S., *The River War*, 465 *(excerpt)*; *The Second World War*, 462 *(excerpt)*
CHWEZI, 272, 273
CINCINNATI, 272, 273
CINQUE, 434
CIRCUMCELLIONS, 114
CIRCUMCISION RITUALS, 46, 301
CIRTA *see* CONSTANTINE
CLAESEN, JOHN, 319
CLEMENT, SAINT, 114
CLEOPATRA, 63, *109*, 109
CLEOPATRA SILENE, 109
CLIMATE, 20
CLOTHING, 107, *175*, 183, 184, 185–86, 188, 235, *500;* Berbers, 107, *130*, 223, 252, *253;* of gold, 182, 183; hides and skins, 43, 45, 57, 107, *271;* trade, 155, 188, 310; *see also* fabrics and textiles
CLOVES, *372*
CLUBS, as tools, 23, 26
COAL, *485*
COAST OF DEAD SHIPS, 374
COETSEE, JACOBUS, 374
COFFEE, 142, *464*
COHEN, RONALD, 225
COINAGE AND CURRENCY, 62, 63, 101, 102, 103, *105*, 106, 108, *120*, 143, 144; cloth, 235; copper, 143, 235; gold, 102, 103, 184, 235, 307, 363; shells, 207, 235, 266, 267; silver, 102, 103, 307
COLBERT, JEAN-BAPTISTE, 364
COLUMBUS, CHRISTOPHER, 357
COMMONWEALTH OF FREE AFRICAN STATES, 499
COMMONWEALTH OF NATIONS, 499, 508, 511
COMORO ISLANDS, 143
COMPANY OF THE ROYAL ADVENTURERS INTO AFRICA, 378–39 *(excerpt)*
CONFERENCE OF INDEPENDENT AFRICAN STATES (CIAS), 499–500, 501
CONFERENCIA DAS ORGANISACOES NACIONALISTAS DAS COLONIAS PORTUGUESAS (CONCP), 509, 510
CONGO (KONGO) (kingdom), 265–69 *passim*, 319, 326, 364, 365, 466; Christian missionaries, 309, 312, 314, *340*, 340, 364; Dutch, *313*, 364, 365; Portuguese, 309, 311, 312, 314, 319, 320, 326, 364, 365, 406; slave trade, 310, 314–15, 317, 318, 334, 364, 384; *see also* Kuba; Luba
CONGO (BRAZZAVILLE), 511; *Conseil National de Libération*, 506–507; independence and warfare, 501–502, 503, 504, 506–507, 509
CONGO (KINSHASA), 464, 507, 509, 511; independence and warfare, 501–502, 503, 504, 506–507, 509; *Organisation Commune Africaine et Malgache*, 507, 511
CONGO, BELGIAN *see* BELGIAN CONGO (CONGO FREE STATE)
CONGO AND CONGO BASIN, 19, 29, 219, 266, 267, 290, 293, 308, 404, 451–52
CONGRESS OF VIENNA, *434*
CONRAD, JOSEPH, 449; *Heart of Darkness*, 449
CONSTANTINE (CIRTA), 106, 107, 145
CONSTANTINOPLE, 110, 114, 115, 353, 358; Eastern Orthodox Church, 63, 65, 114
COPAL, 266, *464*
COPPER, 54, 55, 93, 100, 107, *177*, 189, 316, 452, 462, *485;* currency, 143, 235; searches for, 319–20, 374; trade, 51, 54, 91, 143, 184, 189, 234, 265, 266, 267, 268
COPTIC (lang.), 115
COPTIC ART, *97*, 114, *116*, 116, 117, *135*
COPTIC CHURCH, 63, 114, 115, 116, 134; Palladius on, 126–27 *(quoted)*; Rufinus on, 127–28 *(quoted)*; Saint Anasthasius on,

126 *(quoted)*; Saint Jerome on, 124–25 *(quoted)*; *see also* Eastern Orthodox Church
CORAL, 147, *177*
CORDOVA, 154–55, 355
CORN, 112; *see also* maize
CORREIA DE SA, SALVADOR, 320
CORSIDA, 101, 104
COSMAS INDICOPLEUSTES, 142
COSMOGRAPHIE UNIVERSELLE, by Thevet, *343*
COTTON, 185, 186; in Caribbean and West Indies, 316, 434; trade, 147, 189, *253*, *464*
COUNCIL OF CHALCEDON, 63, 114
COWRY, 207, 208, 245
CREEK TOWN, 327
CRESQUES, ABRAHAM, *175*
CRETACEOUS PERIOD, 19
CRETE, 58
CRO-MAGNON MAN, 28, *39*
CROMWELL, OLIVER, 371
CROSS (state), 326
CROWN, Berber, 106; Egyptian, 53, 77, *84;* Nubian, 64
CRUSADES, 141, 353, 355
CUBA, 434, 511
CUBISM, 8
CUFFEE, PAUL, 403
CULLINAN DIAMOND, *485*
CUOR, 407
CURRANTEE, JOHN, 319
CURRENCY *see* COINAGE AND CURRENCY
CURTIN, PHILIP, 310, 315–16, 326
CUSH *see* NUBIA (KUSH)
CUTTING TOOLS, 23, 28, 29, 31
CUYLER, MAJ. JACOB, 412
CYPRIAN, SAINT, 114
CYRENAICA, 97, 99, 101, 108, 113, *132*, 166
CYRENE, 101

DABULAMANZI, 417
DAGOMBA, 184
DAHLAK ARCHIPELAGO, 141
DAHOMEY (kingdom), 318, 326, 361, *393;* slave trade, 314–15, 318, 326, *346;* *see also* France; West Africa; Yoruba
DAHOMEY (republic), *346*, 504
DAJU, 230
DAMAS, LEON, 467; *Pigments*, "Limbe," 467 *(excerpt)*
DAMBARARE, 322, 407
DANAKIL, 141
DANCE, 8, 29, 33, *35*, 44, 46, 47, 267, *271*, *291*, 301, 301, 388, 392; *see also* masks
DANGALEAT, 255
DAR ES SALAAM, *144*, *171*, 509
DAR TICHITT, 31, 32
DARFUR, 65, 217, 220, 225, *230*, 230, 231, 250, *251*, 256, 266, 267
DARIUS I, 101
DART, RAYMOND, 22
DARWIN, CHARLES, *390*; *The Descent of Man*, 21, 38 *(excerpt)*; *The Origin of Species*, 38
DAUD IBN BWANA SHAYKH, 370
DAURA, 227, 242; legend, 241–42 *(excerpt)*
DAVIDSON, BASIL, 327
DE ASIA, by Barros, 161 *(excerpt)*
DE GAULLE, CHARLES, 463, 500, 501, 515–16
DE LA FOSSE, EUSTACE, 190
DE ROOS, A. J., 418, 419 *(quoted)*
DEATH *see* BURIAL AND FUNERARY CUSTOMS
DECATUR, STEPHEN, *359*
DEGEL, 362
DEIR EL BAHRI, 73
DELACROIX, EUGENE, *482*, 482
DELAFOSSE, MAURICE, 149
DELGADO, CAPE, 370
DEMBO, 406
DENDI, 179, 183, 234
DENHAM, DIXON, *437*
DENKYRA, 326
DENMARK, 434; and Africa, 305, 313
DENON, BARON DOMINIQUE, *482*, 482
THE DESCENT OF MAN, by Darwin, 21, 38 *(excerpt)*

THE DESCRIPTION OF ANIMALS, 140
DESERT, 20, 97, 99, *130*, 130; prehistory, 29, 31, 32
DHLOMO, HERBERT, *Valley of a Thousand Hills*, 384 *(excerpt)*
DIA (DIAKHA), 148
DIAGNE, BLAISE, 460, 461
A DIALOGUE OF NYASALAND, by Mwase, 472 *(excerpt)*
DIAMONDS, 438, *485*, 485
DIARA, 148
DIAS, BARTHOLOMEU, 308, 323, 325, 374
DIAS, DINIS, 307
DIAS DE NOVAIS, PAULO, 319, 320, 404–405
DINGISWAYO, 375
DINIZULU, 418
DINKA, 411
DIOCLETIAN, 112
DIODORUS SICULUS, 121 *(quoted)*
DIOP, BIRAGO, "Mamelles," 479–80 *(excerpt)*
DIOP, DAVID, 467, *Coups de Pilon*, 467 *(excerpt)*
DISEASES AND HEALTH, 7, 465, 491; influenza, 465; medicines and medicine men, 147, 263, 266; smallpox, 324, 325, 418; tsetse fly (sleeping sickness), 30, 32, 219, 231, 233, 264, 363, 465; *see also* liquor and alcoholism
DIULA, 148, 185, 188
DIVINE KINGSHIP, 65, 87, 180; Bantu, 267, *293;* Berbers, 106; Egypt, 52–56 *passim*, 61, 65, 77, 84, 87; Kuba, *293*, 380, 382; Nubia, 61, 76, 77 *(excerpt)*; Saifuwa, 222; Sudan, 181–83, 192, 222, 235, 254; Yoruba, 191, 192
DIVINITIES AND RELIGIOUS BELIEFS, ancestor worship *see* ANCESTOR WORSHIP; animism *see* ANIMISM; anthropolatry, 107; Arabs, 63; Bantu, 47, 263, 267, 268, 269, 270, 273, 274; Berbers, 101, 107, 108, 109, 149; Bushmen, 45, 47, 270; Carthage, 102, 107; Egypt *see* EGYPT; Greece, 102, 108; Nubia, 59, 61, 62, 64; Phoenicia, *101*, 107; Pygmies, 267; Roman, 107; sacrifice of animals, 57, 61, 64, 107, 243; sacrifice of humans, 64, 107, 314; theocracy, 191; Yoruba, 190, 191, 192, 207–208; *see also* burial and funerary customs; Christianity; Islam; Jews; nature, worship of
DJER, 54
DJUBO, Fei Hsin on, 164 *(quoted)*
DOGON, *186*, 388
DOGS, 45, 73, 160; as sacrifice, 64, 243
DOMINGO, CHARLES, 487 *(quoted)*
DOMINICANS, 322
DONATISTS, 113–14, 115, 123
DONGOLA, 114, 115
DONKEY CARAVANS, 91, 184
DOPPER, OLFERT, *343*
DOS SANTOS, JOAO, 322 *(quoted)*
DOUGGA, 110; Temple of Jupiter, *133*
DRA RIVER, 357
DRAKE, SIR FRANCIS, 348
DRAKENSBERG (GREAT ESCARPMENT), 20, 29–30, 46, 414
DRUMS, 140, 181, 182, 183, 301, *330*, *381*
DRYOPITHECINES, 21–22
DRYOPITHECUS ("tree ape"), 21
DRYOPITHECUS AFRICANUS, 22
DU BOIS, FELIX, 376–77 *(quoted)*
DU BOIS, WILLIAM EDWARD BURGHARDT, 316, 460, 461, 464, 467 *(quoted)*, 468; "Address to the Nations of the World," 458 *(excerpt)*; *Atlantic Monthly* essay, 467–69 *(excerpt)*; *Black Reconstruction*, 467
DUFFY, JAMES, 319
DUNAMA I, 224
DUTCH *see* NETHERLANDS
DUTCH EAST INDIA COMPANY, 323, 371, 373
DUTCH WEST INDIA COMPANY, 188
DUYVENDAK, J. J. L., 163–64 *(quoted)*
DWELLINGS, Bantu, *295*, 398; Chad, *256;* Kung, 46; Mauritania, *8;* prehistory, 27,

32, 42–43, 46, 221, 252; Senegal, *331; see also* building construction
DYA WALI, 185
DYAM TENE, 185

EAST AFRICA, 19, 308, 368–71; Arabs, 322, 368, 369, 370, 371, *372;* British *see* BRITISH EAST AFRICA; Germans *see* GERMAN EAST AFRICA; Islam, 137, 139–45, 170, 371; Italians *see* ITALIAN EAST AFRICA; map (1508), *329;* Portuguese, 137, 142, 145, 308, 312, 313, 326, 368–71, 405, 405–407, 456 (*see also* Mozambique); prehistory, 21–29 *passim,* 32, 39, 40; slaves, 141, *144,* 371
EAST AFRICA COMPANY, 422
EAST AFRICAN ASSOCIATION, 461
EAST AFRICAN RIFT (EASTERN RIFT), 19, 29, 32, 264
EAST AND CENTRAL AFRICA STATES, 510
EAST INDIES, Dutch East India Company, 323, 371, 373; foods introduced to Africa, 310; Portuguese, 323
EASTERN ORTHODOX CHURCH, in Alexandria, 62, 112, 114, 141; in Constantinople, 63, 65, 114; Ethiopian Orthodox Church, 134; *see also* Coptic Church
EBONY, 59, 73, 101, 112
EBOUE, FELIX, 463
ECCLESIASTICAL HISTORY, by John of Ephesus, 128 *(excerpt)*
EDEN, RICHARD, 311–12 *(quoted)*
EDO, 191, 193
EDUCATION, 8, *453, 459,* 459, 463, 491, 505; *see also* Christianity, missionaries
EDWARD, LAKE, 28, 30
EGBA, 363
EGYPT, Anglo-Egyptian Sudan *see* ANGLO-EGYPTIAN SUDAN; Aswan Dam, *507;* British, 358, 359, 451, 453, 454, 459, 460, 461, 464; Fatimids, 166, 223, 224; French, *358,* 358–59, *454,* 454, 464, 482; and Israel, 464; Mameluks, 224, 230, 358; Sudan, 184, 185; Suez Canal, *454,* 454, 461, 464; as United Arab Republic, 473, *492,* 497, 499, 503, 504, 507, 509, 511
EGYPT, ANCIENT (MISR), 49–75, 83, 84, 87, 91, 93, 99, 100, 107, 108; agriculture, 30, 49, 51, 52, 59, 65, 82, 83, 110; amulets, 53, 73, 108; architecture and building construction, 49, 53–59 *passim,* 71, 75, 85, 93, 108; Archaic Period, 53–54; barter and currency, 62, 91; boats and ships, 52–53, 74, 90, 91; burial customs, 54–55, 64, 71, 71 *(excerpt),* 87; and Carthage, 107–108; divine kingship *see* pharaoh *below;* divinities and religious beliefs, 30, 54, 54–55, 59, 59, 61, 62, 63, 64, 69–70, 73, 74, 75, 87, 87, 101, 108, 109, 112, *113,* 114, 134, *135,* 140, 173; and Greece, 101; Greek occupation, 59, 61, 62, 63, 112, 114; hieroglyphs, 53, 54, 60, 61, 73, 73, 359; and Hittites, 58, 74; Hyksos, 58, 59, 72–73 *(excerpt),* 73 *(excerpt),* 90; Intermediate Periods, 53; languages, 61, 99, 114; and Levant, 29, 49, 53–54, 55, 57–58; and Libya, 51, 55, 58, 59, 91, 101; Lower Egypt, 53, 84; and Mesopotamia, 52, 53; Middle Egypt, 55; Middle Kingdom, 53, 55, 56–58; music, *72, 93;* New Kingdom, 53, 58–59; and Nubia (Kush), 51, 55–62 *passim,* 75–76 *(excerpt),* 91, 93, 112, 230; Old Kingdom, 31, 52, 53, 54–56; ornament and jewelry, 54, 58–59, 73; painting, 52, 54, 54, 55, 56, 59, 61, 67, 82, 87, 90; and Palestine, 53, 55, 57, 58, 72, 91; people, 32, 52, 87; Persian occupation, 59, 62, 101, 107, 114, 115; pharaoh, 52–56 *passim,* 61, 65, 77, 84, 84, 87; and Phoenicia (Lebanon), 55, 58, 74, 91; pottery, 51, 53, 53, 54, 66, 108; prehistoric and predynastic periods, 21, 29–33 *passim,* 49, 51–53, 65, 180; and Punt, 51, 55, 73–74 *(quoted),* 91; Roman occupation, 59, 61, 63, 84, 108, 109, 110, 112, 113, 114, 122 *(quoted);* sculpture, 31, 54, 55, 56, 57, 59, 59, 68, 69, 72, 73, 85, 87, 91, 108, 109,

135; seals, 53, *73,* 108; slaves, 59; and Syria, 57, 58; tools and utensils, 54, *56;* trade, 51–64 *passim,* 73, 74, 90, 91, 107–108, 112, 220, 223, 233, 234, 266, 267; Upper Egypt, 51, 52, 53, 55, 58, 60, 84; water control, conservation, and irrigation, 51, 61, 62, *82, 83,* 83, 91, *358,* 359; *see also* Nile
EGYPTIAN (lang.), 61, 99
EKOI, *296*
EL BAWITI, Apollo Monastery, icon, *116*
EL FASHASHUYAH, 408
EL OBEID, 409, 410
ELAND, 44, 45, 47
ELEPHANT, *20,* 20, 29, 47 *(excerpt),* 120, *140,* 221; trade, 63, 91, *140;* for warfare, 63, 138; *see also* ivory
ELIZABETH I, QUEEN OF ENGLAND AND IRELAND, 231, 312, 364
ELLIOTDALE, 414
ELMINA, 188, 189, 313, 420; Portuguese, 189, 190, *308, 308,* 309, 313, 367; São Jorge da Mina, 189, 190, *308, 308,* 309, 340, 363
EMBABA, 358
ENCYCLOPEDIA OF ISLAM, on Almoravids, 157–59 *(excerpt);* on Zayd ibn Harithah, 355
ENGLISH ROYAL AFRICAN COMPANY, 318, 378
EQUATORIA, 19, 27, 32
EQUIANO, OLAUDAH (GUSTAVUS VASSA), 403, 424; *The Interesting Narrative of the Life of Olaudah,* 424–26 *(excerpt)*
ERGAMENES *see* ARKAMI
ERITREA, 422, 454, 462; *see also* Italian East Africa
ESHOWE, 418
ETHIOPIA (ABYSSINIA), 32, 63, 64, 65, *126, 135,* 137, 139, 141, *142,* 142, 404, 458, 462, 469, 497; British, 429, 462, 469; and Byzantine empire, 139, 355; Christianity, 63, 95, 112, *126, 134,* 134, *135,* 141, *142,* 164, 170, 230, *254;* Conference of Independent African States, 499; French, 429; Islam, 137, 141, *142,* 142; Italians, 422–23, *445,* 445, 451, 454–55, 462, 469, 491, 491; *Kebra Negast,* 78–79 *(excerpt);* and League of Nations, 462, 469–71 *(excerpt);* myth and legend, 78–79 *(excerpt);* prehistory, 29, 31, 39–40; and South West Africa, 508; and Sudan, 454; and Yemen, 139; *see also* Axum; Ifat; Italian East Africa
ETHIOPIAN CHURCHES, 455, 491
"ETHIOPIAN FAUNA," 20
ETHIOPIAN ROYAL CHRONICLES, 165–66 *(excerpt)*
"ETHIOPIANS" (generic classification), 99, 111, 112, 221
ETRUSCANS, 101
EUESPERIDES (BENGHAZI), 101
EUROPEAN PREHISTORY, 26, 27, 28, 29
EVATT, CAPT. JOHN, 411
EVIAN ACCORDS, 504
EVIL EYE, 107, 118–19, 182
EWEKA, 191–92
EYASI RIFT, LAKE, 30
EZANA, 64, 80 *(quoted),* 112

FABRICS AND TEXTILES, Bantu, 263, 266, 268; bark cloth, 107, 263; Carthage, 107; cloth as currency, 235; Coptic, 97, 116; cotton, 147, 185, 186, 189, *253,* 316, 434, *464;* Dahomey, *346;* flax, 30, 147; Hausa, 227, *246;* hemp, 147; Ibn Khaldun on weaving and tailoring, 157 *(excerpt);* industry in the Americas, 316; industry killed because of cheap exports, 326; linen, 64, 71, 90, 97, 116, 185; Nubia, 61, 64; raffia cloth, 263, 266; satin, 355; silk, 116, 139, 147, 307, 310, 355; Sudan, 185; trade, 91, 106, 107, 147, 185, 270, 306, 310, 340, 355; velvet, 355; weaving and spinning, 185, *267;* wool, 106, 107, 116, 147
FAGE, J. D., 180 *(quoted),* 310, 316, 326, 327
FAIDHERBE, GEN. LOUIS, 421, *442,* 443
FALASHA, 141

FANG, 37, 37–38 *(excerpt),* 267, 296
FANON, FRANTZ, 504
FANTE, 177, 190–91, 420
FANTYN *see* MANKESSIM
FARAS, 230, 251
FAREWELL TRADING COMPANY, 382
FARIM, 406, 407
FARMING *see* AGRICULTURE
FAROUK, 473, *493*
FASHODA (KODOK), 408, 409, 453, 455
FATIMA, 370
FATIMIDS, 166, 223, 224
FAURESMITH CULTURE, 27
FAYUM, *111;* prehistory, 21, 30, 51, 52, 65
FAZA, 369, 370
FAZARI, AL-, 177
FEATHERS, 45, 64, 91, *236, 301*
FEI HSIN, 164 *(quoted)*
FELUPE, 406, 407
FERDINAND, KING OF CASTILE AND ARAGON, 356, 387
FERNANDES, VALENTIN, 190
FERNANDEZ, ANTONIO, 312
FERNANDO, PRINCE OF PORTUGAL, 331
FERNANDO PO, 263, 308, 309
FERTILITY IMAGES AND RITUALS, 53, 107, 267, 301, *376; see also* Apis; Baal; Caelestis; Isis; Osiris; Sarapis; Saturn; Tanit
FETU, 190, 310–11, 319
FEZ, 145, 146, *172–73,* 233, 234, 356, 357
FEZZAN, 99, 103, 111, *130,* 166, 175, 180, 220, 221, 223, 224, 225, 233, 235, 256
FINGO, 414
FIREARMS, 184, 188, 190, 226, 236, 318, 326, 347, 361, *372,* 373, 375, 395, 415, *422,* 423, 484
FIREMAKING, 27, 42, 46
FIRMUS, 113
FIRST WORLD WAR *see* WORLD WAR, I
FISH, 19, 185; trade, 147, 188, 189, 309, 310
FISH RIVER, 308
FISHING, 45, 59, 145, 185, 189, 222, 261, 263; fishhooks, 30, 261; harpoons, 30, 31; prehistory, 29, 30, 43, 52, 180
FLAKE TOOLS, 25, 26, 27, 28, 31, 43, 45
FLATTERS, PAUL, 421
FLAX, 30, 147; *see also* linen
FLINT TOOLS, 31, *53,* 53
FLORENCE, 307
FODI KABBA, 420
FOOD GATHERING, 44, 45, 47, 269; prehistory, 28, 29, 30, 39, 43, 52, 180
FORBES, MAJOR, 419
FOREST, 20, 32; prehistory, 27, 29, 32; rain forest, 20, 32, *261*
FORT BEAUFORT, 413
FORT JESUS, *368,* 369, 370, 371
FORT TERNAN, 22
FOSSILS, 20–28, 39, 40
FOWL *see* BIRDS AND FOWL
FRANCE, in Africa, 305, 312, 313, 314, 429–31 *(excerpt),* 451, 454, 455–56, 458–59, 461, 465, 487, 497, 499, 500; Algeria, 420, *421,* 421, *432,* 443, 443, 457, 463, 499–500, 501, 503, 504; American territory, 358; and Berbers, 421, 443, *491;* and Biafra, 510; Cameroun, 459, 499–500; and Congo (Brazzaville), 511; and Egypt (including Ottoman empire), *358,* 358, 359, 451, *454,* 454, 460, 464, 482; and Ethiopia, 429; the Gambia, 420; and Germany, 451, 459; Ghana, 314; and Great Britain, 358, 453, 464; Guinea, 312, 363; Haiti, *435;* Madagascar *see* MADAGASCAR and MALAGASY (republic); Morocco, 421, 449, 458, 491; and Portugal, 348; prehistory, 26, 27, 28; Second World War, 463; slave trade, 316 *(quoted),* 363, 364, 367; slaves, 401; and South Africa, 323–24; and Togo (Togoland), 459, 506; trade, 312, 323, 348, 363–64; Tunisia, 421, 497; Uganda, 453–54; *Union Français,* 500, 501, 515–16; West Africa (and French West Africa), 348, *349,* 361, 363–64, 421, 429, *442,* 443, 452, 456, 458, 463, 464, 514; *see also* separate listings under French
FRANCIS I, KING OF FRANCE, 363

FRANCISCANS, 309
FRANCO-PRUSSIAN WAR, 451, 459
FRANKINCENSE, 142
FREETOWN, 309, 461
FREMANTLE, ADM. EDMUND, 412
FRENCH EQUATORIAL AFRICA, 463, *464; see also* Central African Republic; Chad; Gabon
FRENCH FOREIGN LEGION, *443, 458, 487,* 491
FRENCH GUINEA, 500, 501, 516; *see also* France, West Africa
FRENCH ROYAL AFRICA COMPANY, 189
FRENCH SUDAN, 361, 429, 453, 458; *see also* France, West Africa; Niger; Senegambia
FRENCH WEST AFRICA, 463, 464, 514; *see also* Dahomey; France, West Africa; French Guinea; French Sudan; Ivory Coast; Mauritania; Niger; Senegal
FRENCH WEST INDIES, 363, 364
FRERE, SIR BARTLE, 417
FROBENIUS, LEO, 273
FRUIT, 180, 310; trade, 132, 147, 155, 355
FULA-PRETO, 406
FULANI (FULBE), 219, *220,* 227, 240, *255,* 362, 388, 420, 421; adages, 380 *(quoted);* and Hausa, 362, 363, 379; jihad, 229, 361, 362–63, 379, *389;* and Portuguese, 406; *see also* Nupe
FUNERARY CUSTOMS *see* BURIAL AND FUNERARY CUSTOMS
FUNJ, 219, 231, *250*
FUNQUR, 409
FUR TRADE, 45
FURA, MOUNT, 407
FUTA JALLON, 362, 431
FUTA TORO, 148, 362, 401
FYNN, HENRY FRANCIS, 382–84 *(quoted)*

GA, 177, 188, 189, 190
GABON, 266, 267, 349, 510; *see also* Fang; French Equatorial Africa
GAIKA, 412, 413
GALAM, 148
GALLA (lang.), 99
GALLA (people), 99, *142*
GAMA, VASCO DA, 308, 312, 323, 325, *329;* on Kilwa, 143 *(quoted),* 342 *(quoted);* on Prester John, 308 *(quoted)*
GAMBARU, 240–41
THE GAMBIA, 313, 315, 420; slave trade, 314–15; *see also* British West Africa; Commonwealth of Nations
GAMBIA RIVER, 177, 307, 363, 420
GAMBLE'S CAVE, 28
GANN, LEWIS, 419–20 *(quoted)*
GAO (AL-KAWKAW), 175, 179–80, 181, 183, 188, 189, 210, 223, 234
GARAMANTES, 99, 103, 111, 115, 180, 220, 221, 222, 223, 233; Herodotus on, 103, 221 *(excerpt)*
GARDINER, ALLEN FRANCIS, *Journey to the Zoolu Country,* 416
GAROUMELE, 240, 241
GARUSI, 23
GARVEY, MARCUS AURELIUS, 460–61, *470,* 470; McKay on, 470–72 *(quoted);* Universal Negro Improvement Association, 460–61, 471
GASTON-MARTIN, G., 316 *(quoted)*
GATSI RUSERE, 407
GAUL, 101, 114
GAZELLE, 31
GEBA RIVER, 407
GEBEL TARIK *see* GIBRALTAR
GE'EZ (lang.), 63
GEIGLER PASHA, 409
GEMS *see* JEWELS
GEMSBOK, 47
GENIE (JINNI), 107, 118
GENOA, 155, 307
GENSERIC, 115
GEOGRAPHY, 19–20
GEOGRAPHY, by Strabo, 66–67 *(excerpt),* 102–103, 112
GEORGE I, KING OF GREAT BRITAIN

AND IRELAND, 367
GERMA, 99
GERMAN EAST AFRICA, *372*, 412, 422, *440*, 449, 456, 459, 485; Maji Maji Rising, 449, 459; *see also* Burundi; Rwanda
GERMAN SOUTH WEST AFRICA, 374, *422*, 422, *440*, 456, 459
GERMANY, in Africa, 305, 313–14, 422, 451, 452, 453, 456, 458; and Belgium, 451; and France, 451; and Great Britain, 451, 456, 457, 459; and Hottentots, 422; and Italy, 451; Kamerun, 422, *440*, 456, 459; and Masai, 422; Nyasaland, 422; and Portugal, 451; and Swahili, *441*; Togo (Togoland), 440, 456, 459; Zanzibar, 422
GERMANY, WEST, 505, 506
GERZA, 52
GEZO, 393
GHADAMES, 99, 232, 234, 256
GHANA (republic), 65, 183, 308, 310, 500, 508, 511, *512*; Africa Bureau, 499; Casablanca Group, 503, 504, 511; Convention Peoples' Party, 465; Conference on Independent African States, 499; and Guinea, union, 500–501; independence, 449, 465, *492, 493*, 497, 499, 500, 512; and Niger, 507; and Togo (Togoland), 504; *see also* Commonwealth of Nations; Gold Coast
GHANA (state), 65, 148, 175, 177, 179–80, 181, 184, 186–87, 210, 219, 356; Al-Bakri on, quoted, 181–82, 183–84, 185; Brandenburgers, 313; British, 314, 320; Christian missionaries, 314; Danes, 313; Dutch, 313; French, 314; gold, 177, 179, 184, 185, 213, 310, 317; Islam, 148, 184, 185; kingship and government, 181–86 *passim*, 182; legend of downfall, 200–201 (*excerpt*): Portuguese, 310–11, 312, 313, 363; slaves and slave trade, 185, 234, 310, 314–15, 317; Swedes, 313; trade, 177, 179, 184, 185, 188, 189, 190, 213, 232, 233, 310, 319; Al-Yaqut on, 185 (*quoted*)
GHAT, 180, 233
GIBRALTAR (GEBEL TARIK), 153–54, 355
GIL EANES, 307
GILDO, 113
GIRAFFE, 26, 29, *35, 437*; as gift, *163*, 163–64, 184
GIUMBO, 164
GIZA, Great Pyramids, 54, *85*, 485
GLASGOW, ROY A., 365
GLASSWARE, 32, 61, 64, 107
GLORY OF KINGS see KEBRA NEGAST
GLOVER, SIR JOHN, 420
GOA, 369, 370, 371
GOAT, 182, 243, 263; domestication of, 31, 52; skins, 142, 232
GOBIR, 227, 229, 247, 361, 362
GODS *see* DIVINITIES AND RELIGIOUS BELIEFS
GOGO, 272
GOLD AND GOLDWORK, 55, 74, 93, 101, 108, 116, 184, 190, *200*, 206–207 (*excerpt*), *207*, 229, 235, 270, 308, 317, 322, *343*, 357, 358, 360, 378, 418, 455, *485*, 485; ceremonial objects, 183, *208, 213*, *420*, 420, 446; clothing, 182, 183; as currency, 102, 103, 184, 235, 307, 365; ornament and jewelry, 61, 103, 182, 184, *208*, 213, 229; searches for, 233, 312, 365; trade, 59, 65, 73, 91, 102–103, 112, 142–43, 144, 145, 146, 155, 160, 170, 175, 177, 179, 185, 188, 189, 190, 206, 213, 215, 233, 234, 245, 270, 307, *308*, 309, 310, 312, 314, 334, 340, 368, 369, 371; utensils, 107, 183, 229
GOLD COAST, 190, 266, 482; British, 310, *348*, 420, 446, 458, 465; Dutch, *348, 348*, 420; Portuguese, 189, 190, *308, 308, 348*, 348; trade, 310; *see also* Akan; Asante; British West Africa; Ga; Ghana (republic)
GOLDIE, SIR GEORGE, 456
GOLE, 407
GOMBE STREAM RESERVE, 25
GONDAR, *8*
GONGO LUTETE, 422
GONNEMA, 412
GONZALVES, ANTAO, 307, 310
GOOD HOPE, CAPE OF, 308

GORDON, GEN. CHARLES GEORGE ("CHINESE"), 410, 411, 428, 453; letter from Muhammad Ahmad, 428–29 (*excerpt*)
GOREE, 313, 443
GORILLA, 21, 22, 24, 39, 41
GOTHS, 115
GOUVEIA, FATHER, 319
GRAAFF-REINET, 412
GRAHAMSTOWN, 412, 413
GRAINS AND CEREALS, 32, 63, 65, *82*, 102, 107, 110, 132, 185, *186*, *231*, 263; domestication of, 30, 31, 180; prehistory, 29, 30, 31; trade, 91, 106, 108, 147, 155, 160, 185, *253, 464*; *see also* barley; millet; rice; sorghum; wheat
GRAIN COAST, 309
GRANADA, 356–57; Alhambra, *386, 387*
GRANT, ULYSSES S., *483*
GRAPES *see* VINEYARDS
GREAT BRITAIN, in Africa, 305, 312, 313, 314, 319, 363, 368, 371, 411, 451, 452, 453, 457, 459, 465, 487, 487, 499, 501; Anglo-Egyptian Sudan *see* ANGLO-EGYPTIAN SUDAN; and Bantu (Xhosa, Zulu), *398*, 398, *401*, 412, 413, 416–17, 417–18, 426 (*excerpt*), *438, 439*; Basutoland, *414*, 414–16; Bechuanaland, 455, 485; Benin, 312, 342, 420; Boer War, 451, *456*, 456–57, 458, *484*, 485; and Boers, 373, 375, 404, 451, 455; British Central Africa (Nyasaland), 420, 452–53, 456, 460, 462, 463, 472, 501; British East Africa *see* BRITISH EAST AFRICA; British Somaliland, 411, 458; British West Africa *see* BRITISH WEST AFRICA; British West Indies, *316*, 316, 364, 420; Cape Colony, 412–14, *439*, 455; Egypt (including Ottoman empire), 358, 359, 451, 453, 454, 459, 460, 461, 464; Ethiopia, 429, 462, 469; and France, 358, 452, 464; and Germany, 451, 456, 457, 459; Ghana, 314, 420; Guinea, 312; and Hottentots, 412, 413; Industrial Revolution, 401, 434; and Portugal, 363; prehistory, 27; Protestantism, 363; Rhodesia *see* RHODESIA and ZAMBIA; Second World War, 463; slave trade, 312, 315, 316 (*excerpt*), 335–36 (*excerpt*), 363, 364, 367–68, 377 (*excerpt*), 378–79 (*excerpt*); slavery and reform movements, 368, 371, *372*, 401, 403, 424, *434*, 434, *435;* South Africa, 372, 373, 375, 404, 408, 412–14, *439*, 451, 455; South Africa, Republic of, 511; South Africa, Union of *see* SOUTH AFRICA, UNION OF; South West Africa, 374; trade, 312, 318, 319, 323, *348*, 348; *see also* Commonwealth of Nations
GREAT ESCARPMENT *see* DRAKENS-BERG
GREAT FISH RIVER, 325, 412, 426
GREAT LAKES, 299
GREAT RIFT VALLEY, 19–20, 264, 267, 271, 273, *299;* prehistory, 20, 23, 28
GREECE, 100, 101–102, 356; divinities and religious beliefs, 102, 108; and Egypt, 101; Egypt occupied by, 59, 61, 62, 63, 112, 114; pottery, 102, 107; trade, 107–108, 137
GREEK (lang.), 62, 63, 114, 115
GREENBERG, JOSEPH, 99
GREGORY VII, POPE, letter to Al-Nasir, 155–56 (*excerpt*)
GREY, SIR GEORGE, 416
GRINDING AND POUNDING IMPLEMENTS, 25, 26, 29, 32, 43, 51, *234*, *253*, *290, 466*
GROBBELAAR, B. J., 44–45 (*quoted*)
GUDU, 362
GUINEA, 32, 190, *343;* British, 312; Dutch, 312; French, 312, 363, 500, 501, 516; Maloe Company, 363; Portuguese, 309, 310 (*see also* Portuguese Guinea); slave trade, 215, 326, 334–35 (*excerpt*), 367, 377 (*excerpt*); trade, 312, 331
GUINEA (republic), 509, 511; Casablanca Group, 503, 504, 511; and Ghana, union, 500–501; Monrovia Group, 504, 505, 506; and Togo (Togoland), 504
GUINEA COMPANY, 367
GUMBO SMART, Macauley on, 336 (*quoted*)

GUMS, 71, 91, 112, 142, 314
GUNGUNYANA, 408
GUNS *see* FIREARMS
GWARI, 227
GWATO, 191, 309
G/WI, 45

H

HABASHAT, 63
HADZA, 30
HADZRAT BILAL IBN RAHAB *see* BILAL
HAFSIDS, 146–47, 224
HAILE SELASSIE (RAS TAFFARI MAKONNEN), 462, 468, 469; appeal to League of Nations, 462, 469–71 (*quoted*)
HAITI, 434, *435*, 510
HAJJ ALI DUNAMA, AL-, 224
HAJJ UMAR, AL-, 421
HAKLUYT, RICHARD, *Voyages*, on Sir John Hawkins, 377 (*excerpt*)
HALAWI, 411
HAMID IBN THWAIN, 411
HAMILCAR BARCA, 104, 119
HAMILTON-BROWNE, COL. G., *A Lost Legionary on South Africa*, 426–28 (*excerpt*)
HAMITIC LANGUAGES, 99, 115, 141
HANNIBAL, 104–105, *105;* Polybius on, 119 (*quoted*)
HANNO, 102
HANOTAUX, GABRIEL, 429–30 (*quoted*)
HAOUZ REGION, 357
HARAR, 141
HARDINGE, SIR ARTHUR, 412
HARKHUF, 73
HARLEM: NEGRO METROPOLIS, by McKay, 470–72 (*excerpt*)
HARPOON, 30, 31, 45
HASAN IBN MUHAMMAD AL-WAZZAN AZ-ZAYYATI, AL- *see* LEO AFRICANUS
HATHOR, 55
HATSHEPSUT, 91, 365; on the Hyksos, 73 (*quoted*); on Punt, 73–74 (*quoted*)
HATTI *see* HITTITES
HATTUSILIS, 74
HAUSA (people), 177, 180, 181, 205–206 (*excerpt*), *217*, 217, 219, 224, 226–27, 228, 229–30, 234, 241, 244, 245, *246*, *256*, 326, 361, 420, *511:* divinities and religious beliefs, 181, 241–45; and Fulani, 362, 363, 379; Leo Africanus on, 228, 229 (*quoted*), 247 (*quoted*); myth, legend, and oral tradition, 241–48 (*excerpts*); trade, 189, 190, 226, 227, 229, *254;* *see also* Kano Chronicle; Nigeria; separate listings under individual groups
HAUSA (lang.), 219, 248
HAWKINS, SIR JOHN, 312, 315, 317, 362, 367, *377*, 377
HAWKINS, WILLIAM, 312, 377
HEAD, HAROLD, 524; autobiography, 524–26 (*excerpt*)
HEART OF DARKNESS, by Conrad, 449
HEBREW (lang.), 99
HEMP, 147
HENNEQUA, JOHN, 319
HENRIQUE, DOM, 309
HENRY IV, KING OF FRANCE, 363
HENRY THE NAVIGATOR, PRINCE OF PORTUGAL, 190, 307, 309, 313, 334, 338
HEPZEFA, 57
HERACLEA, 355
HERAKLEOPOLIS, 55, 56
HERERO (people), 269–70, 325, 373, 374; and Germans, *422*, 422, 459; *see also* Bantu
HERERO (lang.), 44, 269
HERI-HOR, 74
HERODOTUS, *Histories*, 71, 99, 101 (*excerpt*), 102 (*excerpt*), 103 (*excerpt*), 180, 221 (*excerpt*)
HERTZOG, JAMES, 461
HICKS, WILLIAM, 410
HIDES AND SKINS, 27, 29, 32, 35, 43, 45, *140;* as clothing, 43, 45, *271;* as containers, 43, 45, 232; for dwellings, 32, 252; trade, 45–46, 73, 102, 106, 112, 142, 143, 189, 310; *see also* leather
HIERAKONPOLIS, 52, 53; Palette of Narmer, 54, *84, 85*

HIEROGLYPHS, 53, 54, 60, 61, *73*, 73, 359
HILALI (BENI HILAL), 146, *166; Sira Beni Hilal*, 166–68 (*excerpt*)
HINTSA, 413
HIPPO REGIUS (BONE), sermons by Saint Augustine, 123–24 (*quoted*)
HIPPOPOTAMUS, 19, 29, 30, *33*, 222
HISPANIOLA, 315
HISTORIES, by Herodotus, 71, 99, 101, 103; excerpts, 101, 102, 221
HISTORIES, by Polybius, 119 (*excerpt*), 121 (*excerpt*)
HISTORIES, by Procopius, 124
THE HISTORY AND DESCRIPTION OF AFRICA, by Leo Africanus, 228; excerpts, 179, 183, 185, 186, 229, 247
HISTORY OF THE FIRST TEN YEARS OF MAI IDRIS ALOOMA, by Ahmad ibn Fartua, 231; excerpts, 219, 224, 236–39
HISTORY OF THE MONKS IN EGYPT, by Rufinus, 127–28 (*excerpt*)
HISTORY OF THE MOORS IN SPAIN, by Lane-Poole, 154–55 (*excerpt*)
HISTORY OF THE PELOPONNESIAN WAR, by Thucydides, 101 (*excerpt*), 103
HITLER, ADOLPH, 462
HITTITES (HATTI), 54, 58, 60, 74
HLOBANE, 418
HOBSON, JOHN A., *Imperialism: A Study*, 457; *The War in South Africa*, 457
HODGSON, SIR FREDERICK, 420
HOE, *186*, 265
HOFFMAN, JOSIAS, 415
HOMEM, VASCO FERNANDES, 321, 407
HOMINIDS, 22–26 *passim*, 39, 40; *see also* australopithecines
HOMINOIDEA FAMILY, 22
HOMO (species), 23
HOMO ERECTUS, 25, 26, 27, 40
HOMO HABILIS, 24
HOMO SAPIENS, 27, 39, 40, 41
HOMO SAPIENS NEANDERTHALENSIS *see* NEANDERTHAL MAN
HOMO SAPIENS RHODESIENSIS *see* RHODESIAN MAN
HOMO SAPIENS SAPIENS, 27
HONEIN *see* HONO
HONEY, 29, 43, 45, 83, 155
HONEY VAT KLOOT, *484*
HONO (HONEIN), 233
HORDEDEF, 71
HORN, EAST AFRICAN, 27, 32, 99, 160, 220
"HORNS OF THE WORLD," 93
HORSE, 20, 61, 64, 99, 100, 105, 112, 180, 213, 217; cavalry, 184, 188, *210*, 219, *225*, 229, 250; and chariot, 58, *60*, 90, 103, *130*, 180, 221; trade, 106, 112, 155, 185, 235, 310
HORUS, 54, 64, 87, *87*, *135*
HOTTENTOT (lang.), 32, 324
HOTTENTOTS (KHOIKHOI), 28, 30, 32, 44, 46, 269, 270, 271, 294, 295, 299, *324*, 324, 325, 372, 373, 412; and Boers, 325, 373, 412; and British, 412, 413; and Germans, 422
HOUPHOUET-BOIGNY, FELIX, 464, 503, *514*, 514; on French ties, 514–15 (*quoted*)
HOUSEHOLD OBJECTS *see* UTENSILS
HUAMBO, 406
HUGUENOTS, 323, 373
HUILA, 406
HUMAN LIVESTOCK . . . , by d'Auvergne, 335–36 (*excerpt*)
HUMBE, 406
HUNGARY, 307
HUNTING, 19, 30, 40, 44, 45–46, 47, 59, 145, *222*, *231*, 261, 263, 269; agricultural lands encroaching on, 30, 44, 45; poems and prayers, 45 (*excerpt*), 47 (*excerpt*); prehistory, 24–29, 31, 32, 33, *33*, 34–35, 39, 40, 43, 51, 52, 180; in rock art, 33, 33, 34–35, 47; Wilson on, 45–47 (*quoted*); *see also* arrow; bow; spear; stick; stone
HURRY, JAMIESON B., 67–69 (*quoted*)
HYENA, 31, 47
HYKSOS, 58, *59, 90;* Hatshepsut on, 73 (*quoted*); Josephus on, 72–73 (*quoted*)
HYMN TO ATEN, 70 (*excerpt*)
HYMN TO THE NILE, 67 (*excerpt*)

IBERIAN PENINSULA, 100, 101, 103, 104, 105
IBN AL-WARDI, 142, 145
IBN BATTUTA, 161, 185; on copper trade, 189; on Gao, 179 (quoted); on Mali, 179 (quoted), 184 (quoted), 252 (quoted); on Mansa Sulaiman, 182–83 (quoted); on Mogadishu, 161–63 (quoted); on Sudan, 186 (quoted); on Zeila, 142
IBN HAWQAL, 233; Book of Ways and Provinces, 179 (excerpt)
IBN HISHAM, Life of Muhammad (based on Ibn Ishaq), 150–51 (excerpts)
IBN ISHAQ, 150
IBN KHALDUN, 183; Kitab al-Ibar (Universal History), Muqaddimah, excerpts, 153, 155, 156–57
IBN SEIF, 369
IBN TUMART, 146
IBN YASIN (ABD ALLAH IBN YASIN), 146, 157, 158, 356
IBO, 215, 361, 511; Nigerian civil war, 510, 511; slaves, 327; see also Aro; Nigeria
IDOWU, E. BOLAJI, 203–205 (quoted)
IDRIS ALOOMA (IDRIS IBN ALI), 219, 224, 225, 226, 230, 231, 235–36, 241, 361; Ahmad ibn Fartua on, 219 (quoted), 224, 231 (quoted), 236–38 (quoted)
IDRISI, AL-, 145; Kitab Rujar (Book of Roger), 159–60 (excerpt)
IDRISIDS, 173
IFAT, 141, 142, 164
IFE, 177, 188, 189, 191, 192; art and sculpture, 65, 189, 191, 192, 193, 195, 196, 197, 205, 327, 347
IFRIQIYA see TUNIS AND TUNISIA
IGBO, 191
IGBO-UKWU, 191
IGUEGHA, 192
IKEN, 57
ILAN, 166
ILORIN, 227
IMHOTEP, 68, 71; Hurry on, 67–69 (quoted)
IMPERIALISM: A STUDY, by Hobson, 457
IMPERIALISM: THE HIGHEST STAGE OF CAPITALISM, by Lenin, 457
IMPLEMENTS see TOOLS AND IMPLEMENTS
INCENSE, 63, 73, 112; see also gums; spices
INCINHATE, 406
INDIA, 22, 101, 139, 145; trade, 112, 139, 142–43, 145, 307, 371; troops fight with British in Africa, 411, 420
INDIAN OCEAN, trade, 143, 145, 163, 270, 308, 312, 372, 405
INDIGO, 310, 316
INDONESIA, 170
INDUSTRIAL AND COMMERCIAL WORKERS UNION OF AFRICA, 461
INDUSTRIAL REVOLUTION, 401, 434
INFALI SONCO, 407
INHAMBANE, 408
INITIATION RITUALS, 186, 268, 272, 289, 296, 301, 392; see also circumcision rituals
INSECTS, as food, 43, 45, 266; legends about, 247, 247–48 (excerpt); as sacred, 47
THE INSTRUCTIONS FOR HIS SON, MERY-KA-RE, 56 (excerpt)
INTER-AFRICAN AND MALAGASY GROUP (IAMO; Monrovia Group), 504, 505, 506
THE INTERESTING NARRATIVE OF THE LIFE OF OLAUDAH, by Equiano, 424–26 (excerpt)
INTERNATIONAL AFRICAN FRIENDS OF ABYSSINIA, 462
INTERNATIONAL AFRICAN SERVICE BUREAU, 462
INTIM, 406
INYEZANE, 418
IRAMBA, 272
IRAQW, 272
IRON AND IRONWORK, 62, 64, 65, 95, 105, 145, 149, 177, 180, 181, 185, 207–208, 213, 220, 226, 264, 265–66, 272, 293; tools, implements, and utensils, 65, 107,

180, 265–66; trade, 45–46, 143, 147, 160, 265, 272; weapons, 44, 58, 62, 65, 107, 185, 265, 365
ISABELLA, QUEEN OF CASTILE AND ARAGON, 356, 387
ISANDHLWANA, 401, 417, 418
ISIS, 109, 109, 135; Temple, Philae, 64, 112, 113; see also Caelestis; Tanit
ISLAM, 80, 124, 134, 137–49, 180, 181, 185, 186, 190, 217, 219, 220, 222, 223, 224, 226, 227, 230–31, 233, 234, 235, 244, 254, 355–58, 451, 459, 460; Almohads, 146, 159, 356; Almoravids, 146, 148, 149, 157–59 (excerpt), 179, 186, 356, 357; call to worship, 151, 159; Christianity replaced by, 80, 124, 134, 140–41, 173; Covenants, 139; Greek heritage, 356; Hadith, 147; jihads, 140–41, 157, 386, 438 (see also Fulani, jihad; Mahdiyya); justice, administration of, 146, 147, 148, 181, 184, 185, 223; literature and documents, 7; madrasa, 147, 148; Marabouts, 357; pilgrimage (hadj) see MECCA AND MEDINA; Portuguese alliances against, 307, 308, 338, 340, 371; Ramadan, 137, 140; Sharia, 184; and slavery, 141, 152, 318; Sufism, 147–48; zawiya, 148; see also Koran; Muhammad
ISLAMIC ARTS, architecture, 143, 147, 170, 175, 181, 185, 211, 388; miniatures, 150, 151, 168
ISRAEL, 464, 510; see also Palestine
ISTABL ANTAR TEMPLE, inscription, 73 (quoted)
ISTANBUL, 224
ITALIAN EAST AFRICA, 372, 462; see also Eritrea; Ethiopia, and Italians; Italian Somaliland
ITALIAN SOMALILAND, 454, 462, 501
ITALY, in Africa, 422, 445, 454, 459; and Germany, 451; and Hafsids, 146; Libya, 460, 462; and Ottoman empire, 460; trade, 155, 307; Tripolitania, 458
ITINERARIO, by Van Linschoten, 405 (excerpt)
ITURI RIVER FORESTS, 21, 30, 290, 293
IVORY, 101, 192; carving and ornament, 29, 43, 57, 91, 177, 192, 193; trade, 20, 59, 73, 103, 106, 111, 112, 132, 143, 170, 185, 188, 221, 267, 268, 270, 310, 312, 314, 340, 368, 371, 372; utensils, 51, 61, 340, 348
IVORY COAST, 36, 148, 310, 504, 510, 514; Brazzaville Group, 503, 504, 506, 507; French, 348, 421, 446; legend of creation, 36–37 (excerpt); Monrovia Group, 504, 505, 506; see also France, West Africa; Rassemblement Démocratique Africain
IWO ELERU, 28

JABADA, 406
JAGA, 326, 365, 366
JAJA, 420
JAMES II, KING OF GREAT BRITAIN AND IRELAND, 364
JAMESON, LEANDER STARR, 418, 419, 455
JAMESON RAID, 404, 418, 455, 456, 457
JAMESTOWN (Va.), 315
JAVA, 26
JBALA, 118
JEBEL AKHDAR, 28, 97, 99
JEBEL AL-NAFUSA see NAFUSA
JEBEL BARKAL, 59, 75, 76
JEBEL DAR FURNUNG, 230, 230
JEBEL MARRA, 217, 230, 230, 251
JEBEL SEHABA, 29
JEFFERSON, THOMAS, 359
JENNE, 188, 210, 234; mosque, 211, 388
JEREZ, 355
JEROME, SAINT, 124–25 (quoted)
JERUSALEM, 114, 147
JESUITS, 314, 319, 367
JESUS, 135
JEWELRY see ORNAMENT AND JEWELRY
JEWELS, trade in, 103, 106, 107, 147, 307
JEWS, 63, 99, 114, 115, 139, 233
JOBE, 375
JOHANNESBURG, 485

JOHN I, KING OF PORTUGAL, 305, 307
JOHN II, KING
JOHN II, KING OF PORTUGAL, 309, 332, 374
JOHN III, KING OF PORTUGAL, letter from Affonso, 401 (excerpt)
JOHN OF EPHESUS, Ecclesiastical History, 218 (excerpt)
JOHNSON, JAMES, 461
JOHNSON, SAMUEL, 192
JOSEPHUS, 72–73 (quoted)
THE JOURNEY OF WEN-AMON TO PHOENICIA, 74–75 (excerpt)
JOURNEY TO THE ZOOLU COUNTRY, by Gardiner, 416
JUBA II, 108; Pliny the Elder on, 109 (quoted)
JUBA RIVER, 144
JUDA, 349
JUDAR PASHA, 188, 232, 357
JUGURTHA, 108; Sallust on, 108–109 (quoted)
JUKUN, 219, 227, 361
JULIAN, COUNT, 355
JULIUS MATERNUS, 221
JUPITER, 133
JUSTINIAN, 128, 139; Procopius on, 124 (quoted)

KABARENGA, 411
KABKABIA, 230
KABRE, 505–506
KABYLIA, 99, 113
KADALIE, CLEMENTS, 461
KAFFIR WARS, 325–26
KAFUCHE KAMBARA, 405
KAIKUN BEY, 408
KAIROUAN (QAIRAWAN), 145–46, 147; Great Mosque, 145, 147
KAKONDA, 406
KALAHARI DESERT, 20, 21, 30, 31, 45, 373
KALALA ILUNGA, 267
KALAMBO FALLS, 26
KAMBULA, 418
KAMERUN (German), 422, 440, 456, 459
KAMFARA, 227
KAMOSE, 58
KANAPOI, 23
KANEM, 175, 181, 217, 222–26 passim, 233, 234; see also Kanuri
KANEM-BORNU, 177, 180, 219, 224, 231, 235, 250, 361; architecture, 225, 230, 240–41; Bivar and Shinnie on, 240–41 (quoted); Islam, 181, 222, 235, 244; kingship, 222, 224, 226, 227, 229–30, 235, 236, 239, 250; Al-Maqrizi on, 235 (quoted); see also Kanuri
KANEMBU, 241
KANEMI, AL-, 362
KANGABA, 187
KANINI, NGOLA, 320, 406
KANJERA, 27, 28
KANO (people), 8, 175, 181, 225, 227, 229, 236, 242, 244–45, 246, 247, 254, 256, 421; see also Hausa
KANO (city), 362
KANO CHRONICLE, 189, 227, 242–45 (excerpt)
KANURI (people), 180, 181, 219, 222–26 passim, 234; poems and songs, 219 (excerpt), 234–35 (excerpt), 238–40 (excerpt); see also Bornu; Kanem; Kanem-Bornu
KANURI (lang.), 223
KANYANGARA, 274
KAOKOVELD RANGE, 44
KAPANGO, 406
KAPARARIDZE, 322
KARAGWE, 272
KARNAK, 74, 75
KARROO, 20
KASAI RIVER, 268
KASANJE, 320
KASAVUBU, JOSEPH, 501–502, 503, 504, 507
KASENA-GRUSI, 188
KASHTA, 60, 75
KASONKE, 200
KATANGA, 265, 266, 267, 290, 452–53;

secession, 501, 502, 503, 504
KATI, AL-, 188
KATOLE, 406
KATSINA, 227, 229, 245, 247, 256, 362
KAWAR, 223, 233, 256
KEBBI, 227
KEBRA NEGAST (GLORY OF KINGS), 78–79 (excerpt)
KEI RIVER, 412, 413
KEIRA, 230
KEISKAMA RIVER, 413
KENTANI, 414
KENYA, 8, 264, 271, 272, 273, 298, 371; British, 412, 456, 463, 487; East African Association, 461; independence, 493, 506; Kenya Africa Union (K.A.U.), 475; Mau Mau insurrection, 420, 461, 463, 464, 475, 475–79 (excerpt), 476, 493, 493; prehistory, 22, 23, 26, 27; see also British East Africa; Commonwealth of Nations; Kikuyu; Luo
KENYA, by Leys, 460
KENYA, MOUNT, 20
KENYAPITHECUS WICKERI, 22
KENYATTA, JOMO, 461, 464, 475, 493, 507
KERMA, 57, 58
KHARIJITES, 222–23, 224
KHARTOUM, 65, 66, 410–11, 428, 439, 453, 459, 510; prehistory, 28, 30, 52
KHAYR AL-DIN BARBAROSSA, 358
KHOI (lang.), 269
KHOIKHOI see HOTTENTOTS
KHOISAN see BUSHMEN; HOTTENTOTS
KIBINDA ILUNGA, 267
KIKUYU, 298, 412, 461, 475, 493
KILIMANJARO, MOUNT, 20
KILINDINI, 370
KILUANJU, NGOLA, 365
KILWA (QUILOA), 143–44, 170, 170, 270, 313, 326; Barros on, 160–61 (quoted); Vasco da Gama on, 143 (quoted), 342; Great Mosque, 143, 170; Van Linschoten on, 405 (quoted); Portuguese, 312, 313, 405; Shirazi, 143–44; trade, 142, 143, 144–45, 160–61, 170
KILWA CHRONICLE, 143, 160, 161
KILWA KIVINJE, 143
KIMBERLEY, 438
KINGSHIP, CONSTITUTIONAL, 224, 226, 227, 229–30, 236, 239, 250
KINGSHIP, DIVINE see DIVINE KINGSHIP
KINGSHIP, HEREDITARY, 61–62, 105, 106, 181, 233, 269
KINGSHIP, TERRITORIAL, 266, 267
KINSHASA, 510
KIPLING, RUDYARD, 487 (quoted)
KIRINA, battle of, 201
KISSAMA, 405
KITA, 362
KITAB AL-FATTASH, by Mahmud Al-Kati, 186 (excerpt)
KITAB AL-IBAR (UNIVERSAL HISTORY), by Ibn Khaldun, Muqaddimah, excerpts, 153, 155, 156–57
KITAB AL-ZANUJ (CHRONICLE OF THE ZANJ), 143
KITAB RUJAR (BOOK OF ROGER), by Al-Idrisi, 159–60 (excerpt)
KITARA, 272, 273
KITCHENER, SIR HORATIO HERBERT, 411, 411, 453, 485
KLEBER, JEAN-BAPTISTE, 358
KNIFE, 29, 31, 44, 53, 143, 185, 266, 365, 365
KODOK see FASHODA
KOLA TREE AND KOLA NUTS, 155, 185, 188, 189, 190
KOMMENDA, 317, 319
KONG, 148, 188
KONGO see CONGO (KONGO)
KONNY, JOHN, 319
KOOBI FORA, 23
KORAN (QUR'AN), 153; excerpts, 138, 139, 140, 151–52, 152; legal interpretations, 146, 147, 148, 184, 185; study of, 147, 148; teaching, 147, 148, 156, 186, 211, 223
KORDOFAN, 217, 225, 256, 408, 409

KOREISH, 355
KORMANTIN, 190, 420
KOSOKO, 420
KOWIE RIVER, 412
KRELI, 413, 414
KROMDRAAI, 23, 41–42 (excerpt)
KRUGER, PAULUS, 455, 456, 457
KUBA, 293, 364–65, 380, 381; divine kingship, 293, 380, 382; law, 380, 381–82 (excerpt); masks and sculpture, 293, 296, 365; poems and songs, 382 (excerpt)
KUBANIEH, 57
KUCYNSKI, ROBERT R., 316
KUDU, 47
KUFRA, 223
KUMASI, 420, 446
KUMBI SALEH, 179, 210
KUNG, 45, 46
KURMINA, 183
KUSH see NUBIA; SUDAN
KWANGO, 289
KWANGO RIVER, 268
KWANZA RIVER, 268
KWAVI, 273
KWELE, 296

LABAT, JEAN-BAPTISTE, 395
LAGOS, 461
LAING, ALEXANDER GORDON, on Mandingos, 184 (quoted); on Sierra Leone, 327 (quoted)
LAJUWA, 197
LALIBELA, 254; architecture under, 126, 135
LAMPS, 61, 64, 110
LAMTUNA, 148, 158
LAND OF OPHIR, 368
LAND OF PUNT see PUNT
LANE-POOLE, STANLEY, History of the Moors in Spain, 154–55 (excerpt)
LANGENI, 374
LANGUAGES, Adamawa Eastern group, 263, 266; Afro-Asiatic family, 99; Arabic, 99, 130, 141, 146; Bantu see BANTU; Berber, 99, 130, 145; Bush, 32, 324; Coptic, 115; Egyptian, 61, 99; Galla, 99; Ge'ez, 63; Greek, 62, 63, 114, 115; Hamitic, 99, 115, 141; Hausa, 219, 248; Hebrew, 99; Herero, 44, 269; Hottentot, 32, 324; Kanuri, 223; Khoi, 269; Latin, 107; Mande, 148; neo-Punic, 107; Nilotic, 271, 272, 273; Nubian, 115; prehistory, 26, 27, 32; Punic, 107; Sabean, 63; Somali, 99, 141; Tuareg, 99
LANGUEDOC, 146
LATIN (lang.), 107
LAWICK-GOODALL, JANE VAN, 25
LEAD, 100
LEAGUE OF NATIONS, 460, 462, 469–71 (excerpt)
LEAKEY, LOUIS, 22, 23, 42, 42–43 (quoted)
LEAKEY, MARY, 23
LEAKEY, RICHARD, 23
LEATHER AND LEATHERWORK, 42, 43, 51, 57, 142, 147, 227, 246; see also hides and skins
LEBANON, 52–53, 74; see also Phoenicia
LEBDA see LEPTIS MAGNA
LEBU, 100, 105, 130; see also Berbers
LEGEND see MYTH, LEGEND, AND ORAL TRADITION
LENIN, NIKOLAI, Imperialism: The Highest Stage of Capitalism, 457
LEO X, POPE, 228
LEO AFRICANUS (AL-HASAN IBN MUHAMMAD AL-WAZZAN AZ-ZAYATI), 228–29, 247; The History and Description of Africa, excerpts, 183, 185, 186, 229, 247
LEOPARD, 23, 197, 271; skins as trade, 73, 143, 189
LEOPOLD II, KING OF BELGIUM, 452, 453, 453, 459
LEOPOLDVILLE, 501, 504
LEPTIS MAGNA (LEBDA), 105, 110, 221
LESOTHO, 414, 414, 510; see also Basuto and Basutoland; Commonwealth of Nations

LESSEPS, FERDINAND DE, 454
LETTOW-VORBECK, GEN. PAUL, 459
LEVAILLANT, FRANCOIS, 429
LEVANT, 28, 29, 49, 53–54, 55, 57–58, 63
LEWIS ANIABA (HANNIBAL), 314
LEYS, NORMAN, Kenya, 460
LHOTE, HENRI, 33
LIBERIA, 404, 458, 499; founding, 403, 434, 497; Monrovia Group, 504, 505, 506; and South West Africa, 508
LIBREVILLE, 403
LIBYA, 87, 101, 104, 112, 225, 499, 511; Berbers, 100, 105, 112, 130; and Egypt, 51, 55, 58, 59, 91, 101; independence, 497; Italians, 460, 462; prehistory, 28, 31, 32, 35; Sanusiyya, 460, 462; see also Barbary; Berbers; Cyrenaica; Sahara; Tripolitania
LIFE OF MUHAMMAD, by Ibn Hisham, 150–51 (excerpts)
LIMPOPO RIVER, 455
LINEN, 30, 64, 71, 90, 97, 116, 147, 185
LINSCHOTEN, JAN VAN, Itinerario, 405 (excerpt)
LION HUNT, 343
LIPTAKO, 362
LIQUOR AND ALCOHOLISM, 316, 318, 325, 326, 361, 364, 395, 395
LITERATURE, Negritude, 461, 465, 466; see also myth, legend, and oral tradition; separate listings under individual authors and works (also, anthologies appear after every chapter of text)
LOANGO, 266, 268, 395
LITTLE FANTYN, 191
LITTLE POPO, 310
LIVESTOCK, 19, 83, 107; domestication of, 30, 31, 32, 49, 51, 52; as sacrifice, 57, 61, 118; trade, 106; see also ass; cattle; goat; sheep
LIVINGSTONE, DAVID, 403, 430, 436, 437
LOBENGULA, 418, 419, 455
LOMAMI RIVER, 268
LOMAYANI, BERTHA, 518 (quoted)
LOPEZ, CAPE, 363
A LOST LEGIONARY IN SOUTH AFRICA, by Hamilton-Browne, 426–28 (excerpt)
LOST-WAX PROCESS, 65, 191, 192, 195, 205–206 (excerpt)
LOTHAGAM, 23
LOUIS XIII, KING OF FRANCE, 363
LOUIS XIV, KING OF FRANCE, 364, 367
LOURENCO MARQUES, 408
LOZI, 269
LUANDA (SAO PAULO DE LUANDA), 319, 320, 347, 365, 366, 405, 406, 503
LUANZE, 322
LUAPULA RIVER, 268
LUBA, 267–68, 270, 290, 294, 296
LUDERITZ (ANGRA PEQUENA), 374
LUEGE RIVER, 315
LUGARD, SIR FREDERICK, 456, 459, 465
LUKANGA SWAMP, 30
LULUABOURG, 422
LUMUMBA, PATRICE, 501, 502, 503, 517, 518; letter to his wife, 517–18 (excerpt)
LUNDA, 267, 268, 269
LUO, 298, 301
LUSAKA MANIFESTO, 510
LUTHERANS, 373
LUTHULI, ALBERT JOHN, 521; Nobel Prize acceptance speech, 521–22 (excerpt)
LUXOR, 49, 74
LWALWA, 296

MACARTHY, SIR CHARLES, 420
MACAULEY, ZACHARY, 336 (quoted)
MACCALMAN, H. R. 44–45 (quoted)
MACINA, 362, 421
MCKAY, CLAUDE, 470; Harlem: Negro Metropolis, on Garvey, 470–72 (excerpt)
MACLOUTSIE, 418
MACMILLAN, HAROLD, 501 (quoted)
MAHDI see MUHAMMAD AHMAD; SAID MUHAMMAD
MAHDIYYA, 408–11, 411, 428, 428–29 (excerpt), 439, 451, 453, 454, 458
MAGHREB, 28, 97, 99, 100, 101, 107, 113,

114, 115, 132, 184, 185, 223, 388; see also "Africa"; Barbary; Berbers; Carthage
MACTARIS, 122
MAD MULLAH see SAID MUHAMMAD
MADAGASCAR, 143, 482; French, 459, 463, 464; see also Malagasy (people); Malagasy Republic
MADEIRA, 307, 308, 309
MAFIA (island), 143
MAGDA see MAKEDA
MAGE, LT. ABDON, 421
MAHERERO, SAMUEL, 422
MAHMUD AL-KATI, 188; Kitab al-Fattash, 186 (excerpt)
MAHMUD IBN UMAR, 186
MAHMUD IBN ZERGUN, 357–58, 360–61
MAHRA, 142
MAHREM, 63
MAHUEVA, 408
MAIZE, 268, 310; see also corn
MAJI MAJI RISING, 449, 459
MAJUBA HILL, 451, 455
MAKANA, 412–13, 426, 438
MAKAPAN VALLEY, 22, 23
MAKEDA (MAGDA), 78–79 (excerpt)
MAKOMA, 413
MAKURIA, 114, 115, 128, 220, 230, 231
MALAGASY (republic), 503, 504, 506, 507, 510; see also Madagascar
MALAGASY (people), 459, 464
MALAWI, 29, 269, 270, 294, 510; independence, 506; see also Commonwealth of Nations; Nyasaland
MALAWI, LAKE, 20, 270
MALAYA, 373
MALAYSIA, 373
MALCOLM X, 508, 508
MALFANTE, ANTONIO, 233–34 (quoted)
MALI (state), 148, 177, 179–85 passim, 186, 187, 202, 210, 219, 234; gold, 185, 213; Ibn Battuta on, quoted, 179, 182–83, 184, 252; Islam, 148, 181, 184, 185, 186; kingship and government, 182–87 passim, 222; legend, 201–203 (excerpt); Portuguese, 187; serfs and slaves, 184, 185, 234; trade, 184, 185, 188, 213; Al-Umari on, 184 (quoted)
MALI (republic), 511; Casablanca Group, 503, 504, 511; Monrovia Group, 504, 505, 506
MALINDI, 163, 308, 369, 370; Al-Idrisi on, 160 (quoted); Portuguese, 312
MALOE COMPANY OF GUINEA, 363
MAMADU PATE, 406, 407
MAMELUKS, 224, 230, 358
MAMPRUSI, 184
MANDE (people), 180, 181, 183, 187, 188–89, 392; see also Diula; Mandingo; Soninke; Susu
MANDE (lang.), 148
MANDINGOS (MANDINKA), 188, 201, 406, 407, 420, 431, 456; French, 421, 446; Laing on, 184 (quoted)
MANETHO, 53, 72
MANICOLAND, 322
MANIKONGO, 314, 326
MANJACO, 406
MANKASSIM (FANTYN), 190, 191
MANSA KANKAN MUSA, 175, 179, 180, 184, 210, 211; pilgrimage to Mecca, 181, 185
MANSA SULAIMAN, 184, 187; Ibn Battuta on, 182–83 (quoted)
MANSABA, 407
MANSFIELD, WILLIAM MURRAY, EARL OF, 401, 403
MANSOA, 407
MANSOADE, 407
MANSUR, AL- (AHMAD AL-MANSUR), 187–88, 188 (quoted), 232, 357–58, 388
MANSUR ABDURRAHMEN, 361
MANYEMA, 422
MAPS (antique), West Africa (1375), 175; West Africa (1502), 305; East Africa (1508), 329; Kingdom of Prester John (1493), 338; West Africa (1743), 395
MAPS (modern), 18, 50, 98, 138, 178, 218, 262, 306, 354, 402, 450, 498
MAQDISHU see MOGADISHU
MAQRIZI, AL-, 235 (quoted)
MARBLE, 106, 110

MARCHAND, JEAN-BAPTISTE, 453
MAREES, PIETER DE, 188 (quoted), 189 (quoted)
MARENGO, JACOB, 422
MARINIDS, 146, 184, 356
MARITZ, GERT, 416
MARK ANTONY, 109
MARRAKESH, 356, 357
MARRIAGE CUSTOMS, 46, 62, 107, 269, 274
MARSEILLES, 101
MARSHALL, L., 45
MARXISM, influence of, 461, 511
MASAI, 273, 298, 299, 422
MASAPA, 322
MASHONA AND MASHONALAND, 269, 270, 294, 294, 320–22, 326, 407, 418, 419, 455; see also Rhodesia (Northern Rhodesia and Southern Rhodesia)
MASINISSA, 106–107; Polybius on, 121 (quoted)
MASKS, 36, 108, 177, 213, 296, 289, 301, 301
MASMUDA, 146
MASSAESYLINS, 106, 107
MASSANGANO, 405
MASSANGENA, 407
MASSAWA, 422
MASSINA, 148
MASUDI, AL- 65, 143, 144
MASUFA, 158, 233
MASSYLINS, 106–107
MATA, 406
MATABELE AND MATABELELAND, 375, 418–19, 484; see also Rhodesia (Northern Rhodesia and Southern Rhodesia)
MATADI, 464
MATAMBA, 320, 365, 366, 406
MATRILINEAL SUCCESSION, 61–62, 183, 233, 241, 263, 268
MATTING see REEDS AND MATTING
MAU MAU, insurrection, 420, 461, 463, 464, 475, 476, 493, 493; Ngugi on, 475–79 (quoted)
MAURETANIA, 106, 109, 115
MAURETANIA TINGITANA, 109, 113; see also "Africa"
MAURITANIA, 8, 31, 307, 509, 511; see also France, West Africa
MAURITIUS, 510, 511; see also Commonwealth of Nations
MAVURA MHANDE, 407
MBANDI, NGOLA, 320, 365, 404, 405
MBANZAKONGO see SAO SALVADOR
MBONMU, 266
MBOONG, 382
MBOPE KYEEN, 382
MBOPE MABINSHE, 293
MBOPE MOBINJI, 365
MBULAZI, 417
MBUNDU, 320, 326, 406
MBUTI, 293
MECCA, 138, 150; Kaaba, 138, 153; as sacred place of pilgrimage, 140, 147, 148, 157, 168, 181, 223, 232, 235
MECHTA EL ARBI, 28
MEDEA, 145
MEDENINE, 167
MEDINA, as sacred place of pilgrimage, 140, 147, 148
MEDINE, 420, 421
MELANESIA, 422
MELCHITES, 114
MEMPHIS, 53, 55, 58, 67, 76, 84, 108
MEMPHIS, THE FAIR ONE, 67 (excerpt)
MENELIK I, 78
MENELIK II, 423, 429, 445, 454; letter to Abdullahi, 429 (excerpt)
MENESES, DIOGODA, 322
MENKAURE, 85
MENTUHOTEP I, 56
MERCA, 142
MERIMDE, 30, 51
MERNERA, 55
MEROE, 60, 61, 62, 63, 64, 65, 77, 78, 80, 95, 112, 137, 220, 230; architecture, 61, 95, 230; ironworking, 62, 65, 95, 264; Pliny the Elder on, 77–78 (quoted); see also Nubia

MESOPOTAMIA, 52, 53
MESSINA, 104
METALWORK, 147, 340; see also lost-wax process; separate listings under individual metals
METEMMA, 410
METHODISTS, 487; Wesleyans, 455
MHLANGANA, 375
MICHALOWSKI, KASIMIERZ, 251
MICROLITHS, 28, 29
MILIANA, 145
MILLET, 31, 62, 65, 180, 186, 219, 231, 234, 253, 262, 268, 272; trade, 185, 253
MILNER, SIR ALFRED, 456–57
MINERALS AND MINING, 8, 19, 110, 315, 316, 452, 462, 485, 485; pigments from, 33, 44; potassium-argon and radiocarbon dating, 21; trade, 103, 106, 107, 147, 270, 307, 464
MIOCENE EPOCH, 21–22
MITRI, 87
MKWATI, 419
MOBUTU, JOSEPH, 501, 509
THE MODERN TRAVELLER, by Belloc, 456
MOGADISHU (MAQDISHU), 141, 142–43, 144, 160; Ibn Battuta on, 161–63 (quoted)
MOLE-DAGBANE, 177, 188, 189, 190
MOLEMA, S.M., The Bantu Past and Present, 374
MOLI BOIA, 406
MOLITSANE, 415
MOLTENO, 33, 33
MOMBASA, 313, 326, 369, 370, 371; Al-Idrisi on, 160 (quoted); Portuguese, 312, 340, 368, 369, 370–71
MOMBASA CHRONICLE, 369, 371 (excerpt)
MOMPATAZ, 406
MONDLANE, EDUARDO, 510
MONGAZE, 407
MONOMOTAPA, 269, 270, 294, 294, 320–22, 326, 407; see also Mashona and Mashonaland; Rowzi
MONOPHYSITES, 114, 115, 134; see also Coptic Church
MONROVIA, 435, 504
MONROVIA GROUP, 504, 505, 506
MONTEIL, COL. P. L., 421
MOORS, 8, 106, 154, 233, 234; 355–57, 386, 386, 387; Lane-Poole on, 154–55 (quoted)
MORELAND, COL. T. L. N., 421
MORI, FABRIZIO, 35
MOROCCO, 97, 99, 180, 189, 190, 357, 421, 458, 499; Almoravids, 146, 356, 357; Casablanca Group, 503; French, 421, 449, 458, 491; Hafsids, 146–47; Hilali, 146, 166; independence, 497; Islam, 145, 355, 356; Marinids, 146, 184, 356; Ottoman empire, 357, 358; Portuguese, 308, 357, 388; proverbs, 168 (excerpt); and Sudan, 184, 187–88, 210, 232, 357–61 passim, 376, 378; see also Berbers; Mauretania
MOSHOESHOE (MOSHESH), 375, 414, 414–16, 438
MOSSI, 177, 187, 188, 189, 190
MOULOUYA RIVER, 106, 107
MOURI, 313, 314
MOUSSO, 200
MOUSTERIAN CULTURE, 28, 29
MOZAMBIQUE (PORTUGUESE EAST AFRICA), 143, 268, 270, 294, 308, 312, 320–22, 326, 370, 371, 373, 407–408, 423; resistance by FRELIMO, 508, 509, 510; see also Sofala
MOZAMBIQUE (town), 312
MPANDE, 417
MPILA, 365
MSIRI, 452, 453
MTETWA, 374, 375
MU ALLAKAT, 153
MUHAMMAD, PROPHET, 139–40, 141, 151, 355; biography by Ibn Hisham (based on Ibn Ishaq), 150–51 (excerpts); Hadith, 147
MUHAMMAD XI (BOABDIL), 387
MUHAMMAD AHMAD (MAHDI), 408–11, 428, 439, 451, 453; letter to Gordon, 428–29 (excerpt)

MUHAMMAD AL-MAJHILI, 181, 227; The Obligations of Princes, 227, 245 (excerpt)
MUHAMMAD ALI, 359
MUHAMMAD BELO, 363
MUHAMMAD BEY ABU AL-SAUD, 408
MUHAMMAD IBN ABDALLAH, 411
MUHAMMAD IBN SAID AL-MAAMRI, 371
MUHAMMAD RUMFA, 227, 244; in Kano Chronicle, 244–45 (excerpts)
MUHAMMAD SHARIFA, 229
MUHAMMAD TEIRAB, 230, 251
MUISA, 274
MUKITI, 274
MUMMIFICATION, 71, 71
MUQADDIMAH see KITAB AL-IBAR
MURCHISON, RODERICK, 437
MURCHISON FALLS, 437
MUSA IBN NUSAYR, 154, 355
MUSA MOLO, 406
MUSAWWARAT-ES-SUFRA, 61
MUSCAT, 369, 370
MUSGU, 248
MUSIC, 8, 27, 44, 130, 208, 267, 301; instruments, 72, 93, 208, 223, 248, 301; see also drum
MUSLIMS see ISLAM; KORAN
MUSOKA, 274
MUSSOLINI, BENITO, 462, 491
MUTAPA, 143
MUTU-YA-KEVELA, 406
MWANGA, 411
MWARI, 270
MWASE, GEORGE, A Dialogue of Nyasaland, 472 (excerpt)
MWERU, LAKE, 268
MWINDO EPIC, 274, 275–88 (excerpt)
MY LIFE IN THE BUSH OF THE GHOSTS, by Tutuola, 526–27 (excerpt)
MYTH, LEGEND, AND ORAL TRADITION, 6, 7, 330; Arabic, 138; Bantu, 267, 270, 273, 274, 275–88 (excerpt); Berber, 119 (excerpt); Bushmen, 44, 47, 270; Ethiopia, 78–79 (excerpt); Fang, 37–38 (excerpt); Fulani, 380 (excerpt); Ghana, 200–201 (excerpt); Hausa, 241–48 (excerpts); Ivory Coast, 36–37 (excerpt); Kuba, 382 (excerpt); Mali, 201–203 (excerpt); Morocco, 168 (excerpt); Punic, 102; Tunisia, 121 (excerpt); Yoruba, 191–92, 203–208 (excerpt), 526; Zulu, 382 (excerpt), 384, 423, 428 (excerpt)
MZILA, 408
MZILIKAZI, 375
MZINGWANE, 419

NAFUSA (JEBEL AL-NAFUSA), 222, 223
NAMAQUALAND, 323
NAMIB DESERT, 20
NAMIBIA see SOUTH WEST AFRICA
NAMIER, L. B., 316 (quoted)
NANA KWAMENA ANSA, 363
NANAAM, 190
NANDI (people), 273
NANDI (person), 374, 375
NANO WARS, 406
NAPATA, 60, 61, 75, 77, 95, 112
NAPOLEON, 358, 358, 482, 482
NAQA, 62–63, 63
NAQADA, 51, 52, 53
NARMER, 53, 67, 84
NARMER PALETTE see PALETTE OF NARMER
NARON, 44
NASIR IBN MURSHID, 369
NASIR, AL- (ANZIR), letter from Pope Gregory VII, 155–56 (excerpt)
NASSER, GAMAL ABDEL, 464, 473, 492; Philosophy of the Revolution, 473–75 (excerpt)
NASSER IBN ABDULLAH AL-MAZRUI, 370
NATAL, 270, 374, 382, 401, 417, 418, 457, 486; see also South Africa, Republic of; South Africa, Union of; Zulu and Zululand
NATIONAL ASSOCIATION FOR THE ADVANCEMENT OF COLORED PEOPLE, 460, 467
NATIONALISM AND PAN-AFRICAN-

ISM, 455, 457–65 passim, 467, 492, 493, 497, 499–511
NATURAL HISTORY, by Pliny the Elder, 77–78 (excerpt), 109 (excerpt)
NATURE, worship of, 107, 108, 149, 263, 267, 268; see also animism; fertility images and rites; sun, worship of; trees, worship of
NAUKRATIS, 62
NAURUZ, 272
NDABA, 382
NDEBELE, 419, 423, 455, 456
NDEROBO, 30
NDLAMBE, 412, 413
NDONGO, 319, 320, 365–67, 404–405; see also Angola
NDULU, 406
NEANDERTHAL MAN, 27, 28, 39, 40–41
NEFERTITI, 54, 59
NEGRITUDE, 461, 465, 466
NEGROID PEOPLE, 28, 29, 32, 40, 41, 52, 61, 99, 104, 219, 263
NELSON, ADM. HORATIO, 358
NEOLITHIC PERIOD, 31, 32, 180
NEO-PUNIC (lang.), 107
NERO, 77, 112
NE-SU-BA-NEB-DED, 74
NETEKAMANI, 62, 63
NETHERLANDS, in Africa, 305, 312, 313, 314, 319, 320; Angola, 313, 366; Brazil, 313, 365; Congo, 313, 364, 365; Dutch East India Company, 323, 371, 373; Dutch West India Company, 188; Ghana, 313; Gold Coast, 348, 348, 420; gold prospecting, 317; Guinea, 312; Mozambique, 312; and Portugal, 312, 313, 320, 348, 372, 406; Protestantism, 314, 324, 363, 373; São Tomé, 313; slave trade, 315, 316 (excerpt), 363, 373, 390, 391; Sumatra, 420; trade, 188, 312, 313, 319, 323; West Africa, 312–13, 348, 349; see also Boers
NEW AND ACCURATE DESCRIPTION OF THE COAST OF GUINEA, by Bosman, 188–89; excerpts, 206–207, 317, 318–19, 325
NEW GUINEA, 422
NEWTON, JOHN, Thoughts upon the African Slave Trade, 336 (excerpt)
NGOLA see separate listing under following name, as in Mbandi, Ngola
NGONI, 325
NGUGI, JAMES T., 475; Weep Not, Child, 475–79 (excerpt)
NGUNI, 269, 270, 294, 382, 408
N'GURU, 240
NHAMBALAM, 407
NIAGARA MOVEMENT, 467
NIGER, 256, 507; Brazzaville Group, 503, 504, 506, 507; Royal Niger Company, 456; see also France, West Africa; French Sudan; Hausa
NIGER BEND, 103, 148, 180, 188, 190, 326
NIGER RIVER, 99, 180, 189, 217, 223, 266, 313, 326, 356, 357, 360, 404
NIGERIA, 28, 189, 263, 264, 314–15, 336, 361; British, 420–21, 456, 459, 497, 499, 501, 511, 511; coups and civil war, 508, 509, 510–11, 511; independence, 497, 501; Monrovia Group, 504, 505, 506; see also British West Africa; Commonwealth of Nations; separate listings under individual groups and peoples
NIGRITES, 103
NILE, 30, 56, 66, 220, 256, 358; Blue Nile, 66, 217, 219, 231; canals, 62, 82, 83, 91; flooding, 49, 51, 52, 54, 66, 83, 87; hymn to, 67 (excerpt); Murchison Falls, 437; navigation, 51, 62, 91; searches for source, 77, 437; Strabo on, 66–67 (quoted); Upper Nile, 29, 30, 32, 33, 114; White Nile, 66, 217, 271
NILE DELTA, 30, 55, 58, 66, 99, 108, 112
NILE VALLEY, 51, 65, 99, 359; prehistory and predynastic periods, 21, 29, 30, 32, 49, 51, 52, 53, 53
NILOTIC LANGUAGES, 271, 272, 273
NILOTIC PEOPLES, 271–72, 273, 298, 299
NIORO, 148
NIXON, RICHARD M., 497
N'JIMI, 225, 235, 241
NKRUMAH, KWAME, 461, 464, 465

(quoted), 492, 493, 508, 511; depicted on native clothing, 500; "The Motion of Destiny," 512–14 (excerpt)
NKUBA, 274
NKUWU see NZINGA NKUWU
NOBA, 64, 80, 112
NOBATAE (people), 112
NOBATIA (NOBATAE) (kingdom), 114, 115, 128, 251
NOK CULTURE, 65, 180, 181, 191, 193
NONGALAZA, 417
NONGQAUSE, 413, 414
NORTH AFRICA, 97, 99–135 passim, 145–49, 355–59; Islam 137, 145, 146, 166, 173, 175, 355, 356, 451, 459, 460; people, 52, 61, 99, 100; prehistory, 26–30 passim, 32
NORTJE, ARTHUR, 524, 524 (quoted)
NORWAY, 418
NOVUS ATLAS, by Blaeu, 332
NUBA HILLS, 408
NUBIA (KUSH; CUSH), 51, 55, 56–57, 59–65 passim, 61, 93, 95, 112, 114–15, 128, 217, 220, 230–31; architecture, 57, 60, 61, 62, 63, 95, 112, 220, 230; and Axum, 64, 80, 95, 112, 137; burial customs, 57, 61, 62, 64, 112; cattle, 57, 59, 60, 61; divine kingship, 60, 76, 77 (excerpt); divinities and religious beliefs, 59, 61, 62, 64, 65, 80, 114, 115, 128 (excerpt), 134, 170, 230–31; and Egypt, 51, 55–62 passim, 75–76 (excerpt), 91, 93, 112, 230; hereditary kingship, 61–62; and Hyksos, 58; ironwork, 62, 65, 95; languages, 115; painting and sculpture, 60, 61, 63, 230, 251; people, 32, 51, 55, 57, 59, 60–61, 64, 80, 87, 93, 112, 299; and Persian empire, 101; Pliny the Elder on, 77–78 (quoted); pottery, 57, 61, 64, 93, 95, 220; trade, 55, 57, 59, 61, 64, 91, 95, 112; see also Alodia; Makuria; Meroë; Nobatia; Sudan
NUBIAN (lang.), 115
NUMA, 406
NUMIDIA, 102, 106–107, 108, 109, 113, 114, 115; see also "Africa"
NUPE, 197, 219, 227, 361, 421
NUR AL-DIN AL-SHADHILI, 148
NUWAIRI, AL-, 145 (quoted)
NYAMBO KAPARIDZE, 407
NYAMWEZI, 452
NYANDE (JOAQUIN JOSE DA CRUZ), 407
NYANGA, 273; Mwindo epic, 274, 275–88 (excerpt)
NYASALAND (BRITISH CENTRAL AFRICA), 420, 452–53, 456, 460, 462, 463, 472, 501; Federation with Northern and Southern Rhodesia, 463, 506; Germans, 422; see also Malawi
NYIMA, 411
NZELE, 405
NZINGA MBANDI, 320, 365–67, 366, 405
NZINGA NKUWU, 309, 364
NZINGA MVEMBA see AFFONSO

OBA, 191
THE OBLIGATIONS OF PRINCES, by Muhammad al-Majhili, 227
ODUDUWA, 191, 203, 204
ODZI RIVER, 412
OGE, VINCENT, 435
OGISO, 191
OGUN, 207–208
OGUOLA, 192
OHRWALDER, FATHER JOSEPH, 409–10 (quoted)
OIO, 407
OL DOINGO LENGAI, 20
OLDOWAN INDUSTRY, 25, 26
OLDUVAI GORGE, 23–24, 26, 39, 40
OLIOGOCENE EPOCH, 21
OLIVE OIL, 91, 110, 112, 132, 147
OLIVE TREE, cult of, 107, 110
OLIVER, ROLAND, 316
OLYMPIO, SYLVANUS, 504, 505–506
OM DUBREIKAT, 411
OMAN, 369, 371, 372; Portuguese, 313, 369, 370; trade, 143, 372

OMDURMAN, *411*, 411, *439*, *453*
OMER-COOPER, J. D., 374
OMO VALLEY, 23, 27
ONGOE, 322
OPHIR, LAND OF, 368
OPOBO, 326
ORAL TRADITION *see* MYTH, LEGEND, AND ORAL TRADITION
ORANGE FREE STATE, 457; *see also* Boer War; South Africa, Republic of; South Africa, Union of
ORANGE RIVER, 325, 374
ORANGE RIVER SOVEREIGNTY, 415
ORANMIYAN, 191
ORGANISATION COMMUNE AFRICAINE ET MALGACHE (OCAM), 507, 511
ORGANIZATION OF AFRICAN UNITY (OAU), 404, 504, 506, 507, 508, 510, 511; African Liberation Committee, 506, 507–508, 509; Charter, 518–19 *(excerpt)*; and the Congo, 507; creation of, 506; and Nigerian civil war, 510; and Rhodesia, 508
ORIGEN, SAINT, 114
THE ORIGIN OF SPECIES, by Darwin, 38
ORNAMENT AND JEWELRY, 54, 58–59, 73, 108; bone, 29; brass, 189, *298;* copper, 189; enamel, 61; gold, 61, 103, 182, 184, *208, 213,* 229; ivory, 29, 43; leather, 43; ostrich eggshell, 43, 47; prehistory, 29, 43; shell, 29; silver, 182; stone, 61, 65; trade, 73, 143, 189, 266, 270, 310
ORTHODOX CHURCH *see* EASTERN ORTHODOX CHURCH
OSIRIS, *54,* 55, 87, 109
OSTIA, 132
OSTRICH, 47, *53;* eggshell, *31,* 43, 45, 46, 47; plumes, 45, 91
OTTOMAN EMPIRE, 307, 358, 404; in Africa, 142, 369, 388; Barbary Coast states, 357, 358; and British, 358, 359, 451, 453, 454, 459, 460; Egypt, *358,* 358, 359, 451, 453, *454,* 454, 460 *(see also* Anglo-Egyptian Sudan); and French, *358,* 358, 359, 451, *454,* 454, 460; and Italians, 460; Kanem-Bornu, 219, 224, 226, 236; and Portuguese, 313, 369
OUIDAH (OVIDAH), 189, 318, 319; slaves, 317, 318
OUOLOGUEM, YAMBO, *Bound to Violence,* 520 *(excerpt)*
OVAMBA *see* AMBO
OVATJIMBA, 30; MacCalman and Grobbelaer on, 44–45 *(quoted)*
OVIDAH *see* OUIDAH
OVIMBUNDU, 269
OXEN, 110, 112, 180, 213, 233; *see also* cattle
OYO, 177, 188, 189, 190, 191, 192, 326, 363; art and sculpture, 192, 193, 327
OZANEARE, 34; *see also* Tassili caves

P ACHOMIUS, SAINT, Palladius on, 126–27 *(quoted)*
PADMORE, GEORGE, 464
PAINTING, Bantu, *295;* Coptic, *116, 135;* Egypt, 52, 54, 54, 55, 56, 59, 61, 67, *82, 87, 90, 111;* Islamic miniatures, *150, 151, 168;* Nubian, 230, *251;* on ostrich eggshell, 47; painting decoration, 51, 53, 57, 61, 66, 95, *106, 132; see also* rock art
PALANCE, 406
PALESTINE, 27, 30, 53, 55, 57, 58, 72, 91
PALLADIUS, 126–27 *(quoted)*
PALM, 263, *464;* date trade, 147; oil trade, 143, 189, 403
THE PALM WINE DRINKARD, by Tutuola, 526
PALMER, H. R., 240–41
PAN-AFRICAN CONFERENCES, 457–58, 460, 462, 464
PAN-AFRICAN FREEDOM MOVEMENT FOR EAST AND CENTRAL AFRICA (PAFMECA), 501, 503, 506; and southern African parties (PAFMECSA), 506
PAN-AFRICANISM *see* NATIONALISM AND PAN-AFRICANISM

PANTHER, 112
PAPEL, 406, 407
PAPER, 54, 185
PAPUA, 422
PAPYRUS, 51, 54, *90,* 91
PARE MOUNTAIN, 272
PARK, MUNGO, 403
PATE ISLAND, 369, 370, 371
PATTA ISLAND *see* PATE ISLAND
PAUL OF THEBES, SAINT, Saint Jerome on, 124–25 *(quoted)*
PEACE OF UTRECHT, 367
PEARSON, COL. CHARLES, 418
PEMBA, 369–70, 411
PEOPLES OF THE SEA, 58
PEPI I, 72
PEPI II, 55
PEPPER, 309–10, 312, 314, 340
PEREIRA, PACHECO, 308; on trade and West Africa, 188, 189, *(quoted),* 190 *(quoted),* 191 *(quoted)*
PERFUME, 63, 102, 107, 147
PERIPLUS OF THE ERYTHREAN SEA, 79–80 *(excerpt),* 142
PERSIAN EMPIRE, 100, 101, 115, 139, 140, 142, 143–44, 170; Egypt conquered by, 59, 62, 101, 107, 114, 115; trade, 139, 141, 143, 307
PERSON, YVES, 431–32 *(quoted)*
PETITS VOYAGES, by de Bry, *341, 343, 349*
PHARUSIANS, 103
PHILADELPHIA (ship), 359
PHILAE, 64, 112, *113*
PHILIP V, KING OF SPAIN, 367
PHILIPPA, QUEEN OF PORTUGAL, 307
PHILLIPS, J. R., 420
PHILOSOPHY OF THE REVOLUTION, by Nasser, 473–75 *(excerpt)*
PHOENICIA, 55, *100, 101,* 101, 107, *132;* colonies, 100, 101, 103, 108; and Egypt, 55, 58, 74, 91; *see also* Lebanon
PIANKHI, 60, 75; stele, Jebel Barkal, 75, 76
PICKTHALL, MARMADUKE, 152
PICTOGRAPHS, 53, 54; *see also* hieroglyphs; rock art
PIJIGUITI, 406
PINTO, JOAO TEIXEIRA, 407
PISA, 155
PITHECANTHROPINES (PITHECANTHROPUS), 40, 41
PLEISTOCENE EPOCH, 22, 23; Lower Pleistocene, 23, 24, 40; Middle Pleistocene, 23, 25, 26, 27, 40, 41; Upper Pleistocene, 27–28, 30, 31
PLINY THE ELDER, *Natural History,* 77–78 *(excerpt);* 109 *(excerpt)*
PLIOCENE EPOCH, 22, 24
PLOW, 63, 107
POINTS (for arrows and spears), 29, 43, 51
POLITICS, by Aristotle, 119–21 *(excerpt)*
POLYBIUS, *Histories,* 119 *(excerpt),* 121 *(excerpt)*
PONDO, 325; *see also* Bantu
PONGIDAE (PONGIDS), 21, 22, 41; *see also* chimpanzee; gorilla
PORCELAIN TRADE, 143, *171,* 270
PORTUGAL, 305, 307–308; in Africa, 305, 307, 308, 309, *310,* 312, 326, *336, 338,* 338, 355, 404, 405, 406–407, 465, 507–508, 509, 510; Angola *see* ANGOLA; Azores, 308; Benin, 309, 310, 311, 314; Biafra, 510; Brazil, 313, 320, 369; Canary Islands, 308; Cape Verde Islands, 307, 308, 309, 330–31 *(excerpt),* 367, 406; Congo *see* CONGO (KONGO); East Africa, 137, 142, 145, 308, 312, 313, 326, 368–71, 405–407, 456 *(see also* Mozambique); East Indies, 323; Fernando Po, 263, 308, 309; and France, 348; and Germany, 457; Ghana, 310–11, 312, 313, 363; Goa, 369, 370, 371; Gold Coast, 189, 190, 308, 309, *348,* 348; gold trade and search for gold, 310, 321, 365, 369; and Great Britain, 348; Guinea, 309, 310 *(see also* Portuguese Guinea); and Islam, 307, 308, 338, 340, 371; Kilwa, 312, 313, *405;* Madeira, 307, 308, 309; Maghreb, 338; Mali, 187; missionaries, 309, 312, 314, 319, 322, 332,

334, 340, 364, 367, 370, 371; Morocco, 308, 357, 358; and Netherlands, 312, 313, 320, 348, 372, 406; Oman, 313, 369, 370; and Ottoman empire, 313, 369; São Tomé, 308, 309, 312, 313; Sierra Leone, 307, 309; silver, search for, 365; slave trade, 310, 312, 314, 315, 317, 318, 319, 320, 334, 334–35 *(excerpt),* 347, 347, 363, 364, 366, 367, 368, 369, 371, 405; South Africa, 312, 322–23, 324, 325, 372; South West Africa, 373–74; and Spain, 363; trade, 145, 188, 189, 270, 307, 309–10, 312, *315,* 318, 319, 321, 322, 326, 331–32, 340, 348, 364, 368, 369, *405,* 405; West Africa, 179, 189, 190, 215, 308–13, *310, 315,* 348, 349, 363, 364, 367, 406, 452, 456 *(see also* Angola); Wolof, 309, 311; Zanzibar, 312, 369, 370, 371
THE PORTUGUESE CONQUEST OF ANGOLA, by Birmingham, 365 *(excerpt)*
PORTUGUESE EAST AFRICA *see* MOZAMBIQUE
PORTUGUESE GUINEA, 406, 407; resistance by PAIGC, 507–508, 509, 510
PORTUGUESE WEST AFRICA *see* ANGOLA
PORY, JOHN, 229, 247
POTASSIUM-ARGON DATING, 21
POTGIETER, HENDRICK, 416
POTTERY AND CERAMICS, Bantu, 263, 265, 267, 268, 272; Berbers, *106,* 107, 110; Egypt, 51, 53, 53, 54, 66, 108; Greece, 102, 107; Moors, 386; Nubia, 57, 61, 64, 93, 95; potter's wheel, 54; prehistory, 30, 31, 32, 51; Roman, 107; Sèvres service, *482;* shapes borrowed from basketry, 51; trade, 102, 110, 143, *171,* 265, 270, 272
POUNDING IMPLEMENTS *see* GRINDING AND POUNDING IMPLEMENTS
PRA RIVER, 190
PREHISTORIC PERIOD, 19, 21–23, 27, 29, 30, 38–43, 49, 51, 52, 53, 99, 180, 219, 374; agriculture and livestock, 30, 31, 32, 49, 51, 52, 180; burial customs, 27, 29, 32; dancing and music, 27, 29, 33, 35, 44, 47; dwellings, 27, 32, 42–43, 46, 221, 252; firemaking, 27, 42; fishing and hunting, 24–33 *passim,* 33, 34–35, 39, 40, 43, 45, 51, 52, 180; hides and skins, 27, 29, 32, 35, 43; language, development of, 27, *27,* 32; learned behavior, 24, 27, 29; pottery, 30, 31, 32, 51; rock art, 21, 27, 32, 33, 33, *34–35,* 43, 51, 103, 130, 180, 221; tools, implements, and utensils, 23–32 *passim,* 39, 40, 43, 44, 45, 46, 51, 52; weapons, 25–31 *passim,* 39, 40, 43, 51
PREMNIS (QASR IBRIM), 112
PREMPEH, 446, *446*
PRESTER JOHN, 317, 338; Vasco da Gama on, 308 *(quoted);* kingdom shown in map (1493), *338*
PRETORIA, *456,* 485
PRETORIUS, ANDRES, 417
PROCONSUL APE *see* DRYOPITHECUS AFRICANUS
PROCOPIUS, *Histories,* 124; *Secret History (Anecdota),* 124 *(excerpt)*
PROTESTANTS, British, 363; Calvinism, 324, 373; Dutch, 314, 324, 363, 373; Huguenots, 323, 373; Lutherans, 373; Methodists, 455, *487;* Reformation, 363, 386; *see also* Christianity
PROVENCE, 146
PROVIDENCE INDUSTRIAL MISSION, 472
PSAMMETIK III, 60, 62
PSEUDO-SCYLAX, 102
PTOLEMY (astronomer and geographer), 142
PTOLEMY, PHARAOH, 62, 107
PTOLEMY II, 62, 108
PTOLEMY IV, 62
PUBERTY RITUALS, 46; *see also* circumcision rituals
PUNIC (lang.), 107
PUNIC EMPIRE *see* CARTHAGE
PUNIC WARS, 103, 104–105, 107, 108, 119
PUNT (LAND OF PUNT), 51, 55, 63, 73, 91; Hatshepsut on, 73–74 *(quoted)*
PYGMIES, 21, 30, 263, 265, 267, *271,* 273,

293, 293; nature, worship of, 267; poems, 47 *(excerpts)*
PYRAMIDS, 54, 55, 61, 71, 85, 95, 112, *485*

Q ADIR MOUNTAIN, 408, 409
QAIRAWAN *see* KAIROUAN
QASR IBRIM *see* PREMNIS
QUELIMANE, 145
QUILOA *see* KILWA
QUR'AN *see* KORAN
QUSTUL, 64

R ABIH, 458
RADIOCARBON DATING, 21
RAFFIA AND RAFFIA CLOTH, 192, 263, 266
RAIN CEREMONIES, 44, 52, 107, 149
RAMAPITHECUS PUNJABICUS, 22
RAMSES II, 49, 54, 74,
RAMSES III, 58
RAMUSIO, GIOVANNI, 229, 247
RANGER, TERENCE, *Revolt in Southern Rhodesia 1896–7,* 419
RANO, 227
RAS ALULU, 423
RAS MANGASHA, 422
RAS TAFFARI MAKONNEN *see* HAILE SELASSIE
RASHID (person), 408–409
RASHID (ROSETTA) (place), 359
RASSEMBLEMENT DEMOCRATIQUE AFRICAIN (RDA), 464, 499, 500, 514
RAVASCO, RUY, 312
RED SEA, trade, 62, 63, 137, 139, 141, 220
REEDS AND MATTING, 43, 91, 265; for dwellings, 32, 53, *186,* 241, 256; *see also* papyrus
REKMIRE, 56
RELIGION *see* CHRISTIANITY; DIVINITIES AND RELIGIOUS BELIEFS; ISLAM; JEWS; PROTESTANTS; ROMAN CATHOLIC CHURCH
RETIEF, PIETER, 416, 417
REVOLT IN SOUTHERN RHODESIA 1896–7, by Ranger, 419
REYNOLDS, VERNON, 25
RHINOCEROS, 34, 63, 143, 221
RHODES, CECIL, 452–53, 455, *485,* 485; British South Africa Company, 408, 418, 452, 455, 485
RHODESIA (republic), 509–510; Zimbabwe African People's Union (ZAPU), 509, 510
RHODESIA (NORTHERN RHODESIA AND SOUTHERN RHODESIA), 33, 142, 265, 270, 294, 418, 419, 423, 455, 456, 458, 463, 465, 485, 506, 507, 507, 508; Federation with Nyasaland, 463, 506; Mashona and Mashonaland, 269, 270, 294, *294,* 320–22, 326, 407, 418, 419, 455, *484; see also* Zambia; Matabele and Matabeleland, 375, 418–19, 484; *see also* Zambia
RHODESIAN MAN, 27
RICE, 32, 185, *186,* 310, 312; trade, 155, 160, 185, 464
RICHELIEU, CARDINAL, 363
RIEBEECK, JAN VAN, 323, 325 *(quoted),* 371, 372–73
RIF MOUNTAINS, 99, *491*
RIFT VALLEY *see* GREAT RIFT VALLEY
RIO DE ORO, 309
RITUAL AND BELIEF IN MOROCCO, by Westermarck, 118–19 *(excerpt)*
RITUALS AND CEREMONIES, birth, 107; circumcision, 46, 301; death *see* BURIAL AND FUNERARY CUSTOMS; fertility *see* FERTILITY IMAGES AND RITES; initiation, 186, 268, 272, *289,* 296, 301, 392; magic *see* ANIMISM; marriage, 46, 62, 107, 269, 274; medicine men and diviners, 263; prehistory, 27, 44; puberty, 46; rain, 44, 52, 107, 149; sacrifice *see* SACRIFICE; *see also* ceremonial objects; dance; masks
THE RIVER WAR, by Churchill, 465 *(excerpt)*

RIVERS, 19, 149
ROANGA, 314
ROBAH ZOBEIR, 421
ROCK ART, 46, 47, 270; prehistory, 21, 27, 32, 33, 33, 34–35, 43, 51, 103, 130, 180, 221; Willcox on, 43–44 (quoted)
ROCK SHELTERS AND DWELLINGS, 27, 29, 33, 42–43
RODERICK, KING OF SPAIN, 154, 355
ROGER II, KING OF SICILY, 159
ROMAN CATHOLIC CHURCH, 63, 114; Augustinians, 369, 371; and Biafra, 510; Capuchins, 309; Council of Chalcedon, 63, 114; Dominicans, 322; Franciscans, 309; Jesuits, 314, 319, 367; slave trade, 314, 372, 363, 364, 390, 390; see also Christianity
ROMAN EMPIRE, 101, 102, 105, 107, 110, 113, 115; "Africa," 8, 108–15 passim, 122 (excerpt), 132; and Berbers, 106–11 passim, 113; and Carthage, 101, 103, 104–105, 107, 108, 110, 119; Egypt occupied by, 59, 61, 63, 84, 108, 109, 110, 112, 113, 114, 122 (excerpt); see also Byzantine empire
THE ROMANCE OF ANTAR see SIRAT ANTAR
ROME, 63, 114
ROSETTA STONE, 359
ROTBERG, ROBERT, 316
ROWZI, 270, 322, 326
ROYAL NIGER COMPANY, 456
RUANDA-URUNDI, 459; see also Burundi; German East Africa; Rwanda
RUBAGA, 293
RUBBER, 452
RUDOLF, LAKE, 23, 23
RUFIJI RIVER, 143, 422
RUFINUS, History of the Monks in Egypt, 127–28 (excerpt)
RUFISQUE, 313
RUGS, 64, 107
RUREKE, 274
RUVUMA RIVER, 313, 422
RUWENYA RIVER, 407
RUWENZORI RANGE, 20
RUY DE PINA, 308; Chronicle of John II, 332–34 (excerpt)
RWANDA, 271, 272, 273; Organisation Commune Africaine et Malgache, 507, 511; see also German East Africa; Ruanda-Urundi
RWEEJ, 267
RYDER, ALAN, 318

SAADI see BENI SAADI
SABA (SHEBA), 63, 78–79 (excerpt)
SABEAN (lang.). 63
SABR AD-DIN, 164, 165
SACRIFICE, of animals, 57, 61, 64, 107, 118, 243, 269; of humans, 64, 107, 314
SAGRES, 307
SAHARA, 17, 19, 20, 51, 97, 99, 100, 100, 130, 130, 145, 179, 180, 219, 221, 263; prehistory, 28–33 passim, 99; trade, 99, 148, 155, 175, 179, 181, 188, 213, 220–25 passim, 231–35 passim, 245, 250, 252, 253, 326, 359; see also Berbers
SAHEL, 20, 148, 266
SAHILI, AS-, 181
SAHITI, 423
SAID MUHAMMAD (MAD MULLAH), 458
SAIFUWA, 222–27 passim, 234, 235
SAINT CHRISTOPHER COMPANY, 363
SAINT DOMINGUE, 363, 434
ST. LOUIS, 363, 443
SALADIN (SALAH-AL-DIN), 224
SALADO, 172
SALDANHA, ANTONIO DE, 325
SALISBURY, ROBERT GASCOYNE CECIL, MARQUIS OF, 455
SALLUST, 108–109 (quoted)
SALT, 189, 221, 252; dwellings of, 233, 252; trade, 155, 184, 185, 188, 189, 190, 213, 233, 234, 252, 253, 265, 266, 268, 272
SAMORI TOURE, 421, 431, 446, 446, 456; Person on, 431–32 (quoted)
SAN see BUSHMEN

SAN JUAN, 315
SANDILE, 413, 414
SANGOAN CULTURE, 27
SANHAJA, 146, 148, 158, 186; see also Almoravids
SANTO DOMINGO, 315
SANUSIYYA, 460, 462
SAO JOAO (ship), 328–30 (excerpt)
SAO PAULO DE LUANDA see LUANDA
SAO SALVADOR (MBANZAKONGO), 309, 314, 315
SAO TIAGO, 331, 348
SAO TOME, 309, 314; Dutch, 313; Portuguese, 308, 309, 312, 313; slave trade, 312, 315, 319
SAQQARA, Step Pyramid, 67, 85; Temple of Zoser, 85; tombs, 53
SARA, 255
SARAKHOLLE see SONINKE
SARAPIS, 109
SARDINIA, 100, 101, 110
SATIN, 355
SATURN, 107; see also Baal; Sarapis
SAUDI ARABIA, 355
SAVANNA, 16, 19, 20, 180; prehistory, 22, 25, 27, 28, 29, 32, 51
SAY, 455
SAYYID SAID, 372
SCARABS, 73, 108
SCIPIO AFRICANUS (PUBLIUS CORNELIUS SCIPIO), 104
SCRAMBLE FOR AFRICA, 440, 449, 451, 454, 455, 456, 457, 465
SCRAPER, 25, 27, 28, 29, 31, 43
SCULPTURE, bronze see BRONZE, sculpture; copper see BRONZE, sculpture; ivory, 177, 192, 193; terra cotta, 65, 181, 191, 193, 196, 197, 205, 263; wood see WOODWORK AND SCULPTURE; see also separate listings under individual countries and cultures
SEA PEOPLES see PEOPLES OF THE SEA
SEALS, 53, 73, 108
SEBASTIAO, KING OF PORTUGAL, 404
SECOND WORLD WAR see WORLD WAR, SECOND
THE SECOND WORLD WAR, by Churchill, 462 (excerpt)
SECRET HISTORY (ANECDOTA), by Procopius, 124 (excerpt)
SEFAR, 35; seel also Tassili caves
SEGU, 421
SEKU AHMADU see AHMADU IBN TINDANI (AHMADU SEKU)
SELJUKS, 353
SEMNA, 56, 57, 93
SENA, 320, 321, 407, 408
SENEGAL, 148, 314–15, 331; French, 314, 348, 363, 421, 443, 460; see also France, West Africa
SENEGAL RIVER, 177, 180, 307
SENEGAMBIA, 177, 180, 188, 310; see also French Sudan
SENGHOR, LEOPOLD SEDAR, 462, 464, 466; "Black Woman," 466 (excerpt); "For Khalam," 466–67 (excerpt)
SENNAR, 62, 219, 220, 231, 250, 256, 411
SENUWY, 57
SENZANGAKONA, 374, 375
SEPTIMIUS SEVERUS, 110, 111
SEQUEIRA, LOUIS LOPES DE, 320
SERFS, 109, 184, 185
SERPENT, 64; in legend, excerpts, 200–201, 203–205, 241–42
SESOSTRIS III, 56, 57
SETI I, 87
SHABAKO, 60
SHADHILIYYA, 148
SHAHEINAB, 52, 65
SHAKA see CHAKA
SHAMA, 309
SHAMBAA, 272
SHANGANA, 408
SHANGANI RIVER, 418, 419
SHARPEVILLE MASSACRE, 501, 502, 522
SHAYKH AL-AMIN, 363
SHAYKH IBN AHMAD AL-MALINDI, 370–71
SHEBA see SABA
SHEBURUNGU, 274
SHEEP, 26, 31, 32, 263; see also wool

SHELL, as currency, 207, 235, 266, 269; as decoration and ornament, 29, 208; fish-hook and gorge, 30
SHELLFISH, 30, 43, 45, 46
SHERIF AHMAD TAHA, 409
SHILLUK, 408, 409
SHINNIE, PETER L., 240–41 (quoted)
SHIPS see BOATS AND SHIPS
SHIRAZI, 143–44
SHOA, 141
SHOMBA, 365
SHONA see MASHONA AND MASHONALAND; MONOMOTAPA
SHONGO, 364; see also Kuba
SHUKRIA, 409
SICILY, 100, 101–102, 110, 146, 356
SICKLE, 28, 29, 30, 31
SIDAMA, 141
SIDI-BEL-ABBES, 487
SIERRA LEONE, 317, 318, 336 (excerpts); British, 420, 458; founding, 403, 424, 434; Portuguese, 307, 309; see also British West Africa; Commonwealth of Nations
SIGA, 106
SIJILMASA, 179, 222, 223, 233
SIKASSO, 431
SIKEPIR, 418
SIKONYELA, 416
SILK, 116, 139; trade, 147, 307, 310, 355
SILVER AND SILVERWORK, 61, 74, 100, 103, 104, 182, 234, 308, 312, 316; as currency, 102, 103, 307; searches for, 312, 319–30, 365; utensils, 61, 64, 107
SIMONS, ELWYN, 22
SINAI, 51, 91, 99
SIRA BENI HILAL, 166–68 (excerpt)
SIRAT ANTAR (THE ROMANCE OF ANTAR), 152–53 (excerpt)
SIWA OASIS, 99, 101, 108
SKINNER, ELLIOTT P., 527; on policy toward Africa, 527–28 (quoted)
SKINS see HIDES AND SKINS
SLAVE COAST, 310
SLAVE TRADE, 59, 73, 105, 106, 112, 141, 142, 143, 185, 188, 189, 235, 245, 267, 268, 269, 270, 314–20, 326–28, 353, 353, 361–69, 393; Americas (including Brazil, Caribbean and West Indies), 312, 315–18, 316, 316 (excerpt), 317, 320, 327, 335–36 (excerpt), 342, 346, 347, 347, 361, 367, 369, 377, 391, 401, 404, 434, 435; Angola, 312, 319, 320, 323; Arabs, 371, 372; Asante, 326; Benin, 189, 317, 318, 319, 326, 346; Bijagós Islands, 377 (excerpt); Bonny, 326; Brass, 326; British, 312, 315, 316 (excerpt), 335–36 (excerpt), 367, 377 (excerpt); condemned by Congress of Vienna, 434; Congo, 310, 314–15, 317, 318, 334, 364, 384; Creek Town, 326; Cross, 326; Dahomey, 314–15, 318, 326, 346; Dutch, 315, 316 (excerpt), 363, 373, 390, 391; French, 316 (excerpt), 363, 364, 367; the Gambia, 314–15; Ghana, 314–15; Guinea, 215, 326, 334–35 (excerpt), 367, 377 (excerpt); Kenya, 371; Malaya, 373; Nigeria, 314–15; Opobo, 326; Oyo, 326; Portuguese, 310, 312, 314, 315, 317, 318, 319, 320, 334, 334–35 (excerpt), 347, 347, 363, 364, 366, 367, 368, 369, 371, 405; Roman Catholic Church, 314, 327, 363, 364, 390, 390; São Tomé, 312, 315, 319; Senegal, 314–15; Senegambia, 310; Spanish, 315, 363, 364, 367, 368; Tanganyika, 371; Togo, 314–15; Zanzibar, 371, 372; Zimbabwe, 371
SLAVERY, Berbers, 104, 106, 108, 109; Bornu, 226, 229, 235 (excerpt), 239; Carthage, 102, 103, 104, 105; Egypt, 59; France, 401; Ghana, 185, 234, 310, 317; intermarriage, 373; Islam, 141, 152, 153; Kano, 227; Mali, 185, 234; for military purposes, 104, 141, 224, 228, 317, 318, 326, 327, 361; Nubia, 64; Ouidah, 317, 318; reform movements and freedom, 368, 371, 372, 401, 403, 424, 434, 434, 435; Songhai, 185, 234; South Africa, 323, 373, 390; Swahili, 144; United States, 401, 434, 434; Vandals, 115; Yoruba, 317; see also serfs

SLEEPING SICKNESS see TSETSE FLY
SMALLPOX, 324, 325, 418
SMITH, SIR HARRY, 413, 415
SMITH, IAN, 509–10
SMITH, MICHAEL G., 229–30
SMUTS, JAN CHRISTIAAN, 457, 457, 461
SNEFRU, 55, 56
SO, 236, 241
SOBA, 115
SOBAT RIVER, 411
SOFALA (Zanj), 144–45, 270, 312, 322, 368, 408; Barros on, excerpts, 142, 145, 160–61; gold, 142–43, 144, 145, 160; Al-Idrisi on, 145, 159–60 (quoted); Kitab al-Zanuj (Chronicle of the Zanj), 143; trade, 142–43, 144, 145, 160
SOKOTO, 362, 363, 388, 421
SOLEILLET, PAUL, 403
SOLIMANA, 184
SOLOMON, 78, 78–79 (excerpt), 141
SOMABULA FORESTS, 418
SOMALI (people), 99, 142, 144, 437
SOMALI (lang.), 99, 141
SOMALIA (SOMALILAND), 29, 141–43, 144, 511; British Somaliland, 411, 458; Italian Somaliland, 454, 462, 501; see also Italian East Africa
SOMERSET, LORD CHARLES, 412
SOMERSET EAST, 325
SONG OF THE HARPER, 71–72 (excerpt)
SONGHAI, 148, 177, 179, 181, 183–88 passim, 210, 219, 226, 227, 228, 232, 357–61 passim, 376, 388; gold, 185, 213, 357, 358, 360; Islam, 148, 181, 185, 186, 187; kingship and government, 183–87 passim, 222, 230; Leo Africanus on, excerpts, 179, 183, 185, 186; slaves and serfs, 184, 185, 234; trade, 179, 180, 182, 184, 185, 188, 213; see also Gao; Timbuktu
SONINKE (SARAKHOLLE), 148, 177, 181, 187, 200, 219
SORGHUM, 65, 180, 186, 263
SORKO, 185
SOSHANGANA, 408
SOTHO, 46, 270, 294, 325; see also Bantu
SOUS VALLEY, 357
SOUSA, FRANCESCO DE, 407 (quoted)
SOUSA SEPULVEDA, MANOEL DE, 328–30
SOUTH AFRICA, 8, 270, 326, 371–75; Boers see BOERS; British, 372, 373, 375, 404, 408, 412–14, 439, 451, 455; diamonds, 438, 485, 485; engraving (1746), 321; Ethiopian Church, 455; gold, 455, 485, 485; people, 19, 323–24, 373; Portuguese, 312, 322–23, 324, 325, 372; prehistory, 22–23, 25, 27, 29, 33, 39, 323, 373, 390
SOUTH AFRICA, REPUBLIC OF, 294, 501, 507, 510; and Great Britain, 511; protests against apartheid, 423, 508, 510; and Rhodesia, 509–10; and South West Africa, 508, 509, 522; United Nations ban on arms shipments, 511; see also Cape Colony; Natal; Orange Free State; South Africa, Union of; Transvaal
SOUTH AFRICA, UNION OF, 457, 458, 460, 465, 486, 497, 501; Afrikaner National Party, 461–62; apartheid and white superiority, 324, 373, 390, 438, 455, 457, 461–62, 501, 502, 512; United Party, 461, 462; see also Boers; Cape Colony; Natal; Orange Free State; South Africa, Republic of; Transvaal
SOUTH AFRICA COMPANY see BRITISH SOUTH AFRICA COMPANY
SOUTH AFRICAN NATIVE NATIONAL CONGRESS, 461, 509, 510, 511
SOUTH AFRICAN REPUBLIC, 455, 456; see also Boer War; Transvaal
SOUTH SEA COMPANY, 367
SOUTH WEST AFRICA (NAMIBIA), 30, 264, 295, 373–74, 423; controversy over status, 508, 509, 522; German South West Africa, 374, 422, 422, 440, 456, 459; Portuguese, 373–74
SOUTH WEST AFRICA PEOPLES' ORGANIZATION (SWAPO), 510
SOVIET UNION see UNION OF SOVIET SOCIALIST REPUBLICS

SPAIN, 100, 101, 103, 307; and Africa, 305, 355–56, 388, 459; Almohads, 146, 356; Almoravids, 146, 159, 356; Christianity, 356, 386; Greeks, 100, 101; Hafsids, 146; Islam, 172, 356; and Portugal, 363; Moors, 8, 154, 154–55 (excerpt), 305, 355–57, 386, 386, 387; Phoenicians and Carthaginians, 100, 101, 103, 104, 105; Romans, 113; slave trade, 315, 363, 364, 367, 368; War of Spanish Succession, 367; West Indies, 367

SPEAR, 26, 28, 29, 61, 115, 143, 184, 185, 188, 226, 265, 398, 418, 423, 424, 439; spear points, 29, 51; spearheads, 30, 62; see also harpoon

SPEKE, JOHN, 403, 429, 437

SPICES, 63, 71, 147, 307, 355, 372, 405

SPRINGBOK, 45

STANLEY, HENRY M., 403, 436, 437

STANLEY, MOUNT, 20

STANLEY FALLS, 267

STANLEY POOL, 267, 268, 290

STANLEYVILLE, 503, 504, 507

STEEL, 145, 265

STEL, SIMON VAN DER, 323, 374

STELLENBOSCH, 323

STEPPELAND, 19, 20, 29

STERKFONTEIN, 22, 23, 42

STEWART, SIR HERBERT, 410

STICK, as prehistoric utensil and weapon, 25, 26, 29, 39, 43, 45

STONE, 43–44, 62, 106, 110, 116; building construction, 54, 62, 108, 145, 167, 230, 270; in digging stick, 29, 43, 45; ornament and jewelry, 61, 65; tools see TOOLS AND IMPLEMENTS, stone; utensils, 29, 32, 43, 51, 54, 57; as weapon, 25, 39, 139; worship of, 107, 149; see also alabaster; marble

STONE AGE, 28–29, 219; rock art, 21, 33, 43

STRABO, Geography, 66–67 (excerpt), 102–103, 112

STUDENT NONVIOLENT COORDINATING COMMITTEE (SNCC), 508

SUDAN (region), 20, 51, 52, 64–65, 93, 99, 130, 181, 217–59 passim, 263, 266, 355, 359–63; agriculture, 52, 65, 185, 186, 213, 219–20; clothing, 183, 184, 185–86; Islam, 137, 148–49, 175, 254, 356; people, 61, 99, 137, 148, 175, 254, 263, 266, 422; prehistory, 32, 52; trade, 91, 103, 146, 149, 155, 175, 245, 254, 256, 356; see also Anglo-Egyptian Sudan; Bornu; British West Africa; France, West Africa; French Sudan; Ghana (state); Mali (state); Songhai

SUDAN (republic), 465, 497, 499, 504, 511; see also Anglo-Egyptian Sudan

SUDD (aquatic grass), 51, 66

SUEZ, 91, 99

SUEZ CANAL, 454, 454, 461, 464

SUFISM, 147–48

SUGAR AND SUGAR CANE, 308, 310; Caribbean and West Indies, 315, 316, 316, 363, 434; trade, 253, 266, 309, 310; wine, 266

SULAIMAN SOLONG, 230

SULLY, DUC DE, 363

SUMANGURU KANTE, 179; legend, 201–203 (excerpt)

SUMATRA, 420

SUN, worship of, 59, 69, 107, 109; see also Amon-Re; Aten

SUNDAY RIVER, 412

SUNDIATA, 179, 180, 210

SUNNI ALI, 179, 180, 184, 187, 210

SUS, 118

SUSU, 179, 187, 188, 201

SWAHILI, 141, 144, 270, 272, 312, 368, 441

SWANSCOMBE, 27

SWARTKANS, 23

SWAZI AND SWAZILAND, 269, 374, 510

SWEDEN, in Africa, 305, 313

SWORD, 115, 183, 184, 185, 244, 365

SYENE see ASWAN

SYMBOLISM, Bantu, 268; clothing, 183, 184; crook, 54; crown see CROWN; eye, 64, 107, 118–19, 182; flail, 54; moon, 63; ram's head, 64; in rock art, 32, 33; scepter, 77, 87, 183; serpent, 64; staff, 87, 101;

sword, 183; see also ceremonial objects

SYPHAX, 106, 107

SYRACUSE, 102

SYRIA, 57, 114, 224, 473

TABKIN KWOTTO, 362

TABLE BAY, 323, 325

TABLE MOUNTAIN, 371

TACFARINAS, 111; Tacitus on, 122 (quoted)

TACITUS, Annals, 122 (excerpt)

TADA, 197

TAGHAZA, 185, 233, 252, 256

TAHARQA, 60, 62

TAHERT, 222, 223

TAIFARAH, 409

TAKEDDA, 189, 233

TAKRUR, 148, 177, 190, 421

TAMBUSA, 417

TAMENTIT, 233

TANA, LAKE, 462

TANA RIVER, 412

TA-NET-AMON, 74

TANGANYIKA, 23, 264–65, 270, 271, 272, 273, 371, 412; Germans, 440, 449, 459, 485; Maji Maji Rising, 449, 459; see also British East Africa; Kilwa; Tanzania

TANGANYIKA, LAKE, 20

TANGIER, 145, 482

TANIS see AVARIS

TANIT, 107; see also Caelestis; Isis

TANWETAMANI, 60

TANZANIA, 509, 510, 529; see also British East Africa; Commonwealth of Nations; German East Africa; Tanganyika; Zanzibar

TARIK IBN ZAYYAD, 153–54, 355; Lane-Poole on, 154–55 (quoted)

TARIKH AS-SUDAN, by Abd al-Rahman as-Sadi, 186, 359–60 (excerpt)

TARO, 264, 293

TAROUDANT, 149

TARUGA, 65

TASSILI CAVES, 32, 33, 34

TATOG, 272

TAUNG, 22, 23

TCHIYAKA, 406

TEA, 253, 507

TEBU, 221

TEM-BON-DUMBA, 367

TEMBU, 325, 413; see also Bantu

TERNIFINE, 26

TERTIARY PERIOD, 19; Miocene epoch, 21–22; Oligocene epoch, 21; Pliocene epoch, 22, 24

TERTULLIAN, SAINT, 114

TETE, 321, 322, 407

TEXTILES see FABRICS AND TEXTILES

THABA BOSIGO, 415, 416

THEBES, 55, 56, 58, 59, 60, 67, 70, 82; Temple of Amon-Re, 74, 108; Temple of Ramses II, 49, 74; tomb of Seti I, 87; tomb of Tutankhamon, 54, 58–59, 71, 91

THEODORA, BYZANTINE EMPRESS, 128

THEVET, ANDRE, Cosmographie Universelle, 343

THIRD WORLD, 457, 493, 504

THONGA, 294

THOTH, 69, 69

THOTHMES I, 73

THOUGHTS UPON THE AFRICAN SLAVE TRADE, by Newton, 336 (excerpt)

THUCYDIDES, History of the Peloponnesian War, 101 (excerpt), 103

TIBESTI MOUNTAINS, 221

TIE, 240, 241

TIGRE, 423

TILIMSAN see TLEMCEN

TIMBO, 318

TIMBUKTU, 175, 179, 182, 184, 186, 187, 188, 189, 210, 211, 213, 234, 256, 359, 360, 376, 388, 421, 456; Abd al-Rahman as-Sadi on, 359–60 (quoted); Leo Africanus on, quoted, 183, 185, 186; Sankore quarter, mosque and university, 186, 211, 359, 360, 362, 376, 388

TIO, 268

TLEMCEN (TILIMSAN), 145, 146, 233

TIN, 100, 107

TIPPU TIB, 372

TITUS LIVY, 106

TOBACCO, 318, 325; in Americas, 315, 316, 434; introduced to Africa, 310; trade, 45–46

TOBIN, LAKE, 362

TOGO (TOGOLAND), 314–15, 465, 504, 505–506; Brazzaville Group, 503, 504, 506, 507; British, 459, 465; French, 459, 506; Germans, 440, 456, 459; Monrovia Group, 504, 505, 506; Organisation Commune Africaine et Malgache, 507, 511; see also British West Africa; Ghana (republic)

TOIVO JA TOIVO, HERMAN, 522–23 (quoted)

TOLEDO, 356

TOMA, 392

TONDIBI, 188, 357

TONGUE, HELEN, 33

TOOLS AND IMPLEMENTS, adze, 29, 31; axe, 26, 27, 29, 31, 32; blade, 28, 29, 30, 31; bone, 25, 28, 29, 30, 43, 45, 51; bronze, 107; chisel, 29; chopper and cleaver, 23, 25, 26, 44; copper, 54; flake, 25, 26, 27, 28, 31, 43, 45; flint, 31; grinding and pounding, 25, 26, 29, 32, 43, 234, 253; grooving, hollowing, and piercing, 23, 27, 28, 29; hoe, 186, 265; iron, 65, 107, 180, 265–66; knife see KNIFE; microlith, 28, 29; obsidian, 32; plow, 63, 107; point, 29, 43, 51; scraper, 25, 27, 28, 29, 31, 43; sickle, 28, 29, 30, 31; steel, 145; stick, 25, 26, 29, 39, 43, 45; stone as, 25, 29, 43, 45; of stone, 23–32 passim, 39, 40, 43, 44, 45, 51, 52, 56, 65, 181, 263; of wood, 263, 265; for woodworking, 27, 29, 43; see also utensils

TORTOISE SHELL, 46, 63, 143

TORTUGA, 363

TOURE, SAMORI see SAMORI TOURE

TOURE, SEKOU, 464, 500, 516, 516; on African cooperation, 516–17 (quoted)

TOURQUOISE, 91

TOUSSAINT L'OUVERTURE, PIERRE DOMINIQUE, 435

TOWERSON, WILLIAM, 312

TRADE, 403–404; amber, 143, 310; animals, 59, 63, 73, 91, 106, 112, 132, 140, 155, 185, 234, 235, 310; basketry, 265, 272; books, 155, 185, 186; brass, 155, 310; canoes, 266; coffee, tea, and cacao, 142, 253, 464, 507; copal, 266, 464; copper, 51, 54, 91, 143, 184, 189, 234, 265, 266, 267, 268; cotton, 147, 189, 253, 464; fabrics, textiles, and clothing, 91, 106, 107, 147, 155, 185, 188, 266, 270, 306, 310, 340, 355; feathers, 45, 91; fish (dried and salted), 147, 188, 189, 309, 310; fruit, 132, 147, 155; furs, 45; gold see GOLD AND GOLDWORK; grains and cereals, 91, 106, 108, 147, 155, 160, 185, 253, 464; hides, skins, and leather, 45–46, 73, 102, 106, 112, 142, 143, 147, 189, 310; honey, 155; indigo, 310; iron and ironwork, 45–46, 143, 147, 160, 265, 272; ivory see IVORY; jewels, ornament, and jewelry, 73, 103, 106, 107, 143, 147, 266, 270, 307, 310; kola nuts, 155, 185, 188, 189; marble, 106; medicinal plants, 147; metalwork, 147, 340; minerals, 91, 103, 106, 107, 147, 270, 307, 464; olive oil, 91, 110, 112, 132, 147; palm oil, 143, 189, 403; paper and papyrus, 91, 185; pepper, 309–10, 312, 314, 340; perfumes, incense, gums, and spices, 63, 73, 97, 102, 107, 112, 147, 307, 314, 355, 372, 405; pottery, ceramics, and porcelain, 102, 110, 143, 171, 265, 270, 272; reeds and matting, 91, 265; rhinoceros horn, 63, 143; rugs and tapestry, 107, 147; salt see SALT; slaves see SLAVE TRADE; sugar, 253, 266, 309, 310; tobacco, 45–46; tools and utensils, 265, 270; tortoise shell, 63, 143; wax, 147, 310, 314; weapons, 73, 107, 143, 147, 185, 266; wine, 112, 132, 266, 310; wood, 51, 54, 59, 73, 74, 91, 106, 112, 144, 147, 266; see also separate listings under individual countries and peoples

TRANSKEI, 264

TRANSPORTATION, camel see CAMEL; chariot, 58, 60, 90, 103, 130, 180, 221; donkey, 91, 184; horse see HORSE; litters, 343, 405; oxen and bullock, 110, 112, 180, 213, 233; railway, 458, 485; rickshaw, 486; see also boats and ships

TRANSVAAL, 270, 404, 451, 455, 456; gold, 455, 485, 485; prehistory, 22–23, 33, 39; see also Boer War; South Africa, Republic of; South Africa, Union of

TREATY OF VEREENIGING, 457

TREATY OF WICHALE, 423, 454

TREES, worship of, 107, 110, 243, 244, 420

"TRIBALISM," 505

TRIBE see separate listings under individual peoples and groups

TRIMINGHAM, J. SPENCER, 186

TRIPOLI AND TRIPOLITANIA, 97, 99, 109, 113, 115, 166, 180, 234, 235, 359, 458; see also "Africa"; Barbary Coast; Libya

TRISTAO, NUNO, 307, 310

TSETSE FLY (sleeping sickness), 30, 32, 219, 231, 233, 264, 363, 465

TSHOMBE, MOISE, 501, 507, 509

TSWANA, 294, 325; see also Bantu

TUAREG (people), 118, 158, 166, 175, 187, 217, 223, 233, 234, 252, 252, 253, 255, 360, 421; see also Berbers

TUAREG (lang.), 99

TUAT, 233, 360

TUGELA RIVER, 416, 417, 418

TUKOLOR, 421, 431; see also Fulani

TUNIS AND TUNISIA (IFRIQIYA), 97, 99, 102, 107, 110, 115, 145–48, 166, 233, 499; Fatimids, 224; French, 421, 497; Hafsids, 146–47, 224; independence, 497; myth and legend, 121 (excerpt); Ottoman empire, 358; trade, 147, 188, 233, 234; see also "Africa"; Barbary Coast; Berbers

TUNJUR, 230

TUNKA MANIN, 183

TURKANA, 298

TURKS see OTTOMAN EMPIRE; SELJUKS

TUTANKHAMON, 60; tomb, Thebes, 54, 58–59, 71, 91

TUTUOLA, AMOS, 526; My Life in the Bush of the Ghosts, 526–27 (excerpt); The Palm Wine Drinkard, 526

TYALI, 413

TYRE, 100

UBANGI RIVER, 266

UCCIALI, TREATY OF see TREATY OF WICHALE

UGANDA, 264, 272, 411, 480, 511; British, 453–54, 458, 485; French, 453–54; see also British East Africa; Commonwealth of Nations

UJIJI, 437

ULUNDI, 418

UMARI, AL-, 184 (quoted), 186 (quoted)

UMBA RIVER, 422

UMGUNGUNDHLOVU, 416

UMHLAKAZA, 413–14

UMMAYADS, 143

UMME JILMA, 223, 224, 244; song of praise, 234–35 (excerpt)

UNI, 72 (quoted)

UNION AFRICAINE ET MALGACHE (UAM) (Brazzaville Group), 503, 504, 506, 507

UNION AFRICAINE ET MALGACHE DE COOPERATION ECONOMIQUE (UAMCE), 506; see also Organisation Commune Africaine et Malgache

UNION OF SOVIET SOCIALIST REPUBLICS, 493, 502, 507, 511

UNITED ARAB REPUBLIC (UAR), 473, 492, 497, 499, 509, 511; Aswan Dam, 507; Casablanca Group, 503, 504; and Nigerian civil war, 511

UNITED NATIONS, African affairs, 499, 500, 501, 503, 507, 509, 511; African Group, 499, 500; Brazzaville Group, 506; Charter, 463; and South West Africa (Namibia), 508, 522

UNITED STATES, 327, 404, 452, 499; and Africa, 420, 452, 487, 493, 505, 506, 508; African Communities League, 460; American Colonization Society, 403; back-to-Africa movements, 403, 470; and Barbary Coast, 359; Black Muslims, 508; Black Panther Party, 508; Civil Rights Acts, 508; and Congo, 507, 509; French territory, 358; National Association for the Advancement of Colored People, 460; Niagara Movement, 467; and Nigerian civil war, 510, 511; Organization of Afro-American Unity, 508; Pan-African Conference (1900), 457–58, 460; slavery, 401, 434, 434; Student Nonviolent Coordinating Committee (SNCC), 508; Universal Negro Improvement Association, 460–61, 471
UNIVERSAL HISTORY see KITAB AL-IBAR
UNIVERSAL NEGRO IMPROVEMENT ASSOCIATION, 460–61, 471
UPPER VOLTA, Brazzaville Group, 503, 504, 506, 507
UQBA IBN-NAFI, 145, 147
URBAN II, POPE, 353
URBAN VIII, POPE, 390
URSIFAN, 118
URVOY, IVES, 224, 241
USMAN DAN FODIO, 362–63; on Fulani jihad, 379–80 (quoted)
UTENSILS, bone, 51; bronze, 61, 64, 65, 107; calabash, 43; copper, 54; glass, 61, 64; gold, 107, 183, 229; hides and skins (as containers), 43, 45, 232; iron, 107; ivory, 51, 61, 340, 348; ostrich eggshells, 31, 43, 45, 46; prehistory, 27, 29, 32, 43, 45, 46; silver, 61, 64, 107; stone, 29, 32, 43, 51, 54, 57; tortoise carapace, 46, trade, 270; wood, 61, 64; see also pottery and ceramics
UTICA, 105
UYS, PIETER, 416

VALLEY OF A THOUSAND HILLS, by Dhlomo, 384 (excerpt)
VANDALS, 100, 115, 132; Procopius on, 124 (quoted)
VANDELEUR, GEN. JOHN ORMSBY, 412
VANSINA, JAN, 380–81, 381–82, 382 (quoted)
VARELA, 407
VASSA, GUSTAVUS see EQUIANO, OLAUDAH
VENICE, 155, 307
VERWOERD, HENDRIK, 501, 502
VICTORIA, QUEEN OF THE UNITED KINGDOM OF GREAT BRITAIN AND IRELAND, 411, 458
VICTORIA, LAKE, 19, 27, 264, 272, 273
VICTORIA FALLS, 403, 463
VIERVOET, 415
VINEYARDS, 59, 83, 107, 308; grapevine as motif, 117; wine trade, 112, 132, 310
VIRGIN MARY, 109, 135
VISIGOTHS, 355
VITENHAGE, 413
VOLTA RIVER, 190, 191
VOLTA RIVER BASIN, 189
VOLUBIS, 110
VOYAGES, by Hakluyt, 377 (excerpt)

WA, 188
WADAI, 217, 220, 421
WADAN, 309
WADI AJAL, 99
WADSTROM, C. B., 318 (quoted)
WAGADU, 200–201 (excerpt)
WAHEHE, 422
WALATA, 179, 187, 188
WANGARA, 185, 213
WANKIE, 510
THE WAR IN SOUTH AFRICA, by Hobson, 457
WAR OF SPANISH SUCCESSION, 367
WAR OF THE AXE, 413

"WAR OF THE ELEPHANT," 138
WARDEN, MAJ. HENRY, 415
WARFARE, 403; archers, 60, 61, 115, 184, 229; armor, 58, 210, 219, 250; cavalry, 184, 188, 210, 219, 229, 363, 410, 415; elephants used, 63, 138; horse and chariot, 58, 60, 90, 130, 180, 221; mercenaries, 101, 102, 103–104, 107, 108, 115; sacrifice of animals before battle, 118; slaves, 104, 141, 224, 228, 317, 318, 326, 327, 361; see also firearms; weapons; separate listings under individual battles and wars
WARRI, 314
WASHBURN, SHERWOOD L., 22
WATER, worship of, 149; see also rain ceremonies
WATER CONTROL AND CONSERVATION, 61, 62, 82, 83, 91, 110–11, 128, 232, 358, 359, 507; see also Nile, flooding; Suez Canal
WATERBERG MOUNTAINS, 422, 422
WATT, JAMES, 318 (quoted)
WATUSI, 271
WAX, 147, 310, 312, 314
WEAPONS, 44, 58, 62, 65, 102, 107, 145, 185, 265; prehistory, 25–31 passim, 39, 40, 43, 51; trade, 73, 107, 143, 147, 185, 266; see also arrow; bow; firearms; harpoon; knife; spear; sword
WEBBE SHEBELI RIVER, 144
WEENEN, 416
WEEP NOT, CHILD, by Ngugi, 475–79 (excerpt)
WEIGHTS AND MEASURES, 108, 200
WEST AFRICA, 19, 177–215, 356, 363–68; agriculture, 65, 180, 310, 312; British see BRITISH WEST AFRICA; Dutch, 312–13, 348, 349; French see FRANCE, West Africa; Islam, 137, 145, 148, 180, 181, 185, 186, 190, 217, 219, 220, 222, 355; map (1375), 175; map (1502), 305; map (1743), 395; Portuguese, 179, 189, 190, 215, 308–13, 310, 315, 348, 349, 363, 364, 367, 406, 452, 456 (see also Angola); prehistory, 27, 28, 29, 32; slave trade, 310, 314–15, 317, 318, 319, 323, 326, 347, 348, 361, 363, 364, 366, 367; trade, 179, 180, 181, 182, 188–89, 190, 192, 220, 227, 309–10, 312, 314–15, 326; see also Sudan
WEST AFRICAN CONFERENCE (1884–1885), 404, 423, 440–41, 449, 451–52, 452, 453, 454, 459
WEST INDIES see CARIBBEAN AND WEST INDIES
WESTERMARCK, EDWARD, 168 (quoted); Ritual and Belief in Morocco, 118–19 (excerpt)
WHEAT, 30, 31, 32, 51, 65, 83, 101, 109, 110; trade, 106, 108, 155
WHITE NILE, 66, 217, 271
WHITTIER, JOHN GREENLEAF, song of the Bornu slaves, 235 (excerpt)
WHITTING, C. E. J., 380 (quoted)
WILHELM, KAISER, 457
WILLCOCKS, COL. JAMES, 420
WILLCOX, ALEX, 43–44 (quoted)
WILLETT, FRANK, 189, 191, 192
WILLIAMS, ERIC, Capitalism and Slavery, 316
WILLIS, A. J., 322 (quoted)
WILSON, SIR CHARLES, 410 (quoted)
WILSON, MONICA, 45–47 (quoted)
WINE see VINEYARDS
WINE TRADE, 112, 132, 266, 310
WINTERBERG, 413
WINTON, SIR FRANCIS DE, 420
WISSMANN, HERMANN VON, 365
WITBOOI, HENDRIK, 422
WITERWATERSRAND, 455, 485
WOBURN, 413
WOLOF, 177, 188, 189, 190, 309, 342; Fernandes on, 190; Pereira on, 190 (quoted); Portuguese, 309, 311
WOLSELEY, SIR GARNET, 420
WOOD, BRIG. GEN. EVELYN, 418
WOOD, for boats, canoes, and ships, 52–53, 74, 90, 263; building construction, 32, 54, 226, 263, 270; tools, implements, and utensils, 26, 30, 43, 263, 265; trade, 51, 54, 59, 73, 74, 91, 106, 112, 144, 147, 266;

trees worshiped, 107, 110, 243, 244, 420
WOODWORK AND SCULPTURE, 32, 55, 61, 64, 116, 191, 192, 193, 205, 263, 266, 293, 365, 393, 395
WOOL, 106, 107, 116, 147
WORLD WAR I, 451, 457, 458, 459–60, 463
WORLD WAR II, 451, 462, 463
WULI, 421
WYK, WILLIAM VAN, 374
WYNDHAM, THOMAS, 192 (quoted), 312

X-GROUP PEOPLE, 64
XAVIER, 349
XERXES, 101
XHOSA, 325, 413–14, 426, 428, 439; and Boers, 412, 438, 439; and British, 412, 413, 426 (excerpt), 439; cattle complex, 269; and Hottentots, 412; see also Bantu

YAJI, 244 (excerpt)
YAM, 32, 65, 185, 189, 263, 293, 392
YAO, 270
YAQUB AL-MANSUR, 356
YAQUBI, AL-, 179 (quoted)
YAQUT, AL-, 185 (quoted), 232
YAQUT AL-RUMI, 143
YAURI, 227
YEMEN, 63, 64, 137, 138, 139, 142
YOHANNES IV, 422, 454
YORUBA, 189, 190, 191, 227, 361, 420, 511; art and sculpture, 65, 177, 189, 191, 192, 193, 193–99, 205, 205, 215, 266, 310, 346; divine kingship, 191, 192; divinities and religious beliefs, 190, 191, 192, 206 (excerpt), 207–208; oral tradition, 191–92, 203–208 (excerpt), 526; slaves, 317; see also Nigeria
YUSUF AGHA AL-MALIK, 409
YUSUF IBN TASHFIN, 356
YUSUF PASHA AL-SHALLALI, 409

ZAGHAWA, 217
ZAIDITES, 160
ZAMBEZI, 143, 145, 269, 270, 312, 418
ZAMBEZI VALLEY, 19, 293, 294, 322
ZAMBIA, 29, 30, 265, 269, 418, 462, 463, 485, 506, 509, 510; see also Rhodesia (Northern Rhodesia and Southern Rhodesia)
ZANDE, 266
ZANJ (people), 144, 145; Al-Idrisi on, 159–60 (quoted); Kitab al-Zanuj (Chronicle of the Zanj), 143; see also Bantu
ZANJ (place) see SOFALA
ZANZIBAR, 263, 369, 371, 372; British, 372, 411, 456; Germans, 422; Portuguese, 312, 369, 370, 371; slave trade, 371, 372; see also British East Africa; Tanzania
ZARIA, 227, 229, 247, 361, 362
ZAWILA, 222, 223, 224, 235
ZAYD IBN HARITHAH, 355
ZEBRA, 486
ZEILA, 141, 142
ZEUS, 108; see also Amon-Re
ZIMBA, 313, 326
ZIMBABWE, 65, 145, 270, 294, 371, 407
ZIMBABWE AFRICAN PEOPLE'S UNION (ZAPU), 509, 510
ZOGHBY, SAMIR, 232–33 (quoted)
ZOOK, GEORGE F., 378–79 (quoted)
ZOSER, 67, 68, 87; temple and Step Pyramid, Saqqara, 67, 85
ZULU (legendary founder of the Zulu), 382
ZULU AND ZULULAND, 270, 295, 325, 374–75, 382, 398, 416, 416–18, 439, 459; and Boers, 373, 375, 398, 416, 417; British, 398, 398, 401, 416–17, 417–18; cattle, 269, 374; Fynn on, 382–84 (quoted); Hamilton-Browne on, 426–28 (quoted); oral tradition and literature, 382 (excerpt), 384, 423, 428 (excerpt); see also Bantu; Matabele and Matabeleland; South Africa, Republic of; South Africa, Union of
ZUURVELD, 412
ZWAY, LAKE, 141